THE FIRST URBAN CHURCHES 4
ROMAN PHILIPPI

WRITINGS FROM THE GRECO-ROMAN WORLD
SUPPLEMENT SERIES

Clare K. Rothschild, General Editor

Number 13

THE FIRST URBAN CHURCHES 4
ROMAN PHILIPPI

Edited by
James R. Harrison and L. L. Welborn

SBL PRESS

Atlanta

Copyright © 2018 by SBL Press

All rights reserved. No part of this work may be reproduced or transmitted in any form or by any means, electronic or mechanical, including photocopying and recording, or by means of any information storage or retrieval system, except as may be expressly permitted by the 1976 Copyright Act or in writing from the publisher. Requests for permission should be addressed in writing to the Rights and Permissions Office, SBL Press, 825 Houston Mill Road, Atlanta, GA 30329 USA.

Library of Congress Cataloging-in-Publication Data

First urban churches / edited by James R. Harrison and L. L. Welborn.
    volumes cm. — (Society of Biblical Literature. Writings from the Greco-Roman world Supplement series ; Number 7)
    Includes bibliographical references.
    Contents: 1. Methodological foundations.

    ISBN 978-1-62837-102-4 (v. 1 : pbk. : alk. paper) — ISBN 978-1-62837-104-8 (v. 1 : ebook) — ISBN 978-1-62837-103-1 (v. 1 : hardcover : alk. paper)
    ISBN 978-0-88414-111-2 (v. 2 : pbk. : alk. paper) — ISBN 978-0-88414-112-9 (v. 2 : ebook) — ISBN 978-0-88414-113-6 (v. 2 : hardcover : alk. paper)
    ISBN 978-0-88414-234-8 (v. 3 : pbk. : alk. paper) — ISBN 978-0-88414-235-5 (v. 3 : ebook) — ISBN 978-0-88414-236-2 (v. 3 : hardcover : alk. paper)
    ISBN 978-1-62837-226-7 (v. 4 : pbk. : alk. paper) — ISBN 978-0-88414-337-6 (v. 4 : ebook) — ISBN 978-0-88414-336-9 (v. 4 : hardcover : alk. paper)
    1. City churches. 2. Church history—Primitive and early church, ca. 30–600. 3. Cities and towns—Religious aspects—Christianity. I. Harrison, James R., 1952– editor.
 BV637.F57 2015
 270.109173'2—dc23   2015021858

Printed on acid-free paper.

Contents

Abbreviations vii

Excavating the Urban and Country Life of Roman Philippi
and Its Territory
    James R. Harrison 1

Rooted in Heaven and Resident in Philippi, but No ἐκκλησία?
    Kathy Ehrensperger 63

The Social Constituency and Membership of the First Christian
Groups at Philippi: A Literary and Epigraphic Survey
    Julien M. Ogereau 79

Vindolanda Tablet 2.154, *RPC* 1651, and the Provenance
of Philippians
    Paul A. Holloway 123

Polis and *Ekklēsia* at Philippi: A Response to Kathy Ehrensperger,
Paul Holloway, and Julien Ogereau
    Angela Standhartinger 139

First-Century Philippi: Contextualizing Paul's Visit
    Cédric Brélaz 153

Did the Philippian Christ Group *Know* It Was a "Missionary" Society?
    Richard S. Ascough 189

The Imperial Authorities in Paul's Letter to Predominantly Greek
Hearers in the Roman Colony of Philippi
    Peter Oakes 221

"Every Knee Bowed": Jesus Christ as Reigning Lord over
"the Heavenly, the Earthly, and the Subterranean Gods"
(Philippians 2:10)
    Fredrick J. Long and Ryan Kristopher Giffin 239

Rivals, Opponents, and Enemies: Three Kinds of Theological
Argumentation in Philippians
    Samuel Vollenweider 291

From Rome to the Colony of Philippi: Roman Boasting in Philippians
3:4–6 in Its Latin West and Philippian Epigraphic Context
    James R. Harrison 307

Contributors 371
Primary Sources Index 375
Modern Authors Index 395

Abbreviations

General

| | line break
|| | line break every fifth line
{ } | suppressions by the editor, usually due to spelling errors or duplications by the stone mason
< > | additions or substitutions by the epigraphic editor
ca. | circa
l(l). | line(s)
n(n). | note(s)
n.d. | no date
par. | parallel
pl(s). | plate(s)
r. | reigned
s.v. | *sub verbo*, under the word

Primary Sources

1 Esd | 1 Esdras
1 Glor. | Dio Chrysostom, *De gloria 1 (Or. 66)*
1 Macc | 1 Maccabees
1QHa | Hodayota or Thanksgiving Hymnsa
1QSb | Serek Hayaḥad or Rule of the Community
3 Macc | 3 Maccabees
4 Macc | 4 Maccabees
Aen. | Vergil, *Aeneid*
Agr. | Philo, *De agricultura*
Amic. | Cicero, *De amicitia*
An. seni | Plutarch, *An seni respublica gerenda sit*
Ann. | Tacitus, *Annales*

Ant.	Josephus, *Antiquitates judaicae*
Ant. rom.	Dionysius of Halicarnassus, *Antiquitates romanae*
Apocol.	Seneca, *Apocolocyntosis*
Att.	Cicero, *Epistulae ad Atticum*
Aug.	Suetonius, *Divus Augustus*
b. Hag.	Babylonian Talmud Hagigah
B.J.	Josephus, *Bellum judaicum*
Borysth.	Dio Chrysostom, *Borysthenitica* (Or. 36)
Cod. theod.	Codex Theodosianus
Conf.	Philo, *De confusione linguarum*
Congr.	Philo, *De congressu eruditionis gratia*
Cor.	Tertullian, *De corona militis*
De ipsum laud.	Plutarch, *De se ipsum citra invidiam laudando*
De or.	Cicero, *De oratore*
Dom.	Suetonius, *Domitianus*
Ep.	*Epistula(e)*
Epit.	Ausonius, *Epitaphia heroum qui bello Troico interfuerunt*
Fam.	Cicero, *Epistulae ad Familiares*
Gen. an.	Aristotle, *De generatione animalium*
Geogr.	Strabo, *Geographica*
Georg.	Vergil, *Georgica*
Gorg.	Plato, *Gorgias*
H. Ar.	Athanasius, *Historia Arianorum*
Herc. Ot.	Seneca, *Hercules Otaeus*
Hist.	Polybius, *Historiae*; Tacitus, *Historiae*; Thucydides, *Historiae*
Hist. eccl.	Eusebius, *Historia ecclesiastica*; Socrates, *Historia ecclesiastica*
Hist. Rom.	Dio Cassius, *Historia Romana*
Hom. Matt.	John Chrysostom, *Homiliae in Mattheum*
Hom. Phil.	John Chrysostom, *Homiliae in epistulam ad Philippenses*
Id.	Theocritus, *Idylls*
Ign. Trall.	Ignatius, *To the Trallians*
Il.	Homer, *Iliad*
Inst.	Quintilian, *Institutio oratorica*
Interp. Epist. ad Phil.	Theodoret, *Interpretatio Epistulae ad Philippenses*
Jul.	Suetonius, *Divus Julius*

L.A.B.	Liber antiquitatum biblicarum
Laz.	John Chrysostom, *De Lazaro*
Leg.	Philo, *Legum allegoriae*
Legat.	Philo, *Legatio ad Gaium*
Lucil.	Seneca, *Ad Lucilium*
LXX	Septuagint
m. Sanh.	Mishnah Sanhedrin
Marc.	Tertullian, *Adversus Marcionem*
Metam.	Apuleius, *Metamorphoses*; Ovid, *Metamorphoses*
Midr. Ps.	Midrash Psalms
Mor.	Plutarch, *Moralia*
Most.	Plautus, *Mostellaria*
MT	Masoretic Text
Nat.	Pliny, *Naturalis historia*
Nov.	Justinian, *Novellae*
Od.	Homer, *Odyssey*
Onir.	Artemidorus, *Onirocritica*
Phar.	Lucan, *Pharsalia*
Phil.	Cicero, *Orationes Philippicae*; Polycarp, *To the Philippians*
Praec. Ger. rei publ.	Plutarch, *Praecepta gerenda rei publicae*
Praescr.	Tertullian, *De praescriptione haereticorum*
Rep.	Cicero, *De republica*
Res gest.	Res gestae divi Augusti
Sat.	Horace, *Satirae*; Juvenal, *Satirae*: Persius, *Satirae*; Petronius, *Satirae*
Sifre Num.	Sifre Numbers
Sir	Sirach
Somn.	Philo, *De somniis*
Spec.	Philo, *De specialibus legibus*
T. Jud.	Testament of Judah
T. Sol.	Testament of Solomon
Trall.	Ignatius, *To the Trallians*
Tranq. an.	Plutarch, *De tranquillitate animi*
Tusc.	Cicero, *Tusculanae Disputationes*
Verr.	Cicero, *In Verrem*

Secondary Sources

AAA	*Archaeologika Analecta ex Athenon*
ADelt	*Archaiologikon Deltion*
AÉ	Cagnat, René, et al., ed. *L'Année Épigraphique*. Paris: Presses universitaires de France, 1888–.
AGJU	*Arbeiten zur Geschichte des antiken Judentums und des Urchristentums*
AGRW	Ascough, Richard S., Philip A. Harland, and John S. Kloppenborg. *Associations in the Greco-Roman World: A Sourcebook*. Berlin: de Gruyter, 2012.
AJA	*American Journal of Archaeology*
AJEC	*Ancient Judaism and Early Christianity*
AJP	*American Journal of Philology*
AMNG	*Antiken Münzen Nord-Griechenland*
AnAnt	*Anatolia Antiqua*
AnBib	*Analecta Biblica*
AncSoc	*Ancient Society*
AncW	*The Ancient World*
ANRW	Temporini, Hildegard, and Wolfgang Haase, eds. *Aufstieg und Niedergang der römischen Welt: Geschichte und Kultur Roms im Spiegel der neueren Forschung*. Part 2, *Principat*. Berlin: de Gruyter, 1972–.
ArchEph	*Archaiologike ephemeris*
ASAA	*Annuario della Scuola Archeologica di Atene e delle Missioni Italiane in Oriente*
AYB	Anchor Yale Bible
BA	*Biblical Archaeologist*
BAGD	Bauer, Walter, William F. Arndt, F. Wilbur Gingrich, and Frederick W. Danker. *Greek-English Lexicon of the New Testament and Other Early Christian Literature*. 2nd ed. Chicago: University of Chicago Press, 1979.
BCH	*Bulletin de correspondance hellénique*
BCHSupp	Supplements to *Bulletin de correspondance hellénique*
BDAG	Arndt, William, Frederick W. Danker, Walter Bauer, and F. Wilbur Gingrich, eds. *A Greek-English Lexi-*

	con of the New Testament and Other Early Christian Literature. Chicago: University of Chicago Press, 2000.
BE	Bulletin épigraphique
BEB	Elwell, Walter A., ed. Baker Encyclopedia of the Bible. 2 vols. Grand Rapids: Baker, 1988.
BECNT	Baker Exegetical Commentary on the New Testament
BETL	Bibliotheca Ephemeridum Theologicaum Lovaniensium
BFCT	Beiträge zur Förderung christlicher Theologie
BGU	Aegyptische Urkunden aus den Königlichen Staatlichen Museen zu Berlin, Griechische Urkunden. 15 vols. Berlin: Weidmann, 1895–1937.
BHT	Beitrage Zur Historischen Theologie
BibInt	Biblical Interpretation
BMC	R. S. Poole et al., eds. A Catalogue of the Greek Coins in the British Museum. 29 vols. London: British Museum, 1873–1922.
BNP	Cancik, Hubert, ed. Brill's New Pauly: Encyclopedia of the Ancient World. 22 vols. Leiden: Brill, 2002–2011.
BNTC	Black's New Testament Commentaries
BTB	Biblical Theology Bulletin
ByzF	Byzantinische Forschungen
ByzZ	Byzantinische Zeitschrift
BZNW	Beihefte zur Zeitschrift für die neutestamentliche Wissenschaft
CBET	Contributions to Biblical Exegesis and Theology
CBQ	Catholic Biblical Quarterly
CCG	Cahiers du Centre Gustave Glotz
CECNT	Critical and Exegetical Commentary on the New Testament
CHC	Cambridge History of Christianity
CID	Corpus des Inscriptions de Delphes. 4 vols. Paris, 1977–
CIG	Boeckh, August, ed. Corpus Inscriptionum Graecarum. 4 vols. Berlin: Reimer, 1828–1877.
CIL	Corpus Inscriptionum Latinarum. Berlin, 1862–.

CIPh 2.1	Zannis, A., and Ch. Koukouli-Chrysanthaki. *Corpus des inscriptions grecques et latines de Philippes*. Vol. 1: *La cité grecque et macédonienne (inscriptions classiques et hellénistiques*. Athens: École française d'Athènes, forthcoming.
CIPh 2.2	Brélaz, Cédric. *Corpus des inscriptions grecques et latines de Philippes*. Vol. 2: *Le colonies romaine*. Part 1: *La vie publique de la colonie*. Athens: École française d'Athènes, 2014.
CIRB	Struve, V. V., ed. *Corpus Inscriptionum Regni Bosporani*. Moscow: Nauka, 1965.
ClAnt	*Classical Antiquity*
CNT	*Commentaire du Nouveau Testament*
ConBNT	*Coniectanea Neotestamentica*
CP	*Classical Philology*
CPR	*Corpus Papyrorum Raineri*. Vienna: Kaiserlich-königlichen Hof- und Staatsdruckerei, 1895–.
CQ	*Church Quarterly*
CRAI	*Comptes rendus de l'Académie des inscriptions et Belles-Lettres*
DAW	Heberdey, Rudolf, and Adolf Wilhelm. *Reisen in Kilikien*. Kaiserliche [Österreichische] Akademie der Wissenschaften, Philosophisch-historische Klasse, Denkschriften 44.6. Vienna, 1896.
EA	*Epigraphica Anatolica*
EC	*Early Christianity*
ECAM	Early Christianity in Asia Minor
ECL	Early Christianity and Its Literature
EGGNT	Exegetical Guide to the Greek New Testament
ETAM	Laminger-Pascher, G. *Die kaiserzeitlichen Inschriften Lykaoniens*. Fasc. 1: *Der Süden*. Ergänzungsbände zu den Tituli Asiae Minoris 15. Vienna: Österreichische Akademie der Wissenschaften, 1992.
ExpTim	*Expository Times*
F&H	*Food & History*
FD	*Fouilles de Delphes. 3. Épigraphie*. Paris, 1929–.
FRLANT	Forschungen zur Religion und Literatur des Alten und Neuen Testaments
FJTC	Flavius Josephus: Translation and Commentary

GRA	Kloppenborg, John S., Philip A. Harland, and Richard S. Ascough. *Greco-Roman Associations: Texts, Translations, and Commentary*. BZNW 181. Berlin: de Gruyter, 2011–.
HALOT	Koehler, Ludwig, Walter Baumgartner, and Johann J. Stamm. *The Hebrew and Aramaic Lexicon of the Old Testament*. Translated and edited under the supervision of Mervyn E. J. Richardson. 4 vols. Leiden: Brill, 1994–1999.
HDR	Harvard Dissertations in Religion
HNTC	Harper's New Testament Commentaries
HTR	*Harvard Theological Review*
HTS	Harvard Theological Studies
IBC	Interpretation: A Bible Commentary for Teaching and Preaching
ICC	International Critical Commentary
ICG	Breytenbach, Cilliers, Klaus Hallof, Ulrich Huttner, Jennifer Krumm, Stephen Mitchell, Julien M. Ogereau, Erkki Sironen, Marina Veksina, and Christiane Zimmermann, eds. *Inscriptiones Christianae Graecae (ICG): A Digital Collection of Greek Early Christian Inscriptions from Asia Minor and Greece*. Berlin: Edition Topoi, 2016, http://www.epigraph.topoi.org.
IDelos	Roussel, Pierre, and Marcel Launey. *Inscriptions de Délos: Décrets postérieurs à 166 av. J.-C. (nos. 1497–1524). Dédicaces postérieures à 166 av. J.-C. (nos. 1525–2219)*. Académie des Inscriptions et Belles-lettres. Paris: Librairie Ancienne Honoré Champion, 1937.
IDidyma	Rehm, Albert. *Didyma: Zweiter Teil; Die Inschriften*. Edited by Harder, Richard. Berlin: Verlag Gebr. Mann, 1958.
IEph	Engelmann, H., H. Wankel, and R. Merkelbach. *Die Inschriften von Ephesos*. Bonn: Habelt, 1979–1984.
IErythrai	Engelmann, Helmut, and Reinhold Merkelbach. *Die Inschriften von Erythrai und Klazomenai*. Bonn: Rudolf Habelt, 1972.

IG	*Inscriptiones Graecae. Editio Minor*. Berlin: de Gruyter, 1924–.
IGLSyr	*Inscriptiones grecques et latines de la Syrie*. Paris: Geuthner, 1929–.
IGRR	Cagnat, René, et al, ed. *Inscriptiones graecae ad res romanas pertinentes*. 3 vols. Paris: Leroux, 1906–1927.
IGUR	Moretti, L. *Inscriptiones graecae urbis romae*. 4 vols. Studi Pubblicati dall'Istituto Italiano per la Storia Antica 17, 22, 28, 47. Rome: Istututo Italiano per la Storia Antica, 1968.
IJRR	*Interdisciplinary Journal of Research on Religion*
IK	*Inschriften griechischer Städte aus Kleinasien*. Bonn, 1972–.
IKaunos	Marek, Christian. *Die Inschriften von Kaunos*. Vestigia: Beiträge zur alten Geschichte 55. Munich: Beck, 2006.
IKosS	Segre, Mario. *Iscrizioni di Cos*. Monografie della Scuola Archeologica di Atene e delle Missioni Italiane in Oriente 6 and 6.2. Rome: L'Erma di Bretschneider, 1993, 2007.
ILS	Dessau, H., ed. *Inscriptiones Latinae Selectae*. 3 vols. Berlin: Weidmann, 1892–1916.
ILycia	Petersen, Eugen, and Felix von Luschan. *Reisen in Lykien, Milyas und Kibyratien*. Reisen im Südwestlichen Kleinasien 2. Vienna: Codex-Verlag, 1889.
ILydiaHM	Herrmann, Peter, and Hasan Malay. *New Documents from Lydia*. Denkschriften der Österreichische Akademie der Wissenschaften, Philosophisch-Historische Klasse 340. Vienna: Verlag der Österreichischen Akademie der Wissenschaften, 2007.
IMakedD	Demitsas, M. G. Ἡ Μακεδονία ἐν λίθοις φθεγγομένοις καὶ μνημείοις σωζομένοις. Athens: Perre, 1896. Repr., *Sylloge inscriptionum graecarum et latinarum Macedoniae*. Chicago: Ares, 1980.
IMT	Barth, Matthias, and Josef Stauber. *Inschriften Mysia und Troas*. Munich: Leopold Wenger-Institut, 1993.
Int	*Interpretation*

ISmyrna	Petzl, Georg. *Die Inschriften von Smyrna*. 3 vols. Bonn: Habelt, 1982–1900.
JBL	*Journal of Biblical Literature*
JECS	*Journal of Early Christian Studies*
JETS	*Journal of the Evangelical Theological Society*
JFSR	*Journal of Feminist Studies in Religion*
JGRChJ	*Journal of Greco-Roman Christianity and Judaism*
JHS	*Journal of Hellenic Studies*
JÖAI	*Jahreshefte des Österreichischen archäologischen Instituts*
JRA	*Journal of Roman Archaeology*
JRASup	Journal of Roman Archaeology Supplements
JRS	*Journal of Roman Studies*
JSNT	*Journal for the Study of the New Testament*
JSNTSup	Journal for the Study of the New Testament Supplement Series
JTC	*Journal for Theology and the Church*
JTI	*Journal of Theological Interpretation*
KD	*Kerygma und Dogma*
LCL	Loeb Classical Library
LNTS	Library of New Testament Studies
LSJ	Liddell, Henry George, Robert Scott, Henry Stuart Jones. *A Greek-English Lexicon*. 9th ed. with revised supplement. Oxford: Clarendon, 1996.
MAMA	*Monumenta Asiae Minoris Antiqua*. Manchester: Manchester University Press, 1928–1993.
MDAI(A)	*Mitteilungen des Deutschen Archäologischen Instituts, Athenische Abteilung*
MIFAO	Mémoires publiés par les membres de l'Institut français d'archéologie orientale du Caire
MM	Moulton, James H., and George Milligan. *The Vocabulary of the Greek Testament*. London, 1930. Repr., Peabody, MA: Hendrickson, 1997.
NewDocs	Horsley, Greg H. R, and Stephen Llewelyn, eds. *New Documents Illustrating Early Christianity*. North Ryde, NSW: The Ancient History Documentary Research Centre, Macquarrie University, 1981–.
NICNT	New International Commentary on the New Testament

NICOT	New International Commentary on the Old Testament
NIDNTTE	Silva, Moisés, ed. *New International Dictionary of New Testament Theology and Exegesis*. 2nd ed. 5 vols. Grand Rapids: Zondervan, 2014.
NIGTC	New International Greek Testament Commentary
NovT	*Novum Testamentum*
NovTSup	Supplements to Novum Testamentum
NRSV	New Revised Standard Version
NTAbh	Neutestamentliche Abhandlungen
NTD	Das Neue Testament Deutsche
NTOA	Novum Testaumentum et Orbis Antiquus
NTS	*New Testament Studies*
OCM	Oxford Classical Monographs
OGIS	Dittenberger, Wilhelm. *Orientis Graeci Inscriptiones Selectae*. 2 vols. Leipzig, 1903–1905.
P.Col.	*Columbia Papyri*. 11 vols. New York, 1929–1998.
P.Giss.	Eger, O., E. Kornemann, and P. M. Meyer, eds. *Griechische Papyri im Museum des oberhessischen Geschichtsvereins zu Giessen*. Leipzig: Teubner, 1910–1912.
P.Lond.	*Greek Papyri in the British Museum*. 7 vols. London: British Museum Press, 1893–.
P.Oxy.	Grenfell, Bernard P., et al., eds. *The Oxyrhynchus Papyri*. London: Egypt Exploration Fund, 1898–.
P.Paris	Letronne, J. A., W. Brunet de Presle, and E. Egger, eds. *Notices et textes des papyrus du Musée du Louvre et de la Bibliothèque Impériale*. Paris: Institut de France, 1865.
P.Ross.Georg.	Zereteli, G., et al., eds. *Papyri russischer und georgischer Sammlungen*. 5 vols. Amsterdam: Hakkert, 1925–1935.
PAB	Potsdamer Altertumswissenschaftliche Beiträge
PBM	Paternoster Biblical Monographs
PG	Patrologia Graeca [= Patrologica Cursus Completus: Series Graeca]. Edited by Jacques-Paul Migne. 162 vols. Paris, 1857–1886.
PGL	Lampe, Geoffrey W. H. *Patristic Greek Lexicon*. Oxford: Clarendon, 1961.

PGM	Preisendanz, Karl, ed. *Papyri Graecae Magicae: Die griechischen Zauberpapyri.* 2nd ed. Stuttgart: Teubner, 1973–1974.
PRSt	*Perspectives in Religious Studies*
PTMS	Princeton Theological Monograph Series
PW	Wissowa, Georg, and Wilhelm Kroll. *Paulys Real-Enclopädie der classischen Altertumswissenschaft.* New ed. 50 vols. in 84 parts. Stuttgart: Metzler & Druckenmüller, 1894–1980.
RAC	*Reallexikon für Antike und Christentum*
REA	*Revue des études anciennes*
RECAM	Mitchell, S., ed. *Regional Epigraphic Catalogues of Asia Minor.* Vol. 2, *The Ankara District: The Inscriptions of North Galatia.* Oxford: Oxford University Press, 1982.
REG	*Revue des études grecques*
RGRW	Religions in the Graeco-Roman World
RIC	Mattingly, Harold, ed. *The Roman Imperial Coinage.* 10 vols. London: Spink, 1923–1994.
RICM	Feissel, Denis, ed. *Recueil des inscriptions chrétiennes de Macédoine du IIIe au VIe siècle.* BCHSupp 8. Athens: École Française d'Athènes, 1983.
RPC	Burnett, Andrew, et al., eds. *Roman Provincial Coinage.* London: British Museum Press; Paris: Bibliothèque Nationale, 1992–.
SAWW	*Sitzungsberichte des Österreichischen Akademie der Wissenschaften*
SB	Shackleton Bailey
SB	*Sammelbuch griechischer Urkunden aus Aegypten*
SBLDS	Society of Biblical Literature Dissertation Series
SCHNT	Studia ad Corpus Hellenisticum Novi Testamenti
SE	*Studia Evangelica I, II, III*
SEG	*Supplementum Epigraphicum Graecum*
SIG	Dittenberger, Wilhelm, ed. *Sylloge inscriptionum graecarum.* 4 vols. 3rd ed. Leipzig: Hirzel, 1915–1924.
SIRIS	Vidman, Ladislaus. *Sylloge inscriptionum religionis Isiacae et Sarapiacae.* Berlin: de Gruyter, 1969.
SJ	Studia Judaica

SNG ANS	*Sylloge Nummorum Graecorum*, American Numismatic Society
SNG Cop.	*Sylloge Nummorum Graecorum*, Copenhagen
SNG Evelp.	*Sylloge Nummorum Graecorum*, Réna H. Evelpidis
SNG Tüb.	*Sylloge Nummorum Graecorum*, Tübingen
SNTSMS	Society for New Testament Studies Monograph Series
SP	Sacra Pagina
ST	*Studia Evangelica*
Stud.Palmyr.	*Studia Palmyreńskie/Études palmyréniennes*. 10 vols. Warsaw: , 1966–1997.
SVTG	Septuaginta: Vetus Testamentum Graecum
TAM	*Tituli Asiae Minoris*. Vienna: Hoelder, Pichler, Tempsky, 1901–1989.
TAPA	*Transactions of the American Philological Association*
TAPS	Transactions of the American Philosophical Society
TDNT	Kittel, Gerhard, and Gerhard Friedrich, eds. *Theological Dictionary of the New Testament*. Translated by Geoffrey W. Bromiley. 10 vols. Grand Rapids: Eerdmans, 1964–1976.
TENTS	Texts and Editions for New Testament Study
TGST	Tesi Gregoriana, Serie Teologia
THKNT	Theologischer Handkommentar zum Neuen Testament
THNTC	Two Horizons New Testament Commentary
TLG	Berkowitz, Luci, and Karl A. Squitier, eds. *Thesaurus Linguae Graecae: Canon of Greek Authors and Works*. 3rd ed. New York: Oxford University Press, 1990.
TLNT	Spicq, C. *Theological Lexicon of the New Testament*. Translated and edited by J. D. Ernest. 3 vols. Peabody, MA: Hendrickson, 1994.
TNTC	Tyndale New Testament Commentaries
TynBul	*Tyndale Bulletin*
TZ	*Theologische Zeitschrift*
WBC	Word Biblical Commentary
WEC	Wycliffe Exegetical Commentary
WGRW	Writings from the Greco-Roman World

WGRWSup	Writings from the Greco-Roman World Supplement Series
WUNT	Wissenschaftliche Untersuchungen zum Neuen Testament
ZNW	*Zeitschrift für die neutestamentliche Wissenschaft und die Kunde der älteren Kirche*
ZPE	*Zeitschrift für Papyrologie und Epigraphik*

Excavating the Urban and Country Life of Roman Philippi and Its Territory

James R. Harrison

At the outset, this chapter will set forth the results of modern scholarship on the material culture of Philippi (its epigraphy, archaeology, numismatics), the incorporation of the results by New Testament scholars on Philippians, and life in the villages surrounding the Roman colony. From there we will discuss a series of case studies pertinent to the background of the epistle: the imperial cult; indigenous and nonindigenous religions in the city; the elites and nonelites; the associations of Philippi; games, spectacles, and entertainment; and, last, the ticklish issue of where the Praetorian Guard and *familia Caesaris*, both mentioned in the letter, are actually situated. The aim is to help New Testament scholars to appreciate better the great wealth provided by now more than a century's archaeological investigation of ancient Philippi, a repository of invaluable evidence that in recent years is gratifyingly much better utilized in the exegesis of Philippians.

1. Introduction: A Profile of Ancient Philippi and Paul's Letter to the Philippians in Modern Scholarship

1.1. Modern Scholarship on the Material Culture of Philippi and Its Environs

1.1.1. The Inscriptions of Philippi

The history of scholarship on ancient Philippi will remain forever indebted to Paul Collart and Philip Lemerle because of their total mastery of the inscriptional and archaeological evidence relating to Philippi.

After editing significant collections of the Philippian inscriptions early last century, each scholar published his magnum opus on Philippi,[1] works that to this very day remain indispensable for scholars studying the Roman colony. In recent years, however, the pioneering work of Collart and Lemerle has been followed up by two outstanding collections of the epigraphic evidence that have changed the face of Philippian studies.

First, the entire corpus of the Philippian inscriptions, their villages, and the honorific inscriptions of Philippian luminaries from overseas has been collated by Peter Pilhofer.[2] Pilhofer has placed Philippian and classical scholars in his debt because of his German translations of each Latin and Greek inscription, his succinct notes on the texts, and his invaluable nine indexes. The latter provide a mine of information on various motifs, individuals, and geographical locations in the corpus, allowing scholars to identify within Pilhofer's volume the epigraphic evidence and its various editions cited in the secondary literature of the last century. Until Pilhofer, epigraphic publications on Philippi had primarily appeared in

---

1. Paul Collart, "Inscriptions de Philippes, I," *BCH* 56 (1932): 192–231; Collart, "Inscriptions de Philippes, II," *BCH* 57 (1933): 313–79; Collart, "Inscriptions de Philippes, IV," *BCH* 62 (1938): 409–32. For vol. 3 in the series, see Michel Feyel and Jacques Coupry, "Inscriptions de Philippes, III," *BCH* 60 (1936): 37–58. Paul Lemerle, "Inscriptions latines et grecques de Philippes. I. Inscriptions latines," *BCH* 58 (1934): 448–83; Lemerle, "Inscriptions latines et grecques de Philippes. II. Inscriptions latines," *BCH* 59 (1935): 126–64; Lemerle, "Inscriptions latines et grecques de Philippes," *BCH* 61 (1937): 410–20; see also Lemerle, "Le testament d'un Thrace à Philippes," *BCH* 60 (1936): 337–43. For the Christian inscriptions of Philippi, see *RICM*. For further insight into the development of Christianity at Philippi in the later period, see in the essay by Julien Ogereau, "The Social Constituency and Membership of the First Christian Groups at Philippi: A Literary and Epigraphic Survey," in this volume. See also the popular book of Eduard Verhoef, *Philippi: How Christianity Began in Europe; The Epistle to the Philippians and the Excavations at Philippi* (London: Bloomsbury, 2013). Paul Collart, *Philippes et la Macédoine orientale à l'époque chrétienne et byzantine: Recheches d'histoire et d'archéologie* (Paris: de Boccard, 1945). Even though Lemerle's research is not focused on the imperial Philippi of Paul's day, he nevertheless devotes an extensive and valuable discussion to Paul (7–68), before proceeding to the time of Constantine onwards. A series of essays on Pauline Philippi are found in Charalambos Bakirtzis and Helmut Koester, eds., *Philippi at the Time of Paul and after His Death* (Harrisburg, PA: Trinity Press International, 1998). See now the essay of Cédric Brélaz, "First-Century Philippi: Contextualizing Paul's Visit," in this volume.

2. Peter Pilhofer, *Philippi*, vol. 2, *Katalog der Inschriften von Philippi*, 2nd ed., WUNT 119 (Tübingen: Mohr Siebeck, 2009).

the *Bulletin de correspondance hellénique*, now conveniently online for everyone through Perseus Digital Library.

Second, Cédric Brélaz has collected a new edition of the Latin and Greek Philippian inscriptions for Roman Philippi,[3] adding new, unedited texts that have appeared since the publication of Pilhofer's volume, with incisive discussions of each text in its Roman colonial context. Consequently, Brélaz has opened up for classical and New Testament scholars the Thracian and Greek dimensions of the Philippian inscriptions, Philippi's indigenous and imperial gods, the career paths and familial connections of the elites, the slaves at the base of the social pyramid, and the intricate operations of honorific culture, among many other topics. Philippian commentators and scholars now can make use of this rich arsenal of epigraphic evidence for the light it throws on exegetical and social issues.

But how has the archaeological investigation at Philippi proceeded over the last century? Are we better placed to understand the Julio-Claudian context of Paul's letter to the Philippians?

1.1.2. The Archaeology of Philippi

Abandoned in the fourteenth century, Philippi was studied for the first time by Léon Heuzey and Honoré Daumet in 1861.[4] However, systematic excavation of the site officially began with the French School at Athens in 1914, though with two interruptions (1914–1920, 1924–1927). Notwithstanding, there was a long cycle of discovery extending until its last campaign of the school in 1937, when the Second World War provided a definitive interruption. During this period the following sites were excavated.

1. The citadel of the acropolis, the west gate with the streets of the city, and the marsh gate;[5]

---

3. See *CIPh* 2.2. Two more epigraphic volumes will appear. The first is *CIPh* 2.1. A third volume of Philippian inscriptions, edited by C. Brélaz and C. Sarrazanas (*CIPh* 2.3), will review the inscriptions from the paleo-Christian and proto-Byzantine period.

4. Léon Heuzey and Honoré Daumet, *Mission archéologique de Macédonie* (Paris: Firmin-Didot et Cie, 1876).

5. Paul Lemerle and Henri Ducoux, "L'acropole et l'enceinte haute de Philippes," *BCH* 62 (1938): 4–19; Jacques Roger, "L'enceinte basse de Philippes," *BCH* 62 (1938): 20–41; Jacques Coupry "Sondage à l'ouest du forum de Philippes," *BCH* 62 (1938): 42–50.

2. The sanctuary of the Egyptian gods;[6]
3. The sanctuaries and cave reliefs at the acropolis (which were only given definitive publication in 1975 by Paul Collart and Pierre Ducrey);[7]
4. The theater (with the Ephoria of Prehistoric and Classical Antiquities at Kavala only properly restoring the edifice in 1957);[8]
5. The forum (though little was published until the definitive works of Michel Sève and Patrick Weber from 1986 onwards);[9]
6. The *macellum* (commercial market);[10]
7. The Byzantine basilicas;[11]
8. Other diverse finds such as the palestra, with its spectacular latrines at forty-two places, as well as the reliefs of the Maison aux fauves ("House with wild animals") and the (formerly considered Hellenistic but now identified as a Roman) hero monument (*heroon*).[12]

---

6. Paul Collart, "Le sanctuaire des dieux égyptiens à Philippes," *BCH* 53 (1929): 70–100.

7. Paul Collart and Pierre Ducrey, *Philippes I: Les reliefs rupestres*, BCHSupp 2 (Athens: École française d'Athènes, 1975).

8. Paul Collart, "Le theatre de Philippes," *BCH* 52 (1928): 74–124.

9. Michel Sève and Patrick Weber, *Guide du forum de Philippes*, Sites et Monuments 18 (Athens: École française d'Athènes, 2012), with further publication of both authors in the bibliography (87–88), including, especially, Michel Sève and Patrick Weber, "Le côté Nord du Forum de Philippes," *BCH* 110 (1986): 531–81; Michel Sève and Patrick Weber, "Un monument honorifique au forum de Philippes," *BCH* 112 (1988): 467–79. See also E. Lapalus, "Tête de bronze de Philippes (Macédoine)," *BCH* 56 (1932): 360–71; Lapalus, "Sculptures de Philippes," *BCH* 59 (1935): 175–92; Coupry, "Sondage l'ouest du forum de Philippes."

10. Collart, *Philippes*, 364; Georgios Gournaris and Emmanuela Gounari, *Philippi: Archaeological Guide* (Thessalonica: University Studio, 2004), 57–59.

11. For Basilica A, see Gournaris and Gounari, *Philippi*, 39–44; Collart, *Philippes*, 381–412; Lemerle, *Philippes et la Macédoine orientale*, 283–412. For Basilica B, see Gournaris and Gounari, *Philippi*, 51–56; Collart, *Philippes*, 413–513; Lemerle, *Philippes et la Macédoine orientale*, 415–513. For Basilica C, see Gournaris and Gounari, *Philippi*, 89–91; Peter Pilhofer, *Philippi*, vol. 1, *Die erste christliche Gemeinde Europas*, WUNT 87 (Tübingen: Mohr Siebeck, 1995), 24. For the basilica of Philippi outside the walls, see Gournaris and Gounari, *Philippi*, 101–4; Pilhofer, *Philippi*, 1:106. See also Géza Feher, "À propos des inscriptions protobulgares de la basilique de Philippes," *BCH* 59 (1935): 165–74.

12. Paul Lemerle, "Palestre romaine à Philippes," *BCH* 61 (1937): 86–102. On the urban villa called the "House of the wild animals," see *Archaeological Site of Philippi:*

The long rupture caused to the work of French School at Athens at Philippi by World War II finally came to an end when work recommenced at the site in 1968. Researchers have produced new publications on the city again, and the school celebrated its centenary of excavations in 2014.[13] The rebirth of the school's operations was further crowned with honor when the Committee of the UNESCO World Heritage Monuments listed Philippi as a world heritage site at its 2016 meeting (10–17 July) in Istanbul.[14] We have already noted the important recent publications of the French School at Athens by Collart and Ducrey (*Philippes I: Les reliefs rupestres*), Sève and Weber (*Guide du forum de Philippes*), and Sève (*1914–2014: Philippes, ΦΙΛΙΠΠΟΙ, Philippi*). In 2016 another major volume of essays by well-known scholars on the history and archaeology of Philippi was published by the French School at Athens, edited by Julien Fournier.[15] We now await the arrival of a Brill collection of English scholarship covering the sweep of Philippi's social and religious history and archaeology, spanning its transition from a Roman colony to a Christian community, as an English counterpart to Fournier's volume.[16] Last, from 1958 until 1980, the Greek Archaeological Society and Aristotle University of Thessaloniki unearthed the Octagon complex, a bath building, the purported bishop's residence, and—in subsequent excavations by Aristotle University (1988–2002)—early Christian *insulae*, houses and workshops, and possibly some unidentified buildings from the imperial period.[17]

Nomination for Inscription on the UNESCO World Heritage List, ed. Archaeological Lists Fund (Athens: Hellenic Republic—Ministry of Culture and Sports, 2016), 51–52. For the website, see https://tinyurl.com/SBL4216a. On the *heroon*, see Collart, *Philippes*, 177, 369–70; Sève and Weber, "Le côté Nord du Forum *de Philippes*," 536–44; Gournaris and Gounari, *Philippi*, 36–37.

13. For a splendid coverage of the excavations, see Michel Sève, *1914–2014: Philippes, ΦΙΛΙΠΠΟΙ, Philippi; One Hundred Years of French Research* (Athens: École française d'Athènes, 2014).

14. For the detailed application, see the PDF noted above (n. 12): *Archaeological Site of Philippi: Nomination for Inscription on the UNESCO World Heritage List*.

15. Julien Fournier, ed., *Philippes, de la préhistoire à Byzance: études d'archéologie et d'histoire*, BCHSupp 55 (Athens: École française d'Athènes, 2016).

16. Steven J. Friesen et al., eds., *Philippi, from Colonia Augusta to Communitas Christiana: Religion and Society in Transition* (Leiden: Brill, forthcoming).

17. For the Greek publications on these finds, see Emmanouela Gounari, "The Roman Mosaics from Philippi: Evidence of the Presence of the Romans in the City," *Bollettino di Archeologia On Line* (2010): 27 n. 6, https://tinyurl.com/SBL4216b. For the Octagon complex (or *martyrion*), see Gournaris and Gounari, *Philippi*, 66–80;

There remains much to be understood about the material remains of Philippi. But, given the substantial gains above, it could be concluded that we stand in a privileged position for understanding Paul's letter to the house churches in the city because of over one hundred years of exploration of the site. There are real elements of truth to this observation for the Roman colony of the second century CE onwards, but, unfortunately, it is a premature conclusion for our understanding of Paul's Philippi. As Laura Nasrallah has observed, the vast bulk of the archaeological remains at Philippi come from the Antonine period of the second century CE, as opposed to the Julio-Claudian era of the apostle Paul.[18] So, to cite Nasrallah's two examples, the Antonine Forum has the same general plan as its Julio-Claudian counterpart, but nevertheless it has a larger central square; the rock-cut reliefs, valuable evidence for the gods worshiped at Philippi, span an extensive period ranging from the late first century to the third century CE. In other words, there are elements of historical continuity and discontinuity that we must respect in our discussion, rather than naively assuming that we can just read back into Paul's era the social and religious situation from the later Philippian archaeological evidence. We should therefore pay close attention to the first-century CE (and specifically Julio-Claudian) inscriptions, although these are also vastly outnumbered by their second- and third-century CE successors, along with the relevant numismatic evidence from the first-century Roman colony. Then we can reconstruct the historical, social, and religious context of Paul's city with more confidence, even if the portrait is minimalist.

We turn now to the Julio-Claudian numismatic issues from colonial Philippi. What is revealed about the foundation of the Roman colony, and how does the propaganda of Augustus eclipse the pre-Actium claims to

---

Pilhofer, *Philippi*, 1:16–23; Charalambos Bakirtzis, "Paul and Philippi: The Archaeological Evidence," in Bakirtzis and Koester, *Philippi at the Time of Paul*, 37–48. On the baths (the Valaneion), see Gournaris and Gounari, *Philippi*, 81–88; M. Müller-Wiener, "Bischofsresidenz des 4.–7. Jhs. im Östlichen Mittelmeer-Raum," in *Actes du XIe congrès international d'archéologie chrétienne (Lyon, Vienne, Grenoble, Genève, Aoste 1986*, Publications de l'École française de Rome 123 (Rome: École Française de Rome, 1989), 657–67. On the subsequent excavations by Aristotle University (1988–2002), see Gournaris and Gounari, *Philippi*, 92–104.

18. Laura S. Nasrallah, "Spatial Perspectives: Space and Ideology in Roman Philippi," in *Studying Paul's Letters: Contemporary Perspectives and Methods*, ed. Jospeh A. Marchal (Minneapolis: Fortress, 2012), 59–60.

priority made by his triumviral rival for empire after 42 BCE, the Roman general Antony?

1.1.3. The Coinage of Julio-Claudian Philippi

Three coin issues (leaded bronzes) from Julio-Claudian Philippi show the laureate head of Antony on the right side of the obverse of the first coins of the colony (*RPC* 1.1646–49). The legend on this side of the coin shows the letters *AICVP*, which, expanded, is *A[ntonii] I[ussu] C[olonia] V[ictrix] P[hilippensis]* ("by command of Antony, Victory Colony of Philippi"). Undoubtedly, this alludes to the fact that Antony was considered the founder of the colony, who, in 42 BCE, had been victorious over Cassius and Brutus on the marshy plains to the southwest of the city.

The reverse sides of the Antony issues, however, show a variety of important colonial motifs. On the right side of *RPC* 1.1646 we see a man with a veiled head plowing with two oxen. The legend, *Q PAQVIVS RVF C D LEG*, which appears on each Antony issue, represents the name of the issuer of the coin (*Q. Paquius R[ufus]*). The two letters *C D* are more ambiguous in this instance, being viably restored either as *coloniae deducendae* or *coloniam deduxit* (*RPC* 1.307). If the former is correct, the phrase probably alludes to the *triumviri coloniae deducendae* ("three men [charged with the oversight] to found a colony"), whereas, if the latter is correct, it means "he founded the colony." Either way, Antony's pivotal role in founding the colony is underscored, with the plow being a symbol of the *sulcus primigenius*,[19] that is, the first furrow dug at the colony. This furrow marked the foundation of the colony: that is, the groove symbolically marked the divide between the territory within Philippi's boundary and the adjoining lands outside the boundary.[20] Further, the plow symbolism highlights the prosperous agricultural life of the colonists that would emerge over time at Philippi. Moreover, the veiled head of the man plowing—a headdress characteristic of Roman depictions of their

---

19. Szymon Jellonek, "The Coins of Philippi: An Example of Colonial Coinage," in *Pecunia Omnes Vincit: The Coins as an Evidence of Propaganda, Reorganization and Forgery; Conference Proceedings of the Second International Numismatics Conference: Kraków 29–30 May 2015*, ed. Barbara Zajac et al. (Kraków: Institute of Archaeology, Jagiellonian University, 2017), 55.

20. Nasrallah, "Spatial Perspectives," 63.

priests[21]—points to the blessing of the Roman gods on the colony's development. The truncated symbol of the plow on the reverse of *RPC* 1.1648, which bears the identical legend, conveys the same foundational and religious message as the larger portrait of *RPC* 1.1646.

Another Antony issue (*RPC* 1.1647) displays on the reverse a togate figure seated left on a chair holding up a writing board, with an urn at his feet. The editors of *Roman Provincial Coinage* suggest that this is "a scene which may represent the giving out of allotments by lot" to Antony's veterans (*RPC* 1.307–8). The final Antony issue, *RPC* 1.1649, cleverly combines elements of both of the larger obverse portraits in its portraiture.[22] It dispenses with Antony's head on the obverse and replaces it with the obverse image of the urn (*RPC* 1.1647), whereas the reverse shows a victory wreath, an allusion to the victory of Antony at Philippi, given the absence of any mention of the triumvir on the obverse on the coin. These four issues of Antony are remarkable for the integration of Antony's propaganda throughout. The two larger obverse images duplicated in miniature on the two other coins (the plow, the urn), the potent use of symbolism (the plow, the veiled togate figure, the victory wreath as a substitute for Antony's obverse portrait), and foundational colonial rituals (the lot allocation to veterans) convey the message that Rome not only rules Philippi but that Philippi as a colony replicates Rome in miniature in Macedonia. The absence of any of the traditional Greek gods associated with the original establishment of the city under Philipp II (Heracles, Apollo) is telling.[23] As Sophia Kremydi-Sicilianou notes, colonies such as Philippi "were keen on proclaiming their military profile as an aspect of their civic identity … apart from the Thracian Hero Avlonites, no other local cult is found on issues of Philippi."[24]

---

21. An uncertain Philippian issue of Augustus shows two priests plowing on the reverse (*RPC* 1.1656). For a relief of the veiled Augustus as an *augur* with his priestly *lituus*, see Paul Zanker, *The Power of Images in the Age of Augustus*, trans. Alan Shapiro (Ann Arbor: University of Michigan Press, 1988), 125 fig. 101. Additionally, see the veiled bust of Augustus at Corinth (Zanker, *Power of Images*, 301 fig. 232). See also the veiled statue of Tiberius as Pontifex Maximus at the John Paul Getty Museum at https://tinyurl.com/SBL4216c.

22. See also *RPC* 1.308.

23. See n. 19 above.

24. Sophia Kremydi-Sicilianou, "'Belonging' to Rome, "Remaining' Greek: Coinage and Identity in Roman Macedonia," in *Coinage and Identity in the Roman Prov-*

In the case of our single Augustan issue from Philippi (*RPC* 1.1650), the obverse legend shows the laureate head of Augustus to the right. The legend, COL AVG IVL PHIL IVSSV AVG, expanded as *Col*[*onia*] *Aug*[*usta*] *Iul*[*ia*] *Phil*[*ippensis*] *Iussu Aug*[*usti*], means "The Augustan Julian Colony of Philippi, by command of Augustus." Here the Augustan propaganda forcefully asserts that when Octavian was given the honorific "Augustus" in 27 BCE, which further enhanced his extraordinary status after his victory over Antony and Cleopatra at Actium (31 BCE), the name of the colony was changed in three significant ways. The new name reflected (1) Augustus's mediation as Pontifex Maximus with the gods on behalf of Roman citizens at Rome and her colonies (by virtue of the lexical association of *Augustus* with augury); (2) the establishment of his Julian dynasty through his adoptive and apotheosized father, Julius Caesar; (3) the overturning of the command of Antony (*A*[*ntonii*] *I*[*ussu*]) by the superior command of Augustus (*Iussu Aug*[*usti*]). Clearly, then, Augustus was rewriting the history of the colony of Philippi because of his unprecedented victory at Actium over Antony.

In support of this message on the obverse, the reverse of the coin shows three bases, on the middle one of which the statue of Augustus stands in military garb. There the statue of Augustus, identified by *AUG*[*ustus*] *DIVI F*[*ilius*] ("Augustus the son of a God"), is either given a gesture of coronation or saluted by the togate statue of the apotheosized Divus Julius, identified by *DIVO IVL*[*ius*]. Thus the apotheosized Julius brings victory to his adopted son and vice-regent on earth as the *real* victor at Philippi, rebutting the prior claim of Antony in 42 BCE to be the city's founder.[25] The fact that the statues of Augustus and Julius Caesar are presented as being on a single base probably indicates that the same statue was also present on a base in the Julio-Claudian forum at Philippi, given that the other two accompanying bases are empty.[26] Indeed, the cuirassed statue of

---

inces, ed. Christopher Howgego, Volker Heuchert, and Andrew Burnett (Oxford: Oxford University Press, 2005), 100.

25. Jellonek, "Coins of Philippi," 52.

26. Jellonek, "Coins of Philippi," 52. Lewis and Bolden write: "This statue would have been erected in the forum of Philippi in gratitude for Augustus' re-establishment of the colony." Peter E. Lewis and Ron Bolden, *The Pocket Guide to St. Paul* (Kent Town, Australia: Wakefield, 2001), 109.

Augustus, because of its distinctive gait on the coin, could have been modeled in the famous Prima Porta statue of the Roman ruler.[27]

But what type of ritual is being depicted on the obverse? Is it a coronation ritual or an *adlocutio* (i.e., an address given by a general, usually the Roman ruler, to his assembled army and legions)?[28] Since only the hand of Julius Caesar is held above the head of Augustus, with no visible evidence of a wreath being held,[29] the *adlocutio*, in my opinion, is more likely than a coronation, given the Roman rejection of monarchical rule in 510 BCE. The interpretation of this coin remains difficult, and we should not automatically rule out the possibility that Julius Caesar, for example, is giving Augustus instead the *corona civica*, a crown widely depicted in Augustan iconography.[30] However, I would argue, in agreement with the *adlocutio* proposal, that Julius Caesar, as an apotheosized god, is commissioning his adopted son for rule in a public address to the (implied) assembled Philippian citizens in the forum. It is also important to realize that Claudian and Neronian coins replicate the same scene (*RPC* 1.1653–55). Significantly, this is the only issue where a Julian family member appears alongside Augustus in the Philippian coins of the Julio-Claudian period, excluding, of course, the appearance of Tiberius and Drusus in the coins of uncertain Philippian provenance.[31] In sum, the apotheosized Julius Caesar and Augustus remained the legitimating paradigm to be invoked by all subsequent Julio-Claudian rulers in their propaganda in the Roman colony of Philippi.[32]

Last, the obverse of either a Claudian or Neronian coin (*RPC* 1.1651) shows a winged Victory holding a wreath and palm branch, with *VIC[toria]* and *AUG[usti]* respectively on either side of the Victory. Once again the

---

27. Jellonek, "Coins of Philippi," 52.

28. Jellonek, "Coins of Philippi," 52

29. Jellonek, "Coins of Philippi," 53. For the iconography, see Zanker, *Power of Images*, 93.

30. Jellonek is doubtful about the *adlocutio* option interpretatively ("Coins of Philippi," 54). In defense of his stance, we should not forget that a later relief depicts Nero being crowned with a wreath by his goddess-like mother, Agrippina (Zanker, *Power of Images*, 303 fig. 235).

31. Among the uncertain Philippian coins there is reference to Tiberius and Drusus (*RPC* 1.1658–59).

32. To cite the three Flavian examples from the reigns of Vespasian and Domitian (*RPC* 2.343–45), each issue replicates on the reverse the Julius Caesar-Augustan statue discussed above (*RPC* 1.1650).

reestablishment of the colony of Philippi in 27 BCE because of Augustus's victory over Antony and Cleopatra at Actium is emphasized. Lewis and Bolden suggest that because the Victory figure stands on a base, there was probably an identical statue in the Julio-Claudian forum of Philippi.[33] Again, close attention to the numismatic evidence perhaps provides us with unexpected access to the first-century statuary of the Julio-Claudian forum now lost to us at Philippi. Three military standards are also shown, surrounded by the legend COHOR PRAE PHIL, which, expanded, refers to *Cohor*[*tes*] *Prae*[*toriae*] *Phil*[*ippensis*] ("Praetorian Cohorts of Philippi"). Not only is the military nature of the colony reinforced here by this reference to the praetorian cohorts, but also the increasing power of the Praetorian Guard back at Rome, including its ability to make and unmake emperors in the Julio-Claudian period, could have been evoked in the minds of everyday Philippians.[34]

We have seen, then, the powerful contribution that Philippian coinage makes to our understanding of the military ethos of Julio-Claudian Philippi, supplanting the old Greek deities on the coins of Philip II, and, in the case of the Julio-Claudian coins, excising any reference to the indigenous gods. But what has recent New Testament scholarship revealed about the colony of Philippi at the time of Paul's visit?

1.1.4. New Testament Scholarship on the Archaeology, Inscriptions, and Coinage of Philippi and Its Intersection with Acts 16:11–40 and the Epistle to the Philippians

Three seminal coverages of the Roman colony of Philippi have explored the intersection of its documentary, archaeological, numismatic, and literary evidence with Paul's letter to the Philippians in considerable depth. After an exhaustive examination of the archaeological, religious, and colonial context of the city, Pilhofer explores the evidence of Acts, Philippians, and Polycarp for the development of the early Christian community in its urban and village context, insightfully isolating important aspects of Philippian exegesis.[35] By contrast, Lukas Bormann, after discussing the

---

33. Lewis and Bolden, *Pocket Guide to St Paul*, 110.

34. For a discussion of *RPC* 1.651, its relation to Phil 1:13 and Vindolanda Tablet 2.154, and whether it is a coin minted in the Vespasian era, see Paul A. Holloway, "Vindolanda Tablet 2.154, *RPC* 1651, and the Provenance of Philippians," in this volume.

35. Pilhofer, *Philippi*, 1:114–228; on exegesis, see 1:114–52. For the archaeologi-

historical, imperial and cultic background of Philippi, focuses more narrowly on the thank-you letter of Phil 4:10–20, as well as the friendship, patron-client, reciprocity, and *societas* conventions underlying the epistle.[36] Peter Oakes analyzes the social makeup of the believing community at Philippi, estimating the percentages that belonged to the various social groups comprising the city.[37] He concludes that rather than suffering at the hands of fellow townspeople, the "main long-term suffering was likely to be economic" due to poverty (see 2 Cor 8:1–4; Phil 2:4).[38] From there Oakes proceeds to an investigation of Phil 2:5–11 and 3:20–21. He looks at the Philippian imperial context of each pericope, including their numismatic context, concluding that Paul's presentation in 2:5–11 in particular "fits an Imperial figure much more closely than it does any other figure."[39] More generally, Mikael Tellbe and Craig de Vos have usefully provided succinct coverages of the social, religious, and political life of Philippi, focusing on either community conflicts or relations between the state and the Jewish synagogue.[40] Each work throws insight into social relations in the colony.

Other monographs have studied elements of Philippian exegesis intensively, either bringing local evidence to bear or ranging widely across the Greco-Roman inscriptions and papyri in their analysis. We will necessarily be selective in our coverage below.[41] Joseph Hellerman has innovatively

---

cal, religious, and colonial context, see Pilhofer, *Philippi*, 1:15–113. For a response to the essays of Kathy Ehrensperger, Paul Holloway, and Julien Ogereau in this volume, see also the accompanying essay of Angela Standhartinger.

36. Lukas Bormann, *Philippi: Stadt und Christengemeinde zur Zeit des Paulus*, NovTSup 58 (Leiden: Brill, 1995), 11–67, 127–60, 161–205.

37. Peter Oakes, *Philippians: From People to Letter*, SNTSMS 110 (Cambridge: Cambridge University Press, 2001), 1–76. See also the discussion of the social composition of the Philippian church in Davorin Peterlin, *Paul's Letter to the Philippians in the Light of Disunity in the Church*, NovTSup 79 (Leiden: Brill, 1995), 135–70.

38. Oakes, *Philippians*, 211. See Oakes, "The Economic Situation of the Philippian Christians," in *The People beside Paul: The Philippian Assembly and History from Below*, ed. Joseph A. Marchal, ECL (Atlanta: SBL Press, 2015), 63–98.

39. Oakes, *Philippians*, 129–74. For the numismatic context, see 145, 148, 153, 157.

40. Craig Steven de Vos, *Church and Community Conflicts: The Relationships of the Thessalonian, Corinthian, and Philippian Churches with Their Wider Civic Communities*, SBLDS 168 (Atlanta: Scholars Press, 1999), 233–87; Mikael Tellbe, *Paul between Synagogue and State: Christians, Jews, and Civic Authorities in 1 Thessalonians, Romans, and Philippians*, ConBNT 34 (Stockholm: Almqvist & Wiksell, 2001), 141–277.

41. Note, for example, L. Gregory Bloomquist, *The Function of Suffering in Phi-*

approached Phil 2:5–11 against the backdrop of the Philippian honorific inscriptions.[42] Hellerman argues that the apostle Paul, in a radical upending of the traditional *cursus honorum* (course of offices: literally, "course of honors") on the public monuments, depicted Christ's cruciform career in 2:5–11 as a *cursus pudorum* (course of shame). Thus Paul challenged the Philippian believers with a "decidedly subversive and anti-traditional message" by advocating Christ's radical renunciation of status as a nonnegotiable paradigm for their discipleship.[43]

Another seminal piece of Philippian scholarship is Richard Ascough's investigation of the Thessalonian and Philippian house churches from the perspective of the Macedonian association inscriptions.[44] In the case of Philippi, Ascough argues that Paul's gender-inclusive approach to ecclesial leadership (Phil 4:2) reflects association patterns. Furthermore, the titles of ἐπίσκοπος and διάκονος (Phil 1:1) are found in association decrees, along with analogous tendencies toward internal disharmony (2:14), as well as collections for special projects (Phil 4:10–20; see also 2 Cor 8:1–5; 11:9) and the designation of gods as σωτήρ (3:20). While LXX distinctives

---

lippians, JSNTSup 78 (Sheffield: Sheffield Academic, 1993); G. W. Peterman, *Paul's Gift from Philippi: Conventions of Gift Exchange and Christian Giving*, SNTSMS 92 (Cambridge: Cambridge University Press, 1997); Paul A. Holloway, *Consolation in Philippians: Philosophical Sources and Rhetorical Strategy*, SNTSMS 112 (Cambridge: Cambridge University Press, 2001); David E. Briones, *Paul's Financial Policy: A Sociotheological Approach*, LNTS 494 (New York: Bloomsbury, 2013). Two examples of recent PhD dissertations engaging with the Philippian epigraphic context are Gennadi Andreyevich Sergienko, "'Our *Politeuma* Is in Heaven!': Paul's Polemical Engagement with the 'Enemies of the Cross of Christ' in Philippians 3:18–20" (PhD diss., Fuller Theological Seminary, 2011); Dierk Mueller, "Military Images in Paul's Letter to the Philippians" (PhD diss., University of Pretoria, 2013).

42. Joseph H. Hellerman, *Reconstructing Honor in Roman Philippi: Carmen Christi as Cursus Pudorum*, SNTSMS 132 (Cambridge: Cambridge University Press, 2005), 34–109.

43. Hellerman, *Reconstructing Honor in Roman Philippi*, 166.

44. See Richard S. Ascough, *Paul's Macedonian Associations: The Social Context of Philippians and 1 Thessalonians*, WUNT 2/161 (Tübingen: Mohr Siebeck, 2003), 15–109, on the associations, and 110–61, on the Philippian church. See also See Eduard Verhoef, "Collaboration of 'Samothrakiasts' and Christians in Philippi," in Marchal, *People beside Paul*, 83–98, and the response of Ascough in "Response: Broadening the Socioeconomic and Religious Context at Philippi," in Marchal, *People beside Paul*, 99–106. Additionally, see Richard S. Ascough, "Did the Philippian Christ Group Know It Was a 'Missionary' Society?," in this volume.

have to be factored in (e.g., the use of σωτήρ), the considerable similarities between Paul's associations of believers and their Philippian counterparts should not be underestimated.

Julian Ogereau, reassessing the *societas* thesis of Paul J. Sampley,[45] has explored its implications for Philippian studies on the basis of a masterful coverage of the inscriptions and papyri. Ogereau has convincingly argued that the Roman legal model of *societas*—though confined to the Philippian house churches alone—provided Paul with a useful model for his innovative social relations in the city.[46] Accordingly, Paul came to a *societas evangeli* arrangement with the Philippians (Phil 4:10–20), where he provides his labor and skills, and the Philippians financially sponsor the apostle in his evangelistic mission.[47]

Finally, three books have explored the religious place of Philippian women in the Roman colony from the perspective of the indigenous cults, including the epigraphic renderings of the Dionysian mysteries and reliefs of the Diana cult, along with her female worshipers, at the acropolis. The place of Philippian women in the church—Lydia (Acts 16:13–15),[48] Syntyche, and Euodia (Phil 4:2)—demonstrates Paul's interest in women in his missionary outreach and, subsequently, his sponsorship of their role in local ecclesial leadership. In making these decisions, therefore, Paul sociologically reflects in his ministry at Philippi the elevated social, religious, and political status accorded more widely to Macedonian women.[49]

In conclusion, we are seeing here how New Testament scholars have come to an increasing appreciation of the rich and pioneering work of

---

45. Paul J. Sampley, *Pauline Partnership in Christ: Christian Community and Commitment in Light of Roman Law* (Philadelphia: Fortress, 1980).

46. Julien M. Ogereau, *Paul's Koinonia with the Philippians: A Socio-historical Investigation of a Pauline Economic Partnership*, WUNT 2/377 (Tübingen: Mohr Siebeck, 2014), 347.

47. Ogereau, *Paul's Koinonia with the Philippians*, 349.

48. Lilian Portefaix, *Sisters Rejoice: Paul's Letter to the Philippians and Luke-Acts as Received by First-Century Philippian Women*, ConBNT 20 (Stockholm: Almqvist & Wiksell, 1988); Valerie A. Abrahamsen, *Women and Worship at Philippi: Diana/Artemis and Other Cults in the Early Christian Era* (Portland, ME: Astarte Shell, 1995); Jason T. Lamoreaux, *Ritual, Women, and Philippi: Reimagining the Early Philippian Community*, Matrix: The Bible in Mediterranean Context 8 (Eugene, OR: Cascade, 2013). Additionally, see Valerie Abrahamsen, "Priestesses and Other Female Cult Leaders at Philippi in the Early Christian Era," in Marchal, *People beside Paul*, 25–62.

49. Sergienko, "'Our *Politeuma* Is in Heaven!,'" 123–28.

Collart and Lemerle as they undertake exegesis of Philippians. This will continue to grow as scholars make further use of superb epigraphic collections of Pilhofer and Brélaz and learn from the continued work of the French School of Athens at the site of Philippi. The rest of this chapter is devoted to a series of case studies on the material evidence of Philippi and its profitable intersection with Paul's Letter to the Philippians.

2. The Relationship of City to Countryside: The Religious Life of the Villages of Philippi

The relationship of the ancient city to its surrounding countryside and villages has been insufficiently studied as a feature of life in antiquity.[50] This is especially so in the case of early Christianity, where the scholarly focus has heavily concentrated on its urban context, including this current Society of Biblical Literature series on urban Christians.[51] However in the case of Philippi, from Paul Collart onwards scholars have paid close attention to the activities and status of the inhabitants in city's nearby villages.[52] Indeed, the Philippian inscriptions force our attention on the issue, employing Latin and Greek terminology to designate the inhabitants and habitations within Philippian territory (*vicanus* [villager] and κώμη [village]).[53] Collart also refers to the small agglomerations of population

---

50. See John Rich and Andrew Wallace-Hadrill, eds., *City and Country in the Ancient World* (London: Routledge, 1991); A. P. Gregory, "Village Society in Hellenistic and Roman Asia Minor" (PhD diss., Columbia University, 1997); H. Malay and Y. Akkan, "The Village Tar(i)gye and the Cult of Zeus Tar(i)gyenos in the Cayster Valley," *EA* 40 (2007): 16–22. On the hinterland of Ephesus, see R. Meriç, *Das Hinterland von Ephesos: Archäologisch-topographische Forschungen im Kaystros-Tal*, JÖAI 12 (Vienna: ÖAI, 2009).

51. See, however, T. A. Robinson, *Who Were the First Christians? Dismantling the Urban Thesis* (Oxford: Oxford University Press, 2017); James R. Harrison, "An Epigraphic Portrait of Ephesus and Its Villages," in *The First Urban Churches*, vol. 3, *Ephesus*, ed. James R. Harrison and L. L. Welborn, WGRWSup 9 (Atlanta: SBL Press, 2018), 7–12.

52. See Collart, *Philippes*, 285–88; Athanase Rizakis, "Société, institutions, cultes," in Fournier, *Philippes, de la préhistoire à Byzance*, 180–83. For the differing views of Philippian scholars on the extent of the territory of Philippi and its *pomerium*, including its villages, see Pilhofer, *Philippi*, 1:52–73.

53. For *vicanus*, see Pilhofer, *Philippi*, 2.045 (ancient village: Medius [inscription found at modern Philippoi]: undated); 2.048 (ancient village: Satricenus [inscription found at modern Philippoi]: undated); 2.437 (ancient villages unknown due to fragmen-

in the villages of the colony of Philippi, near modern sites (e.g., Berékétli, Sélian, Krifla, Boriani).⁵⁴ The ancient village sites were marked by funerary stelae, sarcophagi, and architectural blocks, marking what was the necropolis outside each city. The modern towns of Doxato and Drama had also emerged from what were originally ancient villages, indicated by the numerous inscribed stones present there.⁵⁵

What, then, are the names of the villages within the territory of Philippi? The ancient villages and their villagers clearly identified by the terminology of *vicanus* and κώμη are (1) Medius; (2) Satricenus; (3) the villagers of Sc[…], Nicaensis, Coreni, and Zcambu[…]; (4) Antheritanus; and (5) Ὀλδηνός. There are other villages mentioned employing the terminology of *vicanus* and κώμη, but due to the fragmentary nature of the inscription or the nonspecification of the actual village name in the text, we do not know their names. Other villages identified as such by Collart (omitting the collection of Antoine Salac),⁵⁶ but whose inscriptions do not use the Latin or Greek terminology, are (1) Καλαμπάκι, (2)

---

tary nature of the inscription [inscription found at modern Doxato]: undated); 2.518 (ancient villages unspecified [inscription found at modern Kobaliste (Κοκκινόγεια)]: undated; 2.519 (ancient villages of Sc[…], Nicaensis, Coreni, Zcambu[…] [inscription found at modern Kobaliste (Κοκκινόγεια): undated); 2.644 (ancient Antheritanus [inscription found at modern Ελευθρούπολις: Παλιόπραβο]: third–fourth century CE). For additional inscriptions from Doxato, see 2.439 (third century CE) and 2.451 (undated). For κώμη, see Pilhofer, *Philippi*, 2.543 (Hellenistic), 2.568 (ancient village: Ὀλδηνός [inscription found at Νέος Σκοπός]: undated). For additional villages, not using "village" terminology in their inscriptions but identified as such by Collart (*Philippes*, 286–87), see Pilhofer, *Philippi*, 2.029 (ancient Καλπαπουρεῖται [situated between modern Philippoi and Kavalla]: second century CE); 2.456 (ancient Προυπτοσουρηνός [modern site not specified in Pilhofer]: undated); 2.512 (ancient village Scarporenus [inscription found at modern Proussotchani]: undated); 2.524 (ancient Tasibastenus [inscription found at modern Reussilova]; second century CE); 2.525 (ancient Tasibastenus [inscription found at modern Reussilova]; undated); 588 (ancient village of Suritanus [inscription found at modern Πρώτη]: undated); 2.597 (ancient Ποδοχώρι: modern Podgora; early third century CE). Additionally, see 414 (ancient Καλαμπάκι [inscription found at modern Kalambaki]: 112 CE): Paul Collart, "Une refection de la 'Via Egnatia' sous Trajan," *BCH* 59 (1935): 395–415.

54. Collart, *Philippes*, 285.
55. Collart, *Philippes*, 285–86.
56. Due to space constrictions, we have confined our investigation to the work of Paul Collart, not incorporating the extra villages mentioned in A. Salac, "Inscriptions du Pangée, de la region Drama-Cavalla et de Philippes," *BCH* 47 (1923): 49–96 (e.g., Pilhofer, *Philippi*, 2.518–20, 523).

Καλπαπουρεῖται, (3) Προυπτοσουργηνός, (4) Scarporenus, (5) Tasibastenus, (6) Suritanus, and (7) Ποδοχώρι. In sum, within the territory of Philippi, there were at least fifteen villages, with others unspecified or unknown due to the fragmentary nature of the epigraphic text.

Modern scholars have pointed to the surprising complexity of the interactions occurring in the texts. As Collart observes, well-known conventions of receiving legacies and disposing of the revenues for the testator operate smoothly at a village level; honorific inscriptions are erected; local divinities are appropriately honored.[57] A fragmentary inscription from Doxato relating to the sales of wine is clearly a decree, with the technical expression (*placuit vicanis* [Resolved by the villagers]) underscoring the decision of the local meeting (i.e., a municipal council, or perhaps an even more basic institution?).[58] Furthermore, as Collart indicates, titles such as ἀντιστράτηγος (the equivalent of duumvir?) and φορολόγος (tax collector) point to more than just a basic level of civic administration.[59] However, as Collart and Rizakis argue, the city of Philippi was ultimately the chief administrative, judicial, and religious center.[60] But what is revealed about daily life by our village inscriptions?

---

57. Rizakis observes that the privileged status of certain indigenous villagers not only "permitted them to receive gifts but equally to have a more role active, as an example of which (was) erecting dedications in honour of benefactors, (and) indeed to take more important decisions" ("Société, institutions, cultes," 182).

58. Collart, *Philippes*, 287–88. See Pilhofer, *Philippi*, 2.437.

59. Collart, *Philippes*, 288. See Pilhofer, *Philippi*, 2.510, ll. 4–5.

60. Collart, *Philippes*, 288. Rizakis argues that there was a social and judicial hierarchy in the colony of Philippi ("Société, institutions, cultes," 181). The preexisting Thracian and Greek villagers (*vici*) living outside the city of Philippi did not have any autonomy, rank, or judicial profile. Rather, "the large decisions in religious, fiscal, and judicial matters, concerning the inhabitants of a *vicus*, emanated from Philippi or elsewhere, the authorities having their headquarters at the chief-place" (182). However, given the inscriptional evidence cited by Collart above, one wonders whether the social hierarchy imposed on the *vici* was quite as unilateral in its operations as Rici suggests. Surely the Romans at Philippi cultivated the cooperation of the outlying Greek and Thracian *vici* by allowing them a measure of administrative and religious independence in day-to-day affairs, even if it was a "very limited autonomy, politically dependent on Philippi"? See Oakes, *Philippians*, 30. See especially Oakes's insightful discussion of the inscription of "Little Hadrianoplis," a Greek-speaking *polis* situated just north of Philippi, having a measure of status in being called a *polis* but certainly not possessing full independence (30–32; see also Pilhofer, *Philippi*, 2.349).

First, the presence of the Rosalia festival at Philippi is mentioned in several inscriptions from the colony of Philippi.[61] These feasts of the dead, originating in Italy, were called Rosalia (day of roses) because the rose played an important role in the funeral cult. Each family and funerary association visited the tomb of the deceased, offering flowers there, above all roses. There the guests took a meal, each crowned with roses (Martial, *Ep.* 10.19.21).[62] The rose symbolized not only the commemoration of the dead but also the return of spring and summer, expressed in the joyous banquet at the tomb of a deceased association member in many cases on one of the days of the Parentalia (February 13–21).[63] The Rosalia were also well known in Roman Philippi and its surrounding area.[64] The festival was probably brought over from Italy to the Roman colony of Philippi. Paul Perdrizet notes that many of the Philippian Rosalia inscriptions congregate around the second century CE, providing more than enough time for the romanization of the indigenous villages since the foundation of the Colonia Iulia Augusta Philippensis in 42 BCE.[65] While this is certainly true, the original military veteran settlers of Philippi would have brought the ritual of Rosalia with them, which were performed by legions for their fallen comrades in battle rather than their family members.[66] Notwithstanding,

---

61. Pilhofer, *Philippi*, 2.045, 512, 644. For an additional Rosalia inscription, see Pilhofer, *Philippi*, 2.529. On the Rosalia festival, see Paul Perdrizet, "Inscriptions de Philippes: Les Rosalies," *BCH* 24 (1900): 229–333; Collart, *Philippes*, 474–85; A. S. Hoey, "Rosaliae Signorum," *HTR* 30 (1937): 22–30; Richard S. Ascough, "Paul's 'Apocalypticism' and the Jesus Associations at Thessalonica and Corinth," in *Redescribing Paul and the Corinthians*, ed. Ron Cameron and Merrill P. Miller, ECL 5 (Atlanta: Society of Biblical Literature, 2011), 164.

62. Perdrizet, "Inscriptions de Philippes," 300.

63. Ascough, "Paul's 'Apocalypticism,'" 164. Note the promise of life beyond the grave pledged by roses, a symbol of spring, in the late empire poet Ausonius (310–395 CE: *Epit.* 31), cited in J. M. C. Toynbee, *Death and Burial in the Roman World* (Baltimore: Johns Hopkins University Press, 1971), 63: "Sprinkle my ashes with pure wine and fragrant oil of spikenard; / Bring balsam too, stranger, with crimson roses. / Tearless my urn enjoys unending spring. / I have not died, but changed my state."

64. Perdrizet, "Inscriptions de Philippes," 304–23.

65. Perdrizet, "Inscriptions de Philippes," 320.

66. The famous Feriale Duranum from Dura-Europos (222–225 CE)—a list of days with prescribed offerings and holy days for the Roman army—assigns the observance of the Rosaliae signorum to May 10 and 31. See Arthur Darby Nock, "The Roman Army and the Roman Religious Year," *HTR* 45 (1952): 187–252; Hoey, "Rosaliae Signorum."

in the case of Philippi, the Rosalia involved the participation of the *viciani* (i.e., associations formed from members of a particular village), who celebrated the festival at the tomb of the deceased.[67]

A particularly revealing Rosalia inscription comes from the village of Scarporenus, located in the territory of the colony of Philippi:

> Cintus, the son of Polola, [a resident from the village of] Scarporenus, has, for himself and for his wife Secis, the daughter of Bithus, provided for the making [of the inscription] during his lifetime. I have left from my inheritance 60 denarii, so that from its interest [the money] might go towards the Rosalia, under the supervision of the Zipas, the son of Mestus, [given for the grave in order to celebrate the meal]. [In the same way I leave] to Diana 250 denarii under [her] supervision [*ad aberterio eius*] of that which is mentioned above.[68]

In the inscription above, a Thracian couple, Cintus and Secis, have bequeathed money from an interest-bearing inheritance for their honorable funeral and have provided money for the continuing annual celebration of the Rosalia at their tomb. Highly intriguing is the statement that this is carried out under the supervision of the goddess Diana. What is being inferred here? Perdrizet argues that in this instance Diana represents the goddess of death, assuming the role of Hekate as ruler over the underworld, along with the likelihood that she has sudden deaths attributed to her agency.[69] Little wonder that the goddess Diana/Hekate had to be placated with further money beyond the death of the couple: Did they fear somehow that they would fall into her postmortem clutches without the provision of a bribe?[70] Would the celebration of the Rosalia, as the later poet Ausonius opined (*Epit.* 31), bring postmortem transformation

---

67. It should be noted that there were tomb rituals other than the Rosalie in the Philippian villages. For example, at Νέος Σκόπος, a bowl was annually filled with wine at the front of the testator's grave, and the grave itself was also crowned (Pilhofer, *Philippi*, 2.568).

68. Pilhofer, *Philippi*, 2.512. For discussion, see Perdrizet, "Inscriptions de Philippes," 310–12; Portefaix, *Sisters Rejoice*, 82–84.

69. Perdrizet, "Inscriptions de Philippes," 311.

70. For another perspective on the operations of the demonic world, note the grave inscription from Philippi (Pilhofer, *Philippi*, 2.296, ll. 4–6: third century CE), which depicts a fighter in animal hunts (*venationes*) speaking thus: "A demon has ordered to me to die on famous ground, in a foundation of Philippi and the emperor Augustus, well-crowned with walls."

and immortality for the Thracian couple?[71] We glean here some precious insights into the folk beliefs of villagers living in the territory of Philippi.

Second, another interesting inscription from a Philippian village, I would argue, further highlights the postmortem fears of everyday Philippians in the villages in relation to Diana. The inscription states:

> For Deana Minervia, who [...] has in order the [following] villagers, the Sc [...], the Nicaenses, the Coreni and the Zcambu[...], [at this place the roof of the te]mple under the *curators* Zaerazistes, the son of the Be ..., Centozaeras, the son of Zipaibes, Cetrilas, the son of the ..., ..., Dizalas, the son of Brassis, and Zipyrus, the son of [Du]les, have restored. Bascilas, the son of Bithus; Cerzus, the son of Dininithus; Caius Corn[elius ...]; ..., the son of Zer[ce]s; Cetrilas, the son of Zeredules; Manta, the daughter of Zerces, the priests (and priestess).[72]

In this inscription, villagers from four communities, two names of which are damaged, have joined together in a common project, supervised by four Thracian officials called "curators,"[73] to fund the restoration of a (damaged?) temple roof of the goddess Deana Minervia. The invocation of "Deana Minervia," Salac claims,[74] is new: but whether the goddess Diana had another surname is unable to be determined due to the fragmentary state of the inscription's first line. Certainly Diana has other epithets at Philippi (Deana Lucifera) and at the village of Doxato (Deana Caszoria), where the goddess is likewise served by a priestess named Valeria Severa.[75] On the stone of our inscription there is a relief to the left of the text representing the cult statue of the goddess in a "primitive form."[76]

It is certainly true, as Salac claims,[77] that the temple "was a religious centre of the countryside." But what precisely is meant by this? Was the

---

71. For a more conventional Rosalia inscription from Philippi, see Pilhofer, *Philippi*, 2.029: "Manta set this up for her own child, Soudios son of Paibilas, twenty-six years old, as a memorial. I bequeath to the Kalpapoureitian grave-diggers 150 denarii. Once a year they shall celebrate the Rosalia" (trans. Ascough, *AGRW* 42).

72. Pilhofer, *Philippi*, 2.519.

73. Salac, "Inscriptions du Pangée," 66.

74. Salac, "Inscriptions du Pangée," 65.

75. Pilhofer, *Philippi*, 2.227, 451.

76. Salac, "Inscriptions du Pangée," 69. For the relief, see the photo of the inscription on p. 64 fig. 5.

77. Salac, "Inscriptions du Pangée."

temple situated in one of the four villages, or was it located elsewhere at a site independent of the villages—a regional cultic center, as it were? Was the Diana cult dominant in each village, providing their collective religious identity? Were there other equally powerful indigenous gods, as one would expect,[78] who also had to be appeased by cult and attended by priestly personnel in each village? Or this attributing too great a religious complexity to village life? Is the cooperation between the four villages primarily dictated by the emergency (?) of the temple's roofing and the necessity of pooling common funds to ensure its prompt resolution? We can answer none of these questions from our text with any certainty.

Furthermore, why were the four villages so careful to resolve this (apparent) emergency through the prompt appointment of curators, a process to be overseen by Diana's priests and priestess lest the goddess might be offended? An important clue is perhaps afforded by the name of the village of the "Coreni." As Lilian Portefaix speculates,[79] "this name may refer to the myth of Hades' abduction of Core to the lower region, which event was thought to have taken place within the colony." Once again we are confronted by indigenous beliefs about the power of Diana as goddess of the underworld, and this helps to explain the great care taken by the four villages in addressing the issue of her temple's roof repair.

Third, the mystery cults also play a role in shaping the postmortem expectations of the villagers living in the nearby countryside of Philippi. A third-century CE inscription from Doxato, 20 km from Philippi, dedicates a remarkable verse epitaph to a young boy who had been an initiate of the Dionysian mysteries:[80]

---

78. Note, for example, the two inscriptions dedicated the god Liber Pater Tasibastenus (Pilhofer, *Philippi*, 2.524–25). The latter inscription, incidentally, is important for our insight into the slave economy of the Philippian villages, being an epitaph of the slave and estate manager (*servus actor*) Lucius, whose master was Caesius Victor.

79. Portefaix, *Sisters Rejoice*, 84.

80. Pilhofer, *Philippi*, 2.439, ll. 11–22. Translated and discussed by Portefaix, *Sisters Rejoice*, 105–6. I have adjusted the translation of Portefaix slightly at several places. See also Abrahamsen, *Women and Worship*, 72. For another Dionysiac mysteries inscription, see Pilhofer, *Philippi*, 2.597 (ancient Ποδοχώρι: modern Podgora; early third century CE [Abrahamsen, *Women and Worship*, 69–70]). Zipas donates 120 denarii in the Rosalia for the mysteries of Dionysius (μύσ[τ]αις [Δι]ονύσου) on behalf of his wife, Kleudis, and their children.

[we are to]rmented, having been overcome with grief, [but you are calm] and restored and living in the Elysian fields. Thus it is resolved by the gods [for you] to live on in everlasting form [a[l]terna vivera forma],[81] which in relation to the heavenly deity is well merited by a distinguished person. The godhead had promised gifts to you for your chaste life, the easy simplicity that had once been ordered by the god. Either the tattooed women initiated into the mysteries of Bromios call you into the flower-bearing meadows of the Satyrs or the basket-bearing Naiads demand [e]qual[ly] that you lead festival bands with flaming torches. Whatever you are boy, whatever your age has determined for you, yet (for your merit you dwell in the blessed fields) [...][82]

The desolation of the grief-stricken parents is contrasted with the joy of the restored life of the initiates in their postmortem state in the Elysian fields. The precise "everlasting form" of the young boy is not specified, but there are strong elements of continuity with the past in that he is invited to lead the Dionysiac festal procession. Notwithstanding, the experience is entirely transformed, reflecting paradisiacal elements, with mythical creatures (Satyrs, Naiads) and dancing tattooed female initiates—which Portefaix suggests were shades of deceased women[83]—populating the idyllic landscape. A fusion of grace and merit-based approaches to the postmortem justification of the deceased is underscored, simultaneously based on the chasteness of the initiate and the promise of divine reward in the afterlife.

Finally, how would Paul's gospel in Philippians have intersected with the religious worldview evinced in the village inscriptions above? We have highlighted the fusion of grace and merit-based understandings of the future hope of the initiates in the Dionysian mysteries. Paul, however, rejects all merit before God, irrespective of whether it was covenant-inherited or performance-based righteousness (Phil 3:4–7), including in this radical critique of human boasting his own current achievements as an apostle (3:8).[84] Against this is poised the gracious gift of God's righteousness (Phil

---

81. At l. 13 Portefaix opts for the restorations of *aeterna* as opposed to *alterna* (Pilhofer, *Philippi*, 2.518 n. 13, see also 516, 517), suggested by Franz Bücheler and Franz Joseph Dölger.

82. At l. 22 of the inscription, Portefaix (*Sisters Rejoice*, 105) includes in her translation the expansion of *dummodo* [...], suggested by Franz Joseph Dölger: *dum mode (pro meritis arva volas)*. See Pilhofer, *Philippi*, 2.518 n. 22 (see 517).

83. Portefaix, *Sisters Rejoice*, 105.

84. See James R. Harrison, "From Rome to the Colony of Philippi: Roman Boast-

3:9a: μὴ ἔχων ἐμὴν δικαιοσύνην τὴν ἐκ νόμου; 3:9b: τὴν ἐκ θεοῦ δικαιοσύνην ἐπὶ τῇ πίστει), secured for humans by the cruciform faithfulness of Christ (3:9b: διὰ πίστεως Χριστοῦ; see also 2:8), the personal experience of which is based on the believer's faith (Phil 3:9b: ἐπὶ τῇ πίστει).

Further, whereas the "eternal form" of the Dionysian initiate in the postmortem Elysian fields is not precisely specified, the believer attains the resurrection of the dead by being conformed through suffering to the death of Christ (Phil 3:10b-11 [v. 10b: συμμορφιζόμενος τῷ θανάτῳ αὐτοῦ]). Not only is the general Jewish hope of the resurrection affirmed in this scenario over against the Dionysian construct of the afterlife, but also the resurrection hope is christologically, soteriologically, and eschatologically redefined in light of Paul's narrative theology. Believers, while experiencing Christ's resurrection power in the present (Phil 3:10a), will nevertheless be conformed to Christ's glorious resurrection body at the eschaton (3:21: σύμμορφον τῷ σώματι τῆς δόξης). Succinctly put, the cruciformity of believers in the present precedes their eschatological glorification (Rom 8:29; 1 Cor 15:42-44, 49; 2 Cor 3:18; 5:17, 21; Phil 3:10-11, 21).[85] This process is patterned on the wider soteriological career of Christ, who, being "in the form of God" (Phil 2:6a: ἐν μορφῇ θεοῦ), assumed "the form of a servant" (2:7a: μορφὴν δούλου) in cruciform obedience to the Father, only to be divinely exalted to the place of unrivaled authority (2:9-11a), to the glory of the Father (2:11b).[86] At each stage, in contrast to the Dionysian mysteries, the Christocentric and paradigmatic "form" of the earthly discipleship and postmortem glorification of believers is spelled out.

Last, while the believer yearns to be with the risen Christ, which is better by far (Phil 1:23), for Paul to remain in the body in Christ in the

---

ing in Philippians 3:4-6 in Its Latin West and Philippian Epigraphic Context," in this volume.

85. Michael J. Gorman, *Inhabiting the Cruciform God: Kenosis, Justification, and Theosis in Paul's Narrative Soteriology* (Grand Rapids: Eerdmans, 2009), 150. Additionally, see R. P. Martin, *Carmen Christi: Philippians 2:5-11 in Recent Interpretation and in the Setting of Early Christian Worship*, SNTSMS 4 (Cambridge: Cambridge University Press, 1967); Ralph P. Martin and Brian J. Dodd, eds., *Where Christology Began: Essays on Philippians 2* (Louisville: Westminster John Knox, 1998).

86. Gerard F. Hawthorne, "In the Form of God and Equal with God (Philippians 2:6)," in Martin and Dodd, eds., *Where Christology Began*, 97-101; Gorman, *Inhabiting the Cruciform God*, 9-39; Larry J. Kreitzer, "'When He at Last Is First!': Philippians 2:9-11 and the Exaltation of the Lord," in Martin and Dodd, eds., *Where Christology Began*, 111-27.

present not only exalts his Lord (1:20b) but also provides the opportunity for continuing fruitful labor among God's people (1:22b, 24–25). Notwithstanding the Dionysian idyllic construal of the postmortem state, the explosion in Paul's language of joy amid the sufferings of his ministry (χάρα: Phil 1:4, 25; 2:2, 29; 4:1: χαίρω: 1:18; 2:17, 18, 28; 3:1; 4:4, 10) challenged the wider pessimism of the ancient world and the indifference of its gods.[87] Above all, the emphasis on Christ's exaltation over the demonic powers (Phil 2:10b: "under the earth")[88] freed the ancients from their fear about the power of Diana over the underworld or about the ability of demons to consign them to death. We are perhaps provided here with a significant clue as to why many ancients, despite the considerable social shame of being attached to the early Christian movement, nevertheless

---

87. Note the comment of L. Gregory Bloomquist: "True, mystery religions and magic promised to bring individual sufferers into contact with the divine and thus enable them to transcend the materiality that brought about suffering. But, the historical evidence suggests that the gods were rarely amenable to this arrangement. Not only were they indifferent to human suffering; they were also ruthlessly committed to their own honor and survival, often at the expense of mortals. Worse, mortals could not escape these capricious and self-absorbed deities even in death." "Subverted by Joy: Suffering and Joy in Paul's Letter to the Philippians," *Int* 61 (2007): 270–82. See Pilhofer, *Philippi*, 1:106–7, for a discussion of the Doxato Dionysiac mystery inscription above (Pilhofer, *Philippi*, 2.439), who also notes the popularity of the Bacchic mysteries in the Roman Empire precisely because they alleviated Roman fears of death through the bliss of an eternal banquet.

88. While "in heaven, on the earth, and under the earth" (Phil 2:10b) is "a conventional description of the universe, following contemporary Jewish and Christian cosmology." Markus Bockmuehl, *The Epistle to the Philippians*, BNTC 11 (Peabody, MA: Hendrickson, 1998), 145. Nevertheless, the phrase καταχθονίων (under the earth) "presumably means both the dead and all the chthonic deities." Paul A. Holloway, *Philippians*, Hermeneia (Minneapolis: Fortress, 2017), 128 n. 116. In addition to a specific Philippian inscriptional reference to a δαίμων (Pilhofer, *Philippi*, 2.296), as well as a reference to Diana/Hekate (512), we must not forget the ubiquitous Philippian epigraphic references to *Dis Manibus* (for the ghost-gods: 079, 080, 136, 277, 384b, 429, 502), *Dis inferis Manibus* (for the underground ghost-gods: 525), *manes inferi* (the underground ghost-gods: 048), and *manes Phaedri* (the ghost-god of Phaedrus: 660), shorthand for the deified souls of the departed and the various gods who lived in the underworld. See also John Reumann, *Philippians: A New Translation with Introduction and Commentary*, AYB 33B (New Haven: Yale University Press, 2008), 357. Additionally, see Fredrick J. Long and Ryan Kristopher Giffin, "'Every Knee Bowed': Jesus Christ as Reigning Lord over 'the Heavenly, the Earthly, and the Subterranean Gods' (Philippians 2:10)," in this volume.

committed themselves to the risen Christ and participated in his eschatological community on earth.

3. The Imperial Cult

The extant archaeological remains of the imperial cult at Philippi belong to the Antonine period. There is a temple dedicated to emperor worship in the northeast corner of the forum courtyard, as well as a base with (probably late first-century) inscriptions of priestesses of the apotheosized Livia that was also found in the forum.[89] We will focus on the inscriptions belonging to the Julio-Claudian and Flavian period,[90] bypassing the references to the apotheosized Julius Caesar and Augustus on the coinage, already discussed above. Overall, the number of Julio-Caudian inscriptions at Philippi honoring the Roman ruler are relatively few.

First, during the reigns of Augustus and his successor, Tiberius, the high-status priests of divine Augustus were commemorated in epitaphs several times.[91] In another well-known feature of the imperial cult, an inscription is also dedicated to a divinized abstraction of Augustus at Philippi as part of the wider cult of virtues, namely, the Aequitas Augusti (the Justice/Equity/Fairness of Augustus).[92] Other members of the house of Augustus are similarly rendered honor by the imperial priests in their epitaphs. For example, in the case of the apotheosized Livia (42 CE), an inscription of the deceased Cornelia Asprila at Kavala mentions self-importantly that the deceased had been "priestess of the divine Augusta."[93] The colony of Philippi, too, consecrates an inscription to the children and grandchildren of Augustus.[94] Moreover, Tiberius and his dead son and

---

89. Even though the forum monument is Antonine, Pilhofer dates the inscriptions of the priestesses on its bases, who are honoring the apotheosized Livia, to the first century CE (Pilhofer, *Philippi*, 2.226). See Peter Oakes, "The Imperial Authorities in Paul's Letter to Predominantly Greek Hearers in the Roman Colony of Philippi," in this volume for further discussion of the imperial context.

90. For references to Antoninus Pius, Caracalla, Commodus, Faustina, Julia Domna, Marcus Aurelius, and Septimius Severus, see Pilhofer, *Philippi*, vol. 2., index, s.v. "IV. Prominente historische Persönlichkeiten."

91. Pilhofer, *Philippi*, 2.031, 241, 531a, 700–703. See also an inscription honoring Octavian (670).

92. Pilhofer, *Philippi*, 2.249.

93. Pilhofer, *Philippi*, 2.002.

94. Pilhofer, *Philippi*, 2.452.

heir, Drusus Julius Caesar (the "Younger"), are honored in an inscription datable to 36/37 CE.[95] But whether Tiberius had actually died (16 March 37 CE) before the time of this epigraphic commemoration is difficult to determine. But possibly the inscription is honoring the death of Tiberius, as well as the earlier death of the "Younger" Drusus (23 CE), as a mark of continuing piety to the Julian house in its Tiberian expression.

Second, in terms of the Claudian epigraphy, a member of the Montanus family is designated in his epitaph a "priest of the divine Claudius in Philippi."[96] In another revealing inscription, the (nondeified) Claudius is honored, but, significantly, the local Hero (Aulonitis?) is also hailed by the worshiper.[97] Thus the importance of the indigenous and imperial cults of the colony is equally recognized in this instance, but this *mutual* recognition of cults is a rare occurrence at Philippi. This stands in marked contrast to Ephesus, where the powerful indigenous goddess, Artemis, routinely precedes the imperial rulers in the inscriptions.[98]

Third, as far as the Flavian dynasty, there is mention of priests of the apotheosized Vespasian.[99] The Philippian clients of Hadrian and Trajan normally ensure that the divine legitimation of the Roman ruler is emphasized at the beginning of the honorific inscriptions of the colony, taking care to mention the apotheosized forebears of Hadrian (i.e., Trajan and Nerva) and Trajan (i.e., Nerva).[100] Last, a fragmentary decree captures well the flattering rhetoric of address employed in approaching the Flavian ruler: "Trajan, the most respected and most admirable, glorious [ἐνδόξως; see Phil 2:11b: εἰς δόξαν τοῦ πατρός]."[101]

---

95. Pilhofer, *Philippi*, 2.282. Another possible inscription of Tiberius is 88: "Caesar, (the son) of the divine Augustus."

96. Pilhofer, *Philippi*, 2.001. Another inscription is dedicated to Drusus the "Elder," with Claudius's name being restored in the inscription (2.232a).

97. Pilhofer, *Philippi*, 2.699.

98. See James R. Harrison, "Ephesian Cultic Officials, Their Benefactors and the Quest for Civic Virtue: Paul's Alternative Quest for Status in Ephesians 1:3–14," in Harrison and Welborn, *First Urban Churches*, 3:258. By contrast, even in the case where the Olympian gods are mentioned in conjunction with emperor worship in the Flavian period at Philippi, Hadrian is still mentioned first (Pilhofer, *Philippi*, 2.208).

99. Pilhofer, *Philippi*, 2.004, 719.

100. Pilhofer, *Philippi*, 2.283, 414, 703. Sometimes there is no reference to the forebears of either Trajan (Pilhofer, *Philippi*, 2.497), Vespasian (2.281), or Nerva (2.559).

101. Pilhofer, *Philippi*, 2.667.

In conclusion, the wealthy priests living at Kavala gained great social prestige in undertaking the ministration of the imperial cult in the Roman colony. The role of upwardly mobile freedmen, the *severi Augustales*, in sponsoring the imperial cult should not be overlooked in this regard (below §5.4).[102] The imperial inscriptions at Philippi reflect the city's numismatic evidence by routinely bypassing any mention of the local cults when honoring the Roman ruler. The apotheosis of various members of the Julio-Claudian and Flavian houses increasingly becomes a vital strut in the legitimation of their rule. In the Philippian numismatic evidence, as we have seen, the Roman rulers similarly assert their connection with Divus Julius and Divus Augustus on the reverse of their coins during the Julio-Claudian and Flavian periods. The worship of the virtues of the Roman ruler as abstractions becomes another potent way of speaking about the presence of the ruler in the colony, highlighting very specific blessings to its citizens as opposed to their more general and routine expressions of beneficence.[103] Thus Paul's proclamation of the divinely exalted Christ as Lord of the entire creation (Phil 2:9–11), who extended his resurrection life and virtue to his grateful dependents in a magnanimous demonstration of overflowing grace, could hardly be seen as anything other than an anti-imperial message in its Philippian context (see Acts 16:20–21).[104]

4. Indigenous and Nonindigenous Cults

At Philippi the traditional Greek and Roman gods are honored in many inscriptions: for example, Aphrodite (Venus), Apollo, Ares, Artemis (Diana), Cupid, Cybele, Dioskouri, Hera, Heracles (Hercules), Jupiter (Zeus), Kabeiroi, Liber Pater (Dionysius/Bacchus), Mercurius, Minerva, Neptune, Nemesis, the Olympian gods, Pan, Poseidon, Silvanus, and Victoria, among others.[105] However, the indigenous Thracian god of the moon

---

102. Pilhofer, *Philippi*, 2.037, 043, 074, 256, 276, 289, 412, 455, 463, 505, 639, 721.

103. Nevertheless, we should not forget the centrality of imperial beneficence in maintaining enthusiasm for the imperial cult. Note, for example, Trajan's restoration of milestones on the road through the province of Macedonia from Dyrrachium to Akontisma (Pilhofer, *Philippi*, 2.414).

104. See Oakes, *Philippians*, 129–74.

105. Numbers refer to Pilhofer, *Philippi*, vol. 2. Aphrodite: 681; Venus: 057; Apollo: 191, 246, 359, 642a, 651, 652, 669, 682; Ares: 161; Artemis: 018, 246; Diana: 174, 512 (there are ninety reliefs of Diana [Artemis] at the acropolis: see Collart and Ducrey, *Philippes I: Les reliefs rupestres*, 8–97); Cupid: 350; Cybele: 054 (see Lam-

and hunting, Bendis, although popularly identified with Artemis (Diana) at Philippi, is also mentioned by herself in the inscriptions.[106] There are also imported Egyptian cults in the form of Isis, Sarapis, and Asclepius.[107] As we will see below (§5.1), the Genius of the city and of the marketplace were also worshiped. Aspects of several of the cults above are worth highlighting.

First, among the various hero cults present at Philippi, there is the local hero cult of Auloneites.[108] The presence of the hero Auloneites finds further confirmation at Philippi on a coin found in the agora of Thasos. On the obverse the divine Augustus is rendered, while on the reverse is this legend: *HEROI AULONITER[es] P[ublicae] C[oloniae] P[hilippensis]*.[109] However, this is, as noted, the only case of a local indigenous cult being identified on a Philippian coin in the early Roman empire.[110] Otherwise the imperial cult dominates numismatically.[111]

Another expression of the worship of the hero at Philippi are seven carvings of Thracian horsemen found on the acropolis.[112] As Valerie Abrahamsen argues, the reliefs were as much a funerary phenomenon as they

---

oreaux, *Ritual, Women, and Philippi*, 84–88; there are three reliefs of Cybele at the acropolis: Collart and Ducrey, *Philippes I: Les reliefs rupestres*, 145–47); Dioskouri: 388, 509e; Hera: 251, 672; Heracles: 650, 660; Hercules: 164, 338–40, 500; Jupiter: 473; Zeus: 568b, 678 (there are five reliefs of Jupiter at the acropolis: Collart and Ducrey, *Philippes I: Les reliefs rupestres*, 138–42); Kabeiroi: 681; Liber Pater: 094, 164, 332, 338–42, 408, 500–501, 524–25; Dionysius: 499, 500a; Bacchus: 529; Mercurius: 094, 164, 225, 485, 514; Minerva: 474 (there are two reliefs of Minerva at the acropolis: Collart and Ducrey, *Philippes I: Les reliefs rupestres*, 143–44); Neptune: 388; Nemesis: 142, 143, 144; Olympian gods: 208; Pan: 545; Poseidon: 161, 439, 509a; Silvanus: 028a, 148, 164, 166; Victoria: 224.

106. Pilhofer, *Philippi*, 2.517.

107. Isis: Pilhofer, *Philippi*, 2.175, 252, 255, 455; Isis Regina: Pilhofer, *Philippi*, 2.132, 506, 581; Serapis: Pilhofer, *Philippi*, 2.191, 192, 252, 307; Asklepios; Pilhofer, *Philippi*, 2.754. On Isis at Philippi, see Portefaix, *Sisters Rejoice*, 114–27.

108. Pilhofer, *Philippi*, 2.580, 622, 624, 625, 703e. See Pilhofer, *Philippi*, 1:88–89, 92–93, 146–47. On the various hero cults, see Pilhofer, *Philippi*, 2.133, 161, 509, 618, 623, 626, 626a, 629, 650 (Heracles), 671a.

109. Cited in *GRA* 312 n. 12.

110. See n. 27 above.

111. Note, however, the identification of the god Mercurius with Augustus ("[This monument] is consecrated to Mercurius Augustus") in Pilhofer, *Philippi*, 2.250.

112. Collart and Ducrey, *Philippes I: Les reliefs rupestres*, 1–7. For discussion, see additionally Collart and Ducrey, *Philippes I: Les reliefs rupestres*, 197–201.

were an expression of traditional votive worship.¹¹³ Thus "the Horseman or Hero (Ἥρως) represented the heroization of the deceased (the rider) as that person ascended to the abode of the Rider God via the horse."¹¹⁴ There are also further representations of horses and warriors riding on horseback at nearby Mount Pangaion and Agitis Gorge.¹¹⁵

Also, in a striking hero cult inscription, the directness of address on one gravestone arrests the reader: "I am a Hero."¹¹⁶ The meaning is not immediately obvious. Does this, for example, point implicitly to the identification of the deceased with the heroes of Homeric epic that we find in some Asia Minor inscriptions?¹¹⁷ However, there is no indication of any Homeric allusion in our text. More likely, the text indicates that the deceased has already entered into the abode of the Rider God. But, equally, the text, it could be argued, highlights the identity and saving presence of the Hero God, stated forcefully for the sake of the readers of the epitaph. Ultimately, is the text deliberately ambiguous in its intention: are the Hero God and the deceased person both speaking to posterity here?

Second, the shrine of Dionysius at Mount Pangaion, 40 km from Kavala, has several Greek inscriptions in honor of the god.¹¹⁸ We have already touched on the Dionysiac mysteries, as practiced at the villages of Ποδοχώρι and Doxato.¹¹⁹ Thus, whether it was the Thracian horseman cult or the Dionysiac mysteries, initiates were translated into a postmortem existence with the god upon their death, however that state might be conceived.

Third, in the case of Artemis (Diana/Bendis), we have already touched on the fact that Artemis was primarily worshiped as the goddess of the

---

113. Note the sculpture of a Thracian horseman on the sarcophagus of a priest of Isis (Pilhofer, *Philippi*, 2.455a).

114. Valerie Abrahamsen, "Christianity and the Rock Reliefs at Philippi," *BA* 51 (1988): 51.

115. George Iliadis, "Iconography of the Hero Horseman and the Continuity of the Imagery of the Horse Rider in the Plain of Philippi and Drama in Northern Greece," 4–5, https://tinyurl.com/SBL4216d.

116. Pilhofer, *Philippi*, 2.547.

117. For example, the identification with the Homeric heroes on the part of the honorand in a Laodicean inscription (*IK* 49.81). For another Homeric epigraphic example, see *IG* 2.3².10051.

118. Pilhofer, *Philippi*, 2.501a, 501b, 501c, 501d. On the cult of Dionysius at Philippi, see Portefaix, *Sisters Rejoice*, 98–114; Lamoreaux, *Ritual, Women, and Philippi*, 76–83.

119. Pilhofer, *Philippi*, 2.597, 439.

underworld, the equivalent of Hekate.[120] But, as Portefaix has observed, the traces of women worshipers of Diana in the reliefs of the acropolis point to their own hope of deification after death by virtue of their association with the goddess.[121]

It is clear, then, as we have already seen (§2), that Paul's resurrection hope, both for himself and his fellow believers at Philippi, played a pivotal role in combatting the strong postmortem expectation of an afterlife in the Philippian cults.

5. The Elites and Nonelites

In speaking about the elites of early imperial society, the dramatic change that had occurred from the time of the unraveling of the late republic and to the establishment of the Julio-Claudian principate needs to be appreciated. In the republican era, the census rank (*ordo*) was based on wealth and political privilege, with senators and equestrians qualifying at the apex of the social pyramid by virtue of their wealth and formal admission to the *ordo*. In the case of the senatorial elites, admission to the *ordo* by the time of Augustus was 250,000 denarii, signified by the *laticlavus* (purple-bordered toga), along with the acquisition of specific offices (the quaestorship, the vigintivirate) and public honors (exclusive seating rights in the theater).[122] By contrast, the entry for the equestrian was one hundred thousand denarii, again with exclusive seating rights provided in the theater.

However, due to the decimation of many of the old senatorial families in the civil war and the inability of the old noble houses to replenish their influence with new clients because of the unparalleled wealth of the Julian house after Actium (31 BCE), the senatorial luminaries under the empire were increasingly dependent on the imperial *cursus honorum* for their social advancement in order to survive. For example, some, such as Hortensius, had to be bailed out by Augustus monetarily if their senatorial

---

120. Collart and Ducrey, *Philippes I: Les reliefs rupestres*, 201–37; Portefaix, *Sisters Rejoice*, 75–98; Abrahamsen, *Women and Worship*, 25–34, 45–68; Lamoreaux, *Ritual, Women, and Philippi*, 43–75.

121. Portefaix, *Sisters Rejoice*, 96. See also Lamoreaux, *Ritual, Women, and Philippi*, 45–51. On the iconographic and epigraphic link between Artemis and the lunar deity, see Lamoreaux, *Ritual, Women, and Philippi*, 89–93.

122. John Matthews, "The Roman Empire and the Proliferation of the Elites," *Arethusa* 33 (2000): 436.

property qualification were to survive intact (Tacitus, *Ann.* 2.37–38). However, others demeaned themselves on the stage or in the gladiatorial arena in the reign of Nero. Whereas the old senatorial nobles were able to promote the military victories of their own houses by means of the traditional triumph at Rome during the republic, by 19 BCE this ritual was confined to Julian house members alone. The traditional quest for military glory, therefore, had been constricted, redefined, and, in the case of the military triumph, replaced with the lesser honor of the *ornamenta triumphalia*.[123]

Simultaneous with these developments, "the growing professionalism of the imperial military elite" spelled the death of the old republican military careers.[124] Previously each army was ultimately the personal client of the Roman noble, with the result that the state inevitably drifted toward civil war as careerists pursued their personal agendas with their own armies.[125] The military *cursus honorum* became *de rigeur* in the early empire as a means of social advancement, especially in Roman colonies such as Pisidian Antioch, Corinth, and Philippi. Consequently, senatorial, equestrian, and military careers at Philippi increasingly owed much to the imperial favor. In the case of Philippi, like the other Roman colonies, the following offices were present: decurio, aedilis, duumvir, and duumvir quinquennalis.[126] Since we will discuss the epigraphic boasting

---

123. T. Itgenshorst argues that Augustus's widespread triumphal monuments changed the occasional nature of the triumphal ceremony during the republic to a divisive and decisive break with the past. See *Tota illa pompa: Der Triumph in der römischen Republik* (Göttingen: Vandenhoeck & Ruprecht, 2005), 9–12, 219–26.

124. Matthews, "Roman Empire," 437. Matthews writes: "Soldiers and lower officers, who had previously been drawn from the farming classes of Italy, but were now recruited without a property qualification, behave and relate to each other, and to their commanders, in a way that reflects their now professional status…. They receive discharge payments and settle locally as leading members of local communities where they are commemorated by thousands of inscribed honours in the cities of the empire with their careers and distinctions set out for all to see" (437).

125. On the decline of the Roman nobility, see Matthias Gelzer, *The Roman Nobility*, trans. Robin Seager (Oxford: Basil Blackwell, 1969), 158–61.

126. Decurio: Pilhofer, *Philippi*, vol. 2, index 7, Philippisches, s.v. "decurio," 1145. On the Philippian elites, see Cédric Brélaz, "Le faciès institutionnel, social et reigieux d'une colonie romaine dans la province de Macédoine," in Fournier, *Philippes, de la préhistoire à Byzance*, 201–5. Aedilis: Pilhofer, *Philippi*, vol. 2, index 7, Philippisches, s.v. "aedilis," 1145. Duumvir: Pilhofer, *Philippi*, vol. 2, index 7, Philippisches, s.v. "duumvir," 1145–46. Duumvir quinquennalis: Pilhofer, *Philippi*, vol. 2, index 7, Philippisches, s.v. "duumvir quinquennalis," 1146.

of equestrian, military, and civic elites at Philippi in my companion essay in this volume, we will commence with two second-century CE senatorial inscriptions, before we sum up the implications of the others in the next section (§5.2 below).

5.1. The Senatorial Elites

In a second-century CE inscription (erected post-171 CE) from the reign of Antoninus Pius,[127] Caius Iulius Maximus Mucianus is identified as a senator by the technical terminology used (*clarissimus*) and the symbolic emblem pertaining to his toga (the purple stripe or *laticlavus*). Mucianus's senatorial status originates with the imperial sponsorship of his career by the Roman ruler. Remarkably, he was exempted, as Brélaz notes,[128] from having to acquire the lower-order positions of a senatorial career. His wider career in the province of Pontus-Bithynia began with the post of quaestor, being part of the senatorial administration in the province. Then he became an aedile Cerialis at Rome, which, by the time of the early imperial age, had become an essentially honorific magistracy, Augustus having stripped the post of its republican powers over the grain supply. On the year of his death, he had acquired the prestigious magistracy of praetor. How did this spectacular rise to senatorial status at Rome commence?

Mucianus had been received into the decurion order at Philippi, having been previously involved in the councils of unnamed cities in the province of Thrace.[129] Brelaz speculates that Mucianis, a Thracian like his brother and a politically ambitious man, approached nearby Philippi on his own initiative, managing to be received into the Roman colony as a decurion and enrolled as a citizen in the prestigious Voltina tribe.[130] It was Mucianus's residence in a Roman military colony that became the springboard for capturing the attention of significant patrons at Rome who could bring his name to the attention of Antoninus Pius for elevation to senatorial status. The full inscription is set out below:

---

127. For a picture of the inscription, see Sève and Weber, *Guide du forum de Philippes*, 46 fig. 22.
128. *CIPh* 2.1.143.
129. The suggestion of Brélaz, *CIPh* 2.1.143.
130. *CIPh* 2.1.144.

To [Caius] Iulius [M]aximus Mucianus, son of Caius, of the tribe Voltina], a most illustrious man [*clarissimus*], honou[r]ed with the purple stripe [*laticlavus*] by the divine [Antoninus] Pius, [quaestor] *pro propraetore* of the province of Pontus-Bithynia, [a]edile Cerialis, praetor designate, as well as decurion at Philippi and in the province of Thrace, aged 35 years, *vac*. Caius Iulius Teres, thraciarch, father of senators, *vac*. to his brother, *vac*. : site *vac*. granted *vac*. by decree *vac*. of the decurions *vac*.[131]

Finally, what is also fascinating is how the Thracian brother of Mucianus, Caius Iulius Teres, sets out his own claim to fame alongside Mucianus: namely, that he belongs, as a father, to a dynasty of senators ("father of senators"), reaching, in the case of one family member, to the consul of Rome itself.[132] As Hellerman has rightly emphasized, the Philippian inscriptions emphasize the inextricable link between significant public honor and kinship within the city.[133]

Another senatorial inscription from the reign of Antoninus Pius shows us the important role that senators played in the role of honoring the gods locally through their beneficence. Rufinianus, who belonged to the senatorial administration of Macedonia (quaestor *pro propraetore*), had previously been a curator (overseer of the local finances) of the municipality (*res publica*) of Philippi.[134] Clearly Rufinianus saw his role as extending to the oversight of the religious well-being of Philippi as much as to its economic administration. In particular, the Romans honored the protective spirit of a place (*genius loci*).[135] So this dedication (161–176 CE) of a statue to the Genius of the Colonia Iulia Augusta Philippensis and its municipality, located in a temple to the Genius in the forum, fitted in well with Rufinianus's conception of his role as curator and local benefactor of the gods: "To the Genius of the Col[onia] Iulia [Aug]ustus Phil[ippensis and of the *res*] *public*[*ca*], [Caius Modiu]s Laet[us] [Rufinianus, quaestor *pro propraetore* of the province of Macedonia], [curator of the *res publica* of the Philippians] … […] has pro[vided for the] [erect]ion in this [temple]."[136]

---

131. *CIPh* 2.1.38. By *vac*. the editor is indicating a space on the stone.

132. *CIPh* 2.1.143–44, 144 n. 9.

133. Joseph Hellerman, "Brothers and Friends in Philippi: Family Honor in the Roman World and in Paul's Letter to the Philippians," *BTB* 39 (2009): 15–25.

134. For a picture of the monument, see Sève and Weber, *Guide du forum de Philippes*, 40 fig. 19.

135. Rizakis, "Société, institutions, cultes," 185–86.

136. *CIPh* 2.1.43.

We know of another dedication to the Genius at the *macellum* ("marketplace") at Philippi.[137] So, it should not surprise us that Rufinianus's dedication to the *genius loci* appears in the Antonine forum, where there was already a temple dedicated to emperor worship in the northeast corner of the courtyard.[138] Furthermore, a base with inscriptions of priestesses of the apotheosized Livia was also found in the forum.[139]

Therefore, once again, was the beneficence of Rufinianus offered in the very center of the imperial cult at Philippi a calculated political move, designed in this instance to gain the attention of the imperial authorities in Macedonia, with a view to securing a future senatorial career? And, given the absence of any first-century senatorial inscriptions at Philippi, did these senatorial opportunists in the city only emerge in the second century? Or did the presence of first-century senatorial inscriptions disappear with the Antonine refurbishment of the earlier Julio-Claudian forum? We simply do not know.

5.2. The Equestrian, Military, and Municipal Elites

The boasting culture of the equestrian, military, and municipal elites in the inscriptions is fully covered in my adjoining essay in this volume. Readers are referred there for full discussion. However, a brief summary is apposite. In the case of equestrians, not only did the Burreni Firmi compete against other equestrian families for status, but members of the same family competed among themselves in order to establish ancestral fame.[140] The importance of imperial patronage is seen in the career of Montanus,[141] reflecting how the traditional republican *cursus honorum* was now reconfigured around the opportunities provided by imperial *cursus honorum*.

---

137. Pilhofer, *Philippi*, 2.251.

138. Sève and Weber, *Guide du forum de Philippes*, 66–67, with statue of Minerva at 70 fig. 47. See, too, the marble head of the small child of Augustus, Caius Caesar, found in the east fountain, perhaps belonging to the earlier Julio-Claudian forum (Sève and Weber, *Guide du forum de Philippes*, 13 fig. 1a–b). For a restoration of the temple, see Sève, *1914–2014*, pl. 185; Sève and Weber, *Guide du forum de Philippes*, 42–43, 68–69.

139. Sève and Weber, "Un monument honorifique." For a picture of the base, see Rizakis, "Société, institutions, cultes," 144 fig. 11. For a restoration, see Sève and Weber, *Guide du forum de Philippes*, 77.

140. Pilhofer, *Philippi*, 2.48, 49.

141. Pilhofer, *Philippi*, 2.53.

However, in the case of "outsiders" such as the Thessalonian Quartus,[142] talent alone was required in order to nudge one's way into the social world of the Philippian luminaries. Ethical qualities are rarely mentioned in the Philippian equestrian inscriptions,[143] in contrast to the Greek inscriptions of the Greek East and Asia Minor, because, seemingly, the acquisition of posts alone is sufficient to secure moral status in the Latin West and in the Roman colonies.

As far as the legionaries and soldiers, the reputation of Maximus,[144] the captor of Decabalus, the last Dacian chieftain, was so towering that those who might have been tempted to excise Domitian's name in a *damnatio memoriae* from his inscription balked at the opportunity. But what is especially significant in the text is its use of rhetorical tropes from the Latin West inscriptions, along with the intersection of its epigraphic content with the relief vignettes on the stone monument itself.

Although the *cursus honorum* of municipal magistrates was confined to civic offices, their monuments were erected from the funds provided by family wills, with the tribal membership being highlighted in the case of one less successful family member.[145] Because of the male-centered nature of family honor in the case of the Philippian inscriptions, the epitaphs of female family members record the achievements of successful male family members,[146] lest family honor should be diminished or impugned in any way. As an addition to our discussion in the companion essay in this volume, it is remarkable that two children are accorded decurion status in their epitaphs: a six-year old child named Annius Atilianus Agricola from the village of Drama, and a five-year-and-nine-months-old child named Caius Vibius Daphnus, also from Drama.[147] Here we see honorific status being accorded to little children, far too young for public life, with a view to enhancing the family's prestige.

Finally, while we have touched on the military elites of Philippi, it is worthwhile highlighting the fame that accrued to veterans in a military colony such as Philippi, especially for one who had fought against Bar Kokhba in the Second Jewish Revolt (132–135 CE). The great diffi-

---

142. Pilhofer, *Philippi*, 2.89.
143. Pilhofer, *Philippi*, 2.68.
144. Pilhofer, *Philippi*, 2.94.
145. Pilhofer, *Philippi*, 2.108.
146. Pilhofer, *Philippi*, 2.133.
147. Pilhofer, *Philippi*, 2.492, 493.

culty of putting down the rebellion of the great messianic Jewish leader, Bar Kokhba ("Son of the Star": Num 24:17), required a Roman general of the quality of Decimus Furius Secundus, whose services were lavishly awarded by Hadrian:

> Decimus Furius Secundus, the son of Decimus, from the Tribus Sergia, from [the state] Cures in Sabinerland, soldier of the of the tenth urban cohort, transferred to the sixth praetorian cohort, *singularis* of the tribune, *beneficiarius* of the tribune, *singularis* of the praetorian prefect, adjutant [*optio*] of the military centuries, standard-bearer, overseer [*curator*] of the money-bag [of the company], aide [*cornicularius*] of the tribune, *evocatus* of Augustus, commander [*centurio*] of the tenth Legion Fretensis, honoured by the deified Hadrian with gifts, awarded with a golden crown for the Jewish war, with neck-chains, with bracelets and with breastplates and promoted by the same emperor, he joined the first Legion Italica, first-centurion [*primipilus*] of that same Legion, appointed decurion in colonies, and honoured with the ornaments of a duumvir in Actia Nicopolis and Ulpia [...]148

Notably, Secundus was appointed, because of his exceptional accomplishments, as decurion of several unspecified Roman colonies, including Philippi. This inscription, while valuable for its intrinsic Jewish interest, also provides us substantial insight into the professionalization of the Roman army and its lucrative rewards under Julio-Claudian and Flavian rule.

5.3. Epigraphic Occupations at Philippi

A variety of occupations are mentioned in the Philippian inscriptions. Although the following list is in no way exhaustive, it ranges from high-status (but not elite) individuals to the humble plebs and high-profile household slaves. We gain thereby a better sense of the social profile of the city.

At the outset, there is a significant reference to a Thyatiran purple-handler in Philippi ("the first of the purple-handlers [τὸν πρῶτον

---

148. Pilhofer, *Philippi*, 2.617. *Singularis* was a junior staff post among the praetorian cohorts. The word *beneficiarius* refers to a soldier who had been promoted by his superiors and freed from routine military duties. However, he was reassigned to higher ranking officers to help them with specialist tasks. *Evocatus* was a soldier who was discharged but who voluntarily reenlisted.

φυροβάφ(ων)], Antiochus, [the son] of Lukos, from Thyateira").[149] This provides an important backdrop to the presence at Philippi of the God-fearer Lydia, who was of freed status and likewise a dealer in purple cloth from the city of Thyatira (Acts 16:14: πορφυρόπωλις πόλεως Θυατείρων).[150] A Thessalonian inscription, also from the province of Macedonia, mentions "an association of purple dyers" (ἡ συνήθεια τῶν πορφυροβάων) of the eighteenth street honoring two members.[151] Although Lydia was not an elite individual and would have been despised as a trader by the provincial hierarchy, she belonged nevertheless to the wealthier echelons of the urban plebs, possessing her own house and being able to extend hospitality (Acts 16:15).[152]

Benefactors also appear in the Philippian inscriptions (*patron*; εὐεργέτης; σωτῆρ),[153] either being priests of the imperial cult, sponsors of the Serapis cult, organizers of the games, or civic benefactors of various unspecified kinds. Other occupations include a teacher, a gymnasiarch, a Latin mime actor, a town crier (or herald) from Philadelphia, a cashier of the bank, an orator, a house steward, a player of the lyre or harp (or, possibly, singer accompanying the musical instrument), clerk of the market, a stone cutter, and, last, a specialist veterinarian for horses.[154] Notwithstanding the complexity of the military organization of the Roman colony of Philippi, revealed in its extensive hierarchy of posts, the sample of occupa-

---

149. Pilhofer, *Philippi*, 2.697. Additionally, Pilhofer, *Philippi*, 2.646 ([*pu*]*rpurari*).
150. G. H. R. Horsley, "The Purple Trade, and the Status of Lydia of Thyatira," *NewDocs 2*: 27–28.
151. *IG* 10.2.1.292 (late second century CE).
152. Peterlin, *Paul's Letter to the Philippians*, 159. For discussion, see Horsley, "Purple Trade"; Peterlin, *Paul's Letter to the Philippians*, 155–60; Richard S. Ascough, *Lydia: Paul's Cosmopolitan Hostess* (Collegeville, MN: Liturgical Press, 2009); Craig Keener, *Acts: An Exegetical Commentary*, vol. 3, *15:1–23:35* (Grand Rapids: Baker, 2014), 2393–2408.
153. Pilhofer, *Philippi*, 2.004, 072, 131, 248, 252, 307, 348, 663, 664.
154. Numbers refer to Pilhofer, *Philippi*, vol. 2: teacher: 071; gymnasiarch: 689 (including a list of *ephebes*, 680, and *neoi* honoring an agoranomos, 665); Latin mime actor: 476; town crier: 301; cashier: 410 (the term "cashier of a bank" is a Greek transliteration of the Latin *arcarius argentarii*; for further examples of the same phenomenon, see Collart, *Philippes*, 304–5; for an excellent example of a Greek transliteration, letter by letter in capitals, of a Latin text at Philippi, see Pilhofer, *Philippi*, 2.048); orator: 098; house steward: 022, 432; lyre or harp player: 647; clerk: 665; stone cutter: 167 (the stonecutter has incised his name: "Bernas has made (the relief and the inscription)"; veterinarian: 322.

tions above is rich and varied, ranging widely across the social echelons of the city.

5.4. Slaves, Freedmen and Agricultural Workers

There is no hint in the epigraphic record of the agricultural poor working outside the city in the wider territory of Philippi. The agricultural day laborers and landless tenant farmers pass unobserved in the epigraphic record, being too poor to leave a tombstone epitaph.[155] Rather, they traveled anonymously from a nearby village or Philippi to their place of work in the countryside when work was actually available. Too often in desperation they would have often been driven by necessity to compete with the urban jobless in the villages, larger towns, or Philippi for whatever unspecialized urban day work may have been available.[156]

But, in the absence of any epigraphic evidence for peasant life at Philippi, it remains to investigate the epigraphic record of slaves (*servus*, δοῦλος, δουλή) and freedmen (*libertus*, *liberta*), some of whom, including those belonging to the prestigious *famila Caesaris* (§8 above),[157] were upwardly mobile and had acquired wealth and status. The important Silvanus association inscriptions,[158] too, will be discussed in the next section. What do we learn about Philippian slaves from the epigraphy?

First, the vast majority of our slave and freedmen inscriptions at Philippi are epitaphs, telling us little else than their master's name, acquisition of freedman/woman status, and family composition.[159] Sometimes the age of the slave is communicated.[160] But, in other cases, substantial status has accrued to those freedmen who became *severi Augustales*.[161] These officials, upon being elected by the municipal senate in the early empire, were expected to give games, restore public works in their own

---

155. Peterlin, *Paul's Letter to the Philippians*, 137.
156. Peterlin, *Paul's Letter to the Philippians*, 138.
157. Pilhofer, *Philippi*, 2.282. Unsurprisingly, the δοῦλος and δουλή terminology is Christian (Pilhofer, *Philippi*, 2:112, 268, 328, 536–37 [see Mark 10:45; Luke 22:26–27; Rom 1:1; 2 Cor 4:5]).
158. Pilhofer, *Philippi*, 2.163–64.
159. Pilhofer, *Philippi*, 2.045.
160. Pilhofer, *Philippi*, 2.392 (seventy-two years old), 528 (twelve years old).
161. Pilhofer, *Philippi*, 2.074b (Titius Cottius, Viriles, freedman of Titus), 721 (Lucius Licinius Euhemerus, freedman of Lucius); see also 037, 505.

towns, and maintain the imperial cult.¹⁶² Obviously, as upwardly mobile freedmen, they had managed to acquire wealth. Another Philippian inscription speaks of Gamicus, freedman of Pontius Novus, who was "the tenant [conduct[or]] for 10 years."¹⁶³ Scholars have speculated what kind of *conductor* Gamicus is. Is he a *conductor metallorum* ("a tenant of a quarry") or a *conductor ferrariarum et marmorum* ("a tenant of an iron and marble mine")?¹⁶⁴ Either way, the freedman has substantial status and significant responsibilities in what was (presumably) his former master's mining interests. Indeed, freedmen were very conscious of the debt they owed to their patron and often dedicated inscriptions to him.¹⁶⁵

Second, issues of religious cult sometimes surface in slave dedications, with some indication of the occupational role of the slave. We see this in a fascinating dedication consecrated to Iuppiter Optimus Maximus, where we find out about a religious vow made by Secundus in response to the direct order of the god: "Secundus, a slave [ser[vus]] of Colonia [col[oniae]] [Philippi] in charge of the water supply, made a vow on god's command [iussi dei]: the priest was a witness."¹⁶⁶ The emphasis on the *iussi dei* is intriguing. The prior divine call of Paul to be an apostle and slave of Jesus Christ also set him apart for the gospel of God (Rom 1:1; Gal 1:1–2a, 15–16 [v. 15a: see Isa 49:1; Jer 1:5; v. 16a: see Isa 42:4b; 49:6b]). However, the apostolic expression of Paul's summons was kerygmatic (Gal 1:16b) and prophetic (1:15a, 16a), as opposed to being cultic, as was the case in our inscription above.

5.5. Conclusion

Finally, brief consideration should be given as to how Paul establishes community in the epistle to the Philippians in a society that was tightly organized around elite hierarchies. In the case of the Roman colony, social prestige based on (1) veteran status, (2) one's Roman census rank (*ordo*), (3) the serendipitous experience of imperial favor, and (4) the acquisition

---

162. See Lily Ross Taylor, "*Augustales, Severi Augustales*, and Severi: A Chronological Study," *TAPA* 45 (1914): 231–53.
163. Pilhofer, *Philippi*, 2.558.
164. Pilhofer, *Philippi*, 2.681.
165. Pilhofer, *Philippi*, 2.582.
166. Pilhofer, *Philippi*, 2.177. The phrase *col(oniae) ser(vus)* might be the Philippian equivalent of *servus publicus* ("public slave").

of military and civic posts in the *cursus honorum*. How did the apostle address the upwardly mobile desires of those converts who desperately wanted to experience higher levels of social status? How did he address the needs of those marginalized by the honor system, with no hope other than continuing humiliation at the hands of the rich and powerful?

Paul's narrative of the elite preexistent Christ (Phil 2:6a: "in the form of God"), who did not cling onto (ἁρπαγμόν) his status of equality before the Father (2:6b) but rather assumed the form of a slave (2:7a), provides the divinely inaugurated paradigm for social leveling in the Philippian church. However, what would have really jarred the status-conscious Philippian believers (Phil 2:3–4) is the numbing depths that the paradigm of the social self-lowering of Christ finally reached (2:5): "even death on a cross" (2:8b).

Furthermore, Christ's socially ignominious but grace-empowering death (Phil 3:9–10a) became the pivotal point of life conformity for the believer (3:10b). It provides the evaluative yardstick for the believer to reject the world's hierarchical boasting in human achievement (3:5–8), while opening up a cruciform and (socially speaking) dishonorable route of upward mobility for the believer toward the future glory of the resurrection (3:11; see also 2:9–11; 3:21). To cite two pertinent examples of this social and theological reevaluative process, (1) it involves the total reconfiguration of the military ethos of the colony, which is now employed metaphorically by Paul for Christian perseverance in the face of suffering (Phil 1:20; 2:19–24, 25–30; 3:12–15; 4:3, 10–19), and (2) the prized Philippian citizenship is supplanted by the believer's current possession of eschatological citizenship in heaven (3:20).[167]

Finally, not only is the social leveling and eschatological elevation of believers christologically and soteriologically articulated by Paul, but also he reconfigures all ecclesial relationships around fictive but socially transformative family bonds (Phil 1:12, 14; 2:25; 3:1, 13, 17; 4:1, 8, 21; see also 2:15). These stand opposed to the status-riddled operations of friendship conventions and the petty rivalries of the elite houses and office

---

167. On the first example, see Mueller, "Military Images," 155–384. On the second example, see Maria Karyakina, "Social Values of Heavenly Society: The Concepts of Honour and Identity in Paul's Letter to the Philippians" (PhD diss., University of Pretoria, 2013). For the prized colonial status of Philippi in the inscriptions, see Pilhofer, *Philippi*, vol. 2, index 7, Philippisches, s.v. "colonia." See also Kathy Ehrensperger, "Rooted in Heaven and Resident in Philippi, but No ἐκκλησία?," in this volume.

holders of the colony.¹⁶⁸ A different understanding of social hierarchy and obligation, family relations, and personal status was now being promoted at Philippi.

6. The Associations of Philippi

6.1. Greco-Roman Associations

Since the Philippian associations and their relationship to the house churches at the colony have been extensively discussed by Ascough,¹⁶⁹ we will only lightly touch on them. The Rosalia festival in the villages of Philippi has been extensively explored above, and attention has been drawn to its relevance for the grave-digger association at Philippi.¹⁷⁰ We have also already mentioned above the two purple-cloth dealer inscriptions at Philippi and their relevance to Lydia in Acts 16:14. Christians were also involved in the purple-dyer profession at Tyre and Corinth later in the empire.¹⁷¹ Purple-dyer associations were present at Philippi, Thessalonica, Hierapolis, and Sagalassos.¹⁷² Given that three of the cities above in which the purple industry flourished had Christian house churches (Philippi, Thessalonica, Hierapolis), one wonders whether there were other believers involved in the purple trade in the first century CE, either as cloth dealers or dyers, and whether common trade connections facilitated communication between the house churches in the three cities and elsewhere.

Two final association inscriptions at Philippi remain to be discussed. In the association inscription of the devotees of Liber (Dionysus), Libera, and Hercules, the female attendants of the god (maenads) brought in

---

168. See Hellerman, "Brothers and Friends in Philippi." Ben Witherington III writes that Paul relates to the Philippians "as family and does not call them friends." See Ben Witherington III, *Paul's Letter to the Philippians: A Socio-rhetorical Commentary* (Grand Rapids: Eerdmans, 2011), 20. The Philippian inscriptions are well aware of ancient friendship conventions: Pilhofer, *Philippi*, 2.199/229 ("well-deserving friend"), 386 ("his friend"). On rivalry at Philippi and the house churches, see Samuel Vollenweider, "Rivals, Opponents, and Enemies: Three Kinds of Theological Argumentations in Philippians," in this volume.

169. Ascough, *Paul's Macedonian Associations*.
170. Pilhofer, *Philippi*, 2.029.
171. Horsley, "Purple Trade," 26.
172. Ascough, *Associations in the Greco-Roman World*, 44, 55, 152, 155, 157, 158, 209.

water at their own cost for the cult.[173] Once again we are reminded of the prominence of women in Macedonian religion and perhaps why women in particular responded to the gospel at Philippi (Lydia) and subsequently held leadership positions in the church (Euodia, Syntyche).

Another association inscription, carved in Latin on the rock face of the acropolis, sets out the contributions of the members to the Temple of Silvanus.[174] Not only is the god Silvanus honored by the construction of the temple and the erection of a bronze statue in the second century CE, but other gods and demigods (Heracles, Mercury, Liber) are also honored with statues. Freedmen belong to the association as much as high-status individuals, such as the city's magistrate of public works (aedile) and various priests. Consequently, the funds offered to the association coffers range from 250 denarii to 50, 25, and 15 denarii; some of these funds are deposited as funeral funds for various members. Finally, bonds of fictive kinship exist to some extent, with leaders being designated *pater* ("father").

We see here interesting organizational correspondences to the early house churches: the use of familial language for apostolic leaders ("father": 1 Thess 2:11; 1 Cor 4:15); the setting aside of differentiated amounts of money for common projects (1 Cor 16:2: "each one of you should set aside a sum of money in keeping with his income"; Phil 2:25–30; 4:10–20); a mix of social classes, including freedmen (see Gal 3:28). Whatever the early church learned organizationally from synagogues as associations, we should not discount the other lessons that may have been learned, as well as avoided in terms of unwelcome ethos, from the ubiquitous Greco-Roman associations.[175]

6.2. The Presence of Jews at Philippi: From προσευχή to συναγωγή

Philo informs us that Jews had settled in Macedonia (*Legat.* 281). But the surprise is that not only is there less evidence for a Jewish presence in Macedonia generally than we would perhaps have expected,[176] but also

---

173. Pilhofer, *Philippi*, 2.029. Translated by Ascough, *Associations in the Greco-Roman World*, 43.

174. Pilhofer, *Philippi*, 2.164–66. Translated by Ascough, *Associations in the Greco-Roman World*, 41 (= Pilhofer, *Philippi*, 2.164). For discussion of the Silvanus cult, see Abrahamsen, *Women and Worship*, 35–38.

175. For full discussion, see Ascough, *Paul's Macedonian Associations*, 191–212.

176. Ascough, *Paul's Macedonian Associations*, 190–212. Additionally, see Pil-

the absence of a significantly sized first-century CE Jewish community at Philippi sits uneasily with the traditional understanding of Judaizing opponents or Jewish missionaries being present in the city, based on Phil 3:1-2. The only evidence for the presence of Jews in the city in the first century CE is Luke's record of a Sabbath προσευχή (place of prayer), consisting only of women attenders (Acts 16:13b), thereby disqualifying it as a synagogue.[177] The size of the actual Jewish community in Pauline Philippi belies the threat posed in Phil 3:1-2.

In response, should we assign a polyvalent understanding to Paul's "dog" imagery in Phil 3:2? Paul, it might be argued, is polemicizing against the Artemis canine imagery on the rock reliefs at the Philippian acropolis,[178] by which image he refers generally to the gentile cults, while also alerting his converts to the potential (but currently *not* actual) threat of Jewish missionaries in the future. In short, there is no concerted Jewish opposition present at Philippi provoking Paul's colored language. Our first evidence for a Jewish synagogue at Philippi significantly postdates the New Testament period (third-fourth century CE): "Nikostratos Aurelios Oxycholios himself furnished this flat tomb/grave [and] if someone lays down [on it] a dead body of others, he will give [a fine] to the synagogue."[179]

Our Jewish name, Nikostratos Aurelios Oxycholios, is a blend of names from different ethnicities, typical of diaspora Jews living in the Roman empire at the time.[180] "Nikostratos" (*praenomen* [first name]) is name Greek; "Aurelios" (*gentilicium* or *nomen gentis* [family name]) is a Roman name (i.e., Aurelius), probably indicating that his Roman citizenship was acquired after Caracalla's 212 CE edict;[181] "Oxycholios" (the *supernomen* or *agnomen* [additional name]) is another Greek name. In particular, the *agnomen* often denoted a significant achievement or

---

hofer (*Philippi*, 1:233-34) on the small size and financial weakness of the Jewish community at Philippi.

177. Ascough, *Paul's Macedonian Associations*, 209. See also Keener, *Acts*, 3:2383-88.

178. See my companion essay in this volume.

179. Pilhofer, *Philippi*, 2.387. Translated by Chaido Koukouli-Chrysantaki, "Colonia Iulia Augusta Philippensis," in Bakirtzis and Koester, eds., *Philippi at the Time of Paul*, 28. A Philippian epitaph ("Simon, the Smyrnan": Pilhofer, *Philippi*, 2.381a) speaks of a Jewish resident of Philippi, originating from another city, but, like our synagogue inscription, it dates to the third century CE.

180. Koukouli-Chrysantaki, "Colonia Iulia Augusta Philippensis," 29-30.

181. Koukouli-Chrysantaki, "Colonia Iulia Augusta Philippensis," 30.

characteristic of the person (or his family). Thus Oxycholios, deriving from the adjective ὀξύχολος (quick-tempered), should not necessarily be construed as "pejorative," as Chaido Koukouli-Chrysantaki suggests,[182] but rather as a semihumorous comment on a well-known family trait (see Mark 3:17). In conclusion, as we have noted, because of the lateness of our evidence, in this instance there exist discontinuities between the first-century context of Philippi and its later third- to fourth-century Jewish expressions.

7. Games, Spectacles, and Entertainment at Philippi

7.1. Games and Spectacles

The ubiquitous culture of athletic games and Roman spectacles for the urban plebs are part of Philippian life. There is mention in a third-century CE honorific inscription of Quintus Flavius Hermadion at Philippi, who was a gymnasiarch (γυμνασίαρχος), high priest, and the games director (ἀγωνοθέτης) of the Great Asklepeia.[183] As a gymnasiarch, he would have seen his young charges wrestling at the *palestra* of Philippi,[184] close to the gymnasium. In regards to the gymnasium, there is a list of the *ephebes*, and the *neoi* honor an *agoranomos*.[185]

Finally, given the refurbishments of the theatre in the second–third century CE for animal fights,[186] it is not surprising that mention of spectacles occurs in the Philippian inscriptions. There is mention, in an inscription (second–third century CE) from outside the territory of Philippi, but whose provenance is unknown, of a gladiator from Philippi.[187] More importantly, there is a verse epitaph (third century CE) of an animal fighter, found in the narthex of Basilica B, who had fought in the *venationes* (animal hunts):

---

182. Koukouli-Chrysantaki, "Colonia Iulia Augusta Philippensis," 31.
183. Pilhofer, *Philippi*, 2.311.
184. The *palestra* is mentioned in Pilhofer, *Philippi*, 2.129. For the archaeological remains, see Lemerle, "Palestre romaine à Philippes." For a reconstruction of the *palestra*, see M. Sève, "Urbanisme, architecture et territoire," in Fournier, ed., *Philippes, de la préhistoire à Byzance*, 148 fig. 16.
185. Pilhofer, *Philippi*, 2.665, 680.
186. Gournaris and Gounari, *Philippi*, 30.
187. Pilhofer, *Philippi*, 2.703.

[…] on behalf of which I—from a glorio[usly] famous family—have completed my fate. A man may enjoy other things—but I [really] like this [career of animal fighting]. A demon ordered me to die on famous ground, [which is] a foundation of Philip and Emperor Augustus, well-crowed with walls. I left the sweet light of the world behind. But if a man puts another in my grave, he should pay the city treasury two thousand denarii.[188]

To the left on the base, large reliefs have been sculpted, seemingly before the inscription was inscribed, the overall effect of which captures the bravery required and danger posed for the fighter. There are two distinct portraits: in the first scene, a completely nude man, struggling with his spear, courageously faces a ferocious beast (possibly a lion?), whereas, in the second scene, another large-maned beast (another lion?) stands behind him, ready to bound in attack.[189]

As far as the content of the inscription, we have already discussed above Philippian beliefs about the demonic and Hades. But what is especially interesting, as a countervailing sentiment to this gloomy reality, is the great honor accorded to a death on the hallowed territory of the city of Philippi articulated in the inscription, given the fame of its two founders, one Greek, the other Roman. The inscription, written in Greek, caters well to the Greek and Roman residents of Philippi by emphasizing both venerable founder traditions of the city.

In sum, there is little doubt, as recent scholarship has shown, that in the Corinthian epistles Paul has been influenced by gladiator imagery.[190] But, in the case of the more general games imagery of Philippians, it can be more ambiguous in its reference. For example, the upward victory call in Christ of the divine ἀγωνοθέτης to the believing spiritual athlete seems clear enough in Phil 3:14 (τῆς ἄνω κλήσεως).[191] However, in the case of

---

188. Pilhofer, *Philippi*, 2.296.

189. Lemerle, "Inscriptions latines et grecques de Philippes. II," 148.

190. See C. W. Concannon, "'Not for an Olive Wreath, but Our Lives': Gladiators, Athletes, and Early Christian Bodies," *JBL* 133 (2014): 193–214; Alan H. Cadwallader, "Paul and the Games," in *Paul in the Greco-Roman World: A Handbook*, ed. J. Paul Sampley (London: Bloomsbury T&T Clark, 2016), 1:363–90; James Unwin, "Subversive Spectacles: The Struggles and Deaths of Paul and Seneca" (PhD diss., Macquarie University, 2017).

191. E.g., J.-F. Collange, *The Epistle of Saint Paul to the Philippians*, BNTC/HNTC (London, 1979), 134; G. F. Hawthorne, *Philippians*, WBC 43 (Waco, TX: Word, 1983), 154–55.

συναθλέω (Phil 1:27; 4:3), whether the reference is military or athletic in its reference is more difficult to determine.[192]

7.2. Mime Troupes

A first-century CE inscription from the village of Drama in the Philippian territory honors an *archimimus* (chief mimic actor) for his entertainment contribution to the Roman colony. For almost two decades Venerianus held the position of *promisthota*, a Latin transcription for the unknown Greek word προμισθώτης. The Greek transliteration is not found in LSJ, but it appears once in a first-century BCE Greek inscription from Thessalia (*SEG* 33.466), the epitaph of a pantomime actor called Spendon. The inscription is erected by Repentinus the προμισθώτης, which the *Supplementum Epigraphicum Graecum* editor takes to be the equivalent of the Latin *locator scenicorum* (contractor for stage scenes). Traveling mime troupes were well known in the early empire, though, from the inscription below, Venerianus seems to be permanently based at Philippi for eighteen years. Therefore, as several scholars have suggested,[193] προμισθώτης is best understood an impresario, a director of theater, or entrepreneur of spectacles. The inscription on the sarcophagus ensures that the great fame of Venerianus and his most worthy wife is not sullied by their heirs recycling the sarcophagus for their own internment:

> Titius Uttiedius Venerianus, for thirty-seven ye[ars] the Latin principal actor in mi[me] and employee [of the city of Philippi], [and] for eighteen ye[ars] the *promisthota*, lived seventy-five years. During his lifetime [he has made the sarcophagus] for himself and for his much deserving wife Alfena Saturnina. Alfena Saturnina, fifty-one ye[ars old]. T[his] sarcopha[gus] does not p[ass] to the heirs.[194]

The relevance of this inscription for Pauline studies is better appreciated when we recall Paul's use of well-known tropes from the mime shows in 1 Cor 1–4 and in the famous Fool's Speech of 2 Corinthians (11:16–

---

192. Dominika Kurek-Chomycz, "Fellow Athletes or Fellow Soldiers? Συναθλέω in Philippians 1:27 and 4:3," *JSNT* 39 (2017): 279–303.

193. Pilhofer, *Philippi*, 2.553–55. The word has been suggested (553) to be the equivalent of the Latin *locator* ("contractor") or *locator a scena* ["contractor for theater"])/*locator scenicorum* ["contractor for stage scenes"]).

194. Pilhofer, *Philippi*, 2.476.

12:10).¹⁹⁵ Paul would have been exposed to the world of mime city by city in the Greek East and in Asia Minor. An even more interesting possibility emerges, if one accepts L. L. Welborn's intriguing suggestion that σκηνοποιός (Acts 18:3: tentmaker) means in its first-century context a "maker of stage properties" for the mime shows.¹⁹⁶ Would an entrepreneur like Venerianus have employed Paul as a prop maker for his mime shows, if the scenario that Welborn proposes is true? Would Aquila and Priscilla have also carried out the same theatrical craft, as Acts 18:3 makes clear? A great deal of interpretative weight rides on the puzzling term σκηνοποιός and its relation to the hermeneutical potential of our first-century Philippian inscription.

7.3. The Circus Relief in the Octagon at Philippi

A badly damaged mosaic of a chariot race in the circus, datable to the fourth century CE, has been unearthed on a pavement in the Octagon of Philippi. Such scenes were very common in the western Provinces, North Africa, and Italy from the first-century BCE onwards.¹⁹⁷ Several stages of the race remain visible around the central circus wall (*spina*), including representations of the *quadrigae* (chariots), charioteers, and horses. The differently colored clothing of the charioteers, one of whom is identified as Alkeides (ΑΛΚΕΙΔΗΣ), indicates the particular faction to which they belong. One of the *quadrigae* of the red faction has met with an accident. Other auxiliary figures of the race (e.g., the *sparsor* who waters the horses; e.g. the *hortator*, a faction employee) are also visible. One of the two turning posts (*metae*)—consisting of three cones, each of which is topped with an egg-shaped decoration—can be seen, along with the lap-counting devices at the eastern and western ends of the stadium. There are also representations of statues (Ceres, Minerva, Roma, Apollo, Hercules),

---

195. L. L. Welborn, "The Runaway Paul," *HTR* 92 (1999): 122–37; Welborn, *Paul, the Fool for Christ: A Study of 1 Corinthians 1–4 in Its Philosophic-Comic Tradition*, JSNTSup 293 (London: T&T Clark, 2005). For an attempt at blunting Welborn's strong case in 2 Cor 11:14–12:10, see Ryan S. Schellenberg, *Rethinking Paul's Rhetorical Education*, ECL 10 (Atlanta: Society of Biblical Literature, 2013), 141–48.

196. Welborn, *Paul, the Fool for Christ*, 111–12.

197. For further mosaic representations in the Roman empire, see John Bradford, *Roman Circuses: Arenas for Chariot Racing* (London: Batsford, 1986), index 3, Representations, s.v. "mosaics." For discussion of the Philippi mosaic, see Gounari, "Roman Mosaics from Philippi." For a representation of the entire mosaic, see 29 fig. 2.

men pouring libations at an altar, a fountain on a base, various prizes, and a monster. Whether chariot racing took place at Philippi is unable to be confirmed, since no remains of a Roman circus have yet been found or references made to it in ancient writers.[198]

8. Philippians 1:13 and 4:22: Paul's Imprisonment and the *Familia Caesaris*

The recent thesis of Michael Flexsenhar III on the slaves of Christ has to be briefly taken into account before we proceed to a consideration of πραιτωρίον in Phil 1:13 and ἐκ τῆς Καίσαρος οἰκίας in 4:22.[199] I will only concentrate on what Flexsenhar says about the *familia Caesaris* in Philippians,[200] leaving aside the rest of his outstanding contribution to historical research. After critiquing the scholarly consensus (e.g., A. von Harnack, J. B. Lightfoot, P. R. C. Weaver) on the upward mobility of the *familia Caesaris* and its relevance for the thesis that early Christians penetrated the upper classes,[201] Flexsenhar argues:

1. That Paul was in prison at Ephesus, not Rome or Caesarea Maritima, when he was writing Philippians (Phil 1:14).[202]
2. That the *praetorium* (πραιτωρίον) mentioned in Phil 1:13 was a provincial administrative building for the proconsul and his staff in Ephesus, not Lightfoot's suggestion of the Praetorian Guard at Rome.[203]

---

198. Gounari, "Roman Mosaics from Philippi," 31 n. 30.
199. Michael A. Flexsenhar III, "Slaves of Christ: Caesar's Household and the Early Christians" (PhD diss., University of Texas at Austin, 2016). The following five paragraphs are drawn from James R. Harrison, *Reading Romans with Roman Eyes: Studies on the Social Perspective of St Paul* (Minneapolis: Fortress, forthcoming), ch. 3.
200. Flexsenhar, "Slaves of Christ," 1–182.
201. On von Harnack, Lightfoot, and Weaver, see Flexsenhar, "Slaves of Christ," 4–11, 113–20, 40–69, respectively. It should be noted that Adolf Deissmann supports the Ephesian hypothesis: "simple Imperial slaves, petty clerks, employed perhaps at Ephesus in the departments of finance or of crown lands." Adolf Deissmann, *Light from the Ancient East* (New York: Hodder & Stoughton, 1910), 160.
202. Flexsenhar, "Slaves of Christ," 112–27.
203. Flexsenhar, "Slaves of Christ," 112–27. Flexsenhar also suggests it could refer to the lodging of Roman officials either traveling or residing outside Ephesus (124).

3. That the believing members of *familia Cesaris* at Ephesus (Phil 4:20) were only involved in the middle to the lower levels of imperial administration (subclerical).[204]
4. That members of the *familia Caesaris* at Ephesus knew key members of the Philippian community via slave social networks (e.g., ethno-geographic, family-household, occupation-labor, cultic).[205]

Flexsenhar's seminal work is characterized by meticulous attention to the epigraphic evidence. He unfolds the meaning of the rare term *familia Casaris* in an excellent discussion of all the relevant epigraphic evidence, helpfully reveals the operations of the imperial family of slaves at Ephesus,[206] outlines the nature of the wide-ranging slave networks, and provides a detailed examination of the meaning of πραιτωρίον, among many other rich contributions. We are so much the richer for Flexsenhar's superb scholarship. But is he correct regarding an Ephesian provenance of Philippians and, concomitantly, the *familia Carsaris* and *praetorium*?

The wording of Phil 1:13, which has been debated since Lightfoot's seminal contribution, does not point to a building (or residential accommodation) but rather to imperial personnel.[207] The phrase "and all the others" (Phil 1:13b: καὶ τοῖς λοιποῖς πᾶσιν), added to ἐν ὅλῳ τῷ πραιτωρίῳ ("in the praetorium"), therefore, must refer to human beings (i.e., soldiers), the reference to humans being contextually supported by the subsequent reference to "most of the brothers in the Lord" (Phil 1:14a).[208] In response Flexsenhar argues from much older traditional readings that the phrase καὶ τοῖς λοιποῖς πᾶσιν means "in all other (places)," verifying that Paul's use of πραιτωρίον has a building in mind.[209] Flexsenhar adds that Paul would not have used the dative singular neuter form of πραιτωρίον if indeed he had wished to indicate a group of soldiers (the Praetorian Guard). Instead the genitive singular (πραιτωριονός) for a guard(s) would have been chosen.[210] But, even if Flexsenhar is correct about the πραιτωρίον denoting a

---

204. Flexsenhar, "Slaves of Christ," 137–46, at esp. 143.
205. For the networks and their applicability to Ephesus and Philippi, see Flexsenhar, "Slaves of Christ," 149–80.
206. Flexsenhar, "Slaves of Christ," 80–92, 129–36.
207. Holloway, *Philippians*, 21–22.
208. Holloway, *Philippians*, 27.
209. Flexsenhar, "Slaves of Christ," 113.
210. Flexsenhar, "Slaves of Christ," 118–19. In 35 n. 119, Flexsenhar cites other examples of the substantive referring to buildings.

building, an Ephesian provenance is not thereby ensured (or a Caesarea Maritima provenance, for that matter). But, in the history of interpretation in a pre-Lightfoot era, various buildings at Rome have been suggested as identifications for our noun: remotely, the imperial palace on the Palatine, but more likely, a small Praetorian barracks attached to the palace or the Praetorian camp itself outside the Colline Gate or Porta Viminalis.[211] In this instance a locative use of the dative πραιτωρίῳ is envisaged. No use of the genitive singular πραιτωριονός is therefore required, since the location itself implies the presence of the Praetorian Guard. If this locative understanding is viable for Rome, as opposed to Ephesus, then καὶ τοῖς λοιποῖς πᾶσιν means something like "a far wider circle," perhaps referring in hyperbolic manner to the Praetorian guards assigned over two years to guard him under his house arrest (Acts 28:16, 30),[212] or to other smaller specialized units of the Praetorian Guard, temporarily and variously assigned as occasion demanded to sites now unknown inside or outside the city.

Assuming, then, that the epistle to the Philippians was written during the imprisonment of Paul with the Praetorian Guard in Rome, in whatever location that may be, it is clear that some believers belonged to the *familia Caesaris* in the capital (Phil 4:22: ἐκ τῆς Καίσαρος οἰκίας).[213] We gain a sense of the important social status of slaves who belonged to the imperial bureaucracy from the intriguing case of an Egyptian free citizen called Herminos, mentioned in a papyrus (early first century CE: P.Oxy. 46.3312), who "went off to Rome and became a freedman of Caesar [ἀπελεύθερος ἐγένετ[ο] Καίσαρος] in order to take appointments."[214] E. A.

---

211. See Reumann, *Philippians*, 171.

212. Reumann, *Philippians*, 171–72.

213. S. K. Stowers, *A Rereading of Romans: Justice, Jews, and Gentiles* (New Haven: Yale University Press, 1994), 76; M. J. Brown, "Paul's Use of ΔΟΥΛΟΣ ΧΡΙΣΤΟΥ ΙΗΣΟΥ in Romans 1:1," *JBL* 120 (2001): 724–25; Holloway, *Philippians*, 190–91. For the most recent defense of the Roman origin of the captivity epistles, see Ben Witherington III, "The Case of the Imprisonment That Did Not Happen: Paul at Ephesus," *JETS* 60 (2017): 525–32. Additionally, see Bockmuehl, *Epistle to the Philippians*, 25–32.

214. G. H. R. Horsley, "Joining the Household of Caesar," *NewDocs* 3:7–9; Flexsenhar, "Slaves of Christ," 165–67. For examples from the literary evidence of freedmen seeking power by entering the imperial service as slaves, each unauthorized attempts, see Pliny, *Nat.* 12.12; Tacitus, *Hist.* 2.92. Cited in P. R. C. Weaver, *Familia Caesaris: A Social Study of the Emperor's Freemen and Slaves* (Cambridge: Cambridge University Press, 1972), 36. See, too, Peter Oakes's cautionary comments about not overstating the case for the "upward social mobility" of slaves from a limited sample of

Judge has correctly noted that an attempt by an imperial slave to go Rome for the same purpose would need strong prior patronal support from within Caesar's household for it to be successful (was he successful at all?), as well as considerable funds for the journey and the cost of his manumission.[215] Normally this would imply that direct entry into the *familia Caesaris* was a very difficult route for the upwardly mobile seeking greater status on their own initiative. However, this papyrus is seemingly blithely ignorant of all of this, perhaps implying either that our knowledge of entry into the *familia Caesaris* is deficient and there were unexpected opportunities for talented entrepreneurs to squeeze their way in, or that this particular individual has access to patronal connections invisible to us but that are well known to the senders and recipients of the letter.[216] But, in the case of the Roman believers who belonged to the *familia Caesaris* in the capital, their entry into service of Caesar would probably have occurred in the early Julio-Claudian age from the outside, particularly during the reigns of Augustus and Tiberius, facilitated by gift, bequest, or legacy, or by the ruler's purchase or confiscation.[217] Their conversion took place considerably later.

On the basis of our slender evidence, we cannot specify what roles urban believing slaves might have fulfilled in the imperial administration. Certainly the tombstones of slaves in the *familia Casaris* at Rome are usually clear about their important status, but we have no way of knowing whether believers could have filled any of these more prestigious posts.[218] Or were some of the believers slave-owned slaves (*servi vicarii*),

---

slaves in the *family Caesaris*. Peter Oakes, *Reading Romans in Pompeii: Paul's Letter at Ground Level* (Minneapolis: Augsburg Fortress, 2010), 78–79.

215. See Edwin A. Judge, "Rank and Status in the World of the Caesars and St Paul," in *Social Distinctives of the Christians in the First Century: Pivotal Essays by E. A. Judge*, ed. David M. Scholer (Peabody, MA: Hendrickson, 2008), 148.

216. Judge, "Rank and Status," 148.

217. Weaver, *Familia Caesaris*, 199.

218. B. K. Harvey, *Roman Lives: Ancient Roman Life as Illustrated by Latin Inscriptions*, Focus Classical Sources (Newburyport, MA: Focus Publishing/Pullins, 2004), 67 [*CIL* 5.5188]: "in charge of the Greek library in the temple of Apollo"; Harvey, *Roman Lives*, 69 [*CIL* 5.5195]: "chamberlain of the second level"; Harvey, *Roman Lives*, 70 [*CIL* 6.4226]: "steward of the Lollian warehouses"; Harvey, *Roman Lives*, 81; Arthur E. Gordon, in collaboration with Joyce S. Gordon, *Album of Dated Latin Inscriptions*, 4 vols. (Berkeley, University of California Press, 1958–1965), 1:122: "imperial secretary."

recruited as personal slaves of the imperial slave administrators?[219] Or did some slaves belong to the houses of powerful imperial freedmen at Rome, a distinct possibility if the reference to the "household of Narcissus" (ἐκ τῶν Ναρκίσσου) is indeed the powerful freedman in the Claudian bureaucracy (Rom 16:11b; see Tacitus, *Ann.* 13.3; Dio Cassius, *Hist. Rom.* 60.3)?[220] Alternatively, were some believers members of the "non-clerical, non-financial, non-professional" retinue of slaves serving on the domestic staff of the imperial palace?[221] Unfortunately, we cannot speak with any precision.

Returning to the epigraphic context of Philippi, there are a few references to soldiers belonging to the Praetorian cohort at Philippi,[222] in addition to the numismatic evidence noted above (*RPC* 1.1651). Flexsenhar correctly notes that there would have been interaction between the *familia Caesaris* at Ephesus and Philippi, particularly in the form of imperial couriers (*tabellarii*) carrying formal correspondence.[223] The Philippians themselves would have known of representatives from the *familia Caesaris* in their city, as an inscription in honor of Tiberius and Drusus in Basilica B in Philippi demonstrates. But this stands in contrast to the large amount of *familia Caesaris* inscriptions at Ephesus. Our sole inscribed monument at Philippi was erected by three freedmen of Caius

---

219. For a fine example of an inscription from Rome of a *servus vicarii*, see the inscription of Musicus Scurranus, slave of the Roman ruler Tiberius (Harvey, *Roman Lives*, 68 [*CIL* 6.5197]). The *vicarii* mentioned hold the following positions: salesman, administrator of household expenses, three secretaries, doctor, two financial advisers, wardrobe, chamberlain, two manservants, two cooks, minor chamberlain. The diverse skills of the *vicarii* are especially worthy of note. Moreover, Harvey observes that the inscription "demonstrates the surprisingly independent lifestyles some slaves enjoyed, despite their servile status" (*Roman Lives*, 102). If some of the believing slaves belonging to the *familia Caesaris* were *vicarii*, it allows us to see how their specialized gifts could possibly be used in the body of Christ, as well as the freedom that they would have had before 64 CE in attending the meetings of believers within the capitol.

220. See Brown, "Paul's Use of ΔΟΥΛΟΣ ΧΡΙΣΤΟΥ ΙΗΣΟΥ," 36.

221. Weaver, *Familia Caesaris*, 227. For example, Harvey, *Roman Lives*, 78 [*CIL* 6.8958]: "hairdresser"; Harvey, *Roman Lives*, 79 [*CIL* 6.9037]: "seamstress"; Harvey, *Roman Lives*, 80 [*CIL* 6.9097]: "masseuse."

222. Pilhofer, *Philippi*, 2.202 (96 CE), 429 (undated), 617 (138 CE). See Flexsenhar, "Slaves of Christ," 119 n. 38.

223. Flexsenhar, "Slaves of Christ," 172–73. For a list of the Ephesian inscriptions referring to the *famila Caesaris* at Ephesus and Asia more widely, see Flexsenhar, "Slaves of Christ," 133–36.

Iulius Augustus, namely, Cadmus, Atimetus, and Martialis.[224] Whatever the truth of the provenance of Philippians, the imperial slave networks would have provided opportunities for believers to communicate with each other across the eastern Mediterranean basin.

9. Conclusion

The material culture of Philippi has been extensively excavated for more than a century now, with immense benefit to New Testament and classical scholars in terms of the epigraphy, archaeology, numismatics, and iconography unearthed. The main challenge remaining for New Testament scholars interested in Paul's Philippi is that the bulk of our evidence, documentary and archaeological, dates from the second century CE onwards. The key methodological issue is how to determine from this later evidence what might be continuous or discontinuous with Paul's much-loved epistle to his congregation in the first century CE.

Bibliography

Abrahamsen, Valerie A. "Christianity and the Rock Reliefs at Philippi." *BA* 51 (1988): 46–56.

———. "Priestesses and Other Female Cult Leaders at Philippi in the Early Christian Era." Pages 25–62 in *The People beside Paul: The Philippian Assembly and History from Below*. Edited by Joseph A. Marchal. ECL. Atlanta: SBL Press, 2015.

———. *Women and Worship at Philippi: Diana/Artemis and Other Cults in the Early Christian Era*. Portland, ME: Astarte Shell, 1995.

Archaeological Lists Fund, ed. *Archaeological Site of Philippi: Nomination for Inscription on the UNESCO World Heritage List*. Athens: Hellenic Republic—Ministry of Culture and Sports, 2016.

---

224. Pilhofer, *Philippi*, 2.282. Out of the seventeen *libertus* and six *liberta* inscriptions in the Philippian corpus, this is the only case of freedmen from the *familia Caesaris* at Philippi. Pilhofer concludes regarding the inscriptional evidence: "Other members of the *familia Caesaris* have not yet appeared in Philippi" (344). Did the freedmen belong to the *familia Caesaris* at Ephesus and migrate to Philippi in Augustus's reign? Or did they come directly from Rome itself? Or from another Roman cony entirely (e.g., Corinth, Pisidian Antioch)? The occasion of and reason for their arrival at Philippi is lost to us.

Ascough, Richard S. *Lydia: Paul's Cosmopolitan Hostess*. Collegeville, MN: Liturgical Press, 2009.

———. "Paul's 'Apocalypticism' and the Jesus Associations at Thessalonica and Corinth." Pages 151–86 in *Redescribing Paul and the Corinthians*. Edited by Ron Cameron and Merrill P. Miller. ECL 5. Atlanta: Society of Biblical Literature, 2011.

———. *Paul's Macedonian Associations: The Social Context of Philippians and 1 Thessalonians*. WUNT 2/161. Tübingen: Mohr Siebeck, 2003.

———. "Response: Broadening the Socioeconomic and Religious Context at Philippi." Pages 99–106 in *The People beside Paul: The Philippian Assembly and History from Below*. Edited by Joseph A. Marchal. ECL. Atlanta: SBL Press, 2015

Bakirtzis, Charalambos. "Paul and Philippi: The Archaeological Evidence." Pages 37–48 in *Philippi at the Time of Paul and after His Death*. Edited by Bakirtzis, Charalambos, and Helmut Koester. Harrisburg, PA: Trinity Press International, 1998.

Bakirtzis, Charalambos, and Helmut Koester, eds. *Philippi at the Time of Paul and after His Death*. Harrisburg, PA: Trinity Press International, 1998.

Bloomquist, L. Gregory. *The Function of Suffering in Philippians*. JSNTSup 78. Sheffield: Sheffield Academic, 1993.

———. "Subverted by Joy: Suffering and Joy in Paul's Letter to the Philippians." *Int* 61 (2007): 270–82.

Bockmuehl, Markus. *The Epistle to the Philippians*. BNTC 11. Peabody, MA: Hendrickson, 1998.

Bormann, Lukas. *Philippi: Stadt und Christengemeinde zur Zeit des Paulus*. NovTSup 58. Leiden: Brill, 1995.

Bradford, John. *Roman Circuses: Arenas for Chariot Racing*. London: Batsford, 1986.

Brélaz, Cédric. *Corpus des inscriptions grecques et latines de Philippes*. Vol. 2: *Le colonies romaine*. Part 1: *La vie publique de la colonie*. Athènes: École Française d'Athènes, 2014.

———. "Le faciès institutionnel, social et reigieux d'une colonie romaine dans la province de Macédoine." Pages 199–214 in *Philippes, de la préhistoire à Byzance: Études d'archéologie et d'histoire*. Edited by Julien Fournier. BCHSupp 55. Athens: École française d'Athènes, 2016.

Briones, David E. *Paul's Financial Policy: A Socio-theological Approach*. LNTS 494. New York: Bloomsbury, 2013.

Brown, M. J. "Paul's Use of ΔΟΥΛΟΣ ΧΡΙΣΤΟΥ ΙΗΣΟΥ in Romans 1:1." *JBL* 120 (2001): 723–37.
Cadwallader, Alan H. "Paul and the Games." Pages 363–90 in vol. 1 of *Paul in the Greco-Roman World: A Handbook*. Edited by J. Paul Sampley. London: Bloomsbury T&T Clark, 2016.
Collange, J.-F. *The Epistle of Saint Paul to the Philippians*. BNTC/HNTC. London: Epworth, 1979.
Collart, Paul. "Inscriptions de Philippes, I." *BCH* 56 (1932): 192–231.
———. "Inscriptions de Philippes, II." *BCH* 57 (1933): 313–79.
———. "Inscriptions de Philippes, IV." *BCH* 62 (1938): 409–32.
———. "Le sanctuaire des dieux égyptiens à Philippes." *BCH* 53 (1929): 70–100.
———. "Le theatre de Philippes." *BCH* 52 (1928): 74–124.
———. "Une refection de la 'Via Egnatia' sous Trajan." *BCH* 59 (1935): 395–415.
Collart, Paul, and Pierre Ducrey. *Philippes I: Les reliefs rupestres*. BCHSupp 2. Athens: École française d'Athènes, 1975.
Concannon, C. W. "'Not for an Olive Wreath, but Our Lives': Gladiators, Athletes, and Early Christian Bodies." *JBL* 133 (2014): 193–214.
Coupry, Jacques. "Sondage à l'ouest du forum de Philippes." *BCH* 62 (1938): 42–50.
Deissmann, Adolf. *Light from the Ancient East*. New York: Hodder & Stoughton, 1910.
Feher, Géza. "À propos des inscriptions protobulgares de la basilique de Philippes." *BCH* 59 (1935): 165–74.
Feyel, Michel, and Jacques Coupry. "Inscriptions de Philippes, III." *BCH* 60 (1936): 37–58.
Flexsenhar, Michael A., III. "Slaves of Christ: Caesar's Household and the Early Christians." PhD diss., University of Texas at Austin, 2016.
Fournier, Julien, ed. *Philippes, de la préhistoire à Byzance: Études d'archéologie et d'histoire*. BCHSupp 55. Athens: École française d'Athènes, 2016.
Friesen, Steven J., et al., eds. *Philippi, from Colonia Augusta to Communitas Christiana: Religion and Society in Transition*. Leiden: Brill, forthcoming.
Gelzer, Matthias. *The Roman Nobility*. Translated by Robin Seager. Oxford: Basil Blackwell, 1969.

Gorman, Michael J. *Inhabiting the Cruciform God: Kenosis, Justification, and Theosis in Paul's Narrative Soteriology*. Grand Rapids: Eerdmans, 2009.

Gordon, Arthur E., in collaboration with Joyce S. Gordon. *Album of Dated Latin Inscriptions*. 4 vols. Berkeley, University of California Press, 1958–1965.

Gounari, Emmanouela. "The Roman Mosaics from Philippi: Evidence of the Presence of the Romans in the City." *Bollettino di Archeologia On Line* (2010): 27–38.

Gournaris, Georgios, and Emmanuela Gounari. *Philippi: Archaeological Guide*. Thessalonica: University Studio, 2004.

Gregory, A. P. "Village Society in Hellenistic and Roman Asia Minor." PhD diss., Columbia University, 1997.

Harrison, James R. "Ephesian Cultic Officials, Their Benefactors and the Quest for Civic Virtue: Paul's Alternative Quest for Status in Ephesians 1:3–14." Pages 253–97 in *Ephesus*. Vol. 3 of *The First Urban Churches*. Edited by James R. Harrison and L. L. Welborn. WGRWSup 9. Atlanta: SBL Press, 2018.

———. "An Epigraphic Portrait of Ephesus and Its Villages." Pages 1–67 in *Ephesus*. Vol. 3 of *The First Urban Churches*. Edited by James R. Harrison and L. L. Welborn. WGRWSup 9. Atlanta: SBL Press, 2018.

———. *Reading Romans with Roman Eyes: Studies on the Social Perspective of St Paul*. Minneapolis: Fortress, forthcoming.

Harvey, B. K. *Roman Lives: Ancient Roman Life as Illustrated by Latin Inscriptions*. Focus Classical Sources. Newburyport, MA: Focus Publishing/Pullins, 2004.

Hawthorne, Gerard F. "In the Form of God and Equal with God (Philippians 2:6)." Pages 97–101 *Where Christology Began: Essays on Philippians 2*. Edited by Ralph P. Martin and Brian J. Dodd. Louisville: Westminster John Knox, 1998.

———. *Philippians*. WBC 43. Waco, TX: Word, 1983.

Hellerman, Joseph H. "Brothers and Friends in Philippi: Family Honor in the Roman World and in Paul's Letter to the Philippians." *BTB* 39 (2009): 15–25.

———. *Reconstructing Honor in Roman Philippi: Carmen Christi as Cursus Pudorum*. SNTSMS 132. Cambridge: Cambridge University Press, 2005.

Heuzey, Léon, and Honoré Daumet. *Mission archéologique de Macédonie*. Paris: Firmin-Didot et Cie, 1876.

Hoey, A. S. "Rosaliae Signorum." *HTR* 30 (1937): 22–30.
Holloway, Paul A. *Consolation in Philippians: Philosophical Sources and Rhetorical Strategy*. SNTSMS 112. Cambridge: Cambridge University Press, 2001.
———. *Philippians*. Hermeneia. Minneapolis: Fortress, 2017.
Horsley, G. H. R. "Joining the Household of Caesar." *NewDocs* 3:7–9.
———. "The Purple Trade, and the Status of Lydia of Thyatira." *NewDocs* 2:25–32.
Iliadis, George. "Iconography of the Hero Horseman and the Continuity of the Imagery of the Horse Rider in the Plain of Philippi and Drama in Northern Greece." *Revista Santuários*. https://tinyurl.com/SBL4216d.
Itgenshorst, T. *Tota illa pompa: Der Triumph in der römischen Republik*. Göttingen: Vandenhoeck & Ruprecht, 2005.
Jellonek, Szymon. "The Coins of Philippi: An Example of Colonial Coinage." Pages 51–60 in *Pecunia Omnes Vincit: The Coins as an Evidence of Propaganda, Reorganization and Forgery; Conference Proceedings of the Second International Numismatics Conference: Kraków 29–30 May 2015*. Edited by Barbara Zając et al. Kraków: Institute of Archaeology, Jagiellonian University, 2017.
Judge, Edwin A. "Rank and Status in the World of the Caesars and St Paul." Pages 137–56 in *Social Distinctives of the Christians in the First Century: Pivotal Essays by E. A. Judge*. Edited by David M. Scholer. Peabody, MA: Hendrickson, 2008.
Karyakina, Maria. "Social Values of Heavenly Society: The Concepts of Honour and Identity in Paul's Letter to the Philippians." PhD diss., University of Pretoria, 2013.
Koukouli-Chrysantaki, Chaido. "Colonia Iulia Augusta Philippensis." Pages 4–36 in *Philippi at the Time of Paul and after His Death*. Edited by Charalambos Bakirtzis and Helmut Koester. Harrisburg, PA: Trinity Press International, 1998.
Kreitzer, Larry J. "'When He at Last Is First!': Philippians 2:9–11 and the Exaltation of the Lord," Pages 111–27 *Where Christology Began: Essays on Philippians 2*. Edited by Ralph P. Martin and Brian J. Dodd. Louisville: Westminster John Knox, 1998.
Kremydi-Sicilianou, Sophia. "'Belonging' to Rome, "Remaining' Greek: Coinage and Identity in Roman Macedonia." Pages 95–106 in *Coinage and Identity in the Roman Provinces*. Edited by Christopher Howgego, Volker Heuchert, and Andrew Burnett. Oxford: Oxford University Press, 2005.

Kurek-Chomycz, Dominika. "Fellow Athletes or Fellow Soldiers? Συναθλέω in Philippians 1:27 and 4:3." *JSNT* 39 (2017): 279–303.

Lamoreaux, Jason T. *Ritual, Women, and Philippi: Reimagining the Early Philippian Community*. Matrix: The Bible in Mediterranean Context 8. Eugene, OR: Cascade, 2013.

Lapalus, E. "Sculptures de Philippes." *BCH* 59 (1935): 175–92.

———. "Tête de bronze de Philippes (Macédoine)." *BCH* 56 (1932): 360–71.

Lemerle, Paul. "Inscriptions latines et grecques de Philippes." *BCH* 61 (1937): 410–20.

———. "Inscriptions latines et grecques de Philippes. I. Inscriptions latines." *BCH* 58 (1934): 448–83.

———. "Inscriptions latines et grecques de Philippes. II. Inscriptions latines." *BCH* 59 (1935): 126–64.

———. "Le testament d'un Thrace à Philippes." *BCH* 60 (1936): 337–43.

———. "Palestre romaine à Philippes." *BCH* 61 (1937): 86–102.

———. *Philippes et la Macédoine orientale à l'époque chrétienne et byzantine. Recheches d'histoire et d'archéologie*. Paris: de Boccard, 1945.

Lemerle, Paul, and Henri Ducoux. "L'acropole et l'enceinte haute de Philippes." *BCH* 62 (1938): 4–19.

Lewis, Peter E., and Ron Bolden. *The Pocket Guide to St. Paul*. Kent Town, Australia: Wakefield, 2001.

Malay, H., and Y. Akkan. "The Village Tar(i)gye and the Cult of Zeus Tar(i)gyenos in the Cayster Valley." *EA* 40 (2007): 16–22.

Martin, R. P. *Carmen Christi: Philippians 2:5–11 in Recent Interpretation and in the Setting of Early Christian Worship*. SNTSMS 4. Cambridge: Cambridge University Press, 1967.

Martin, Ralph P., and Brian J. Dodd, eds. *Where Christology Began: Essays on Philippians 2*. Louisville: Westminster John Knox, 1998.

Matthews, John. "The Roman Empire and the Proliferation of the Elites." *Arethusa* 33 (2000): 429–46.

Meriç, R. *Das Hinterland von Ephesos: Archäologisch-topographische Forschungen im Kaystros-Tal*. JÖAI 12. Vienna: ÖAI, 2009.

Mueller, Dierk. "Military Images in Paul's Letter to the Philippians." PhD diss., University of Pretoria, 2013.

Müller-Wiener, M. "Bischofresidenz des 4.–7. Jhs. im Östlichen Mittelmeer-Raum." Pages 651–709 in *Actes du XIe congrès international d'archéologie chrétienne (Lyon, Vienne, Grenoble, Genève, Aoste 1986.*

Publications de l'École française de Rome 123. Rome: École Française de Rome, 1989.

Nasrallah, Laura S. "Spatial Perspectives: Space and Ideology in Roman Philippi." Pages 53–74 in *Studying Paul's Letters: Contemporary Perspectives and Methods*. Edited by Joseph A. Marchal. Minneapolis: Fortress, 2012.

Nock, Arthur Darby. "The Roman Army and the Roman Religious Year." HTR 45 (1952): 187–252.

Oakes, Peter. "The Economic Situation of the Philippian Christians." Pages 63–82 in *The People beside Paul: The Philippian Assembly and History from Below*. Edited by Joseph A. Marchal. ECL. Atlanta: SBL Press, 2015.

———. *Philippians: From People to Letter*. SNTSMS 110. Cambridge: Cambridge University Press, 2001.

———. *Reading Romans in Pompeii: Paul's Letter at Ground Level*. Minneapolis: Augsburg Fortress, 2010.

Ogereau, Julien M. *Paul's Koinonia with the Philippians: A Socio-historical Investigation of a Pauline Economic Partnership*. WUNT 2/377. Tübingen: Mohr Siebeck, 2014.

Perdrizet, Paul. "Inscriptions de Philippes: Les Rosalies." BCH 24 (1900): 229–333.

Peterman, G. W. *Paul's Gift from Philippi: Conventions of Gift Exchange and Christian Giving*. SNTSMS 92. Cambridge: Cambridge University Press, 1997.

Peterlin, Davorin. *Paul's Letter to the Philippians in the Light of Disunity in the Church*. NovTSup 79. Leiden: Brill, 1995.

Pilhofer, Peter. *Philippi*. Vol. 1, *Die erste christliche Gemeinde Europas*. WUNT 87. Tübingen: Mohr Siebeck, 1995.

———. *Philippi*. Vol. 2, *Katalog der Inschriften von Philippi*. 2nd ed. WUNT 119. Tübingen: Mohr Siebeck, 2009.

Portefaix, Lilian. *Sisters Rejoice: Paul's Letter to the Philippians and Luke-Acts as Received by First-Century Philippian Women*. ConBNT 20. Stockholm: Almqvist & Wiksell, 1988.

Reumann, John. *Philippians: A New Translation with Introduction and Commentary*. AYB 33B. New Haven: Yale University Press, 2008.

Rich, John, and Andrew Wallace-Hadrill, eds. *City and Country in the Ancient World*. London: Routledge, 1991.

Rizakis, Athanase. "Société, institutions, cultes." Pages 175–97 in *Philippes, de la préhistoire à Byzance: Études d'archéologie et d'histoire*. Edited by Julien Fournier. BCHSupp 55. Athens: École française d'Athènes, 2016.

Robinson, T. A. *Who Were the First Christians? Dismantling the Urban Thesis*. Oxford: Oxford University Press, 2017.

Roger, Jacques. "L'enceinte basse de Philippes." *BCH* 62 (1938): 20–41.

Salac, A. "Inscriptions du Pangée, de la region Drama-Cavalla et de Philippes." *BCH* 47 (1923): 49–96.

Sampley, Paul J. *Pauline Partnership in Christ: Christian Community and Commitment in Light of Roman Law*. Philadelphia: Fortress, 1980.

Schellenberg, Ryan S. *Rethinking Paul's Rhetorical Education*. ECL 10. Atlanta: Society of Biblical Literature, 2013.

Sergienko, Gennadi Andreyevich. "'Our *Politeuma* Is in Heaven!': Paul's Polemical Engagement with the 'Enemies of the Cross of Christ' in Philippians 3:18–20." PhD diss., Fuller Theological Seminary, 2011.

Sève, Michel. *1914–2014: Philippes, ΦΙΛΙΠΠΟΙ, Philippi; One Hundred Years of French Research*. Athens: École française d'Athènes, 2014.

———. "Urbanisme, architecture et territoire." Pages 131–50 in *Philippes, de la préhistoire à Byzance: Études d'archéologie et d'histoire*. Edited by Julien Fournier. BCHSupp 55. Athens: École française d'Athènes, 2016.

Sève, Michel, and Patrick Weber. *Guide du forum de Philippes*. Sites et Monuments 18. Athens: École française d'Athènes, 2012.

———. "Le côté Nord du Forum de Philippes." *BCH* 110 (1986): 531–81.

———. "Un monument honorifique au forum de Philippes." *BCH* 112 (1988): 467–79.

Stowers, S. K. *A Rereading of Romans: Justice, Jews, and Gentiles*. New Haven: Yale University Press, 1994.

Taylor, Lily Ross. "*Augustales, Severi Augustales*, and *Severi*: A Chronological Study." *TAPA* 45 (1914): 231–53.

Tellbe, Mikael. *Paul between Synagogue and State: Christians, Jews, and Civic Authorities in 1 Thessalonians, Romans, and Philippians*. ConBNT 34. Stockholm: Almqvist & Wiksell, 2001.

Toynbee, J. M. C. *Death and Burial in the Roman World*. Baltimore: Johns Hopkins University Press, 1971.

Unwin, James. "Subversive Spectacles: The Struggles and Deaths of Paul and Seneca." PhD diss., Macquarie University, 2017.

Verhoef, Eduard. "Collaboration of 'Samothrakiasts' and Christians in Philippi." Pages 83–98 in in *The People beside Paul: The Philippian Assembly and History from Below*. Edited by Joseph A. Marchal. ECL. Atlanta: SBL Press, 2015.

———. *Philippi: How Christianity Began in Europe; The Epistle to the Philippians and the Excavations at Philippi*. London: Bloomsbury, 2013.

Vos, Craig Steven de. *Church and Community Conflicts: The Relationships of the Thessalonian, Corinthian, and Philippian Churches with Their Wider Civic Communities*. SBLDS 168. Atlanta: Scholars Press, 1999.

Weaver, P. R. C. *Familia Caesaris: A Social Study of the Emperor's Freemen and Slaves*. Cambridge: Cambridge University Press, 1972.

Welborn, L. L. *Paul, the Fool for Christ: A Study of 1 Corinthians 1–4 in Its Philosophic-Comic Tradition*. JSNTSup 293. London: T&T Clark, 2005.

———. "The Runaway Paul." *HTR* 92 (1999): 122–37.

Witherington, Ben, III. "The Case of the Imprisonment That Did Not Happen: Paul at Ephesus." *JETS* 60 (2017): 525–32.

———. *Paul's Letter to the Philippians: A Socio-rhetorical Commentary*. Grand Rapids: Eerdmans, 2011.

Zanker, Paul. *The Power of Images in the Age of Augustus*. Translated by Alan Shapiro. Ann Arbor: University of Michigan Press, 1988.

Rooted in Heaven and Resident in Philippi, but No ἐκκλησία?

Kathy Ehrensperger

There is a widely shared consensus that particular contextual factors pertaining to Philippi as a Roman colony as well as to Paul's imprisonment are clearly reflected in Paul's Letter/s to the Philippians.[1] However, the fact that the Christ followers are not addressed anywhere in this letter as ἐκκλησία, as well as the absence of any references by Paul to himself (or anybody else) as an apostle, is not considered in the same vein as other peculiar aspects of this letter. If it is assumed to be Pauline, then there must be reasons for both of these omissions here, despite the fact that the absence of the designation ἐκκλησία is shared with Romans.

In this contribution I will briefly consider the absence of the designation *apostle* and then focus mainly on possible reasons for the absence of the designation ἐκκλησία for the Christ-following group in Philippi.

1. The Absence of Paul's Self-Reference as Apostle

It has been argued that the absence of the label *apostle* most likely has something to do with the cordial relationship between Paul and the

---

1. I assume the literary unity of the letter. See also Samuel Vollenweider, "Politische Theologie im Philipperbrief," in *Paulus und Johannes*, ed. Dieter Sanger and Ulrich Mell, WUNT 198 (Tübingen: Mohr Siebeck 2006), 458. The absence of ἐκκλησία and apostle in the opening verse could of course be explained by the fragmentary character of a letter that is composed of parts of longer letters. This argument based on the hypothesis of the composite character of Philippians is of course possible, but since the two labels are of such importance for the Christ movement, why then would a redactor not have added them in the first place? Hence I presuppose Philippians to be one letter and proceed in my analysis on this assumption.

Philippians; the letter seems to imply this whether it is classified in the category of friendship letter or not.² Other proposals have focused on the competitive honor discourse prevalent in the *colonia*,³ as is evident from the many titles in honorific inscriptions over against which Paul would have wished to emphasize the service character of leadership in this movement rather than claims to superiority. Another hypothetical option might be that Paul was not the founder of this community and accepted his secondary role, which could be implied by the reference to Epaphroditos as ὑμῶν ἀπόστολον (although one might consider this a rather unlikely scenario, given that Acts 16 so clearly depicts Paul in the role of the founder). Whether Paul was the founder of the Christ-following group in Philippi or not, it is noteworthy that not only is the term *apostle* with reference to himself absent, but whenever he refers to others in leading roles, he refers to them as "coworker," "brother," "fellow fighter," or "companion" rather than as apostles (as, e.g., in 1 Cor 9:5; 12:28–29).⁴ These terminological peculiarities may not be accidental and when taken together with the fact that Paul accepted material support only from the Philippians are indications that their relationship differed significantly from that between Paul and other groups of Christ followers.⁵

There is plausibility and legitimacy in all of these explanations, but the reason for the absence of this leadership designation could also lie in the mere fact that there is no indication that Paul's apostleship has been challenged among the Philippian Christ followers or by someone in their context. It seems Paul did not have to defend his position as apostle here. In this respect Philippians certainly differs from the Corinthian correspondence and from Galatians, where obviously his apostleship is challenged, whether internally or externally. Moreover, in Romans Paul explains why he considers it his right to address the Christ followers in Rome as their

---

2. See, e.g., Lukas Bormann, *Philippi: Stadt und Christengemeinde zur Zeit des Paulus*, NovTSup 58 (Leiden: Brill, 1995), 200.

3. See Joseph H. Hellerman, *Reconstructing Honor in Roman Philippi: Carmen Christi as Cursus Pudorum*, SNTSMS 132 (Cambridge: Cambridge University Press, 2005), 34–109.

4. See Kathy Ehrensperger, *Paul and the Dynamics of Power: Communication and Interaction in the Early Christ-Movement* (London: T&T Clark, 2007), 37–50.

5. See Julien Ogereau, "Paul's κοινωνία with the Philippians: *Societas* as a Missionary Funding Strategy," *NTS* 60 (2104): 360–78; and also his *Paul's Koinonia with the Philippians: A Socio-historical Investigation of a Pauline Economic Partnership*, WUNT 2/377 (Tübingen: Mohr Siebeck, 2014).

apostle despite the fact that he has not founded any of the Christ-following groups there, and in 1 Thessalonians he uses *apostle*, although not in the opening address, for himself and Silvanus and Timothy (1 Thess 2:7), who most likely were the two cofounders of this ἐκκλησία.[6] So a pattern in Paul's reference to himself as apostle emerges, which indicates that the frequency of and emphasis on this label is related to disputes concerning his leadership role or their absence in particular places. The high frequency of the label in the Corinthian correspondence and the stern claim that he is an apostle not through the activity of human beings but Christ Jesus and God himself in Galatians demonstrate this clearly. In Romans and 1 Thessalonians there is no indication of such a struggle, hence the label is only used twice in Romans as a self-reference (Rom 1:1; 11:13) and once in 1 Thess 2:7, referring corporately to himself, Silvanus, and Timothy. Thus the absence of the label *apostle* as a self-reference in Philippians may well be an indication of the undisputed position of Paul in this community.

In addition to this unquestioned position, Paul's imprisonment may have played a part in the avoidance of certain designations.[7] If there were a high likelihood that others than the intended addressees would read the letter, Paul may have tried to avoid any formulation that might have put the addressees at risk or could have given a reason for further suspicion on the part of the local authorities who held him captive. The term *apostle* implies a meditating or go-between role, and such a role could have been considered problematic. A prisoner who designated himself as a go-between could have been seen as signaling an intention to transmit communication if not goods, especially since a person loyal to him carried the letter. The label *apostle* implies a specific relationship between the parties involved, with the apostle acting on behalf of someone else. Outsiders could have interpreted the addressees thus as those on whose behalf Paul acted. Whatever he was accused of and imprisoned for, this could have drawn unwanted attention to the addressees. To designate himself as apostle in conjunction with addressing a group whose legal

---

6. See Ehrensperger, *Paul and the Dynamics of Power*, 50–51.

7. See Standhartinger, who argues that the reference to himself and Timothy as *douloi Christou* possibly indirectly indicates that as slaves, they were not free, and that they have to deal with pressure, fear, persecution, and contempt. Angela Standhartinger, "Aus der Welt eines Gefangenen: Die Kommunikationsstruktur des Philipperbriefs im Spiegel seiner Abfassungssituation," *NovT* 55 (2013): 147.

status was not quite clear was potentially dangerous.[8] Slave language may have raised fewer questions on the part of the authorities. This leads me to consider the other designation that is avoided for the people addressed by Paul.

2. No ἐκκλησία in Philippi?

The less noticed peculiarity in the letter to the Philippians is the absence of any explicit reference to the Christ followers there via the term ἐκκλησία. The passage in Phil 3:6 clearly refers to the Christ followers in Judea (Gal 1:22–23) rather than the Philippians. The note that when Paul left Macedonia (4:15), no ἐκκλησία shared "in the matter of giving and receiving except you alone," is a reference to Christ followers other than the Philippians. Where Paul addresses them directly in the plural he uses other terms, such as "saints" (1:1), "beloved" (1:12; 4:8), "brothers/siblings" (3:1, 17; 4:1), Philippians (4:15); when he addresses particular members, he uses their names (Euodia and Syntyche, 4:2), or mentions a rather mysterious "local companion" (4:2). He also explains to them that their πολίτευμα is in heaven, and when he refers to them as being in Philippi he uses the strange form Φιλιππήσιοι (4:15)—a term that almost appears to be a Pauline creation, as it combines the name of a Greek city with a Latin ending, a very unusual combination indeed.[9]

The absence of the term ἐκκλησία is, of course, already noteworthy in the letter opening (1:1), but as noted above, this absence permeates the entire letter. I consider two perspectives in interpretations relevant here, which are, however, not mutually exclusive. Angela Standhartinger has argued that the letter as a whole (or at the least the parts which she considers to be Pauline) has something to do with Paul's personal situation and that this has implications for the Philippians, that is, that the "public transcript" includes a "hidden transcript," with ambiguities and double meaning being the means for a hidden communication.[10] Thus the absence of the term ἐκκλησία for Christ followers in Philippi may have something

---

8. Bormann, *Philippi*, 220.

9. Such a use of a Latin ending for a Greek term is not unique, but such an ending for the inhabitants of Philippi is without any parallel literary or epigraphic evidence. Peter Pilhofer, *Philippi*, vol. 1, *Die erste christliche Gemeinde Europas*, WUNT 87 (Tübingen: Mohr Siebeck, 1995), 116.

10. Standhartinger particularly draws attention to the risk of written communi-

to do with this hidden transcript the letter represents. The omission may also have something to do with the sociopolitical context in Philippi itself. The two aspects are not two sides of the same coin, but they are also not necessarily completely separate.

3. Paul's Context—in Prison

Paul's imprisonment may have led to special caution in the use of words and arguments in this letter, as it possibly would have been read not only by the intended addressees. In agreement with Standhartinger's focus on the communicative structure of the letter in light of the implications this situation may have had, Hans Föster and Patrick Sänger in a recent article have presented thorough arguments for this as the decisive contextual factor for Paul's use of the term πολίτευμα—implying that Paul tried to present a double image of the movement that would not appear suspicious to Roman authorities.[11] Similar to Standhartinger, they argue that an openly anti-imperial letter would have constituted a high risk for the author(s) as well as for the addressees, and thus Pilhofer's identification of anti-imperial trajectories, although not wrong, must have been formulated in the ambiguous vein of a hidden transcript.[12] I am not convinced by Föster's and Sänger's arguments that Paul attempted to depict the Christ movement as actually Jewish, that is, by reference to his Jewish credentials in 3:4–6 and to them as "the circumcision," and hence as a *religio licita* that would pose no threat to Roman law and order.[13] Nevertheless, their attention to the potential risk in writing a letter from prison is noteworthy. If Paul had to write with a view to hostile Roman coreaders, it might actually have proved necessary to formulate in a nonsuspicious way, which meant he had to avoid certain potentially suspicious terms.

---

cation, which could be used against the accused ("Aus der Welt eines Gefangenen," 157–60).

11. Hans Förster and Patrick Sänger, "Ist unsere Heimat im Himmel? Überlegungen zur Semantik von πολίτευμα in Phil 3.20," *EC* 5 (2014): 149–77.

12. Föster and Sänger, "Ist unsere Heimat im Himmel?," 168–75.

13. This argument raises questions on a number of levels, not least the widely refuted assumption of the notion of a *religio licita*. On this see Görge K. Hasselhoff and Meret Strothmann, eds., *"Religio Licita?" Rom und die Juden*, SJ 84 (Berlin: de Gruyter, 2017).

It thus could be envisaged that the mentioning of an ἐκκλησία by a prisoner in the hands of Rome could have given rise to Roman suspicion that this ἐκκλησία by the fact of being associated with a potential criminal should be classified as a criminal group. To be a member of such a group would have rendered the members potential criminals by association rather than by what they actually did or did not do.[14] By mentioning ἅγιοι, followed by ἐπίσκοποι and διάκονοι, Paul could have indirectly hinted at them as an assembly, in that where there are ἐπίσκοποι in particular there must be something to oversee, and if there are διάκονοι, there must be something in relation to which to serve. Hence the mentioning of these two functions, rather than being an indication of some organizational peculiarity in Philippi, and certainly not an early use of established offices, would be a coded indication that Paul was actually addressing them as a group, as an ἐκκλησία, with members and local leaders, without using any ἐκκλησία-oriented terminology. The absence of the term ἐκκλησία and the presence of the terms ἐπίσκοποι and διάκονοι would thus be two sides of the same coin, namely, an attempt by the imprisoned Paul to protect the addressees from potentially life-threatening suspicions on the part of the Roman authorities.

Whilst I consider it possible that Paul's personal situation, that is, his imprisonment, contributed to the avoidance of certain terms, I think there are also significant reasons to consider the local situation of the addressees as the reason for the absence of the term ἐκκλησία in Philippians.

4. The Philippians' Context: The Colonia Julia Augusta Philippensis

The Roman colony of Philippi, certainly after its second founding in 42 BCE as Colonia Julia Augusta Philippensis, was to a high degree a Roman city, more so than most cities or even colonies of the Roman East. In their thorough analyses of archaeological and literary evidence, Pilhofer and others have convincingly demonstrated that the public life of the colony at that time was dominated by Roman architecture, inscriptions, and institutions, and that the governance of the city was entirely in the hands of Roman citizens. Although Peter Oakes has argued that this does not mean

---

14. Borman more specifically thinks that Paul's relationship with the Philippians is actually a patron-client relationship. A new group, i.e., a *collegia*, needed the approval by the authorities and must have been considered useful to the city (*utilitas civitatis*), which can hardly be envisaged for the Christ followers in Philippi (*Philippi*, 222).

that the majority of the inhabitants were Roman, but that, according to his estimate, about 60 percent of the population was Greek,[15] the dominating control of running the *colonia* was firmly in Roman hands. There also is no evidence of an interaction of a Greek elite with Roman rule in the vein similar to what is known from other *coloniae* or cities in the East. For Aphrodisias, for instance, it can be asserted the local elite "understood the power of the emperors within the rubric of their deity Aphrodite.... They maintained identity and pride by defining Roman power within their view of cosmic power, an action essential for their political and social identity."[16] There is no evidence of a Greek elite surviving for the time under discussion in Philippi, and this means that there is no evidence of interaction with Roman domination and ideology from within a Greek perception, that is, from within a local Greek symbolic and social universe. The power of definition, politically, socially, and ideologically, was exclusively in Roman hands. We find here a Roman minority dominating all aspects of life, as far as can be assumed, of a majority of Greeks, and possibly Thracians, who did not have elite status.[17] The integration of Roman domination and ideology into a Greek perception of the cosmos from their own perspective, however, was highly significant because it enabled the Greek population under Roman domination to maintain the power of their local deities for their own particular social and political identity, as seen in the example of Aphrodisias.[18] The absence of evidence for such a perspective and of an actual affirmation of the value and power of Greek and Thracian identity in Philippi must have constituted problems, if not clear alienation of at least part of the Greek and Thracian population from Roman domination. They were second-class inhabitants of the city, with no opportunity to participate in civic public live and no opportunity to participate in the exercise of power in their own city, as most of them did not have the highly

---

15. Peter Oakes, *Philippians: From People to Letter*, SNTSMS 110 (Cambridge: Cambridge University Press, 2001), 55–76.

16. Douglas R. Edwards, *Religion and Power: Pagans, Jews and Christians in the Greek East* (New York: Oxford University Press 1996), 19.

17. No evidence of Thracians living within the precepts of the city has been found, although their presence in the surrounding rural areas is well documented. See Oakes, *Philippians*, 32.

18. That this was normally the Roman way of ruling has been convincingly demonstrated by Clifford Ando, "The Rites of Others," in *Roman Literary Cultures: Domestic Politics, Revolutionary Poetics, Civic Spectacles*, ed. Jonathan Edmondson and Alison Keith (Toronto: University of Toronto Press, 2016), 254–77.

valued Roman citizenship, as is documented in the exceedingly high percentage of Latin inscriptions of the period. The fact that Roman citizenship is so frequently attested in inscriptions could indicate a need on the part of Romans to assert themselves over against the Greek and Thracian majority. Could it be that this Roman domination and all pervasive visibility was not just accepted as the norm but inherently challenged by some locals? We do not know of any unrest in the city, but the Latin inscriptions give way to an overwhelming number of Greek inscriptions from the second century onwards. Latin could not hold its position as the dominant language, and if this is an indication to go by, other aspects of Roman life could not hold their grip over the Greek population long term either.

Be this as it may, in the first century the Greek and Thracian population was excluded from citizenship in their own city; city citizenship in Philippi was bound up with Roman citizenship, that is, citizenship in a city far away, through the allocation of the Roman citizens resident in Philippi to the *tribus Voltinia*. One could only be a *civis Philippensis* as a *civis Romanus*, and thus the citizenship in the city of Philippi had its roots or origins in another place, in a city some distance away, possibly unfamiliar to many of its colonial citizens. This was combined with the *ius Italicum*, which granted great privileges to the Roman population (exemption from taxes, tributes, and duties; the right to prosecute civil lawsuits [vindication]; acquire [*manicipatio*], own [*usucapio*], and transfer [*in iure cession*] property). Joseph Hellerman has argued that this points to a clear distinction between citizens and noncitizens, with respective status difference and all its implications.[19] If we consider negatively, then, what noncitizens, that is, the majority of the population, were unable to attain, a rather grim situation emerges. Not only were they not able to participate in the governing of their own city, and to acquire honor and status according to the *cursus honorum*, but they actually had to carry the financial burden of the city, did not have equal standing before the law, and could not freely deal with property. This may well have resulted in an economic situation where it was difficult to meet the needs of everyday life, a possibility that is indicated by Paul's reference to the contribution of the Macedonians to the collection despite their "deep poverty" (ἡ κατὰ βάθους πτωχεία αὐτῶν;

---

19. Hellerman, *Reconstructing Honor*, 115. Note also his reference (114) to the loss of citizenship by Dio Chrysostom (*1 Glor.* 66.15): "To the disenfranchised, life seems with good reason not worth living, and many choose death rather than life after losing their citizenship."

2 Cor 8:1-2). Thus we find in Philippi a population constituted partly of citizens, but whose citizenship was rooted and had its origin far away in Rome, and partly of Greeks and Thracians, who from a Roman perspective were aliens in their own city. Rights, status, and to a significant extent also economic means were unequal goods distributed along those citizenship lines. Although possibly local Greek associations granted some kind of status and organizational means for self-identification, their function was limited and cannot be compared to the power, privileges, and status of the Roman citizenship body in the city. Moreover, the right to set up associations (*collegiae*) and hold assemblies was granted by the Roman magistrates, and their existence was only granted if considered useful for the *colonia*, meaning that even such groups of potential self-identification could only exist by the mercy of Roman rule.

The Colonia Julia Augusta Philippensis thus did not have a civic assembly (ἐκκλησία) of its city citizens, as did other Greek cities (πόλεις) in the Roman East, nor did it have a Greek elite that could transmit aspects of a Greek perception of Roman domination on their own terms. The Greek population did not have any public, legitimate means, whether political, social, economic, or ideological, to publicly assert their own identity under these circumstances. Not to be able to deal with difficult experiences in life on one's own terms, from one's own perspective, and to integrate these into one's own narrative of identity and belonging has traumatic implications, leading to disorientation and loss of meaning.[20] To deny someone or some group of people the possibility of self-identification is an extreme form of domination, which, combined with violence (and the foundation of a Roman colony was an act of violence against the local population in this case), is traumatic.

The Greek and Thracian population at the time of Paul was not in a position to have their perspective integrated into the grand narrative of the colony. At the public level they had no opportunity to express their perspective or negotiate it in relation to Roman domination. In this realm they did not have a voice. No cultural translation process between the Greek or Thracian and the Roman perception of the world took place, certainly not at the public level. Thus for Paul's early "saints in Philippi" the

---

20. See Kathy Ehrensperger, *Paul at the Crossroads of Cultures: Theologizing in the Space-Between*, LNTS 456 (London: T&T Clark, 2013), 150–51; Anathea Portier-Young, *Apocalypse against Empire: Theologies of Resistance in Early Judaism* (Grand Rapids: Eerdmans 2011), 11–12.

term ἐκκλησία may have had little or no meaning, as they were not familiar anymore with ἐκκλησίαι of Greek πόλεις because such a form of communal participation did not exist in Philippi.

Whether the term could have been mediated via a Jewish community is an open question. Although the lack of evidence for any significant Jewish presence in Philippi should not be taken as evidence for the absence of such a presence, it renders arguments based on such a presence difficult. At least the narrative of Acts presents as a historically plausible scenario the presence of a Jewish place of prayer or synagogue outside the city walls, and the presence of some Godfearers (who must have had some contact, even if only occasionally, with Jews) there (Acts 16:13). The presence of Godfearers only makes sense in conjunction with the presence of Jews. In the world of Acts such a presence is considered possible, even though the historicity of this scene may be doubtful. Hence it cannot be entirely ruled out that the term ἐκκλησία could have been familiar to the Philippians via Jewish presence in the *colonia*. However, the absence of a civic assembly is the context that provides most likely the reasons for the absence of the term ἐκκλησία.

If the term and concept were unfamiliar to the addressees, then the absence of the term in Philippians is an indication of Paul's ability as a transcultural/bicultural mediator. Familiar with more than one social and cultural context, he was able to mediate and relate in a way to the addresses that is meaningful from within their social and cultural world. Paul then may not have used this term because it did not resonate with any cultural code they were familiar with, and as such it is an example of his ability to become all things to all people (1 Cor 9:22). It can thus be seen as a semantic indication pointing to the very specific contextualization of the message of Christ in the particularity of a local situation.

But Paul could also have avoided this term for more specific political reasons. As mentioned above, the reference to ἐπίσκοποι and διάκονοι and the absence of the title *apostle* could be another indication that Paul was aware of coreaders who could have interpreted such terms as a reference to some Greek subversion of the Roman form of government in the city, an attempt at establishing a Greek assembly, even if only of an association (*collegia*) alongside the exclusive Roman form of rule. It could have been regarded as subversive because any form of association would have required Roman approval, as noted above. If this was the case, Paul again appears as a skilled cultural-political mediator with a high level of contextual political sensitivity. The use of the term ἐκκλησία would have put not only himself but also the letter carrier and the addressees at risk; it would have been dangerous to use when suspicious readers were listening into this conversation. Paul in a different but in no ways less sophisticated vein proves his ability to become all things to all people: to those under domination like one under domination. The emphasis on sharing in this letter may have wider ramifications than the financial support and the sharing of joy; the sharing in the suffering might indicate something specific in the circumstances in which they lived. Paul's chains and the restrictions of the Greek population in this Roman colony may have been perceived by Paul as an analogous although not identical experience: there is an analogy between *Graeca capta*, or in this case *Macedonia capta*, and Paul in chains, as both are inflicted by imperial domination.

The absence or avoidance of the term ἐκκλησία, then, is clearly contextual in my view, whether the Philippians are not familiar with it or whether they are fully conversant with it and it is thus too dangerous to be used. But it leaves the community with no term to refer to themselves as a Christ-following group like, for example, the Corinthians, who are ἐκκλησία τοῦ θεοῦ τῇ ὄυσῃ ἐν Κορίνθῳ (1 Cor 1:2). The implications of this absence for the identity formation of this Christ-following group and their self-perception require further analysis that is beyond the scope of this article, but it is evident that Paul holds them in high esteem. Unlike the Corinthians, at least some of them are regarded as mature by Paul (3:15), he trusts them, and they are exemplary in their ways in Christ. Thus their embodiment of the values and ways of life in Christ is apparently not dependent on the designation ἐκκλησία.

5. No ἐκκλησία but a πολίτευμα?

Paul nevertheless may have sensed that some sort of communal term might be helpful or appropriate for them. The unique use of the term πολίτευμα in this letter (3:20), like the absence of the term ἐκκλησία, relates rather well to the local situation of Philippi. I assume that "the saints" must have been familiar with the Roman concept of citizenship (*civitas Romana*). Thus the link of the Philippian citizenship with Rome, that is, a place far away from the actual place of living, could have provided a pattern for Paul to create an analogy for the Christ followers of that colony. Although they are deprived of belonging to the Roman citizenship body, and thus of a collective body of belonging in which they could actively participate, Paul assures them that they do have a realm of belonging. Although it too is located somewhere beyond the boundaries of their local place of living, it is nevertheless as real as the Philippian civic belonging of Roman citizens that had its origin in Rome.[21] The assertion that they too are part of and actively participate in a civic community seems in tune with the lack of such possibilities for Greeks and Thracians in the Roman social and symbolic universe of the city.[22] Since active participation in the social, political, and cultic public affairs of their city was not an option available to the majority of the population, the term πολίτευμα could have provided Greek and Thracian Christ followers with an alternative to the Roman status of belonging that freeborn men as Roman citizens of the colony

---

21. I think the proposal of Föster and Sänger to translate ὑπάρχω as "has its roots/ or origin" is more appropriate than translating it with "is" ("Ist unsere Heimat im Himmel?," 165).

22. Whether πολίτευμα refers to citizenship per se or rather to a communal body is controversially debated. Arzt-Grabner has argued that here the term means "citizenship." Peter Arzt-Grabner, "Die Stellung des Judentums in neutestamentlicher Zeit anhand der Politeuma-Papyri und anderer Texte," in *Papyrologie und Exegese: Die Auslegung des Neuen Testaments im Lichte der Papyri*, ed. Jens Herzer, WUNT 2/341 (Tübingen: Mohr Siebeck, 2012), 127–58. Niebuhr is of the view that for Paul it has its origin in the Jewish πολίτευμα concept. Karl-Wilhelm Niebuhr, *Heidenapostel aus Israel: Die jüdische Identität des Paulus nach ihrer Darstellung in seinen Briefen*, WUNT 62 (Tübingen: Mohr Siebeck, 1992), 102. Angela Standhartinger has recently presented strong arguments against the notion of citizenship implicit in the term, noting that according to political theory and practice of antiquity the term designates a body of citizens with political rights. Belonging to a πολίτευμα implies *per definitionem* that the person is actively involved in the politics of the respective group. See Angela Standhartinger, "Apocalyptic Thought in Philippians," in *The Jewish Apocalyptic Tradition and the Shaping of New Testament Thought*, ed. Benjamin E. Reynolds and Loren Stuckenbruck (Minneapolis: Fortress, 2017), 239. Wojtkowiak argues that it can be translated as both "Gemeinwesen" or "Bürgerschaft," which in his view does not exclude the notion of citizenship. See Heiko Wojtkowiak, *Christologie und Ethik im Philipperbrief: Studien zur Handlungsorientierung einer frühchristlichen Gemeinde in paganer Umwelt* (Göttingen: Vandenhoeck & Ruprecht, 2012), 209. For an in-depth analysis of the function of the concept see also Thomas Kruse, "Ethnic *Koina* and *Politeumata* in Ptolemaic Egypt," in *Private Associations and the Public Sphere*, ed. Vincent Gabrielsen and Christian A. Thomsen (Copenhagen: Det Kongelige Danske Videnskabernes Selskab, 2015), 270–300. The main point for my argument is the expression of a place of belonging; whether this is expressed as citizenship or a form of accepted civic organization, the crucial point is that with the term πολίτευμα a collective aspect of belonging is expressed.

enjoyed.²³ With the term πολίτευμα Paul refers to a collective entity that has active rights within a city to manage their internal affairs.²⁴ Although not (yet) evident for everyone in the here and now, these Philippian Christ followers are given assurance of status and belonging to a collective body in analogy to the Roman model, but clearly distinct from it, if not as a clear alternative to it.

Read in the wider context of the letter, it is part of Paul's attempt to teach these former pagans the way of life in Christ in their particular Roman-dominated context, which excludes them as Greek and Thracian noncitizens from active participation in civic life, and thus deprives them of the possibility of finding a place in the narrative of belonging as well as the power structures of the colony. Paul tries to show them that the ways and means by which such integration and belonging to the colony could be achieved would be contrary to the ways in Christ, in that the Roman elite values of competing for honor and status at the expense of others, and through inflicting suffering and alienation on others, was contrary to life in Christ. They were part of a πολίτευμα that was rooted beyond the realm of Philippi, but unlike the Roman colonists' *tribus Voltinia*, their group was not rooted in Rome but ἐν οὐρανοῖς. They were part of a πολίτευμα, and thus they had a place where they belonged. Excluded from the dominating narrative of belonging and deprived of their own voice in the civic and public affairs of the colony, Paul assures them of their own voice and their specific way of life as followers of Christ. That they are admonished to μόνον ἀξίως τοῦ εὐαγγελίου τοῦ Χριστοῦ πολιτεύεσθε (1:27) is thus related to this realm of belonging, to this πολίτευμα that is rooted ἐν οὐρανοῖς. This is the realm that should provide them with orientation for their lives in the here and now. As rooted in this heavenly realm, they are empowered to become agents of their own lives in Christ, despite living under the conditions of domination imposed by colonial rule. If these conditions lead to suffering

---

23. The fact that, e.g., in the association of the cult of Silvanus Roman designations for office holders were used indicates that alternatives for active participation and the acquisition of status and honor were aspired to by those who were hindered from ever climbing the respective ladder of the Roman *cursus honorum*. As Hellermann notes, "Titular mimicry is … indicative of the social value replication characteristic of non-elite groups in the Roman world" (*Reconstructing Honor*, 102).

24. Thomas Kruse, "Das jüdische Politeuma von Herakleopolis in Aegypten," in *Volk und Demokratie im Altertum*, ed. Vera V. Dement'eva and Tassilo Schmidt (Göttingen: Vandenhoeck & Ruprecht, 2010), 97.

and hardship, this is not due to their deprived status in the colony, and thus not to be eschewed or valued as being dishonoring or shameful but rather the opposite. As members of the πολίτευμα rooted ἐν οὐρανοῖς, such struggles precisely are evidence of God's grace (Phil 1:28–30).

6. Conclusions

The absence of the term ἀπόστολος with reference to himself, as well as the absence of the term ἐκκλησία for the Philippian Christ followers, and the peculiar use of the term πολίτευμα, in my view are deliberate contextual choices by Paul out of concern for the addressees. They are more than mere linguistic peculiarities but rather encompass cultural codes relevant for and decipherable specifically by these addressees. They are possible indications for a hidden transcript of power, for an implicit alternative to the attempt on the part of the imperial dominating power at depriving those who were different from their own perspective, of their own narrative of belonging, and of their own way of rendering meaning to their life experience. Paul's avoidance of a term that in other letters is of such high importance out of concern for those addressed is speaking a clear, culturally and politically aware language, particularly relevant for those addressed in the letter opening as πᾶσιν τοῖς ἁγίοις ἐν Χριστῷ Ἰησοῦ τοῖς οὖσιν ἐν Φιλίπποις. There is not merely one perspective, one language, one discourse through which narratives of meaning and belonging to Christ can be, even should be told. Paul adapts to the context, varies language, and diversifies perceptions and cultural codes in order to empower those in Christ. The absence of the terms ἀπόστολος and ἐκκλησία is thus evidence that Paul is not engaging in a monolingual monologue but in a multilingual conversation.

Bibliography

Ando, Clifford. "The Rites of Others." Pages 254–77 in *Roman Literary Cultures: Domestic Politics, Revolutionary Poetics, Civic Spectacles*. Edited by Jonathan Edmondson and Alison Keith. Toronto: University of Toronto Press, 2016.

Arzt-Graber, Peter. "Die Stellung des Judentums in neutestamentlicher Zeit anhand der Politeuma-Papyri und anderer Texte." Pages 127–58 in *Papyrologie und Exegese: Die Auslegung des Neuen Testaments im Lichte der Papyri*. Edited by Jens Herzer. WUNT 2/341. Tübingen: Mohr Siebeck, 2012.

Bormann, Lukas. *Philippi: Stadt und Christengemeinde zur Zeit des Paulus.* NovTSup 58. Leiden: Briil, 1995.

Edwards, Douglas R. *Religion and Power: Pagans, Jews and Christians in the Greek East.* New York: Oxford University Press, 1996.

Ehrensperger, Kathy. *Paul and the Dynamics of Power: Communication and Interaction in the Early Christ-Movement.* London: T&T Clark, 2007.

———. *Paul at the Crossroads of Cultures: Theologizing in the Space-Between.* LNTS 456. London: T&T Clark, 2013.

Förster, Hans, and Patrick Sänger. "Ist unsere Heimat im Himmel? Überlegungen zur Semantik von πολίτευμα in Phil 3.20." *EC* 5 (2014): 149–77.

Hasselhoff, Görge K., and Meret Strothmann, eds. *"Religio Licita?" Rom und die Juden.* SJ 84. Berlin: de Gruyter, 2017.

Hellerman, Joseph H. *Reconstructing Honor in Roman Philippi: Carmen Christi as Cursus Pudorum.* SNTSMS 132. Cambridge: Cambridge University Press, 2005.

Kruse, Thomas. "Das jüdische Politeuma von Herakleopolis in Aegypten." Pages 93–106 in *Volk und Demokratie im Altertum.* Edited by Vera V. Dement'eva and Tassilo Schmidt. Göttingen: Vandenhoeck & Ruprecht, 2010.

———. "Ethnic *Koina* and *Politeumata* in Ptolemaic Egypt." Pages 270–300 in *Private Associations and the Public Sphere.* Edited by Vincent Gabrielsen and Christian A. Thomsen. Copenhagen: Det Kongelige Danske Videnskabernes Selskab, 2015.

Niebuhr, Karl-Wilhelm. *Heidenapostel aus Israel: Die jüdische Identität des Paulus nach ihrer Darstellung in seinen Briefen.* WUNT 62. Tübingen: Mohr Siebeck, 1992.

Oakes, Peter. *Philippians: From People to Letter.* SNTSMS 110. Cambridge: Cambridge University Press, 2001.

Ogereau, Julien M. *Paul's Koinonia with the Philippians: A Socio-historical Investigation of a Pauline Economic Partnership.* WUNT 2/377. Tübingen: Mohr Siebeck, 2014.

———. "Paul's κοινωνία with the Philippians: *Societas* as a Missionary Funding Strategy." *NTS* 60 (2104): 360–78.

Pilhofer, Peter. *Philippi*, Vol. 1, *Die erste christliche Gemeinde Europas.* WUNT 87. Tübingen: Mohr Siebeck, 1995.

Portier-Young, Anathea. *Apocalypse against Empire: Theologies of Resistance in Early Judaism.* Grand Rapids: Eerdmans, 2011.

Standhartinger, Angela. "Apocalyptic Thought in Philippians." Pages 233–43 in *The Jewish Apocalyptic Tradition and the Shaping of New Testament Thought*. Edited by Benjamin E. Reynolds and Loren Stuckenbruck. Minneapolis: Fortress, 2017.

———. "Aus der Welt eines Gefangenen: Die Kommunikationsstruktur des Philipperbriefs im Spiegel seiner Abfassungssituation." *NovT* 55 (2013): 140–67.

Vollenweider, Samuel. "Politische Theologie im Philipperbrief?" Pages 457–69 in *Paulus und Johannes*. Edited by Dieter Sänger and Ulrich Mell. WUNT 198. Tübingen: Mohr Siebeck, 2006.

Wojtkowiak, Heiko. *Christologie und Ethik im Philipperbrief: Studien zur Handlungsorientierung einer frühchristlichen Gemeinde in paganer Umwelt*. Göttingen: Vandenhoeck & Ruprecht, 2012.

The Social Constituency and Membership of the First Christian Groups at Philippi: A Literary and Epigraphic Survey

Julien M. Ogereau

1. Introduction

It is now more than fifty years since Edwin A. Judge published his little but insightful essay on the social patterns of the early Christians, in which he explored the social composition of the early church and its relation to the dominant social institutions of the day.[1] Judge wanted to challenge the then-popular view that the first Christians were mostly from a lower social

---

This paper was written while I was a research associate on the project "Authorization of Early Christian Knowledge Claims in Greece" with the Excellence Cluster 264 Topoi (B-5-3) at Humboldt-Universität zu Berlin. Its revision and completion were partly made possible through a Junior Research Fellowship at the Macquarie University Ancient Cultures Research Centre, Sydney, Australia, in 2015. I would also like to thank the Greek archaeological services of Kavala, in particular D. Malamidou and C. Koukouli-Chrysanthaki, for their kind support and assistance during a field trip in July 2015, as well as D. Feissel, C. Brélaz, and P. Pilhofer for practical help and stimulating conversations on the history and epigraphy of Philippi.

1. Edwin A. Judge, *The Social Pattern of Christian Groups in the First Century: Some Prolegomena to the Study of New Testament Ideas of Social Obligation* (London: Tyndale, 1960). Other important essays by Judge include "The Early Christians as a Scholastic Community," in *The First Christians in the Roman World: Augustan and New Testament Essays*, ed. James R. Harrison, WUNT 229 (Tübingen: Mohr Siebeck, 2008), 526–52; Judge, "The Social Identity of the First Christians: A Question of Method on Religious History," in *Social Distinctives of the Christians in the First Century: Pivotal Essays by E. A. Judge*, ed. David M. Scholer (Peabody, MA: Hendrickson, 2008), 117–35; Judge, "Cultural Conformity and Innovation in Paul: Some Clues from Contemporary Documents," *TynBul* 35 (1984): 3–24.

and economic class and that early Christianity should be understood as a revolutionary proletarian movement whose aim was to do away with classical civilization and its established social order.² Rather provocatively, he proposed instead that "far from being a socially depressed group…, if the Corinthians are at all typical, the Christians were dominated by a socially pretentious section of the population of the big cities."³ Thereby Judge wanted to emphasize that, in contrast with contemporary unofficial associations, the first Christian groups were in fact much more heterogeneous socially and economically than previously thought. They drew on a "broad constituency" made up of "the household dependents of the leading members," dependents who represented "by no means the most debased section of society" in comparison with the peasants and slaves, the "most underprivileged classes."⁴ Indeed, as he would later argue, the first churches established by the apostle Paul in Asia Minor and Greece appeared to be "societies sponsored to a socially heterogeneous membership by local notabilities."⁵ In sum, Judge contended that, until at least the end of the first century, when it began to penetrate the rural inland of Asia Minor (see Pliny, *Ep.* 10.96), Christianity was "a socially well backed movement of the great Hellenistic cities."⁶

Those familiar with the history of scholarship on the topic would know that Judge's thesis provoked a small revolution in the field of early Christian studies. It prompted a debate that lasted several decades, during which appeared several significant contributions by well-known scholars such as Martin Hengel, Gerd Theissen, Abraham Malherbe, Wayne

---

2. Judge, *Social Pattern*, 51. Judge accepted the idea that many early Christians were from the "lower classes," whatever might have been meant by this anachronistic category, but rejected the explanation that Christianity succeeded *because* it was a movement from the lower classes. Judge should be read within its original historical context as a reaction to the works of K. Kautsky and A. Kalthoff and their socialistic agenda. See especially Judge, *Social Pattern*, 49–61; Judge, "Scholastic Community," 530–31; Judge, "Cultural Conformity," 1–5.

3. Judge, *Social Pattern*, 60. The word *pretentious* appears to be key here. Judge understood 1 Cor 1:26 "as a piece of impassioned rhetoric" and not as "a factual statement": "It leaves no doubt that in their own opinion, and presumably also in that of their contemporaries, [the Corinthians] were anything but a collection of unintelligent nonentities" (59).

4. Judge, *Social Pattern*, 60.
5. Judge, "Scholastic Community," 530.
6. Judge, *Social Pattern*, 61.

Meeks, Justin Meggitt, and, most recently, Alexander Weiß.[7] At the turn of the twenty-first century, the focus then shifted from qualitative surveys to quantitative studies designing and employing socioeconomic scales aimed at improving simplistic binary models and at delineating more precisely, if it were at all possible, the social stratification of the early church.[8] These studies, and the sociological methodologies and models they have employed, have not been without their critics, however.[9] Some have found them to rely too heavily on what they consider to be anachronistic and predeterministic models (rather than on the primary sources themselves), while others have disagreed on the social categories they introduce, some of which might have been altogether foreign to Roman society or simply distort the ancient reality.[10]

---

7. Martin Hengel, *Property and Riches in the Early Church* (London: SCM, 1974); Gerd Theissen, *The Social Setting of Pauline Christianity* (Edinburgh: T&T Clark, 1982), which is a translated compilation of earlier essays; Abraham J. Malherbe, *Social Aspects of Early Christianity* (Baton Rouge: Louisiana State University Press, 1977); Wayne A. Meeks, *The First Urban Christians* (New Haven: Yale University Press, 1983), esp. 51–73; Justin J. Meggitt, *Paul, Poverty and Survival* (Edinburgh: T&T Clark, 1998); Alexander Weiß, *Soziale Elite und Christentum: Studien zu ordo-Angehörigen unter den frühen Christen* (Berlin: de Gruyter, 2015). A full review of scholarship is beyond the scope of this essay. Most of the literature is summarized in Judge, "Social Identity," 118–27; Weiß, *Soziale Elite*, 5–22; and more succinctly in Julien M. Ogereau, *Paul's Koinonia with the Philippians: A Socio-historical Investigation of a Pauline Economic Partnership*, WUNT 2/377 (Tübingen: Mohr Siebeck, 2014), 42–47.

8. Most prominent are Steven J. Friesen, "Poverty in Pauline Studies: Beyond the So-Called New Consensus," *JSNT* 26 (2004): 323–61; Bruce W. Longenecker, "Exposing the Economic Middle: A Revised Economy Scale for the Study of Early Urban Christianity," *JSNT* 31 (2009): 243–78. See also, more generally, Ekkehard W. Stegemann and Wolfgang Stegemann, *The Jesus Movement: A Social History of Its First Century* (Edinburgh: T&T Clark, 1999), 53–95 (esp. 72), 288–316 (esp. 301, 313). For an attempt at modeling the Philippian church specifically, see Davorin Peterlin, *Paul's Letter to the Philippians in the Light of Disunity in the Church*, NovTSup 79 (Leiden: Brill, 1995), 136–70; Peter Oakes, *Philippians: From People to Letter*, SNTSMS 110 (Cambridge: Cambridge University Press, 2001), 55–76.

9. Most notoriously, see John M. G. Barclay, "Poverty in Pauline Studies: A Response to Steven Friesen," *JSNT* 26 (2004): 363–66.

10. Judge had already warned against this danger in the early 1960s. See Judge, *Social Pattern*, iii, 7, 51; Judge, "Scholastic Community," 527–28. See more generally Judge, "Social Identity," 127–30; Weiß, *Soziale Elite*, 23–28 (on the question of the definition of *soziale Elite* and *Oberschichtigen*). For a recent critique of binary and pyramidal stratification models of Roman society, and the alternative proposal (already

This is not the place to offer a detailed critique of these studies, which can be useful insofar as they help us conceptualize and visualize the position of the first Christians on the Roman social ladder. One can nonetheless regret that since Judge's seminal work too many studies have been either too broad in their scope, generalizing global trends without paying much attention to local particularities, or too narrow, focusing mainly on the first two to three generations of Christians depicted in the New Testament. They have also been too discriminating vis-à-vis the primary sources they have examined, concentrating primarily on literary sources while often ignoring epigraphic evidence from subsequent centuries.[11] The present volume, which represents a noteworthy attempt to study early Philippian Christianity in the light of all the available literary, documentary, and archaeological evidence, thus provides us with an opportunity to begin to redress this situation and to tackle the question of the social constituency and membership of the early church from the perspective of one particular urban context, the Colonia Iulia Augusta Philippensis.[12] It will also allow

---

envisaged by Judge, *Social Pattern*, iii) to consider it in terms of concentric circles, see Henrik Mouritsen, "Status and Social Hierarchies: The Case of Pompeii," in *Social Status and Prestige in the Graeco-Roman World*, ed. Annika B. Kuhn (Stuttgart: Steiner, 2015), 87–113 (esp. 101–5).

11. For a similar critique vis-à-vis the study of early Christianity as an urban phenomenon, see the introduction and rationale to the whole series by James R. Harrison, "Introduction," in *Methodological Considerations*, vol. 1 of *The First Urban Churches*, ed. James R. Harrison and L. L. Welborn, WGRWSup 7 (Atlanta: SBL Press, 2015), 2–3. This remark of course does not apply to Werner Eck, "Das Eindringen des Christentums in den Senatorenstand bis zu Konstantin d. Gr.," *Chiron* 1 (1971): 381–406; Gary J. Johnson, "A Christian Business and Christian Self-Identity in Third/Fourth Century Phrygia," *VC* 48 (1994): 341–66; Paul McKechnie, "Christian City Councillors in the Roman Empire before Constantine," *IJRR* 5 (2009): 1–20; and Weiß, *Soziale Elite*.

12. There does exist a rich scholarly tradition on the history of Philippi and its first churches, however. Standard studies remain those by Collart and Lemerle (both now dated, but fundamental), as well as by Bormann, Pilhofer, and Oakes. See Paul Collart, *Philippes: Ville de Macédoine depuis ses origines jusqu'à la fin de l'époque Romaine* (Paris: de Boccard, 1937); Paul Lemerle, *Philippes et la Macédoine orientale à l'époque chrétienne et byzantine* (Paris: de Boccard, 1945); Lukas Bormann, *Philippi: Stadt und Christengemeinde zur Zeit des Paulus*, NovTSup 78 (Leiden: Brill, 1995); Peter Pilhofer, *Philippi*, vol. 1, *Die erste christliche Gemeinde Europas*, WUNT 87 (Tübingen: Mohr Siebeck, 1995); Oakes, *Philippians*. See also the small volume edited by Charalambos Bakirtzis and Helmut Koester, *Philippi at the Time of Paul and after His Death* (Harrisburg, PA: Trinity Press International, 1998). Also crucial will be the collection

us to reflect on possible avenues through which we may further research the topic and improve our understanding of early Christian social history.

2. The First Generation of Christians (ca. 50–90s CE)

An attempt to analyze the social constituency of the first two to three generations of Christians at Philippi leaves the social historian with no other option but to turn to the New Testament, and in particular to the letter, or collection of letters,[13] of the apostle Paul written to the community he founded in the very late 40s CE. Thankfully, the Epistle to the Philippians provides us with suggestive internal evidence that draws us into the social world of the apostle and his disciples.

As exegetes have long noted,[14] the final part of the canonical letter, verses 4:15–20, is characterized by an unusual concentration of what appears to be commercial terms and expressions such as ἀπέχω (4:18), πληρόω (4:18), κοινωνέω (4:15), and εἰς λόγον δόσεως καὶ λήμψεως (4:15). A detailed examination of such technical language in the light of contemporary literary and documentary sources confirms a reader's first impression: Paul employs the jargon of the marketplace and of business partnership to acknowledge his receipt of the Philippians' material and/or financial assistance.[15] He does so in a way that strikingly resembles the contractual formulae used in leases, receipts, and partnership agreements from the same period.[16]

---

of essays edited by Steven J. Friesen et al., *Philippi, from Colonia Augusta to Communitas Christiana: Religion and Society in Transition* (Leiden: Brill, forthcoming).

13. A number of hypotheses on the literary composition of Philippians have been argued. For a condensed review of scholarship, see Ogereau, *Paul's Koinonia*, 223–34.

14. E.g., Heinrich A. W. Meyer, *Critical and Exegetical Handbook to the Epistles to the Philippians and Colossians*, CECNT (Edinburgh: T&T Clark, 1875), 221; J. B. Lightfoot, *St Paul's Epistle to the Philippians* (London: Macmillan, 1913), 165; Marvin R. Vincent, *A Critical and Exegetical Commentary on the Epistles to the Philippians and to Philemon*, ICC (Edinburgh: T&T Clark, 1897), 148; Harry A. A. Kennedy, "The Financial Colouring of Philippians iv. 15–18," *ExpTim* 12 (1900): 43–44.

15. So much so that Koester considered 4:10–20 to be a separate receipt (*Quittung*), in which Paul acknowledged the Philippians' gift, and which was later appended to the series of letters composing canonical Philippians. Helmut Koester, *Introduction to the New Testament*, vol. 2, *History and Literature of Early Christianity*, 2nd ed. (Berlin: de Gruyter, 2000), 136.

16. For a detailed examination of Paul's commercial language in the light of docu-

Nevertheless, most commentators have generally interpreted Paul's speech in 4:15–20 in a more figurative way. He resorted to such commercial language to express metaphorically his gratitude to the Philippians and to emphasize his friendship with them, they have argued.[17] Or, as others have suggested, Paul thereby attempted to hide his embarrassment for his receipt of their gift, which somewhat challenged his sense of self-sufficiency (see 4:10–14), and which would have placed him in a socially uncomfortable position vis-à-vis the Philippians, that is, as someone dependent on their patronage.[18]

The main arguments against a figurative interpretation of the passage have been articulated in a recent publication and therefore need not be reviewed in depth here.[19] Suffice it to say that a metaphorical reading of this section is confronted with a major difficulty: Paul has actually received some concrete form of support, a material donation and/or a financial contribution, which he duly acknowledges, and not some intangible form of affection for which he might have expressed his gratitude, or sense of indebtedness, by means of an accounting metaphor, as Plautus, Cicero, or Seneca might have done.[20]

What is in any case more relevant to our immediate concern is the question of the purpose, function, or even appropriateness of Paul's commercial language in this passage. What does it tell us about the socioeconomic location of Paul and the Philippians? Undoubtedly, Paul's

---

mentary sources, see "Part One: A Philological Survey," in Ogereau, *Paul's Koinonia*, 51–221. See also Ogereau, "The Earliest Piece of Evidence of Christian Accounting: The Significance of the Phrase εἰς λόγον δόσεως καὶ λήμψεως (Phil 4:15)," *Comptabilité(S)* 6 (2014): 1–16.

17. This is the main thrust of Peterman's study, for instance. Gerald W. Peterman, *Paul's Gift from Philippi: Conventions of Gift-Exchange and Christian Giving*, SNTSMS 92 (Cambridge: Cambridge University Press, 1997). See Peter Marshall, *Enmity in Corinth: Social Conventions in Paul's Relationship with the Corinthians*, WUNT 2/33 (Tübingen: Mohr Siebeck, 1987), 157–64; Pilhofer, *Philippi*, 1:147–52.

18. See, e.g., C. H. Dodd, *New Testament Studies* (Manchester: Manchester University Press, 1967), 71–72. In a similar vein, Marshall and Welborn have suggested that Paul rejected the Corinthians' offer of friendship in the form of a gift so as not to become entrapped by the social demands of "unequal patronal friendships." See Marshall, *Enmity*, 233, 257; L. L. Welborn, *An End to Enmity: Paul and the "Wrongdoer" of Second Corinthians* (Berlin: de Gruyter, 2011), 368, 398–400.

19. See Ogereau, *Paul's Koinonia*.

20. E.g., Plautus, *Most.* 1.3.304; Cicero, *Amic.* 16.58; Seneca, *Lucil.* 81.18. See Ogereau, *Paul's Koinonia*, 276.

controlled use of technical terms indicates a strong familiarity with not only the contractual business language of his time but also with the socioeconomic conventions of Roman society. It reveals that Paul was as comfortable in the marketplace doing business with his contemporaries as he was dispensing theological and ethical instruction to his disciples in private houses or as he was discoursing with philosophers in the Athenian agora, as Acts relates. It shows that Paul, in addition to having a brilliant theological intellect, also had a sharp business mind, which, remarkably enough, he could put to use in his dealings with fellow Christ believers. As has been argued elsewhere in great detail, he had indeed a clear business strategy when it came to funding his missionary activities, which "enabled him to circumvent the negative effects of patronage, maximise his limited human and financial resources, and ensure the practical involvement of his communities in the work of his mission."[21]

This perspective on Paul, one has to admit, might be difficult to accept for those who view him as the theologian par excellence of the early church and as the founder of Western Christianity. Yet, we ought not to forget that Paul was first and foremost a man of his world, an artisan from the grass roots of Roman society, a provincial plebeian who could work long hours in a dusty and grimy workshop, which, Ronald Hock convincingly demonstrated more than three decades ago, he could also use as a platform for his ministry.[22] He was as much steeped in the Scriptures and traditions of his Jewish forefathers as he was accustomed to the socioeconomic conventions and language of his Greco-Roman cultural environment. These two aspects of Paul's identity simply cannot be dissociated from each other, nor should one facet be emphasized over the other. They must be held in tension if we are to understand Paul fully and if we are to make proper sense of this passage in Philippians.

This having been acknowledged, it must further be noted that Paul's proficient use of commercial *termini technici* gives his discourse a markedly economic resonance that is highly suggestive of the Philippians' sociocultural milieu. It locates it within a particular economic register, a

---

21. See especially "A Socio-economic Analysis of Paul's Κοινωνία with the Philippians," in Ogereau, *Paul's Koinonia*, 310–47 (citation on 349). For a concise summary of this thesis, see Ogereau, "Paul's Κοινωνία with the Philippians: Societas as a Missionary Funding Strategy," *NTS* 60 (2014): 360–78.

22. Ronald F. Hock, *The Social Context of Paul's Ministry: Tentmaking and Apostleship* (Philadelphia: Fortress, 1980).

register that, it is fair to assume, must have been suitable for the occasion and vis-à-vis his audience. As Davorin Peterlin has rightly remarked, Paul's business language not only demonstrates that he was "sufficiently well-versed in terminology of financial transactions" but that he also "clearly expected them to comprehend the terminology."[23] Echoing Peterlin, Roman historian Robert Knapp has likewise recognized that "Paul's letter to the Philippians uses language that is extensively mercantile" and has accordingly concluded: "Not only does this indicate Paul's own background as a man of commerce, but also that the audience was operating in this exchange and business environment, and felt positive about it."[24]

In other words, unless one assumes that Paul was an unskilled communicator who misjudged his audience's ability to understand this technical language, the Philippians must have clearly grasped what he meant. This must be because they shared his experience of the marketplace, his fluency with its commercial jargon, as well as his familiarity with its sociocultural codes and conventions. This recognition then helps us situate Paul and the Philippians among the free and servile working classes of Roman society, among the commercial and artisan *plebs media*, as Paul Veyne labeled them,[25] that populated the *fora* and *stoae* of the Roman Greek East, among the craftsmen and traders who have been brought to light in a number of recent epigraphic studies.[26] In contrast with the Corinthians, who overall appear to have been relatively wealthier (see 1 Cor 1:26; 2 Cor 8:2—all rhetorical exaggeration duly considered), the Philippians indeed comprised, as Richard Ascough likewise concluded, "predominantly non-

---

23. Peterlin, *Philippians*, 153.

24. Robert Knapp, *Invisible Romans* (London: Profile Books, 2011), 8.

25. Paul Veyne, "La 'plèbe moyenne' sous le Haut-Empire romain," *Annales* 55 (2000): 1169–99.

26. Pierre Sodini, "L'artisanat urbain à l'époque paléochrétienne (IVe–VIIe s.)," *Ktema* 4 (1979): 71–119; Guy Labarre and Marie-Thérèse Le Dinahet, "Les métiers du textile en Asie Mineure de l'époque hellénistique à l'époque impériale," in *Aspects de l'artisanat du textile dans le monde méditerranéen (Égypte, Grèce, monde romain)*, Collection de l'institut d'archéologie et d'histoire de l'antiquité, Université Lumière-Lyon 2 (Paris: de Boccard, 1996), 49–116; Onno M. van Nijf, *The Civic World of Professional Associations in the Roman East* (Amsterdam: Gieben, 1997), esp. 18–23, 42; Nicolas Tran, *Dominus tabernae: Le statut de travail des artisans et des commerçants de l'Occident romain (Ier siècle av. J.-C.–IIIe siècle ap. J.-C.)* (Rome: École Française de Rome, 2013).

elites, either slaves or freed and free persons, for whom participation in the marketplace was an everyday experience and an integral part of their social world."[27]

In sum, they were people of modest or moderate means whose living standards would have depended on the nature of their trade, on the products they manufactured or commerced, and on their professional status (i.e., whether they ran independent workshops and/or small businesses, or whether they were employed or exploited as slaves to manage the affairs and/or estates of wealthier patrons),[28] and who, if they were successful enough, might have gained a certain degree of socioeconomic and political influence over their local community.[29] From the profits they made in their daily business activities, they could then support Paul in his missionary endeavors and even participate in the collection for the poor in Jerusalem.

3. Subsequent Generations of Christians (ca. second–fifth centuries CE)

This having been established, what may be said about the social constituency of the Philippian Christians in subsequent decades and centuries? How did it evolve? How did it differ from earlier generations? Unfortu-

---

27. Richard S. Ascough, *Paul's Macedonian Associations: The Social Context of Philippians and 1 Thessalonians*, WUNT 2/161 (Tübingen: Mohr Siebeck, 2003), 122. This in turn gives some weight to Oakes's thesis that the Philippians' suffering was primarily economic, their newly found faith having possibly severed local commercial ties and ostracized them from business acquaintances, networks, and professional associations. See Oakes, *Philippians*, 77–102.

28. See Albert F. Norman, "Gradations in Later Municipal Society," *JRS* 48 (1958): 80–83 (mostly relying on the evidence from Libanius); Sodini, "L'artisanat urbain," 111, 118–19; Labarre and Le Dinahet, "Les métiers," 64–67; Tran, *Dominus tabernae*, 4–5, 77–101, 255–315.

29. On the political involvement and influence of artisans and traders, some of whom rose to the level of the local elite, see for example Sodini, "L'artisanat urbain," 117–18; Van Nijf, *Civic World*, 22; Tran, *Dominus tabernae*, 2–5. Oakes is generally more pessimistic regarding the relative prosperity of the original Philippian church, arguing that its suffering was primarily of an economic nature. See Oakes, *Philippians*, 63–70, 77–96. See Peter Oakes, "Leadership and Economic Suffering in the Letters of Polycarp and Paul to the Philippians," in *Trajectories through the New Testament and the Apostolic Fathers*, vol. 2 of *The New Testament and the Apostolic Fathers*, ed. Andrew F. Gregory and Christopher M. Tuckett (Oxford: Oxford University Press, 2005), 335–73.

nately, none of these questions can be answered easily due to the paucity of our sources about the Philippian community, which, in contrast with the increasingly more significant church of Thessalonica, the capital of Illyricum from the fourth century, progressively faded away from the historical record.[30]

Very little information that would be relevant to our topic indeed transpires in the book of Acts or in Polycarp's letter, leaving us with a very sketchy portrait of the community in the late first century and early second century CE.[31] The author of Acts simply confirms what is already apparent in Paul's epistle, namely, that the original congregation comprised members from the merchant class such as Lydia the purple-seller (πορφυρόπωλις; Acts 16:14), as well as low-level public servants or officials such as the jailer (Acts 16:33).[32] Polycarp's admonition against the love of money (φιλαργυρία/avaritia; Polycarp, *Phil.* 4.1; 11.1–4),[33] on the other hand, suggests that avarice was a real temptation for the Philippians and needed to be addressed.[34] This in turn implies that some probably had

---

30. See Jean-Pierre Sodini, "L'architecture religieuse de Philippes, entre Rome, Thessalonique et Constantinople," *CRAI* 2014 (2016): 1509, 1513.

31. For a tentative reconstruction of the early history of the first Christian community at Philippi, see Pilhofer, *Philippi*, 1:229–58.

32. A detailed discussion of the social status of the jailer and of Lydia is found in Peterlin, *Philippians*, 144–50, 155–60. See Pilhofer, *Philippi*, 1:174–82, 187–98. But see Oakes, *Philippians*, 65, on the status of the jailer.

33. Only chapters 1–9 and 13 (found in Eusebius, except for the last sentence) of the Greek text have been preserved. The missing chapters 9–12 are known to us from a complete but imperfect Latin translation. See Philipp Vielhauer, *Geschichte der urchristlichen Literatur: Einleitung in das Neue Testament, die Apokryphen und die Apostolischen Väter* (Berlin: de Gruyter, 1975), 557. For a more detailed discussion, see William R. Schoedel, "Polycarp of Smyrna and Ignatius of Antioch," *ANRW* 27.1:273–85; Paul Hartog, ed., *Polycarp's Epistle to the Philippians and the Martyrdom of Polycarp: Introduction, Text, and Commentary* (Oxford: Oxford University Press, 2013), 26–32.

34. Valens's moral shortcoming was likely one of the main reasons prompting Polycarp's letter, which aimed to promote the theological unity, ethical purity, steadfastness, and cohesion of the community. See Harry O. Maier, "Purity and Danger in Polycarp's Epistle to the Philippians: The Sin of Valens in Social Perspective," *JECS* 1 (1993): 229–47; Paul Hartog, *Polycarp and the New Testament: The Occasion, Rhetoric, Theme, and Unity of the Epistle to the Philippians and Its Allusions to New Testament Literature*, WUNT 2/134 (Tübingen: Mohr Siebeck, 2002), 108; Hartog, *Polycarp's Epistle*, 49–51. See also Roman Garrison, "The Love of Money in Polycarp's Letter to the Philippians," in *The Graeco-Roman Context of Early Christian Literature* (Sheffield: Sheffield Academic Press, 1997), 74–79.

the capacity to earn substantial sums of money through their economic activities, or that they might have been tempted to acquire money through less honest means.³⁵ Indeed, the presbyter Valens was himself enticed by his own greed and became embroiled in some financial scandal (Polycarp, *Phil.* 11.1-4). Virtually nothing is known about the matter, but what can be inferred is that Valens had abused his office and position of authority in the church (*quod sic ignoret is locum qui datus est ei*; 11.1). It is likely that he had done so either by pursuing private economic activities with a view to accumulating wealth for himself, or worse by stealing from the community's common fund.³⁶ Not much else can be deduced from these (and other) literary sources, which forces the social historian to turn to documentary and archaeological evidence in search for traces that the Philippian Christians might have left on their urban environment.³⁷

Just as in Rome or in Asia Minor, it is funerary epigraphy that proves to be the most insightful, providing us with modest but suggestive glimpses into the life and social composition of the community.³⁸ While a

---

35. *Pace* Maier, Oakes is of the opinion that Polycarp's admonition against φιλαργυρία was meant to encourage the Philippians not to be "drawn back into relational networks, economic networks, that involved some Greco-Roman religious practice or other activity anathema to the Christian," and which would have led to apostasy. Maier, "Purity," 238; Oakes, "Leadership and Economic Suffering," 368.

36. See Walter Bauer, *Die Briefe des Ignatius von Antiochia und der Brief des Polykarp von Smyrna*, ed. Henning Paulsen, 2nd rev. ed. (Tübingen: Mohr Siebeck, 1985), 123-24; Maier, "Purity," 236-38; Pilhofer, *Philippi*, 1:218-24; Hartog, *Polycarp's Epistle*, 50, 76-78, 141-42. Meinhold's idea that Valens had done so by receiving a *donatio* from Marcion is not convincing. See Peter Meinhold, "Polykarpos," PW 1.42:1686.

37. For a succinct review of the literary sources, see Dimitris J. Kyrtatas, "Early Christianity in Macedonia," in *Brill's Companion to Ancient Macedon: Studies in the Archaeology and History of Macedon, 650 BC-300 AD*, ed. Robin J. Lane Fox (Leiden: Brill, 2011), 587-99.

38. A classic study for Rome remains Sandra R. Joshel, *Work, Identity, and Legal Status at Rome: A Study of the Occupational Inscriptions* (Norman: University of Oklahoma Press, 1992). See also Jean-Sodini, "L'artisanat urbain"; Nicolas Tran, "La mention épigraphique des métiers artisanaux et commerciaux en Italie centro-méridionale," in *Vocabulaire et expression de l'économie dans le monde antique*, ed. Jean Andreau and Véronique Chankowski (Paris: de Boccard, 2007), 119-41. For Christian funerary evidence from Asia Minor, see, for instance, Konstantinas P. Mentzu, Συμβολαί εἰς τὴν μελέτην τοῦ οἰκονομικοῦ καὶ κοινωνικοῦ βίου τῆς πρωίμου βυζαντινῆς περιόδου (Athens: Diatribe epi Didaktoria, 1975); Elsa Gibson, *The "Christians for Christians" Inscriptions of Phrygia*, HTS 32 (Missoula, MT: Scholars Press, 1978); Ste-

detailed survey of Christian epigraphy at Philippi should be carried out in the comparative light of the entire dossier of Christian and non-Christian inscriptions of the colony,[39] and indeed of the whole province, for the sake of conciseness we shall focus in what follows on a very limited sample of early Christian documents, namely, those that contain information of a socioeconomic nature. At Philippi, these amount to a mere handful of inscriptions, which can be dated approximately between the early fourth century and the late fifth or early sixth centuries CE.[40]

What may well be one of the earliest Christian occupational inscriptions consists of a large circular hopscotch game measuring 1 meter in diameter and adorned with two simple crosses: † Ἰωάννου | † μαγ[ί]ρου.[41] It was found in the northern hall of the *macellum*, south of the *forum*,[42] where Ioannes, a cook or, rather, a butcher or meat dealer, as a rare defini-

---

phen Mitchell, *Anatolia: Land, Men, and Gods in Asia Minor*, vol. 2 (Oxford: Oxford University Press, 1993); Johnson, "Christian Business"; McKechnie, "Christian Councillors"; Sylvain Destephen, "La christianisation de l'Asie Mineure jusqu'à Constantin: Le témoignage de l'épigraphie," in *Le problème de la christianisation du monde antique*, ed. Hervé Inglebert, Sylvain Destephen, and Bruno Dumézil (Paris: Picard, 2010), 171–75; Cilliers Breytenbach and Christiane Zimmermann, *Early Christianity in Lycaonia and Adjacent Areas*, ECAM 2 (Leiden: Brill, 2018).

39. For a similar recommendation, see Louis Robert, "L'épigraphie," in *L'histoire et ses méthodes*, ed. Charles Samaran (Paris: Gallimard, 1961), 462–63; Mitchell, *Anatolia*, 2:58.

40. No Christian inscription from eastern Macedonia can be dated with certainty prior to the reign of Constantine, except perhaps that of Aurelius Capiton, the "new presbyter of the catholic church" (πρεσβύτερος νέος τῆς καθολεικῆς ἐκλησίας), which could be dated to 262/3 CE (following the provincial-era dating), although it is more likely dated to 379/80 (following the colonial-era dating; *RICM* 233 = *ICG* 3254). See Lemerle, *Philippes*, 84, 94–101; *RICM*, p. 196.

41. *RICM* 229 = *ICG* 3250; fourth–fifth centuries CE: "(Hopscotch game) of Ioannes, (the) butcher." The words Ἰωάννου and μαγ[ί]ρου are written in circular fashion around the game, one letter per slot. See Jacques Coupry, "Un joueur de marelle au marché de Philippes," *BCH* 70 (1946): 104–5; Peter Pilhofer, *Philippi*, vol. 2, *Katalog der Inschriften von Philippi*, 2nd ed., WUNT 119 (Tübingen: Mohr Siebeck, 2009), 247. Its date is not entirely certain (ca. fourth–fifth centuries CE), though unlikely to be earlier than the fourth century CE. The destruction of the *macellum* to make way for the Basilica B in the middle of the sixth century provides a safe *terminus ante quem*. See Coupry, "joueur de marelle," 104.

42. For a brief description of the *macellum* (53 × 27 m.), see Claire De Ruyt, *Macellum: Marché alimentaire des Romains* (Louvain-la-Neuve: Institut supérieur d'archéologie et d'histoire de l'art, Collège Érasme, 1983), 133–37.

tion of μάγειρος by Artemidorus suggests (*Onir.* 3.56),⁴³ presumably had a shop or a stall, and where people could have played the game seated.⁴⁴ One of several board games scattered around the *forum* and the *macellum*,⁴⁵ its exact purpose is not entirely clear. It may have been meant as a piece of advertisement for Ioannes's nearby Christian meat shop or stall, or it may have simply been intended to entertain bored customers and passersby (or the shop owner himself).⁴⁶ What is certain is that Ioannes is one of the few rare known Christian μάγειροι from Greece and Asia Minor,⁴⁷ a profession that is in any case seldom encountered in inscriptions during the Roman era, though more commonly attested in papyri.⁴⁸

While this inscription raises more questions than it gives information about the first Philippian Christians (especially regarding their dietary habits and their attitude toward meat sold in the *macellum*, which had been potentially sacrificed to pagan deities),⁴⁹ it is quite suggestive of the

---

43. Artemidorus, *Onir.* 3.56: Οἱ δὲ ἐν ἀγορᾷ μάγειροι οἱ τὰ κρέα κατακόπτοντες καὶ πιπράσκοντες. See Coupry, "Joueur de marelle," 104; Louis Robert, "Études sur les inscriptions et la topographie de la Grèce Centrale: VI. Décrets d'Akraiphia," *BCH* 59 (1935): 448 n. 4. See also Edwin M. Rankin, *The Role of the ΜΑΓΕΙΡΟΙ in the Life of the Ancient Greeks, as Depicted in Greek Literature and Inscriptions* (Chicago: University of Chicago Press, 1907), 64–66.

44. On this particular type of board games, see Hans Lamer, "*Lusoria tabula*," PW 1.26:1987–88 (n. 45).

45. See Collart, *Philippes*, 362; Coupry, "Joueur de marelle," 102 n. 5; Michel Sève and Patrick Weber, *Guide du forum de Philippes*, Sites et Monuments 18 (Athens: École Française d'Athènes, 2012), 74–75.

46. The two crosses are particularly intriguing, their use being quite rare in public inscriptions before the fourth century CE (so Lemerle). Could they have been meant to reassure potential customers that the meat sold met Christian dietary standards (i.e., that it had not been sacrificed to pagan deities)? On the apotropaic significance of the other crosses carved on the rock of the acropolis, on the eastern gate itself, and on an altar to Isis found by the eastern gate, see Lemerle, *Philippes*, 85–86 (with add., p. 519).

47. See, e.g., *IG* 2².13343 (= *ICG* 1921; Athens, fifth–sixth centuries CE); *MAMA* 3.82 (Diocaesarea; fourth–sixth centuries CE?); *IG* 12.8.595 (Thasos; date?). See Mentzu, Συμβολαί, 118–19.

48. The term is more frequently observed in the Delphic temple accounts from the Hellenistic period, in which it refers to a sacrificer (e.g., *FD* 3.4.77, 5.19, 5.23; *CID* 2.31, 34). See Rankin, ΜΑΓΕΙΡΟΙ, 55–64; Kurt Latte, "Μάγειρος," PW 1.27:393–95; LSJ, s.v. "μάγειρος." For papyri, see, e.g., P.Oxy. 1.108; *BGU* 1.34; *CPR* 9.77; P.Giss. 1.101.

49. Archaeological evidence from the nearby island of Thasos and elsewhere suggests that *macella* remained directly connected to cultic places well into the late Roman period. So much so that it seems appropriate to speak of a "circuit de la viande"

social location and economic role of some believers in the fourth or fifth century, a decisive time for Christianity. It also provides us with some insight into their self-representation in the public sphere, their interaction with competing visual discourses of social identification and self-promotion, and their subtle transformation of public spaces, the *macellum* in this case, where, in earlier times, the *Fortuna* and the *Genius macelli*, *Mercurius Augustus*, as well as the *Aequitas Augusti*, had been revered.[50]

As with many of the other Christian inscriptions from Philippi, Ioannes's board game strikes by its modesty. It lacks the pretentiousness and aesthetic refinements of other non-Christian inscriptions set up around the forum and the *macellum*,[51] which, it is often overlooked, was a major public building that could sometimes be expensively decorated with ornate marble *mensae lapidae* and statuary.[52] This in itself is quite indicative of Ioannes's lower socioeconomic position in the colony as a μάγειρος, whose "status was among the lowest on the job market."[53] Had he been wealthier and/or wanted to be more socially assertive, he could have for instance erected an honorific inscription or sponsored and dedicated a mosaic pavement. The inscription only features two simple crosses, which, however discreet they might have been initially (they have now almost completely faded), nonetheless give the impression that Ioannes thereby sought to claim a place for himself as a Christian in the social and economic center of Philippi. "Jean aura lui-même (sans

---

in Roman cities, whereby temples functioned as the main suppliers of meat to *macella*. The crosses on the hopscotch game may have thus been meant to signal to Christian customers that the meat sold met Christian dietary standards and complied with Paul's instructions in 1 Cor 10:25–33. On meat production and distribution in Roman cities, see, e.g., William Van Andringa, "Du sanctuaire au macellum: Sacrifices, commerce et consommation de la viande à Pompéi," *F&H* 5 (2007): 47–72; Jean-Yves Marc, "Le macellum de Thasos," *Collegium Beatus Rhenanus* 16 (2013): 18–20 (see esp. the bibliography in nn. 3–5).

50. On *Fortuna* and the *Genius macelli*, see Pilhofer, *Philippi*, 2.251 (first–second century CE). On *Mercurius Augustus*, see *CIPh* 2.1.132 (= Pilhofer, *Philippi*, 2.250; first century CE). On *Aequitas Augusti*, see *CIPh* 2.1.117 (= Pilhofer, *Philippi*, 2.249; first century CE). See also the measuring tables probably dedicated to the emperor (*CIPh* 2.1.32; ca. 50s CE, *inedita*).

51. For the inscriptions from the *macellum* specifically, see Pilhofer, *Philippi*, 2.245–58.

52. Claire De Ruyt, "Les produits vendus au macellum," *F&H* 5 (2007): 136, 145–46.

53. Nicolas Tran, "Le statut de travail des bouchers dans l'Occident romain de la fin de la République et du Haut-Empire," *F&H* 5 (2007): 151.

doute!) avec application voulu éterniser son personnage de chrétien," notes Jacques Coupry.⁵⁴ Without a doubt, this would have been a bold move prior to Constantine's tolerance edict of 313, or even shortly afterward. For, although the edict did make life easier for Christians, their relation with their non-Christian contemporaries could still sometimes be tense throughout the fourth and fifth centuries and could lead to sporadic, violent clashes, especially over the appropriation of public spaces.⁵⁵ Whatever the case may have been, this inscription is a rare and potentially early testimony of the subtle, yet subversive, penetration of Christianity in Philippian society and of the progressive transformation of its public spaces, transformation that became much more assertive from the end of the fourth century.⁵⁶

Ioannes is unlikely to have been the only Christian artisan active in the colony in the fourth or fifth century, even though little evidence has survived of the commercial activities of other church members, who perhaps populated the artisanal quarter southwest of the city.⁵⁷ For example, one epitaph, which was found in the Turkish cemetery of Raktcha but is now lost, mentions a πραγματευτής named Aurelius Severos: Αὐρήλιος | Σεβῆρος | πραγματευ|τὴς ἐποίησ[α]|| τὸ χαμοσόρ[ιον] B || τοῦτο ἐμαυ[τῷ]|| καὶ τῇ συμβ[ίῳ]| μου Αὐρ(ηλίᾳ) Κλαυδίᾳ| καὶ τοῖς γλυ[κυτά]|τοις μου τέκν[οι] ς·|| ἰ δέ τις τολμήσι ἔτε|ρον σκήν<ω>μα κατα{ι}|θέσθαι, δώσι τῷ ἱερ[ω]||τάτῳ ταμίῳ χρυσοῦ| λίτραν μίαν.⁵⁸ Severos, whom the original editors thought to

---

54. Coupry, "Joueur de marelle," 104–5.

55. See, e.g., Christophe J. Goddard, "Un principe de différenciation au coeur des processus de romanisation et de christianisation: Quelques réflexions autour du culte de Saturne en Afrique romaine," in *Le problème de la christianisation du monde antique*, ed. Hervé Inglebert, Sylvain Destephen, and Bruno Dumézil (Paris: Picard, 2010), 132–35. See Ramsay MacMullen, "Religious Toleration around the Year 313," *JECS* 22 (2014): 499–517. See also "Part IV: Religious Violence," in Harold A. Drake, ed., *Violence in Late Antiquity: Perceptions and Practices* (Burlington, VT: Ashgate, 2006), 265–342.

56. As Provost and Boyd have noted, all the *intra muros* churches at Philippi were constructed in prominent public locations where religious or civic edifices formerly stood. See Samuel Provost and Michael Boyd, "Application de la prospection géophysique à la topographie urbaine: II. Philippes, les quartiers Ouest," *BCH* 126 (2002): 473 n. 56.

57. Samuel Provost and Michael Boyd, "Application de la prospection géophysique à la topographie urbaine: I. Philippes, les quartiers Sud-Ouest," *BCH* 125 (2001): 468, 472.

58. *RICM* 232 = *ICG* 3253; fourth century CE: "I, Aurelius Severos, an (estate)

be a *negotiator*, was more likely an estate manager or overseer (*actor*) similar to those attested in several Greek and Latin inscriptions from Philippi.[59]

---

manager, made this [second?] tomb for myself and my wife Aurelia Claudia, and my dearest children. If anyone dares to lay another corpse [here], he/she shall pay one pound of gold to the most sacred treasury." See Collart, *Philippes*, 290 n. 4; Pilhofer, *Philippi*, 2.83. The verisimilitude between *RICM* 231 (= *ICG* 3252) and *RICM* 232 (= *ICG* 3253) makes it very likely that both inscriptions were produced by the same workshop. It is not certain that Severos was Christian, but the metaphorical use of σκήνωμα (l. 12) is a strong hint (see 2 Pet 1:13–14). The term is otherwise rare in inscriptions and appears to be used exclusively in Christian epitaphs. See *RICM* 123 (= *ICG* 3141; Thessalonica; fourth century CE?); Yiannis E. Meimaris and Kalliope I. Kritikakou-Nikolaropoulou, eds., *The Greek Inscriptions from Ghor Es-Safi (Byzantine Zoora)*, vol. 1 of *Inscriptions from Palaestina Tertia*, Meletemata 41 (Athens: Research Centre for Greek and Roman Antiquity, National Hellenic Research Foundation, 2005), 180–83 n. 89 (405 CE); G. H. R. Horsley and Stephen Mitchell, eds., *The Inscriptions of Central Pisidia* (Bonn: Habelt, 2000), 82–83 n. 56 (σκηνωμάτων; third-fourth centuries CE); Dietrich Berges and Johannes Nollé, eds., *Tyana: Archäologisch-historische Untersuchungen zum südwestlichen Kappadokien* (Bonn: Habelt, 2000), 1:269–71 n. 108 (ca. fourth century CE); *SEG* 59.1713 (Jerusalem, fourth–fifth centuries CE). See also *PGL*, s.v. σκήνωμα; G. H. R. Horsley, "σκήνωμα," *NewDocs* 4:172 n. 85.

59. E.g., Pilhofer, *Philippi*, 2.22, 248, 333, 344, 432, 525. See Paul Perdrizet, "Inscriptions de Philippes: Les Rosalies," *BCH* (1900): 313; Collart, *Philippes*, 289; *RICM*, p. 197. See also Mentzu, Συμβολαί, 103–4; Louis Robert and Jeanne Robert, *BE* (1980): 439 n. 412; Mitchell, *Anatolia*, 1:162–64; Jean-Jacques Aubert, *Business Managers in Ancient Rome: A Social and Economic Study of Institores, 200 B.C.–A.D. 250* (Leiden: Brill, 1994), 186–96; Thomas Corsten, "Estates in Roman Asia Minor: The Case of Kibyratis," in *Patterns in the Economy of Roman Asia Minor*, ed. Stephen Mitchell and Constantina Katsari (Swansea: The Classical Press of Wales, 2005), 7–13. Another Christian πραγματευτής named Nikandros is known at Philippi, but his epitaph has yet to be published. See Charalambos Bakirtzis, "Ἔκθεση Παλαιοχριστιανικῶν ἀρχαιοτήτων στὸ Μουσεῖο Φιλίππων," *AAA* 13 (1980): 95; *RICM*, p. 18 n. 84 bis. For additional evidence of Christian πραγματευταί from Macedonia and Asia Minor, see, e.g., *RICM* 111 (= *ICG* 3129; Thessalonica, fifth–sixth centuries CE); *MAMA* 6.222 (= *ICG* 960; Apamea, 247/8 CE); *IK* 67.111 (= *ICG* 1346; Antiocheia, fifth century CE). More generally, see Pantelis M. Nigdelis, Ἐπιγραφικὰ Θεσσαλονίκεια: Συμβολὴ στην πολιτικὴ καὶ κοινωνικὴ ιστορία τῆς Ἀρχαίας Θεσσαλονίκης (Thessalonica: IMXA, 2006), 226–29. For the original editors' opinion that Severos was a negotiator, see Léon Heuzey and Pierre G. H. Daumet, *Mission Archéologique de Macédoine* (Paris: Librairie de Firmin-Didot, 1876), 94. See Margaritis G. Dimitsas, Ἡ Μακεδονία ἐν λίθοις φθεγγομένοις καὶ μνημείοις σωζομένοις (Athens: Perre, 1896), 2:732 n. 929 (ἔμπορος). The term πραγματευτής could certainly mean "negotiator." See Koenraad Verboven, "Ce que *negotiari* et ses dérivés veulent dire," in *Vocabulaire et expression de l'économie dans le monde antique*, ed. Jean Andreau and Véronique Chankowski (Paris: de Boccard, 2007), 93–94.

He must have therefore held relatively important responsibilities either running a business or overseeing the production and financial administration of an estate, and thus presumably enjoyed a relatively better standard of living than independent artisans or small local farmers.[60] Judging from his *praenomen*, he must have also commanded greater social respectability than most πραγματευταί (especially if he was managing a large estate), who, for the great majority, seem to have been slaves or freedmen.[61]

The same might be true of Alexandros, a fifth-century builder (οἰκοδόμος) who could afford a sizable marble tombstone for himself, his wife, and his mother: Μνῆμα| Ἀλεξάν|δρου οἰ|κοδόμου καὶ τῆ<ς> συν||βίου αὐτοῦ| ἅμα τῇ γλυ|κυτάτη μη|τρ{ρ}ί {ι}.[62] The title of his occupation remains somewhat ambiguous, as it could refer to a wide range of building activities and implies varying levels of theoretical knowledge, practical qualifications, and experience as a builder.[63] Alexandros might thus have been a simple builder with basic training and no significant responsibility on construction sites. Or he might have been one of the accomplished workers or foremen from Constantinople or Thessalonica who were employed to build one of the seven or eight basilicas erected in Philippi between the fourth and sixth centuries.[64]

---

60. See Paul Perdrizet, "Voyage dans la Macédoine première," *BCH* 21 (1897): 531; Collart, *Philippes*, 289.

61. On the social conditions and legal status of πραγματευταί, see in particular Louis Robert, *Hellenica: Recueil d'épigraphie, de numismatique et d'antiquités grecques* (Paris: Adrien-Maisonneuve, 1955), 10:83; Robert, *Hellenica: Recueil d'épigraphie, de numismatique et d'antiquités grecques* (Paris: Adrien-Maisonneuve, 1965), 13:105; Louis and Jeanne Robert, *BE* (1963): 177–78 n. 263; Aubert, *Business Managers*, 193–94, 417–19. See Norbert Ehrhardt, "Eine neue Grabinschrift aus Iconium," *ZPE* 81 (1990): 186–87.

62. *RICM* 248 = *ICG* 3269; fifth–sixth centuries CE: "Tomb of Alexandros, architect (or builder), and of his wife, as well as of his dearest mother." See *SEG* 30.584; Pilhofer, *Philippi*, 2.116.

63. See Sodini, "L'artisanat urbain," 79. On the significance and usage of the term, see also Anastasios K. Orlandos and Ioannes N. Travlos, *Lexicon archaion architektonikon horon* (Athens: Archaiologike Hetaireia, 1986), s.v. "οἰκοδόμος"; Marie-Christine Hellmann, *Recherches sur le vocabulaire de l'architecture grecque, d'après les inscriptions de Délos* (Paris: de Boccard, 1992), 296–97. Mentzu seems to understand the term to refer to private entrepreneurs (εἰς τοὺς ἰδιωτικῶς ἐξασκοῦντας τὸ ἐπάγγελμα). Mentzu, Συμβολαί, 169.

64. These are the Octagon basilica (late fourth–fifth centuries CE), which was built next to the episcopal palace and on top of the basilica of Paul dedicated by the

Still more intriguing is the "receiver" (ὑποδέκτης) and linen merchant or manufacturer (ὀθονίτης)[65] Ioannes, who was buried with a certain Agathe, one of only two known deaconesses at Philippi: † Κυμιτίριον | διαφέροντα | Ἀγάθης δια|κόνου καὶ Ἰω|άν<ν>ου ὑποδέ||κτου κὲ ὠθο|νιτοῦ †.[66] The exact nature of his activities and responsibilities as an ὑποδέκτης are unclear and difficult to determine precisely in the absence of any specific context and comparable epigraphic evidence.[67] Given the mention of his involvement in the linen industry as a second vocation, Peter Pilhofer (following Valerie Abrahamsen perhaps) concluded that Ioannes must have held the office of church treasurer ("Kassierer ['Kirchmeister'?]"),[68] even though no mention of the church is made, and the terms more

---

bishop Porphyrios (by far the earliest Christian building at Philippi—ca. 340s), the basilica *extra muros* excavated by Pelekanidis (fourth–fifth centuries CE), the small basilica 300 m. south of the basilica *extra muros* excavated by Pennas, the two large Basilicas A (fifth century CE) and B (sixth century CE) erected on either side of the forum and studied by Lemerle, the partially excavated Basilica C on the southwestern slopes of the acropolis next to the museum (fifth–sixth centuries CE), and a yet-to-be excavated Basilica D (early sixth century CE?) further to the west that was identified by Provost and Boyd (see fig. 3, n. 13, in Sodini). See Lemerle, *Philippes*, 281–513, 517–18; Stylianos Pelekanidis, "Ἡ ἔξω τῶν τειχῶν παλαιοχριστιανικὴ βασιλικὴ τῶν Φιλίππων," *ArchEph* 1955 (1961): 114–79; Charalambos Pennas, "Early Christian Burials at Philippi," *ByzF* 21 (1995): 215–27; Provost and Boyd, "I. Philippes," 492–96; Provost and Boyd, "II. Philippes," 460–69. See Sodini, "L'architecture religieuse." The excavation reports for the Octagon complex are too numerous to be listed here but are conveniently summarized in Sodini, "L'architecture religieuse," 1516–17 nn. 14–16.

65. The noun derives from ὀθόνη, i.e., "fine linen or cloth," but gives no indication of any specific role in the production or distribution stages (as ὀθονιοπώλης does). See LSJ, s.v. "ὀθόνη"; *PGL*, s.v. "ὀθόνη"; Mentzu, Συμβολαί, 107–8; Sodini, "L'artisanat urbain," 90–92; Labarre and Le Dinahet, "Les métiers," 59. Feissel understands him to be a "marchand de toile." *RICM*, p. 18 n. 84 bis. In any case, Philippi was never a production center for the textile industry.

66. Pilhofer, *Philippi*, 2.115 = ICG 3381; fifth century CE: "Tomb belonging to Agathe the deaconess and to Ioannes the 'receiver' and linen-worker." The stone was first mentioned in Bakirtzis, "Ἔκθεση Παλαιοχριστιανικῶν," 95. For the epitaph of the deaconess Poseidonia and the *kanonike* Pancharia, see *RICM* 241 (= ICG 3262; fourth–fifth centuries CE).

67. The term is rarely attested in comparison to ἀποδέκτης, which is commonly found in Attic inscriptions from the classical and Hellenistic periods (e.g., *IG* 1³.84, *IG* 2².212; see *IG* 12.Supp.438, Thasos, third–fourth centuries CE).

68. Pilhofer, *Philippi*, 2.115, p. 122. See Valerie Abrahamsen, "Women at Philippi: The Pagan and Christian Evidence," *JFSR* 3 (1987): 23 (n. 22): "treasury official."

commonly used to designate administrators of sacred or public treasuries (ταμιεῖον) were ταμίας (*quaestor* in Latin) or οἰκονόμος (for the church especially).[69] If such was the case, he would have presumably been responsible for collecting donations and bequests, or perhaps funerary fines (in case of the desecration of a tomb).[70] But Ioannes could have equally been a "receiver" of imported products at a textile depot or, more likely, a tax collector,[71] such as those attested in papyri from the fourth century onward who had the charge of exacting (mainly grain) taxes (e.g., P.Col. 7.150, 161; Karanis, 347-351 CE).[72] Being a Christian or a cleric from the lower ranks would have been no obstacle (e.g., the διάκονος and ὑποδέκτης of Stud.Palmyr. 8.958; fifth-sixth centuries CE).[73] Whatever the case may have been, Ioannes is likely to have come from the slightly more educated and wealthier sections of Philippian society, to have been involved in some measure in the administration and political life of the colony,[74] and seems

---

69. See LSJ, s.v. "ταμίας"; *PGL*, s.v. "οἰκονόμος" 3; Hugh J. Mason, *Greek Terms for Roman Institutions: A Lexicon and Analysis* (Toronto: Hakkert, 1974), 91; Arnold H. M. Jones, *The Later Roman Empire, 284-602: A Social Economic and Administrative Survey* (Oxford: Blackwell, 1964), 902; Ewa Wipszycka, *Les ressources et les activités économiques des églises en Égypte du IVe au VIIIe siècle* (Brussels: Fondation Égyptologique Reine Élisabeth, 1972), 135-41. But see Lampe, who renders (quite rightly) ὑποδέκτης by "treasury official" on the basis of two texts (Athanasius, *H. Ar.* 75: ὑποδέκτην ἐν Κωνσταντινουπόλει ταμιακῶν γενόμενον; John Chrysostom, *Hom. Matt.* 85.4: οἱ δὲ, ὑπὲρ ὧν ὑποδέκται καὶ φορολόγοι καὶ λογισταὶ καὶ ταμίαι μεριμνῶσιν [PG 58.762: *exceptores, quaestores, rationarii et pecuniarii curare coguntur*]). *PGL*, s.v. "ὑποδέκτης."

70. E.g., *RICM* 231 (= *ICG* 3252); *RICM* 232 (= *ICG* 3253); *SEG* 45.795 (= *ICG* 3289 A). On the administration of church finances in late antiquity, see especially Jones, *Later Roman Empire*, 894-910.

71. Feissel understands him to be a "percepteur," which is the sense more commonly encountered in literary sources (e.g., John Chrysostom, *Laz.* 4.4 [PG 48.988: *exactor*]; John Chrysostom, *Hom. Matt.* 85.4 [PG 58.762: *exceptores*]; Justinian, *Nov.* 163.2 [Schoell: *susceptor*]). See *RICM*, p. 18 n. 84 bis. See *PGL*, s.v. "ὑποδέκτης."

72. See Friedrich Oertel, *Die Liturgie: Studien zur ptolemäischen und kaiserlichen Verwaltung Ägyptens* (Leipzig: Teubner, 1917), 222-25; Jacqueline Lallemand, *L'administration civile de l'Égypte de l'avènement de Dioclétien à la création du diocèse (284-382): Contribution à l'étude des rapports entre l'Égypte et l'Empire à la fin du IIIe et au IVe siècle* (Brussels: Palais des Académies, 1964), 212-15.

73. See Wipszycka, *Les ressources*, 168.

74. Lallemand notes that many ὑποδέκται were recruited among "la bourgeoisie des cités." Some of them actually belonged to the *curia* or were former municipal magistrates (Lallemand, *L'administration*, 215).

to have felt no social embarrassment in mentioning his unpopular occupation on his epitaph.[75]

The Philippian Christians did not confine themselves to the commercial world, however, for they were involved in the educational and medical sectors as well, as is indicated by two additional epitaphs from the fourth or fifth century. The first one makes mention of a διδάσκαλος named Aurelius Kyriakos, who was likely a schoolteacher (rather than a cleric in charge of instructing young catechumens),[76] and whose marble tombstone was discovered in the vicinity of the eastern necropolis at Dikili-Tasch. It reads: Αὐρήλιος | Κυριακὸς διδ[άσ]|καλος ἐποίησ[α]|τὸ χαμοσόρ[ιον] | τ[ο]ῦτο ἐ[μαυτῷ]|| κ[αὶ τῇ συμβίῳ]| μου [Α]ὐρη[λία]|| Μαρκελλίνῃ| καὶ τέκνοις·| εἰ δέ τις τολ||μήσι ἕτερον σκή|νωμα καταθέσ|θαι, δώσει τῷ | ἱερωτάτῳ τα|[μ]είῳ χρυσοῦ|| [λί]τραν μίαν.[77] The second funerary plate was engraved in memory of a certain Paul, the priest and doctor of the Philippians, who was buried in the northern aisle of the basilica *extra muros* (tomb A),[78] a fourth- or fifth-century structure of major

---

75. But neither did many *publicani*. See Onno van Nijf, "The Social World of Tax Farmers and Their Personnel," in *The Customs Law of Asia*, ed. Michel Cottier et al. (Oxford: Oxford University Press, 2008), 279–311.

76. *RICM*, p. 195. See Mentzu, Συμβολαί, 27. Contra Jacques Coupry and Michel Feyel, "Inscriptions de Philippes," *BCH* 60 (1936): 53–54; *AE* 1937.19 n. 49; Lemerle, *Philippes*, 94. Another "newly-baptised Christian teacher" (διδασκάλλος χρηστιανός νεοφωτείστος) is attested at Thessalonica (*RICM* 123 = *ICG* 3141; fourth century CE).

77. *RICM* 231 = *ICG* 3252; fourth century CE: "I, Aurelius Kyriakos, teacher, made this tomb for [myself and] my [wife] Aurelia Marcelline, and for [our] children. If anyone dares to lay another corpse [here], he/she shall pay one pound of gold to the most sacred treasury." See Lemerle, *Philippes*, 94; Pilhofer, *Philippi*, 2.71. Along with the term σκήνωμα (l. 11; see n. 51 above), the cognomen Κυριακός is the only other hint of Aurelius's possible Christian faith, though not a definitive clue. See Denis Feissel, *BE* (1987): 358 n. 432 (correcting *RICM*, p. 195).

78. The basilica, which is located in the eastern necropolis in the village of Krenides, included sixteen tombs (Α–Π) scattered throughout its floor and delivered no fewer than a dozen epitaphs, which represents about a third of all the Christian inscriptions recovered on the territory of the Roman colony. Its first phase is dated by Pelekanidis toward the beginning of the fourth century (based on numismatic evidence), possibly during Constantine's reign (p. 177), but Pallas places it in the fifth or early sixth century. For a detailed report of the excavations conducted in the mid-1950s, see Pelekanidis, "Ἡ παλαιοχριστιανικὴ βασιλική." For a summary description in English (but with many mistakes with respect to the inscriptions), see Ralph F. Hoddinott, *Early Byzantine Churches in Macedonia and Southern Serbia: A Study of the Origins and the Initial Development of East Christian Art* (London: Macmillan, 1963),

importance that has delivered some of the best-preserved and more precisely dated burials. It reads: Κοιμητήριον Πα[ύλου]‖ πρεσβ(υτέρου) καὶ ἰατροῦ| Φιλιππησίων.| Κ(ύρι)ε Ἰ(ησο)ῦ Χ(ριστ)ὲ ὁ θ(εὸ)ς ὁ ποιήσας| ἀπὸ τῶν μὴ ὄντων εἰ<ς>‖ εἶναι, ἐν τῇ ἡμέρᾳ τῆ<ς>| κρίσεως μὴ μνησθῇς| τῶν ἁμαρτιῶν μου, ἐλ[έ]|ησόν με.[79]

Kyriakos's inscription is a good illustration of the increasingly prominent and influential role Christians played in education (even if only at an elementary level)[80] in the third and fourth centuries (even in peripheral urban centers such as Philippi), a role that would eventually prompt Julian's *School Edict* of 362 CE, banning Christian pedagogues from using Greek classical literature and imposing financial sanctions on Christian schools (see Cod. theod. 13.3.5; Julian, *Ep.* 42).[81] Paul's epitaph, on the other hand, provides further evidence that clerics could have two vocations and combine their ecclesiastical functions with other unrelated economic (or noneconomic) activities (see Cod. theod. 13.1.1, 5; 16.2.8, 10, 14–15).[82] Each case thus offers a good example of a Christian pushing the

---

99–106. See Demetrios I. Pallas, *Les monuments paléochrétiens de Grèce découverts de 1959 à 1973* (Rome: Pontificio Istituto di Archeologia Christiana, 1977), 107–10; *RICM*, pp. 17–18.

79. *RICM* 237 = *ICG* 3258; fourth-fifth centuries CE: "Tomb of Paul, presbyter and doctor of the Philippians. Lord Jesus Christ, God who brought into being that which was not, do not remember my sins in the day of judgment, have mercy on me!" See *SEG* 19.440; Pilhofer, *Philippi*, 2.100; Évelyne Samama, *Les médecins dans le monde grec: Sources épigraphiques sur la naissance d'un corps médical* (Geneva: Librairie Droz, 2003), 189–90 n. 089.

80. In Egypt, the term διδάσκαλος mostly identified "elementary instructors," although "it can refer to teachers at various stages" as well. See Raffaella Cribiore, *Gymnastics of the Mind: Greek Education in Hellenistic and Roman Egypt* (Princeton: Princeton University Press, 2001), 50–51.

81. See, e.g., Henri-Irénée Marrou, *Histoire de l'éducation dans l'Antiquité*, vol. 2, *Le monde romain* (Paris: Seuil, 1948), 139–41; Glen W. Bowersock, *Julian the Apostate* (Cambridge: Harvard University Press, 1978), 83–85; Rowland Smith, *Julian's Gods: Religion and Philosophy in the Thought and Action of Julian the Apostate* (London: Routledge, 1995), 212–14; Thomas M. Banchich, "Julian's School Laws: *Cod. Theod.* 13.5.5 and *Ep.* 42," *AncW* 24 (1993): 5–14.

82. Priests or deacons practicing medicine are indeed rather well attested throughout the empire. See the examples adduced in *RICM*, p. 201; Samama, *Les médecins*, 026, 027, 070, etc.; Mentzu, Συμβολαί, 32–45. More generally on the professional vocations of clerics in late antique Egypt and Asia Minor, see Wipszycka, *Les ressources*, 154–73. See Destephen, "La christianisation," 173–74.

boundaries of participation in society and attaining a certain degree of respectability, though without reaching the level of the local elites. Both are indeed more than likely to have been well educated, to have sat higher up the social ladder than artisans and traders, and also perhaps to have enjoyed greater socioeconomic stability, even though the social conditions of teachers could vary considerably depending on their terms of employment, the subjects they taught, and their sources of income.[83]

From the fourth century onward, Christians of higher social status begin to make their appearance in the epigraphic record.[84] Three inscriptions in particular stand out from the rest by the occupations and honorific titles they mention. One of the earliest epitaphs, the first of only two Latin Christian inscriptions discovered at Philippi,[85] commemorates a *vir clarissimus* and *ex comite* named Mauricius: † *Hic in pace requies|c[i]t in nomine| [C]hristi Mauriçi|[us] vir clarissi|[mus] ex comite*.[86] Both the location of the tomb (tomb Θ, west of the diaconicon, in the basilica *extra muros*),[87] and the physical features of the stone itself (a reused and neatly engraved

---

83. On the superior social status and mobility of doctors and the political and administrative role they could play in civic life, see, e.g., Samama, *Les médecins*, 61–64, 66–68. See Norman, "Gradations," 82; Masao Kobayashi, "The Social Status of Doctors in the Early Roman Empire," in *Forms of Control and Subordination in Antiquity*, ed. Toru Yuge and Masaoki Doi (Leiden: Brill, 1988), 416–19. On teachers, see Norman, "Gradations," 82; Robert A. Kaster, "The Social Status of the Grammarians," in *Guardians of Language: The Grammarian and Society in Late Antiquity* (Berkeley: University of California Press, 1997), 100–136; Cribiore, *Gymnastics*, 45–73 (esp. 59–65); Lisa Maurice, "The Social Status of the Teacher," in *The Teacher in Ancient Rome: The Magister and His World* (Plymouth, UK: Lexington Books, 2013), 143–78.

84. The same phenomenon is observed in Thessalonica. See Efthymios Rizos, "The Making of a Christian Society in the Late Antique Civil Diocese of Macedonia—Archaeological Evidence on Christianisation from Modern Greece," in *Christianisierung Europas: Entstehung, Entwicklung und Konsolidierung im archäologischen Befund*, ed. Orsolya Heinrich-Tamaszka, Niklot Krohn, and Sebastian Ristow (Regensburg: Schnell & Steiner, 2012), 320–21. See (more generally) Jones, *Later Roman Empire*, 895–96.

85. Pilhofer also noted the presence of a "seemingly unpublished Christian Latin inscription" lying next to the epitaph of Theodora found in the Basilica B (*RICM* 246 = *ICG* 3267; fourth–fifth centuries CE). See Pilhofer, *Philippi*, 2.268, p. 332.

86. *RICM* 251 = *ICG* 3272; fourth century CE: "Here rests in peace, in the name of Christ, Mauricius, a *vir clarissimus*, ex-count." See Pilhofer, *Philippi*, 2.111.

87. Pelekanidis, "Ἡ παλαιοχριστιανικὴ βασιλική," 161. Tomb H in Hoddinott, *Early Byzantine Churches*, 104.

tabula ansata made of fine white marble), indicate that Mauricius was a person of some importance in the community. This is further made evident by the titles *vir clarissimus* and *ex comite* (which are rarely attested at Philippi),[88] which, even if only meant honorifically,[89] help identify Mauricius as one of the local elites, possibly a high military or civic official of senatorial status who was likely in close contact with the imperial palace at Constantinople,[90] and who may have also been a patron of the church— hence his burial in the floor of the basilica.

Andreas, the "young faithful tribune of the notaries" (ὁ πιστὸς τριβοῦνος νοταρίων),[91] is another high-profile, Christian layman interred in the basilica *extra muros* (tomb Δ by the narthex): † Ἐνθάδε κῖται Ἀνδρέας | οὗ τὸ ἐπίκλην Κομιτᾶ ὁ | πιστὸς τριβοῦνος νο|ταρίων, συνετὸς ὤν, ἡλι|κία, κάλλος καὶ εὐγένια||{α} πολλὴ ἦν παρ' αὐτῷ·| οὗτος δ' ἐτελεύτα ἐτῶν | δέκα ὀκτώ παρὰ μῆ(να) α' ἡμ(έρας) ϛ'.[92] Since he was buried at the age of eighteen, it is unlikely that Andreas held any tribunitian or notarial responsibilities, the military and administrative offices of *tribunus* and *notarius* being usu-

---

88. See *CIPh* 2.1, 37, 38, 41, 42.

89. See *AE* 1983.252 n. 890. From the fifth century CE, the title *clarissimus* ceases to indicate effective membership of the Senate (Jones, *Later Roman Empire*, 8, 104–5, 379).

90. See Otto Seeck, "Clarissimi viri," PW 1.6:2628; Seeck, "Comites," PW 1.7:622–32; Adolf Berger, "Clarissimus," in *Encyclopedic Dictionary of Roman Law*, TAPS 43.2 (Philadelphia: American Philosophical Society, 1953), 390; Berger, "Comites," in *Encyclopedic Dictionary of Roman Law*, 397. See also Jones, *Later Roman Empire*, 8, 104–5, 379, 528–31; Alexander Demandt, *Die Spätantike: Römische Geschichte von Diocletian bis Justinian, 284–565 n. Chr.*, vol. 6.3 of *Handbuch der Altertumswissenschaft* (Munich: Beck, 1989), 76, 250, 273–74, 278, 281–82, 405.

91. Mentzu-Meimare here understands πιστός "im Sinne des getauften Christen und Mitglieds der Kircher," and suggests placing a comma after the adjective (i.e., "the young believer, a tribune of the notaries"). Konstantina Mentzu-Meimare, review of *Recueil des inscriptions chrétiennes de Macédoine du IIIe au VIe siècle*, by Denis Feissel, *ByzZ* 77 (1984): 324. But see "Andreas," in *The Prosopography of the Later Roman Empire*, vol. 2, *395–527*, ed. John R. Martindale (Cambridge: Cambridge University Press, 1980), 87: *Andreas qui et Comitas v(ir) d(evotus), tribunus et notarius*. See *RICM*, p. 208.

92. *RICM* 247 = *ICG* 3268; fifth century CE: "Here lies Andreas, nicknamed Komitas, the faithful tribune of the notaries, an intelligent [man]. Youth, beauty, and great nobility were his. He died at eighteen years of age, minus one month and six days." See *SEG* 19.444; Pilhofer, *Philippi*, 2.104.

ally attributed as honorary titles to sons of important officers.[93] Andreas, who was also praised for his beauty (κάλλος) and great nobility (see εὐγένια πολλή, ll. 5–6),[94] and who was remembered with a smoothly polished and neatly carved marble tombstone, is yet another clue of the presence of well-to-do and distinguished Christian families at Philippi in later antiquity.

There is, in fact, ample evidence from the Roman province of Macedonia,[95] and indeed from the rest of the empire, that by the fourth century such honorific titles were no longer rare for Christians to hold.[96] At Philippi, this is further indicated by a late boundary stone of white marble found fortuitously in the environs of Argyroupolis, some 20 km. northwest of the city (but within the territory of the colony),[97] which was used to demarcate the property of the *vir magnificentissimus* Maurentios

---

93. See *RICM*, p. 208. On the offices of *tribunus* and *notarius*, see Jones, *Later Roman Empire*, 573–75; Demandt, *Spätantike*, 241. For equally young *notarii*, see Jones, *Later Roman Empire*, 1235 n. 21.

94. The themes of beauty and nobility are not uncommon in Christian hagiography. See *RICM*, p. 208.

95. See, e.g., the *viri clarissimi / magnificentissimi / perfectissimi* and *comes* mentioned in *RICM* 64 (= *ICG* 3074; fifth century CE), *RICM* 86 (= *ICG* 3095; Thessalonica, fourth century CE), *RICM* 120 (= *ICG* 3138; Thessalonica, fourth century CE), *RICM* 132 (= *ICG* 3152; Thessalonica, sixth century CE), and *RICM* 267 (= *ICG* 3303; Heraclea Lyncestis, fifth–sixth centuries CE). Not all of them can be surely identified as Christian, however.

96. E.g., ETAM 15.141–42 (= *ICG* 724–25; Lycaonia; fourth–fifth centuries CE); *MAMA* 6.13 (= *ICG* 952; Phrygien; fourth century CE); *IG* 4.3.1491 (= *ICG* 2973; Corinth, fourth–fifth centuries CE). See Eck, "Eindringen des Christentums"; McKechnie, "Christian Councillors"; Weiß, *Soziale Elite*, 188–208.

97. On the delineation of the territory of the colony, see especially Athanasios D. Rizakis, "Le territoire de la colonie romaine de Philippes: Ses limites au Nord-Ouest," in *Autour des libri coloniarum: Colonisation et colonies dans le monde romain; Actes du Colloque International (Besançon, 16–18 octobre 2003)*, ed. Antonio Gonzales and Jean-Yves Guillaumin (Besançon: Presses Universitaires de Franche-Comté, 2006), 123–30; Georges Tirologos, "Les recherches sur les cadastres romains du territoire colonial de Philippes (Macédoine orientale—Grèce): Bilan et perspectives," in Gonzales and Guillaumin, *Autour des libri coloniarum*, 131–49; Athanasios D. Rizakis, "Une *praefectura* dans le territoire colonial de Philippes: Les nouvelles données," in *Colons et colonies dans le monde romain*, ed. Ségolène Demougin and John Scheid (Rome: École française de Rome, 2012), 87–105; Cédric Brélaz and Georges Tirologos, "Essai de reconstitution du territoire de la colonie de Philippes: Sources, méthodes et interprétations," in *Espaces et territoires des colonies romaines d'Orient*, ed. Hadrien Bru, Guy Labarre, and Georges Tirologos (Besançon: Presses Universitaires de Franche-Comté, 2016), 119–89.

from the church's estate: (A) [–] |[[δι]α[φ]έρο[ν]]| Μαυρεν|τίου.| † μ(εγαλο)π(ρεπεστάτου).†| (B) [–] ΜΕΓΕΟ . . N| διαφέ[ρ(ον)] τῇ| Φιλιππισ(ίων)| ἁγ(ίᾳ) ἐκκλ(ησίᾳ).[98] Maurentios, who was likely a high official of senatorial status at the imperial court in the fifth or sixth century,[99] and not the Metropolite of Philippi, as Eutychia Kourkoutidou-Nikolaidou concluded by (mis-)reading Α(ΡΧΙ)Ε(ΠΙΣΚΟΠΟΥ) on the first line of face A,[100] should thus be counted among the few known elite members of the local Christian community, who may have also acted as one of its patrons by donating land and/or by sponsoring the construction of edifices.[101] What is clear is that, by the fifth or sixth century, the church at Philippi had grown sufficiently large and wealthy to own some kind of estate side by side with those of local elites such as Maurentios[102] and actually stored substantial amounts of food (oil, wine, grain) in the episcopal complex (next to the Octagon church), probably with a view to feeding the poor and the local clergy.[103]

Significantly, however, none of these inscriptions and monuments particularly stands out by their physical characteristics or ornamentation, for they remain overall relatively modest in their general outlook,[104]

---

98. *RICM* 224 = *ICG* 3245; fifth–sixth centuries CE: "(A) … belonging to Maurentios, a *vir magnificentissimus*; (B) … belonging to the holy church of the Philippians." See *SEG* 27.259; Pilhofer, *Philippi*, 2.528.

99. See Paul Koch, *Die byzantinischen Beamtentitel von 400 bis 700* (Jena: Neuenhahn, 1903), 45–58. See *RICM*, p. 191; Jones, *Later Roman Empire*, 543–44; Demandt, *Spätantike*, 199–200.

100. Eutychia Kourkoutidou-Nikolaidou, "Μακεδονία-Θράκη," *ADelt* 27 B.2 (1972): 575. See *RICM*, p. 191.

101. On the patronage of Christian buildings throughout the province, see, e.g., Kara Hattersley-Smith, "The Early Christian Churches of Macedonia and Their Patrons," *ByzF* 21 (1995): 229–34. See William Bowden, "A New Urban Élite? Church Builders and Church Building in Late-Antique Epirus," in *Recent Research in Late-Antique Urbanism*, ed. Luke Lavan, JRASup 42 (Portsmouth, RI: Journal of Roman Archaeology, 2001), 64–67.

102. It may have acquired the estate through a donation, as became increasingly common after Constantine. See Jones, *Later Roman Empire*, 895–96, 904–5; Wipszycka, *Les ressources*, 34–37.

103. See Sodini, "L'architecture religieuse," 1518. On the upkeep of the clergy, see, e.g., Jones, *Later Roman Empire*, 906–9.

104. For a typology and catalogues of Roman Macedonian funerary stelae, see Maria Lagogianni-Georgakarakos, *Die Grabdenkmäler mit Porträts aus Makedonien* (Athens: Akademie von Athen, 1998); Ioanna Spiliopoulou-Donderer, *Kaiserzeitliche*

while the *cursus honorum* of the deceased is generally omitted or reduced to a succinct summary of the main offices and/or honorific titles held or received.[105] This mode of self-representation contrasts rather starkly with the pomposity of non-Christian inscriptions, be they honorific or funerary, which were more commonly used as social media to assert one's prestige in the community.[106] It is also striking that only a handful of Christian sarcophagi have actually been found throughout Macedonia, none of which features elaborate sculpted decorations.[107] Sarcophagi being an expensive commodity that, at Philippi, were used almost exclusively by equestrian and senatorial families,[108] it is thus very likely that few Philippian Christians ranked among the top elite of Roman society.[109]

Grabaltäre Niedermakedoniens: Untersuchungen zur Sepulkralskulptur einer Kunstlandschaft im Spannungsfeld zwischen Ost und West (Mannheim: Bibliopolis, 2002); P. Adam-Veleni, ΜΑΚΕΔΟΝΙΚΟΙ ΒΩΜΟΙ (Athens: TAP, 2002), 150, 152–65, 170, 175–76, 298–99, etc. (with corresponding plates). For sarcophagi, see Thea Stefanidou-Tiveriou, *Die lokalen Sarkophage aus Thessaloniki* (Ruhpolding, Germany: Rutzen, 2014).

105. This is a general trend throughout Macedonia. For more details, see Julien M. Ogereau, "Authority and Identity in the Early Christian Inscriptions from Macedonia: An Overview," in *Authority and Identity in Emerging Christianities in Asia Minor and Greece*, ed. Cilliers Breytenbach and Julien M. Ogereau, AJEC 103 (Leiden: Brill, 2018).

106. See esp. the two honorific inscriptions in Pilhofer, *Philippi*, 2.240 and 357 (= *CIPh* 2.1.37–38; second century CE), or the enormous monumental funerary altar (3.78 × 2.74 m.) prominently erected at a crossroad on the Via Egnatia east of Philippi (*CIPh* 2.1.63 = Pilhofer, *Philippi*, 2.58; first century CE). For a survey and explanation of the phenomenon, see in particular Werner Eck, *Monument und Inschrift: Gesammelte Aufsätze zur senatorischen Repräsentation in der Kaiserzeit*, ed. Walter Ameling and Johannes Heinrichs (Berlin: de Gruyter, 2010), 311–31, 383–99.

107. E.g., *RICM* 116, 117, 238 (= *ICG* 3134, 3135, 3259; third–fifth centuries CE)—*RICM* 117 is now on display at the Byzantine Museum of Thessaloniki. On the question of the social status of sarcophagi owners (at Thessalonica), see in particular Thea Stefanidou-Tiveriou, "Social Status and Family Origin in the Sarcophagi of Thessalonikē," in *From Roman to Early Christian Thessalonikē: Studies in Religion and Archaeology*, ed. Laura S. Nasrallah, Charalambos Bakirtzis, and Stephen J. Friesen, HTS 64 (Cambridge: Harvard University Press, 2010), 178–84.

108. On the use of sarcophagi by the elites at Philippi, see *CIPh* 2.1.59–61. The same is also the case at Thessalonica (Stefanidou-Tiveriou, "Social Status," 152–53).

109. A significant amount of material evidence may have also been destroyed in the meantime, just as in Thessalonica (Stefanidou-Tiveriou, "Social Status," 152).

Interestingly, the only (marble) Christian sarcophagus so far discovered at Philippi, which was found in the floor of the basilica *extra muros* (tomb H, northern aisle),[110] did not contain the remains of a local notable but of the "first presbyter" (πρωτοπρεσβύτερος) Paul, the highest-ranking cleric after a bishop (whom he could replace in his absence).[111] His tomb illustrates particularly well the (increasingly) powerful position and prestige of clerics in later antiquity (bishops especially),[112] which here seem to be further emphasized by a stern warning in the final clause of the epitaph not to reuse the presbyter's "single-body sarcophagus" (μονόσωμον).[113]

This said, the scarcity of Christian sarcophagi at Philippi (and Thessalonica) could also be explained by a different reason, namely, a local preference for larger vaulted tombs in which several family members could be buried together, such as those unearthed in the eastern and western necropoleis,[114] in the basilica *extra muros* (tombs B and Γ),[115] and in the vast burial complex excavated by Charalambos Pennas in the mid-1970s

---

110. Tomb G in Hoddinott, *Early Byzantine Churches*, 104.

111. See Socrates, *Hist. eccl.* 6.9.3. See also *PGL*, s.v. ἀρχιπρεσβύτερος, πρωτοπρεσβύτερος; Pelekanidis, "Ἡ παλαιοχριστιανικὴ βασιλική," 166–67; *RICM*, p. 203. For other examples of πρωτοπρεσβύτερος, see *MAMA* 7.89 (= *ICG* 554; Lycaonia, fourth century CE), *CIG* 4.8822 (= *ICG* 2310; Galatia, fourth century CE), *RECAM* 2.449 (= *ICG* 2466; Galatia, fourth century CE).

112. On the power of bishops, see, e.g., Claudia Rapp, "The Elite Status of Bishops in Late Antiquity in Ecclesiastical, Spiritual, and Social Contexts," *Arethusa* 33 (2000): 379–99; Raymond Van Dam, "Bishops and Society," in *Constantine to c. 600*, ed. Augustine Casiday and Frederick W. Norris, CHC 2 (Cambridge: Cambridge University Press, 2007), 343–66.

113. *RICM* 238 (= *ICG* 3259; fourth–fifth centuries CE): † Κυμητήριον Παύλου| πρεσβοιτέρου τῆς Φι|λιππισίων ἁγίας τοῦ| θεοῦ ἐκλησίας· ἤ τις δὲ| μετὰ τὴν ἐμὴν κατάθε||σιν ἐπιχειρήσει ἐνθάδε ἔτε|ρον θεῖναι νεκρόν, λόγον δώ|σει τῷ θεῷ· ἔστιν γὰρ μονό|σωμον πρωτοπρεσβοιτέρου †, i.e., "Tomb of Paul, presbyter of the holy church of God of the Philippians. Whoever attempts to lay another corpse here after my burial shall give an account unto God. For this is the 'single tomb' of a first presbyter." See *SEG* 19.443; Pilhofer, *Philippi*, 2.103. For similar examples of the term μονόσωμον at Thessalonica, see *RICM* 153 and 170 (= *ICG* 3173 and 3191; fifth–sixth centuries CE). See *RICM*, p. 202; Louis and Jeanne Robert, *BE* (1965): 72 n. 2.

114. See *RICM* 234 (= *ICG* 3255; fourth century CE) and below. New vaulted tombs were discovered underneath one of the streets opposite the basilica *extra muros* in the yet-to-be-reported 2015 excavation season.

115. Several skeletons and eighteen skulls (of clerics?) were discovered in the two tombs. See Pelekanidis, "Ἡ παλαιοχριστιανικὴ βασιλική," 153–54, 157 (photos 34, 40–43). See Hoddinott, *Early Byzantine Churches*, 103–4.

some 300 m. south of the basilica *extra muros*.[116] The fourth- (or early fifth-) century complex comprised a central courtyard hedged by porticoes, around which were built a basilica (south), storage rooms (north), and a 100 sq. m. structure (east), which may have been used as a place of worship or as a *hagiasma*, and under which a sizable burial chamber was constructed.[117] In total, nine vaulted tombs (some of which have marble walls), a rectangular tomb, twenty tile graves, several lead coffins, and nineteen skeletons (oriented toward the east) were discovered onsite. In addition, two funerary epigrams commemorating the founders of the burial chamber were found engraved and painted in red letters on the revetment of the entrance and southern wall of the south chamber.[118]

Originally from Pontus, Flavius Gorgonios and Glykeris, who is identified as the daughter of a *vir clarissimus* (λαμπρότατος), had settled in Philippi and built a tomb (ἡρῷον, l. 5) for themselves and their dependents: Φλάβιος Γοργόνιος ὁ Κρατεροῦ | καὶ ἡ Γλυκερὶς ἡ Ἀνδρονείκου τοῦ λ(α)μ(προτάτου) | ἐκ πατρίδος Πόντου, οἰκήσαντες | ἐν Φιλίπποις, ἑαυτοῖς καὶ τοῖς τέκνοις | κατεσκεύασαν τὸ ἡρώιον, παρανγέ||λοντες μηδὲν ἐπεισφέρειν σκήνωμα | ἀλλότριον τοῦ γένους. Εἰ δέ τις τολ|μήσιεν δώσει{ι} προστείμου, τῇ μὲν | ἁγιωτάτῃ ἐκκλησίᾳ χρυσοῦ | λείτρας δύο, τῷ δὲ ἱερωτάτῳ || ταμείῳ χρυσοῦ λείτρας πέντε.[119] Nothing else is known of the affluent and illustrious couple, who, despite Pennas's reservations, must have been Christian.[120] The fact that they insisted on mentioning Glykeris's filiation with the *cla-*

---

116. Pennas, "Burials."

117. The complex is approximately dated to the second half of the fourth century (after 364–367 CE) based on numismatic evidence. See Pennas, "Burials," 215.

118. Pennas, "Burials," 217–18.

119. Pilhofer, *Philippi*, 2.125a = *ICG* 3289 A; fourth–fifth centuries CE: "Flavius Gorgonios, son of Krateros, and Glykeris, daughter of the *vir clarissimus* Androneikos, from their homeland Pontus, lived in Philippi, and built this tomb for themselves and their children, ordering that no one should bury another corpse from another family [here]. But if someone dares [to do so], he/she shall pay a fine of two pounds of gold to the most holy church, and of five pounds of gold to the most sacred treasury." See *SEG* 45.795; Denis Feissel, *BE* (1998): 703 n. 631; Pilhofer, *Philippi*, 2.125a. Another, smaller epigram dedicated to Glykeris was also found in the south chamber. See Pilhofer, *Philippi*, 2.125b (= *ICG* 3289 B).

120. The metaphorical usage of the term σκήνωμα, and the notice to pay fines to the church as well as, remarkably enough, to the imperial *fiscus* (ἱερώτατον ταμεῖον), are very strong indications that the senior members of the household were Christians. Pennas and Pilhofer remain unsure, even though it is very improbable that non-Christians would have been (or felt) compelled to have tomb desecrators pay fines to the

rissimus Androneikos, whom Pennas (very improbably) thought to be the friend of Libanius, the once-governor of Bithynia and vicar of Thrace (365/366 CE),[121] gives away their attachment to their elevated social origins and status. Added to the sheer dimensions of the complex, the abundant use of marble revetment, and the size of the household, there can be little doubt that Gorgonios and Glykeris were among the prominent families of the colony in the late fourth or early fifth century.

Surprisingly, though, none of the vaulted tombs excavated in this complex features the kind of richly decorated murals discovered in the eastern Christian necropolis at Thessalonica.[122] At least three to four such hypogea have so far been excavated at Philippi.[123] The two most important are the tomb B of the presbyters Faustinos and Donatos, located in the southern aisle of the basilica *extra muros*, on whose walls were painted four Latin crosses in elegant wreaths;[124] and the vaulted tomb found in

---

church in the second half of the fourth century. See Pennas, "Burials," 220; Pilhofer, *Philippi*, 2.125a, pp. 134–36.

121. Pennas, "Burials," 219. See "Andronicus 3," in *The Prosopography of the Later Roman Empire*, vol. 1, *260–395*, ed. Arnold H. M. Jones et al. (Cambridge: Cambridge University Press, 1971), 64–65.

122. Some of these tombs are now on display at the Byzantine Museum of Thessaloniki, e.g., the fourth-century tomb of Eustorgia and her husband (*RICM* 124 = *ICG* 3142). See Efterpi Marki, Η νεκρόπολη της Θεσσαλονίκης στους υστερορωμαϊκούς και παλαιοχριστιανικούς χρόνους (μέσα του 3ου έως μέσα του 8ου αι. μ.Χ.) (Athens: TAP, 2006), 123–204 (with many drawings), pls. 1–26. See Stylianos Pelekanidis, *Gli affreschi paleocristiani ed i piu antichi mosaici parietali di Salonicco* (Ravenna: Dante, 1963), 8–12; Pelekanidis, "Die Malerei der Konstantinischen Zeit," in *Studien zur frühchristlichen und byzantinischen Archäologie* (Thessalonica: Institute for Balkan Studies, 1977), 75–96; Pamela Bonnekoh, *Die figürlichen Malereien in Thessaloniki vom Ende des 4. bis zum 7. Jahrhundert: Neue Untersuchungen zur erhaltenen Malereiausstattung zweier Doppelgräber, der Agora und der Demetrios-Kirche* (Oberhausen: Athena, 2013). For a detailed survey of the eastern Christian necropolis of Thessalonica, see Marki, Η νεκρόπολη.

123. Two other tombs discovered in the vicinity of the basilica *extra muros* and in the western necropolis (by the village of Lydia) also featured some crosses. See Chaido Koukouli, "Αρχαιότητες και μνημεία Ανατολικήως Μακεδονίας," *ADelt* 23, B.2 (1968): 353–54; Koukouli, "4. Λυδία ('Υδρόμυλοι)." *ADelt* 24, B.2 (1969): 347–48.

124. *RICM* 235 = *ICG* 3256; mid-fourth century CE. The blue cross on the western side was ornate with pearls and precious stones. See Pelekanidis, "'Η παλαιοχριστιανικὴ βασιλική," 152–53, 155, 157 (photos 40–43); Hoddinott, *Early Byzantine Churches*, 103. Similar painted crosses have been found at Thessalonica. See Pelekanidis, "'Η παλαιοχριστιανικὴ βασιλική," 155 n. 1.

the eastern necropolis by the public fountain of the modern village of Krenides, in which a large enwreathed Latin cross with peacocks on either side was painted within a semicircular band on which a plea to be resurrected (Κύριε ... ἀνάστησον ἡμᾶς) was inscribed.[125] While the occupants of the latter remain unidentified, the sophisticated ornamentation strongly suggests that they were also of substantial means, being able to afford a large and lavishly decorated tomb, and of a higher social standing than the average Christian population.

These few epitaphs and funerary monuments thus provide us with additional insight into the social constituency of the Philippian church in the fourth and fifth centuries, which drew its membership from a progressively broader social spectrum. It comprised members from the lower levels of society such as Herakleon, Kyriakos and Nikandra, Philokyrios and Eutychiane, or Euodiane and Dorothea,[126] who could only afford roughly cut, grossly engraved, and poorly decorated epitaphs,[127] as well as a few members from the local nobility who were buried in the basilica *extra muros*, in ornate vaulted tombs, or in the imposing burial complex excavated by Pennas. This development is not particularly surprising, it must be said, but accords quite well with a general pattern of social diversification and upward mobility among Christians observed throughout the rest of the empire (e.g., Eusebius, *Hist. eccl.* 7.15.1, 7.16.1).[128]

---

125. *RICM* 234 = *ICG* 3255; fourth century CE. See the commentary (with photos) in Stylianos Pelekanidis, "Παλαιοχριστιανικός τάφος εν Φιλίπποις," in *Studien zur frühchristlichen und byzantinischen Archäologie* (Thessalonica: Institute for Balkan Studies, 1977), 67–76. See Pilhofer, *Philippi*, 2.99; Pallas, *Les monuments*, 106–7.

126. Heraklon: *RICM* 250 (= *ICG* 3271; fifth–sixth centuries CE): † Ἐρακλέ|ωνο[ς]| μιμό[ριον]| ἐν τω[...], i.e., "Monument of Herakleon...." See *SEG* 19.450; Pilhofer, *Philippi*, 2.110.

Kyriakos and Nikandra: *RICM* 243 (= *ICG* 3264; fourth–fifth centuries CE): † Κοιμητή|ριον Κυρια|κοῦ καὶ Νικ[ά]|νδρας, i.e., "Tomb of Kyriakos and Nikandra." See Lemerle, *Philippes*, 102 n. 4; Pilhofer, *Philippi*, 2.274.

Philokyrios and Eutychiane: *RICM* 249 (= *ICG* 3270; fifth–sixth centuries CE): Μεμόριον| Φιλοκυρί|ου καὶ Εὐ|τυχιανῆς, i.e., "Funerary monument of Philokyrios and Eutychiane." See Lemerle, *Philippes*, 102 n. 5; Pilhofer, *Philippi*, 2.308. Another Philokyrios is attested in Pilhofer, *Philippi*, 2.123 (= *ICG* 3382; fifth–sixth centuries CE).

Euodiane and Dorothea: Pilhofer, *Philippi*, 2.114 (= *ICG* 3380; fifth century CE): † Κυμ(ητήριον) Εὐοδι|ανῆς κέ Δω|ροθέας, i.e., "Tomb of Euodiane and Dorothea."

127. Most of these tombstones were reused as building material in the Basilica B and the basilica *extra muros*.

128. See, e.g., Jones, *Later Roman Empire*, 71, 895; Eck, "Eindringen des Chris-

One will note that the role and presence of slaves in the Christian community at Philippi remains difficult to determine. Hardly anything indeed transpires in the epigraphic record, even though four persons identify themselves as δοῦλοι or *servi*.[129] While it would be tempting to conclude that these individuals died in slavery, the context always points explicitly or implicitly to a metaphorical usage of the term with Christ or God as point of reference.[130] It is obvious, for example, that Theodora, the δούλη τοῦ Θεοῦ and wife of the centurion Agroikios, was not a slave.[131] Whether her husband was Christian or not is not clear. If indeed he was, he would be one of the very few Christian military officers attested in Macedonia.[132]

Whatever the case may be, the few impressive funerary monuments reviewed above certainly attest to the growing importance Christians assumed in Philippian society from the fourth century onward. It must have been under the patronage of such prominent local figures, of pow-

---

tentums"; Timothy D. Barnes, "Statistics and the Conversion of the Roman Aristocracy," *JRS* 85 (1995): 135–47; McKechnie, "Christian Councillors"; Weiß, *Soziale Elite*, 188–208.

129. *RICM* 227–28 (= *ICG* 3248–49; fourth–fifth centuries CE), *RICM* 246 and 252 (= *ICG* 3267 and 3273; fourth–fifth centuries CE).

130. *RICM* 227–28 consist of invocations to Christ inscribed on a mosaic floor of the basilica of Paul (originally located underneath the Octagon) and carved out on a western stylobate of the Octagon complex. At Thessalonica, slaves of prominent households identify themselves as οἰκέται. See *RICM* 159–60 (= *ICG* 3180–81; fifth–sixth centuries CE), although see *RICM* 161 (= *ICG* 3182; fifth century CE).

131. *RICM* 246 (= *ICG* 3267; fourth–fifth centuries CE): † Ἐνθάδε κῖτε| ἡ δούλη τοῦ Θ(εο)ῦ| Θεοδώρα γαμητὴ| Ἀγρυκίου κεντυ|ρίωνος, i.e., "Here lies the servant of God, Theodora, wife of Agroikios, a centurion." See *AÉ* 1936.16 n. 49; Lemerle, *Philippes*, 102 n. 2; Pilhofer, *Philippi*, 2.268.

132. A *protector*, who may have been an officer of the imperial guard and who was awarded the *comitiva* upon retiring, is known at Berea. Loukretia Gounaropoulou and Miltiades B. Hatzopoulos, eds., *Επιγραφές κάτω Μακεδονίας, τεύχος Α΄: Επιγραφές Βέροιας* (Athens: Institute of Historical Research, 1998), 374 n. 438 (= *ICG* 3643; 545 CE), while an *eparchos* (ἔπαρχος), i.e., a commander of a military unity (rather than a prefect), is attested at Edessa. See Loukretia Gounaropoulou and Miltiades B. Hatzopoulos, eds., *Επιγραφές κάτω Μακεδονίας, τεύχος Β΄* (Athens: Institute of Historical Research, 2015), 451–52 n. 336 = *ICG* 3602; fifth–sixth centuries CE. A number of Christian soldiers are also known at Edessa (*RICM* 26–29 = *ICG* 3034–37; fifth–sixth centuries CE), Berea (*RICM* 70 = *ICG* 3080; fifth–sixth centuries CE), and Thessalonica (*RICM* 153–54, 205 = *ICG* 3173–74, 3226; fifth–sixth centuries CE), but none are of superior ranks.

erful ecclesiastical figures (about whom so little is known),[133] and of the Christian emperors that a sizable Christian community thrived in the late Roman and early Byzantine eras and that the octagonal church complex (with the adjacent *episkopion*), the basilica *extra muros*, and the large Basilicas A, B, C, and (probably) D—buildings of seemingly disproportionate size for a small provincial city—were erected between the end of the fourth century and the sixth century.[134]

4. Concluding Remarks

As stated earlier, a comprehensive survey of Christian epigraphy at Philippi should be carried out in the comparative light of the entire dossier of inscriptions of the colony, which is too ambitious a project for this succinct overview. This selective examination has nonetheless proven insightful and suggestive in a number of respects. Not least, it has underlined once again the historical importance of epigraphic evidence, which complements literary sources that are very lacunose from the second century onward. Indeed, the inscriptions herein examined, which represent about a third of the available evidence at Philippi and its environs, help us bring back to life the long-extinguished voices of the Philippian Chris-

---

133. So far only eighteen to nineteen members of the lower and upper clergy are known to us from the epigraphical record: three readers (*RICM* 221, 225, 242 = *ICG* 3242, 3246, 3263), two deaconesses and one *kanonike* (*RICM* 241 = *ICG* 3262; Pilhofer, *Philippi*, 2.115 = *ICG* 3381), eight presbyters (*RICM* 233, 235–39 = *ICG* 3254, 3256–60), including a proto-presbyter (*RICM* 238 = *ICG* 3259), and one bishop named Porphyrios, who dedicated the basilica of Paul (underneath the Octagon) around 340 CE (*RICM* 226 = *ICG* 3247). The clerical status of the Andreas found buried in the nave of the basilica excavated by Pennas, south of the basilica *extra muros*, is unclear (Pilhofer, *Philippi*, 2.125 = *ICG* 3290). Three more priests were found buried in the basilica located near the sanctuary of Heros Auloneites at Kipia, south of Philippi (Pilhofer, *Philippi*, 2.630–32 = *ICG* 3294–96). Several skeletons and eighteen skulls (of clerics?) were also found in tomb Γ in the nave of the basilica *extra muros*. See Pelekanidis, "Ἡ παλαιοχριστιανικὴ βασιλική," 154 (photo 34).

134. See Hattersley-Smith, "Churches of Macedonia"; Rizos, "Making of Christian Society," 331–32; Bowden, "New Urban Élite?" The sheer number and dimension of the churches at Philippi, which seem out of proportion with the size of the local Christian population, strongly indicate that Philippi functioned as some kind of pilgrimage center in later antiquity. See esp. Sodini, "L'architecture religieuse," 1541. See Charalambos Bakirtzis, "Paul and Philippi: The Archaeological Evidence," in Bakirtzis and Koester, *Philippi at the Time of Paul and after His Death*, 37–48.

tians. They allow us to reconstruct the contours of a once-vibrant Christian community and to determine its social composition with slightly greater precision than the extant literary evidence. To be sure, this portrait will forever remain hazy and impressionistic for lack of more accurate primary data. Inscriptions are in any case merely illustrative, documenting what once was in a very discriminate manner, and fail to give us an exact and full picture of the ancient reality.[135]

The remaining question confronting us, therefore, is to what extent such empirical studies could or should be generalized. How representative of the bigger picture is this brief glimpse of a local community over several centuries? It is perhaps advisable to err on the side of caution until we have a better understanding of the social characteristics of the early Christians in the rest of the Macedonian province, and indeed in the whole of the Greek East. This calls for the pursuit of similar epigraphic surveys in the light of literary and archaeological sources, and for the development of tools that will facilitate the collection, curation, and analysis of a large body of epigraphic material. One such tool might take the form of the database of early Christian inscriptions that has been developed by the Excellence Cluster 264 Topoi at Humboldt-Universität zu Berlin, in cooperation with the *Inscriptiones Graecae* of the Berlin-Brandenburg Academy of Sciences and Humanities.[136] In time, this database, and the monograph series deriving from it, will allow us to reconstruct a much more precise sociological profile of the early Christians in Greece and Asia Minor during the first five centuries CE and to analyze in more detail Christianity's socioeconomic impact and transformation of the Roman empire.[137]

---

135. See Julien M. Ogereau, "Methodological Considerations in Using Epigraphic Evidence in Determining the Socioeconomic Context of the Early Christians," in Harrison and Welborn, *First Urban Churches*, 1:250–56.

136. The database can be accessed and searched online at http://www.epigraph.topoi.org. It includes original texts of the inscriptions with English or German translations, short commentaries and descriptives, and bibliographic references, as well as images, whenever available.

137. The first volume in the series focused on the Lycus Valley, while the second volume covers Lycaonia. In addition, several volumes on early Christianity in Phrygia, Macedonia, Galatia, Ionia, Attica, and Corinthia are in preparation. For now see Ulrich Huttner, *Early Christianity in the Lycus Valley*, ECAM 1 (Leiden: Brill, 2013); Breytenbach and Zimmermann, *Early Christianity in Lycaonia*.

Bibliography

Abrahamsen, Valerie. "Women at Philippi: The Pagan and Christian Evidence." *JFSR* 3 (1987): 17–30.

Adam-Veleni, Polyxeni. *ΜΑΚΕΔΟΝΙΚΟΙ ΒΩΜΟΙ*. Athens: TAP, 2002.

Ascough, Richard S. *Paul's Macedonian Associations: The Social Context of Philippians and 1 Thessalonians*. WUNT 2/161. Tübingen: Mohr Siebeck, 2003.

Aubert, Jean-Jacques. *Business Managers in Ancient Rome: A Social and Economic Study of Institores, 200 B.C.–A.D. 250*. Leiden: Brill, 1994.

Bakirtzis, Charalambos "'Έκθεση Παλαιοχριστιανικῶν ἀρχαιοτήτων στὸ Μουσεῖο Φιλίππων." *AAA* 13 (1980): 90–98.

———. "Paul and Philippi: The Archaeological Evidence." Pages 37–48 in *Philippi at the Time of Paul and after His Death*. Edited by Charalambos Bakirtzis and Helmut Koester. Harrisburg, PA: Trinity Press International, 1998.

Bakirtzis, Charalambos, and Helmut Koester, eds. *Philippi at the Time of Paul and after His Death*. Harrisburg, PA: Trinity Press International, 1998.

Banchich, Thomas M. "Julian's School Laws: *Cod. Theod.* 13.5.5 and *Ep.* 42." *AncW* 24 (1993): 5–14.

Barclay, John M. G. "Poverty in Pauline Studies: A Response to Steven Friesen." *JSNT* 26 (2004): 363–66.

Barnes, Timothy D. "Statistics and the Conversion of the Roman Aristocracy." *JRS* 85 (1995): 135–47.

Bauer, Walter. *Die Briefe des Ignatius von Antiochia und der Brief des Polykarp von Smyrna*. Edited by Henning Paulsen. 2nd rev. ed. Tübingen: Mohr Siebeck, 1985.

Berger, Adolf. *Encyclopedic Dictionary of Roman Law*. TAPS 43.2. Philadelphia: American Philosophical Society, 1953.

Berges, Dietrich, and Johannes Nollé, eds. *Tyana: Archäologisch-historische Untersuchungen zum südwestlichen Kappadokien*. Bonn: Habelt, 2000.

Bonnekoh, Pamela. *Die figürlichen Malereien in Thessaloniki vom Ende des 4. bis zum 7. Jahrhundert: Neue Untersuchungen zur erhaltenen Malereiausstattung zweier Doppelgräber, der Agora und der Demetrios-Kirche*. Oberhausen: Athena, 2013.

Bormann, Lukas. *Philippi: Stadt und Christengemeinde zur Zeit des Paulus*. NovTSup 78. Leiden: Brill, 1995.

Bowden, William. "A New Urban Élite? Church Builders and Church Building in Late-Antique Epirus." Pages 57–68 in *Recent Research in Late-Antique Urbanism*. Edited by Luke Lavan. JRASup 42. Portsmouth, RI: Journal of Roman Archaeology, 2001.

Bowersock, G. W. *Julian the Apostate*. Cambridge: Harvard University Press, 1978.

Brélaz, Cédric, and Georges Tirologos. "Essai de reconstitution du territoire de la colonie de Philippes: Sources, méthodes et interpretations." Pages 119–89 in *Espaces et territoires des colonies romaines d'Orient*. Edited by Hadrien Bru, Guy Labarre, and Georges Tirologos. Besançon: Presses Universitaires de Franche-Comté, 2016.

Breytenbach, Cilliers, and Julien M. Ogereau, eds. *Authority and Identity in Emerging Christianities in Asia Minor and Greece*. AJEC 103. Leiden: Brill, 2018.

Breytenbach, Cilliers, and Christiane Zimmermann. *Early Christianity in Lycaonia and Adjacent Areas: From Paul to Amphilochius of Iconium*. ECAM 2. Leiden: Brill, 2018.

Collart, Paul. *Philippes: Ville de Macédoine depuis ses origines jusqu'à la fin de l'époque Romaine*. Paris: de Boccard, 1937.

Corsten, Thomas. "Estates in Roman Asia Minor: The Case of Kibyratis." Pages 1–51 in *Patterns in the Economy of Roman Asia Minor*. Edited by Stephen Mitchell and Constantina Katsari. Swansea: The Classical Press of Wales, 2005.

Coupry, Jacques. "Un joueur de marelle au marché de Philippes." *BCH* 70 (1946): 102–5.

Coupry, Jacques, and Michel Feyel. "Inscriptions de Philippes." *BCH* 60 (1936): 37–58.

Cribiore, Raffaella. *Gymnastics of the Mind: Greek Education in Hellenistic and Roman Egypt*. Princeton: Princeton University Press, 2001.

Demandt, Alexander. *Die Spätantike: Römische Geschichte von Diocletian bis Justinian, 284–565 n. Chr*. Vol. 6. 3 of *Handbuch der Altertumswissenschaft*. Munich: Beck, 1989.

Destephen, Sylvain. "La christianisation de l'Asie Mineure jusqu'à Constantin: Le témoignage de l'épigraphie." Pages 171–75 in *Le problème de la christianisation du monde antique*. Edited by Hervé Inglebert, Sylvain Destephen, and Bruno Dumézil. Paris: Picard, 2010.

Dimitsas, Margaritis G. Ἡ Μακεδονία ἐν λίθοις φθεγγομένοις καὶ μνημείοις σωζομένοις. Athens: Perre, 1896.

Dodd, C. H. *New Testament Studies*. Manchester: Manchester University Press, 1967.

Drake, Harold A., ed. *Violence in Late Antiquity: Perceptions and Practices*. Burlington, VT: Ashgate, 2006.

Eck, Werner. "Das Eindringen des Christentums in den Senatorenstand bis zu Konstantin d. Gr." *Chiron* 1 (1971): 381–406.

———. *Monument und Inschrift: Gesammelte Aufsätze zur senatorischen Repräsentation in der Kaiserzeit*. Edited by Walter Ameling and Johannes Heinrichs. Berlin: de Gruyter, 2010.

Ehrhardt, Norbert. "Eine neue Grabinschrift aus Iconium." *ZPE* 81 (1990): 185–88.

Friesen, Steven J., et al., eds. *Philippi, from Colonia Augusta to Communitas Christiana: Religion and Society in Transition*. Leiden: Brill, forthcoming.

———. "Poverty in Pauline Studies: Beyond the So-Called New Consensus." *JSNT* 26 (2004): 323–61.

Garrison, Roman. "The Love of Money in Polycarp's Letter to the Philippians." Pages 74–79 in *The Graeco-Roman Context of Early Christian Literature*. Sheffield: Sheffield Academic Press, 1997.

Gibson, Elsa. *The "Christians for Christians" Inscriptions of Phrygia*. HTS 32. Missoula, MT: Scholars Press, 1978.

Goddard, Christophe J. "Un principe de différenciation au coeur des processus de romanisation et de christianisation: Quelques réflexions autour du culte de Saturne en Afrique romaine." Pages 115–45 in *Le problème de la christianisation du monde antique*. Edited by Hervé Inglebert, Sylvain Destephen, and Bruno Dumézil. Paris: Picard, 2010.

Gounaropoulou, Loukretia, and Miltiades B. Hatzopoulos, eds. *Επιγραφές κάτω Μακεδονίας, τεύχος Α': Επιγραφές Βέροιας*. Athens: Institute of Historical Research, 1998.

———. *Επιγραφές κάτω Μακεδονίας, τεύχος Β'*. Athens: Institute of Historical Research, 2015.

Harrison, James R. "Introduction." Pages 1–40 in *Methodological Considerations*. Vol. 1 of *The First Urban Churches*. Edited by James R. Harrison and L. L. Welborn. WGRWSup 7. Atlanta: SBL Press, 2015.

Hartog, Paul, ed. *Polycarp and the New Testament: The Occasion, Rhetoric, Theme, and Unity of the Epistle to the Philippians and Its Allusions to New Testament Literature*. WUNT 2/134. Tübingen: Mohr Siebeck, 2002.

———. *Polycarp's Epistle to the Philippians and the Martyrdom of Polycarp: Introduction, Text, and Commentary*. Oxford: Oxford University Press, 2013.

Hattersley-Smith, Kara. "The Early Christian Churches of Macedonia and Their Patrons." *ByzF* 21 (1995): 229–34.

Hellmann, Marie-Christine. *Recherches sur le vocabulaire de l'architecture grecque, d'après les inscriptions de Délos*. Paris: de Boccard, 1992.

Hengel, Martin. *Property and Riches in the Early Church*. London: SCM, 1974.

Heuzey, Léon, and Pierre G. H. Daumet. *Mission Archéologique de Macédoine*. Paris: Librairie de Firmin-Didot, 1876.

Hock, Ronald F. *The Social Context of Paul's Ministry: Tentmaking and Apostleship*. Philadelphia: Fortress, 1980.

Hoddinott, Ralph F. *Early Byzantine Churches in Macedonia and Southern Serbia: A Study of the Origins and the Initial Development of East Christian Art*. London: Macmillan, 1963.

Horsley, G. H. R. "σκήνωμα." *NewDocs* 4:172.

Horsley, G. H. R., and Stephen Mitchell, eds. *The Inscriptions of Central Pisidia*. Bonn: Habelt, 2000.

Huttner, Ulrich. *Early Christianity in the Lycus Valley*. ECAM 1. Leiden: Brill, 2013.

Johnson, Gary J. "A Christian Business and Christian Self-Identity in Third/Fourth Century Phrygia." *VC* 48 (1994): 341–66.

Jones, Arnold H. M. *The Later Roman Empire, 284–602: A Social Economic and Administrative Survey*. Oxford: Blackwell, 1964.

Jones, Arnold H. M., et al., eds. *The Prosopography of the Later Roman Empire*, Vol. 1, *260–395*. Cambridge: Cambridge University Press, 1971.

Joshel, Sandra R. *Work, Identity, and Legal Status at Rome: A Study of the Occupational Inscriptions*. Norman: University of Oklahoma Press, 1992.

Judge, Edwin A. "Cultural Conformity and Innovation in Paul: Some Clues from Contemporary Documents." *TynBul* 35 (1984): 3–24.

———. "The Early Christians as a Scholastic Community." Pages 526–52 in *The First Christians in the Roman World: Augustan and New Testament Essays*. Edited by James R. Harrison. WUNT 229. Tübingen: Mohr Siebeck, 2008.

———. "The Social Identity of the First Christians: A Question of Method on Religious History." Pages 117–35 in *Social Distinctives of the Chris-*

tians in the First Century: Pivotal Essays by E. A. Judge. Edited by David M. Scholer. Peabody, MA: Hendrickson, 2008.

———. *The Social Pattern of Christian Groups in the First Century: Some Prolegomena to the Study of New Testament Ideas of Social Obligation.* London: Tyndale, 1960.

Justinian. *Corpus iuris civilis.* Vol. 3: *Novellae.* Edited by R. Schoell and W. Kroll. Berlin: Weidmann, 1895.

Kaster, Robert A. "The Social Status of the Grammarians." Pages 100–136 in *Guardians of Language: The Grammarian and Society in Late Antiquity.* Berkeley: University of California Press, 1997.

Kennedy, Harry A. A. "The Financial Colouring of Philippians iv. 15–18." *ExpTim* 12 (1900): 43–44.

Knapp, Robert. *Invisible Romans.* London: Profile Books, 2011.

Kobayashi, Masao. "The Social Status of Doctors in the Early Roman Empire." Pages 416–24 in *Forms of Control and Subordination in Antiquity.* Edited by Toru Yuge and Masaoki Doi. Leiden: Brill, 1988.

Koch, Paul. *Die byzantinischen Beamtentitel von 400 bis 700.* Jena: Neuenhahn, 1903.

Koester, Helmut. *History and Literature of Early Christianity.* Vol. 2 of *Introduction to the New Testament.* 2nd ed. Berlin: de Gruyter, 2000.

Koukouli, Chaido. "Ἀρχαιότητες καὶ μνημεῖα Ἀνατολικῆως Μακεδονίας." *ADelt* 23, B.2 (1968): 353–54.

———. "4. Λυδία (Ὑδρόμυλοι)." *ADelt* 24, B.2 (1969): 347–48.

Kourkoutidou-Nikolaidou, Eutychia. "Τυχαία ευρήματα." *ADelt* 27 B.2 (1972): 575.

Kyrtatas, Dimitris J. "Early Christianity in Macedonia." Pages 587–99 in *Brill's Companion to Ancient Macedon: Studies in the Archaeology and History of Macedon, 650 BC–300 AD.* Edited by Robin J. Lane Fox. Leiden: Brill, 2011.

Labarre, Guy, and Marie-Thérèse Le Dinahet. "Les métiers du textile en Asie Mineure de l'époque hellénistique à l'époque impériale." Pages 49–116 in *Aspects de l'artisanat du textile dans le monde méditerranéen (Égypte, Grèce, monde romain).* Collection de l'institut d'archéologie et d'histoire de l'antiquité, Université Lumière-Lyon 2. Paris: de Boccard, 1996.

Lagogianni-Georgakarakos, Maria. *Die Grabdenkmäler mit Porträts aus Makedonien.* Athens: Akademie von Athen, 1998.

Lallemand, Jacqueline. *L'administration civile de l'Égypte de l'avènement de Dioclétien à la création du diocèse (284–382): Contribution à l'étude des rapports entre l'Égypte et l'Empire à la fin du IIIe et au IVe siècle*. Brussels: Palais des Académies, 1964.

Lamer, Hans. "*Lusoria tabula*." PW 1.26:1987–88.

Latte, Kurt. "Μάγειρος." PW 1.27:393–95.

Lemerle, Paul. *Philippes et la Macédoine orientale à l'époque chrétienne et byzantine: Recherches d'histoire et d'archéologie*. Paris: de Boccard, 1945.

Lightfoot, J. B. *St Paul's Epistle to the Philippians*. London: Macmillan, 1913.

Longenecker, Bruce W. "Exposing the Economic Middle: A Revised Economy Scale for the Study of Early Urban Christianity." *JSNT* 31 (2009): 243–78.

MacMullen, Ramsay. "Religious Toleration around the Year 313." *JECS* 22 (2014): 499–517.

Maier, Harry O. "Purity and Danger in Polycarp's Epistle to the Philippians: The Sin of Valens in Social Perspective." *JECS* 1 (1993): 229–47.

Malherbe, Abraham J. *Social Aspects of Early Christianity*. Baton Rouge: Louisiana State University Press, 1977.

Marc, Jean-Yves. "Le *macellum* de Thasos." *Collegium Beatus Rhenanus* 16 (2013): 18–20.

Marki, Efterpi. *Η νεκρόπολη της Θεσσαλονίκης στους υστερορωμαϊκούς και παλαιοχριστιανικούς χρόνους (μέσα του 3ου έως μέσα του 8ου αι. μ.Χ.)*. Athens: TAP, 2006.

Marrou, Henri-Irénée. *Histoire de l'éducation dans l'Antiquité*. Vol. 2, *Le monde romain*. Paris: Seuil, 1948.

Marshall, Peter. *Enmity in Corinth: Social Conventions in Paul's Relationship with the Corinthians*. WUNT 2/33. Tübingen: Mohr Siebeck, 1987.

Martindale, John R., ed. *The Prosopography of the Later Roman Empire*. Vol. 2, *395–527*. Cambridge: Cambridge University Press, 1980.

Mason, Hugh J. *Greek Terms for Roman Institutions: A Lexicon and Analysis*. Toronto: Hakkert, 1974.

Maurice, Lisa. "The Social Status of the Teacher." Pages 143–78 in *The Teacher in Ancient Rome: The Magister and His World*. Plymouth, UK: Lexington Books, 2013.

McKechnie, Paul. "Christian City Councillors in the Roman Empire before Constantine." *IJRR* 5 (2009): 1–20.

Meeks, Wayne A. *The First Urban Christians*. New Haven: Yale University Press, 1983.

Meggitt, Justin J. *Paul, Poverty and Survival*. Edinburgh: T&T Clark, 1998.

Meimaris Yiannis E. and Kalliope I. Kritikakou-Nikolaropoulou, eds. *The Greek Inscriptions from Ghor Es-Safi (Byzantine Zoora)*. Vol. 1 of *Inscriptions from Palaestina Tertia*. Meletemata 41. Athens: Research Centre for Greek and Roman Antiquity, National Hellenic Research Foundation, 2005.

Meinhold, Peter. "Polykarpos." PW 1.42:1686.

Mentzu, Konstantinas P. Συμβολαὶ εἰς τὴν μελέτην τοῦ οἰκονομικοῦ καὶ κοινωνικοῦ βίου τῆς πρωίμου βυζαντινῆς περιόδου. Athens: Diatribe epi Didaktoria, 1975.

———. Review of *Recueil des inscriptions chrétiennes de Macédoine du IIIe au VIe siècle*, by Denis Feissel. *ByzZ* 77 (1984): 324.

Meyer, Heinrich A. W. *Critical and Exegetical Handbook to the Epistles to the Philippians and Colossians*. CECNT. Edinburgh: T&T Clark, 1875.

Mitchell, Stephen. *Anatolia: Land, Men, and Gods in Asia Minor*. 2 vols. Oxford: Oxford University Press, 1993.

Mouritsen, Henrik. "Status and Social Hierarchies: The Case of Pompeii." Pages 87–113 in *Social Status and Prestige in the Graeco-Roman World*. Edited by Annika B. Kuhn. Stuttgart: Steiner, 2015.

Nigdelis, Pantelis M. Ἐπιγραφικά Θεσσαλονίκεια: Συμβολή στην πολιτική και κοινωνική ιστορία της Αρχαίας Θεσσαλονίκης. Thessalonica: IMXA, 2006.

Nijf, Onno M. van. *The Civic World of Professional Associations in the Roman East*. Amsterdam: Gieben, 1997.

———. "The Social World of Tax Farmers and Their Personnel." Pages 279–311 in *The Customs Law of Asia*. Edited by Michel Cottier et al. Oxford: Oxford University Press, 2008.

Norman, Albert F. "Gradations in Later Municipal Society." *JRS* 48 (1958): 80–83.

Oakes, Peter. "Leadership and Economic Suffering in the Letters of Polycarp and Paul to the Philippians." Pages 335–73 in *Trajectories through the New Testament and the Apostolic Fathers*. Vol. 2 of *The New Testament and the Apostolic Fathers*. Edited by Andrew F. Gregory and Christopher M. Tuckett. Oxford: Oxford University Press, 2005.

———. *Philippians: From People to Letter*. SNTSMS 110. Cambridge: Cambridge University Press, 2001.

Oertel, Friedrich. *Die Liturgie: Studien zur ptolemäischen und kaiserlichen Verwaltung Ägyptens*. Leipzig: Teubner, 1917.

Ogereau, Julien M. "Authority and Identity in the Early Christian Inscriptions from Macedonia." Pages 217–39 in *Authority and Identity in*

Emerging Christianities in Asia Minor and Greece. Edited by Cilliers Breytenbach and Julien M. Ogereau. AJEC 103. Leiden: Brill, 2018.

———. "The Earliest Piece of Evidence of Christian Accounting: The Significance of the Phrase εἰς λόγον δόσεως καὶ λήμψεως (Phil 4:15)." *Comptabilité(S)* 6 (2014): 1–16.

———. "Methodological Considerations in Using Epigraphic Evidence in Determining the Socioeconomic Context of the Early Christians." Pages 250–56 in *Methodological Considerations*. Vol. 1 of *The First Urban Churches*. Edited by James R. Harrison and L. L. Welborn. Atlanta: SBL Press, 2015.

———. *Paul's Koinonia with the Philippians: A Socio-historical Investigation of a Pauline Economic Partnership*. WUNT 2/377. Tübingen: Mohr Siebeck, 2014.

———. "Paul's Κοινωνία with the Philippians: Societas as a Missionary Funding Strategy." *NTS* 60 (2014): 360–78.

Orlandos, Anastasios K., and Ioannes N. Travlos. *Lexicon archaion architektonikon horon*. Athens: Archaiologike Hetaireia, 1986.

Pallas, Demetrios I. *Les monuments paléochrétiens de Grèce découverts de 1959 à 1973*. Rome: Pontificio Istituto di Archeologia Christiana, 1977.

Pelekanidis, Stylianos. *Gli affreschi paleocristiani ed i piu antichi mosaici parietali di Salonicco*. Ravenna: Dante, 1963.

———. "Ἡ ἔξω τῶν τειχῶν παλαιοχριστιανικὴ βασιλικὴ τῶν Φιλίππων." *ArchEph* 1955 (1961): 114–79.

———. "Die Malerei der Konstantinischen Zeit." Pages 75–96 in *Studien zur frühchristlichen und byzantinischen Archäologie*. Thessalonica: Institute for Balkan Studies, 1977.

———. "Παλαιοχριστιανικός τάφος εν Φιλίπποις." Pages 67–76 in *Studien zur frühchristlichen und byzantinischen Archäologie*. Thessalonica: Institute for Balkan Studies, 1977.

Pennas, Charalambos. "Early Christian Burials at Philippi." *ByzF* 21 (1995): 215–27.

Perdrizet, Paul. "Inscriptions de Philippes: Les Rosalies." *BCH* (1900): 299–323.

———. "Voyage dans la Macédoine première." *BCH* 21 (1897): 416–45.

Peterlin, Davorin. *Paul's Letter to the Philippians in the Light of Disunity in the Church*. NovTSup 79. Leiden: Brill, 1995.

Peterman, Gerald W. *Paul's Gift from Philippi: Conventions of Gift-Exchange and Christian Giving*. SNTSMS 92. Cambridge: Cambridge University Press, 1997.

Pilhofer, Peter. *Philippi*. Vol. 1, *Die erste christliche Gemeinde Europas*. WUNT 87. Tübingen: Mohr Siebeck, 1995.

———. *Philippi*. Vol. 2, *Katalog der Inschriften von Philippi*. 2nd ed. WUNT 119. Tübingen: Mohr Siebeck, 2009.

Provost, Samuel, and Michael Boyd. "Application de la prospection géophysique à la topographie urbaine: I. Philippes, les quartiers Sud-Ouest." *BCH* 125 (2001): 453–521.

———. "Application de la prospection géophysique à la topographie urbaine: II. Philippes, les quartiers Ouest." *BCH* 126 (2002): 431–88.

Rankin, Edwin M. *The Role of the ΜΑΓΕΙΡΟΙ in the Life of the Ancient Greeks, as Depicted in Greek Literature and Inscriptions*. Chicago: University of Chicago Press, 1907.

Rapp, Claudia. "The Elite Status of Bishops in Late Antiquity in Ecclesiastical, Spiritual, and Social Contexts." *Arethusa* 33 (2000): 379–99.

Rizakis, Athanasios D. "Le territoire de la colonie romaine de Philippes: Ses limites au Nord-Ouest." Pages 123–30 in *Autour des libri coloniarum: Colonisation et colonies dans le monde romain; Actes du Colloque International (Besançon, 16–18 octobre 2003)*. Edited by Antonio Gonzales and Jean-Yves Guillaumin. Besançon: Presses Universitaires de Franche-Comté, 2006.

———. "Une *praefectura* dans le territoire colonial de Philippes: Les nouvelles données." Pages 87–105 in *Colons et colonies dans le monde romain*. Edited by Ségolène Demougin and John Scheid. Rome: École française de Rome, 2012.

Rizos, Efthymios. "The Making of a Christian Society in the Late Antique Civil Diocese of Macedonia—Archaeological Evidence on Christianisation from Modern Greece." Pages 319–42 in *Christianisierung Europas: Entstehung, Entwicklung und Konsolidierung im archäologischen Befund*. Edited by Orsolya Heinrich-Tamaszka, Niklot Krohn, and Sebastian Ristow. Regensburg: Schnell & Steiner, 2012.

Robert, Louis. "Études sur les inscriptions et la topographie de la Grèce Centrale: VI. Décrets d'Akraiphia." *BCH* 59 (1935): 438–52.

———. *Hellenica: Recueil d'épigraphie, de numismatique et d'antiquités grecques*. Vol. 10. Paris: Adrien-Maisonneuve, 1955.

———. *Hellenica: Recueil d'épigraphie, de numismatique et d'antiquités grecques*. Vol. 13. Paris: Adrien-Maisonneuve, 1965.

———. "L'épigraphie." Pages 462–63 in *L'histoire et ses méthodes*. Edited by Charles Samaran. Paris: Gallimard, 1961.

Ruyt, Claire De. "Les produits vendus au macellum." *F&H* 5 (2007): 135–50.

———. *Macellum: Marché alimentaire des Romains*. Louvain-la-Neuve: Institut supérieur d'archéologie et d'histoire de l'art, Collège Érasme, 1983.

Samama, Évelyne. *Les médecins dans le monde grec: Sources épigraphiques sur la naissance d'un corps medical*. Geneva: Librairie Droz, 2003.

Schoedel, William R. "Polycarp of Smyrna and Ignatius of Antioch." *ANRW* 27.1:273–85.

Seeck, Otto. "*Clarissimi viri.*" PW 1.6:2628.

Sève, Michel, and Patrick Weber. *Guide du forum de Philippes*. Sites et Monuments 18. Athens: École Française d'Athènes, 2012.

Smith, Rowland. *Julian's Gods: Religion and Philosophy in the Thought and Action of Julian the Apostate*. London: Routledge, 1995.

Sodini, Pierre. "L'artisanat urbain à l'époque paléochrétienne (IVe–VIIe s.)." *Ktema* 4 (1979): 71–119.

Spiliopoulou-Donderer, Ioanna. *Kaiserzeitliche Grabaltäre Niedermakedoniens: Untersuchungen zur Sepulkralskulptur einer Kunstlandschaft im Spannungsfeld zwischen Ost und West*. Mannheim: Bibliopolis, 2002.

Stefanidou-Tiveriou, Thea. *Die lokalen Sarkophage aus Thessaloniki*. Ruhpolding, Germany: Rutzen, 2014.

———. "Social Status and Family Origin in the Sarcophagi of Thessalonikē." Pages 178–84 in *From Roman to Early Christian Thessalonikē: Studies in Religion and Archaeology*. Edited by Laura S. Nasrallah, Charalambos Bakirtzis, and Stephen J. Friesen. HTS 64. Cambridge: Harvard University Press, 2010.

Stegemann, Ekkehard W., and Wolfgang Stegemann. *The Jesus Movement: A Social History of Its First Century*. Edinburgh: T&T Clark, 1999.

Theissen, Gerd. *The Social Setting of Pauline Christianity*. Edinburgh: T&T Clark, 1982.

Tirologos, George. "Les recherches sur les cadastres romains du territoire colonial de Philippes (Macédoine orientale—Grèce): Bilan et perspectives." Pages 131–49 in *Autour des libri coloniarum: Colonisation et colonies dans le monde romain; Actes du Colloque International (Besançon, 16–18 octobre 2003)*. Edited by Antonio Gonzales and Jean-Yves Guillaumin. Besançon: Presses Universitaires de Franche-Comté, 2006.

Tran, Nicolas. *Dominus tabernae: Le statut de travail des artisans et des commerçants de l'Occident romain (Ier siècle av. J.-C.–IIIe siècle ap. J.-C.).* Rome: École Française de Rome, 2013.

———. "La mention épigraphique des métiers artisanaux et commerciaux en Italie centro-méridionale." Pages 119–41 in *Vocabulaire et expression de l'économie dans le monde antique.* Edited by Jean Andreau and Véronique Chankowski. Paris: de Boccard, 2007.

———. "Le statut de travail des bouchers dans l'Occident romain de la fin de la République et du Haut-Empire." *F&H* 5 (2007): 151–67.

Van Andringa, William. "Du sanctuaire au macellum: Sacrifices, commerce et consommation de la viande à Pompéi.'" *F&H* 5 (2007): 47–72.

Van Dam, Raymond. "Bishops and Society." Pages 343–66 in *Constantine to c. 600.* Edited by Augustine Casiday and Frederick W. Norris. CHC 2. Cambridge: Cambridge University Press, 2007.

Verboven, Koenraad. "Ce que *negotiari* et ses dérivés veulent dire." Pages 89–118 in *Vocabulaire et expression de l'économie dans le monde antique.* Edited by Jean Andreau and Véronique Chankowski. Paris: de Boccard, 2007.

Veyne, Paul. "La 'plèbe moyenne' sous le Haut-Empire romain." *Annales* 55 (2000): 1169–99.

Vielhauer, Philipp. *Geschichte der urchristlichen Literatur: Einleitung in das Neue Testament, die Apokryphen und die Apostolischen Väter.* Berlin: de Gruyter, 1975.

Vincent, Marvin R. *A Critical and Exegetical Commentary on the Epistles to the Philippians and to Philemon.* ICC. Edinburgh: T&T Clark, 1897.

Weiß, Alexander. *Soziale Elite und Christentum: Studien zu ordo-Angehörigen unter den frühen Christen.* Berlin: de Gruyter, 2015.

Welborn, L. L. *An End to Enmity: Paul and the "Wrongdoer" of Second Corinthians.* Berlin: de Gruyter, 2011.

Wipszycka, Ewa. *Les ressources et les activités économiques des églises en Égypte du IVe au VIIIe siècle.* Brussels: Fondation Égyptologique Reine Élisabeth, 1972.

Vindolanda Tablet 2.154, *RPC* 1651, and the Provenance of Philippians

Paul A. Holloway

I would like to consider two pieces of material evidence relevant to the interpretation of Philippians. The first is Vindolanda Tablet 2.154, a troop-strength report from the Roman garrison at Vindolanda in the north of England dating from between 92 to 97 CE. It was kindly brought to my attention by Sandra Bingham of the University of Edinburgh in a personal email this past April. The second is *RPC* 1651, a small copper coin that was issued at Philippi for much of the first and second centuries CE. The first piece of evidence will clarify a point of language in Paul's letter. The second will say something about Philippi itself. Both pieces of evidence promise to cast light on the provenance of the letter.

1. On the Occasion of Philippians

It was not uncommon for ancient letters to indicate the date when they were written—or more correctly the date when they were sent—and in a few instances also the place. Peter White estimates about 15 percent of Cicero's letters contain a dateline, while Cicero himself remarks that Atticus included a dateline in nearly all of his letters (Cicero, *Att.* 3.23.1).[1]

This paper was read at the Annual Meeting of the Society of Biblical Literature in San Diego in November 2014. This essay borrows from, adapts, and expands on material discussed in greater detail in my commentary on Philippians for the Hermeneia series: Paul A. Holloway, *Philippians*, Hermeneia (Minneapolis: Fortress, 2017). Gratitude is due to the editors of Fortress Press for permission to adapt and reuse this material.

1. See Peter White, *Cicero in Letters* (Oxford: Oxford University Press, 2010), 75–76.

According to Suetonius, Augustus included not only the date but the hour in which a letter was sent (*Aug.* 50). The typical form a dateline took can be illustrated from Cicero, *Fam.* 12.16, which concludes *D[ata] VIII Kal[endas] Iun[ias] Athensis*, "Mailed May 25th from Athens."

The modern interpreter of Paul's letters is, of course, not so lucky. Paul never included a dateline in any of his letters, and we are only sometimes able to assign a place of writing (though never a firm date) on the basis of internal evidence. Here then is the relevant evidence from Philippians, most of which will be familiar enough. Paul is in prison awaiting trial on capital charges. The city in which he is being held has an established community of Christ believers. Most of these are supportive, but a number are opposed to Paul. The latter, Paul claims, have stepped up their efforts at proclamation, he says, out of jealousy and spite, "imagining that they raise up affliction to my bonds" (Phil 1:15–17).[2]

Paul has apparently been in prison for some time—a point often overlooked by commentators—since he complains that the Philippians have been slow in sending to his aid, a delay of sufficient length to have caused offense were it not for the fact that they "lacked opportunity" (Phil 4:10), presumably meaning that they could not find a trustworthy carrier.[3] Part of the reason for the delay may also have lain in the length and difficulty of the journey from Philippi, since Epaphroditus, the person finally charged with carrying the Philippians' gift, fell ill along the way but pressed on becoming critically ill in the process.[4] Epaphroditus has since recovered,

---

2. Unless otherwise indicated, all biblical translations are mine.

3. The difficulty in finding a reliable carrier for a letter, not to mention for money and other goods, is well known; see, for instance, the evidence collected in John L. White, *Light from Ancient Letters* (Philadelphia: Fortress, 1986), 215. Prisoners in Roman custody typically paid for their own upkeep. Jens-Uwe Krause, *Gefängnisse im römischen Reich* (Stuttgart: Steiner, 1996); S. Arband, W. Macheiner, and C. Colpe, "Gefangenschaft," *RAC* 9:318–45; see Brian Rapske, *The Book of Acts and Paul in Roman Custody* (Grand Rapids: Eerdmans; Carlisle, UK: Paternoster, 1994) 209–16; Richard J. Cassidy, *Paul in Chains: Roman Imprisonment and the Letters of St. Paul* (New York: Crossroads, 2001), 124–42.

4. Most commentators simply assume that Epaphroditus fell ill after arriving in the city of Paul's imprisonment. But according to 2:27, 30, Epaphroditus's initial illness as well as its critical worsening were due to his efforts to reach Paul with the Philippians' gift, implying that Epaphroditus fell ill on the way and then continued on at some risk to his health. It is also noteworthy that while the Philippians had received word of Epaphroditus's condition (2:26), they did not know just how bad it

and Paul is sending him back with the present letter (Phil 2:25, 27). Paul plans to send Timothy when he knows something more definite about his case (Phil 2:19, 23), and he claims to be "confident in the Lord" that he will himself be free to visit Philippi in the near future—which in this case probably means "I doubt you'll ever see me again" (Phil 2:24).[5]

2. Three Traditional Views regarding the Letter's Provenance

The traditional view is that Paul wrote Philippians in Rome, but Caesarea Maritima has also been reasonably proposed. According to Acts, Paul was imprisoned awaiting trial in both of these cities, and while much of Acts is novelistic, there is good reason to accept these claims, since Paul in Roman custody does little to support the author of Acts's larger thesis that Paul received a positive reception from gentiles.[6] There would also have been opposition to Paul from other Christ believers in either of these locations, though perhaps the alleged motives of jealousy and spite noted above fit better with Rome, where Paul was by his own admission an interloper (Rom 15:20). That said, deciding between Rome and Caesarea probably makes little actual difference for the interpretation of Philippians, since in either case Philippians will be one of Paul's last letters, and since for all practical purposes Caesarea and Rome were merely two phases in the same lengthy incarceration beginning in Judea and ending in Rome.

There is also a case to be made that Paul was imprisoned for a time in Ephesus.[7] This has been a particularly attractive alternative to scholars who

---

had become (2:27a), suggesting that someone traveling in the opposite direction had passed Epaphroditus on the road when he was in the initial stages of his illness and had brought news of this back to Philippi. This fact is important in determining the distance between Paul and Philippi. It is also important in calculating the number of implied trips between Paul and Philippi, as we shall see below.

5. Paul's plan to send Timothy may be taken at face value. However, his professed confidence in the Lord that he himself will be able to visit soon should be read as an echo of his earlier effort at 1:25–26 to allay the Philippians' fears that he may be executed—effectively withdrawn at 1:27 and then explicitly contradicted at 2:17–18.

6. Richard Pervo, *Acts*, Hermeneia (Minneapolis: Fortress, 2009), 552–53.

7. The principal arguments for an Ephesian provenance were set forth at the beginning of last century by Paul Feine, *Die Abfassung des Philipperbriefes in Ephesus mit einer Anlage über Röm 16,3–20 als Epheserbrief*, BFCT 20.4 (Gütersloh: Bertelsmann, 1916); Adolf Deissmann, "Zur ephesinischen Gefangenschaft des Apostel Paulus," in *Anatolian Studies Presented to Sir William Mitchell Ramsey*, ed. W. H. Buck-

partition Philippians, since the more exchanges between Paul and the Philippians one assumes—John Reumann manages to discover ten!⁸—the more difficult it is to imagine Paul as far away as Rome or Caesarea. But even if one allows for a lengthy Ephesian imprisonment, which must remain uncertain, it is unlikely that Philippians was written there, since the letter contains no reference to the Jerusalem collection, which was foremost on Paul's mind during his stay in Ephesus, and to which the Macedonian churches were to make a significant contribution (1 Cor 16:1–4; 2 Cor 8–9; Gal 2:10; see also Rom 15:25–28). The difficulty in finding a letter carrier and the resulting delay in sending to Paul's support, as well as the difficulties of Epaphroditus's journey also argue against an Ephesian provenance. Other locations are theoretically possible, since Paul claims to have been jailed on multiple occasions (2 Cor 11:23), although it is doubtful that any of these was a lengthy imprisonment in anticipation of a capital trial as Philippians requires.⁹

3. On the Meaning of πραιτώριον in Phil 1:13

A key piece of evidence in determining the provenance of Philippians is Paul's boast in 1:13 that his witness has spread ἐν ὅλῳ τῷ πραιτωρίῳ, "in the whole πραιτώριον." The Greek πραιτώριον transliterates the Latin *praetorium*, which was originally used to refer to a Roman general's tent or camp headquarters and then by extension to members of his staff such as his military council or personal bodyguard. By the late Republic the term was used to refer to a military governor's residential compound as well as its guardsmen. Eventually, of course, it denoted the imperial guard in Rome established by Augustus.¹⁰

---

ler and W. M. Calder (Manchester: Manchester University Press, 1923), 121–27; and G. S. Duncan, *St. Paul's Ephesian Ministry: A Reconstruction with Special Reference to the Ephesian Origin of the Imprisonment Epistles* (London: Hodder & Stoughton; New York: Scribners, 1930). While by no means impossible, the evidence for an Ephesian imprisonment remains circumstantial (1 Cor 15:32; 2 Cor 1:8–10; for the former, see Abraham Malherbe, "The Beasts at Ephesus," *JBL* 87 [1968]: 71–80).

8. John Reumann, *Philippians: A New Translation with Introduction and Commentary*, AYB 33B (New Haven: Yale University Press, 2008), 7. On the relationship of the Ephesian hypothesis to certain partition theories, see, e.g., Jean-François Collange, *L'épître de saint Paul aux Philippiens*, CNT 10A (Neuchâtel: Delachaux & Niestlé, 1973).

9. See Paul's short imprisonment in Acts 16 and Peter's in Acts 12.

10. Sandra Bingham, *The Praetorian Guard: A History of Rome's Elite Special Forces* (London: Tauris, 2013).

It has been suggested that πραιτώριον in Phil 1:13 refers to an official building, such as the residence of a provincial governor, as it does, for instance, in Acts 23:35 (see also Matt 27:20; Mark 15:16; John 18:28, 33; 19:9). If this is the case, then Philippians was almost certainly written from Caesarea, since it is unthinkable that imperial buildings in Rome during the early principate would have borne military names implying that Rome was an occupied city.[11] It is unlikely, however, that πραιτώριον here refers to a building, since the whole expression reads ἐν ὅλῳ τῷ πραιτωρίῳ καὶ τοῖς λοιποῖς πᾶσιν, "in the whole πραιτώριον and all the rest," where "all the rest," given Paul's usage elsewhere, is most naturally interpreted as a reference not to other buildings but to other personnel.[12] This would imply that πραιτώριον is also a reference to personnel.[13] This interpretation also makes excellent sense of 1:14, where Paul continues: "and the majority of the brothers in the Lord ... are daring more and more to speak the word without fear." Taken together, verses 13–14 would then describe the effect of Paul's imprisonment first on those outside the church and then on those inside.

That τοῖς λοιποῖς πᾶσιν likely refers to other personnel has been taken by some to favor a Roman provenance but not all are convinced. For, as already indicated, during the late Republic a provincial governor's personal guard was also known as his *praetorium*. If this nomenclature continued in

---

11. J. B. Lightfoot, *St. Paul's Epistle to the Philippians: A Revised Text with Introduction, Notes, and Dissertations* (London: Macmillan, 1868), 99–104.

12. 1 Thess 4:13 ("that you not grieve as the rest [οἱ λοιποί]") and 5:6 ("let us not sleep as the rest [οἱ λοιποί]"); 1 Cor 7:8–12 ("to the unmarried and widows ... to those married ... to the rest [τοῖς λοιποῖς]"); 2 Cor 13:2 ("I warned those who sinned previously and all the rest [τοῖς λοιποῖς πᾶσιν]"); Rom 11:7 ("the elect obtained, but the rest [οἱ λοιποί] were hardened"); see also Wilhelm Michaelis, *Der Briefe des Paulus an die Philipper*, THKNT 11 (Leipzig: Deichert, 1935), 51. Chrysostom, however, understands both expressions locally. He first equates τὸ πραιτώριον with τὰ βασιλεία, anachronistically assuming that someone of Paul's stature was detained in the "imperial palace," not in the *castra praetoria*, after which he is forced to interpret καὶ τοῖς λοιποῖς πᾶσιν locally: οὐδὲ ἐν τῷ πραιτωρίῳ μόνον, ἀλλὰ καὶ ἐν τῇ πόλει ... πάσῃ, "and not in the *praetorium* [= palace] only, but also in all the *city*" (*Hom. Phil.* 2 [PG 62:192b.14–16]); see also Theodoret, *Interp. Epist. ad Phil.* 1:12–13 (PG 82:564A).

13. Similar expressions in which ὅλος ("whole"), which is often used of buildings, refers to people include: "the whole Sanhedrin" (Matt 26:59; Mark 15:1); "the whole people" (Acts 2:47); "the whole church" (Acts 15:22; Rom 16:23; 1 Cor 14:23); "the whole civilized world" (Rev 3:10; 12:9). "the whole household" (Heb 3:2–5; Titus 1:11); "the whole city" (Mark 1:33; Acts 21:30); "the whole world" (1 John 2:2; 5:19).

the empire after the establishment of the imperial guard at Rome, then it is possible that ἐν ὅλῳ τῷ πραιτωρίῳ at Phil 1:13 refers not to the imperial cohorts but to a smaller detachment of provincial guardsmen assigned to a governor's residential compound. Here the commentary tradition reaches something of an impasse, for all the evidence that Roman governors were protected by a contingent of "praetorians" comes from the late Republic before the establishment of the Praetorian Guard in Rome (e.g., Cicero, *Verr.* 4.65; 5.92). One is therefore left to speculate whether this terminology continued after the establishment of the imperial guard. Neither option is without potential embarrassment.

4. Vindolanda Tablet 2.154

This brings me Vindolanda Tablet 2.154, which as I have already indicated is a troop-strength report from the Roman outpost at Vindolanda in northern England. Vindolanda is about 30 mi. west of Newcastle and 1 mi. south of Hadrian's Wall.[14] It seems that writing materials were in short supply on the British frontier at this time and that records were written in ink on small oak tablets a little bit larger than a postcard. Writing tablets of this sort were unknown prior to the excavations at Vindolanda, where several hundred were recovered. It is my understanding that a few have now been found elsewhere. The tablets at Vindolanda were buried under a layer of clay that preserved them. Restoring them was quite a technical feat, since in situ they had the consistency of wet tissue paper.

Vindolanda Tablet 2.154[15] begins with a date (month and day, not year) and the name of the cohort's *praefectus*, Julius Verecundus, whose service, however, can be dated to between 92 and 97 CE. Next the cohort's total strength is reported, which at the time was 752. At this point the list is divided into two parts: those absent from the fort on assignment elsewhere and those still attached to the main garrison, about twenty of whom were either ill or wounded. We are interested in those absent. Most of these, 337, to be precise, had been sent to reinforce the nearby fort at Coria. But at line five we learn that forty-six had been sent to London to serve in the governor's bodyguard. The text reads: *ex eis absentes singulares legati xlvi*.

---

14. Alan K. Bowman, *Life and Letters on the Roman Frontier: Vindolanda and Its People*, 2nd ed. (London: British Museum Press, 2004).

15. https://tinyurl.com/SBL4216e.

This is interesting for a couple of reasons. For instance, it indicates that in at least some cases provincial governors recruited their bodyguards from auxiliary units in their province. But what is especially interesting for our purposes is that those guardsmen are not here called *praetoriani*, as one would expect if that title were still being applied to provincial guardsmen at this time, but *singulares*. In other words, while provincial governors continued to have a contingent of guardsmen under their direct control, these guards were no longer called *praetoriani* but *singulares*.

To be sure, this tablet dates from the end of the first century, but the most likely cause for this change in terminology—from *praetorianus* to *singularis*—would be the establishment of the imperial Praetorian Guard in Rome by Augustus. As is well known, this guard quickly increased in importance over the course of the first century, so that by the time of Nero it not only had its own permanent camp, built by Tiberius in 23 (Tacitus, *Ann.* 4.2; Suetonius, *Tib.* 37.1) but had been increased to twelve cohorts with a nominal strength of six thousand.[16] To my knowledge, this change in terminology has not yet been adduced in interpreting Paul's expression in Phil 1:13. I at least was unaware of it before Sandra Bingham brought it to my attention.

But there is more. Shortly after Bingham brought the Vindolanda evidence to my attention, I came across Michael Speidel's *Guards of the Roman Imperial Armies*, which examines in detail some eighty-three pieces of mostly epigraphic evidence regarding provincial *singulares*. Despite its title, the evidence Speidel reviews is for both imperial and senatorial provinces.[17] This evidence ranges over the first four centuries CE, and much of it is a bit late for our purposes. However, several pieces of evidence fall within our period, and they would all appear to support the conclusion I have drawn from Vindolanda Tablet 2.154.[18]

---

16. *AE* 1978.286. Vitellius strengthened the Praetorian Guard to sixteen cohorts of one thousand (Tacitus, *Hist.* 2.93.2); see also *BNP* 11:773–76.

17. Michael Speidel, *Guards of the Roman Imperial Armies: An Essay on the Singulares of the Provinces*, Antiquitas 1 (Bonn: Habelt, 1978), 15.

18. For evidence that the term *praetorium* may have continued on occasion to be used for a governor's guards, see Speidel, *Guards*, 20 and n. 97, who cites as the principal evidence for this *IG* 12.5.697: στρατιώτηρ ἐκ τῶν τοῦ πραιτωρίου τοῦ ἀνθυπάτου, "a soldier of those of the πραιτώριον of the governor (of Achaia)"; however, R. Egger interprets this as a reference to the governor's residence. See "Das Praetorium als Amtssitz und Quartier römischer Spitzenfunktionäre," *SAWW* 250 (1966): 26. Speidel also cites *AE* 1933.57, which speaks of a governor's *princeps praetorio*, but this may simply mean

I cannot discuss this evidence in detail, but here is a representative list. First is *CIL* 13.7709, which speaks of the *singulares* of Achilius Strabo, governor of Germania inferior, datable to the 70s CE.[19] Second is B. and H. Galsterer, *Die römischen Steininschriften aus Köln*, number 260, the funerary inscription of Titus Flavius Tullio, who identifies himself as a *singularis* also serving in Germania inferior, presumably from the Flavian period (between 70 and 89 CE).[20] Third is Jules Baillet, *Inscriptions grècques et latines des tombeaux des rois où syringes à Thèbes*, graffito 1688, by a certain Ammonios, a *singularis* of C. Minicius Italus, prefect of Egypt in 103–104 CE.[21] Fourth is *Greek Papyri in the British Museum* 2851, a troop-strength report that lists the *singulares* of Fabius Justius, governor of Moesia inferior in 105 CE. Judging from Baillet, graffito 1688, which is in Greek, the term *singularis* was simply transliterated in Greek as σινγουλαρίος,[22] though Josephus (*B.J.* 3.120), speaking of general Vespanian's military guard, translates ἐπίλεκτοι. Speidel writes, "Army commanders in the Empire were denied a praetorian cohort.... Praetorian guards became an imperial prerogative." Instead of a *"cohors* or *ala praetoriana"* they now possessed "less formally a *numerus* of *pedites* and *equites singulares*."[23]

Again, none of this evidence is referenced in the commentaries on Philippians that I have consulted, but it seems to me that it argues strongly that by the time Paul wrote Philippians *praetoriani* referred exclusively to the

---

the officer in charge of "headquarters." See Boris Rankov, "The Governor's Men: The *Officium Consularis* in Provincial Adminstration," in *The Roman Army as a Community*, ed. Adrian Goldsworthy and Ian Haynes, JRASup 34 (Portsmouth, RI: Journal of Roman Archaeology, 1999), 19. A *praetorianus* is mentioned in *CIL* 3.6085, 7135, and 7136 serving as a *stationarius* (police officer) near Ephesus, but this can simply mean that he was a *former* imperial guardsman. See also F. F. Bruce, *Philippians* (San Francisco: Harper & Row, 1989), xxii. For a *singularis* similarly employed, see *AE* 1937.250.

19. See also *AE* 1923.33.

20. B. Galsterer and H. Galsterer, *Die römischen Steininschriften aus Köln* (Cologne: Wissenschaftliche Katalogue des Römisch-Germanischen Museums, 1975), 260.

21. Jules Baillet, *Inscriptions grècques et latines des tombeaux des rois où syringes à Thèbes*, MIFAO 42 (Cairo: L'Institut Français d'Archéologie Orientale du Caire, 1926), graffito 1688.

22. See *IG* 10.2.384, 495, 583; *IGRR* 3.394; *AE* 1937.250; 1940.216 (= IGLSyr 7.4037); 1969–1970.602; 1973.538; Balliet, graffito 1473 (= *SB* 6638.1); P.Oxy. 20.2284; and P.Ross.Georg. 3.1 (collected by Speidel, *Guards*); see also Michael Speidel, "Two Greek Graffiti in the Tomb of Ramses V," *CdE* 49 (1974): 384–86.

23. Speidel, *Guards*, 5–6.

imperial guard at Rome and—assuming Phil 1:13 refers to personnel—that Philippians can therefore be reliably assigned to a Roman imprisonment.

5. *RPC* 1651

Let me turn now to my second piece of material evidence, *RPC* 1651, which does not speak directly to the provenance of Paul's letter but to Philippi itself and especially to a possible point of civic pride that might have caused Paul to mention his guards in the first place, something he does not do in Philemon, for instance—or for that matter in Colossians, if Colossians is indeed one of Paul's authentic letters, which I doubt. *RPC* 1651 is a small copper coin (*semis*[24]) reading *VIC*[*toria*] *AUG*[*usta*] on the front and *COHOR*[*s*] *PRAE*[*toria*] *PHIL*[*ippensis*] on the back. An unusually large number of these (approximately 150) have so far been recovered.[25]

Coins of this sort, commonly called "semi-autonomous," are notoriously difficult to date because they do not name the current emperor. Philippe Collart dated this coin to the reign of Augustus and interpreted it as commemorating Augustus's victory over Antony in 31 BCE and his settlement at Philippi of a cohort of praetorians when he refounded the colony in 30 BCE, an interpretation consistent with the literary evidence but not required by it.[26] This interpretation went largely unchallenged

---

24. Roman coins tended to decrease in nominal value by halves. The nominal unit was the *as*, half of which was the *semis* (half), and a quarter of which was the *quadrans* (quarter), not unlike the American dollar, half-dollar, and quarter-dollar. During the early principate, two *asses* equaled a *dupondius*, two *dupondii* a *sesterius*, and four *sesterii* a *denarius*. The gold *aureus* was worth twenty-five *denarii*.

25. *RPC* 1 lists eighty-five specimens held in various Western museums; Katerina Chryssanthaki-Nagle, *L'histoire monétaire d'Abdère en Trace (VIes. av. J.-C.-IIe s. ap. J.-C.)*, Meletemata 51 (Athens: de Boccard, 2007), 795–98, lists another forty-five found in Abdera; Sophia Kremydi-Sicilianou, *Multiple Concealments from the Sanctuary of Zeus Olympios at Dion: The Roman Provincial Coin Hoards*, Meletemata 35 (Athens: de Boccard, 2004), 85–89, lists two from Amphipolis 1998; one from Ierissos 1976; seven from Dion 1999 (cat. nos. 1508–14); one from Dion 1998 (cat. no. 77). Coins of this type have also been found in the Agora of Athens: J. H. Kroll, *The Athenian Agora*, vol. 26 in *Greek Coins* (Princeton: Princeton University Press, 1993) 184, no. 476.

26. Philippe Collart, *Philippes: Ville de Macédoine, depuis ses origines jusqu'à la fin de l'époque romaine* (Paris: de Boccard, 1937), 1:231–35; 2: pl. 30.8–11, whose arguments were accepted in subsequent *Sylloge*: SNG Evelp., 1275–77; SNG ANS, 674–81; SNG Cop., 305–6; SNG Tüb., 1031. The literary evidence mentions Octavian and

RPC 1651 struck in the first century or early second century CE. Courtesy of Forum Ancient Coins

until the publication of the first volume of *Roman Provincial Coins*, which based on the coin's copper composition dated it no earlier than the reign of Claudius, though still allowing a reference to an early settlement of praetorians by Augustus.[27]

This redating has not been taken into account in subsequent interpretations of Philippians, which still rely exclusively on Collart, if they mention the coin at all.[28] It seems to me, however, that if this redating is accepted it casts considerable light on the interpretation of Philippians, since it not only dates the striking of the coin closer to the time of Paul's letter but, more importantly, attests to Philippi's continuing pride in its praetorian foundations, a fact that Paul, now a prisoner of the guard, would presumably to be alluding to at Phil 1:13. Further evidence of the continuing importance of the Praetorian Guard for the civic self-understanding of the Philippians are several military *diplomata* (official retirements papers) witnessed by one or more imperial guardsmen from Philippi, as well as a number of inscriptions connected in one way or another to Philippi in which guardsmen are named.[29] Particularly intrigu-

---

Anthony adding eight thousand praetorians after Philippi (Appian 5.1.3). It does not mention where they were settled when their service was completed, but that a cohort was settled at Philippi is a reasonable guess (Res gest. 28.1).

27. *RPC* 1:288, 308. M. Durry, "Sur une monnaie de Philippes," *REA* 42 (1940): 412–16, had already dated the coin to the reign of Claudius, while H. Gaebler, *AMNG* 3.2:102–3 nos. 14–15, simply dated it to "Imperial times."

28. E.g., Reumann, *Philippians*. Other New Testament scholars still following Collart include: Lukas Bormann, *Philippi: Stadt und Christengemeinde zur Zeit des Paulus*, NovTSup 78 (Leiden: Brill, 1995), 22 n. 67; Peter Oakes, *Philippians: From People to Letter*, SNTSMS 110 (Cambridge: Cambridge University Press, 2001), 13, 25; Laura S. Nasrallah, "Spatial Perspectives: Space and Archaeology in Roman Philippi," in *Studying Paul's Letters: Contemporary Perspectives and Methods*, ed. Joseph Marchal (Minneapolis: Fortress, 2012), 53–74.

29. For the *diplomata*, see Peter Pilhoffer, *Philippi*, vol. 1, *Die erste christliche Gemeinde Europas*, WUNT 87 (Tübingen: Mohr Siebeck, 1995; rev. ed., 2009 [not

ing is *CIPh* 2.1.6, a large dedicatory inscription honoring the imperial family datable to the reign of Claudius. *CIPh* 2.1.6 was commissioned by L. Atiarius Schoenias most likely on the occasion of his election to civic office. Unfortunately, *CIPh* 2.1.6 is fragmentary and cannot be reconstructed with certainty, but one possible rendering identifies Schoenias not only as an important civic patron but as a former "tribunus cohortium praetoriarum VII et VIII."

Additional arguments for a later dating of the coin have been proposed by Sophia Kremydi-Sicilianou.[30] Recent coin finds at Dion (1998), Amphipolis (1998), Ierissos (1976), and especially the large datable circulation hoard found at Dion in 1999, indicate that the coin, which appears in a variety of subtypes (e.g., Victoria standing on a globe, on a pedestal, or simply walking), continued in production as late as the reign of Antoninus Pius.[31] The content of these finds also suggests that the subtype in which Victoria is depicted standing on a globe mark the coin's earliest issues, since this iconography does not appear on the coins that are datable to the second century. From this Kremydi-Sicilianou theorizes, reasonably in my view, that the Victoria on a globe was intended to evoke the Victoria that Augustus placed in the renovated Curia in 29 BCE, which Victoria was also on a globe and became a widely circulated symbol of Roman imperial domination throughout the first century.[32] But, as she goes on to observe, the Victoria in the Curia was initially called Victoria Romana and so far as

---

seen by me]), index, s.v. *cohors*; Pilhoffer, *Philippi*, vol. 2: *Katalog der Inschriften von Philippi*, WUNT 119 (Tübingen: Mohr Siebeck, 2001; 2nd ed., 2009 [not seen by me]), index, s.v. *cohors*. See further T. Sarikakis, "Des soldats Macedoniens dans l'armée romaine," in *Ancient Macedonia* (Thessalonica: Institute of Balkan Studies, 1977), 2:431–63; F. Papazoglou, "Quelques aspects d l'histoire de la province Macédoine," *ANRW* 2.7.1:302–69, esp. 338–52. For the inscriptions, see *CIPh* 2.1, index, s.v. *cohors*.

30. Sophia Kremydi-Sicilianou, "*Victoria Augusta* on Macedonian Coins: Remarks on Dating and Interpretation," Τεκμήρια 7 (2002): 63–84; Kremydi-Sicilianou, *Multiple Concealments*, 85–89; more generally, Kremydi-Sicilianou, "'Belonging' to Rome, 'Remaining' Greek: Coinage and Identity in Roman Macedonia," in *Coinage and Identity in the Roman Provinces*, ed. Christopher Howgego, Volker Heuchert, and Andrew Burnett (Oxford: Oxford University Press, 2007), 95–106.

31. Kremydi-Sicilianou, "*Victoria Augusta*," 64.

32. Kremydi-Sicilianou, "*Victoria Augusta*," 69. See Paul Zanker, *The Power of Images in the Age of Augustus*, translated by Alan Shapiro, Jerome Lectures 16 (Ann Arbor: University of Michigan Press, 1988), 79–85. A large statue of Victory on a globe was also set up in the Athenian Agora.

we know only began to be referred to as Victoria Augusta in the reign of Claudius, after which it became an especially important piece of imperial propaganda in the reign of Vespasian, who was anxious to style himself as a new Augustus in an effort to establish a new dynasty after the civil wars of 69–70.[33] Kremydi-Sicilianou proposes that *RPC* 1651 was therefore first struck by Vespasian near the beginning of his reign.[34] However, a striking in the reign of Claudius also fits the evidence.

A question raised by Kremydi-Sicilianou's proposed dating of the coin is whether the settlement of praetorians at Philippi referred to on the reverse of *RPC* 1651 might actually have taken place not in the reign of Augustus but early in the reign of Vespasian, when large numbers of soldiers were decommissioned after the civil wars that elevated him to emperor. This is possible, but if *RPC* 1651 was a commemorative issue linking Vespasian to Augustus, then a reference to an earlier settlement by Augustus—a point of continuing civic pride now exploited by Vespasian— still remains the best explanation, even if Vespasian himself also settled guardsmen there, which at this point, like most theories surrounding this fascinating coin, must remain uncertain.[35]

Bibliography

Arband, S., W. Macheiner, and C. Colpe. "Gefangenschaft." *RAC* 9:318–45.

Baillet, Jules. *Inscriptions grècques et latines des tombeaux des rois où syringes à Thèbes*. MIFAO 42. Cairo: L'Institut Français d'Archéologie Orientale du Caire, 1926.

---

33. Kremydi-Sicilianou, "*Victoria Augusta*," 73.

34. Kremydi-Sicilianou, "*Victoria Augusta*," 76–79.

35. That Vespasian staffed the ranks of his army with recruits from Philippi is reasonable, and that at least some of these became part of his imperial guard is consistent with the military *diplomata* published by Pilhofer, three of which (030A, 202 [see 203], and 705) date from Vespasian's reign. However, one of these *diplomata* (item 705) can be dated to the first year of Vespasian's reign, making it likely that in at least this case we have a Philippian who was a member of the guard before Vespasian came to power, a possibility made more likely if the Shoenias of *CIPh* 2.1.6 was also a retired guardsman. For Kremydi-Sicilianou's claim that Vespasian renamed Philippi "colonia victrix" ("*Victoria Augusta*," 77), based on Philhofer's reconstruction of *CIL* 3.1.660, see Brélaz's alternative explanation at *CIPh* 2.1.151. (I wish to thank Prof. Brélaz for a private email exchange regarding *CIPh* 2.1.151, in which he kindly shared his expertise with me.)

Bingham, Sandra. *The Praetorian Guard: A History of Rome's Elite Special Forces*. London: Tauris, 2013.
Bormann, *Philippi: Stadt und Christengemeinde zur Zeit des Paulus*. NovTSup 78. Leiden: Brill, 1995.
Bowman, Alan K. *Life and Letters on the Roman Frontier: Vindolanda and Its People*. New ed. London: British Museum Press, 2003.
Bruce, F. F. *Philippians*. San Francisco: Harper & Row, 1989.
Cassidy, Richard J. *Paul in Chains: Roman Imprisonment and the Letters of St. Paul*. New York: Crossroads, 2001.
Chryssanthaki-Nagle, Katerina. *L'histoire monétaire d'Abdère en Trace (VIes. av. J.-C.-IIe s. ap. J.-C.)*. Meletemata 51. Athens: de Boccard, 2007.
Collange, Jean-François. *L'épître de saint Paul aux Philippiens*. CNT 10A. Neuchâtel: Delachaux & Niestlé, 1973.
Collart, Philippe. *Philippes: Ville de Macédoine, depuis ses origins jusqu'à la fin de l'époque romaine*. 2 vols. Paris: de Boccard, 1937.
Deissmann, Adolf. "Zur ephesinischen Gefangenschaft des Apostel Paulus." Pages 121–27 in *Anatolian Studies presented to Sir William Mitchell Ramsey*. Edited by W. H. Buckler and W. M. Calder. Manchester: Manchester University Press, 1923.
Duncan, G. S. *St. Paul's Ephesian Ministry: A Reconstruction with Special Reference to the Ephesian Origin of the Imprisonment Epistles*. London: Hodder & Stoughton; New York: Scribner's, 1930.
Durry, M. "Sur une monnaie de Philippes." *REA* 42 (1940): 412–16.
Egger, R. "Das Praetorium als Amtssitz und Quartier römischer Spitzenfunktionäre." *SAWW* 250 (1966): 1–47.
Feine, Paul. *Die Abfassung des Philipperbriefes in Ephesus mit einer Anlage über Röm 16,3–20 als Epheserbrief*. BFCT 20.4. Gütersloh: Bertelsmann, 1916.
Gaebler, H. *AMNG* 3.2.102–3, nos. 14–15.
Galsterer, B., and H. Galsterer. *Die römischen Steininschriften aus Koln*. Cologne: Wissenschaftliche Katalogue des Römisch-Germanischen Museums, 1975.
John Chrysostom. *In Epistolam ad Philippenses*. PG 62.
Krause, Jens-Uwe. *Gefängnisse im römischen Reich*. Stuttgart: Steiner, 1996.
Kremydi-Silicianou, Sophia. "'Belonging' to Rome, 'Remaining' Greek: Coinage and Identity in Roman Macedonia." Pages 95–106 in *Coinage and Identity in the Roman Provinces*. Edited by Christopher Howgego,

Volker Heuchert, and Andrew Burnett. Oxford: Oxford University Press, 2007.

———. *Multiple Concealments from the Sanctuary of Zeus Olympios at Dion: The Roman Provincial Coin Hoards.* Meletemata 35. Athens: de Boccard, 2004.

———. "Victoria Augusta on Macedonian Coins: Remarks on Dating and Interpretation." Τεχμήρια 7 (2002): 63–84.

Kroll, J. H. *The Athenian Agora.* Vol. 26 of *Greek Coins.* Princeton: Princeton University Press, 1993.

Lightfoot, J. B. *St. Paul's Epistle to the Philippians: A Revised Text with Introduction, Notes, and Dissertations.* London: Macmillan, 1868.

Malherbe, Abraham. "The Beasts at Ephesus." *JBL* 87 (1968): 71–80.

Michaelis, Wilhelm. *Der Briefe des Paulus an die Philipper.* THKNT 11. Leipzig: Deichert, 1935.

Nasrallah, Laura S. "Spatial Perspectives: Space and Archaeology in Roman Philippi." Pages 53–74 in *Studying Paul's Letters: Contemporary Perspectives and Methods.* Edited by Joseph Marchal. Minneapolis: Fortress, 2012.

Oakes, Peter. *Philippians: From People to Letter.* SNTSMS 110. Cambridge: Cambridge University Press, 2001.

Papazoglou, F. "Quelques aspects d l'histoire de la province Macédoine." *ANRW* 2.7.1:302–69.

Pervo, Richard. *Acts.* Hermeneia. Minneapolis: Fortress, 2009.

Pilhofer, Peter. *Philippi.* Vol. 1, *Die erste christliche Gemeinde Europas.* 2nd ed. WUNT 87. Tübingen: Mohr Siebeck, 2009.

———. *Philippi.* Vol. 2, *Katalog der Inschriften von Philippi.* WUNT 119. Tübingen: Mohr Siebeck, 2001. 2nd ed., 2009.

Rankov, Boris. "The Governor's Men: The *Officium Consularis* in Provincial Adminstration." Pages 15–34 in *The Roman Army as a Community.* Edited by Adrian Goldsworthy and Ian Haynes. JRASup 34. Portsmouth, RI: Journal of Roman Archaeology, 1999.

Rapske, Brian. *The Book of Acts and Paul in Roman Custody.* Grand Rapids: Eerdmans; Carlisle, UK: Paternoster, 1994.

Reumann, John. *Philippians: A New Translation with Introduction and Commentary.* AYB 33B. New Haven: Yale University Press, 2008.

Sarikakis, T. "Des soldats Macedoniens dans l'armée romaine." Pages 431–63 in vol. 2 of *Ancient Macedonia.* Thessalonica: Institute of Balkan Studies, 1977.

Speidel, Michael. *Guards of the Roman Imperial Armies: An Essay on the Singulares of the Provinces*. Antiquitas 1. Bonn: Habelt, 1978.
———. "Two Greek Graffiti in the Tomb of Ramses V." *CdE* 49 (1974): 384–86.
Theodoret. *In Epistolam ad Philippenses*. PG 82.
White, John L.. *Light from Ancient Letters*. Philadelphia: Fortress, 1986.
White, Peter. *Cicero in Letters*. Oxford: Oxford University Press, 2010.
Zanker, Paul. *The Power of Images in the Age of Augustus*. Translated by Alan Shapiro. Jerome Lectures 16. Ann Arbor: University of Michigan Press, 1988.

Polis and *Ekklēsia* at Philippi: A Response to Kathy Ehrensperger, Paul Holloway, and Julien Ogereau

Angela Standhartinger

Depending on the dating of Paul's first visit to Galatia (Gal 4:13–18; Acts 16:6), Philippi was the first or second place Paul headed off to after his rift with the Antiochian missionary center on account of the Antiochian incident (Gal 2:11–14). In any event, the city on the Via Egnatia, connecting the Balkans to Rome, seems to have been the first urban center in which Paul and a small group of fellows—presumably Titus, Silvanus, and Timothy—succeeded in making some friends. The assembly of the Philippesioi formed a "partnership in the gospel" and perhaps also a formal *societas unius rei*, as Ogereau has recently argued.[1] As Phil 4:15–16 states, the assembly funded Paul's missionary efforts in Thessalonica and perhaps also in Corinth (2 Cor 11:7–9). From the letter to the Thessalonians we also learn that at the end of their first stay in Philippi, the group around Paul suffered and were shamefully mistreated (1 Thess 2:2–3). While we do not know what exactly happened, Paul insinuates in Philippians that outsiders caused suffering and distress to the assembly (Phil 1:28–30).

This paper of Angela Standhartinger was delivered in response to the original papers of Kathy Ehrensperger, Paul Holloway, and Julian Ogereau, each of which are included revised in this volume, at the *Polis* and *Ekklēsia* session at the Annual Meeting of the Society of Biblical Literature, San Diego (22–25 November 2015). The quotes from Ehrensperger and Ogereau cited below come from the original drafts of their papers presented at the session.

1. Julien M. Ogereau, "Paul's *Koinōnia* with the Philippians: *Societas* as a Missionary Funding Strategy," *NTS* 60 (2014): 360–78. See also Ogereau, *Paul's Koinonia with the Philippians: A Socio-historical Investigation of a Pauline Economic Partnership*, WUNT 2/377 (Tübingen: Mohr Siebeck, 2014).

We know just as little about how the relationship between the Philippians and the Pauline group developed. One can assume that they formed part of the Macedonian assemblies, which contributed to the Jerusalem collection "during a severe ordeal of affliction" and "despite extreme poverty" (2 Cor 8:1–2). When Paul was imprisoned, the Philippians "revived" their concern for him (Phil 4:10). This revival of interest suggests that there had been an interruption in their financial support of Paul's missionary efforts. But now Paul formally confirms his receipt of a large gift, presumably money, through Epaphroditus (Phil 4:18). This Epaphroditus also served Paul during his imprisonment as "the apostle" of the Philippians and at some point became deathly ill (Phil 2:25–30). In Phil 1 Paul expresses his gratitude for the Philippians' support of him while he was in prison and hopes to be delivered through their prayers (Phil 1:5, 7, 19). These are virtually all the hard facts that we know about the Philippian assembly in Christ from Paul's letters.

Since the 1990s New Testament scholars endeavored to supplement our understanding of Paul's community at Philippi with archaeological data.[2] The site is relatively well known because archaeological excavation has been more or less continuously conducted there since 1914, and today around 15 percent of the city center has been unearthed.[3] The city was founded by settlers from Thassos and was renamed Philippi by Philipp II, the father of Alexander the Great, in the fourth century BCE. The settlers

---

2. Peter Pilhofer, *Philippi*, vol. 1, *Die erste christliche Gemeinde Europas*, WUNT 87 (Tübingen: Mohr Siebeck, 1995); Lukas Bormann, *Philippi: Stadt und Christengemeinde zur Zeit des Paulus*, NovTSup 78 (Leiden: Brill, 1995); Valerie A. Abrahamsen, *Women and Worship at Philippi: Diana/Artemis and Other Cults in the Early Christian Era* (Portland, ME: Astarte Shell, 1995); Craig S. de Vos, *Church and Community Conflicts: The Relationships of the Thessalonian, Corinthian, and Philippian Churches with Their Wider Civic Communities*, SBLDS 168 (Atlanta: Scholars Press, 1999); Peter Oakes, *Philippians: From People to Letter*, SNTSMS 110 (Cambridge: Cambridge University Press, 2001); Mikael Tellbe, *Paul between Synagogue and State: Christians, Jews, and Civic Authorities in 1 Thessalonians, Romans, and Philippians*, ConBNT 34 (Stockholm: Almqvist & Wiksell, 2001); Richard S. Ascough, *Paul's Macedonian Associations: The Social Context of Philippians and 1 Thessalonians*, WUNT 2/161 (Tübingen: Mohr Siebeck, 2003).

3. For an archaeological overview see Chaido Koukouli-Chrysantaki, "Colonia Iulia Augusta Philippensis," in *Philippi at the Time of Paul and after His Death*, ed. Charalambos Bakirtzis and Helmut Koester (Harrisburg, PA: Trinity Press International, 1998), 5–35; Michel Sève and Patrick Weber, *Guide du forum de Philippes*, Sites et Monuments 18 (Athens: École Française d'Athènes, 2012).

came mostly from Ionia and Thassos but also from Thrace. The Hellenistic city had a theater that was renovated and Romanized in the second century CE.[4] However, by 167 BCE Philippi seems to have been only a small town (Strabo, *Geogr.* 7.41). It was integrated into the administrative district of Amphipolis in the Roman province of Macedonia. In 42 BCE Octavian and Antony battled here against Cassius and Brutus. Whether the city was devastated during this battle is disputed among scholars.[5] After his victory, Antony formed the core of the first Roman colony by settling Roman veterans there, as the earliest bronze coins minted by the city indicate.[6] It was Augustus who, after his victory over Antony in 31 BCE, formally refounded Philippi as a Roman colony, organized according to *ius italicum*. The Roman settlers were veterans and tradesmen, who, judging from the majority of the inscriptions, remained Latin speaking until the beginning of the third century CE.[7] Some have called the city therefore a "miniature Rome."[8]

These facts are both helpful and challenging with regard to our understanding of Paul's mission in Philippi, which the papers of Kathy Ehrensperger, Paul Holloway, and Julien Ogereau presented here demonstrate. To whom were Paul and Timothy writing in Greek, in a city where most of the inscriptions inside the city walls were written in Latin up to the end of the third century? Was it addressed to the Roman elite based in

---

4. G. Karadedos and Chaido Koukouli-Chrysanthaki, "From the Greek Theatre to the Roman Arena: The Theatres at Philippi, Thasos and Maroneia," in *Thrace in the Graeco-Roman World: Proceedings of the Tenth International Congress of Thracology. Komotini—Alexandroupolis 18–23 October 2005*, ed. Athena Iakonidou (Athens: National Hellenic Research Foundation, Centre for Greek and Roman Antiquity; Hellenic Ministry of Culture, XVIIIth Ephorate of Prehistoric and Classical Antiquities, Komotini, Greece, 2007), 273–90.

5. See Bormann, *Philippi*, 11–29; *pace* Oakes, *Philippians*, 3–40.

6. See Chaido Koukouli-Chrysanthaki, "Philippi," in *Brill's Companion to Ancient Macedon: Studies in the Archaeology and History of Macedon 650 BC–300 AD*, ed. Robin J. Lane Fox (Leiden: Brill, 2011), 447.

7. In the new edition of 225 inscriptions pertaining to the civic life of the colony by Cédric Brélaz, *CIPh* 2.1, 215 are written in Latin. Eight of nine Greek inscriptions originated in the third century or later. The only early Greek inscription remembers a Thracian king and ally of Brutus and Cassius (*CIPh* 1 = Peter Pilhofer, *Philippi*, vol. 2, *Katalog der Inschriften von Philippi*, 2nd ed., WUNT 119 [Tübingen: Mohr Siebeck, 2009], 53).

8. Franca Landucci, "Philippi," in *The Encyclopedia of Ancient History* (Malden, MA: Wiley-Blackwell, 2013), 5260.

the city center or to farmers (or even day laborers) living in small villages outside the city wall? Are they Romans, Greeks, Thracians, or descendants of the Judeans, or a mixture of these groups? Is the particular Roman character and political status of the Colonia Iulia Augusta Philippensis reflected in the letter, and if so, how? To what extent was loyalty to Caesar and Rome at stake here? Where should we place Paul's assembly on the religious landscape of this particular city?

The three papers examined here address some of these issues. Ehrensperger observes that Paul does not call himself an apostle in Philippians. She suggests that this title, which translates as "messenger" or "envoy," might have been dangerous for someone who, at the time of the writing, was a Roman prisoner. Strikingly, the assembly is also not addressed as *ekklēsia* but as "holy ones with their bishops and deacons" or, more literally translated, "supervisors" and "servants." These two functions might openly point to a hierarchy—something that, as Mary Beard, John North, and Simon Price have argued, has to be maintained by all religions—and only indirectly point to an organizational structure.[9] Greeks are not represented in the forum in Philippi, nor does any Greek hold a political office. Therefore, in Ehrensperger's view, the political term *ekklēsia*, the assembly of the political body of a city, had no meaning to them. Moreover, as Ehrensperger supposes, the Greek term might have been understood by outsiders as provocative in attempting to establish "a Greek assembly ... alongside the exclusively Roman form of rule."[10] When Paul speaks of the heavenly *politeuma*, a term Ehrensberger translates as "citizenship," he promises the Greek-speaking community citizenship in heaven, despite their lack of Roman citizenship. Thus the absence of the terms *apostle* and *ekklēsia* points to deeper layers of communication that convey a hidden message.

---

9. Mary Beard, John North, and Simon Price write: "Sacrifices and other religious rituals were concerned with defining and establishing relationship of power. Not to place oneself within the set of relationship between emperor, gods, élite and people was effectively to place oneself outside the mainstream of the whole world and the shared Roman understanding of humanity's place within that world. Maintenance of the social order was seen by the Romans to be dependent on maintenance of this agreed set of symbolic structures which assigned a role to people at all levels." Mary Beard, John North, and Simon Price, *Religions of Rome*, vol. 1, *A History* (Cambridge: Cambridge University Press, 1998), 361.

10. For the quotation, see p. 72 above.

I agree with the assumption of some coded communication in this letter or, more precisely, these letters.[11] But as this ciphering was designed to obfuscate, it is more than likely that we will not be able crack the code easily or unambiguously. I also ask myself whether the expression from Phil 4:15 οὐδεμία ... ἐκκλησία ... εἰ μὴ ὑμεῖς μόνοι ("no *ekklēsia* ... except you alone") rules out that the assembly in Philippi called itself an *ekklēsia*. However, I am grateful to Ehrensperger for bringing up the question of how the terms *ekklēsia* and *politeuma* relate to each other. I was only able to look briefly into Plutarch's political writings, where *ekklēsia* refers to the actual assembly where politicians deliver speeches, while *politeuma* is used always in the plural for governmental actions.[12] Recently some have argued that Phil 3:20 asserts a heavenly citizenship for Christians in opposition to Roman *civitas*, while others see an opposition to a constituted body of the Jewish ethnos.[13] But both theories are problematic. Kurt Aland has shown that the Latin translation of πολίτευμα is *municipatus* rather than *civitas*, and the presence of Jews in Philippi before the fourth century CE has not been demonstrated by archaeological evidence.[14] In Aristotle's writings *politeuma* describes a constitution, governmental action, and the body of politically active members of a given community.[15] Like Phil 3:20,

---

11. I still argue that the canonical letter to the Philippians is a compilation made by the congregation at the beginning of the second century out of three letters, sent to them by Paul over few months. See Angela Standhartinger, "'Join in Imitating Me' (Philippians 3.17): Towards an Interpretation of Philippians 3," *NTS* 54 (2008): 417–35.

12. See for ἐκκλησία Plutarch, *An. seni* 794C, 796C; *Praec. ger. rei publ.* 803D, 810D; for πολίτευμα Plutarch, *An seni* 784D, 793B, 793C, 796B; *Praec. ger. rei publ.* 818D.

13. Pilhofer, *Philippi*, 1:127–39; Peter Arzt-Grabner, "Die Stellung des Judentums in neutestamentlicher Zeit anhand der Politeuma-Papyri und anderer Texte," in *Papyrologie und Exegese: Die Auslegung des Neuen Testaments im Licht der Papyri*, ed. Jens Herzer, WUNT 2/341 (Tübingen: Mohr Siebeck, 2012), 127–58; Karl-Heinrich Ostmeyer, "Politeuma im Neuen Testament und die Politeuma-Papyri von Herakleopolis," in Herzer, *Papyrologie und Exegese*, 159–71; Hans Förster and Patrick Sänger, "Ist unsere Heimat im Himmel? Überlegungen zur Semantik von πολίτευμα in Phil 3,20," *EC* 5 (2014): 149–77.

14. See Tertullian, *Marc.* 3.24.3; *Cor.* 13.3–4. See Kurt Aland, "Die Christen und der Staat nach Phil. 3,20," in *Kurt Aland, Supplementa zu den neutestamentlichen und den kirchengeschichtlichen Entwürfen*, ed. Beate Köster, Hans-Udo Rosenbaum, and Michael Welte (Berlin: de Gruyter, 1990), 192–204. For the only known Jewish inscription from Philippi, see Koukouli-Chrysantaki, "Colonia," 28–35.

15. Walter Ruppel, "Politeuma," *Philologus* 82 (1927): 272–75, 433–54.

Platonic-Stoic philosophy speaks of a heavenly *politeuma*.[16] On the one hand, it portrays the heavens as the ultimate example of political order, which is to be imitated by humankind. On the other hand, heaven is also the true home of the wise, from which they have come and to which they shall return after their educational sojourn on earth.[17] In Philippians, the body of active political citizens already exists in heaven and consists most likely of the assembly of angels.[18] They are going to act on behalf of those whom Paul calls "us" in Phil 3:20. They are going to act, as many ancient *politeumata* did, by sending a savior to rescue their exiled members from a dangerous situation.[19] Philippians 3:20, in my view, does not promise citizenship to those who might not hold it but rather promises salvation from a hostile environment of suffering and humiliation. But Ehrensperger is right that Paul presupposes political understanding and democratic ideas on the part of his intended readers.

I am also grateful to Ehrensperger for pointing out the many offices that are referred to in Philippians. Alongside bishops or supervisors (Phil 1:1), deacons, servants, and envoys (Phil 1:1), there is an apostle—not Paul but Epaphroditus—as well as a *leitourgos* or public servant and ambassador of the community (Phil 2:25–30). In line with Ogereau's recent observation that the Philippians form a *societas unus rei* with Paul, in which Paul performs the work while the Philippians contribute the money, one can ask, who commissioned whom to do what here? Might it be that Paul continued to develop further the missionary strategy in which, according

---

16. Dio Chrysostom, *Borysth.* 22–23, 29–32. See also Philo, *Spec.* 1.13–15; 2.45.

17. See Philo, *Conf.* 77–78: "For this reason all the wise men mentioned in the books of Moses are represented as sojourners, for their souls are sent down from heaven upon earth as to a colony; and on account of their fondness for contemplation, and their love of learning, they are accustomed to migrate to the terrestrial nature. Since therefore having taken up their abode among bodies, they behold all the mortal objects of the outward senses by their means, then they subsequently return back from thence to the place from which they set out at first, looking upon the heavenly country in which they have the rights of citizens as their native land" (ἐπανέρχονται ἐκεῖσε πάλιν, ὅθεν ὡρμήθησαν τὸ πρῶτον, πατρίδα μὲν τὸν οὐράνιον χῶρον ἐν ᾧ πολιτεύονται [trans. Yonge]). See Philo, *Somn.* 1.181; *Agr.* 65.

18. For a similar perception of humans being members of a heavenly council of angels, see 1QH^a 19 XI, 11–14; 11 II, 19–22; 1QS^b 4, 24–26; etc.

19. See the many examples collected from inscriptions by Franz Jung, ΣΩTHP: *Studien zur Rezeption eines Hellenistischen Ehrentitels im Neuen Testament*, NTAbh 39 (Münster: Aschendorff, 2002), 54–62, 112–69, and throughout.

to Acts, he was trained in Antioch, namely, that he intended for Philippi to be his new missionary center? That the Philippians sent Paul out to preach Christ in Thessalonica, Athens, and Corinth? That they saw his imprisonment as a breach of agreement? We can only speculate here, but the different language in Philippians might point to special relationship between this community and Paul.[20]

Holloway is the first scholar to bring the firsthand military reports from the Roman frontier in England, the Vinolanda Tablets, into the discussion of Philippians. From Tablet 2.154 he learns that the bodyguards of the provincial governor in London are no longer called *praetoriani*, as they were in the time of the Roman republic, but *singulari leg(ati)*. Therefore Holloway suggests that the phrase ἐν ὅλῳ τῷ πραιτωρίῳ must refer to the *preaetoriani* as the bodyguards of Augustus and his successors in Rome. A second piece of evidence is the copper coin *RPC* 1651 from Philippi, testifying to the presence of a Praetorian Guard at Philippi. This coin had previously been regarded by many as proving the presence of a Praetorian Guard at Philippi as early as the time of Augustus.[21] However, on the basis of a qualitative metal analysis, the coin has recently been redated to the rein of Claudius or Nero. I am especially grateful for this updating. For Holloway, the redated coin proves "Philippi's continuing pride in its praetorian foundations," therefore also explaining the fact that "Paul, now a prisoner of the guard, alludes to them in Phil 1:13."[22] However, as Holloway himself concedes, Sophia Kremydi-Sicilianou has redated the coin a second time on the basis of two hoard finds and now places it in the reign of Vespasian.[23] This date concurs with the epigraphic testimonies of *praetoriani* at Philippi, which do not predate the seventh decade of the first century. She explains the release of this coin in terms of the support, also documented elsewhere, of the Philippians for Vespasian and his takeover of power in Rome. This sounds reasonable to me and would seem to contradict Holloway's claim that Paul appeals to the *praetoriani* connection.

I also have some questions to the notion that the expression ἐν ὅλῳ τῷ πραιτωρίῳ ("in the whole praetorium," Phil 1:13), refers to a group of people. Of the 209 references to the term ἐν ὅλῳ listed in the *Thesaurus*

---

20. See Ogereau, *Paul's Koinonia*.
21. *RPC* 1:307.
22. For the quotation, see p. 132 above.
23. Sophia Kremydi-Sicilianou, "Victoria Augusta on Macedonian Coins: Remarks on Dating and Interpretation," *Tekmeria* 7 (2003): 63–84.

Linguae Graecae and the Searchable Inscription database up to the second century CE, none links it to a group of people.[24] Instead, the entries combine ὅλος with corpora, for example, the body, a house, writings, life, and other temporal expressions. When a whole body of people is referred to, the expression is ἐν παντὶ τῷ λαῷ. The interpretation of ἐν ὅλῳ τῷ πραιτωρίῳ as referring to members of the Praetorian Guard seems to extrapolate from the image of Paul's imprisonment described in Acts. However, this part of the narrative of Acts is historically implausible. Even if Paul had had Roman citizenship, he was still "an artisan from the grass roots of Roman society," in the words of Ogereau.[25] The form of free house arrest, *libera custodia*,

---

24. Of the 201 entries for the expression ἐν ὅλῳ τῷ in the *TLG* from literature from the eighth century BCE to the second century CE, none refer unambiguously to a body of people. Instead, medical writers such as Hippocrates and Galen use in eighty-five instances the expression ἐν ὅλῳ τῷ σώματι (in the whole body). We have also frequently expressions of time, such as "in the whole year" (ὅλῳ τῷ ἔτει or ἐν ὅλῳ τῷ ἐνιαυτῷ, eight instances) or "in the whole life" (ἐν ὅλῳ τῷ βίῳ, ten instances). Both expressions appear also eight times on inscriptions. Sometimes ἐν ὅλῳ is related to corpora of writings, such as ἐν ὅλῳ τῷ λόγῳ (six instances), ἐν ὅλῳ τῷ γράμματι (two instances), ἐν ὅλῳ τῷ βιβλίῳ (two instances). Finally, we find the spatial phrase ἐν ὅλῳ τῷ κόσμῳ (Rom 1:8; in all twenty instances). The expression ἐν ὅλῳ τῷ οἴκῳ is to be found only two times in the Septuagint. In Gen 35:31 Laban searches for idols but could not find them in whole of the house. More ambivalent is God's speech to Aaron and Miriam in Num 12:6–8: "When there are prophets among you, I the LORD make myself known to them in visions.... Not so with my servant Moses; he is entrusted with all my house. With him I speak face to face." Here ἐν ὅλῳ τῷ οἴκῳ might refer to the tent of meeting or temple, called the house of God, but it could refer to the people of Israel as well. However, the expression ἐν παντὶ τῷ refers more often to a body of people, such as ἐν παντὶ τῷ λαῷ (Melito, *Peri Pascha* 414; Neh 9:10, 38; Judg 14:3); ἐν παντὶ τῷ ἔθνει (Josephus, *B.J.* 1.648; see ἐν παντὶ <τῷ> γένει; Aristotle, *Gen. an.* 755b36). So if Paul had wanted to refer obviously to a body of people, he might have said ἐν παντὶ τῷ πραιτωρίῳ.

25. For Ogereau's quote, see p. 85 above. In the first century, Roman citizenship was quite rare in the provinces, especially among Jews. Even municipal elites who were heavily involved in the imperial cult did not usually have it. Freedmen and freedwomen in Rome and veterans received, if anything, Italic but not Roman citizenship. Acts uses citizenship as a narrative device in order to protect Paul from the customary torture (Acts 16:38; 22:20) and to place him on the same footing as the officials. See Wolfgang Stegemann, "War der Apostel Paulus ein römischer Bürger?," *ZNW* 78 (1987): 200–229; Karl Leo Noethlichs, "Der Jude Paulus—Ein Tarser oder Römer?," in *Rom und das himmlische Jerusalem: Die frühen Christen zwischen Anpassung und Ablehnung*, ed. Raban von Haehling (Darmstadt: Wissenschaftliche Buchgesellschaft, 2000), 53–84; Richard I. Pervo, *Acts*, Hermeneia (Minneapolis: Fortress, 2009), 389–

referred to in Acts was a privilege of the Roman senatorial class and the very highest-ranking provincial elites.[26] Paul's case is scarcely comparable to that of the Jewish prince Agrippa.[27] But the conditions of Paul's imprisonment described in Acts appear more comfortable than what Josephus tells us about Agrippa's arrest in the time of Caligula. Therefore I think one should be critical of amplifying the enigmatic insinuations from Phil 1:13 with information taken from Acts.[28] In this verse, I detect a hidden transcript, a message of which we can no longer decipher its concrete meaning. But I still think the *praetorium* of Phil 1:13 is most plausibly the palace of the provincial governor, which served as a courtroom in which hearings were held. Therefore I opt that Paul wrote Philippians either in Ceasarea (see Acts 23:35) or, in my view more probably, Ephesus, where, according to 2 Cor 1:8, he faced a death sentence.

Ogereau focuses on the much-discussed social location of Paul's communities in this concrete urban context and highlights the commercial "marketplace" language used in Phil 4:15–20. This helps him to situate Paul and the Philippians among the free and servile working classes of Roman society, people of moderate means who ran workshops and small businesses, employed some personnel, and who might even have owned slaves.[29] He further examines the evidence from the subsequent centuries. Polycarp's letter, charging a presbyter Valens with some financial scandal, proves somewhat informative, although the details remain obscure (Poly-

---

90; *pace* Heike Omerzu, *Der Prozess des Paulus: Eine exegetische und rechtshistorische Untersuchung der Apostelgeschichte*, BZNW 115 (Berlin: de Gruyter, 2002), 19–51.

26. Jens-Uwe Krause, *Gefängnisse im Römischen Reich* (Stuttgart: Steiner, 1996), 183–88.

27. Josephus, *Ant.* 18.192–236; only after some time and because a member of the Tiberian family intervened for him did Agrippa's conditions change. Then he was placed in charge "of a humane centurion" and was allowed to take a daily bath and "to have assistance from his friends" (*Ant.* 18.203; see Acts 27:1–3). The *liberia custodia* at home (Acts 28:16–31) is conceded to Agrippa only in the very last days of his custody (*Ant.* 18.235).

28. See Angela Standhartinger, "Letter from Prison as Hidden Transcript: What It Tells Us about the People at Philippi," in *The People beside Paul: The Philippian Assembly and History from Below*, ed. Joseph A. Marchal, ECL 17 (Atlanta: SBL Press, 2015), 107–40; Standhartinger, "Aus der Welt eines Gefangenen: Die Kommunikationsstruktur des Philipperbriefs im Spiegel seiner Abfassungssituation," *NovT* 55 (2013): 140–67.

29. See Ogereau at p. 87 above.

carp, *Phil.* 11.1–2). Ogereau goes on to scrutinize the earliest Christian inscriptions from the early fourth to the late fifth century CE. Here he finds an inscription of Ioannes, a meat dealer at the market place; Severos, a negotiator or estate manager; Alexandros, an architect; Aurelius Kyriakos, a school teacher; and Paul, the *presbyteros* or elder and physician. A *vir clarissimus* perhaps with senatorial status and an artfully decorated grave, on the one hand, and some poorly decorated epitaphs, on the other, document the social spread of the Christian communities in the fourth and fifth centuries.

Again, I am grateful for this empirical, long-term study, which combines qualitative and quantitative data on the concrete social structure of the community. But what I find most intriguing in Ogereau's paper is what he merely implies: that there are no Christian inscriptions to be found in the inner city until the fourth century. To say it with Charalampos Tsochos, there are almost no Christian symbols apart from two engraved crosses up to the fifth century.[30] This is striking because the community promoted its letter and sent it to Antioch already in the middle of the second century, as one can learn from Polycarp (*Phil.* 13). Already around 150 they were famous for housing five future martyrs (*Phil.* 9.1). The mosaic-pavement of the Church of Paul demonstrates that still in the fourth century they were proud of their special relationship with the apostle.[31] But where did they live in the first, second, and third centuries? Where were they been buried? Did they remain invisible because they were too poor to leave anything behind for posterity? Or did they fear persecution or dwell in those areas of the city that are still unearthed or even lie outside the city walls in the more rural areas on the city's outskirts?

As to the question of social stratification of the community in Philippi, I am more skeptical about assuming that the use of the commercial formula εἰς λόγον δόσεως καὶ λήμψεως (in the matter of giving and receiving) requires formal training, or at least more education than a farming or gardening woman who went to the city to sell her goods in the market would have had. I wonder why Ogereau does not take into account the fact that

---

30. Charalampos Tsochos, *Die Religion in der römischen Provinz Makedonien*, PAB 40 (Stuttgart: Steiner, 2012), 49–50, 122.

31. The inscription on the mosaic floor of this "basilica" reads: Πο[ρφύ]ριος ἐπίσκοπος τὴ[ν κ]έντησιν τῆς βασιλικῆς Παύλο[υ ἐπ]οίησεν ἐν Χρ(ιστ)ῷ ("Porphyrios, the bishop, created in Christ the mosaic of the Basilica of Paul"). See *RICM* 226 = Pilhofer, *Philippi*, 2.329/G472.

Paul and his fellows also worked at Thessalonica in order to avoid burdening the local assembly (1 Thess 2:9). The funds from Philippi must have been extremely limited, or at least not sufficient to meet the needs of two or three missionaries. Compared to Corinth, the Macedonian assemblies were also described as poor later on (2 Cor 8:1). Because of these "facts" I am still inclined to place the Philippians, at least in the time of Paul, in the lower strata of the city's society.

The three papers have proven that it is extremely productive to read Philippians in its urban environment and against the backdrop of the local archaeological data. These readings help us to ask some new questions as well as to notice where our traditional perceptions might lack evidence or are historically and socially unlikely. Together, they challenge us to rethink and reframe our understanding of Paul's theology as well as of the two narratives about his mission, in his letters and in Acts, and to bring them down to earth.

Bibliography

Abrahamsen, Valerie A. *Women and Worship at Philippi: Diana/Artemis and Other Cults in the Early Christian Era*. Portland, ME: Astarte Shell, 1995.

Aland, Kurt. "Die Christen und der Staat nach Phil. 3,20." Pages 192–204 in *Kurt Aland, Supplementa zu den neutestamentlichen und den kirchengeschichtlichen Entwürfen*. Edited by Beate Köster, Hans-Udo Rosenbaum, and Michael Welte. Berlin: de Gruyter, 1990.

Arzt-Grabner, Peter. "Die Stellung des Judentums in neutestamentlicher Zeit anhand der Politeuma-Papyri und anderer Texte." Pages 127–58 in *Papyrologie und Exegese: Die Auslegung des Neuen Testaments im Licht der Papyri*. Edited by Jens Herzer. WUNT 2/341. Tübingen: Mohr Siebeck, 2012.

Ascough, Richard S. *Paul's Macedonian Associations: The Social Context of Philippians and 1 Thessalonians*. WUNT 2/161. Tübingen: Mohr Siebeck, 2003.

Beard, Mary, John North, and Simon Price. *Religions of Rome*. Vol. 1, *A History*. Cambridge: Cambridge University Press, 1998.

Bormann, Lukas. *Philippi: Stadt und Christengemeinde zur Zeit des Paulus*. NovTSup 78. Leiden: Brill, 1995.

Förster, Hans, and Patrick Sänger. "Ist unsere Heimat im Himmel? Überlegungen zur Semantik von πολίτευμα in Phil 3,20." *EC* 5 (2014): 149–77.

Jung, Franz. *ΣΩΤΗΡ: Studien zur Rezeption eines hellenistischen Ehrentitels im Neuen Testament*. NTAbh 39. Münster: Aschendorff, 2002.

Karadedos, G., and Chaido Koukouli-Chrysanthaki. "From the Greek Theatre to the Roman Arena: The Theatres at Philippi, Thasos and Maroneia." Pages 273–90 in *Thrace in the Graeco-Roman World: Proceedings of the Tenth International Congress of Thracology; Komotini—Alexandroupolis 18–23 October 2005*. Edited by Athena Iakonidou. Athens: National Hellenic Research Foundation. Centre for Greek and Roman Antiquity; Hellenic Ministry of Culture. XVIIIth Ephorate of Prehistoric and Classical Antiquities, Komotini, Greece, 2007.

Koukouli-Chrysantaki, Chaido. "Colonia Iulia Augusta Philippensis." Pages 5–35 in *Philippi at the Time of Paul and after His Death*. Edited by Charalambos Bakirtzis and Helmut Koester. Harrisburg, PA: Trinity Press International, 1998.

———. "Philippi." Pages in 437–52 in *Brill's Companion to Ancient Macedon: Studies in the Archaeology and History of Macedon 650 BC–300 AD*. Edited by Robin J. Lane Fox. Leiden: Brill, 2011.

Krause, Jens-Uwe. *Gefängnisse im Römischen Reich*. Stuttgart: Steiner, 1996.

Kremydi-Sicilianou, Sophia. "Victoria Augusta on Macedonian Coins: Remarks on Dating and Interpretation." *Tekmeria* 7 (2003): 63–84.

Landucci, Franca. "Philippi." Pages 5260–62 in *The Encyclopedia of Ancient History*. Malden, MA: Wiley-Blackwell, 2013.

Noethlichs, Karl Leo. "Der Jude Paulus—Ein Tarser und Römer?" Pages 53–84 in *Rom und das himmlische Jerusalem: Die frühen Christen zwischen Anpassung und Ablehnung*. Edited by Raban von Haehling. Darmstadt: Wissenschaftliche Buchgesellschaft, 2000.

Oakes, Peter. *Philippians: From People to Letter*. SNTSMS 110. Cambridge: Cambridge University Press, 2001.

Ogereau, Julien M. *Paul's Koinonia with the Philippians: A Socio-historical Investigation of a Pauline Economic Partnership*. WUNT 2/377. Tübingen: Mohr Siebeck, 2014.

———. "Paul's *Koinōnia* with the Philippians: *Societas* as a Missionary Funding Strategy." *NTS* 60 (2014): 360–78.

Omerzu, Heike. *Der Prozeß des Paulus: Eine exegetische und rechtshistorische Untersuchung der Apostelgeschichte*. BZNW 115. Berlin: de Gruyter, 2002.

Ostmeyer, Karl-Heinrich. "Politeuma im Neuen Testament und die Politeuma-Papyri von Herakleopolis." Pages 159–71 in *Papyrologie und*

Exegese: Die Auslegung des Neuen Testaments im Licht der Papyri. Edited by Jens Herzer. WUNT 2/341. Tübingen: Mohr Siebeck, 2012.
Pervo, Richard I. *Acts.* Hermeneia. Minneapolis: Fortress, 2009.
Philo. *The Works of Philo: Complete and Unabridged.* Translated by C. D. Yonge. Peabody, MA: Hendrickson, 1993.
Pilhofer, Peter. *Philippi.* Vol. 1, *Die erste christliche Gemeinde Europas.* WUNT 87. Tübingen: Mohr Siebeck, 1995.
———. *Philippi.* Vol. 2, *Katalog der Inschriften von Philippi.* 2nd ed. WUNT 119. Tübingen: Mohr Siebeck, 2009.
Ruppel, Walter. "Politeuma." *Philologus* 82 (1927): 268–312, 430–55.
Sève, Michel, and Patrick Weber. *Guide du forum de Philippes.* Sites et Monuments 18. Athens: École Française d'Athènes, 2012.
Standhartinger, Angela. "Aus der Welt eines Gefangenen: Die Kommunikationsstruktur des Philipperbriefs im Spiegel seiner Abfassungssituation." *NovT* 55 (2013): 140–67.
———. " 'Join in Imitating Me' (Philippians 3.17): Towards an interpretation of Philippians 3." *NTS* 54 (2008): 417–35.
———. "Letter from Prison as Hidden Transcript: What It Tells Us about the People at Philippi." Pages 107–40 in *The People beside Paul: The Philippian Assembly and History from Below.* Edited by Joseph A. Marchal. ECL 17. Atlanta: SBL Press, 2015.
Stegemann, Wolfgang. "War der Apostel Paulus ein römischer Bürger?" *ZNW* 78 (1987): 200–229.
Tellbe, Mikael. *Paul between Synagogue and State: Christians, Jews, and Civic Authorities in 1 Thessalonians, Romans, and Philippians.* ConBNT 34. Stockholm: Almqvist & Wiksell, 2001.
Tsochos, Charalampos. *Die Religion in der römischen Provinz Makedonien.* PAB 40. Stuttgart: Steiner, 2012.
Vos, Craig S. de. *Church and Community Conflicts: The Relationships of the Thessalonian, Corinthian, and Philippian Churches with Their Wider Civic Communities.* SBLDS 168. Atlanta: Scholars Press, 1999.

First-Century Philippi: Contextualizing Paul's Visit

Cédric Brélaz

Along with Pisidian Antioch, Lystra, Iconium, Alexandria Troas, and Corinth, Philippi is, according to the narrative of the Acts of the Apostles, one of the many Roman colonies visited by the apostle Paul during his journeys through Asia Minor and Greece.[1] It is, however, together with Corinth, by far the most well-known colony among the nearly thirty similar settlements founded by Roman power in the eastern Mediterranean in the second half of the first century BCE.[2] Thanks to systematic excavations, which were first launched by the French School of Archaeology at Athens more than one hundred years ago, and to the discovery of hundreds of inscriptions on stone, such as honorific texts, dedications, and epitaphs (a significant part of them being still unpublished), we have a better sense of what the city of Philippi looked like in antiquity—especially with regard to public life, society and cults—than for any other Roman colony in the Greek-speaking provinces of the empire.[3] On the other hand, the passage

---

This study was completed during my fellowship at Harvard University's Center for Hellenic Studies, Washington, DC. I would like to thank the conveners and the attendees of the Philippi sessions at the 2014 Annual Meeting of the Society of Biblical Literature in San Diego, as well as Steven Friesen (University of Texas at Austin), Daniel Gerber, and Michel Matter (University of Strasbourg), for their valuable remarks and suggestions.

1. Marie-Françoise Baslez, "Paul et l'émergence d'un monde 'gréco-romain' Réflexions sur la romanité de l'apôtre," in *Paul's Graeco-Roman Context*, ed. Cilliers Breytenbach (Leuven: Peeters, 2015), 29–45.

2. Maurice Sartre, "Les colonies romaines dans le monde grec. Essai de synthèse," in *Roman Military Studies*, ed. Edward Dąbrowa (Kraków: Jagiellonian University Press, 2001), 111–52.

3. Michel Sève, *1914–2014: Philippes, ΦΙΛΙΠΠΟΙ, Philippi; 100 ans de recherches françaises* (Athens: École française d'Athènes, 2014); Pierre Ducrey, "100 ans de

of Acts devoted to Paul's stay at Philippi (16:12–40), in a brief but dense account, provides a lot of information on the institutions, on the society, and on the religious life in the colony that would otherwise have remained unknown to us. This chapter will situate Paul's visit in its local context—material, social, political, and religious at the same time—by relying on what we can infer from the archaeological and epigraphic evidence.

In what follows, four main issues regarding Paul's presence in first-century Philippi will be addressed:

1. What was the urban context of Paul's visit, and what did the town of Philippi look like in the mid-first century?
2. What were the main ethnic and social groups in Roman Philippi, and how does this affect our understanding of Paul's audience?
3. How did the political and legal institutions of the Roman colony operate, and what does this tell us about the accuracy of the depiction of the apostle's arrest and flogging in Acts?
4. What were the major deities worshiped in Roman Philippi, and what might have been the place of the Christian group founded by Paul among the various cultic associations attested in the colony?

This chapter does not intend to discuss the reliability of the narrative of Acts regarding Paul's visit. It will look, rather, at the archaeological and epigraphic evidence in order to allow us to reconstruct the mid-first-century urban, social, cultural, religious, and legal background of Paul's visit, preaching, and creation of the first Christian group.[4] This paper will show how the social, cultural, and legal context of Philippi might have influenced Paul's actions and, conversely, will reassess what impact the apostle's

---

fouilles et de recherches de l'École française d'Athènes à Philippes (1914–2014)," *CRAI* 2014: 1449–62.

4. Previous studies include Paul Lemerle, *Philippes et la Macédoine orientale à l'époque chrétienne et byzantine: Recherches d'histoire et d'archéologie* (Paris: de Boccard, 1945), 1:7–112; Peter Pilhofer, *Philippi*, vol. 1, *Die erste christliche Gemeinde Europas*, WUNT 87 (Tübingen: Mohr Siebeck, 1995); L. Michael White, "Visualizing the 'Real' World of Acts 16: Toward Construction of a Social Index," in *The Social World of the First Christians: Essays in Honor of Wayne A. Meeks*, ed. L. Michael White and O. Larry Yarbrough (Minneapolis: Fortress, 1995), 234–61; Laura S. Nasrallah, "Spatial Perspectives: Space and Archaeology in Roman Philippi," in *Studying Paul's Letters: Contemporary Perspectives and Methods*, ed. Joseph A. Marchal (Minneapolis: Fortress, 2012), 53–74.

stay in Philippi and the emerging Christian community might have had on the colony. It will argue that society in first-century Philippi can only be fully understood through the combined investigation of the archaeological/epigraphic and New Testament evidence.

1. The Urban Context of Paul's Visit in Mid-First-Century Philippi

In the aftermath of the battle fought between the republicans and Caesar's heirs on the plain in front of Philippi, the foundation of a Roman colony in 42 BCE on the site of the former Greek city led to the settlement of hundreds, if not thousands, of soldiers originating from Italy.[5] By settling veterans of the battle there, Mark Antony's intention was to take advantage of the land around Philippi, hoping both to solve the recurrent problem of lack of land in the Italian Peninsula and to secure the strategic position of Philippi on the Egnatian Way. The colony was reinforced and founded again a dozen years later, in 30 BCE, when Octavian settled Roman citizens in Philippi who—because of their support to Mark Antony, who had just been defeated in Actium—were expelled from Italy so that their estates could be seized and given to Octavian's own soldiers (Dio Cassius, *Hist. Rom.* 51.4.6). Therefore, the Hellenistic city of Philippi ceased to exist in 42 BCE when a new political constitution was set up by Roman power.

Although it caused dramatic changes with respect to demography, social structure, ethnic and cultural interactions, land ownership, and political institutions, the replacement of the Greek city of Philippi by a Roman colony did not instantaneously affect the physical organization of the town. Some of the most fundamental features of the town planning dating back to the foundation of the city by the Macedonians in the fourth century BCE were kept by the Roman colonists, such as the delimitation of the town by walls, the grid pattern of streets and blocks, and one of the major public buildings in the classical and Hellenistic city, the theater, which stood on the slopes of the acropolis.[6] Despite the reinforce-

---

5. Paul Collart, *Philippes: Ville de Macédoine, depuis ses origines jusqu'à la fin de l'époque romaine* (Paris: de Boccard, 1937), 223–57; Chaido Koukouli-Chrysanthaki, "Philippi," in *Brill's Companion to Ancient Macedon: Studies in the Archaeology and History of Macedon, 650 BC–300 AD*, ed. Robin J. Lane Fox (Leiden: Brill, 2011), 437–52.

6. Cédric Brélaz and Julien Demaille, "Traces du passé macédonien et influences de l'hellénisme dans les colonies de Dion et de Philippes," in *L'héritage grec des colonies*

ment (and the formal refoundation) of the colony thanks to Octavian in 30 BCE, no substantial public works seem to have been carried out in the colony during the first three or four decades of its existence. This was in no way specific to Philippi. Roman colonies typically initiated public building projects after they had been established for at least half a century at the earliest, by which point the local elite had become wealthy enough to fund such works.[7] Yet various archaeological and epigraphic evidence suggests that a public space such as a square, which was required for official activities and celebrations (including dedications to the emperors), did already exist in Philippi under the Julian emperors, probably as early as the Augustan period.[8]

On the other hand, when Paul visited Philippi in the late 40s, ninety years or so after it was refounded as a Roman colony, the city had been undergoing considerable remodeling for the past few years with regard to town planning and public building projects. The archaeological analysis of the forum has shown that the earliest monumental stage of the public space should be dated to the second quarter of the first century CE, maybe under the reign of Claudius.[9] At the time when Paul arrived at Philippi, the colony had just been provided with a brand-new forum, which must have already had the general shape it would keep during the next centuries (with the exception of the later restructuring works that were carried out at different times, in particular the mid-second century). This was a monumental square surrounded by various public buildings sheltering the civic life of the colony, including (at least from the mid-second century onwards) a council hall, a judicial basilica, an archives building, a public library, a temple for the imperial cult, a speakers' podium, and porticoes. The southern part of the forum, where shops stood, served as a marketplace. In the Hellenistic period, above this flat area, on the slopes of the acropolis, there was a terrace with temples where copies of the most

---

romaines d'Orient: Interactions culturelles dans les provinces hellénophones de l'empire romain, ed. Cédric Brélaz (Paris: de Boccard, 2017), 119–56.

7. Rebecca J. Sweetman, ed., *Roman Colonies in the First Century of Their Foundation* (Oxford: Oxbow, 2001).

8. Michel Sève and Patrick Weber, *Guide du forum de Philippes*, Sites et Monuments 18 (Athens: École française d'Athènes, 2012), 11–17; Cédric Brélaz, "Le *Corpus des inscriptions grecques et latines de Philippes*: Apports récents et perspectives de recherche sur une colonie romaine d'Orient," *CRAI* 2014: 1476–77.

9. Sève and Weber, *Guide du forum de Philippes*, 12–17.

important public documents of the Greek city were displayed on stone. This terrace now served as the Capitolium found in most Roman colonies all over the empire, that is, the sanctuary devoted to the main tutelary gods of the Roman state, as on the Capitoline Hill in Rome.[10] This whole monumental and architectural layout looked very Roman indeed, even though the building material and the construction techniques were mostly Greek. This implies that Greek architects and craftsmen were hired for the works. Unlike in Corinth, where much more of the architectural heritage of the Greek city was preserved (even if transformed and reinterpreted by the Roman colonists),[11] the city center of Philippi was drastically modified to ensure compliance with the Roman pattern.

This monumentalizing display of Romanness was the urban environment in which Paul's deeds in Philippi took place, as the narrative of Acts—especially the episode of the apostle's arrest and flogging—suggests (see §3 below). The forum is referred to in Acts 16:19 by the generic Greek word meaning a public square, ἀγορά.[12] Several significant monuments were erected in the forum or in its immediate surroundings shortly before Paul's visit. A very long inscription (nearly 20 m) made of huge bronze letters of 62 cm (the biggest inscription ever in all Latin epigraphy after the dedication of the Pantheon in Rome!) was engraved on the floor of the square to commemorate the paving of the newly inaugurated forum by a man who had been a priest of the deified Augustus.[13] Only the fixing holes of the bronze letters have survived to the present (as is the case for the much-discussed inscription naming the *aedilis* Erastus in Corinth),[14] but this inscription filling the whole central portion of the forum—long,

---

10. Josephine Crawley Quinn and Andrew Wilson, "Capitolia," *JRS* 103 (2013): 117–73.

11. Benjamin W. Millis, "The Local Magistrates and Elite of Roman Corinth," in *Corinth in Contrast: Studies in Inequality*, ed. Steven J. Friesen, Sarah A. James, and Daniel N. Schowalter, NovTSup 155 (Leiden: Brill, 2014), 38–53.

12. It should not to be confused with μάκελλον, the "marketplace," as in 1 Cor 10:25. The ἀγορά in Philippi is also referred to in a third-century CE Greek inscription. Peter Pilhofer, *Philippi*, vol. 2, *Katalog der Inschriften von Philippi*, 2nd ed., WUNT 119 (Tübingen: Mohr Siebeck, 2009), 133, l. 15.

13. *CIPh* 2.1.66.

14. Steven J. Friesen, "The Wrong Erastus: Ideology, Archaeology, and Exegesis," in *Corinth in Context: Comparative Studies on Religion and Society*, ed. Steven J. Friesen, Daniel N. Schowalter, and James C. Walters, NovTSup 134 (Leiden: Brill, 2010), 231–56.

big, and shining as it was—must have looked very impressive to anyone visiting the city center of Philippi at that time, especially when seen from the upper terrace. In the northeastern corner of the forum, an honorary monument supporting statues of the emperor Claudius and his relatives was erected.[15] A few years earlier, a long base displaying the statues of the first emperors and their heirs who had been granted the tribunician power, presumably from Augustus onwards, was erected by freedmen of emperor Gaius, probably on the upper terrace of the forum where the Capitolium stood.[16] A huge (5 m long) dedication to the imperial family was carved on the front wall of a bathhouse in the center of the city. It was probably in honour of Claudius and his adopted son, Nero, whose name was deliberately erased because he had suffered *abolitio memoriae*. It commemorates the benefactions of the man who refurbished the baths, erected statues to the gods, and gave donations to the whole population of the colony, not just to the citizens (*populus*), nor only to the *Augustales*—an order of distinguished freedmen devoted to the worship of the emperor—but he also gave donations to the local councillors (*decuriones*) and their wives and children, and even to the people who did not belong to the civic elite, living in the countryside (*pagani*), many of them not even Roman citizens.[17]

We should keep in mind, however, that, because of changes to the forum brought by the Antonine works of the mid-second century, many earlier inscriptions were removed from their initial location or were even destroyed so that we only have a partial understanding of what the public square actually looked like at the time of Paul's visit.[18] Furthermore, several other monuments, though dating to the first century CE, did not yet stand in the forum at the time when Paul visited Philippi, contrary to what some recent scholarship suggests.[19] In particular, the statue base for the priestesses of the deified Livia standing before the temple of the imperial cult, as well as the inscriptions referring to the soldier L. Tatinius Cnosus

---

15. *CIPh* 2.1.5.
16. *CIPh* 2.1.8a.
17. *CIPh* 2.1.6.
18. Michel Sève, "Le destin des honneurs pour les empereurs et les notables à Philippes: Note d'épigraphie et de topographie," in *Mémoire et histoire: Les procédures de condamnation dans l'Antiquité romaine*, ed. Stéphane Benoist (Metz: CRULH, 2007), 139–52; *CIPh* 2.1.32–35, 66–67.
19. Pilhofer, *Philippi*, 1:118–21.

on the other side of the square,[20] were not erected until the Flavian period. Moreover, the blocks mentioning two prominent families of the colony, the Mucii and the Decimii, although they were found in the fountains on the northern side of the public square, originally belonged to funerary monuments that formerly stood outside the city. Those monuments were later demolished and removed from one of the necropolises of the city so that they could be used as building material during the reconstruction works that took place in the forum in late antiquity.[21] Unlike the Mucii and Decimii monuments, which were probably erected during the reign of Claudius, the huge funerary altar to the equestrian officer C. Vibius Quartus, which stands next to the Egnatian Way and is still visible today in what was the eastern necropolis of the city in a place called "Dikili Tash"—after its Turkish name, which means the "standing stone" because of the presence of the Roman monument—is of a later date. This was erected under the reign of Nero at the earliest and thus could not have been seen by Paul on his way from Neapolis to Philippi, unlike all of the later travelers until the nineteenth century.[22]

2. Society, Ethnicity, and Language: The Audience of Paul's Preaching

Philippi during the first century CE was an elite-dominated community. Most of these elites, who were monopolizing public offices and governing the colony, were descendants of the first colonists at the time when Paul visited Philippi about one hundred years after Mark Antony's foundation. This is shown by their names (*gentilicia*), some of which were typical of a specific region in Italy. Unlike in some other Roman colonies in Macedonia and Greece, such as Dium, Buthrotum, and especially Corinth, there were no freedmen among the first officials of the colony in Philippi (freedmen were able to run for public offices until the *lex Visellia* was passed in 24 CE), nor individuals coming from the Roman families who had already been doing business for a long time in the eastern Mediterranean.[23]

---

20. *CIPh* 2.1.126, 84–85.
21. *CIPh* 2.1.59, 119.
22. *CIPh* 2.1.63.
23. Brélaz, "Apports," 1486–1501. See Athanasios D. Rizakis, "Recrutement et formation des élites dans les colonies romaines de la province de Macédoine," in *Les élites et leurs facettes: Les élites locales dans le monde hellénistique et romain*, ed. Mireille

Like Patras and Pisidian Antioch, Philippi was a military colony, as they were called by Augustus in the Res gestae divi Augusti (28.1); that is, a colony primarily made of discharged soldiers. Compared to other Roman colonies in the East, where foreigners, having gained Roman citizenship under the Julio-Claudian or Flavian emperors, had the chance to enter local councils and in some cases even at a very early stage, the colonists in Philippi were very reluctant to integrate foreigners. For three centuries, from the creation of the colony in 42 BCE to the middle of the third century CE, the same group retained power in Philippi. This is a symptom of the very conservative spirit of the local elites in Philippi. The Roman citizens kept asserting their Italian and Latin cultural identity for centuries. In particular, Latin remained the official language of the colony much longer than in most Roman colonies established in the eastern provinces, where Greek began to be used for public purposes during the second century CE, as early as the reign of Hadrian in Corinth.[24]

Epigraphic evidence shows that Philippian elites were very keen on self-representation and self-promotion. Numerous honorific dedications engraved on statue bases displayed in the center of the city and epitaphs recorded their names and deeds. There are dozens of extant inscriptions mentioning the political career (or *cursus honorum*) of Philippians and the role they played in the civic life of the colony through public offices and benefactions to their fellow citizens. These inscriptions suggest that the local elites' main concern was the acquisition of social prestige for themselves and their family. Commitment for the common good, generosity towards the community, local patriotism, and pride in their social status are some of the values for which local elites used to compete.[25] Joseph Hellerman argued that Paul's intention, in praising Jesus's humility in Phil 2:5–11 (in the so-called Christ Hymn), was to denounce implicitly the

---

Cébeillac-Gervasoni and Laurent Lamoine (Rome: École française de Rome, 2003), 107–30; Benjamin W. Millis, "The Social and Ethnic Origins of the Colonists in Early Roman Corinth," in Friesen, Schowalter, and Walters, *Corinth in Context*, 13–35.

24. Athanasios D. Rizakis, "Le grec face au latin: Le paysage linguistique dans la péninsule balkanique sous l'empire," in *Acta colloquii epigraphici Latini Helsingiae 3.–6. sept. 1991 habiti*, ed. Heikki Solin, Olli Salomies, and Uta-Maria Liertz (Helsinki: Societas Scientiarium Fennica, 1995), 373–91.

25. See, in particular, *CIPh* 2.1.68, where the benefactor is praised for his love toward his fellow citizens (*amor eius in cives*), for his kindness (*benevolentia*), and for his generosity (*liberalitas*).

vanity of the local elites in the colony.²⁶ Hellerman is correct in pointing out that honor was a core value within the ethical framework of the upper classes in Philippi. We should not, however, be surprised that Philippians were so eager to get fame and social promotion. This was not specific to Philippi. Similar inscriptions, proudly proclaiming careers and ranks, were to be found everywhere throughout the Roman Empire at that time, and what we have just said about the values of the upper classes in Philippi is consistent with the aristocratic mentalities of local elites in the Greco-Roman world from the late Hellenistic period onwards.²⁷ The elites' concern for glory was not deeper in Philippi than in the other Roman colonies or Greek cities visited by Paul. The same could be said for Ephesus, where the local elites usually followed a given order to access the highest offices in the city, although the order was not as rigid there as in the Roman colonies.²⁸ Therefore, it does not seem that Paul's intention through the Christ Hymn was to blame specifically the Philippians for their attitude toward public life. Moreover, in comparison with Ephesus or even Pisidian Antioch, another Roman colony visited by Paul, local elites in Philippi were of a much lower level. While we know of seven families of senatorial rank in Antioch,²⁹ we have only one instance for a senator in Philippi. Furthermore, this man was not a descendant of Italian colonists but originated from the Thracian royal dynasty.³⁰ No family in Philippi was as wealthy and as influential as the most elite families in Pisidian Antioch, where the family of the governor of Cyprus Sergius Paullus, whom Paul met according to Acts 13:6–12, was well established, or in Corinth, where

---

26. Joseph H. Hellerman, *Reconstructing Honor in Roman Philippi: Carmen Christi as Cursus Pudorum*, SNTSMS 132 (Cambridge: Cambridge University Press, 2005).

27. Mireille Cébeillac-Gervasoni and Laurent Lamoine, *Les élites et leurs facettes*; Jens Bartels, *Städtische Eliten im römischen Makedonien: Untersuchungen zur Formierung und Struktur* (Berlin: de Gruyter, 2008).

28. François Kirbihler, "Un *cursus honorum* à Éphèse? Quelques réflexions sur la succession des magistratures de la cité à l'époque romaine," in *Folia Graeca in honorem Edouard Will, Historica*, ed. Paul Goukowsky and Christophe Feyel (Nancy: ADRA, 2012), 67–107.

29. Helmut Halfmann, "Italische Ursprünge bei Rittern und Senatoren aus Kleinasien," in *Tra Oriente e Occidente: Indigeni, Greci e Romani in Asia Minore*, ed. Gianpaolo Urso (Pisa: Edizioni ETS, 2007), 165–87.

30. *CIPh* 2.1.37–38.

the most powerful families of the province of Achaia settled to be close to the proconsul.

All of the Roman citizens of Philippi did not belong to the dominant group we have been describing so far. Furthermore, the Italians themselves were only a fraction of the whole population living in the city of Philippi and its surrounding territory. As shown by many inscriptions, a very high percentage of the population of Philippi in the first century CE—which unfortunately cannot be accurately estimated due to the lack of any reliable figure—was made up of Greeks and Thracians. Although they had lost much of their land to the creation of the colony in 42 BCE, the local population of the former Greek city of Philippi was allowed to stay in the territory of the new community as foreign residents, or *incolae*, as they were called in Latin.[31] They no longer enjoyed civic rights in what became a part of the Roman state, but they still belonged to the colony from an administrative point of view. Among the *incolae*, who were foreigners with respect to Roman citizenship, Thracians can easily be recognized in the inscriptions thanks to their distinctive names.[32] They were in Philippi as descendants of the native population, since the Thracians were the first settlers of the area—even before the coming of Thasians and other Greeks to eastern Macedonia in the archaic and classical periods.[33] Although the Thracians continued to speak their own language during the Roman imperial period, they nevertheless used Greek or sometimes even Latin to engrave inscriptions, since the Thracian language was not written. The use of the Latin language by foreign residents is an infrequent phenomenon among the Roman colonies settled in Greek-speaking provinces, and only Thracians are mentioned in such inscriptions. Greeks, by contrast, did not use Latin in any of Philippi's inscriptions. This willingness of some Thracians to use the language of the Roman colonists suggests that eastern Macedonia in the imperial period was not fully hellenized.[34]

---

31. Athanasios D. Rizakis, "*Incolae-paroikoi*: Populations et communautés dépendantes dans les cités et les colonies romaines de l'Orient," *REA* 100 (1998): 599–617.

32. Dan Dana, *Onomasticon Thracicum: Répertoire des noms indigènes de Thrace, Macédoine orientale, Mésies, Dacie et Bithynie*, Meletemata 70 (Athens: National Hellenic Research Foundation, 2014).

33. Angelos G. Zannis, *Le pays entre le Strymon et le Nestos: Géographie et histoire (VIIe–IVe siècle avant J.-C.)*, Meletemata 71 (Athens: National Hellenic Research Foundation, 2014).

34. Cédric Brélaz, "La langue des *incolae* sur le territoire de Philippes et les contacts linguistiques dans les colonies romaines d'Orient," in *Interpretatio: Traduire*

We understand that, in mid-first-century Philippi, society was, from a cultural point of view, divided into three main ethnic groups. First, there were Roman citizens, who were the Latin-speaking descendants of the first Italian colonists who enjoyed civic rights in the public life of the colony. In the 40s and 50s of the first century during Paul's visit, they must have been the third or the fourth generation after the coming of the first colonists. There were also Thracians, who, being the native population in eastern Macedonia, probably represented the vast majority of the people living in the countryside. Finally, there were people who can be described as culturally Greek, who were either descendants—not only of the Macedonians settled in the city by King Philip II in 356 BCE but also of the Thasians and Athenians who were already present in the area—or they were people coming from other parts of the Greek world to settle in Philippi during the Hellenistic and early Roman period.

Among which of these three groups did Paul find his first followers? The prosopography of the Pauline community in Philippi, short though it is, shows that the first Christians mainly bore Greek names: Lydia, Epaphroditus, Euodia, Syntyche. Even Clement must have been a foreigner bearing as a single name a Roman *cognomen*, as is very common in the Greek-speaking provinces. Some of them could have been freedmen or even slaves.[35] Scholarship has often questioned the reliability of the whole passage regarding the figure of Lydia, both because her name—which is in fact an ethnic—is very uncommon and because there is no other evidence for a Jewish community in Philippi before the middle of the third century CE, when a synagogue is referred to in an epitaph for the first time.[36] Although archaeological or epigraphic evidence for a Jewish community in Philippi in the first century CE is lacking, there is no reason to reject the information given by Acts 16:13–14 that there were some Jews or at least some Jewish sympathizers in the colony. The narrative of Acts provides

---

l'altérité culturelle dans les civilisations de l'Antiquité, ed. Frédéric Colin, Olivier Huck, and Sylvie Vanséveren (Paris: de Boccard, 2015), 371–407.

35. Richard S. Ascough, *Paul's Macedonian Associations: The Social Context of Philippians and 1 Thessalonians*, WUNT 2/161 (Tübingen: Mohr Siebeck, 2003), 122–28.

36. Pilhofer, *Philippi*, 2.387a. For possible Semitic names in Philippi, see Pilhofer, *Philippi*, 2.381a; *CIPh* 2.1.23. For redactional versus historical elements in Lydia's story, see Jean-Pierre Sterck-Degueldre, *Eine Frau namens Lydia: Zu Geschichte und Komposition in Apostelgeschichte 16,11–15.40*, WUNT 2/176 (Tübingen: Mohr Siebeck, 2004); Richard S. Ascough, *Lydia: Paul's Cosmopolitan Hostess* (Collegeville, MN: Liturgical Press, 2009).

the only evidence for Jewish communities at the time of Paul's journeys for other cities as well, such as Thessalonica, Berea, and Corinth;[37] but unlike its accounts of these cities, and unlike its accounts of Pisidian Antioch and Athens as well (Acts 13:14; 17:1, 10, 17; 18:4), Acts makes no specific reference to Jews as a group or to a synagogue in Philippi, but only to Lydia as a Godfearer and to a modest "place of prayer," which probably was an outdoor meeting place located outside the city gate where Jewish sympathizers gathered on the Sabbath (whose existence Paul was not even sure of when he first entered Philippi according to Acts 16:13, οὗ ἐνομίζομεν προσευχὴν εἶναι). Lydia's characterization as a Godfearer (σεβομένη τὸν θεόν) in Acts 16:14 is consistent with similar descriptions of Judaizing pagans involved in the life of the local Jewish communities in Thessalonica, Athens, and Corinth (Acts 17:4, 17; 18:7). Therefore, one must admit that the Jewish community in the colony—if any—was probably very small.[38]

It, therefore, seems that the first Christian group in Philippi was chiefly made of Greek foreign residents settled in the Roman colony and included women, some of them being perhaps Jewish sympathizers coming from Asia Minor, as we are told about Lydia coming from Thyatira. This is consistent with the epigraphic evidence concerning the origin of foreign residents who settled in Philippi, primarily for commercial purposes, as Lydia did as a seller of purple. Philippi was integrated in a regional economic network corresponding to the northern shores of the Aegean basin extending from Thessalonica to the northwestern/western part of Asia Minor along the most used land (in this case the Egnatian Way) and sea routes.[39] Paul himself participated in this network when he sailed from Alexandria Troas (another Roman colony) to Neapolis-Kavala, crossing from Asia Minor into Macedonia. The fact that Paul's audience during his earliest preaching in Macedonia was made up of pagan Greeks—rather than Jews, as had chiefly been the case in Asia Minor—might explain, as James Ware argues, why the apostle put such

---

37. Ascough, *Associations*, 192–202.

38. Cédric Brélaz, "'Outside the City Gate': Center and Periphery in Paul's Preaching in Philippi," in *The Urban World and the First Christians*, ed. Steve Walton, Paul Trebilco, and David Gill (Grand Rapids: Eerdmans, 2017), 123–40.

39. Cédric Brélaz, "Philippi: A Roman Colony within Its Regional Context," in *Les communautés du Nord égéen au temps de l'hégémonie romaine: Entre ruptures et continuités*, ed. Julien Fournier and Maria-Gabriella G. Parissaki, Meletemata 77 (Athens: National Hellenic Research Foundation, 2018), 163–82.

an emphasis on the "mission of the church" to deliver the gospel to the gentiles in his letter to the Philippians.[40]

Two groups seem to have been excluded from Paul's preaching: the native Thracians and the Italian colonists. Most of the Thracians belonging to the colony of Philippi were settled in the countryside, as shown by dozens of inscriptions referring to Thracian names and to Thracian rural communities known in Latin as *vici*, or "villages," found throughout the assumed colonial territory.[41] The fact that Paul predominantly met Greeks involved in manufacture and trade activities among the foreign residents in Philippi and, perhaps, especially with people active in the textile sector (as would also be the case in Corinth, where the apostle worked as a tentmaker according to Acts 18:2–3) confirms that Pauline Christianity was essentially an urban phenomenon. Paul does not, however, seem to have had an audience among the Roman colonists, although these must have represented a significant part of the inner-city population. Paradoxically enough, the only interaction Paul had with the Italian elites of the colony was when he was arrested and flogged by the duumvirs after the master of the prophetess complained before them about Paul's preaching (see §3 below). Although he was a Roman citizen like the colonists, as he referred to it himself in order to be freed from jail (Acts 16:37), he and the Italian colonists came from to different cultural and social backgrounds. Furthermore, there is no unquestionable evidence that Paul did know Latin.[42] As a Jew raised in a Greek city in the Roman East, Paul was keen to address a Greek-speaking audience, whether they were Jewish or not. In first-century Philippi Greek was not yet widespread among the Italian colonists. While some of them may have been fluent in Greek already, there was no systematic bilingualism among the local elites at that time. We cannot be sure that the officials who ordered the apostle to be put in jail were able to speak Greek, but it is likely that their officers, the ῥαβδοῦχοι or lictors

---

40. James P. Ware, *The Mission of the Church in Paul's Letter to the Philippians in the Context of Ancient Judaism*, NovTSup 120 (Leiden: Brill, 2005).

41. Cédric Brélaz and Georges Tirologos, "Essai de reconstitution du territoire de la colonie de Philippes: Sources, méthodes et interprétations," in *Espaces et territoires des colonies romaines d'Orient*, ed. Hadrien Bru, Guy Labarre, and Georges Tirologos (Besançon: Presses Universitaires de Franche-Comté, 2016), 119–89.

42. Peter van Minnen, "Paul the Roman Citizen," *JSNT* 56 (1994): 43–52; Stanley E. Porter, "Did Paul Speak Latin?," in *Paul: Jew, Greek, and Roman*, ed. Stanley E. Porter, Pauline Studies 5 (Leiden: Brill, 2008), 289–308.

(usually Roman citizens of lower social status)—the ones who probably flogged Paul and Silas and who were then sent to the prison to tell them they were free (Acts 16:35-38)—could speak Greek, and the "prison guard" (δεσμοφύλαξ) who was converted (Acts 16:23-36), too, this task being often assigned to public slaves.[43]

3. The Political and Legal Institutions in Philippi and the Context of Paul's Arrest

Scholarship has rightly pointed out how accurate the description of Philippi in Acts 16:12 as being a Roman colony is—with the use of the term κολωνεία, transliterated from Latin, rather than the more customary Greek word ἀποικία, which is used, for instance, by Strabo to refer to Roman colonies as well (*Geogr.* 12.3.6, 11).[44] None of the other Roman colonies visited by Paul is specified as such in Acts (Pisidian Antioch, Lystra, Iconium, Alexandria Troas, Corinth). The mention of the first "district" (μερίς) of the Roman province of Macedonia, to which Philippi belonged, also stresses the administrative framework of the colony. Peter Pilhofer has convincingly argued that the *lectio difficilior* in the textual transmission of the passage (ἥτις ἐστὶν πρώτης μερίδος τῆς Μακεδονίας πόλις, κολωνεία rather than ἥτις ἐστὶν πρώτη τῆς μερίδος Μακεδονίας πόλις, κολωνεία, meaning that Philippi was "a city of the first district of Macedonia"), should be preferred since it provides information that more accurately reflects the administrative realities of Roman Macedonia.[45] Some scholars, including Pilhofer, have argued that the accuracy of the description of Philippi's status suggests that the author of Acts (possibly Luke, as has been suggested) was himself from Macedonia and consequently possessed deep knowledge about the province.[46] One should note, however, that this was in no way specific to Philippi in Acts and that

---

43. Cédric Brélaz, *La sécurité publique en Asie Mineure sous le Principat (Ier–IIIe s. ap. J.-C.): Institutions municipales et institutions impériales dans l'Orient romain* (Basel: Schwabe, 2005), 74–85, 177–79.

44. See Athanasios D. Rizakis, *Achaïe, II: La cité de Patras; Épigraphie et histoire*, Meletemata 25 (Athens: National Hellenic Research Foundation, 1998), no. 363.

45. Pilhofer, *Philippi*, 1:159–65. For an opposite interpretation, see Richard S. Ascough, "Civic Pride at Philippi: The Text-Critical Problem of Acts 16.12," *NTS* 44 (1998): 93–103.

46. Pilhofer, *Philippi*, 1:153–59.

the author of the narrative, whoever he was, employed the same attention to detail in his referring to the exact titles of local officials in Thessalonica (Acts 17:6–8) and in Ephesus (Acts 19:35), as well as in his depictions of how justice operated in the provinces of the Roman Empire in general (Acts 18:12–17; 25:8–12; 26:30–32). To further complicate matters, there is the added possibility that the word κολωνεία was an interpolation, since it stands in apposition to πόλις. It could have been added as a comment on Philippi's status in order to make it clear that, unlike most other local communities in the Greek-speaking provinces, Philippi was a part of the Roman state.[47]

As a political entity and local community, the colony of Philippi generally referred to itself in public inscriptions as a *res publica*.[48] After Greek started to be used in public contexts in the middle of the third century CE, the words πόλις or even δῆμος were used to express the same concept. The former was the most common term in Greek to refer to any political entity, whatever its precise status was, and the latter refers to a community.[49] Since πόλις was such a common term, Philippi was referred to as such in Acts 16:12 and 16:20. Contrary to what Pilhofer assumed, there is no need to see an implicit reference to the colony in Phil 3:20, where Paul asserts that the true "community" (πολίτευμα) for the Christians was in heaven and not on earth.[50] Although the term πολίτευμα can refer to a political entity, it usually describes a body lacking the formal institutions of a city, such as an association, an ethnic community (such as the Jews in Alexandria) or, during the Hellenistic period, a group of soldiers.[51] Instead of interpreting the passage as a comment on the local conditions in Philippi as a political community, the whole passage could, rather, be interpreted as a general condemnation of the attachment to earthly goods (Phil 3:19), emphasizing the significance of the afterlife for Christians and their claim that they will become a community of their own. Furthermore, Paul's assertion of his belonging to the tribe of Benjamin in Phil 3:5 should not be understood as implicit criticism of the identity of the local elites in Philippi, on the grounds that the colonists—like every Roman citizen, including Paul (although his tribe

---

47. For the reasons that might have led to this specification, see below.
48. See, e.g., *CIPh* 2.1.16, 29, 43, 45.
49. See, e.g., Pilhofer, *Philippi*, 2.22, 119, 301; *CIPh* 2.1.47, 64, 129.
50. Pilhofer, *Philippi*, 1:118–34.
51. Hans Förster and Patrick Sänger, "Ist unsere Heimat im Himmel? Überlegungen zur Semantik von πολίτευμα in Phil 3,20," *EC* 5 (2014): 149–77.

remains unknown to us)—belonged instead to a Roman electoral tribe, namely, the Voltinia. In this passage, the apostle states rather that his pride in his own Jewish identity and in being a Hebrew of the tribe of Benjamin vanished as soon as he acknowledged Christ.

Epigraphic evidence clearly shows that, since its refoundation as a colony, Philippi possessed the same Roman institutions that could be found in any other Roman colony throughout the empire. The colony of Philippi must have received bylaws by central power in Rome defining how local institutions should work, as we know from a copy of a such charter issued for the Caesarian colony of Urso in Baetica, southern Spain.[52] As soon as the first century CE, many inscriptions mentioning the political careers of the local elites refer to the various offices held by them and common to all of the Roman colonies, such as the offices of duumvirs, aediles, and quaestors. Few inscriptions explicitly refer to the concrete duties of local officials. One such inscription is the dedication by the two active aediles of a bronze statue of the personification of the Fairness of the Emperor (Aequitas Augusti) made of metal coming from counterfeit measuring instruments the two officials had seized and melted.[53] This illustrates the aediles' duties to police the marketplace. Among the recently published material, there are two more inscriptions involving duumvirs found in the sanctuary of the Thracian Rider-God (Hero Aulonites) located on the plain lying at the bottom of Mount Pangaion in Kipia. They seem to show that this most important sanctuary devoted to a native deity was to some extent run by the colony's officials, although the worship was not performed by public priests and its participants were, strictly speaking, not members of an official cult in the colony.[54]

Of special interest is the information given by epigraphic evidence about the careers of local elites. The inscriptions mentioning a *cursus honorum* are numerous enough to allow us to reconstruct how careers were usually shaped, and this a unique opportunity as far as Roman colonies in the East are concerned. A closer examination of the evidence allows insights into the sociology of local elites. It turns out that, in Philippi, local elites did not form a homogeneous group and that various types of careers

---

52. Michael H. Crawford, ed., *Roman Statutes* (London: Institute of Classical Studies, 1996), 1:393–454, no. 25. A new fragment of the charter has been recently added: *AE* 2006.645.

53. *CIPh* 2.1.17.

54. *CIPh* 2.1.158, 168.

were achieved at the same time by different people. Even if the greatest share of power was in the hands of a relatively small number of families, most of them descendants of the first Italian settlers, the people among them who met the property qualification required to enter the local council were numerous enough to make the integration of individuals of foreign or freeman origin unnecessary. The colonists did not need to open widely the council to new citizens to maintain the number of members, which may have been about one hundred. This could be an indication of the local demographics whereby a high number of Roman citizens were settled in Philippi from the beginning.[55] The competition in seeking offices, with only two new positions corresponding to the aediles available every year for junior officials, was so intense among local elites that most of the individuals elected in the council would in the end remain simple decuriones and would have no chance to hold an office. The major offices, especially the office of duumvir, were reserved for the members of the wealthiest and most prominent families. Before they reached the legal age to become full members of the council, the young men coming from those families were often given the title of an honorary decurio in order for them to gain early recognition as potential candidates and to be preselected for subsequent political careers.[56] We observed above that some inscriptions mention the people as a civic body in the colony (*populus*) as well as the "citizens" (*cives*).[57] Although no reference is made to electoral groups (the *curiae* or tribes) in the inscriptions from Philippi, there is no reason to doubt that public life in the colony, as in its counterparts elsewhere in Italy and in the provinces, both in the West and in the East, included the division of the

---

55. One should be very cautious in this regard when using demographic projections such as those provided by Barbara Levick, *Roman Colonies in Southern Asia Minor* (Oxford: Clarendon, 1967), 43–45, 92–96, 161–62; Peter Oakes, *Philippians: From People to Letter*, SNTSMS 110 (Cambridge: Cambridge University Press, 2001), 40–50. On the methodology and limits of demographic modeling, see Rinse Willet, "Whirlwind of Numbers—Demographic Experiments for Roman Corinth," *AncSoc* 42 (2012): 127–58.

56. Cédric Brélaz and Athanasios D. Rizakis, "Le fonctionnement des institutions et le déroulement des carrières dans la colonie de Philippes," *CCG* 14 (2003): 155–65; Cédric Brélaz, "Philippes: Le faciès institutionnel, social et religieux d'une colonie romaine dans la province de Macédoine," in *Philippes, de la Préhistoire à Byzance: Études d'archéologie et d'histoire*, BCH Supp 55, ed. Julien Fournier (Athens: École française d'Athènes, 2016), 199–214.

57. *CIPh* 2.1.6, 68.

citizens into such groups so that they could take part in the appointment of local officials during popular assemblies.[58] The narrative of Acts 16:22 also refers to the meeting of the people in the forum of Philippi, but this was a spontaneous gathering, not a formal popular assembly: the people running to the forum to see Paul and Silas is characterized in Acts as "a crowd" (ὁ ὄχλος), and this took place without any legal procedure.

The arrest, flogging, and imprisonment of Paul and Silas by the colony's officials in Acts 16:19–40 form, together with the conversion of Lydia, one of the two most emblematic scenes of the narrative about the apostle's visit to Philippi. The passage provides us with detailed information about the political and legal institutions in the colony and several other aspects that would have remained otherwise undocumented. The title of the highest officials of the colony, the *duumviri*, is properly translated into Greek as στρατηγοί in Acts 16:20, while in Acts 16:19 the word ἄρχοντες generically refers to local officials on the whole, to local "authorities," as it were.[59] As is made clear by epigraphic evidence, the exact title of the duumvirs in Philippi was *duumuir iure dicundo*, which means that those officials were responsible for the highest jurisdiction in the colony. Yet, Paul and Silas were ordered to be flogged and put into prison by the duumvirs without any trial (Acts 16:37: ἀκατακρίτους). In this case, the duumvirs were encouraged to act quickly because of the unexpected turn of events. After Paul exorcised an alleged prophetess he had met on his way to the place of prayer (Acts 16:16–19), her masters, who were furious at the apostle because they had lost their source of income, brought Paul and Silas before the duumvirs in the forum. Presumably, the duumvirs stood in one of the official buildings surrounding the square at that time, perhaps in the building lying on the western side of the forum, which has been identified—at least after the remodeling of the forum in the mid-second century—as a civil basilica, a building dedicated to the administrative and judicial activities of local officials.[60] Before the duumvirs, the masters of the prophetess complained about Paul's and Silas's preaching, referring to

---

58. Umberto Laffi, "La struttura costituzionale nei municipi e nelle colonie romane: Magistrati, decurioni, popolo," in *Gli Statuti Municipali*, ed. Luigi Capogrossi Colognesi and Emilio Gabba (Pavia: IUSS, 2006), 120–31.

59. Compare οἱ πρῶτοι τῆς πόλεως, referring to the local elites of the colony in Pisidian Antioch in Acts 13:50.

60. Michel Sève and Patrick Weber, "Peut-on parler d'une basilique civile au forum de Philippes?," in *Basiliques et agoras de Grèce et d'Asie Mineure*, ed. Laurence

them as Jews and blaming them for spreading foreign—namely, Jewish—customs that Roman citizens would have been forbidden to follow and for disrupting public order in the colony.[61] A crowd then started gathering in the forum because of the commotion and, having been incited against them, started shouting at Paul and Silas. The officials' decision to have Paul and Silas flogged and put in jail was a matter of law enforcement rather than jurisdiction (Acts 16:22-23). The duumvirs wanted above all to avoid a riot, as happened in many cities visited by Paul owing to the hostility of the local Jewish community (see, e.g., Acts 13:44-50; 17:5-9; 18:12-17). Civic life in the local communities of the Roman Empire was deeply influenced by the role of the mob. The people in the form of a crowd were able to put pressure on local elites and to express their will through shouting during formal popular assemblies as well as during informal gatherings in public spaces such as squares and theaters, such as when they requested benefactions from them or took part in the punishment of criminals in cases of mob justice.[62] The duumvirs' prompt reaction in Philippi should be compared to the decision of the secretary of the people in Ephesus when he dismissed the spontaneous gathering of the crowd in the theater when the goldsmiths rioted against the apostle, saying that such a gathering was illegal and that the only authority qualified to judge Paul, if he turned out to be guilty of sacrilege, was actually the Roman governor (Acts 19:29-40). The fact that the duumvirs ordered Paul to be freed the following morning demonstrates their primary concern with public order in Philippi. Paul's imprisonment was not meant as a punishment (and jail never was considered as such in Roman criminal law) but as a way to prevent unrest. The duumvirs' attitude was in no way unusual. Evidence from other sources shows that arbitrary arrests, physical violence, and corporal punishments due to Roman soldiers as well as local officials were a common phenomenon and were a regular part of law

---

Cavalier, Raymont Descat, and Jacques des Courtils (Bordeaux: Ausonius, 2012), 91-106.

61. For the interpretation of what these customs were, see Pilhofer, *Philippi*, 1:189-93. Craig S. de Vos argues that Paul and Silas were rather accused of practicing magic. Craig S. de Vos, "Finding a Charge That Fits: The Accusation against Paul and Silas at Philippi (Acts 16.19-21)," *JSNT* 74 (1999): 51-63.

62. Christina T. Kuhn, "Emotionality in the Political Culture of the Graeco-Roman East: The Role of Acclamations," in *Unveiling Emotions: Sources and Methods for the Study of Emotions in the Greek World*, ed. Angelos Chaniotis (Stuttgart: Steiner, 2012), 295-316.

enforcement during the policing stages of the legal criminal procedure in the Roman Empire.[63]

Despite the decision of the duumvirs to release Paul and Silas from jail the day after they had them arrested, the apostle refused to leave the jail and requested that the duumvirs come and apologize for what they had done. On that occasion, Paul mentioned that he was a Roman citizen and, as such, he could not be beaten or put to jail without any trial (Acts 16:37). From a legal point of view, Paul's argument was absolutely correct, just as it would be again when he was arrested in Jerusalem and then appealed in Caesarea to the emperor's court (Acts 22:25–29; 25:10–12).[64] Paul's legal arguments and emphasis on respecting procedure, regardless of any religious consideration, played a key role in his defense toward Roman authorities. These passages are some of the most explicit evidence for the legal privileges of being a Roman citizen.[65] The closest parallels for Paul's legal arguments can be found in one instance of martyrological literature, namely the Martyrdom of Pionius. During the persecution ordered by emperor Trajan Decius in 250, Pionius also contested the judicial procedure's lawfulness when he was unjustly arrested and questioned by a local official in Smyrna rather than by a governor's envoy.[66] The trend of apologetic Christian literature to demonstrate that the prosecution of martyrs by Roman authorities had no valid legal bases was intended to prove that Christians were doing no harm and that they were rather victims of the Roman judicial system's arbitrariness.[67] The whole passage about the arrest of Paul in Philippi might well have been fabricated by the author of Acts in order to enhance the alleged impact of the apostle's

---

63. Brélaz, *Sécurité*, 56–64, 271–75.

64. See Heike Omerzu, *Der Prozess des Paulus: Eine exegetische und rechtshistorische Untersuchung der Apostelgeschichte*, BZNW 115 (Berlin: de Gruyter, 2002). For the legal procedure leading to Paul's appeal, see Mariangela Ravizza, "Καίσαρα ἐπικαλοῦμαι: L'appello di Paolo di Tarso all'imperatore," in *Eparcheia, autonomia e civitas Romana: Studi sulla giurisdizione criminale dei governatori di provincia (II sec. a.C.–II d.C.)*, ed. Dario Mantovani and Luigi Pellecchi (Pavia: IUSS, 2010), 113–31.

65. Ekkehard Weber, "Das römische Bürgerrecht des Apostels Paulus," *Tyche* 27 (2012): 193–207.

66. Louis Robert, Glen W. Bowersock, and Christopher P. Jones, *Le martyre de Pionios, prêtre de Smyrne* (Washington, DC: Dumbarton Oaks Research Library and Collection, 1994), 41–43, §15.

67. Ari Z. Bryen, "Martyrdom, Rhetoric, and the Politics of Procedure," *ClAnt* 33 (2014): 243–80.

preaching in the cities he visited and to add dramatic events into the narrative. Nevertheless, this narrative is, from an institutional and legal point of view, perfectly consistent with what we know from other sources about the civic life in the colonies and about how law was enforced in the local communities of the Roman Empire. This shows, once again, the accuracy of the information regarding administration the author of Acts chose to put in his narrative and the great attention he was paying to the realities of power in the Roman Empire. In this respect, one wonders whether the characterization of Philippi as a Roman colony in the very beginning of the passage regarding the apostle's journey to Macedonia in Acts 16:12, perhaps an interpolation, as mentioned above, was not meant to make the arbitrary decision, coming later in the narrative, of local officials to put Paul in jail even more obvious. In any other Greek city local authorities would of course have been allowed neither to flog nor to imprison Roman citizens like Paul and Silas without trial.[68] But the fact that this occurred in a Roman colony, where the local magistrates themselves were Roman citizens too and were supposed to observe Roman law carefully, made the event even more outrageous and the whole story more striking.

4. The First Christian Group and the Religious Landscape of the Roman Colony

Epigraphic and archaeological evidence informs us about dozens of deities who were worshiped by the local population in Roman Philippi. Most evidence dates back to the second and third century CE, but we can confidently assume that many cults were already present at the time of Paul's visit. One can roughly divide the deities worshiped and the types of cults in the colony into three different groups, corresponding to each one of the main ethnic and cultural categories known among local population in Roman Philippi.

First, there were cults brought to Philippi by the Italian settlers at the time when the colony was founded. This is especially true for typically Italic agrarian deities, who are very scarcely documented in the provinces, especially in the East, such as Silvanus and Vertumnus.[69] The refoundation

---

68. Julien Fournier, *Entre tutelle romaine et autonomie civique: L'administration judiciaire dans les provinces hellénophones de l'empire romain (129 av. J.-C.–235 apr. J.-C.)* (Athens: École française d'Athènes, 2010), 364–65.

69. Pilhofer, *Philippi*, 2.28a, 148, 163–66, 515.

of Philippi as a Roman colony also implied the creation of a sacred area where the worship of the tutelary gods of the Roman state occurred. As mentioned above, this area was located in Philippi on the upper terrace of the forum, where several temples presumably stood. Dedications to Jupiter, and in particular to Jupiter Optimus Maximus, illustrate the introduction of the Roman pantheon to the colony.[70] The earliest evidence for imperial cult in Philippi dates from the time of Claudius.[71] At the time of Paul's visit, a place devoted to the worship of the emperor and his relatives seems to have already stood in the northeastern corner of the lower terrace in the forum (where the base supporting the statues of the priestesses of deified Livia would be built in the Flavian period, and later in the Antonine age the temple of the imperial cult), as suggested by a dedication to emperor Claudius's father found in this area.[72] However, the imperial cult should not be considered a specifically Italian phenomenon. Even if Roman citizens—either of Western origin or foreigners having gained citizenship—seem to have been involved in the launch of the imperial cult in Greek cities in Asia Minor, the imperial cult was spread throughout the Roman East as early as the early 20s BCE.[73]

Second, there were Greek gods who had been imported in eastern Macedonia by the first Thasian settlers of the area during the archaic period and later by the Macedonians after King Philip II seized the Thasian settlement of Krenides. One of these gods was Apollo.[74] Isis together with the so-called Egyptian gods could be included with the Greek deities as well, since these cults, in spite of their Egyptian origin, were reshaped by Greeks and spread during the Hellenistic period.[75] One might add the evidence from Acts to the Greek cults that are known to us thanks to archaeology and to the inscriptions. Apart from a group of Judaizing pagans, the narrative, as mentioned above, refers to a prophetess who allegedly had divinatory skills. Even if we cannot be sure of the reliability of the story

---

70. Pilhofer, *Philippi*, 2.178, 186, 223, 384, 473, 514, 588; *AE* 2012.1377; *CIPh* 2.1.225.

71. *CIPh* 2.1.6, 66.

72. *CIPh* 2.1.5.

73. François Kirbihler, "César, Auguste et l'Asie: Continuités et évolutions de deux politiques," in *César sous Auguste*, ed. Olivier Devillers and Karin Sion-Jenkins (Bordeaux: Ausonius, 2012), 125–44.

74. Pilhofer, *Philippi*, 2.191, 246, 359, 509b, 642a (see *CIPh* 2.1, app. 1, 368–69); *SEG* 59:691.

75. Pilhofer, *Philippi*, 2.175, 190–93, 255, 506, 581; *CIPh* 2.1.23, 54–55, 134, 193.

regarding the prophetess in Acts, the invocation of the "Highest God" (Acts 16:17: ὁ θεὸς ὁ ὕψιστος) in Philippi is still likely, since the cult of Zeus Hypsistos, for instance, seems to have originated in Macedonia. The fact that the prophetess recognized in Paul and Silas worshipers (or "slaves," δοῦλοι) of the "Highest God" may be seen as another confirmation of the theory that this name could also be given a Judaizing interpretation in some instances and that empirical syncretism could connect the Almighty God worshiped by Paul with monotheistic trends within paganism.[76]

Finally, there were the native Thracian cults. The major native deity in Philippi was the so-called Thracian Rider-God, as he is usually called in scholarship, who was named Hero Aulonites in the votive inscriptions—Aulonites being a local or regional epithet—or Dominus (or Deus Magnus) Rincaleus in the rock reliefs on the acropolis. This god, whose cult was widespread throughout the culturally Thracian region, from the Balkans to northwestern Anatolia, was very often depicted on gravestones because of his chthonian attributes. A sanctuary in Kipia at the bottom of the Mount Pangaion was specifically dedicated to him.[77] Because of a historical and cultural change, which can be verified in all of the Roman colonies in the East, this regional deity started to be depicted on coins minted by the colony in the middle of the third century CE, when this type replaced the traditional Roman iconography that had been used thus far.[78]

This brief characterization of the deities according to the cultural background to which they originally belonged does not imply that there were no interactions between these cults, nor that there was a specialization of the cults depending on who was the worshiper and on ethnicity, nor even that religious life in Roman Philippi was made of hermetic and homogeneous cultural and social groups.[79] On the contrary, syncretism

---

76. Stephen Mitchell, "Further Thoughts on the Cult of Theos Hypsistos," in *One God: Pagan Monotheism in the Roman Empire*, ed. Stephen Mitchell and Peter van Nuffelen (Cambridge: Cambridge University Press, 2010), 167–208.

77. *CIPh* 2.1, pp. 52–55.

78. Michel Amandry, "Le monnayage de la Res Publica Coloniae Philippensium. Nouvelles données," in *Fides: Contributions to Numismatics in Honor of Richard B. Witschonke*, ed. Peter G. van Alfen, Gilles Bransbourg, and Michel Amandry (New York: American Numismatic Society, 2015), 495–507. See also Constantina Katsari and Stephen Mitchell, "The Roman Colonies of Greece and Asia Minor: Questions of State and Civic Identity," *Athenaeum* 96 (2008): 221–49.

79. Cédric Brélaz, "Thracian, Greek, or Roman? Ethnic and Social Identities of Worshippers (and Gods) in Roman Philippi," in *Philippi, from Colonia Augusta to*

was a very common phenomenon in Philippi, and Thracian deities in particular were often assimilated to their Greek or Roman counterparts. For that reason, in order to be able to assess the cultural identity of a god in all its aspects, we have to pay attention to the epithets given to the gods as well as to the deities' attributes as they are depicted in iconography, which usually impart much about the local reception of the deities and about the specific form in which they were worshiped. For instance, the god who was worshiped by Thracians since the Hellenistic period in a dedicated sanctuary in the ancient settlement located on the site of the modern town of Drama was named Dionysos in Greek dedications but Liber Pater in Latin. In some instances in the colony's territory, Liber Pater bore an additional Thracian epithet, Tasibastenus.[80] This suggests that, in the cult of Liber Pater in eastern Macedonia, rather than the Italic god, the corresponding indigenous deity was worshiped, who was recognized at an early stage as Dionysos by the Greeks, who themselves claimed a Thracian origin for this god. In the same way, the detailed study of the iconography of the goddess who was named Diana on the dedications accompanying the reliefs carved on the acropolis has shown that the model for the depiction of the deity, in spite of some regional features borrowed from the attributes of the Thracian deity Bendis, was in reality the Greek Artemis, who was already worshiped in Philippi in the fourth century BCE.[81]

On the other hand, worshiping Thracian deities was not peculiar to natives nor limited to the countryside, where the native population was predominant. The Hero God was depicted on several reliefs in the acropolis as well as on many funerary stelae and sarcophagi in the urban necropolises of Philippi, including tombs belonging to the elites of Italian origin, because of the eschatological dimension of the cult.[82] The sanctuary of the Hero Aulonites in Kipia was also visited by Italian colonists and by Roman soldiers passing by.[83] Conversely, typical Roman deities were also worshiped outside the city, and not only by Roman citizens. Dedications to Jupiter, in this case together with an indigenous deity called

---

Communitas Christiana: Religion and Society in Transition, ed. Steven J. Friesen et al. (Leiden: Brill, forthcoming).

80. Pilhofer, *Philippi*, 2.338–39, 341–42, 408, 417, 501b, 501c, 524, 525.

81. Paul Collart and Pierre Ducrey, *Philippes I: Les reliefs rupestres*, BCHSupp 2 (Athens: École française d'Athènes, 1975), 222–25.

82. See, e.g., *CIPh* 2.1.112, 114, 144, 193.

83. Pilhofer, *Philippi*, 2.580, 619, 621; *CIPh* 2.1.76, 78, 81, 111, 158, 168.

Myndrytus, and even to the Italic agrarian god Vertumnus were erected by Thracians in the territory of the colony, as far as the valley of Prossotsani or the area of the Pangaion.[84] The funerary ceremonies known as the Rosalia and the Parentalia, commemorating the deceased, which were imported to eastern Macedonia from Italy by the Roman colonists, were adopted by the native population as well.[85] All of this suggests that there was no segmentation of religious practice in the Roman colony of Philippi along the lines of ethnic or cultural categorization. Deities and cults were not brought together in groups formed on the basis of their supposed cultural origins, nor reserved for categories of worshipers presenting the same cultural characteristics. Neither the deities attested in the colony nor the worshipers were divided into distinctly homogeneous and exclusive groups. As time went on, during the second and especially the third century CE, the division between the different categories of deities, such as the division between the different ethnic and cultural groups forming the society in Philippi, became smoother owing to interaction and mutual influence. During the first hundred years or so after the colony was founded, however, the various deities must have had stronger identities, and, at the time when the apostle Paul visited Philippi, there was most likely a sharper distinction between the cults that the Roman settlers had just brought to Philippi from Italy (e.g., Jupiter Optimus Maximus or Silvanus) and the gods who had already been worshiped for a long time in the area, either by the Greeks (e.g., Artemis) or by the native population (e.g., the Hero God), or by both of them (e.g., Dionysos).

Apart from the rites that were performed by official priests (pontiffs, augurs, flamines) on behalf of the public as a whole and, as in any other Roman colony, were part of the official life of the community, in Roman Philippi religion was a private matter.[86] Cultic associations, which were part of the Greco-Roman conception of togetherness and social relations,[87] played a major role in that sphere. Many inscriptions refer to the existence of such clubs in Philippi, using various names (*collegium, consacrani, cultores, thiasus,* θρησκευταί, μύσται), as well as to their internal structure and

---

84. Pilhofer, *Philippi*, 2.514–15.

85. See, e.g., Pilhofer, *Philippi*, 2.29, 133, 512, 524, 597, 636, 644; *AE* 2012.1382.

86. Audrey Bertrand, *La religion publique des colonies dans l'Italie républicaine et impériale* (Rome: École française de Rome, 2015).

87. Paulin Ismard, *La cité des réseaux: Athènes et ses associations VIe–Ier siècle av. J.-C.* (Paris: Publications de la Sorbonne, 2010).

management, especially regarding the grants made to them by individuals. As recent scholarship on early Christianity has convincingly argued, the first group established by Paul in Philippi was originally organized in a way similar to the non-Christian cultic and occupational associations.[88] As stated by the apostle himself in the letter to the Philippians, the community had its own officials and managed the financial resources that would help sustain Paul during his journeys.[89] The cultic associations attested in the colony that were most similar to the Christian group with respect to the social background of its members were certainly the brotherhood of Silvanus in Philippi and the brotherhood of Apollo in Drama.[90] Both gathered Roman citizens, freedmen, foreigners (Thracians and Greeks), and, in the case of the Silvanus club, even slaves belonging to individuals as well as to the colony. The cognomina borne by the Roman citizens show that most of them were the descendants of foreigners or of freedmen. Thus, the upper class of the colonists did not take part in these two associations, and their members—even if they were of very different status (Roman citizens, freedmen, free foreigners, slaves)—all represented the middle to middle-lower levels of the Philippian society. The social composition of these two cultic associations might illustrate what could also have been the audience of the early Christian group in Philippi, except that, as mentioned above, no Thracians are known among the first followers of Paul, and most of them were Greeks. The apparent absence of Thracians among Christians in Philippi even in later times might be surprising, given that some of the native cults attested in eastern Macedonia during the Roman Imperial period seem to have shared common concerns with the Christian message and had similar theological beliefs, such as the eschatological prospects included in the cult of the Hero God or the initiation rites performed by the Dionysiac/Orphic clubs.[91] The absence of Thracians highlights the Christian group's focus on the Greeks settled in the town of Philippi.

---

88. Ascough, *Associations*; Julien M. Ogereau, *Paul's Koinonia with the Philippians. A Socio-historical Investigation of a Pauline Economic Partnership*, WUNT 2/377 (Tübingen: Mohr Siebeck, 2014).

89. Lemerle, *Philippes*, 52–56; Pilhofer, *Philippi*, 1:140–47, 226–27; Ascough, *Associations*, 129–61.

90. Pilhofer, *Philippi*, 2.163–66, 509b (= *AE* 2006.1339).

91. Collart, *Philippes*, 413–23; Pilhofer, *Philippi*, 2.166a (= *AE* 2006.1337), 340, 439, 535, 568, 597. See Pilhofer, *Philippi*, 1:240–45.

Furthermore, the Silvanus and Apollo brotherhoods differed from the Christian group in several crucial respects: (1) as suggested by the epigraphic catalogs listing the names of their members, their size probably exceeded the first community comprising Paul's followers by a large margin; (2) these brotherhoods, although they included people from different social statuses, apparently did not welcome women; (3) these associations used Latin to display their member lists (certainly because the worship of Silvanus was introduced to the colony by Italian settlers and because most members of the brotherhood of Apollo in Drama were originally natives and were not reluctant to use the language of the colonists), whereas the Christian group in Philippi was exclusively Greek-speaking.[92] On the other hand, by describing the groups he had formed around him in Philippi, just as he had in other places in Greece and Asia Minor, as ἐκκλησίαι (Phil 4:15), Paul was deliberately distinguishing them from other cultic associations. The term *ekklēsia* was rather unusual for private associations, and, during Roman imperial times, it continued to refer to popular assemblies in Greek cities.[93] In borrowing this word from the lexicon of the civic and political institutions, Paul's intention was probably to emphasize the uniqueness of the Christian message. The Christian groups were not intended to be associations like any other cultic club. On the contrary, they were meant to become a community on their own or a πολίτευμα, as stated by Paul in Phil 3:20, which would be able to challenge the ordinary secular institutions.[94]

Conclusion: Why Philippi?
Philippian and Christian Connectivity within the Roman East

According to Acts, Philippi has apparently been a very emblematic place for early Christianity, and as such it has received much attention from New

---

92. We only know of two Christian inscriptions in Latin of a later date (Pilhofer, *Philippi*, 2.111–12).

93. Henri-Louis Fernoux, *Le Demos et la Cité: Communautés et assemblées populaires en Asie Mineure à l'époque impériale* (Rennes: Presses Universitaires de Rennes, 2011); Cédric Brélaz, "Democracy and Civic Participation in Greek Cities under Roman Imperial Rule: Political Practice and Culture in the Post-Classical Period," *CHS Research Bulletin* 4 (2016): https://tinyurl.com/SBL4216f.

94. Anna C. Miller, *Corinthian Democracy: Democratic Discourse in 1 Corinthians*, PTMS 220 (Eugene, OR: Pickwick, 2015); Young-Ho Park, *Paul's Ekklesia as a Civic Assembly: Understanding the People of God in Their Politico-social World*, WUNT 2/393 (Tübingen: Mohr Siebeck, 2015).

Testament scholarship. The significance Philippi gained as a city in the early Byzantine Empire has often been retrospectively considered a justification for Paul visiting the colony in the mid-first century. Still, it is worth asking: Why Philippi? According to Strabo, Philippi was a "small settlement" (κατοικία μικρά) in late Hellenistic times until the battle of 42 BCE (*Geogr.* 7, frag. 17a).[95] Even if it "grew" (ηὐξήθη) after it was refounded as a Roman colony, as recognized by Strabo, the city remained a medium-sized local community in the eastern Mediterranean. Philippi was not a world-class city like Corinth, which, only a hundred years after it was rebuilt by Caesar, had regained its historical position as a major commercial hub and leading city in mainland Greece, hosting the proconsul of Achaia's headquarters and resuming the Isthmian games, which the city used to organize until its destruction in 146 BCE. Neither was Philippi as thriving and powerful as the Roman colony of Pisidian Antioch, which had a close relationship with the emperors (as shown by the fact that, unlike in Philippi, the office of duumvir had been several times offered to the emperor and his relatives in order to honor them during the first century CE),[96] and where we know of seven families of senatorial rank and many knights who reached key positions in the imperial administration. As lavish as the monumentalized city center may have appeared to visitors in the mid-first century CE, Philippi should rather be compared to other Eastern Roman colonies of a similar size, such as Dyrrachium, Dium, Patras, Alexandria Troas, or Berytus. Philippi was undoubtedly an important city, but its influence was limited to a regional scale in eastern Macedonia, and the colony could compete neither with Thessalonica, which served as the proconsul of Macedonia's headquarters, nor with Berea, which was the capital city of the Macedonian *koinon*.

Moreover, there was no significant Jewish community at that time in Philippi. Unlike in most cities he had visited, Paul did not find a synagogue in Philippi, and the first people he met in the colony happened to be not native Jews but Godfearers. In some cases, Paul passed over cities, as important as they might have been, probably because there was no significant Jewish community there. This seems to have been the case in neighboring Amphipolis. This free city lay, like Philippi, on the Egnatian

---

95. Strabo, *Strabons Geographica*, vol. 2, *Buch V–VIII: Text und Übersetzung*, ed. S. Radt. Göttingen (Vandenhoeck & Ruprecht, 2003).

96. Michel Christol and Thomas Drew-Bear, "Un nouveau notable d'Antioche de Pisidie et les préfets de *duumviri* de la colonie," *AnAnt* 10 (2002): 277–89.

Way. Amphipolis had been a very important city in late Hellenistic times. It was the capital of the first district of the Roman province of Macedonia, and a large community of Roman citizens had settled there for commercial reasons, taking advantage of its harbor. Still, Paul only passed through the city on his way from Philippi to Thessalonica (Acts 17:1). The main reason why Paul stayed in Philippi is that the city was the first stop on the Egnatian Way for travelers, like Paul, who were coming by boat from Asia Minor to Macedonia via Neapolis. By this fortuitous reason alone, we could not have predicted the importance that Paul's visit would have for the apostle's missions on the whole and for the future of Christianity in Greece. As time progressed, the community in Philippi had become by the second century crucial for interactions between early Christian groups of Asia Minor and of mainland Greece.[97]

In mid-first-century Philippi, the two or maybe three visits of the apostle must have had a limited impact on the life of the colony, apart from, perhaps, the unrest caused by Paul's exorcism of the prophetess and by his hearing led by the duumvirs in the forum, if the story is reliable. Through his appearances in front of the highest local officials in Philippi's public square—the heart of the Roman colony—the apostle was suddenly given a centrality that he had been previously denied in the narrative, in contrast to Paul's first meeting "outside the city gate" with Godfearers (Acts 16:13). By writing about Paul in this way, the author of Acts intended to suggest that the apostle and the Christian message ultimately reached a public dimension, and—paradoxically enough—almost gained an official recognition through the apostle's flogging and imprisonment in Philippi. This was part of the author's strategy in trying to prove the immediate significance of Paul's preaching in the cities as soon as he visited them in the mid-first century.[98] In the religious landscape of Philippi and among the numerous cultic associations known at the time of Paul's visit, however, the Christian *ekklēsia*, at first, involved only very few people. Still, this small community played a major role in the success of Paul's missions in Greece. On several occasions, Paul himself highlighted the remarkable faithfulness that the first Christian group he founded in Macedonia had toward him, and the material and financial support he always received from it (Phil 1:7–8; 2:25; 4:10–18; 2 Cor 8:1–5). These

---

97. Brélaz, "Colony."
98. Brélaz, "Gate."

strong ties between the Philippians and the apostle were pointed out by Polycarp, bishop of Smyrna, and Tertullian as early as the second century (Polycarp, *Phil.* 3; 9.1; Tertullian, *Praescr.* 36.1–2). Long after Paul's visits, in a time when Christianity would become the predominant religion of the Roman Empire, at the beginning of the fourth century, the Philippian church continued to capitalize on the memory of the apostle and openly claimed its apostolic origins, as made clear by the fact that the first cathedral church was dedicated to Paul and that a martyrial cult was launched in his honor.[99]

Bibliography

Amandry, Michel. "Le monnayage de la Res Publica Coloniae Philippensium: Nouvelles données." Pages 495–507 in *Fides: Contributions to Numismatics in Honor of Richard B. Witschonke*. Edited by Peter G. van Alfen, Gilles Bransbourg, and Michel Amandry. New York: American Numismatic Society, 2015.

Ascough, Richard S. "Civic Pride at Philippi: The Text-Critical Problem of Acts 16.12." *NTS* 44 (1998): 93–103.

———. *Lydia: Paul's Cosmopolitan Hostess*. Collegeville, MN: Liturgical Press, 2009.

———. *Paul's Macedonian Associations: The Social Context of Philippians and 1 Thessalonians*. WUNT 2/161. Tübingen: Mohr Siebeck, 2003.

Bartels, Jens. *Städtische Eliten im römischen Makedonien: Untersuchungen zur Formierung und Struktur*. Berlin: de Gruyter, 2008.

Baslez, Marie-Françoise. "Paul et l'émergence d'un monde 'gréco-romain' Réflexions sur la romanité de l'apôtre." Pages 29–45 in *Paul's Graeco-Roman Context*. Edited by Cilliers Breytenbach. Leuven: Peeters, 2015.

---

99. Jean-Pierre Sodini, "L'architecture religieuse de Philippes, entre Rome, Thessalonique et Constantinople," *CRAI* 2014: 1509–42; Cédric Brélaz, "Entre Philippe II, Auguste et Paul: La commémoration des origines dans la colonie romaine de Philippes," in *Une mémoire en actes: Espaces, figures et discours dans le monde romain*, ed. Stéphane Benoist, Anne Daguet-Gagey, and Christine Hoët-van Cauwenberghe (Lille: Presses Universitaires du Septentrion, 2016), 119–38; Cédric Brélaz, "The Authority of Paul's Memory and Early Christian Identity at Philippi," in *Authority and Identity in Emerging Christianities in Asia Minor and Greece*, ed. Cilliers Breytenbach and Julien M. Ogereau (Leiden: Brill, 2018), 240–66.

Bertrand, Audrey. *La religion publique des colonies dans l'Italie républicaine et impériale*. Rome: École française de Rome, 2015.

Brélaz, Cédric. "The Authority of Paul's Memory and Early Christian Identity at Philippi." Pages 240–66 in *Authority and Identity in Emerging Christianities in Asia Minor and Greece*. Edited by Cilliers Breytenbach and Julien M. Ogereau. Leiden: Brill, 2018.

———. "Democracy and Civic Participation in Greek Cities under Roman Imperial Rule: Political Practice and Culture in the Post-Classical Period." *CHS Research Bulletin* 4.2 (2016): https://tinyurl.com/SBL4216f.

———. "Entre Philippe II, Auguste et Paul: La commémoration des origines dans la colonie romaine de Philippes." Pages 119–38 in *Une mémoire en actes: Espaces, figures et discours dans le monde romain*. Edited by Stéphane Benoist, Anne Daguet-Gagey, and Christine Hoët-van Cauwenberghe. Lille: Presses Universitaires du Septentrion, 2016.

———. "La langue des *incolae* sur le territoire de Philippes et les contacts linguistiques dans les colonies romaines d'Orient." Pages 371–407 in *Interpretatio: Traduire l'altérité culturelle dans les civilisations de l'Antiquité*. Edited by Frédéric Colin, Olivier Huck, and Sylvie Vanséveren. Paris: de Boccard, 2015.

———. *La sécurité publique en Asie Mineure sous le Principat (Ier–IIIe s. ap. J.-C.): Institutions municipales et institutions impériales dans l'Orient romain*. Basel: Schwabe, 2005.

———. "Le *Corpus des inscriptions grecques et latines de Philippes*: Apports récents et perspectives de recherche sur une colonie romaine d'Orient." *CRAI* 2014: 1463–1507.

———. "'Outside the City Gate': Center and Periphery in Paul's Preaching in Philippi." Pages 123–40 in *The Urban World and the First Christians*. Edited by Steve Walton, Paul Trebilco, and David Gill. Grand Rapids: Eerdmans, 2017.

———. "Philippes: Le faciès institutionnel, social et religieux d'une colonie romaine dans la province de Macédoine." Pages 199–214 in *Philippes, de la Préhistoire à Byzance: Études d'archéologie et d'histoire*. Edited by Julien Fournier. BCH Supp 55. Athens: École française d'Athènes, 2016.

———. "Philippi: A Roman Colony within Its Regional Context." Pages 163–82 in *Les communautés du Nord égéen au temps de l'hégémonie romaine: Entre ruptures et continuités*. Edited by Julien Fournier and

Maria-Gabriella G. Parissaki. Meletemata 77. Athens: National Hellenic Research Foundation, 2018.

———. "Thracian, Greek, or Roman? Ethnic and Social Identities of Worshippers (and Gods) in Roman Philippi." In *Philippi, from Colonia Augusta to Communitas Christiana: Religion and Society in Transition.* Edited by Steven J. Friesen et al. Leiden: Brill, forthcoming.

Brélaz, Cédric, and Julien Demaille. "Traces du passé macédonien et influences de l'hellénisme dans les colonies de Dion et de Philippes." Pages 119–56 in *L'héritage grec des colonies romaines d'Orient: Interactions culturelles dans les provinces hellénophones de l'empire romain.* Edited by Cédric Brélaz. Paris: de Boccard, 2017.

Brélaz, Cédric, and Athanasios D. Rizakis. "Le fonctionnement des institutions et le déroulement des carrières dans la colonie de Philippes." *CCG* 14 (2003): 155–65.

Brélaz, Cédric, and Georges Tirologos. "Essai de reconstitution du territoire de la colonie de Philippes: Sources, méthodes et interprétations." Pages 119–89 in *Espaces et territoires des colonies romaines d'Orient.* Edited by Hadrien Bru, Guy Labarre, and Georges Tirologos. Besançon: Presses Universitaires de Franche-Comté, 2016.

Bryen, Ari Z. "Martyrdom, Rhetoric, and the Politics of Procedure." *ClAnt* 33 (2014): 243–80.

Cébeillac-Gervasoni, Mireille, and Laurent Lamoine, eds. *Les élites et leurs facettes: Les élites locales dans le monde hellénistique et romain.* Rome: École française de Rome, 2003.

Christol, Michel, and Thomas Drew-Bear. "Un nouveau notable d'Antioche de Pisidie et les préfets de *duumviri* de la colonie." *AnAnt* 10 (2002): 277–89.

Collart, Paul. *Philippes: Ville de Macédoine, depuis ses origines jusqu'à la fin de l'époque romaine.* Paris: de Boccard, 1937.

Collart, Paul, and Pierre Ducrey. *Philippes I: Les reliefs rupestres.* BCHSupp 2. Athens: École française d'Athènes, 1975.

Crawford, Michael H., ed. *Roman Statutes.* 2 vols. London: Institute of Classical Studies, 1996.

Dana, Dan. *Onomasticon Thracicum: Répertoire des noms indigènes de Thrace, Macédoine orientale, Mésies, Dacie et Bithynie.* Meletemata 70. Athens: National Hellenic Research Foundation, 2014.

Ducrey, Pierre. "100 ans de fouilles et de recherches de l'École française d'Athènes à Philippes (1914–2014)." *CRAI* 2014: 1449–62.

Fernoux, Henri-Louis. *Le Demos et la Cité: Communautés et assemblées populaires en Asie Mineure à l'époque impériale*. Rennes: Presses Universitaires de Rennes, 2011.

Förster, Hans, and Patrick Sänger. "Ist unsere Heimat im Himmel? Überlegungen zur Semantik von πολίτευμα in Phil 3,20." *EC* 5 (2014): 149–77.

Fournier, Julien. *Entre tutelle romaine et autonomie civique: L'administration judiciaire dans les provinces hellénophones de l'empire romain (129 av. J.-C.–235 apr. J.-C.)*. Athens: École française d'Athènes, 2010.

Friesen, Steven J. "The Wrong Erastus: Ideology, Archaeology, and Exegesis." Pages 231–56 in *Corinth in Context: Comparative Studies on Religion and Society*. Edited by Steven J. Friesen, Daniel N. Schowalter, and James C. Walters. NovTSup 134. Leiden: Brill, 2010.

Halfmann, Helmut. "Italische Ursprünge bei Rittern und Senatoren aus Kleinasien." Pages 165–87 in *Tra Oriente e Occidente: Indigeni, Greci e Romani in Asia Minore*. Edited by Gianpaolo Urso. Pisa: Edizioni ETS, 2007.

Hellerman, Joseph H. *Reconstructing Honor in Roman Philippi: Carmen Christi as Cursus Pudorum*. SNTSMS 132. Cambridge: Cambridge University Press, 2005.

Ismard, Paulin. *La cité des réseaux: Athènes et ses associations VIe–Ier siècle av. J.-C*. Paris: Publications de la Sorbonne, 2010.

Katsari, Constantina, and Stephen Mitchell. "The Roman Colonies of Greece and Asia Minor: Questions of State and Civic Identity." *Athenaeum* 96 (2008): 221–49.

Kirbihler, François. "César, Auguste et l'Asie: Continuités et évolutions de deux politiques." Pages 125–44 in *César sous Auguste*. Edited by Olivier Devillers and Karin Sion-Jenkins. Bordeaux: Ausonius, 2012.

———. "Un *cursus honorum* à Éphèse? Quelques réflexions sur la succession des magistratures de la cité à l'époque romaine." Pages 67–107 in *Folia Graeca in honorem Edouard Will, Historica*. Edited by Paul Goukowsky and Christophe Feyel. Nancy: ADRA, 2012.

Koukouli-Chrysanthaki, Chaido. "Philippi." Pages 437–52 in *Brill's Companion to Ancient Macedon: Studies in the Archaeology and History of Macedon, 650 BC–300 AD*. Edited by Robin J. Lane Fox. Leiden: Brill, 2011.

Kuhn, Christina T. "Emotionality in the Political Culture of the Graeco-Roman East: The Role of Acclamations." Pages 295–316 in *Unveiling Emotions: Sources and Methods for the Study of Emotions in the Greek World*. Edited by Angelos Chaniotis. Stuttgart: Steiner, 2012.

Laffi, Umberto. "La struttura costituzionale nei municipi e nelle colonie romane: Magistrati, decurioni, popolo." Pages 120–31 in *Gli Statuti Municipali*. Edited by Luigi Capogrossi Colognesi and Emilio Gabba. Pavia: IUSS, 2006.

Lemerle, Paul. *Philippes et la Macédoine orientale à l'époque chrétienne et byzantine: Recherches d'histoire et d'archéologie*. Paris: de Boccard, 1945.

Levick, Barbara. *Roman Colonies in Southern Asia Minor*. Oxford: Clarendon, 1967.

Miller, Anna C. *Corinthian Democracy: Democratic Discourse in 1 Corinthians*. PTMS 220. Eugene, OR: Pickwick, 2015.

Millis, Benjamin W. "The Local Magistrates and Elite of Roman Corinth." Pages 38–53 in *Corinth in Contrast: Studies in Inequality*. Edited by Steven J. Friesen, Sarah A. James, and Daniel N. Schowalter. NovTSup 155. Leiden: Brill, 2014.

———. "The Social and Ethnic Origins of the Colonists in Early Roman Corinth." Pages 13–35 in *Corinth in Context: Comparative Studies on Religion and Society*. Edited by Steven J. Friesen, Daniel N. Schowalter, and James C. Walters. NovTSup 134. Leiden: Brill, 2010.

Minnen, Peter van. "Paul the Roman Citizen." *JSNT* 56 (1994): 43–52.

Mitchell, Stephen. "Further Thoughts on the Cult of Theos Hypsistos." Pages 167–208 in *One God: Pagan Monotheism in the Roman Empire*. Edited by Stephen Mitchell and Peter van Nuffelen. Cambridge: Cambridge University Press, 2010.

Nasrallah, Laura S. "Spatial Perspectives: Space and Archaeology in Roman Philippi." Pages 53–74 in *Studying Paul's Letters: Contemporary Perspectives and Methods*. Edited by Joseph A. Marchal. Minneapolis: Fortress, 2012.

Oakes, Peter. *Philippians: From People to Letter*. SNTSMS 110. Cambridge: Cambridge University Press, 2001.

Ogereau, Julien M. *Paul's Koinonia with the Philippians: A Socio-historical Investigation of a Pauline Economic Partnership*. WUNT 2/377. Tübingen: Mohr Siebeck, 2014.

Omerzu, Heike. *Der Prozess des Paulus: Eine exegetische und rechtshistorische Untersuchung der Apostelgeschichte*. BZNW 115. Berlin: de Gruyter, 2002.

Park, Young-Ho. *Paul's Ekklesia as a Civic Assembly: Understanding the People of God in Their Politico-Social World*. WUNT 2/393. Tübingen: Mohr Siebeck, 2015.

Pilhofer, Peter. *Philippi*. Vol. 1, *Die erste christliche Gemeinde Europas*. WUNT 87. Tübingen: Mohr Siebeck, 1995.

———. *Philippi*. Vol. 2, *Katalog der Inschriften von Philippi*. 2nd ed. WUNT 119. Tübingen: Mohr Siebeck, 2009.

Porter, Stanley E. "Did Paul Speak Latin?" Pages 289–308 in *Paul: Jew, Greek, and Roman*. Edited by Stanley E. Porter. Pauline Studies 5. Leiden: Brill, 2008.

Quinn, Josephine Crawley, and Andrew Wilson. "Capitolia." *JRS* 103 (2013): 117–73.

Ravizza, Mariangela. "Καίσαρα ἐπικαλοῦμαι: L'appello di Paolo di Tarso all'imperatore." Pages 113–31 in *Eparcheia, autonomia e civitas Romana: Studi sulla giurisdizione criminale dei governatori di provincia (II sec. a.C.–II d.C.)*. Edited by Dario Mantovani and Luigi Pellecchi. Pavia: IUSS, 2010.

Rizakis, Athanasios D. *Achaïe, II: La cité de Patras; Épigraphie et histoire*. Meletemata 25. Athens: National Hellenic Research Foundation, 1998.

———. "*Incolae-paroikoi*: Populations et communautés dépendantes dans les cités et les colonies romaines de l'Orient." *REA* 100 (1998): 599–617.

———. "Le grec face au latin: Le paysage linguistique dans la péninsule balkanique sous l'empire." Pages 373–91 in *Acta colloquii epigraphici Latini Helsingiae 3.–6. sept. 1991 habiti*. Edited by Heikki Solin, Olli Salomies, and Uta-Maria Liertz. Helsinki: Societas Scientiarium Fennica, 1995.

———. "Recrutement et formation des élites dans les colonies romaines de la province de Macédoine." Pages 107–30 in *Les élites et leurs facettes: Les élites locales dans le monde hellénistique et romain*. Edited by Mireille Cébeillac-Gervasoni and Laurent Lamoine. Rome: École française de Rome, 2003.

Robert, Louis, Glen W. Bowersock, and Christopher P. Jones. *Le martyre de Pionios, prêtre de Smyrne*. Washington, DC: Dumbarton Oaks Research Library and Collection, 1994.

Sartre, Maurice. "Les colonies romaines dans le monde grec: Essai de synthèse." Pages 111–52 in *Roman Military Studies*. Edited by Edward Dąbrowa. Kraków: Jagiellonian University Press, 2001.

Sève, Michel. "Le destin des honneurs pour les empereurs et les notables à Philippes: Note d'épigraphie et de topographie." Pages 139–52 in *Mémoire et histoire: Les procédures de condamnation dans l'Antiquité romaine*. Edited by Stéphane Benoist. Metz: CRULH, 2007.

———. *1914–2014: Philippes, ΦΙΛΙΠΠΟΙ, Philippi; 100 ans de recherches françaises*. Athens: École française d'Athènes, 2014.

Sève, Michel, and Patrick Weber. *Guide du forum de Philippes*. Sites et Monuments 18. Athens: École française d'Athènes, 2012.

———. "Peut-on parler d'une basilique civile au forum de Philippes?" Pages 91–106 in *Basiliques et agoras de Grèce et d'Asie Mineure*. Edited by Laurence Cavalier, Raymont Descat, and Jacques des Courtils. Bordeaux: Ausonius, 2012.

Sodini, Jean-Pierre. "L'architecture religieuse de Philippes, entre Rome, Thessalonique et Constantinople." *CRAI* 2014: 1509–42.

Sterck-Degueldre, Jean-Pierre. *Eine Frau namens Lydia: Zu Geschichte und Komposition in Apostelgeschichte 16,11–15.40*. WUNT 2/176. Tübingen: Mohr Siebeck, 2004.

Strabo. *Strabons Geographica*. Vol. 2, *Buch V–VIII: Text und Übersetzung*. Edited by S. Radt. Göttingen: Vandenhoeck & Ruprecht, 2003.

Sweetman, Rebecca J., ed. *Roman Colonies in the First Century of Their Foundation*. Oxford: Oxbow, 2001.

Vos, Craig S. de. "Finding a Charge That Fits: The Accusation against Paul and Silas at Philippi (Acts 16.19–21)." *JSNT* 74 (1999): 51–63.

Ware, James P. *The Mission of the Church in Paul's Letter to the Philippians in the Context of Ancient Judaism*. NovTSup 120. Leiden: Brill, 2005.

Weber, Ekkehard. "Das römische Bürgerrecht des Apostels Paulus." *Tyche* 27 (2012): 193–207.

White, L. Michael. "Visualizing the 'Real' World of Acts 16: Toward Construction of a Social Index." Pages 234–61 in *The Social World of the First Christians: Essays in Honor of Wayne A. Meeks*. Edited by L. Michael White and O. Larry Yarbrough. Minneapolis: Fortress, 1995.

Willet, Rinse. "Whirlwind of Numbers—Demographic Experiments for Roman Corinth." *AncSoc* 42 (2012): 127–58.

Zannis, Angelos G. *Le pays entre le Strymon et le Nestos: Géographie et histoire (VIIe–IVe siècle avant J.-C.)*. Meletemata 71. Athens: National Hellenic Research Foundation, 2014.

Did the Philippian Christ Group *Know* It Was a "Missionary" Society?

Richard S. Ascough

Introduction

According to Paul, the Philippian Christ adherents formed the only group that entered into a partnership with Paul—"You Philippians indeed know that in the early days of the gospel, when I left Macedonia, no church shared with me in the matter of giving and receiving, except you alone" (Phil 4:15).[1] From the extant Pauline letters there is no indication that any other group established a reciprocal relationship quite like the one Paul had with the Philippians. The nature of this relationship—this κοινωνία—between Paul and the recipients of Philippians has been given much attention by scholars, who have attempted to determine just what it involved. Although there is no universal agreement, many interpreters view it as a contractual relationship in which the Philippians provided the finances for Paul, who, in exchange, preached the gospel. He thus became their agent abroad, and in writing to them encourages them to act in a similar fashion by proclaiming the message of Christ locally.

In my own reading of the text, I do think it is clear that a contractual relationship had been established between Paul and the Philippians and that money had flowed from them to him. Given my arguments elsewhere that the Philippian Christ group bore organizational features typical of associations, even while differing in some practices,[2] this is somewhat surprising at first glance. Although members of the Christ group would have been aware that founder figures were deserving of honors, more typically the

---

1. Unless otherwise stated, all biblical translations follow the NRSV.
2. Richard S. Ascough, *Paul's Macedonian Associations: The Social Context of Philippians and 1 Thessalonians*, WUNT 2/161 (Tübingen: Mohr Siebeck, 2003), 110–61.

money flowed from the founder and/or a patron to the group, not the other way around.[3] Just as puzzling is why a contractual relationship would be set up for beneficial exchange when nothing of substance was gained by the Philippians themselves. As far as I know, there are no precedents for a group funding a newly met founder to depart quickly in order to found other groups in other locales. At the same time, there are some extant inscriptions that do record persons acting as ambassadors on behalf of associations. In these cases, the delegate was dispatched to Roman imperial authorities, sometimes the emperor himself, in order to negotiate benefits on behalf of the association. The inscriptions we have are set up to recognize the successes of such embassies, noting the positive impact on the group and sometimes on the city itself. In some cases, the group recognizes that the ambassador himself funded the trip and honors him for his largesse, suggesting that the expectation is that the group would normally bear the financial burden itself.

In light of such data, I will argue that the Philippians contracted with Paul to approach the Roman authorities on their behalf in order to secure for them some privilege. Although more speculatively, I will suggest that given their struggles in the *polis*, what they were seeking was Roman citizenship or at least formal recognition as an association. Unfortunately, Paul's embassy did not go well. Either as a direct result of his intercession on their behalf, or perhaps more likely, his own sense of the need to evangelize, Paul was arrested and imprisoned (1:7).[4] When he writes to the Philippians he is clear that he fell afoul of Roman authorities, although he is now making some connections with the Roman Praetorian Guard (1:13) and members of "Caesar's household" (4:22). Paul, naturally, wants to turn

---

3. For a lengthy and sustained argument that Paul's status among the communities to which he wrote was that of founder of an association, see James Constantine Hanges, *Paul, Founder of Churches: A Study in Light of the Evidence for the Role of "Founder-Figures" in the Hellenistic-Roman Period*, WUNT 292 (Tübingen: Mohr Siebeck, 2012), esp. 378–433 and 451–64. For the argument for Paul as founder figure at Philippi specifically, see Markus Öhler, "Gründer und ihre Gründung: Antike Vereinigungen und die paulinische Gemeinde in Philippi," in *Der Philipperbrief des Paulus in der hellenistisch-römischen Welt*, ed. Jörg Frey and Benjamin Schließer, WUNT 353 (Tübingen: Mohr Siebeck, 2015), 121–51.

4. I see Paul's task (and eventual arrest) reflected in Philippians as a very different context from the purported appeal to Caesar recorded in Acts 25:10–12, where Paul has already been arrested and is in trial before the Judean procurator Felix (see Acts 28:19).

this failure into a success, and dispatches his letter to the Philippians to assure them that their citizenship is secured but it is of a heavenly sort (3:20; 1:27). Rather than negotiate with the emperor or his representative on such menial matters as earthly citizenship, Paul managed to proclaim a message of much greater importance (1:12–18). The Philippians' support in this, although not directly intentional, has gained them great benefits (4:19). As he concludes the letter, he recognizes their most recent payment for his services and conveys to them that it is to be the last—the contract is terminated (4:18).[5]

In a nutshell, I am suggesting that the Philippians did not know that they were funding a recruitment drive when they established a contractual relationship with Paul. It is only in light of his *failure* to carry out the duties for which he was initially contracted that Paul reframes the relationship in an attempt to present it to them in the best possible light, smoothing the way for his next visit with them (1:26).

The Philippian Christ Group as an Association

Philippi and its surrounding area is one of the most extensive deposits of association inscriptions in Macedonia (second only to Thessalonica). Sixteen association inscriptions are attested at Philippi, with another nine from the surrounding villages and four from nearby Amphipolis and Eidomene.[6] A diversity of deities and a variety of names are attested in these

---

5. For an overview of the sequence of events I am proposing, see appendix 1.
6. Philippi: *GRA* 1.71 = Peter Pilhofer, *Philippi*, vol. 2, *Katalog der Inschriften von Philippi*, 2nd ed., WUNT 119 (Tübingen: Mohr Siebeck, 2009), 340/L589 (first–second centuries CE); *GRA* 1.68 = *CIL* 3.633 (second century CE); Pilhofer, *Philippi*, 2.524/L103 (second century CE); *AGRW* 42 = Pilhofer, *Philippi*, 2.029/G215 (second century CE); *GRA* 69 = Pilhofer, *Philippi*, 2.133/G441 (second–third centuries CE); *GRA* 1.70 = Pilhofer, *Philippi*, 2.142/G562 (second–third centuries CE); Pilhofer, *Philippi*, 2.143/G563 (second–third centuries CE); Pilhofer, *Philippi*, 2.144/G298 (second–third centuries CE); *SIRIS* 122 (second–third centuries CE); *SIRIS* 123 (third century CE); *SIRIS* 124 (third century CE); *AGRW* 44 = Pilhofer, *Philippi*, 2.697/M580 (date uncertain); Pilhofer, *Philippi*, 2.350/L448 (date uncertain); Pilhofer, *Philippi*, 2.209/L468 (date uncertain); Pilhofer, *Philippi*, 2.525/L104 (date uncertain); Pilhofer, *Philippi*, 2.529/L106 (date uncertain). Reussilova: *CIL* 3.703, 704 (both uncertain date); Proussotchani: *CIL* 3.707 (date uncertain); Alistrati: IMakedD 1104 (third century CE?); Podgora: IMakedD 920 (early third century CE); Kalambaki: Pilhofer, *Philippi*, 2.410/G258 (date uncertain); Raktcha: Pilhofer, *Philippi*, 2.091/L360 (second–third cen-

Greek and Latin inscriptions. Some of the associations found a divine patron in deities that were dominant at Philippi (Diana, Silvanus, Dionysus, and Serapis and Isis), although not all worshipers of these deities were necessarily part of an association, nor was the association necessarily directly linked to the sanctuary dedicated to these deities. Although this evidence for associations at Philippi and its environs tends to postdate the formation of the Christ group at Philippi, it can still be instructive for understanding the group dynamics reflected in the Pauline letter addressed to the Philippians, particularly when set within the broader associative practices in the Roman period.

My earlier work on Philippians has argued in detail that the Christ group to which Paul and Timothy wrote shared organizational features with an array of religious associations. The Christ group was a gender-inclusive association, with women holding some leadership positions.[7] Throughout the letter, the Philippians are addressed in language similar to that used by associations in inscriptions. At the same time, Paul and Timothy contrast how the Philippians are to act with practices typical of associations. For example, the Philippians are to focus on humility (Phil 2:3) rather than the "zeal for honor" that is so often highlighted in the association texts. Characteristic of antiassociation polemic in antiquity is the description of those whose "god is their belly" and who "glory ... in their shame," with minds set on "earthly things" (Phil 3:18–21). It is employed in the letter as a contrast to the type of group the Philippians are to be, namely, one that does not seek self-honor, nor revel in raucous banquets. Yet, that the letter itself reflects organizational and behavioral features of associations indicates that the recipients think of themselves as an association, as do Paul and Timothy when writing to them.

In turning my attention once again to Philippi, I intend to demonstrate further that association texts, broadly construed, are helpful for understanding the situation of the Christ group at Philippi, if only to challenge dominant interpretations of Philippians. It may be that at the end of the day the dominant interpretation prevails and will be stronger for the

---

turies CE); Pilhofer, *Philippi*, 2.095/L346 (date uncertain); Selian: Pilhofer, *Philippi*, 2.045/L042. Amphipolis: W. R. Paton, *The Greek Anthology*, 5 vols., LCL (Cambridge: Harvard University Press, 1916), 2:264 (late third century BCE); *AGRW* 33 = *SEG* 48.716 ter. (90/89 BCE); *AGRW* 34 = *SIG* 3.1140 (Roman period). Eidomene: *SEG* 19.483 (41–44 CE).

7. Ascough, *Paul's Macedonian Associations*, 160–61.

challenge, or it may be that association texts help us rethink the received understandings of the letter and, ultimately, get us to the core concern of the SBL seminar, that is, how the *ekklēsia* intersects with the *polis*. Of course, I am in support of the latter view.

The Contractual Relationship

Paul brackets his letter to the Philippian Christ group with twofold references to κοινωνία. In the opening thanksgiving he recalls for them their "sharing in the gospel [τῇ κοινωνίᾳ ὑμῶν εἰς τὸ εὐαγγέλιον] from the first day until now" (1:5). A few sentences later he uses the same root word to describe how the Philippians "share in God's grace" (συγκοινωνούς τῆς χάριτος) with him, both in his imprisonment and in his apology for the gospel (ἐν τῇ ἀπολογίᾳ καὶ βεβαιώσει τοῦ εὐαγγελίου; 1:7). Later, as he brings the letter to a close, he again uses the compound to note how the Philippians share in his distress (συγκοινωνήσαντές τῇ θλίψει; 4:14). In the very next sentence he employs the verbal form of the root to note how the Philippians were the only ones to share with him "in the matter of giving and receiving" (ἐκοινώνησεν εἰς λόγον δόσεως καὶ λήμψεως; 4:15). These four instances are very different in their employment of κοινωνία. As David Briones observes, "Constituting their κοινωνία is a mutual sharing in gospel advancement, grace, suffering, and finances; a strange combination, to say the least, but one which positively distinguishes the Philippians from any other Pauline community."[8] Yet, coming as they do at the beginning and conclusion of the letter, these uses of κοινωνία reflect the importance of some shared relationship between Paul and the Philippians.

Recently, Julian Ogereau has argued that the κοινωνία that Paul shares with the Philippians is predicated on a relationship in which Paul supplies the skill and labor while the Philippian Christ group provides the funding.[9] This is a "strategic economic partnership" (a *societas*, in Latin) that brings together Paul and the Philippians in the work of evangelistic ministry.[10]

---

8. David E. Briones, *Paul's Financial Policy: A Socio-theological Approach*, LNTS 494 (London: Bloomsbury, 2013), 63.

9. Julien M. Ogereau, *Paul's Koinonia with the Philippians: A Socio-historical Investigation of a Pauline Economic Partnership*, WUNT 2/377 (Tübingen: Mohr Siebeck, 2014), 349. The argument is summarized concisely in Ogereau, "Paul's κοινωνία with the Philippians: *Societas* as a Missionary Funding Strategy," *NTS* 60 (2014): 360–78.

10. Ogereau, *Paul's Koinonia*, 15, 219, 348; Ogereau, "Paul's κοινωνία," 363.

Drawing on a data set of one hundred inscriptions and 370 papyri that includes contracts, receipts, leases, decrees, honorific inscriptions, and private letters, Ogereau convincingly demonstrates how κοινων- cognates are used with an economic meaning, in particular in contexts of accounting. Turning to Philippians, particularly 1:3–11 and 4:14–20, Ogereau argues that Paul's expressions of his κοινωνία with the Philippians reflect this economic partnership—"mutual involvement in a common enterprise," which is the proclamation of the gospel.[11] The business terms employed throughout the letter are not to be taken metaphorically but refer to the giving and receiving of money in a commercial transaction. A common fund has been set up with the Philippians, "whereby money was regularly allocated to provide for the costs associated with his missionary activities," such a foundation being "the most effective way to collect, manage, and utilize finances to fund Paul's missionary activities."[12] Yet, the relationship is not a straightforward commercial transaction, which normally would involve fee for service with some profit as its aim. Rather, "Paul's κοινωνία consisted of a *societas unius rei*, whose primary, non-profitable objective or course of action (*res*) was the εὐαγγέλιον, i.e., the proclamation of the gospel. Rather than labeling Paul's κοινωνία εἰς τὸ εὐαγγέλιον as a *societas Christi*, it may therefore be best described as a *societas evangelii*."[13]

On the whole, I think Ogereau is correct in his observations about the nature of the language used by Paul (and his cowriter) in his correspon-

---

Ogereau's argument confirms the earlier work of J. Paul Sampley, *Pauline Partnership in Christ: Christian Community and Commitment in Light of Roman Law* (Philadelphia: Fortress, 1980), esp. 51–77 (see Ogereau, *Paul's Koinonia*, 219). See also Brian J. Capper, "Paul's Dispute with Philippi: Understanding Paul's Argument in Phil 1–2 from His Thanks in 4:10–20," *TZ* 49 (1993): 193–214; Hans Dieter Betz, *Studies in Paul's Letter to the Philippians*, WUNT 343 (Tübingen: Mohr Siebeck, 2015), 11, 118–19, 124–29. John Reumann rejects contractual obligation theories, noting, "Would Roman authorities have allowed such status [i.e., *societas*] for the (Philippian) church in Roman law? More likely they were viewed as a guild or *collegia* (Meeks) or persecuted like other eastern cults." John Reumann, *Philippians*, AYB 33B (New Haven: Yale University Press, 2008), 147. On the latter point, it is not at all clear that Eastern cults were persecuted at Philippi; certainly the cult of Isis was accepted by the second century CE, and probably earlier, as was the cult of the Great Mother (Cybele).

11. Ogereau, "Paul's κοινωνία," 372.
12. Ogereau, *Paul's Koinonia*, 289.
13. Ogereau, *Paul's Koinonia*, 338; see 280–89; see also Ogereau, "Paul's κοινωνία," 376.

dence with the Philippian Christ adherents. At the same time, I am not as convinced that we can accept at face value that "Paul must have found *societas* to be a legitimate and effective means to sponsor his mission," as Ogereau claims.[14] This is to take Paul's rhetorical flourishes as an accurate reflection of the situation. Yet, as Ogereau himself acknowledges, the situation is somewhat unprecedented, and even Ogereau seems to struggle with explicating what advantage the Philippians gained from such a nonprofitable arrangement; there is no *mutual* benefit, except for a vague notion of "a shared sense of accomplishment and significance."[15] In Ogereau's view, Paul convinces a recently formed association to enter into a formal, commercial partnership in which they pay for services that are enacted in a geographically distant locale among persons unknown, with no economic or even social benefits (in the form of honors) to themselves. This would indeed be a hard sell for Paul!

Elsewhere, Paul tells the Corinthian association that he "robbed other churches by accepting support from them in order to serve you" (ἄλλας ἐκκλησίας ἐσύλησα λαβὼν ὀψώνιον πρὸς τὴν ὑμῶν διακονίαν; 2 Cor 11:8). This seems an odd way to speak about a group or groups who have willingly provided support, or even entered into a contractual obligation, in which Paul evangelizes on their behalf—the thing Paul claims he has been doing among the Corinthians. On the other hand, without wanting to be overly literal, this odd statement may express Paul's frustration of knowing that, having been contractually commissioned by the Philippians for one task, he has actually been diverted to a different task (evangelism) and thus has "robbed" the other groups since he has knowingly not delivered services for which he was commissioned. Even more tellingly, Paul seems intent to point out that he did not externally finance his recruitment efforts, preferring to work with his hands, supplemented only occasionally with outside donations (1 Thess 2:9; 1 Cor 4:12; 2 Cor 6:5; see also Acts 18:3).[16]

So, building on Ogereau's premise that a partnership has been formed (for which I think he has provided ample evidence), I will suggest that the nature of the contract is much different than Ogereau and others presume. For, while there are few precedents for κοινωνία/*societas* relationships to be

---

14. Ogereau, "Paul's κοινωνία," 378.
15. Ogereau, *Paul's Koinonia*, 346; see further 339–42.
16. Peter Oakes, *Philippians: From People to Letter*, SNTSMS 110 (Cambridge: Cambridge University Press, 2001), 68–69.

formed for which there are not *mutual* benefits, there is evidence among the data set from Greco-Roman associations for a local association sending an emissary to imperial officers in order to secure favors for themselves. We will examine briefly a few such examples from inscriptions, before using these data to suggest that this was the original intention of Paul's commission. He was not successful, however, and as a result ended up being imprisoned.

It is also noteworthy that his confinement put him in contact with the Praetorian Guard and the imperial household:

> 1:13: So that it has become known throughout the whole imperial guard [ὅλῳ τῷ πραιτωρίῳ] and to everyone else that my imprisonment is for Christ.

> 4:22: All the saints greet you, especially [μάλιστα] those of the emperor's household [οἱ ἐκ τῆς Καίσαρος οἰκίας].

The Praetorian Guard was the emperor's personal bodyguard, which maintained a strong presence at Rome itself and accompanied the emperor during his travels.[17] By the mid-first century the originally small division had grown substantially, so much so that while the bulk of the soldiers could remain with the emperor's residence in Rome, detachments could be stationed throughout major urban centers, guarding the governor's palace or residence, or a military headquarters.[18] The very mention of them here clearly indicates that Paul is imprisoned in close proximity to imperial authorities, if not the emperor himself.

The "household of Caesar" is a reference to the *familia Caesari*, which was composed primarily of slaves and freedpersons of the imperial household, which numbered in the thousands and was spread throughout the Roman Empire. It was divided into two branches, one focused on the domestic sphere and managing imperial landholdings, the other involved in widespread civil service posts in which they administered the empire.[19]

---

17. See the summary in Mikael Tellbe, *Paul between Synagogue and State: Christians, Jews, and Civic Authorities in 1 Thessalonians, Romans, and Philippians*, ConBNT 34 (Stockholm: Almqvist & Wiksell, 2001), 243–44.

18. Reumann, *Philippians*, 196.

19. See further Paul Weaver, *Familia Caesaris: A Social Study of the Emperor's Freedmen and Slaves* (Cambridge: Cambridge University Press, 1972).

There is no way to know exactly to which of these branches Paul refers in 4:22.[20] Since members of the *familia Caesaris* would have been present at Ephesus or at Caesarea Maritima as well as at Rome, their being with Paul does not allow us to identify the location of his imprisonment, although it does nudge toward Rome given the larger percentage of such persons there, along with the Praetorian Guard mentioned in 1:13.[21]

Paul draws specific attention to this group through the word μάλιστα, which has been taken to suggest a previous acquaintance between those with Paul and the Christ adherents at Philippi.[22] The intent could just as easily be interpreted to be underlining that Paul has made inroads into the imperial network, albeit not in the way the Philippians had hoped. Given his circumstances, Paul writes to the Philippian Christ group, but rather than simply explain that the original work for which he has been contracted has not gone according to plan, Paul legitimizes his failure and his current circumstances by framing it according to the advancement of the gospel. This evangelism is his own project, not that of the Philippians, yet he links his own situation to theirs in order to redefine the nature of their partnership so that they are fellow sufferers with him (συγκοινωνήσαντές μου τῇ θλίψει; 4:14).

---

20. Wilhelm Michaelis rightly notes that members of the *familia Caesaris* in a given location, particularly slaves and freedpersons, may well have been part of an association before adhering to the Christ cult. Wilhelm Michaelis, *Der Brief des Paulus an die Philipper*, THKNT 11 (Leipzig: Deichert, 1935), 75. Adolf Deissmann points to this fact by arguing this common membership would have been the basis for the forming of a household-based Christ group, rather than imagining that random freedpersons gathered together. Adolf Deissmann, *Light from the East: The New Testament Illustrated by Recently Discovered Texts of the Greco Roman World*, 2nd ed. (New York: Doran, 1927), 441, cited in Reumann, *Philippians*, 740.

21. So Gordon D. Fee, *Paul's Letter to the Philippians*, NICNT (Grand Rapids: Eerdmans, 1995), 459–60. I recognize that my argument may have implications for locating Paul during this imprisonment and the writing of Philippians. In an earlier publication I reviewed briefly the possible locales, concluding that Ephesus was the most likely place. Richard S. Ascough, "Philippians," in *The Oxford Encyclopedia of the Books of the Bible*, ed. Michael D. Coogan (Oxford: Oxford University Press, 2011), 2:167–68. In light of rethinking (in this essay) Paul's relationship with the Philippians, I find myself leaning toward incarceration in Rome. The argument I am making herein, however, does not hinge on Paul being in any specific place.

22. Bonnie B. Thurston and Judith M. Ryan, *Philippians and Philemon*, SP 10 (Collegeville, MN: Liturgical Press, 2005), 161; Gerald F. Hawthorne, *Philippians*, WBC 43 (Dallas: Word, 1983), 216.

Associations and Delegations[23]

Evidence suggests that associations could send delegates to undertake business on their behalf. For example, we have a fragmentary inscription giving a list of delegates sent to the sanctuary of Theoi Megaloi on Samothrace by different Ionian cities, including the names of official delegates of the Ionian-Hellespontine association of Dionysiac *technitai* (*IG* 12.8.163; first century BCE). Another text involving the Ionian Dionysiac *technitai*, this time from the island of Kos, records the content of a letter from Sulla concerning privileges for the group, which he sent to the civic leaders (IKosS, side A; 81–82 BCE):[24]

> Lucius Cornelius Sulla Epaphrodeitos, son of Lucius, dictator, to the civic leaders, Council and People of the Koans, greetings. I have granted to Alexandros, citizen of Laodikeia, lyre-player, a noble and good friend of ours, ambassador [πρεσβευτῇ] from the association [κοινόν] of performers [τεχνῖται] gathered around Dionysos who are from Ionia and the Hellespont and of the performers gathered around Dionysos Kathegemon ["Dionysos the Leader"], permission to set up a monument in the most conspicuous place in your midst with the privileges granted by me to the performers inscribed on it. Since, having been its ambassador [πρεσβεύσαντος] to Rome, the senate passed a decree concerning these things, I want you, therefore, to provide a most conspicuous place in your midst where the monument concerning the performers will be set up. I attach … copies of my letter and the decree [?] … of the senate.

The letter notes that the permission to erect a monument within the local civic landscape has been granted by Sulla directly to Alexandros, who is acting as ambassador (πρεσβευτής) on behalf of the association.

Most of the evidence for associations sending ambassadors involves the delegation approaching political authorities on behalf of the group. For example, a stela set up by an association of immigrant shippers and merchants from Tyre in Phoenicia decrees honors for a fellow member of the association, noting that Patron son of Dorotheos undertook numerous benefactions on behalf of the group (*AGRW* 223 = IDelos 1519; 153/152

---

23. For full translations of most of the following texts see appendix 2 below. The Greek texts are available online at the *AGRW* website: http://philipharland.com/greco-roman-associations/.

24. Trans. Philip A. Harland, https://tinyurl.com/SBL4216g.

BCE). It continues to note how he not only bankrolled an embassy (πρεσβεία) to go to Athens and appeal to the "People of the Athenians"—at the time the de facto rulers over Delos—but also accepted the commission to act as ambassador (πρεσβευτής) on their behalf in the delegation. As a result of his appearing before the Athenian civic council, the association was given permission to build a sanctuary for Heracles, bringing honor not only to the group, the inscription tells us, but also honor for the gods. In this case, in order to engage in a civic building project on Delos, the association needed to gain permission from authorities external to the island itself, thus necessitating a delegation be sent, and, of course, be funded for the trip.

From the Roman period we have a text in which the *technitai* from Asia working at the temple in Didyma honor a man whose accomplishments include, among other things, having thrice been victorious in the Didymeian games and acting as gymnasiarch (*AGRW* 180 = IDidyma 107; 37–41 CE). The dedicators single out a particular accomplishment in which the honoree served as "ambassador to Augustus [πρεσβεύσαντα πρὸς τὸν Σεβαστὸν] with respect to the inviolability of Didymean Apollo and the privileges of the city." The association here highlights how one of their own members was instrumental in negotiating with the emperor on behalf of the city itself, and in so doing secured their own place within the civic landscape, insofar as they too are aligned with this man of royal descent who has also been honored "by Asia, by the People of the Milesians, and by the elders' council [*gerousia*] with golden images and statues and with other great honors."

Later in the first century an association of leather cutters erected a monument recording honors for a Roman citizen who acted for six months as market overseer "in a vigorous and extravagant manner" and served as "curator of the association [*conventus*] of Romans" and was the priest of Artemis (*AGRW* 131 = *TAM* 5.2.1002; Thyatira, late first century CE). Among these duties he also was "ambassador to the emperor in Rome [πρεσβεύσαντα πρὸς τὸν Σεβαστὸν εἰς Ῥώμην] three times, legal representative in the laborious cases concerning the Attaleians at his own expense, and priest of Artemis." It is not clear whether his legal representation is linked to his delegations to Rome, nor is he singled out has having acted as ambassador of either the leather cutters' association or the association of Romans, as was the case in the previous inscriptions we cited above. Nevertheless, what does stand out is that, from the perspective of the occupational association that erected the monument (and it is no accident that I chose one affiliated with leather working!), they saw the honorees' role as ambassador as having implications for their own well-being within Thyatira itself, insofar as they are willing to act on behalf of his daughters in commissioning the stela and seeing to its placement. As part of their own civic posturing, they link themselves to a man who has served his city and dealt directly with imperial authorities in Rome.

The following three examples certainly postdate the time of Paul but serve to demonstrate that the practice of associations sending delegates to Rome continued in the second and third century. The first example comes from Nysa and again involves the Dionysiac *technitai*. The Ephesian branch honors Aelius Alcibiades for his many years of benefaction to the association, both locally and in Rome, by committing to a number of honorifics such as the erection of golden images and statues dedicated to him in imperial temples, the setting up of inscribed transcriptions of decrees honoring him in temples and civic public space, crowning him with a golden crown during the contests, and making a public announcement in his honor during every meeting (*AGRW* 184 = IEph 22 = *GRA* 2.144 side A only; ca. 142 CE). The inscription concludes by noting that copies of the decrees will be sent to Nysa in the hands of three highly regarded ambassadors and, furthermore, "copies of the inscription will be sent by an embassy of elders to the greatest emperors and to the synod in Rome for the sake of acknowledging together what the benefactor Alkibiades has done."

In Thyatira, the bakers honor a man who has served as contest director, asiarch, high priest, and market director and distributor (*AGRW* 138 = *TAM* 5.2.966 = *GRA* 2.125; second-third century CE). He also acted as "ambassador to the emperors [πρεσβεύσαντα πρὸς τὸν αὐτοκράτορα] at his own expense with success for the greatest homeland." Again we see the link between ambassadorial appointment and resulting civic benefit, although the nature of these benefits remains unstated. Even more understated is the inscription, also from Thyatira, in which the woolworkers honor the athlete C. Perelius Aurelius Alexandros, who was "the anointed ambassador" (τὸν ἄλειπτον πρεσβευτὴν), either for the games or in undertaking a delegation to Rome (*AGRW* 141 = *TAM* 5.2.1019; ca. 218–222 CE).

As a final example, we turn to Egypt, where civil strife in Alexandria involving Judeans and Greeks led to each side sending delegations to plead their case before the emperor Caligula.[25] According to Josephus, "Three

---

25. For a summary of details of the event and the context of the visit, see Andrew Harker, "The Jews in Roman Egypt: Trials and Rebellions," in *The Oxford Handbook of Roman Egypt*, ed. Christina Riggs (Oxford: Oxford University Press, 2012), 281–82.

delegates [πρεσβευταὶ] were chosen by each of the factions [στάσεως] and appeared before Gaius" (*Ant.* 18.257 [Feldman]). One of these delegates was Philo, who recounts in great detail the events that transpired at the meetings. According to Philo, Caligula summoned the delegations "to take part in the contention about our citizenship [περὶ τῆς πολιτείας]" (*Leg.* 44 [Colson]). The Judean delegation requested Caligula reassert rights granted to the Judeans by the Ptolemies and reaffirmed by Augustus, while the Greek delegation "scurrilously reviled the Jews, asserting ... that they neglected to pay the honors due to the emperor" (Josephus, *Ant.* 18.257 [Feldman]). Despite their efforts, the Judean delegation was not only unsuccessful, but their visit also resulted in Caligula's increased annoyance with the Judeans, not only in Alexandria but also in Judea itself, where he dispatched a force to set up his image in the Jerusalem temple (*Ant.* 18.261–268).

Paul's Reconfiguration of the Contract

In all but the final example above, the embassy resulted in some positive outcome for the group represented by the ambassadors. This is what one would expect from epigraphic evidence. If there were delegations that failed in their efforts, it would hardly be commemorated in stone. If Paul's role is that of a delegate, its outcome is rather more akin to that of Philo's, although with less national impact. In Paul's case, it is clear that he has been imprisoned, for that is the context he points to early in the letter (1:7). In dispatching Epaphroditus to the Philippians with letter in hand, Paul seems to be addressing what could be a breach of contract between himself and the Philippians. Brian Capper suggests: "The reason for the interruption of the flow of support from the Philippians to Paul, evident in the 'thankless thanks' of 4.10, was Paul's imprisonment itself. The Philippians had viewed this as a breach of their initial contract with Paul, and had in consequence cut the flow of funds."[26] In Capper's view, the contract breeched involved their direct support of Paul preaching the gospel.

Yet, as Paul describes his efforts to promote the advance of the gospel, the tone seems less apologetic for not having preached than presenting preaching as a *better alternative* to what they had commissioned him to

---

Harker notes other delegations of Alexandrian Judeans sent to Rome to meet with Claudius and another to meet with Nero.

26. Capper, "Paul's Dispute with Philippi," 209.

undertake on their behalf. As John Reumann notes, in the section 1:12–18a, "Paul says little or nothing in what follows about 'what has happened to me' (NRSV). He dwells instead on interpreting the outcome positively for the gospel."²⁷ Paul claims that his arrest "has actually [μᾶλλον] helped to spread the gospel" (1:12). The adverb μᾶλλον is a comparative term, indicating "more than might have been expected," which Ware takes to indicate more success in the spread of the gospel.²⁸ Yet as Reumann points out, according to BAGD it could also indicate "for a better reason, rather" and as such suggests the reverse of what might have been anticipated, and it can also carry the weight of "other than" expected (LSJ).²⁹ That is, Paul is suggesting that, although he was sent for one purpose, another outcome was the result, which Paul now attempts to sell to the Philippians as better than the originally intended goal. It thus becomes ex post facto a legitimation of things having gone badly.

This, of course, begs the question as to the initial purpose of Paul's contract with the Philippians. In a number of instances in which an association sent a delegation to external authorities, they were seeking to secure some recognition of their own place within the local civic context—for example, permission to erect a statue or build a temple, or assurances of better treatment. As noted above, in the case of the Philippians, Paul seems particularly concerned to assure them that despite his imprisonment, something good is happening, both for him and for the Philippian Christ group. It is striking that Paul twice references the Philippians' citizenship:

---

27. Reumann, *Philippians*, 193.

28. James Ware, *The Mission of the Church in Paul's Letter to the Philippians in the Context of Ancient Judaism*, NovTSup 120 (Leiden: Brill, 2005), 174 n. 35; see Hawthorne, *Philippians*, 43.

29. BAGD, s.v. "μᾶλλον"; LSJ, s.v. "μᾶλλον." Marvin R. Vincent, *A Critical and Exegetical Commentary on the Epistles to the Philippians and to Philemon*, ICC (Edinburgh: T&T Clark, 1897), 16; Peter T. O'Brien, *Commentary on Philippians*, NIGTC (Grand Rapids: Eerdmans, 1991), 90; Fee, *Philippians*, 110–11; Thurston and Ryan, *Philippians and Philemon*, 56–57; Ben Witherington III, *Paul's Letter to the Philippians: A Socio-rhetorical Commentary* (Grand Rapids: Eerdmans, 2011), 76. These commentators generally understand the verse to be contrasting the imprisonment, which would clearly hinder the gospel preaching, with Paul's emphasis on continued proclamation. I suggest that Paul's emphasis on proclamation is in contrast to a *different* initial purpose that did not involve preaching. Reumann suggests that Paul's emphasis is on personal moral development (*Philippians*, 194).

1:27: Live your life [πολιτεύομαι] in a manner worthy of the gospel of Christ.

3:20: Our citizenship [πολίτευμα] is in heaven, and it is from there that we are expecting a Savior, the Lord Jesus Christ.

As O'Brien notes, "most commentators have rightly observed that πολιτεύομαι is not Paul's customary word to describe Christian conduct or behaviour," and thus the expression is either a synonym for the more typical περιπατέω or is a term distinctive to the context of Philippi.[30] At root it is an overtly political term and thus can be linked to both civic and imperial engagement, and the positioning of the two words to frame the body "sets the letter in a distinct political context."[31] Πολίτευμα is "a technical term for an institution within a polis" and as such "stands for the ruling class as a sovereign body with specific rights, voting procedures, etc."[32] Thus, in 3:20 Paul seems to be arguing that "our state and constitutive government is in heaven."[33] John Dickson suggests that the word πολιτεύομαι (1:27) "has primarily to do with one's social conduct as a citizen of the gospel community" but is used in order to "contrast the Philippians' sense of belonging to a Roman colony with the assurance of their heavenly citizenship."[34] That is, it is difficult to see Paul's invocation of heavenly citizenship here as anything but a contrast to civic citizenship.

There is, however, no basis for assuming the Philippians already have Roman citizenship. Prosopographical study of the few names mentioned

---

30. O'Brien, *Philippians*, 146.
31. Tellbe, *Synagogue and State*, 243.
32. Gert Lüderitz, "What Is the Politeuma?," in *Studies in Early Jewish Epigraphy*, ed. J. W. van Henten and P. W. van der Horst, AGJU 21 (Leiden: Brill, 1994), 187–88.
33. Andrew T. Lincoln, *Paradise Now and Not Yet: Studies in the Role of the Heavenly Dimension in Paul's Thought with Special Reference to His Eschatology*, SNTSMS 43 (Cambridge: Cambridge University Press, 1981), 100.
34. John P. Dickson, *Mission-Commitment in Ancient Judaism and in the Pauline Communities*, WUNT 2/159 (Tübingen: Mohr Siebeck, 2003), 104 and n. 56. Dickson is referring to Phil 1:27. I have made a similar argument for Paul's use of πολίτευμα in 3:20 (Ascough, *Paul's Macedonian Associations*, 146–49). I think the word πολίτευμα can invoke the civic context and also serve as a contrast with other associations that claim πολίτευμα within their own group (see Ascough, *Paul's Macedonian Associations*, 148–49). See also Tellbe, *Synagogue and State*, 239–43, and Bruce W. Winter, *Seek the Welfare of the City: Christians as Benefactors and Citizens* (Grand Rapids: Eerdmans, 1994), 82–85.

in Philippians indicates that they were not high-status members of the *polis*.³⁵ They were, it would seem, among the majority of the civic population that were neither Roman nor citizens and likely worked in "service industries" (e.g., craft workers, shopkeepers, slaves) or were farmers who lived in the city while farming rented land in the area.³⁶ This would have proven to be quite a disadvantage at Philippi; "under the provisions of the Roman form of constitutional government conferred on the city by Octavian in 42 B.C., Philippi was 'governed as if it was on Italian soil and its administration reflected that of Rome in almost every respect.'"³⁷ After the Third Macedonian War, Roman citizens were exempt from direct taxation, and only the non-Romans paid taxes.³⁸ As was the case empire-wide, "Discrimination in favour of citizens as opposed to aliens was ... a permanent feature of the Roman judicial system. It was practised in all spheres of the law where aliens were technically excluded, as from the *ius civile*, and where they were not, as in criminal law as administered by the *cognitio* procedure."³⁹ Anyone without citizenship living in Philippi would be at a distinct social and economic disadvantage, since they would be barred from access to the honorable social circles and prevented from purchasing land⁴⁰ and thus raising their status within the *polis*. Epigraphic texts from Philippi clearly show that honor and status was played out in elite and nonelite circles as people vied for the *cursus honorum*—esteem and recognition through public office.⁴¹ In sum, it seems likely that members of the Philippian Christ group occupied a

---

35. Ascough, *Paul's Macedonian Associations*, 122–29.

36. Oakes, *Philippians*, 76. Oakes suggests that the pattern of civic development at Philippi "means that the majority of the population of the town were probably not Romans and not citizens" and were certainly not veterans (54). He suggests a proportion of 40 percent Romans to 60 percent Greeks (76).

37. O'Brien, *Philippians*, 461, citing Lincoln, *Paradise Now*, 100.

38. Clifford Ando, "The Administration of the Provinces," in *A Companion to the Roman Empire*, ed. David S. Potter, Blackwell Companions to the Ancient World (Malden, MA: Blackwell, 2006), 185.

39. Peter Garnsey, *Social Status and Legal Privilege in the Roman Empire* (Oxford: Clarendon, 1970), 262, cited by Oakes, *Philippians*, 73.

40. Oakes, *Philippians*, 72–73.

41. Joseph H. Hellerman, *Reconstructing Honor in Roman Philippi: Carmen Christi as Cursus Pudorum*, SNTSMS 132 (Cambridge: Cambridge University Press, 2005), esp. 64–109.

lower status in a context in which civic pride and public display of honor loomed large.[42]

This lack of status provides sufficient explanation for the Philippians' troubles within the city. In 1:30 Paul notes for the Philippians, "you are having the same struggle [ἀγών] that you saw I had and now hear that I still have," which is often taken to indicate that they were suffering as a result of preaching the gospel. Yet as Dickson points out, Paul's emphasis here is on the experience—the suffering—not the cause: "To infer from the phrase τὸν αὐτὸν ἀγῶνα that the *cause* of the suffering—namely, the preaching of the gospel—was the same in both cases is to push Paul's language too far."[43] The Philippian Christ adherents are indeed experiencing local opposition, but it is not clearly linked to any sense that they are themselves involved in recruitment efforts. A more likely explanation, as Oakes demonstrates, of the nature of their suffering is that it results from their lack of income, with their low status exacerbated by their new commitment to Christ. As a result of the latter, many of their normal social, and thus economic, activities would be curtailed, albeit somewhat differently for various subgroups—for example, withdrawal of facilities by fellow craftspeople, withdrawal of custom, cancellation of tenancy, foreclosure of debt, breaking of patron-client relationships, and so on. Thus, their civic status, rather than their aberrant beliefs and practices, proves sufficient explanation for their suffering.[44] The overall effect of the

---

42. See Richard S. Ascough, "Civic Pride at Philippi: The Text-Critical Problem of Acts 16.12," *NTS* 44 (1998): 96–103.

43. Dickson, *Mission-Commitment*, 106.

44. See Richard S. Ascough, "Broadening the Socio-economic and Religious Context at Philippi: A Response to Oakes, Abrahamsen, and Verhoef," in *People beside Paul: The Philippian Assembly and History from Below*, ed. Joseph Marchal, ECL (Atlanta: SBL Press, 2015), 99–106. This is not antithetical to theories of religious persecution linked to the Christ adherents' noninvolvement in civic cults and/or the imperial cult; so Tellbe, *Synagogue and State*, 231–50; Craig Steven de Vos, *Church and Community Conflicts: The Relationships of the Thessalonian, Corinthian, and Philippian Churches with Their Wider Civic Communities*, SBLDS 168 (Atlanta: Scholars Press, 1999), 262–75. See also Jason T. Lamoreaux, who places the emphasis on the tangible economic issues that are at stake. Jason T. Lamoreaux, *Ritual, Women, and Philippi: Reimagining the Early Philippian Community*, Matrix: The Bible in Mediterranean Context 8 (Eugene, OR: Cascade, 2013), 117–18. Oakes demonstrates how positing the Philippians providing financial resources need not necessarily lead to the presumption that the Christ group there was wealthy. The "amounts of money that would make a substantial difference to an itinerant missionary accustomed to hardship need

social and economic hardship caused tension and ruptures in the unity of the church, which Paul addresses at length in the body of the letter.[45]

There would be much at stake for a small group of noncitizens making the attempt to increase their profile in the civic landscape. The Philippian Christ adherents may have hoped that through contracting with Paul to appeal to the imperial authorities, perhaps even the emperor himself, they would be granted such status. Having failed in this attempt, Paul assures them of their true citizenship—a consolation prize of sorts for his failed effort to secure for them the tangible benefits of real citizenship.

The Philippians' Role in Evangelism

In this final section, we turn our attention to Paul's rhetoric concerning the Philippians' role in the spread of the gospel message. Many commentators presume that the Philippians are engaged in local evangelism. For example, Mark Keown argues that Paul expects the Philippian Christ adherents to evangelize in both Philippi and the surrounding regions, seen in his encouragement around contending for the faith (1:27–30), unity and ethical living (2:14–16a), exemplars such as Timothy and Epaphroditus (2:19–30), and especially his thanksgiving for the Philippian involvement in evangelistic mission (1:3–7) and urging for imitation (4:9).[46] Similarly, James Ware examines evidence for Paul's use of Isaiah traditions to encourage the Philippian church to promote the gospel among nonbelievers.[47] Yet for both these exegetes, Paul's promotion of the Philippians as evangelists is not at all clear. Keown rightly admits the lack of any direct appeal to evangelism in the letter, and despite his extensive exploration of the Jewish notion of the eschatological conversion of the gentiles, Ware continually points out "the uniqueness of the early Christian mission."[48]

---

not be great," and 2 Cor 8:2–3 points to at least some financial hardship among the Macedonian Christ adherents (*Philippians*, 69).

45. On the links between civic struggle and unity within the group see Winter, *Seek the Welfare*, 98–104.

46. Mark J. Keown, *Congregational Evangelism in Philippians: The Centrality of an Appeal for Gospel Proclamation to the Fabric of Philippians*, PBM (Milton Keynes, UK: Paternoster, 2008).

47. Ware, *Mission of the Church*.

48. Keown, *Congregational Evangelism*, 1; see Robert L. Plummer, *Paul's Understanding of the Church's Mission: Did the Apostle Paul Expect the Early Christian Com-*

Such special pleading suggests there is another way to understand the texts than that they indicate an evangelistic thrust.

For example, in the opening thanksgiving Paul cites his fond memories of the Philippians, grounded in "your sharing in the gospel [τῇ κοινωνίᾳ ὑμῶν εἰς τὸ εὐαγγέλιον] from the first day until now" (1:5). As noted, many interpreters understand this to be a financial sharing in Paul's gospel mission.[49] Linked to his recognition in 4:15 of their involvement in "meeting his needs," Paul here recognizes their long-term commitment. The grammar is somewhat awkward, however: "κοινωνία + εἰς with εὐαγγέλλιον distances the subjects slightly from the activity denoted by 'gospel'. Paul is saying that the Philippians' 'partnership' was *for* the preaching of the gospel, not *in* the task of preaching itself."[50] This certainly makes sense of the temporal aspects indicated by Paul. It is a "partnership" insofar as they pay for Paul's efforts. It does not, however, suggest that they themselves preached. Nor are the Philippians likely to have participated in Paul's evangelistic efforts among themselves "from the first day," as they themselves had not yet aligned with Christ. This phrase is generally taken to be marking the formation of the contractual relationship that began with Paul's departure from Philippi.[51] Alternatively, in keeping with common practice, they may well have *paid* Paul for his teaching, as would be typical with any itinerant philosopher that came to town.[52] From the first time they met him, they had some type of a contractual relationship with him. In either case, the phrasing is awkward, and the slight grammatical distancing of *gospel* from *partnership* noted by Dickson may also anticipate his *apologia* for having shifted the terms of the formal contract with the Philippians when he departed, as we noted above in discussing 1:12.

Paul returns to this theme again at the conclusion of the letter, reminding the Philippians that "in the early days of the gospel, when I

---

munities to Evangelize? (Milton Keynes, UK: Paternoster, 2006), 134; Ware, *Mission of the Church*, 287.

49. For example, Sampley, *Pauline Partnership*; Capper, "Paul's Dispute with Philippi," 193–214; Peter Pilhofer, *Philippi*, vol. 1, *Die erste christliche Gemeinde Europas*, WUNT 87 (Tübingen: Mohr Siebeck, 1995), 246, 360–78; Ogereau, *Paul's Koinonia*, 309; Ogereau, "Paul's κοινωνία," 371; Betz, *Studies*, 124–29.

50. Dickson, *Mission-Commitment*, 125, his emphasis.

51. See Capper, "Paul's Dispute with Philippi," 204–5.

52. As Pilhofer notes, the precise meaning of the phase is not clear, although it certainly indicates that Paul's time at Philippi marked a turning point in his work (*Philippi*, 1:246).

left Macedonia, no church shared with me in the matter of giving and receiving [ἐκοινώνησεν εἰς λόγον δόσεως καὶ λήμψεως], except you alone" (4:15). The reciprocity of "giving and receiving" rightly suggests to Ogereau and others that this is a reference to their contractual relationship.[53] What is striking is the reciprocity. Interpreters have struggled to give a clear indication of how Paul's preaching elsewhere has a direct bearing on the Philippians.[54] Even more striking, in the next verse he extrapolates that they are funding his needs rather than his work. Paul makes three references in the letter to his needs and how they have been addressed by money sent by the Philippians, using χρεία in 2:25 and 4:16, and ὑστέρησις in 4:11. Elsewhere, he tells the Corinthians that the Philippians (and perhaps the Thessalonians[55]) sent funds for his "needs/wants" (ὑστέρημα in 2 Cor 11:9). In the case of the two uses of χρεία in Philippians, the definite article "probably indicates 'the need at the time.'"[56] This suggests Paul's recognition that the Philippians' financial support is helping him with the immediate practical aspects of his travels such as food and accommodation ("the necessities of life")[57] rather than being

---

53. Ogereau, *Paul's Koinonia*, 289.

54. The Philippians are understood here to be "receiving" spiritual goods and instruction in faith (O'Brien, *Philippians*, 534–35; Reumann, *Philippians*, 663) or simply just the written receipt itself (Hawthorne, *Philippians*, 270). Reumann rightly notes that giving and receiving "characterized *collegia* and other societies," pointing to the Rosalia festival and memorial banquets at Philippi (*Philippians*, 663; see Ascough, *Paul's Macedonian Associations*, 26–28). He goes on to say that "Paul appeals to Christians, with their *politeuma* in heaven, not to invest in fountains or festivals but Paul and mission." While he and I agree here that heavenly citizenship is what Paul gives back to the Philippians, we differ in the timing. Reumann assumes that this deal reflects what was initially brokered, while I am arguing that it is offered as a consolation prize. That it is a business deal can be seen in the language of "strict accounting" in which expenditures and receipts are "carefully recorded" (Hawthorne, *Philippians*, 270).

55. "The plural in 2 Cor 11,8 may also point to the congregation of Thessalonica supporting Paul in Corinth together with the Philippians, but this is not certain." L. J. Lietaert Peerbolte, *Paul the Missionary*, CBET 34 Leuven: Peeters, 2003, 222.

56. Fee, *Philippians*, 447 n. 30, his emphasis. Fee also notes that while ὑστέρησις can indicate "what is lacking," it also can be used synonymously with χρεία for "need."

57. Fee, *Philippians*, 276 n. 21. In 2:25 Paul's recognition that Epaphroditus was the Philippians' ἀπόστολον καὶ λειτουργὸν τῆς χρείας μου might suggest that the "need" also has a personal aspect beyond the necessities of life, but the latter were first and foremost the reason for sending Epaphroditus to Paul (see O'Brien, *Philippians*, 331–33).

directly linked to recruitment work he is undertaking at Thessalonica and elsewhere.

Having drawn the thanksgiving to an end (1:26), Paul opens the body of the letter with reference to "striving side by side with one mind for the faith of the gospel" (1:27), placing the emphasis on the Philippians themselves. The dative in τῇ πίστει τοῦ εὐαγγελίου is "probably implying advantage" and thus is not the faith produced in others as a result of gospel preaching but is rather the Philippians' own life of faith that arises from their own earlier interactions with Paul.[58] The need for unity is to provide one another with mutual support in living up to the standards set by Paul, particularly in the face of the civic "distress" discussed earlier.[59]

Following his hymnic exemplar of the humility of Christ (2:6–11), Paul urges the Philippians to ethical action so they can "shine like stars in the world" amid a "crooked and perverse generation" (2:15). In the following verse Paul notes λόγον ζωῆς ἐπέχοντες (2:16). Ἐπέχω is best translated not as "holding forth" but "holding fast"; as such, it is not a reference to outreach. I will not repeat here the arguments of Dickson,[60] with whom I am largely in agreement. He concludes that the verse does not refer to recruitment efforts on the part of the Christ group but rather "concerns the Philippians' devotion to the life of obedience, an obedience which according to Paul will shine amidst a corrupt world."[61] While "shining forth" suggests they can be an example, it has more to do with ethics than evangelism. This seems to be the key passage. Without the "holding forth" translation of the verb here, there is little else to suggest that the Philippians themselves are involved in local evangelism, nor that the suffering they are experiencing is directly linked to such activities. This counters the position of Plummer and others who assume the suffering is linked to evangelism and then extrapolate "one of the most significant reasons that we do not find more explicit injunctions to evangelism in Paul's letters" is

---

58. Dickson, *Mission-Commitment*, 105–6.

59. See Winter, *Seek the Welfare*, 82–104. It is noteworthy that Paul here employs an athletic metaphor (συναθλέω), which is repeated in 4:3 in describing the work of Eudoia, Syntyche, Clement, and others. Although often taken as a reference to evangelism, Paul's most extensive use of the athletic metaphor in the letter occurs in 3:12–14, where he describes his personal quest for righteousness, not his evangelistic duties. It is the former, rather than the latter, that I see behind the words of 1:27 (and also 4:3).

60. Dickson, *Mission-Commitment*, 107–14.

61. Dickson, *Mission-Commitment*, 114.

due to Paul "consistently assuming this to be the case."[62] Yet this is circular; if *we* assume Paul assumes it and then project this onto the letters, we can then *assume* there is no need for Paul to command it—an argument not so much from silence but from presumption!

A final piece of evidence cited as indicative of missionizing proclivities among the Philippians is Paul's imperatives to emulate his own behavior, which he invokes twice in the letter:

> 3:17: Join in imitating me, and observe those who live according to the example you have in us.

> 4:9: Keep on doing the things that you have learned and received and heard and seen in me.

In neither instance, however, is there any direct link to Paul's recruitment efforts. In the first, most explicit call for imitation the context focuses on ethical behavior, with Paul advocating that the Philippians behave differently from the "enemies" of the cross, whose primary activity seems to be banqueting. In the second occurrence, the context is even more clearly ethical admonition, and reads much like general epistolographic paraenetic material rather than a directive specific to the Philippians' circumstances.[63] In this regard, Paul's example is not his own missionary work per se but the ethical life that he leads, as the Philippians have both seen and heard. As part of this general admonition, Paul urges, "let your gentleness [ἐπιεικής] be known to everyone" (4:5). Citing usage in Josephus, Dickson suggests that Paul's use of ἐπιεικής here stands in direct contrast with persons who would typically involve themselves in civic affairs in a manner that could be constituted "public meddling."[64] The Philippians are instead to attend to private affairs and civil peace (see 1 Thess 4:11–12), yet another indication that for the Christ adherents, civic belonging and citizenship is (now) a secondary aspiration.

---

62. Plummer, *Paul's Understanding*, 134.

63. The virtues listed in 4:8 are drawn from Greco-Roman moralists and would be advocated well beyond a Christian context (see Reumann, *Philippians*, 638–40), although they do fit into a christological perspective when used by Paul (Fee, *Philippians*, 415–19).

64. Dickson, *Mission-Commitment*, 273–74.

Conclusion

It seems that there are no clear instances in which the Philippians are urged to undertake or continue recruitment efforts of their own. They are not a local missionary community. Together with arguments that the formal contractual κοινωνία is predicated on fee for services that lie outside the realm of evangelism, it seems unlikely that the Philippian Christ group would self-identify as a "missionary" congregation. That said, in the letter, Paul attempts to reframe the κοινωνία contractual relationship to suggest that although the Philippians funded him to secure for them civic rights and privileges from the Roman authorities, they in fact funded something greater, the proclamation of the good news of Jesus Christ. In so doing, they get something greater in return—the granting of *heavenly* citizenship by God and a guarantee that in future all their *needs* will be fulfilled. Thus, the letter attempts to demonstrate how Paul's failure to secure citizenship for the Philippians is actually not a bad thing, since they have a better citizenship—instead of getting what they paid for, they funded his proclamation, so now their needs will be fulfilled. Yet, up to this point, the Philippians have not been a missionary group, either at home or abroad, and I imagine they would have been surprised to find out that this was the de facto nature of what they had been funding in providing support for Paul. Yet, even in reframing the relationship, Paul nowhere clearly advocates that they undertake such activities themselves.

Having so reframed the κοινωνία he has with the Philippian Christ group, as he concludes the letter, Paul recognizes their most recent payment for his services and conveys to them that it is to be the last—the contract is terminated (4:18). In Roman law, "the contract of a partnership (*societas*) might be ended or dissolved in a conservable variety of ways and circumstances," including the "fulfilment of the object of the partnership, as where the partnership had been formed for a particular transaction" (Justinian, *Corpus Iuris Civilis* 3.25.6; see also *Digest* 17.2.65.10) or the occurrence "of an event that rendered impossible the accomplishment of the object of the partnership" (*Digest* 17.2.63.10).[65] In Paul's case, either or both of these circumstances seem to apply. His imprisonment means that it is unlikely that he will be able to negotiate anything on behalf of the

---

65. R. D. Melville, *A Manual of the Principles of Roman Law Relating to Persons, Property, and Obligations* (Edinburgh: Green & Son, 1915), 399–400.

Philippians, yet in his letter he redefines the nature of their partnership such that it has been accomplished insofar as in partnering with him in the spread of the gospel they have achieved heavenly citizenship. Thus, Paul writes that he has "been paid in full" (4:17–18) and no longer has any needs/wants (ὑστέρησις; 4:11). It is not the end of the relationship, however, as he still plans to return to Philippi to see them again (1:26), but their formal business relationship is concluded.

My reading of the situation at Philippi is not focused on Paul's perceptions of the κοινωνία with the Philippians rather than its reality[66] but, more importantly, on how Paul is attempting to *shift* the perception of the relationship to *fit* his own reality. The Philippians sent money to Paul on various occasions not as gifts but payments for services to be rendered on their behalf. Although unable to deliver the contracted services, Paul presents his alternative delivery of services—namely, evangelism—as having benefits surpassing the original contract—namely, heavenly citizenship—before going on to terminate the contract as having been filled (4:10–14).

Appendix 1: Proposed Chronology of Events

Paul in Philippi (Phil 1:5)
    perhaps receives funds for teaching, as per an itinerant philosopher
Paul establishes κοινωνία with the Philippians (Phil 1:5; 4:15)
    perhaps to broker citizen rights for them with imperial authorities?
En route to Rome Paul stops at Thessalonica
Philippians send economic support for his "needs" (χρεία; Phil 4:16)
    Macedonia contributed to the *poor* in Jerusalem (see Rom 15:26)
En route to Rome Paul stops in Corinth
Philippians (and Thessalonians?) send funds for Paul's "needs/wants" (ὑστέρημα; 2 Cor 11:9)
In Rome (?) Paul attempts to negotiate on behalf of the Philippians
Paul is arrested, either as a result of negotiations or for preaching or both
Philippians send Epaphroditus with money for Paul's "needs" (χρεία; Phil 2:25b; 4:18)
Paul sends Epaphroditus back with the letter recognizing final payment and notifying Philippians of termination of contract (Phil 2:25, 28–29)

---

66. As is the case with Briones, *Paul's Financial Policy*, 128.

Paul writes that he has "been paid in full" = contract fulfilled (Phil 4:17–18)
Paul no longer has "needs/wants" (ὑστέρησις; Phil 4:11)
God will satisfy their "needs" (χρεία; Phil 4:19)

Appendix 2: Associations and Delegations

AGRW 223 = IDelos 1519 (Delos, 153/152 BCE)

When Phaidrias was civic leader [*archōn*, in Athens] on the eighth of the month of Elaphebolion, during an assembly [*ekklēsia*] in the temple of Apollo:

Dionysios son of Dionysios the head of the society [*archithiasitēs*] said: Since Patron son of Dorotheos, who is a member of the synod [*synodos*], approached the assembly and reaffirmed his existing goodwill towards the synod, and because he has fulfilled numerous needs without hesitation and continues to speak and do what is advantageous both for the association [*koinon*] and for the synod all the time in accordance with his own existing goodwill toward everyone of the merchants and shippers who sail on the sea. Now adding even more goodwill with the goodwill of the gods, he invited the association to dispatch an embassy [πρεσβείαν] to the People of the Athenians in order that it might grant to them a place in which to build a sanctuary of Herakles, the cause of the greatest good things that happen to people and the founder of our original homeland. Being chosen ambassador [πρεσβευτὴς] to the Council and the People of the Athenians, he sailed, readily taking upon himself the expenses from his own resources and demonstrating the goodwill of the synod towards the People. In this way he accomplished the will of the society members [*thiasitai*] and increased honor for the gods, just as it suited him. He spoke often and in a manner demonstrating love of humanity at suitable times and he also spoke appropriate things on the synod's behalf at the most pressing moment with every kindness and with love of honor, and he received the society [*thiasos*] for two days on behalf of his son.

All translations are from Richard S. Ascough, Philip A. Harland, and John S. Kloppenborg, *Associations in the Greco-Roman World: A Sourcebook* (Waco, TX: Baylor University Press, 2012).

Therefore, in order that he may provide in the future without being asked and the synod may display its consideration for people who show goodwill toward it by returning appropriate favours to benefactors, and in order that still other people may become zealous admirers of the synod because of the thanks shown towards that person and in order that those who show love of honor may compete for the favour of the synod: For good fortune! It was resolved by the association of the Tyrian Herakleists of merchants and shippers to praise Patron son of Dorotheos and to crown him with a gold crown each year during the performance of the sacrifices to Poseidon on account of the virtue and goodness which he continues to have towards the association of the Tyrian merchants and shippers. It was also resolved to set up a painted image of him in the sanctuary of Herakles and in another place where he decides. Let him be free of paying his share and free from service with regard to everything that happens in the synods. Let the appointed leaders of the society, the treasurers, and the secretary take care of proclaiming the following proclamation during the sacrifices as they are taking place and in the synods: "The synod of the Tyrian merchants and shippers crown Patron son of Dorotheos, the benefactor." Let them write this decree on a stone plaque and let them set it up in the sanctuary of Herakles, and let the treasurer and the head of the society share the cost of this.

This was done when Dionysios son of Dionysios was leader of the society and Patron son of Dorotheos was priest.

The People of Athens. The synod of Tyrian merchants and shippers.

AGRW 180 = IDidyma 107 (Miletos area, Didyma, 37–41 CE)

The performers [*technitai*] from Asia working at the temple in Didyma honored Meniskos Melanos son of Zopyros, sacred-victor, who was thrice victor at the Didymeia games; he was their foremost head of the gymnasium who accomplished the remaining things with extreme love of glory; and, he was ambassador to Augustus [πρεσβεύσαντα πρὸς τὸν Σεβαστὸν] with respect to the inviolability of Didymean Apollo and the privileges of the city. He has also been honored by Asia, by the People of the Milesians, and by the elders' council [*gerousia*] with golden images and statues and with other great honors, being a descendant of king Lykomedes. They dedicated this to the Didymean god [i.e., Apollo] and to Pythian Artemis [i.e., sister of Apollo] on account of his virtuous behaviour and good-will towards them.

AGRW 131 = *TAM* 5.2.1002 (Thyatira, Lydia, late first century CE)

The leather-cutters [*skytotomoi*] honored T. Flavius Alexandros son of Metrophanes of the tribe of Quirina, who was market-overseer in a vigorous and extravagant manner for six months, curator of the association [*conventus*] of Romans, ambassador to the emperor in Rome [πρεσβεύσαντα πρὸς τὸν Σεβαστὸν εἰς Ῥώμην] three times, legal representative in the laborious cases concerning the Attaleians [?] at his own expense, and priest of Artemis in a manner displaying piety and love of honor. This was set up on behalf of Flavia Alexandra and Flavia Glykinne, his daughters.

AGRW 184 = IEph 22 = *GRA* 2.144 (side A only) (Nysa, ca. 142 CE)

On the proposal of Publius Aelius Pompeianus Paion of Side, Tarsus and Rhodes, winner of many poetic contests, composer of songs and rhapsodist of god Hadrian, theologian of the temples which are in Pergamon, appointed director of contests of the Augustan Pythian games, and by the vote of P. Aelius ... of Kyzikos, harpist, unexpected winner of the Capitolinian games and Olympian games: Since Aelius Alcibiades is an educated and generous man, excelling in other virtues, providing for a long time continuously, even twelve years, doing good for the musicians, receiving honor and magnificence together with the synod [*synodos*], and displaying love of honor in many matters both for us and for the common good. Furthermore, since he honored the sacred precinct of the world-wide performers [*technitai*] at the temple of Rome by donating excellent books, and since he granted magnificent gifts of properties, including stabling facilities, from which we reap the continuous, everlasting rent, distributing the rents among ourselves annually on the birthday of god Hadrian. In response, the performers at Rome reciprocated with favour, voted on other honors for him, appointed him highpriest through all eternity, and thought him worthy to be honored along with the company of the other highpriests by having his name inscribed first on the plaques. For, on the one hand, he adorned the imperishable memory of Hadrian and, on the other, he has made known the highly regarded synod through his gifts. As a result, the synod participates in magnificent parades and carries out costly religious services during holidays.

Because of these things and for good fortune, the game-conquering and crown-winning world-wide performers associated with Dionysos and emperor Caesar T. Aelius Hadrian Antoninus Augustus Pius and the fellow-contestants whom they met during the quinquennial contests of the great Ephesian games in the greatest and first metropolis of Asia—the city of the Ephesians, twice temple-warden of the Augusti [*Sebastoi*]—have passed a resolution that, in addition to the honors decreed to the man, they will vote for a well-balanced favour of exchange by doing the following: They will set up golden images and statues in the holy temples of the emperors in Asia and in Nysa, the emperor-loving homeland of Alcibiades. They will inscribe the voted decrees on a monument [*stela*] in the temple of Apollo, as well as in the rest of his public works and throughout all the cities, in order that it may be a good memorial of both Alcibiades' generosity and his well-received favours. They will publicly honor him with a gold crown in services and libations during the contest. And they will make a public announcement and honor him during each meeting [*synlogos*]. A copy of the decrees will be sent out to his brilliant fatherland, the city of Nysa—by way of the elders P. Aelius Pompenianus Paion of Side, Tarsus and Rhodes, winner of many poetic contests, composer of songs and rhapsodist of god Hadrian, theologian of the temples which are in Pergamon, appointed director of contests of the Pythian Augustan games, and Aristides son of Aristides Pergaion of Pergamon, incredible poet.

Copies of the inscription will be sent by an embassy of elders to the greatest emperors and to the synod in Rome for the sake of acknowledging together what the benefactor Alkibiades has done [σ[τεῖ]|λαί τε πρεσβείαν καὶ παρὰ τὸν μέγιστον α[ὐτο]|κράτορα καὶ πρὸς τὴν ἐν Ῥώμῃ σύνοδον [χάριν] | ὁμολογοῦσαν ὑπὲρ τῶν πεπραγμένων [τῷ εὐ]||εργέτῃ Ἀλκιβιάδῃ].

AGRW 138 = *TAM* 5.2.966 = *GRA* 2.125 (Thyatira Lydia, second–third century CE)

For good fortune! The bakers [*artokopoi*] set this up from their own resources to honor Gaius Julius Julianus Tatianus, who was director of contests, Asiarch, highpriest for life, distributor [*triteutēs*] and director of the market in the same year, and ambassador to the emperors [πρεσβεύσαντα πρὸς τὸν αὐτοκράτορα] at his own expense with success for the greatest homeland. He was son of C. Julius Hippianos and Cornelia Secunde the highpriests of Asia, grandson of Flavius Moschios the highpriest, descendent of Flavius Hippianos and Flavia Tatia who, like their ancestors, acted as highpriests with their kin, contributed to public buildings, and displayed love of honor all the time, and were founders of the homeland.

Lesbios Philotas the supervisor set up the statue and the altar with his son Asklepiades from their own resources.

AGRW 141 = *TAM* 5.2.1019 (Thyatira, Lydia, ca. 218–222 CE)

C. Perelius Aurelius Alexandros, the outstanding and foremost member of the eternal and immortal athletes of the world-wide competitions of the Pythian Augusteian games and the anointed ambassador [τὸν ἄλειπτον πρεσβευτὴν] The wool-workers [*lanarioi*] set this up in his honor when Aurelius Moschianos son of Ammianos was supervisor.

Bibliography

Ando, Clifford. "The Administration of the Provinces." Pages 177–92 in *A Companion to the Roman Empire*. Edited by David S. Potter. Blackwell Companions to the Ancient World. Malden, MA: Blackwell, 2006.

Ascough, Richard S. "Broadening the Socio-economic and Religious Context at Philippi: A Response to Oakes, Abrahamsen, and Verhoef." Pages 99–106 in *People beside Paul: The Philippian Assembly and History from Below*. Edited by Joseph Marchal. ECL. Atlanta: SBL Press, 2015.

———. "Civic Pride at Philippi: The Text-Critical Problem of Acts 16.12." *NTS* 44 (1998): 96–103.

———. *Paul's Macedonian Associations: The Social Context of Philippians and 1 Thessalonians*. WUNT 2/161. Tübingen: Mohr Siebeck, 2003.

———. "Philippians." Pages 167–70 in vol. 2 of *The Oxford Encyclopedia of the Books of the Bible*. Edited by Michael D. Coogan. Oxford: Oxford University Press, 2011.

Betz, Hans Dieter. *Studies in Paul's Letter to the Philippians*. WUNT 343. Tübingen: Mohr Siebeck, 2015.

Briones, David E. *Paul's Financial Policy: A Socio-theological Approach*. LNTS 494. London: Bloomsbury, 2013.

Capper, Brian J. "Paul's Dispute with Philippi: Understanding Paul's Argument in Phil 1–2 from His Thanks in 4:10–20." *TZ* 49 (1993): 193–214.

Deissmann, Adolf. *Light from the East: The New Testament Illustrated by Recently Discovered Texts of the Greco Roman World*. 2nd ed. New York: Doran, 1927.

Dickson, John P. *Mission-Commitment in Ancient Judaism and in the Pauline Communities*. WUNT 2/159. Tübingen: Mohr Siebeck, 2003.

Fee, Gordon D. *Paul's Letter to the Philippians*. NICNT. Grand Rapids: Eerdmans, 1995.

Garnsey, Peter. *Social Status and Legal Privilege in the Roman Empire*. Oxford: Clarendon, 1970.

Hanges, James Constantine. *Paul, Founder of Churches: A Study in Light of the Evidence for the Role of "Founder-Figures" in the Hellenistic-Roman Period*. WUNT 292. Tübingen: Mohr Siebeck, 2012.

Harker, Andrew. "The Jews in Roman Egypt: Trials and Rebellions." Pages 277–87 in *The Oxford Handbook of Roman Egypt*. Edited by Christina Riggs. Oxford: Oxford University Press, 2012.

Hawthorne, Gerald F. *Philippians*. WBC 43. Dallas: Word, 1983.

Hellerman, Joseph H. *Reconstructing Honor in Roman Philippi: Carmen Christi as Cursus Pudorum*. SNTSMS 132. Cambridge: Cambridge University Press, 2005.

Josephus. *Jewish Antiquities*. Vol. 8, Books 18–19. Translated by Louis H. Feldman. LCL. Cambridge: Harvard University Press, 1965.

Keown, Mark J. *Congregational Evangelism in Philippians: The Centrality of an Appeal for Gospel Proclamation to the Fabric of Philippians*. PBM. Milton Keynes, UK: Paternoster, 2008.

Lamoreaux, Jason T. *Ritual, Women, and Philippi: Reimagining the Early Philippian Community*. Matrix: The Bible in Mediterranean Context 8. Eugene, OR: Cascade, 2013.

Lincoln, Andrew T. *Paradise Now and Not Yet: Studies in the Role of the Heavenly Dimension in Paul's Thought with Special Reference to His Eschatology*. SNTSMS 43. Cambridge: Cambridge University Press, 1981.

Lüderitz, Gert. "What Is the Politeuma?" Pages 183–225 in *Studies in Early Jewish Epigraphy*. Edited by J. W. van Henten and P. W. van der Horst. AGJU 21. Leiden: Brill, 1994.

Melville, R. D. *A Manual of the Principles of Roman Law Relating to Persons, Property, and Obligations*. Edinburgh: Green & Son, 1915.

Michaelis, Wilhelm. *Der Brief des Paulus an die Philipper*. THKNT 11. Leipzig: Deichert, 1935.

Oakes, Peter. *Philippians: From People to Letter*. SNTSMS 110. Cambridge: Cambridge University Press, 2001.

Oates, J. F., R. S. Bagnall, and W. H. Willis. *Checklist of Editions of Greek Papyri and Ostraca*. 5th ed. BASP Supplements 9. Oakville, CT: American Society of Papyrologists, 2001.

O'Brien, Peter T. *Commentary on Philippians.* NIGTC. Grand Rapids: Eerdmans, 1991.

Ogereau, Julien M. *Paul's Koinonia with the Philippians: A Socio-historical Investigation of a Pauline Economic Partnership.* WUNT 2/377. Tübingen: Mohr Siebeck, 2014.

———. "Paul's κοινωνία with the Philippians: *Societas* as a Missionary Funding Strategy." *NTS* 60 (2014): 360–78.

Öhler, Markus. "Gründer und ihre Gründung: Antike Vereinigungen und die paulinische Gemeinde in Philippi." Pages 121–51 in *Der Philipperbrief des Paulus in der hellenistisch-römischen Welt.* Edited by Jörg Frey and Benjamin Schließer. WUNT 353. Tübingen: Mohr Siebeck, 2015.

Paton, W. R. *The Greek Anthology.* 5 vols. LCL. Cambridge: Harvard University Press, 1916.

Peerbolte, L. J. Lietaert. *Paul the Missionary.* CBET 34. Leuven: Peeters, 2003.

Philo. *On the Embassy to Gaius.* Translated by F. H. Colson. LCL. Cambridge: Harvard University Press, 1962.

Pilhofer, Peter. *Philippi.* Vol. 1, *Die erste christliche Gemeinde Europas.* WUNT 87. Tübingen: Mohr Siebeck, 1995.

———. *Philippi.* Vol. 2, *Katalog der Inschriften von Philippi.* 2nd ed. WUNT 119. Tübingen: Mohr Siebeck, 2009.

Plummer, Robert L. *Paul's Understanding of the Church's Mission: Did the Apostle Paul Expect the Early Christian Communities to Evangelize?* Milton Keynes, UK: Paternoster, 2006.

Reumann, John. *Philippians.* AYB 33B. New Haven: Yale University Press, 2008.

Sampley, J. Paul. *Pauline Partnership in Christ: Christian Community and Commitment in Light of Roman Law.* Philadelphia: Fortress, 1980.

Tellbe, Mikael. *Paul between Synagogue and State: Christians, Jews, and Civic Authorities in 1 Thessalonians, Romans, and Philippians.* ConBNT 34. Stockholm: Almqvist & Wiksell, 2001.

Thurston, Bonnie B., and Judith M. Ryan. *Philippians and Philemon.* SP 10. Collegeville, MN: Liturgical Press, 2005.

Vincent, Marvin R. *A Critical and Exegetical Commentary on the Epistles to the Philippians and to Philemon.* ICC. Edinburgh: T&T Clark, 1897.

Vos, Craig Steven de. *Church and Community Conflicts: The Relationships of the Thessalonian, Corinthian, and Philippian Churches with Their Wider Civic Communities.* SBLDS 168. Atlanta: Scholars Press, 1999.

Ware, James. *The Mission of the Church in Paul's Letter to the Philippians in the Context of Ancient Judaism*. NovTSup 120. Leiden: Brill, 2005.

Weaver, Paul. *Familia Caesaris: A Social Study of the Emperor's Freedmen and Slaves*. Cambridge: Cambridge University Press, 1972.

Winter, Bruce W. *Seek the Welfare of the City: Christians as Benefactors and Citizens*. Grand Rapids: Eerdmans: Paternoster, 1994.

Witherington, Ben, III. *Paul's Letter to the Philippians: A Socio-rhetorical Commentary*. Grand Rapids: Eerdmans, 2011.

The Imperial Authorities in Paul's Letter to Predominantly Greek Hearers in the Roman Colony of Philippi

Peter Oakes

Philippians is notable for including direct references to Roman imperial institutions. As many scholars have argued, there are probably also several less direct allusions to the Roman authorities. There are also authority claims for Christ that could be seen as impinging on those of Rome. On top of all this, the context of the writing of the letter is Paul's imprisonment by the Roman authorities, an issue to which he makes extended reference. A common approach to the presence of Rome-related material in Philippians has been to observe that Philippi was a Roman colony, to infer from that that Paul's audience were Roman citizens, and to explain the Roman references as relating somehow to issues facing them as Christian Roman citizens in Philippi. However, as Peter Pilhofer argues, it was unlikely that there was a majority of Roman citizens in Philippi at the time when Paul wrote,[1] and, as I have argued, the proportion of Roman citizens among the Christians in Philippi would probably have been lower than the proportion in the town's population. If most of Paul's hearers were Greek, what were Paul's rhetorical aims in referring to the Roman imperial authorities in the letter?

We will first review two types of approach that do see Paul's hearers as Romans and that interpret the letter in the light of that. We will then summarize arguments on the questions of whether Paul's hearers in Philippi were mainly veteran soldiers and, if they were not mainly veteran soldiers, whether they were still mainly Roman citizens. Having answered both of

---

1. Peter Pilhofer, *Philippi*, vol. 1, *Die erste christliche Gemeinde Europas*, WUNT 87 (Tübingen: Mohr Siebeck, 1995), 92.

these in the negative, we will gather the texts in Philippians that could be seen as relating to the imperial authorities, then consider how we should understand the elements of the letter's rhetoric that relate to Roman institutions, if the expected hearers of the letter were probably not mainly Roman citizens.

1. Philippians for Romans

In a recent book on Paul, Marvin Pate argues that the imperial cult was one of the two "key religious beliefs that sparked Paul's letter."[2] An effect of this cult was to "notably contribute to the suffering of Paul and the Philippian believers."[3] Pate sees Paul responding in various ways in his letter. In Phil 4:7, Paul promises that "the peace of God that surpasses all understanding will guard your hearts and your minds in Christ Jesus." For Pate, Phil 4:7 "asserts that what people need is the peace of God (implied), not *pax Romana*."[4] Pate reads Phil 2:9–11 in a related way. He writes, "One of the themes that forms the backdrop to Philippians 2:9–11 is the imperial cult. Paul's talk about Jesus being given universal authority, such that all who bow before him experience salvation, alludes to Caesar Augustus bringing peace and salvation to the world through submission to him."[5] Pate relates Paul's use of the titles "Lord" and "Savior" to their usage in relation to the Roman emperor.[6] He sees Paul as encouraging "the Philippian church to be faithful to the gospel despite persecution from the imperial cult."[7] By this, Pate means that the Christian assembly is facing "persecution because it does not submit to the worship of Caesar."[8] Pate envisages all this as happening in a strongly colonial social context. He writes, "Paul himself alludes to Philippi as a Roman colony in Philippians 3:20 (cf. 1:27), for the word 'citizenship'/'commonwealth' (πολίτευμα) tapped into the Philippians' pride that their city was 'Rome' away from Rome, a little Italy, since its members were Roman citizens with all due

---

2. C. Marvin Pate, *Apostle of the Last Days: The Life, Letters, and Theology of Paul* (Grand Rapids: Kregel Academic, 2013), 183.
3. Pate, *Apostle of the Last Days*, 183.
4. Pate, *Apostle of the Last Days*, 184.
5. Pate, *Apostle of the Last Days*, 185.
6. Pate, *Apostle of the Last Days*, 185.
7. Pate, *Apostle of the Last Days*, 192.
8. Pate, *Apostle of the Last Days*, 190.

rights."[9] Pate's reading of these issues is a nice example because it is boldly stated and compact. It is representative of many recent approaches in that it draws attention to the Roman colonial identity of the letter's hearers, then uses that to interpret key elements of the letter as being *opposed* to elements of Roman ideology.

Although this is common in recent scholarship, if we go back a bit further, the typical story is very different. Far from seeing Paul as challenging Roman religious or political institutions, scholars such as Gerhard Friedrich draw attention to Roman aspects of the Philippian context and Paul's letter in order to argue that Paul shapes his language in order to appeal to his Roman military audience. For Friedrich, Philippi was "very much a town of soldiers."[10] So, when Paul uses "political and military" terms in Phil 1:27–30, "That is a language that the old soldiers in Philippi understand."[11] In contrast to Pate, Friedrich's reading of key sections of the text such as Phil 2:5–11 is not conducted with reference to political-religious issues.

Neither of these characterizations of the rhetoric of Philippians in relation to the Roman imperial authorities is convincing. The imperial cult is unlikely to be a significant issue shaping Paul's letter (see below). Philippi was not, in Paul's day, a town full of veteran soldiers, and his hearers were unlikely to have been mainly Roman citizens.

2. Where Have All the Soldiers Gone? The Relationship between the Veteran Settlement and the Population of Philippi in Circa 60 CE

Lynn Cohick recently wrote that Philippi "was populated by landed Roman farmers and military veterans, perhaps sons of men who fought in the decisive battle on the nearby plains between Octavian and Marc Antony, on the one hand, and Brutus and Cassius on the other in 42 BCE."[12] Strictly speaking, there has never been a town anywhere that could be described as

---

9. Pate, *Apostle of the Last Days*, 185.

10. Gerhard Friedrich, "Der Brief an die Philipper," in *Die kleineren Briefe des Apostels Paulus*, ed. H. W. Beyer et al., NTD 9th ed. 8 (Göttingen: Vandenhoeck & Ruprecht, 1962), 92, my translation: "eine ausgesprochene Soldatenstadt."

11. Friedrich, "Brief an die Philipper," 106, my translation: "Das ist eine Sprache, die die alten Soldaten in Philippi verstehen."

12. Lynn H. Cohick, "Philippians and Empire: Paul's Engagement with Imperialism and the Imperial Cult," in *Jesus Is Lord, Caesar Is Not: Evaluating Empire in New Testament Studies*, ed. Scot McKnight and Joseph B. Modica (Downers Grove, IL: IVP Academic, 2013), 166.

"populated by landed ... farmers and military veterans." Who would do the laundry? In the case in point, who did the laundry in Philippi? As Andrew Wallace-Hadrill points out, even in elite houses the great majority of the inhabitants are nonelite.[13] This is a particularly important for interpretation of Paul's letters because the expected hearers will be particularly likely to have included all the kinds of people left invisible by characterizing a population as "landed ... farmers and military veterans." It is very hard to imagine circumstances, other than a post-Constantinian church in a military camp, in which Friedrich's vision of the hearers of a New Testament text as mainly soldiers (or retired soldiers) would be at all likely to be accurate.

The Roman colonial settlement at Philippi in 42 BCE was indeed military and large. Coin evidence shows Mark Antony's settling of a substantial number—probably a couple of thousand—of his veteran soldiers at Philippi after the battle.[14] Further coinage shows the process of allocation of land parcels to the retiring soldiers.[15] Octavian/Augustus organized a further settlement there around 30 BCE after his defeat of Antony at Actium. This probably involved about a thousand praetorians and a large number of Antony's supporters in Italy (Dio Cassius, *Hist. Rom.* 51.4.6). However, even 30 BCE is ninety years before Paul is writing, in either early sixties or mid-fifties CE. If there were still a numerically substantial presence of veteran soldiers in Philippi at that point, it would have required either continual new veteran settlement there or for almost all the grandsons and great-grandsons of the original veteran colonists to have also served in the army, then returned to Philippi.

The dynamics of a major veteran settlement such as Philippi would mean that a very large area of farmland was divided into rectangles and allocated at the time of the colony's foundation. A second foundation, such as Octavian's at Philippi in 30 BCE, would have required extensive further allocation of land beyond the original grid. By this time, the area of allocated land would have extended a long way from the walls of the city. There was not scope for this to continue as a process over the subsequent century. As J. C. Mann writes, "Most of the veterans known in the pre-Hadrianic colo-

---

13. Andrew Wallace-Hadrill, *Houses and Society in Pompeii and Herculaneum* (Princeton: Princeton University Press, 1994), 103.

14. *RPC* 1.1646: Antony/Q Paquius Ruf(us) C D LEG, man plowing; 1648: A I C V P/Q Paq. Ruf, plow; 1656–60 (probably Philippi): Augustus, Tiberius, Drusus, or Claudius/two priests plowing.

15. *RPC* 1.1647; see also 1649.

nies were probably men who had returned home. Such colonies also, and more especially those away from the military areas, must soon have become settled communities with little to offer a veteran who was not a native."[16]

From inscriptions, we do know of a number of veteran soldiers who settled at Philippi well after the two initial colonizations.[17] They would probably have continued to play a major role in the politics of the colony in Paul's time.[18] However, it is extremely unlikely that they formed a substantial percentage of the population at that time. It is even more unlikely that a significant proportion of Paul's hearers were veteran soldiers.[19]

3. Were Most of Paul's Philippian Hearers Roman Citizens?

It sounds undeniable. They were Philippians. Philippi was a Roman colony. The citizens of a Roman colony were citizens of Rome. However, the argument does not work. It is quite likely that Roman citizens were in a minority in the population of Philippi even right after colonization. The Roman colonists in 42 BCE were veteran soldiers who were given land to act as farmers. It would be a strange model of a town's population that saw such a group as forming more than 50 percent of the population. We do not need to go anywhere near as far as Bruce Malina, whose preindustrial city model is of up to 20 percent elite combined with 80 percent craft workers,[20] to conclude that farmers would rarely make up more than half the population of a town. The rest must have been people other than farmers: people other than the Roman colonists. A key source of these other people is indicated by Susan Alcock, who argues that peasant land loss typically leads to the dispossessed moving into towns.[21] Such disposses-

---

16. J. C. Mann, *Legionary Recruitment and Veteran Settlement during the Principate*, ed. M. M. Roxan, Occasional Publication 7 (London: Institute of Archaeology, 1983), 18.

17. E.g., Peter Pilhofer, *Philippi*, vol. 2, *Katalog der Inschriften von Philippi*, 2nd ed., WUNT 119 (Tübingen: Mohr Siebeck, 2009), no. 218.

18. Lukas Bormann, *Philippi: Stadt und Christengemeinde zur Zeit des Paulus*, NovTSup 78 (Leiden: Brill, 1995), 150.

19. For a fuller discussion see Peter Oakes, *Philippians: From People to Letter*, SNTSMS 110 (Cambridge: Cambridge University Press, 2001), 50–54.

20. Bruce J. Malina, *The New Testament World: Insights from Cultural Anthropology* (London: SCM, 1983), 72–73. The extreme-sounding figures are moderated by Malina seeing 90 percent of the population residing beyond the town itself, so, for instance, the elite make up 2 percent of the region's overall population.

21. Susan E. Alcock, *Graecia Capta: The Landscapes of Roman Greece* (Cambridge: Cambridge University Press, 1993), 93–128.

sion would have happened on a substantial scale to the local Greeks when the Roman colony was formed. Over the period between colonization and Paul's letter, the economic vitality of the colony (evidenced by building work) would have continued to draw Greeks and others into Philippi. Lydia, the purple trader of Acts 16, is indicative of this kind of movement. There would also have been a growing number of slaves in the population: another group who were not Roman citizens.

In most Roman colonies in the Greek East the result of such processes was that Roman culture became secondary to Greek culture, as indicated, for instance, by the language used in inscriptions.[22] This was not the case in Philippi in the first two centuries of its life as a Roman colony. Political control remained solely in Roman hands. In contrast to Corinth,[23] for instance, there were no Greek magistrates at Philippi in that period. There were also strong efforts at broader cultural control, seen for instance in the presence of a Latin public library and in the uniquely attested civic employment of the leader of a group of Latin-speaking mime actors.[24] An effect of all this is that, when inscriptions from Philippi first became available to New Testament scholars, they gave an impression of an overwhelmingly Roman population. However, since collection of material has moved a good way beyond the forum, into more peripheral areas of Philippi, the impression has been somewhat corrected.[25] Overall, Pilhofer, having done extensive study of Philippian epigraphy, concludes, "Certainly the Romans were not numerically in the majority."[26]

Just as with veteran soldiers, we can argue that the proportion of Romans in the Christian assembly at Philippi was likely to have been lower than the proportion in the general population. Since Romans were proba-

---

22. See, for instance, Barbara Levick, *Roman Colonies in Southern Asia Minor* (Oxford: Clarendon, 1967), 161-62.

23. Anthony J. S. Spawforth, "Roman Corinth: The Formation of a Colonial Elite," in *Roman Onomastics in the Greek East: Social and Political Aspects; Proceedings of the International Colloquium on Roman Onomastics, Athens, 7-9 September 1993*, ed. A. D. Rizakis, Meletemata 21 (Athens: Institouton Hellenikes kai Romaikes Archaiotetos Ethnikon Hidryma Ereunon, 1996), 173.

24. On the public library, see Paul Collart, *Philippes, Ville de Macédoine: Depuis ses origines jusqu'à la fin de l'époque romaine* (Paris: de Boccard, 1937), 338-39, 359. On the mime actors, see 272-73.

25. Oakes, *Philippians*, 35-40.

26. Pilhofer, *Philippi*, 1:92, my translation: "Gewiß waren die Römer zahlenmäßig nicht in der Mehrheit."

bly in a minority (although a sizable and powerful minority) in the general population, they were very probably in a minority among Paul's hearers. This point is further reinforced by the observation that, of the four Philippians whom the letter itself names, three are Greek (Euodia, Syntyche, 4:2, and Epaphroditos, 2:25),[27] and only one is Roman (Clement, 4:3). If this is a random set of names in the assembly, the likelihood of this pattern occurring would be much higher if there were a majority of Greeks in the assembly than if there were a majority of Romans.

If most Philippian Christians were Greek, might they not still have been Roman citizens, hence citizens of Philippi? The answer is, in general, no. As Adrian Sherwin-White argues, citizenship was hardly ever given to local people at the creation of this kind of colony.[28] P. A. Brunt doubts that Philippi (among a list of other towns with a similar legal constitution) "admitted [to citizenship] more than a handful of provincials."[29] The same political and economic factors that would have tended to shut Greeks out of citizenship at the time of colonization—by taking the land and the political power, the Romans dismantled the local Greek elite—also appear to have continued in operation in the first and second centuries CE. Otherwise Greeks would have appeared among the lists of magistrates, since that was the clearest route to citizenship short of joining the army or being a freed slave.[30] The great majority of Greeks in the Philippian Christian assembly would not have been citizens of Rome or of Philippi.

4. Texts in Philippians Directly or Indirectly Relating to the Imperial Authorities

The texts that could be argued to be relevant fall into three types: texts directly referring to Roman institutions or to processes in which they are involved; texts making authority claims that could be seen as restricting

---

27. Leaving aside the uncertain matter of whether Syzygus (4:3) is a personal name.

28. Adrian N. Sherwin-White, *The Roman Citizenship*, 2nd ed. (Oxford: Clarendon, 1973), 352.

29. P. A. Brunt, *Italian Manpower: 225BC–AD14* (Oxford: Oxford University Press, 1971, 1987), 253.

30. Peter Garnsey, *Social Status and Legal Privilege in the Roman Empire* (Oxford: Clarendon, 1970), 266.

that of the Roman Empire; and texts that may be alluding to the empire, the emperor, or their actions or attributes.

4.1. Texts Referring to Roman Institutions or Processes Involving Them

Most refer to Paul's imprisonment and the possibility of execution:

> 1:13: ὥστε τοὺς **δεσμούς** μου φανεροὺς ἐν Χριστῷ γενέσθαι **ἐν ὅλῳ τῷ πραιτωρίῳ** καὶ τοῖς λοιποῖς πάσιν, 14 καὶ τοὺς πλείονας τῶν ἀδελφῶν ἐν κυρίῳ πεποιθότας τοῖς **δεσμοῖς** μου ... 20 ... μεγαλυνθήσεται Χριστὸς ἐν τῷ σώματί μου, εἴτε διὰ ζωῆς **εἴτε διὰ θανάτου**. 21 Ἐμοὶ γὰρ ... τὸ **ἀποθανεῖν** κέρδος. 23 ... τὴν ἐπιθυμίαν ἔχων εἰς **τὸ ἀναλῦσαι** καὶ σὺν Χριστῷ εἶναι

> 1:13: so my **chains** are apparent as being for Christ, **in the whole praetorium** and to all the others, 14 and most of the brothers and sisters, trusting in the lord on account of my **chains** ... 20 ... Christ will be magnified in my body, whether through life **or through death**. 21 For me ... **to die** is gain. 23 ... having the desire **to depart** and be with Christ

> 2:17: ... εἰ καὶ **σπένδομαι** ἐπὶ τῇ θυσίᾳ καὶ λειτουργίᾳ τῆς πίστεως ὑμῶν

> 2:17: ... even if **I am being poured out** on the sacrifice and service of your faith

Most of these are clear references to either imprisonment or execution. There is continued debate about the sense of "praetorium,"[31] but on any reading it alludes to Paul's custody by specifically Roman authority.

Also specifically relating to Roman power is the note on the mode of Jesus's death:

> 2:8: θανάτου δὲ **σταυροῦ**

> 2:8: death on a **cross**

---

31. For a recent view see Michael A. Flexsenhar III, "Echoes in the Praetorium: People, Place, and Prospects in Phil 1:13," in *Philippi, From Colonia Augusta to Communitas Christiana: Religion and Society in Transition*, ed. Steven J. Friesen, Daniel Schowalter, and Michalis Lychounas (Boston: Brill, forthcoming).

The final specific reference to Roman institutions is the surprising greeting:

4:22: ἀσπάζονται ὑμᾶς πάντες οἱ ἅγιοι, μάλιστα δὲ **οἱ ἐκ τῆς Καίσαρος οἰκίας**

4:22: All the holy ones greet you, especially **those of Caesar's household**

It has also been argued that the reference to the audience as Φιλιππήσιοι (4:15) is inherently a reference to a Roman institution because it is a Latin loanword, hence especially appropriate to a Roman colony—and an audience of citizens.[32] However, the Latin name for the colony, which lies behind the transliterated Latin term here, was so commonly used as a designation for the town that Paul's use of Φιλιππήσιοι looks unlikely to carry any specific political sense.[33]

4.2. Texts Making Authority Claims That Could Be Seen as Restricting That of the Roman Empire

These are assertions about the extent of authority and power granted to Christ that appear to infringe on what would generally be seen as the realm of the empire that controlled most of the civilized world known to the writer. We do need a degree of caution in this argument, because there were many deities in the Roman world who had something akin to universal authority ascribed to them in literature or epigraphy but whose cults were part of the public sphere, without that usually being perceived as a threat to Rome. An example would be the cult of Isis in many cities of the empire. However, such claims, whether by Paul or the followers of other cults, undoubtedly did have some rhetorical force among their audiences. Irrespective of whether actual Roman authorities would have seen authority claims about Isis or Christ as impinging on Roman rule, these claims would have functioned among the followers of those cults partly because the claims would have been seen by those followers as impinging on the Roman realia of their situation.

2:9: διὸ καὶ ὁ θεὸς αὐτὸν ὑπερύψωσεν
καὶ ἐχαρίσατο αὐτῷ τὸ ὄνομα τὸ ὑπὲρ πᾶν ὄνομα,

---

32. E.g., Peter T. O'Brien, *Commentary on Philippians*, NIGTC (Grand Rapids: Eerdmans, 1991), 531.
33. Oakes, *Philippians*, 66–68.

10 ἵνα ἐν τῷ ὀνόματι Ἰησοῦ **πᾶν γόνυ κάμψῃ**
ἐπουρανίων καὶ **ἐπιγείων** καὶ καταχθονίων
11 καὶ **πᾶσα γλῶσσα** ἐξομολογήσηται ὅτι **κύριος** Ἰησοῦς Χριστὸς
εἰς δόξαν θεοῦ πατρός.

2:9: Therefore God highly exalted him
and granted him **the name that is above every name**,
10 so that at the name of Jesus **every knee should bend**,
of those in heaven and **of those on earth** and of those under the earth,
and **every tongue** should confess that Jesus Christ is **lord**
to the glory of God the father.

3:20: ἐξ οὗ καὶ **σωτῆρα ἀπεκδεχόμεθα κύριον** Ἰησοῦν Χριστόν, 21 ὃς μετασχηματίσει τὸ σῶμα τῆς ταπεινώσεως ἡμῶν σύμμορφον τῷ σώματι τῆς δόξης αὐτοῦ κατὰ **τὴν ἐνέργειαν τοῦ δύνασθαι αὐτὸν καὶ ὑποτάξαι αὐτῷ τὰ πάντα**.

3:20: **from where** also **we eagerly await a saviour**, the **lord** Jesus Christ, 21 who will transform our lowly bodies into the likeness of his glorious body, in accordance with **the power that also enables him to subject all things to himself**.

4.3. Texts That May Be Alluding to the Empire or the Emperor

The last of the examples above also contains several potential allusions to the emperor as a point of comparison for the description of Christ: "savior," "lord," the one with power to "subject all things to himself." More broadly, Christ fits the picture of the rescuer of his people, coming to them in Philippi from the πολίτευμα to which they really belong.[34] Although πολίτευμα is not, as far as I know, a term used of Rome in relation to its colonies, the general idea of the rescuer from the mother community certainly fits the ideology of the emperor's defense of Roman colonists.

The word πολίτευμα has itself been seen as a possible allusion to Roman citizenship.[35] I argue elsewhere that usage in papyri and in other texts suggests this to be incorrect. A more likely understanding is as

---

34. Oakes, *Philippians*, 139.
35. E.g., Richard J. Cassidy, *Paul in Chains: Roman Imprisonment and the Letters of St. Paul* (New York: Crossroad, 2001), 194–95.

a governing institution that regulates behavior and acts as a source of redress for difficulties. However, this does still impinge on the imperial authorities because it means that Phil 3:20 depicts the Philippian Christians as being under the guidance and protection of an institution beyond the reach of Rome.[36] Links to Roman citizenship have been also been suggested for the term πολιτεύεσθε in 1:27.[37] Although "live as citizens" is a rather unlikely translation of πολιτεύεσθε, there is a potential allusion to Rome in the clause as a whole and its function in the letter:

1:27: Μόνον ἀξίως τοῦ εὐαγγελίου τοῦ Χριστοῦ πολιτεύεσθε,

1:27: Only, **conduct yourselves [publicly?] in a way worthy of the gospel** of Christ

The idea of a way of life grounded in what is "worthy" in relation to a governing narrative does sound somewhat allusive of living in a way worthy of Roman identity.[38] The possible link is somewhat strengthened by the political nature of πολιτεύεσθε and maybe εὐαγγέλιον. Standing firm as a citizen body has also been suggested by Timothy Geoffrion as shaping the subsequent phrasing,[39]

στήκετε ἐν ἑνὶ πνεύματι, μιᾷ ψυχῇ συναθλοῦντες τῇ πίστει τοῦ εὐαγγελίου

stand firm in one spirit, striving together with one soul for the faith of the gospel

The richest seam of potential allusions to Rome has been the depiction of Christ in 2:6–11. The points of comparison with the Roman emperor in verses 9–11 are very compelling. At the very least, Christ is depicted as an emperor of some kind: a figure before whom people (and other beings)

---

36. Peter Oakes, "The Christians and Their Politeuma in Heaven: Philippians 3:20 and the Herakleopolis Papyri," in *In the Crucible of Empire: The Impact of Roman Citizenship upon Greeks, Jews and Christians*, ed. Katell Berthelot and Jonathan Price, Interdisciplinary Studies in Ancient Culture and Religion (Leuven: Peeters, forthcoming).

37. R. R. Brewer, "The Meaning of *Politeuesthe* in Philippians 1.27," *JBL* 73 (1954): 76–83.

38. Oakes, *Philippians*, 138, citing Cicero, *De legibus* 2.2.5.

39. Timothy C. Geoffrion, *The Rhetorical Purpose and the Political and Military Character of Philippians: A Call to Stand Firm* (Lewiston, NY: Mellen, 1993), 24.

from everywhere bow down. In first-century Philippi, this would appear extremely likely to have been visualized by the hearers in terms of the Roman emperor. In 2:9-11, the picture is complicated by the text being in part a citation of Isa 45:23. In that text, the figure on the throne is God. However, God himself is being depicted in that text in imperial terms, accepting the obeisance of the nations. So, when Paul places Jesus on that throne, seeing God as exercising authority through Jesus, this is a depiction of Jesus both as divine agent and imperial figure.[40] The Philippians are bound to have perceived the imperial element, whether or not they also perceived the divine one.

More contestable suggestions have been made about allusions to the emperor in 2:6-8. The most plausible of these would be a deliberate contrast with the Roman emperor's imperial self-aggrandizement, particularly over issues such as τὸ εἶναι ἴσα θεῷ, "having equality with God" (2:6).[41]

A further suggested allusion to Rome is Pilhofer's view that Paul's designating of himself as φυλῆς Βενιαμίν, "of the tribe of Benjamin," in 3:5, the only place he does this, is an allusion to the fact of Philippian citizens belonging to a Roman voting tribe, specifically the *tribus Voltinia*.[42] This appears hard to demonstrate.

5. The Imperial Cult, Other Cults, and the Lived Reality of Rome in Philippi

For Pate and various other scholars such as Gordon Fee,[43] the key explanation of this kind of data is that the Philippians were facing persecution on account of refusal to participate in imperial cult activities. However, for most Greeks, and indeed most nonelite Romans, the process of "turn[ing] to God from idols" (1 Thess 1:9) would have been likely to have caused trouble in many more immediate and pressing places than the imperial cult. Domestic cults and trade-related cults are two areas where a sharp drop in piety would have tended to produce serious tension between the convert and people who were in a position to cause the convert difficulties.

---

40. Oakes, *Philippians*, 169-70.

41. D. Karl Bornhäuser, *Jesus imperator mundi (Phil 3, 17-21 u. 2,5-12)* (Gütersloh: Bertelsmann, 1938), 17.

42. Pilhofer, *Philippi*, 1:123-27.

43. Gordon D. Fee, *Paul's Letter to the Philippians*, NICNT (Grand Rapids: Eerdmans, 1995), 31-32.

The imperial cult would have come into the picture at certain points, but it would be unlikely to have been among the earliest points of difficulty.

Sometimes an attempt is made to show that the imperial cult would have been particularly significant at Philippi. This was true up to a point. However, as in Roman colonies in general, the temple of the cult of the imperial family was not actually the most prominent in the city. Nor is it clear that being a colony would have made the imperial cult more pressing for Greeks than would have been the case elsewhere. In fact, the reverse is probably true. In noncolonial cities such as Ephesus, Greeks were heavily involved in promotion of the imperial cult. There was nowhere near such a level of involvement by Greeks in the cult in the Roman colony at Philippi.

Fee writes that Phil 2:9–11 "places Christ in bold contrast to 'lord Nero', whose 'lordship' they have refused to acknowledge" in the imperial cult.[44] It appears correct that Christ's authority is being depicted as beyond that of the emperor, but, especially if we link it with the letter's other points relating to the authorities, the point looks to be wider than specifically a cultic one.[45]

The role of Rome in the lives of the Greek inhabitants of Philippi was much broader. In their daily lives they were reminded of Rome's authority in many ways. Visually, the most striking of these was the predominant view from the forum. If you stand in the forum, you are overlooked by the hill on which the acropolis stands. But this is not what you would have noticed in the Roman period. What you would have seen, immediately up the hill and looming over the forum, is the set of temples of the Capitoline Triad, the key gods of Rome: Jupiter, Juno, and Minerva.[46] The topography of Philippi exaggerated the architectural effect that a Roman colony sought to achieve: to recreate the Capitoline Hill at the head of the Forum in Rome. In many colonies, such as Pompeii, the best they could do was to build a platform for the temples. But at Philippi, every time you walked into the forum, you saw Rome and its power.

This visual effect is representative of the broader phenomenon that, in Philippi, power and wealth were strongly assigned along Roman/non-Roman lines. In other cities such as Thessalonica, this was not true to at all the same extent. There, many Greeks had political power and wealth.

---

44. Fee, *Philippians*, 197.

45. Oakes, *Philippians*, 204–8.

46. Michel Sève and Patrick Weber, "Le côté Nord du forum de Philippes," *BCH* 110 (1986): 531–81.

In Philippi there were indeed some better-off Greeks (as indicated by epigraphy), but, in general, the leading positions and possessions were allocated along citizenship lines. In Philippi, Rome represented the local power structures.

From this conclusion, if we consider Paul's presentation of the imperial authorities from a sociological standpoint, a couple of probable effects of the rhetoric are apparent.

6. The Powerless Authorities in Paul's Rhetoric

In Philippians, Paul's direct and implicit references to the Roman authorities consistently represent them as powerless: in his imprisonment, in the situation of the Philippian Christians, and on a global and indeed cosmic scale.

According to 1:13, even the act of imprisoning Paul brings home the inability of the authorities to resist the gospel. The result of the imprisonment is that the name of Christ has penetrated the entirety of even the Praetorium (whether that is the guard at Rome or a governor's residence or other building elsewhere). Looking beyond that, in 1:20, the authorities are unable to bring about a shameful death for Paul. He knows that, if he dies, it will be in a way that glorifies Christ. The authorities are unable to bring about a bad outcome for Paul: death is at least as advantageous to him as life (1:21–23). However, more striking than all this is that, according to Paul, even the decision as to whether he dies is not in the authorities' hands. He weighs up the benefits of death and life then concludes that, since his survival is better for the Philippians, that is what will happen (1:24–25).

The authorities' weakness goes beyond Paul's imprisonment. Philippians 1:28 discusses the outcome of suffering that the Philippian Christians are undergoing. Paul declares that the Philippians will be protected by God and that those who are causing suffering to them will be destroyed. If the authorities are involved, as they probably are to some extent, in the suffering that the Philippians are described as undergoing, then the authorities will be caught up in the destruction. Similarly, in 3:18–19, if the authorities are among the "enemies of the cross of Christ" they will face destruction. Systemically, the empire lacks authority over the Christians because they belong to a πολίτευμα, a community that makes and implements decisions, that is beyond the empire's reach (3:20).

In 2:8–9, the attempt by the authorities to bring shame on Christ by the manner of his death is overturned by God, who grants him supreme status. This granting of status then has further implications. Any political or cultic claimants to having "the name above every name" have now lost it (2:9). The imperial authorities, like everything else in heaven, earth, and the underworld, must bow to Christ (2:10). Jesus is the one who will be acclaimed by every creature in the cosmos as Lord, eclipsing any other claims to that title (2:11). Philippians 3:20–21 recapitulates and applies these points. It is Christ who is the powerful σωτήρ who comes from the πολίτευμα to rescue the Christians from any threat. All things are subjected to Christ's authority.

In token of the present scope of Christ's authority, the greeting of 4:22 indicates that his gospel has penetrated the very heart of the empire. There is a Christian community in the imperial household.

7. Weakening the Authorities to Sustain a Deviant Group

Where Paul presents a rhetoric of weakened imperial authorities, that has the effect, in Philippi, for a Greek audience but also for Romans among them, of weakening the Roman colonial authorities in Philippi. To weaken the central authorities is, in this case, to weaken the local authorities.

A rhetoric of weak authority structures helps sustain a deviant group. There are various senses in which the Christian group in Philippi could have been seen as deviant, whether through refusal to honor various gods or through the formation of unusual social structures. Luke even narrates Paul's visit to Philippi in a way that stresses the difference between his message and the customs of Romans who could impose their will in the forum (Acts 16:21).

Whether the Philippian Christians faced pressure from the colonial authorities or from their neighbors, Greek or Roman, the sense of danger to the group would have been diminished if they were convinced by Paul that, when placed in comparison with the group's protecting deity, the colonial authorities had no power. Any trouble from neighbors would have derived a significant amount of its force from the fact that beyond the upset neighbors lay Philippian authorities who would take the neighbors' side if matters got to the stage of coming into the public realm.

Paul's rhetoric reverses the situation for the Philippian Christians, representing as all-powerful the beings with whom they were linked. Paul also represents God and Christ as being actively committed to the welfare of the Philippian Christian group.

8. Weakening the Authorities to Lower an Intragroup Barrier

A second probable social effect of Paul's rhetoric would be to lower a key intragroup barrier. Even though a majority of Christians were probably Greek, there was probably a significant number of Romans other than Clement in the group. In fact, the Philippian assembly is quite likely to have had a higher proportion of Romans than any of the others that Paul wrote to. The distinction between Romans and Greeks would have been one of the sharpest within the assembly. This would be particularly so because the colonial situation of Philippi made this distinction of citizenship one of strongest predictors of difference in political power and in wealth. In this situation, a rhetoric that disempowers the imperial authorities would have devalued this key distinction, lowering the height of a key barrier within the assembly.

Conclusion

Paul is unlikely to have written Philippians for a predominantly Roman audience (although there may have been a larger minority of Roman citizens than in the audience of any other of his letters). However, the strong Roman control of the colony of Philippi means that his depiction of the imperial authorities would have had strong implications for the nature of the authority (and status) structures experienced by his audience there. The rhetoric of this depiction offered strengthening of the Christian group, both in the face of pressure from outside and in terms of internal cohesion.

Bibliography

Alcock, Susan E. *Graecia Capta: The Landscapes of Roman Greece.* Cambridge: Cambridge University Press, 1993.

Bormann, Lukas. *Philippi: Stadt und Christengemeinde zur Zeit des Paulus.* NovTSup 78. Leiden: Brill, 1995.

Bornhäuser, D. Karl. *Jesus imperator mundi (Phil 3, 17–21 u. 2,5–12).* Gütersloh: Bertelsmann, 1938.

Brewer, R. R. "The Meaning of *Politeuesthe* in Philippians 1.27." *JBL* 73 (1954): 76–83.

Brunt, P. A. *Italian Manpower: 225BC–AD14.* Oxford: Oxford University Press, 1971.

Cassidy, Richard J. *Paul in Chains: Roman Imprisonment and the Letters of St. Paul*. New York: Crossroad, 2001.

Cohick, Lynn H. "Philippians and Empire: Paul's Engagement with Imperialism and the Imperial Cult." Pages 166–82 in *Jesus Is Lord, Caesar Is Not: Evaluating Empire in New Testament Studies*. Edited by Scot McKnight and Joseph B. Modica. Downers Grove, IL: IVP Academic, 2013.

Collart, Paul. *Philippes, Ville de Macédoine: Depuis ses origines jusqu'à la fin de l'époque romaine*. Paris: de Boccard, 1937.

Fee, Gordon D. *Paul's Letter to the Philippians*. NICNT. Grand Rapids: Eerdmans, 1995.

Flexsenhar, Michael A., III. "Echoes in the Praetorium: People, Place, and Prospects in Phil 1:13." In *Philippi, from Colonia Augusta to Communitas Christiana: Religion and Society in Transition*. Edited by Steven J. Friesen, Daniel Schowalter, and Michalis Lychounas. Boston: Brill, forthcoming.

Friedrich, Gerhard. "Der Brief an die Philipper." *Die kleineren Briefe des Apostels Paulus*. Edited by H. W. Beyer et al. NTD 9th ed. 8. Göttingen: Vandenhoeck & Ruprecht, 1962.

Garnsey, Peter. *Social Status and Legal Privilege in the Roman Empire*. Oxford: Clarendon, 1970.

Geoffrion, Timothy C. *The Rhetorical Purpose and the Political and Military Character of Philippians: A Call to Stand Firm*. Lewiston, NY: Mellen, 1993.

Levick, Barbara. *Roman Colonies in Southern Asia Minor*. Oxford: Clarendon, 1967.

Malina, Bruce J. *The New Testament World: Insights from Cultural Anthropology*. London: SCM, 1983.

Mann, J. C. *Legionary Recruitment and Veteran Settlement during the Principate*. Edited by M. M. Roxan. Occasional Publication 7. London: Institute of Archaeology, 1983.

Oakes, Peter. "The Christians and Their *Politeuma* in Heaven: Philippians 3:20 and the Herakleopolis Papyri." In *In the Crucible of Empire: The Impact of Roman Citizenship upon Greeks, Jews and Christians*. Edited by Katell Berthelot and Jonathan Price. Interdisciplinary Studies in Ancient Culture and Religion. Leuven: Peeters, forthcoming.

"The Christians and Their *Politeuma* in Heaven: Philippians 3:20 and the Herakleopolis Papyri." In *Citizenship*. Edited by Katell Berthelot. Interdisciplinary Studies in Ancient Culture and Religion. Leuven: Peeters, forthcoming.

———. *Philippians: From People to Letter.* SNTSMS 110. Cambridge: Cambridge University Press, 2001.

O'Brien, Peter T. *Commentary on Philippians.* NIGTC. Grand Rapids: Eerdmans, 1991.

Pate, C. Marvin. *Apostle of the Last Days: The Life, Letters, and Theology of Paul.* Grand Rapids: Kregel Academic, 2013.

Pilhofer, Peter. *Philippi.* Vol. 1, *Die erste christliche Gemeinde Europas.* WUNT 87. Tübingen: Mohr Siebeck, 1995.

———. *Philippi.* Vol. 2, *Katalog der Inschriften von Philippi.* 2nd ed. WUNT 119. Tübingen: Mohr Siebeck, 2009.

Sève, Michel, and Patrick Weber. "Le côté Nord du forum de Philippes." *BCH* 110 (1986): 531–81.

Sherwin-White, Adrian N. *The Roman Citizenship.* 2nd ed. Oxford: Clarendon, 1973.

Spawforth, A. J. S. "Roman Corinth: The Formation of a Colonial Elite." Pages 167–82 in *Roman Onomastics in the Greek East: Social and Political Aspects; Proceedings of the International Colloquium on Roman Onomastics, Athens, 7–9 September 1993.* Edited by A. D. Rizakis. Meletemata 21. Athens: Institouton Hellenikes kai Romaikes Archaiotetos Ethnikon Hidryma Ereunon, 1996.

Wallace-Hadrill, Andrew. *Houses and Society in Pompeii and Herculaneum.* Princeton: Princeton University Press, 1994.

"Every Knee Bowed":
Jesus Christ as Reigning Lord over "the Heavenly, the Earthly, and the Subterranean Gods" (Philippians 2:10)

Fredrick J. Long and Ryan Kristopher Giffin

Introduction

Religious devotion to the gods was everywhere present in the Roman world. James B. Rives surveys traditional Greco-Roman religious practices and shows how myth—the traditional tales about the deeds of the gods—flourished in public contexts throughout the empire. These tales were represented, for example, in the prayers and hymns of public festivals, in temple adornments and decorations in other public buildings, and in the plots for the mass entertainments presented in the theaters and amphitheaters of the Roman Empire.[1] Just how well we moderns receive and evaluate such information is debatable. In this regard, John Scheid in his *The Gods, the State, and the Individual* has programmatically confronted modern presuppositions about historical research into ancient religion: "If we think purely through abstractions, working from syntheses or general studies far removed from the sources, or by means of theories not continually subjected to empirical verification, we inevitably impose ideas and concepts of today on the civilizations of the past"; moreover, Scheid articulates the fundamental methodological principle of alterity, that is, "the obligation to take the otherness of the ancients as a point of departure."[2] This is no less true of New Testament texts such as Phil 2:6–11 that reflect the profound merger of religious and political ideas for the

---

1. James B. Rives, *Religion in the Roman Empire* (Malden, MA: Blackwell, 2007), 28–32.
2. John Scheid, *The Gods, the State, and the Individual: Reflections on Civic Reli-*

benefit of the fledging Christian movement in relation to similar and alternative religious ideas.³

The so-called Christ Hymn of Phil 2:6–11, which has been characterized as the apostle Paul's "Master Story,"⁴ encapsulates early Christian affirmations about the religiopolitical narrative of Jesus, the Christ, as Lord within the context of the more prevalent Roman religious-political narratives of victory, political ascendency, and acquired divine status, especially as found in Philippi.⁵ The Christ Hymn narrates the story of Christ in two acts. The downward movement of Christ is described in 2:6–8. Being "in the form of God" and possessing "equality with God," Christ Jesus "did not consider equality with God as something to be used for his own advantage" (2:6). Instead of exploiting his divine status, Christ "emptied himself" and "humbled himself and became obedient even to the point of death—even death on the cross" (2:7–8). A transition into the second act comes in 2:9. Because Christ Jesus did not exploit the advantages of his status, but chose instead to act with self-emptying humility for the sake of others, "God highly exalted him and gave him the name above all names" (2:9). The text reaches a dramatic climax in 2:10–11.

---

gion in Rome, trans. Clifford Ando (Philadelphia: University of Pennsylvania Press, 2016), 6.

3. The use of the term *Christian* here is not anachronistic but acknowledges the fundamental political nature of the term in its first-century context. See Fredrick J. Long, "Ephesians: Paul's Political Theology in Greco-Roman Political Context," in *Christian Origins and Classical Culture: Social and Literary Contexts for the New Testament*, ed. S. E. Porter and A. W. Pitts, TENTS 9, Early Christianity in Its Hellenistic Context 1 (Leiden: Brill, 2013), 255.

4. Michael J. Gorman, *Cruciformity: Paul's Narrative Spirituality of the Cross* (Grand Rapids: Eerdmans, 2001), 88. Gorman argues that Paul's spirituality of the cross is a narratively shaped spirituality, and Phil 2:6–11 is the master narrative that shapes his spirituality. We will refer to Phil 2:5–11 as the hymn throughout this paper because it is common to do so, not because we are convinced it is a hymn. Serious debate ensues whether form-critically this pericope is a hymn; for summary discussions of this issue see Gordon D. Fee, *Paul's Letter to the Philippians*, NICNT (Grand Rapids: Eerdmans, 1995), 193 n. 4, and Stephen E. Fowl, *Philippians*, THNTC (Grand Rapids: Eerdmans, 2005), 108–13.

5. On the social ascendency, see Joseph H. Hellerman, *Reconstructing Honor in Roman Philippi: Carmen Christi as Cursus Pudorum*, SNTSMS 132 (Cambridge: Cambridge University Press, 2005).

Although quite debated, it seems more likely that the hymn is Paul's creation, and if not, that it enjoyed his full endorsement.[6] Moreover, most likely writing from Rome, Paul's awareness of things imperial and their impact on Philippi seems quite probable.[7] Typically, interpreters evaluate the Christ Hymn in terms of the imperial cult generally, or specifically and rightly the climactic acclamation that Jesus Christ is "Lord" (κύριος).[8] However, arguably the hymn supplants more specifically the Roman imperial narrative that its politicians, like the heroes, were descended from the gods and were from heaven, and thus rightly at death return to the heavenly stars seated as gods through *consecratio* (Greek ἀποθέωσις), what can be called imperial astral afterlife. At the same time, the hymn subverts "imperial paganism" that encouraged the worship of the gods to maintain the *pax deorum*.[9] This imperial paganism in religious conception both

---

6. The scholarly literature on the subject is vast. The poetic nature of this text (among other things) has led the majority to the position that 2:6–11 is a pre-Pauline fragment that Paul has adopted into his letter. Although possible, a number of scholars find this proposal ultimately unconvincing, including, e.g., N. T. Wright, *The Climax of the Covenant: Christ and the Law in Pauline Theology* (Minneapolis: Fortress, 1993), 57; Peter T. O'Brien, *The Epistle to the Philippians*, NIGTC (Grand Rapids: Eerdmans, 1991), 198–202; Dean Flemming, *Philippians: A Commentary in the Wesleyan Tradition*, New Beacon Bible Commentary (Kansas City, MO: Beacon Hill, 2009), 106; Fowl, *Philippians*, 110–12; Paul A. Holloway, *Philippians*, Hermeneia (Minneapolis: Fortress, 2017), 115. The close link between the text and the rest of the epistle are enough to convince us that Paul himself wrote the poem and that, even if he did not, it certainly says what he wanted it to, so that we may safely assume that he chose to use these precise words even if they did exist in prior form—a form that, if it did exist, is wholly unknown to us.

7. The traditional view is Rome. Ephesus and Caesarea have been suggested as the most viable alternatives to Rome. In light of the dissatisfaction with the arguments for Ephesus and Caesarea, and in light of the epistle itself, we affirm Rome as the most probable place where the epistle was crafted. For a full discussion of the issues involved and positions taken in deciding Paul's location see Holloway, *Philippians*, 19–24; O'Brien, *Epistle*, 19–26. What scholars agree on is that Paul was indeed in detainment of some sort (1:7; 12–14, 17), that Paul's place of writing had members of "Caesar's household" (4:22), that extensive evangelistic efforts were taking place wherever he was in detainment (1:14–18), that he was awaiting trial and the possibility of his execution was very real (1:19–30; 2:17), and that in the face of all of this the Epistle to the Philippians is Paul's most joyous letter.

8. See especially the review of positions in Peter Oakes, *Philippians: From People to Letter*, SNTSMS 110 (Cambridge: Cambridge University Press, 2001), 129–38.

9. The origin of the expression "imperial paganism" may (possibly) be traced to

undergirded Rome's and the emperor's right to rule and directed Rome's ruling rightly by upholding the worship of the gods. This religious foundation and prerogative belonged fundamentally to the state (see, e.g., Cicero, *De legibus*) and was the responsibility of the various priesthoods exemplified by the emperor himself as *pontifex maximus*.[10]

After discussing select religious-political features of Philippi as a Roman colony, this essay explores the religious language of "the heavenly ones, the earthly ones, and the subterranean ones" (Phil 2:10) as a reference to pagan deities. Sufficient and diverse evidence exists that these substantival adjectives referred to the gods who occupied these realms. Second, we will explore the exaltation of Christ against the concurrent Roman religious belief of *consecratio*/ἀποθέωσις celebrated in the imperial cult. Cicero and subsequent imperial writers described this religious view of astral afterlife celebrating the imperial gods seated among the gods. Third, taken together in Phil 2:10–11 Paul depicted a submission scene in which every knee of the gods would submit to the victorious Christ as Lord.

William J. Irons, "The Transition from Heathen to Christian Civilization, from the Time of the Antonines to the Fall of the Western Empire," *Transactions of the Royal Historical Society* 7 (1878): 163–75. Irons (172) does not define the term but uses it one time to describe the precise moment of transition from paganism to Christianity: "We have now arrived at the accomplished change from Imperial paganism to Christianity in the Roman world. The pagan Sacrifices and the gladiatorial shows had been abolished by Theodosius and his son Honorius. But the Empire itself was gone." See also Franz Cumont, *The Mysteries of Mithra*, trans. Thomas J. McCormack, 2nd rev. ed. (Chicago: Open Court, 1903), 177. Cumont used the expression to describe the pull to incorporate the traditional pantheon of gods into the mystery practices of Mithraism. Our use here acknowledges the centralizing pull of the imperial cult around the emperor, who as *pontifex maximus* espoused the proper worship of all divinities, especially those central to the life and preservation of the (Roman) state.

10. E.g., see the remarkable statement of Cicero to open his work *De domo suo*, "Gentlemen of the Pontifical College: Among the many divinely-inspired expedients of government established by our ancestors, there is none more striking than that whereby they expressed their intention that the worship of the gods and the vital interests of the state should be entrusted to the direction of the same individuals, to the end that citizens of the highest distinction and the brightest fame might achieve the welfare of religion by a wise administration of the state, and of the state by a sage interpretation of religion" (Watts). On the seriousness of the emperor's role as *pontifex maximus*, consider Res gest. 19–21, in which Augustus interweaves his construction/enlargement of state buildings (senate house, the portico at the Flaminian circus, roads, bridges, theater, etc.) with temple/cult sites, noting eighty-two temples rebuilt.

The context of Philippians as a whole and importantly the intertextuality of Isa 45:23 supports this interpretation, since Isaiah depicted Yahweh's defeat of the pagan gods and their nations, such that their idol gods would bow down (Isa 46:1). Paul in Philippians, then, intended Christians to live worthily as citizens in view of Jesus's example of servanthood, whom God exalted as Lord.

Colonia Iulia Augusta Philippensis

Philippi maintained close legal and social ties with Rome as its colony.[11] After the victory of Antony and Octavian over Cassius and Brutus in 42 BCE, Philippi was named Colonia Victrix Philippensium and was later renamed Colonia Iulia Augusta Philippensis by Augustus in 27 BCE with his military victory at Actium (30 BCE).[12] Victory altars at Philippi and the subsequent coinage of Augustus memorialized Philippi "as the location at which Augustus began his career as imperator—a career which would have far-reaching implications for the whole known world."[13] The fertile land around Philippi made it a choice location for a colony. Roman military veterans were resettled there as full Roman citizens, thus deposing previous landholding residents. These colonists included initially Antony's legionaries and then Octavian's cohort of Praetorians.[14] Retired military veterans subsequently may have continued to resettle there, although in fewer numbers. One statue at a gravesite along the Egnatian Way outside the city heralded a soldier's list of honorific names and accomplishments, "Gaius Vibius Quartus, son of Gaius, from the tribe Cornelia, soldier of the Fifth Legion Macedonica, decurion of the ala Scubulorum, prefect of the Third Cohort Cyreneica, military tribune of the Second Legion Augusta."[15]

The military victories of Rome continued to impress on the minds of those living in Philippi. Shortly after defeating Britannia, Claudius annexed

---

11. Interacting with the extensive archaeological work on Philippi, see the excellent work of Oakes, *Philippians*, chs. 1–2.

12. Oakes, *Philippians*, 13.

13. Hellerman, *Reconstructing Honor*, 68. For the altars established after the victory of 42 BCE, see Oakes, *Philippians*, 13.

14. Oakes, *Philippians*, 25.

15. Quotation and description from Hellerman, *Reconstructing Honor*, 79. He cites Peter Pilhofer, *Philippi*, vol. 2, *Katalog der Inschriften von Philippi*, WUNT 119 (Tübingen: Mohr Siebeck, 2000), 65, no. 058/L047.

neighboring Thrace, in 46 CE. Despite the more numerous and diverse Greek and Thracian populations, Roman influence remained dominant, as seen in its control of the land, its cultural influence (e.g., the active Latin drama troupe there), its substantial public library, the civic inscriptions, and subsequent coinage.[16]

Religiously, Philippi was diverse, merging local deities with the traditional Greek and Roman pantheon. In addition to the presence of the Isis cult, "residents honored Roman gods such as Jupiter, Neptune, Mercury, and Silvanus."[17] Artemis/Diana was also worshiped at Philippi throughout the imperial period, as was Dionysius, no doubt in association with the active theater troupe.[18] Particularly important were the cults addressing matters of life after death, as Chaido Koukouli-Chrysantaki summarizes: "It is evident that the cults that, through initiation and purification ceremonies, promised people a better life after death were gaining ground. The cults of Dionysos and the hero horseman had a special place near those of the Kabiroi, the Egyptian gods, and the great goddess Cybele and her companion Attis."[19]

Importantly, the colony embraced the hero cults; the Macedonians were well acquainted with such cults modeled on the example of Heracles.[20] Specifically, a very prominent cult of the Thracian hero Αὐλωνείτης existed and then merged with the emperor cult of Augustus.[21] One coin with the legend R[es] P[ublica] C[oloniae] P[hilippensis] above a Thracian Rider

---

16. Oakes, *Philippians*, 74–75. For the impact of coinage, see Sophia Kremydi-Sicilianou, "'Belonging' to Rome, 'Remaining' Greek: Coinage and Identity in Roman Macedonia," in *Coinage and Identity in the Roman Provinces*, ed. Christopher Howgego, Volker Heuchert, and Andrew Burnett (Oxford: Oxford University Press, 2007), 95–106.

17. For Isis, see Oakes, *Philippians*, 14, 38. Quotation is from Hellerman, *Reconstructing Honor*, 66.

18. Peter Pilhofer, *Philippi*, vol. 1, *Die erste christliche Gemeinde Europas*, WUNT 87 (Tübingen: Mohr Siebeck, 1995), 93.

19. Chaido Koukouli-Chrysantaki, "Colonia Iulia Augusta Philippensis," in *Philippi at the Time of Paul and after His Death*, ed. Charalambos Bakirtzis and Helmut Koester (Harrisburg, PA: Trinity Press International, 1998), 26.

20. See, e.g., J. P. V. D. Balsdon, "The 'Divinity' of Alexander," *Historia* 1 (1950): 377.

21. So powerful was this cult that subsequent Christian martyrs received syncretized cults. See Eduard Verhoef, "Syncretism in the Church of Philippi," *HTS* 64 (2008): 697–714.

identified as HEROI AULONITE (reverse) with the emperor Augustus (obverse) depicted and identified as DIVO AUGUSTO has been found at Thasos.[22] Provincial coinage continued to stress the divinity of deceased emperors.[23] Under Claudius, coins were minted showing Divus Julius and Divus Augustus.[24] Under Nero, Augustus on the platform inscribed with DIVUS AUG is crowned by Victory.[25] Then, too, under Claudius Philippi had received the cult of the divinized Livia, and it is likely that a cult of Claudius also existed in the time of Paul.[26] The extension of deified status to imperial family members was not unusual.[27] Moreover, Fernando Lozano maintains, "Imperial cult practice, in its Roman or provincial variety, turned out to be one of the most widespread religious manifestations throughout the Roman empire. Thus, in honor of the rulers of the Mediterranean and their families, festivals were created, sacrifices were celebrated, and imperial priests were appointed."[28] As we will show, the religious environment of Philippi stressing victory, hero cult, and the worship of divinized imperial family members among the gods provides the context to interpret Phil 2:10–11.

The Problem of the Heavenly, Earthly, and Subterranean in Interpretation

Despite the enormous attention given to Phil 2:5–11, one portion of the passage has not been properly contextually accounted for, the triadic phrase found in 2:10c: ἐπουρανίων καὶ ἐπιγείων καὶ καταχθονίων, "of the heavenly ones/things and of the earthly ones/things and of the subterranean one/things."[29] This geographic list of genitive substantive adjectival modifiers

---

22. Pilhofer, *Philippi*, 1:97. The coin was found at the Agora in Thasos. Pilhofer regrets that this coin is not yet published.
23. Kremydi-Sicilianou, "'Belonging' to Rome," 99.
24. *RPC* 1:1653–54 (Claudius).
25. *RPC* 1:1655 (Nero).
26. Koukouli-Chrysantaki, "Colonia Iulia Augusta Philippensis," 25–26. On Livia, see Peter Oakes, "Re-mapping the Universe: Paul and the Emperor in 1 Thessalonians and Philippians," *JSNT* 27 (2005): 308. He cites Michel Sève and Patrick Weber, "Un monument honorifique au forum de Philippes," *BCH* 112 (1988): 467–79.
27. See Fernando Lozano, "*Divi Augusti* and *Theoi Sebastoi*: Roman Initiatives and Greek Answers," *CQ* 57 (2007): 139–52.
28. Lozano, "*Divi Augusti*," 140.
29. Unless otherwise noted, all translations of Scripture in this paper are original,

is syntactically prominent due to polysyndeton (stressing each entity) and by being discontinuous with its head noun ("every knee") located after the verb ("will bow").[30] Moreover, the items are lexically prominent as technical terms referring to a pagan regional taxonomy (see discussion below).[31] These substantive adjectives are curiously inserted in the hymn where interpreters universally recognize the strong allusion to Isa 45:23 (LXX): πᾶν γόνυ κάμψη ... καὶ πᾶσα γλῶσσα ἐξομολογήσηται ("every knee will bow ... and every tongue confess").[32]

Two critical questions are identifying the triadic referents and why this has been inserted prominently in the middle of the strong allusion. Bible translations reflect the diversity of viewpoints, translating the substantives as neuter "things" (KJV, ASV, Young's), merely as geographic indicators (RSV, NRSV, NIV, NET, NLT), or personal entities, "those who" (Luther, NASB, HCSB).[33] The most vigorous proponent of "things" was J.

---

based on the critical editions of the Greek texts (NA[28] and LXX). For two seminal pieces of scholarship on the passage (each reprinted), see Ralph P. Martin, *Carmen Christi: Philippians ii. 5–11; In Recent Interpretation and in the Setting of Early Christian Worship*, SNTSMS 4 (Cambridge: Cambridge University Press, 1967); Martin, *A Hymn of Christ: Philippians 2:5–11 in Recent Interpretation and in the Setting of Early Christian Worship*, 3rd ed. (repr., Downers Grove, IL: InterVarsity Press, 1997); and Otfried Hofius, *Der Christushymnus Philipper 2,6–11: Untersuchungen Gestalt und Aussage eines urchristlichen Psalms*, WUNT 2/17 (Tübingen: Mohr Siebeck, 1976; 2nd ed., 1991).

30. On discontinuous elements and polysyndeton, see Fredrick J. Long, *Koine Greek Grammar: A Beginning-Intermediate Exegetical and Pragmatic Handbook*, Accessible Greek Resources and Online Studies (Wilmore, KY: GlossaHouse, 2015), 77–78, 280–82, respectively.

31. Importantly, too, this taxonomy is also found in Rev 5:3, 13 (discussed below) and is even more ancient, seen in the Ten Commandments forbidding idolatry (Exod 20:4; Deut 5:8).

32. The relevant portion of the Gottingen text of LXX Isa 45:23 reads: κάμψει πᾶν γόνυ καὶ ἐξομολογήσεται πᾶσα γλῶσσα τω θεω. Although the echo is obviously not verbatim, the shared vocabulary makes it clear enough that Phil 2:6–11 adopts the language of Isa 45:23 (LXX), as the apparatus in the outer margin of NA[28] notes and as virtually every commentary on Philippians acknowledges. For the Gottingen LXX of Isa 45:23 see Joseph Zeigler, *Isaias* SVTG 14 (Gottingen: Vandenhoeck & Ruprecht, 1967), 294–95.

33. Unfortunately, the Latin does not resolve between neuter and masculine referents, since *caelestium et terrestrium et infernorum* may be either masculine or neuter in form.

B. Lightfoot,[34] but subsequent interpreters have rightly understood that agencies, not things, are in view. Similarly, some interpreters refrain from any attempts at specification except to note the universal scope of the homage paid to Jesus.[35] Concerning the geography, nearly all interpreters acknowledge that the language of Phil 2:10c reflects the commonly held ancient view of a three-tiered universe: the heavens, the earth, and the subterranean regions.[36] Whatever the adjectives of Phil 2:10c might refer to, what is clear is that the language of this text reflects a common ancient understanding of how the universe was spatially structured.[37] Concerning

---

34. In view of Paul's "all creation" in Rom 8:22 (see also Rev 5:13; Eph 1:20–22) and similar references in the apostolic fathers (Ignatius, *Trall.* 9.1; Polycarp, *Phil.* 2) J. B. Lightfoot argued, "It would seem therefore that the adjectives here are neuter; and any limitation to intelligent beings, while it detracts from the universality of the homage, is not required by the expressions. The personification of universal nature offering its praise and homage to its Creator in the 148th Psalm will serve to illustrate St Paul's meaning here. If this view be correct, all endeavours to explain the three words of different classes of intelligent beings; as Christians, Jews, heathens; angels, men, devils; the angels, the living, the dead; souls of the blessed, men on earth, souls in purgatory, etc., are out of place." J. B. Lightfoot, *Saint Paul's Epistle to the Philippians*, Classic Commentaries on the Greek New Testament (London: Macmillan, 1913), 115.

35. So Flemming, *Philippians*, 121; Fowl, *Philippians*, 103. Moisés Silva even cautions against attempting to identify specific referents, although he acknowledges what he considers the "least objectionable" view: spirits in heaven, people on earth, and the dead in Sheol. Moisés Silva, *Philippians*, 2nd ed., BECNT (Grand Rapids: Baker Academic, 2005), 116.

36. See, for example, John Reumann, *Philippians: A New Translation with Introduction and Commentary*, AYB (New Haven: Yale University Press, 2008), 357; Bonnie B. Thurston and Judith M. Ryan, *Philippians and Philemon*, SP (Collegeville, MN: Liturgical Press, 2005), 84; Gerald F. Hawthorne and Ralph P. Martin, *Philippians*, rev. ed., WBC 43 (Nashville: Nelson, 2004), 128; Markus Bockmuehl, *The Epistle to the Philippians*, BNTC 11 (Peabody, MA: Hendrickson, 1998), 145; O'Brien, *Epistle*, 244; I. Howard Marshall, *The Epistle to the Philippians* (London: Epworth, 1991), 56–57; Fred B. Craddock, *Philippians*, Interpretation (Atlanta: John Knox, 1985), 42. Peter T. O'Brien notes that the totality of this three-storied universe was often expressed by phrases that included all three without inquiring too closely into the content of the separate compartments of that universe (O'Brien, *Epistle*, 244, citing Homer, *Od.* 5.184–186, as evidence).

37. This point, too, is commonly made in reference to the work of Erik Peterson, *Heis Theos: Epigraphische, Formgeschichtliche und Religionsgeschichtliche Untersuchungen*, FRLANT 24 (Göttingen: Vandenhoeck & Ruprecht, 1926); repr., Erik Peterson, *Heis theos: Epigraphische, formgeschichtliche und religionsgeschichtliche Untersuchungen zur antiken "Ein-Gott"-Akklamation: Nachdruck der Ausgabe von Erik Peterson

personal agencies, I-Jin Loh and Eugene A. Nida consider the two remaining views:

> [Although the] *KJV* and *ASV* understand the adjectives to be neuter, that is, "things" ... it is more likely that the reference is to rational beings.... It is not necessary to identify these rational beings exclusively as "spirits." It is quite possible that *beings in heaven* refers to the angels, and those *on earth* to human beings. *The world below* refers most likely to the residence of the dead known as Hades. Its equivalent in the Old Testament is Sheol. In ancient times, people believed that there was an underworld where the spirits of the dead carried on a shadowy existence. In any case, the author intends to show that the lordship of Jesus Christ is cosmic and universal (cf. Eph 4:10; Rev 5:3, 13).[38]

Theirs reflects a majority view of the agents referred to: heavenly angels, earthly people, and the dead souls (or possibly evil spirits) in Hades, but the main point is Christ's cosmic lordship. The alternative view is that the triad refers to evil (astral) "spirits" over whom Christ has gained the victory. Martin Dibelius, Ernst Käsemann, Ralph Martin, Frank W. Beare, and others hold this view.[39] According to Peter O'Brien, Otfried Hofius

---

1926 mit Ergänzungen und Kommentaren von Christoph Markschies, Henrik Hildebrandt, Barbara Nichtweiß u.a. 2012, ed. Christoph Markschies, Henrik Hildebrandt, and Barbara Nichtweiss, Ausgewählte Schriften 8 (Würzburg: Echter, 2012). For example, Ernst Käsemann says, "Peterson called attention to the fact that the rule over the tripartite cosmos is ascribed especially to deities whose cult has absorbed astronomical elements, and thus particularly to the sun God." Ernst Käsemann, "Critical Analysis of Philippians 2:5–11," *JTC* 5 (1968): 81, citing Peterson, *Heis Theos*, 259 n. 2, 262–63, 236–37.

38. I-Jin Loh and Eugene A. Nida, *A Handbook on Paul's Letter to the Philippians*, UBS Handbook Series (New York: United Bible Societies, 1995), 63–64.

39. Martin Dibelius, *Die Geisterwelt im Glauben des Paulus* (Göttingen: Vandenhoeck & Ruprecht, 1909), 107–9; Käsemann, "Critical Analysis," 45–88; Frank W. Beare, *The Epistle to the Philippians*, HNTC (Peabody, MA: Hendrickson, 1959), 86, and for others, see Martin, *Carmen Christi*, 258–65. Beare argues, "It is not *human* adoration which the hymn describes, as if the threefold phrase meant 'the blessed dead in heaven, the living on earth, and the souls in purgatory'; all this would be the language of a later age. The reference here is certainly to *spirits*—astral, terrestrial, and chthonic" (emphasis original). Part of Beare's argument hinges on his position that the Greek verb ἐξομολογέω, "confess," in 2:11 "has no reference to a confession of faith in Jesus on the part of the *church*," and therefore Paul cannot have human beings in view here. Instead Beare concludes, "What is depicted here is an Enthronment—the Enthron-

and Wesley Carr have provided the definitive responses.[40] However, both Hofius and Carr are too restrictive in the evidence that they evaluate. These will be treated in turn here.

Carr surveys mainly evidence from the apostolic and church fathers (Ignatius, Polycarp, Justin, and Ignatius) and Scripture; much more evidence outside these sources exists. One text that Carr must contend with is Ignatius, *Trall.* 9.1, since it contains the exact same concert of substantive adjectives, ἐπουρανίων καὶ ἐπιγείων καὶ ὑποχθονίων.

> 9.1 Κωφώθητε οὖν, ὅταν ὑμῖν χωρὶς Ἰησοῦ Χριστοῦ λαλῇ τις, τοῦ ἐκ γένους Δαυίδ, τοῦ ἐκ Μαρίας, ὃς ἀληθῶς ἐγεννήθη, ἔφαγέν τε καὶ ἔπιεν, ἀληθῶς ἐδιώχθη ἐπὶ Ποντίου Πιλάτου, ἀληθῶς ἐσταυρώθη καὶ ἀπέθανεν, βλεπόντων τῶν ἐπουρανίων καὶ ἐπιγείων καὶ ὑποχθονίων· (2) ὃς καὶ ἀληθῶς ἠγέρθη ἀπὸ νεκρῶν, ἐγείραντος αὐτὸν τοῦ πατρὸς αὐτοῦ, ὃς καὶ κατὰ τὸ ὁμοίωμα ἡμᾶς τοὺς πιστεύοντας αὐτῷ οὕτως ἐγερεῖ ὁ πατὴρ αὐτοῦ ἐν Χριστῷ Ἰησοῦ, οὗ χωρὶς τὸ ἀληθινὸν ζῆν οὐκ ἔχομεν.[41]

> 9. Be deaf, therefore, whenever anyone speaks to you apart from Jesus Christ, who was of the family of David, who was the son of Mary; who really was born, who both ate and drank; who really was persecuted under Pontius Pilate, who really was crucified and died while those in heaven and on earth and under the earth looked on; (2) who, moreover, really was raised from the dead when his Father raised him up, who—his Father, that is—in the same way will likewise also raise us up in Christ Jesus who believe in him, apart from whom we have no true life.[42]

---

ment of Jesus Christ as the King of all God's creation, visible and invisible; and the acclamation of the spirits who surround his throne." Beare is not clear about the nature of these mighty astral spirits. His claim that these spirits "rule" over the three realms of the universe indicates that he might equate "spirits" with the various deities of the Greco-Roman world, but this cannot be concluded with any certainty from his comments. Neither can it be discerned whether he would include angels among or *as* these astral spirits. In the end, Beare offers no comment on the precise nature of the spirits, only that spirits are in view here behind all three adjectives and human beings are not.

40. O'Brien, *Philippians*, 245; Hofius, *Christushymnus*, 20–40; Wesley Carr, *Angels and Principalities: The Background, Meaning, and Development of the Pauline Phrase Hai Archai Kai Hai Exousiai*, SNTSMS 42 (Cambridge: Cambridge University Press, 1981), 86–89.

41. Michael William Holmes, *The Apostolic Fathers: Greek Texts* (Grand Rapids: Baker, 1999), 164.

42. Michael William Holmes, *The Apostolic Fathers: English Translations* (Grand Rapids: Baker, 1999), 165.

Carr argues that, because Ignatius elsewhere uses the adjectives ἐπουράνιος and ἐπίγειος in the neuter (e.g., Ignatius, *Trall.* 5.2) and similarly so does Polycarp (Polycarp, *Phil.* 2.1), therefore at *Trall.* 9.1 we should also understand these adjectives as neuter such that "the reference is not so much to beings that inhabit the three regions as to the overall notion of universality of homage to God. The best parallel is Psalm 148."[43] There are at least two problems with this line of reasoning. First, the contexts of *Trall.* 5.2 and *Phil.* 2.1 are significantly different from *Trall.* 9.1; and even in *Trall.* 5.2 Ignatius acknowledges the reality of angelic and other spiritual entities. Second, the texts that Carr appeals to—*Trall.* 5.2, *Phil.* 2.1, and Ps 148—all lack the third region signified by καταχθόνιος.[44] Thus, this difference must be accounted for.

As it stands, Ignatius assumes rather than explicates the identity of these entities in *Trall.* 9.1 except to say that they "see" Christ crucified and by implication also Christ resurrected. Ignatius clearly alludes to Phil 2:10 but connects the heavenly, earthly, and subterranean ones with Christ's death by "seeing" it; thus, they are agents and not things. But how are we to interpret them? Other Pauline passages speak of Christ's death and resurrection as occurring in view of important agents, especially rulers (1 Cor 2:6–8) or rulers and authorities (Col 2:14–15; see also Eph 3:10). Thus, in 1 Cor 2:6–8 Paul affirms that "the rulers of this age" had not understood God's plan and ignorantly put Christ, "the Lord of glory," to death. Significantly, however, these rulers are human governing officials and not supernatural beings.[45] In Col 2:14–15, Christ's death and resurrection are done in view of "the rulers and the authorities" (τὰς ἀρχὰς καὶ τὰς ἐξουσίας): "By disarming the rulers and authorities, he made a public display of them, triumphing over them in the cross." Such an affirmation builds on the prior one that in Christ all Deity dwells fully in bodily form (2:9) and that Christ is "head over all rule and authority" (2:10). Impor-

---

43. Carr, *Angels and Principalities*, 87.

44. Psalm 148 is bipartite in its conception of the created order of "heaven and earth." It has three movements: 148:1–6, "Praise the Lord from the Heavens," and then particularized; 148:7–12, "Praise the Lord from the Earth," and then particularized; 148:13–14, "His glory is above earth and heaven," as the conclusion.

45. See the excellent treatment of Gordon D. Fee, *New Testament Exegesis: A Handbook for Students and Pastors*, 3rd ed. (Louisville: Westminster John Knox, 2002), 84–93, and the earlier work of Gene Miller, "ΑΡΧΟΝΤΩΝ ΤΟΥ ΑΙΩΝΟΣ ΤΟΥΤΟΥ: A New Look at 1 Corinthians 2:6–8," *JBL* 91 (1972): 522–28; and Wesley Carr, "The Rulers of This Age: 1 Corinthians 2:6–8," *NTS* 23 (1976): 20–35.

tantly, in 2:15 "the rulers and the authorities" (τὰς ἀρχὰς καὶ τὰς ἐξουσίας) are differentiated in that each has its own article (as in Eph 3:10). In fact, a study of the Pauline usage of rule/ruler and authority/authorities supports understanding the first group of "rulers" on a human scale and the second group of "authorities" as nonhuman entities.[46] For Ignatius, then, the meaning is indeterminate except that the entities are personal agents; one must understand from the religious milieu whom these adjectives signify in view of the original context of Philippians.

Hofius treats Jewish apocryphal texts (e.g., T. Sol. 18.3; 21.1), Porphyry (through Servius's commentary on Virgil's *Bucolics*), and Scripture, and finally evaluates the later magical papyri.[47] These latter references, although speaking of (demonic) beings in these three realms, Hofius discounts as too unlike the context of Phil 2:10. It will be instructive to consider the magical evidence in view of religious trends. Although there was increasing interest in transcending to the heavenly domains (see, e.g., Lucian's *Parliament of the Gods*), "the hundreds of *defixiones* from around the Mediterranean attest the continued popularity and power of Persephone, Hermes, Hecate, and various underworld demons and ghosts during the late imperial periods."[48] A third-century CE inscription from

---

46. See the review of the evidence in Fredrick J. Long, "Roman Imperial Rule under the Authority of Jupiter-Zeus: Political-Religious Contexts and the Interpretation of 'the Ruler of the Authority of the Air' in Ephesians 2:2," in *The Language of the New Testament: Context, History and Development*, ed. S. E. Porter and A. W. Pitts, Linguistic Biblical Studies 6; Early Christianity in its Hellenistic Environment 3 (Leiden: Brill, 2013), 124–33.

47. Hofius quotes Servius poem 5.66 (referring readers also to Apuleius, *Metam.* 11.5.1; 25.3): *sed constat secundum Porphyrii librum, quem Solem appellavit, triplicem esse Apollinis potestatem, et eundem esse Solem apud superos, Liberum patrem in terris, Apollinem apud inferos*. "But it is evident, according to Porphyry's book, which he called 'Sun,' that the power of Apollo is threefold, and he was the same Sun in the world above, the Free Father on the earth, and Apollo in the infernal regions" (my translation). The Latin text is from the PHI Latin database: http://latin.packhum.org/loc/2349/6/315#315.

48. Christopher A. Faraone, "The Collapse of Celestial and Chthonic Realms in a Late Antique 'Apollonian Invocation' (PGM I 262-347)," in *Heavenly Realms and Earthly Realities in Late Antique Religions*, ed. Ra'anan S. Boustan and Annette Yoshiko Reed (Cambridge: Cambridge University Press, 2004), 214. See also R. L. Gordon and Francisco Marco Simón, eds., *Magical Practice in the Latin West: Papers from the International Conference Held at the University of Zaragoza, 30 Sept.–1 Oct. 2005*, RGRW 168 (Leiden: Brill, 2010).

Carthage (*IGRR* 1.945) speaks to the power of Hermes, who traverses the different realms of the gods with different names:[49]

> *IGRR* 1.945
> ὁρκίζω σε τὸν θεὸν τὸν νεκυαγωγὸν τὸν ἅγιον Ἑρμῆν, τὸν οὐράνιον Αων κρειφτὸν ἐπίγειον ἀλέον [— —]βνιν, τὸν χ[θό]νιον Αρχφησον·

> I adjure you by god, the dead-leading holy Hermes, the heavenly Aeon, enfleshed earthly crazed [— —] βνιν, the subterranean Archphesus.

James Hope Moulton and George Milligan related P.Lond. 46 (fourth century CE) to Phil 2:10. Lines 164–71 include the following:

> ὑπόταξόν μοι πάντα τὰ δαιμόνια ἵνα μοι ἦν ὑπήκοος πᾶς δαίμων οὐράνιος καὶ αἰθέριος καὶ ἐπίγειος καὶ ὑπόγειος καὶ χερσαῖο[ς] καὶ ἔνυδρος καὶ πάσᾳ ἐπιπομπῇ καὶ μάστιξι θεοῦ καὶ ἔσται σοι τὸ δαιμόνια πάντα ὕπηκοα.[50]

> obey me all demons in order that to me would be subject every daemon, heavenly and ethereal and earthly and subterranean and land-dwelling and living in water, and for every punishment and scourging of God also all the daemons will be subject to you.

Adolf Deissmann recognized the relationship of the third-century CE P.Paris 574.3037–45 to Phil 2:10 but adds in a footnote to his translation, "In spite of the resemblance to Phil. 2:10, Eph. 2:2, 3:10, 6:12, this is not a quotation from St. Paul. The papyrus and St. Paul are both using familiar Jewish categories."[51]

> 3037 ....ὁρκί-
> ζω σε, πᾶν πνεῦμα δαιμόνιον, λαλῆσαι ὁποῖ-
> ον καὶ ἂν ᾖς, ὅτι ὁρκίζω σε κατὰ τῆς σφραγῖ-
> 3040 δος ἧς ἔθετο Σολομὼν ἐπὶ τὴν γλῶσσαντοῦ

---

49. The following inscriptional texts were found at https://epigraphy.packhum.org. Translations are our own.

50. F. G. Kenyon, ed., *Greek Papyri in the British Museum* (London: British Museum, 1893), 1:70, as cited in "ἐπίγεος," MM, 236. Our translation.

51. Adolf Deissmann, *Light from the Ancient East: The New Testament Illustrated by Recently Discovered Texts of the Graeco-Roman World*, trans. L. R. M. Strachan, 2nd ed. (London: Hodder & Stoughton, 1910), 257 n. 11. The Greek text is from p. 253 and his translation from p. 257.

Ἰηρεμίου καὶ ἐλάλησεν. καὶ σὺ λάλησον
ὁποῖον ἐὰν ᾖς ἐπεουράνιον ἢ ἀέριον
εἴτε ἐπίγειον εἴτε ὑπόγειον ἢ καταχθόνιον
ἢ Ἐβουσαῖον ἢ Χερσαῖον ἢ Φαρισαῖον.

3037..I adjure
thee, every daemonic spirit, say whatsoever
thou art. For I adjure thee by the seal
3040 which Solomon laid upon the tongue
of Jeremiah and he spoke. And say thou
whatsoever thou art, in heaven, or of the air,
or on earth, or under the earth or below the ground,
or an Ebusaean, or a Chersaean, or a Pharisee.[52]

Three more passages are found in *PGM* 12.67–72, 12.325–31, and 17a.2–6.[53]

PGM 12.67–72

λόγος γ' ἐπὶ τῆς αὐτῆς θυσίας·ἐπικαλοῦμαι ὑμᾶς, θεοὶ οὐράνιοι καὶ ἐπίγειοι
καὶ ἀέρ<ι>οι καὶ ἐπιχθόνιοι, καὶ ἐξορκίζω κατὰ τοῦ κατέχοντος τὰ δ' θεμέλια
ἐπιτελέσαι μοι, τῷ δεῖνα (ἢ τῇ δεῖνα), τόδε πρᾶγμα καὶ δοῦναί μοι χάριν,
ἡδυγλωσσίαν, ἐπ[αφ]ροδισίαν πρὸ[ς] πάντας ἀνθρώπους καὶ πάσας γυναῖκας
τὰς ὑπὸ τὴν κτίσι[ν], ἵνα μοι ὦσι ὑποτεταγμένοι εἰς πάντα, ὅσα ἐ[ὰν] θέλω,
ὅτι δοῦλός εἰμι τοῦ ὑψίστου θε[ο]ῦ [τ]οῦ κατέχοντο[ς] τὸν κόσμον καὶ
παντοκρ[ά]τορος.

Third formula for the same offering: I call upon you, gods of heaven and gods of earth, gods aerial and gods terrestrial. And I conjure you by the one who controls the 4 foundations, to accomplish for me, the man NN [or the woman NN] such-and-such a matter and to give me favor, sweet speech, charm with all men I and all women under creation, that they may be submissive to my every wish, inasmuch as I am the slave of the most high god, the almighty who controls the universe.

---

52. Deissmann comments on these last three items: "This remarkable trio of daemons obviously comes from LXX Gen. 15:20, Exod. 3:8, 17, etc., where we find Χετταῖοι (who have become Χερσαῖοι, *i.e.* 'land daemons'), Φερεζαῖοι (who have become the more intelligible 'Pharisees'), and Ἰεβουσαῖοι. Χερσαῖος, which also occurs elsewhere as a designation applied to a daemon…, has here no doubt the force of an adjective derived from a proper name" (*Light from the Ancient East*, 257 n. 12).

53. Translations are from Hans Dieter Betz, *The Greek Magical Papyri in Translation, Including the Demotic Spells* (Chicago: University of Chicago Press, 1986), 155, 165, 253, respectively.

PGM 12.325–331

Ἠνοίγησαν αἱ πύλαι τοῦ οὐρανοῦ, ἠνοίγησαν αἱ πύλαι τῆς γῆς.
ἠνοίγη <ἡ> ὅδευσις τῆς θαλάσσης, ἠνοίγη ἡ ὅδευσις τῶν ποταμῶν,
ἠκούσθη μου τὸ πνεῦμα ὑπὸ πάντων θεῶν καὶ δαιμόνων,
ἠκούσθη μου τὸ πνεῦμα ὑπὸ πνεύματος οὐρανοῦ,
ἠκούσθη μου τὸ πνεῦμα ὑπὸ πνεύματος ἐπιγείου,
ἠκούσθη μου τὸ πνεῦμα ὑπὸ πνεύματος θαλασσίου,
ἠκούσθη μου τὸ πνεῦμα ὑπὸ πνεύματος ποταμίου.

The gates of heaven were opened. The gates of earth were opened.
The route of the sea was opened. The route of the rivers was opened.
My spirit was heard by all gods and daemons.
My spirit was heard by the spirit of heaven.
My spirit was heard by the terrestrial spirit.
My spirit was heard by the marine spirit.
My spirit was heard by the riverine spirit.

PGM 17a.2–6

Ἄνουβι, θεὲ ἐπίγε[ιε κ]αὶ ὑπόγειε καὶ οὐρ[ά]νιε,
κύον, κύον, κύο[ν, ἀ]νάλαβε σεαυτοῦ τὴν πᾶσαν
ἐξουσίαν καὶ πᾶς[α]ν δύναμιν κατὰ τῆς Τιγηροῦ,
ἣν ἔτεκεν Σοφία· <ἀ>νάπαυσον αὐτὴν τῆς ὑπερηφανείας
καὶ τ[οῦ] λογισμοῦ καὶ τῆς αἰσχύνης.

Anubis, god on earth and under earth and heavenly;
dog, dog, dog, assume all your authority
and all your power against Tigerous,
whom Sophia bore. Make her cease from
her arrogance, calculation, and her shamefulness.

What these texts demonstrate is little uniformity except in their geographic descriptions. However, the diversity of all the descriptors makes any appeal to a demonic background of spirits to explain Phil 2:10 problematic. It is largely this lack of uniformity and amalgamation of additional descriptors beyond the geographic heavenly/aerial, earthly, and subterranean that leads Hofius to dismiss this background altogether.[54] However, these magical texts are extremely eclectic and reflect the broad spectrum of religious belief, experience, and practice. These descriptors along with others in a variety of expressions are precisely what we should expect.

---

54. Hofius, *Christushymnus*, 20–21.

Nevertheless, their reference to virtually the same geographic regions betrays another early source. What is this other source?

In this regard, Dibelius briefly considered a much more promising line of research at the conclusion of his analysis of "in the heavenlies" from Eph 3:10: "In Homer only the gods are called ἐπουράνιος (e.g., Z₁₂₉, ₁₃₁, ₅₂₇); later the adjective becomes the noun: οἱ ἐπουράνιοι the gods (Theocr., Id. 205)."[55] It is in this direction also that our major lexicons have pointed interpreters of Phil 2:10, namely, to the gods.[56] So, too, Craig S. Keener has noted when commenting on 2:10 that the Greeks worshiped gods in the heavens, earth, sea, and the underworld, although not favoring this interpretation.[57]

Evidence for the Heavenly, Earthly, and Subterranean Gods

Below we will survey references to the heavenly, earthly, and subterranean gods as are found in the lexicon of Julius Pollux, scholia, inscriptions, and other diverse classical literature. How early are the gods associated with the heavenly, earthly, and subterranean spaces? Homer acknowledges the regional gods in *Od.* 5.184–186, when Calypso makes an oath to Odysseus by reference to their domains:

ἴστω νῦν τόδε γαῖα καὶ οὐρανὸς εὐρὺς ὕπερθε
καὶ τὸ κατειβόμενον Στυγὸς ὕδωρ, ὅς τε μέγιστος
ὅρκος δεινότατός τε πέλει μακάρεσσι θεοῖσι,
μή τί τοι αὐτῷ πῆμα κακὸν βουλευσέμεν ἄλλο.

---

55. Dibelius, *Geisterwelt*, 232: "Bei Homer heißen nur die Götter ἐπουράνιος (z. B. Z₁₂₉, ₁₃₁, ₅₂₇); später wird das Adjektiv zum Substantiv: οἱ ἐπουράνιοι die Götter (Theocr. *Id.* 205)."

56. BDAG, s.v. "ἐπουράνιος," 2.b.β; BDAG, s.v. "ἐπίγειος," 1.b.β; BDAG, s.v. "καταχθόνιος." The same is true of LSJ, s.v. "ἐπουράνιος"; see also the reference to gods under LSJ, "καταχθόνιος" (although here readers are not referred to Phil 2:10). In LSJ, s.v. "ἐπίγειος," no mention is made of gods or Phil 2:10.

57. Craig S. Keener, *IVP Bible Background Commentary: New Testament* (Downers Grove, IL: InterVarsity Press, 1993), 560. He says, "Those 'in heaven' would include the angels, probably the rebellious angels who rule the pagan nations (see comment on Eph 1:19-23). Greeks worshiped gods in the heavens, earth, sea and underworld; traditional Greek mythology also placed the shadowy existence of departed souls in the underworld. Paul announces that whatever categories of beings there are, they must acknowledge Christ's rule, because he is exalted above them. One often bowed the knee in obeisance before a ruler or deity."

> Know this, by earth and by heaven far reaching above
> and by the Styx flowing downward, which is the greatest
> and most dreadful oath approaching the blessed gods,
> that I mean you no sort of harm. (our translation)

However, since it is generally accepted that the heavens, earth, and subterranean regions reflect an ancient conceptualization of space, we must show how such spaces were in fact understood commonly in relation to the gods such that the (substantive) adjectives ἐπουράνιοι καὶ ἐπίγειοι καὶ καταχθόνιοι could be found in tandem in fact to refer to the gods.

Importantly, this regional taxonomy of gods corresponds to that found in Julius Pollux, second-century CE Egyptian Greek grammarian and sophist, who lists Attic synonyms and phrases by subject matter and identifies each of these four regional deities of heavenly, earthly, marine, and subterranean at the start of his description (1.23.4–24.10). Below, the text is given in its original sequence with only our comments added in brackets:

> [heavenly =] θεοὶ ὑπερουράνιοι, ἐνουράνιοι, ἐπουράνιοι, ἐναιθέριοι, ἐναέριοι· [earthly =] ἐπίγειοι, οἱ αὐτοὶ καὶ ἐπιχθόνιοι· [marine =] ἐνάλιοι, θαλάττιοι, οἱ αὐτοὶ καὶ ἐνθαλάττιοι, [subterranean =] ὑπόγειοι, χθόνιοι καὶ ὑποχθόνιοι καὶ καταχθόνιοι, [various gods =] ἑστιοῦχοι [house-guarding], πολιοῦχοι [city-guarding], πατρῷοι [ancestral], ξένιοι [foreign], φίλιοι [friendly], ἑταιρεῖοι [fellowship], φράτριοι [clan], ἀστεροπηταί [lightning], ἀγοραῖοι [of the agora], ἐρίγδουποι [thundering], ἐφέστιοι, ἐπικάρπιοι, στράτιοι, τροπαιοῦχοι, ἱκέσιοι, τρόπαιοι, ἀποτρόπαιοι, λύσιοι, καθάρσιοι, ἁγνῖται, φύξιοι, σωτῆρες, ἀσφάλειοι, παλαμναῖοι, προστρόπαιοι, γενέθλιοι, γαμήλιοι, φυτάλιοι, προτρύγαιοι. [further explanation =] τὰ πολλὰ δὲ τούτων ὡς ἴδιά ἐστι τοῦ Διός, ὥσπερ ὁ ὑέτιος [the one bringing rain] καὶ ὁ καταιβάτης [one bringing thunder], καὶ παρ' Ἀθηναίοις φράτριος. τὸ γὰρ νεφεληγερέτης [cloud gatherer] καὶ ὅσα τοιαῦτα ἐπὶ τοῦ Διός, ὥσπερ καὶ τὸ ἐννοσίγαιος [earth shaker] καὶ τὸ ἐνοσίχθων [earth shaker] καὶ τὰ ὅμοια ἐπὶ τοῦ Ποσειδῶνος, ποιηταῖς ἀνείσθω.

Several things are noteworthy. First, as we would expect, Pollux describes the variety of terms available for the first major groupings of the gods—heavenly, earthly, marine, and subterranean—before moving to the household, city, ancestral gods, and so on. Second, the taxonomy is prioritized by the most important spaces. Third, marine gods are listed, yet searching for lists of these regional gods reveals that the marine gods are not as commonly listed with the others; it seems that they may be grouped with either the earthly gods or subterranean gods. Fourth, the adjectives can function substantively such that θεοί, "gods," need not be explicit.

Many scholia on ancient texts give explanatory comments that not simply show a tripartite universe but refer to gods as identified by such spaces. It is impossible to date these works, but the older portions (designated *vetera*) reflect ancient commentary dating as early as the fourth century BCE.[58] A good sampling of scholia will be presented here. In the older (*vetera*) scholia of Homer, *Od.* 5.418.7–11, we see the divisions of the world according to the three brother gods of Zeus (heavens), Poseidon (sea), and Pluto (subterranean parts), with the earthly parts not parceled out but acknowledged as belonging, probably because the earth is included with the sea and the discussion pertains to Amphitrite, the wife of Poseidon.

Ἀμφιτρίτη λέγεται ἡ θάλασσα. ἀδελφὰ γάρ εἰσι τὰ στοιχεῖα ὁ Ποσειδῶν, ὁ Ζεὺς, καὶ ὁ Πλούτων. τῷ μὲν Διὶ ἔλαχεν ἡ τρίτη μοῖρα, ἤγουν τὰ οὐράνια, τῷ δὲ Ποσειδῶνι ὡσαύτως ἡ θάλασσα, τῷ δὲ Πλούτωνι ὡσαύτως ἡ τρίτη, ἤγουν τὰ καταχθόνια. ἡ γῆ δέ ἐστι καὶ τῶν τριῶν.

Amphitrite is called the sea. For the brothers are the elements, Poseidon, Zeus, and Pluto. A third part is apportioned to Zeus, as they say, the heavens, and to Poseidon likewise the sea, and to Pluto likewise a third, they say, the subterranean parts. Moreover, the earth is also [included] in the three parts.

The *vetera Scholia in Homerum* (revised) on the *Il.* 3, verse 278, line 2, explains the text:

[καὶ οἳ ὑπένερθε] ἐκφοβῶν δὲ τοὺς Τρῶας τοὺς οὐρανίους θεοὺς καὶ ἐπιγείους καὶ ὑπογείους καλεῖ.

---

58. For an understanding of the dating and format of scholia, we are particularly indebted to the fine work of Eleanor Dickey, *Ancient Greek Scholarship: A Guide to Finding, Reading, and Understanding Scholia, Commentaries, Lexica, and Grammatical Treatises, from Their Beginnings to the Byzantine Period* (Oxford: Oxford University Press, 2010). The Greek texts are from the Thesaurus Linguae Graecae database. All translations are ours.

καὶ οἳ ὑπένερθε: And fearing the Trojans, he called the heavenly and earthly and subterranean gods.

The *vetera Scholia in Pindarum* Ode 8, 106g1–4, concerns the proper identification of Hermes in relation to the regions.

ὅτι δὲ ὁ Ἑρμῆς καὶ ἐπουράνιος καὶ
ἐπίγειος καὶ ὑποχθόνιος δηλονότι καὶ κῆρυξ θεῶν ἐν οὐρανῷ
καὶ ἐν γῇ· καὶ ὅτι ὑποχθόνιος, μαρτυρεῖ Ὅμηρος (ω1)·
Ἑρμῆς δὲ ψυχὰς Κυλλήνιος ἐξεκαλεῖτο.

Now, that Hermes is heavenly and earthly and subterranean clearly even being the herald of the gods in heaven and in earth. And that he is subterranean, Homer testifies, "Cyllenian Hermes calls out [for himself] souls." (*Od.* 24.1)

In the *vetera Scholia in Lycophronem* (edited by Isaac and John Tzetzes) at 679.15–16, in the midst of discussing the statue at Athens called Τ.[ρικέφαλος] Νωνακριάτης ὁ Ἑρμῆς (see LSJ, s.v. "τρικέφαλος"), the statue's three heads are given explanation first in the older scholia and then the alternative ("OR") as edited by one of the Tzetzes brothers:

<τρικέφαλος> δὲ ὁ αὐτὸς ἢ ὅτι ἐστὶν οὐράνιος καὶ θαλάσσιος καὶ καταχθόνιος
ἢ διὰ τὸ φυσικὸν καὶ λογικὸν καὶ ἠθικόν.

"Three headed" is either that he is heavenly and of sea and subterranean, OR, because of the physical and logical and ethical.

Also revised by one of the Tzetzes, the *Scholia in Aristophanem* on verse 1126, line 2, provides an explanatory comment on the nature of Hermes:

<Ἑρμῆ χθόνιε:> ὁ Ἑρμῆς καὶ οὐράνιος καὶ ἐπίγειός ἐστι καὶ καταχθόνιος.

Ἑρμῆ χθόνιε: Hermes is heavenly and earthly and subterranean.

In the *vetera Scholia in Aeschylum in Persas* (also edited by Thomas Magister and Demetrius Triclinius) on verse 499b, line 2 (see also 497, line 12), we have the brief explanation:

γαῖαν οὐρανόν τε] ἤγουν τοὺς ἐπιγείους καὶ οὐρανίους θεούς.

γαῖαν οὐρανόν τε: that is to say, the earthly and the heavenly gods

Thus, ancient interpreters of a wide variety of important classical works expressed a framework of explanation that associated the gods to their geographic domains.

The epigraphic evidence is also instructive especially because of the diversity of locations and dating.[59] The adjectives (or equivalents)— ἐπουράνιος, ἐπίγειος, καταχθόνιος—are often plural, occurring with or without θεός as substantives alone or in some combination with some frequency. Consider these examples of the adjective ἐπουράνιος alone.

1. Zeus Savior and Hera Savior are θεοί ἐπουράνιοι, "heavenly gods" (*CIRB* 36 from the north Black Sea, 275–79 CE).
2. "Heavenly Zeus" (*SB* 1:4166 from Egypt, n.d.).

Many of these inscriptions do not name the particular "heavenly god(s)": *IK* 56.73 (Cilicia, early first century CE); *DAW* 38.94 (Cilicia, second century CE); *IK* 10.1115 and 1114 (from Bithynia, third and fourth century CE, respectively); *ASAA* 41–42 (1963-1964), no. 351 (Phrygia, n.d.); *IG* 12.Supp.165 (Melos during the reign of Nero); and *EA* 27.11.4 (Hierapolis, ca. 166–215 CE).

Many mention the "heavenly" (ἐπουράνιοι or οὐράνιοι) and "subterranean" (καταχθόνιοι, ὑποχθόνιοι) gods:[60] *TAM* 2.521 (Lycia at Pinara, Roman period); *TAM* 2.613 (Lycia at Tlos, Roman imperial period); *TAM* 5.2.1731 (Magnesia on Sipylos, n.d.); *TAM* 5.2.1096 (Thyatira, n.d.); *IMT* Kyz Kapu Dağ 1825 (Mysia, n.d.); *JÖAI* (1915), 45 (Cilicia, n.d.); *JHS* 18 (1898), 307.3 (Cilicia and Isauria, n.d.); and *IK* 56.135 (Cilicia, 101 CE).

With slight variations (οὐράνιοι, χθόνιοι, or κατὰ γῆς), there are several more:[61] ILycia 2.9.16 (Lycia, n.d. with κ[α]τ[α]χθονί[οις καὶ οὐραν]ίοις [θε]οῖς); ISmyrna 643 (οἵ τε θεοὶ οἱ οὐράνιοι καὶ οἱ κατὰ γῆς δαίμονες, imperial period); *EA* 27.11.4 = *ASAA* 41–42 (1963-1964), number 351 (Hierapolis, late second century CE with χθονίοις); *MAMA* 6, list 150.186 (Phrygia,

---

59. Use of the Packard Humanities Institute's searchable Greek Inscriptions is subject to agreement. The searchable Greek Inscriptions is available at https://epigraphy.packhum.org/. The Greek text supplied below is from this database.

60. E.g., Demeter, Persephone, the Erinyes, and Hades/Pluto (the *katachthonian* Zeus); in Latin, *di manes*. For numerous ancient references, see LSJ, s.vv. "χθόνιος," "καταχθόνιος," and "ὑποχθόνιος."

61. See Dionysius of Halicarnassus, *Ant. rom.* 2.72.8, l. 8 (ἐπικαλεσάμενος τούς τε οὐρανίους καὶ καταχθονίους θεούς), and 6.89.4, l. 8 (τοὺς θεοὺς τοὺς οὐρανίους ἵλεως εἶναι καὶ δαίμονας τοὺς καταχθονίους).

n.d.; τοὺς οὐρανίους θεοὺς καὶ καταγαίους); *MAMA* 3.77 (Cilicia, Roman period; τοὺς οὐρανίους θεοὺς καὶ τοὺς καταχθονίους); and *SEG* 21.815 = *MDAI(A)* 67 (1942), 73.128 (Attica, first/second century CE) has χθόνιός τε οὐράνιός τε δράκων.

One inscription differentiates "heavenly" and "subterranean" from "terrestrial gods" (ἐπίγειοι) and "marine gods" (ἐνάλιοι):[62] θεούς ... ἐπουρανίους τε καὶ ἐπιγείους καὶ ἐναλίους καὶ καταχθονίους (ILydiaHM 7.1 from Mysia, second century CE).

In the inscriptional record, the adjectives for "subterranean" occur too frequently to account for separately; ὑποχθόνιος occurs thirty-eight times and καταχθόνιος 751 times, over five hundred of which are in Sicily, Italy, and the West, and 441 in Rome and its environment. The vast majority are undated funerary inscriptions that may date after the first century CE. Most will abbreviate Θ. Κ. for Θεοῖς Καταχθονίοις. For example, across seven lines of text the inscription *IGUR* 3.1309 reads, Θ[εοῖς] Κ[αταχθονίοις] ἐνθάδε κεῖται ἀνὴρ πολλῶν ἀντάξιος ἄλλων, Πομπήιος Διοκλῆς τέρματ' ἔχων σοφίης, "To the subterranean gods, Here lies a man worth as much as many others, Pompeius Diocles, having supremacy of wisdom."

Two conclusions may be drawn from this survey of the inscriptional evidence. First, combinations of the adjectives often occur together. Second, the subterranean deities were particularly important in the West. Each conclusion informs what we observe in Phil 2:10 since Roman religious ideas impacted Philippi.

As far as other literary works, Aelius Aristides from Asia Minor in his encomium "For Zeus" (Εἰς Δία), delivered circa 149 CE at Smyrna, described four regions of the gods—heaven, air, sea, and earth—by design of Zeus.

> And he gave the four regions to the gods, so that nothing anywhere might be without gods, but that they might everywhere attend upon all things which are and all things which are coming into being, having divided up among themselves, like prefects and satraps, first as their homeland the region of heaven and then that in the air and in the sea and on the earth

---

62. See Strabo, *Geogr.* 6.2.11, l. 32, who refers to τοῖς τε καταχθονίοις θεοῖς καὶ τοῖς θαλαττίοις. This classification of god is also found in Auguste M. H. Audollent, *Defixionum tabellae quotquot innotuerunt, tam in Graecis Orientis quam in totius Occidentis partibus praeter Atticas in Corpore Inscriptionum Atticarum editas* (Paris, 1904), 242, l. 11 (Carthage, third century CE) and possibly *IGUR* 3.1203, l. 4 (Rome, n.d.).

[τὴν δὴ πρώτην πατρίδα τὴν οὐράνιον καὶ τὴν κατ' ἀέρα καὶ τὴν ἐν θαλάττῃ καὶ τὴν ἐπὶ γῆς]. (18)[63]

We see in Aristides a distinction that develops later: heaven as "aether" is differentiated from "air" (see Artemidorus below and the magical inscriptions above). Also, oddly missing here are the subterranean gods, although this may reflect more Aristides's strategy to best praise Zeus. The second century showed the increasing popularity of the subterranean gods alongside the heavenly gods.[64] As we have seen, in the catalogued inscriptions, references to subterranean gods in Italy and the West account for a large majority of their occurrences, mostly on epitaphs.

Another late second-century CE author, Artemidorus, wrote his *Onirocriticon*, "The Interpretation of Dreams," in which the gods are identified by name by geographical location. Self-identified as Artemidorus of Daldis in Lydia, Asia Minor, he was actually trained in Ephesus. In 2.34.1–26 below Artemidorus provides a representative view of how the deities were geographically classified. His discussion starts with the Olympian gods in the aether realm before going to the other realms of heavenly, earthly, marine, and subterranean.

> Of the gods, we say that some belong to Olympus (or similarly to the aether), some to the heavens, some to the earth, some to the sea and the rivers, and some to the underworld [οὓς καὶ αἰθερίους καλοῦμεν, τοὺς δὲ οὐρανίους, τοὺς δὲ ἐπιγείους, τοὺς δὲ θαλασσίους καὶ ποταμίους, τοὺς δὲ χθονίους]. Zeus, Hera, Aphrodite Ourania, Artemis, Apollo, Aetherial Fire, and Athena are reasonably said to belong to aether. Helios, Selene, the Stars, the Clouds, the Winds, … and Iris belong to the heavens; all these are perceptible by the senses. Of the gods who belong to the earth, those perceptible by the senses are Hekate, Pan, Ephialtes, and Asklepios (who at the same time is also said to be perceptible by the intellect); those perceptible by the intellect are the Diokouroi, Herakles, Dionysos, Hermes, Nemesis, Aphrodite Pandemos, Tyche, Peitho, the Graces, the Hours, the Nymphs, and Hestia. The sea gods perceptible by the intel-

---

63. Translation and provenance are from Aelius Aristides, *P. Aelius Aristides: The Complete Works*, vol. 1, *Orations I–XVI*, trans. Charles Allison Behr (Leiden: Brill, 1981).

64. Christopher A. Faraone is correct to state, "The Greeks in archaic and classical times tend to divide up the supernatural into two fairly distinct categories, each with their own forms of ritual and address: (1) the Olympian or celestial, and (2) the chthonian" ("Collapse of Celestial and Chthonic Realms," 213).

lect are Poseidon, Amphitrite, Nereus, the Nereids, Leukothea, and Phorkys; those perceptible by the senses are Thalassa itself, the Waves, the Seashores, the Rivers, the Marshes, the Nymphs, and Acheloös. The underworld gods are Pluto, Persephone, Demeter, Kore, Iakkhos, Sarapis, Isis, Anubis, Harpokrates, underworld Hekate, the Furies, the *daimones* who attend them, and Phobos and Deimos, whom some call the sons of Ares. (Artemidorus Daldianus, *Onir.* 2.34)[65]

One sees a clear demarcation moving from one realm of the gods to the next. In 2.34.31 a transition occurs to discuss the Olympian gods in more detail until 2.35.48, where the transition occurs to discuss the heavenly gods (περὶ δὲ τῶν οὐρανίων ἑξῆς ἐροῦμεν). This detailed discussion "in order" (ἑξῆς) extends until the next transition, from the heavenly to the earthly gods, at 2.36.153–154 (ταῦτα μὲν περὶ τῶν οὐρανίων· περὶ δὲ τῶν ἐπιγείων θεῶν ὧδε κρίνειν προσήκει); the transition to the marine gods occurs at 2.37.155–156 (περὶ δὲ θαλασσίων καὶ ποταμίων θεῶν ἕκαστα ὧδε ἔχει); and the transition to the subterranean gods occurs at 2.38.25–26 (ἐπειδὴ δὲ περὶ τούτων κατὰ τὸ ἐνδεχόμενον εἴρηται, λοιπὸν ἂν εἴη περὶ χθονίων θεῶν εἰπεῖν καὶ τῶν πέριξ <τούτων>). The discussion then turns to Ocean and Tethys at 2.39.45 before a discussion of heroes and demons at 2.40.1 (Περὶ δὲ Ἡρώων καὶ Δαιμόνων).

The taxonomy of gods by space—heavenly gods, earthly gods, marine gods, and subterranean gods—is reflected also in Vergil, who sought to praise the emperor Augustus. He praised Octavian by appeal to the fourfold pattern of identifying him with the earth, sea, and sky gods but rejecting the gods of the lower realms (*Georg.* 1.25–39).[66]

> and you too, Caesar, who, in time, will live among a company
> of the gods, which ones unknown, whether you choose
> to watch over cities and lands, and the vast world
> accepts you as bringer of fruits, and lord of the seasons,
> crowning your brows with your mother Venus's myrtle,
> or whether you come as god of the vast sea, and sailors

---

65. The English translation is from R. J. White, *The Interpretation of Dreams* (Park Ridge, NJ: Noyes, 1975). See also the translation of Daniel E. Harris-McCoy, *Artemidorus' Oneirocritica: Text, Translation, and Commentary* (Oxford: Oxford University Press, 2012).

66. On this basis, Gertrude Hirst argues for the earlier dating of Horace. "A Discussion of Some Passages in the Prologue to the Georgics. (l. 14, 15 and 27)," *Transactions and Proceedings of the American Philological Association* 59 (1928): 19–32, esp. 28–30.

worship your powers, while furthest Thule serves you,
and Tethys with all her waves wins you as son-in-law,
or whether you add yourself to the slow months as a Sign,
where a space opens between Virgo and the grasping claws,
(Even now fiery Scorpio draws in his pincers for you,
and leaves you more than your fair share of heaven):
whatever you'll be (since Tartarus has no hope of you as ruler,
and may such fatal desire for power never touch you,
though Greece might marvel at the Elysian fields,
and Proserpine, re-won, might not care to follow her mother),
grant me a fair course, and agree to my bold beginning.[67]

It is as if Vergil were musing, "It is doubtful which society of gods you are to join, gods of earth, of sea, or of sky (certainly not gods of the underworld)."[68]

Although the acclamation of the living emperor as a god is less evidenced in Rome than in the eastern provinces,[69] Vergil reveals the extent to which flatterers of the emperor Augustus were willing to affirm him as divine while still alive. But after death, there was no such difficulty even to affirm Augustus as a "heavenly god." Thus, the *demos* of Erythrai (a coastal Ionian city of Asia Minor) makes this dedication: "The Demos to Gaius Julius Augustus Caesar heavenly god" (ὁ δῆμος Γαίωι Ἰουλίωι Σεβαστῶι Καίσαρι θεῶι ἐπουρανίωι; IErythrai 63, n.d.). Similarly, in Pontus and Paphlagonia during Claudius's reign (45–54 CE) another inscription acknowledges the peace (εἰρήνη) of Augustus, honors Caesar Claudius, and affirms Gaius Aquila as "the high priest of the heavenly god Augustus" (ὁ τοῦ ἐπουρανίου θεοῦ Σεβαστοῦ ἀρχιερεύς) (IKaunos 1.c; see also 1.a). But how did Augustus attain the status of a heavenly one among the gods?

Becoming a "God": *Consecratio*/Ἀποθέωσις

The most analogous and relevant religious affirmation to the claim of God's exceedingly great exaltation (ὑπερυψόω) of Jesus Christ in Phil 2:9 would have been the deification (ἀποθέωσις/*consecratio*) of deceased Caesars and their family members, transporting them into "heavenly places"

---

67. The translation by A. S. Kline and is available at https://tinyurl.com/SBL4216h.
68. So summarizes Hirst, "Discussion," 28–29.
69. See the chart detailing this difference in Lozano, "*Divi Augusti*," 142.

among the gods.[70] Overall, in the first century five emperors and seven of their family members were officially recognized as apotheosized by the senate.[71] From Augustus's death (14 CE) through Constantine's (337 CE) "thirty-six of the sixty emperors ... and twenty-seven members of their families were apotheosized and received the title of *divus* ('divine')."[72] Those officially deified at Rome postmortem by the end of Nero's reign at 68 CE included in chronological order Julius Caesar (died in 44 BCE and deified in 42 BCE under dramatic circumstances involving a dream and comet[73]), Augustus (14 CE under Tiberius), Drusilla (sister of Caligula, 38 CE under Caligula), Livia Augusta (wife of Augustus, died in 29 CE and deified in 42 CE under Claudius), Claudius (54 CE under Agrippina and Nero), and the two members of Nero's family—his daughter Claudia in 63 CE and wife, Poppaea Augusta, in 65 CE. The list of imperial family members recognized as deified in Athens included seventeen persons, most of whom were so recognized while still alive.[74]

In Rome, eyewitnesses who saw the soul taken heavenward by Jupiter's eagle testified to the ascension of the deceased emperor.[75] The dead body

---

70. See the section on "'Heavenly Honours Decreed by the Senate': From Emperor to Divus" in Ittai Gradel, *Emperor Worship and Roman Religion*, OCM (Oxford: Clarendon, 2002), 261–371.

71. S. R. F. Price, "Gods and Emperors: The Greek Language of the Roman Imperial Cult," *JHS* 104 (1984): 83.

72. S. R. F. Price, "From Noble Funerals to Divine Cult: The Consecration of Roman Emperors," in *Rituals of Royalty: Power and Ceremonial in Traditional Societies*, ed. David Cannadine and S. R. F. Price, Past and Present Publications (Cambridge: Cambridge University Press, 1987), 57.

73. Suetonius records that Julius dreamed the night before his assassination that he soared above the clouds and shook hands with Jupiter (*Jul.* 81.3). Also the belief of Julius's apotheosis was secured when on the eve of the first day of the games celebrating his apotheosis, sponsored by Octavian, a comet appeared in the sky lasting seven days and was thought to represent his soul elevated to heaven (Suetonius, *Jul.* 88), as represented on coins. For discussion see Larry Kreitzer, "Apotheosis of the Roman Emperor," *BA* 53 (1990): 213–15. For a discussion of the historical phenomenon and its political exploitation, see John T. Ramsey and A. Lewis Licht, *The Comet of 44 B.C. and Caesar's Funeral Games*, APA American Classical Studies 39 (Atlanta: Scholars Press, 1997).

74. See discussion and chart in Lozano, "*Divi Augusti*," 142.

75. Augustus's apotheosis was attested by "an ex-praetor who took oath that he had seen the form of the Emperor, after he had been reduced to ashes, on its way to heaven" (Suetonius, *Aug.* 100.4); the ex-praetor is identified as Numerius Atticus (Cas-

was ignited on a funerary pyre with an eagle released flying skyward. The event is depicted as such in iconography in prominent ways (e.g., the apotheosis of Titus on the underside of the arch dedicated to him by Domitian in Rome, 81 CE) or with the divinized soul riding the *quadriga* (four-horse chariot) heavenward. Julius Caesar is often thus represented, or by a shining star representing his comet (BMC 323).[76]

With an official consecration by the Senate, the deceased ruler or family member could establish for themselves a Roman cult with temples, priests, and sacrificial liturgies. Gertrude Grether describes how this played out for Livia, the wife of the divine Augustus, whose statue upon her consecration was joined with Augustus's in his temple in Rome (Dio Cassius, *Hist. Rom.* 60.5.2).[77] However, deification was also proclaimed by an emperor unofficially for other (deceased) household members or self-proclaimed (by Caligula for himself).[78] For instance, several princes of the Julian imperial household are depicted in reliefs and artwork as deified figures, for example Germanicus, the elder Drusus, and Marcellus.[79]

The earliest extant Roman political treatise to feature apotheosis is Cicero's *De republica* (ca. 54 BCE). Cicero had fully endorsed the belief by recounting the tradition found in Ennius surrounding Romulus, the founder of a "new people" (*novum populum*; 2.11.21), and by depicting the divinization of other subsequent worthy Roman political rulers/lead-

---

sius Dio, *Hist. Rom.* 56.46.2; see also 56.42.3). The deification of Drusilla, the sister of Caligula, was attested by Livius Geminus of the senatorial class (Dio Cassius, *Hist. Rom.* 59.11.4). The custom of producing witnesses is mocked in Seneca, *Apocol.* 9.

76. In the conclusion to Ovid's *Metamorphoses* at 15.843–850, Jupiter orders Venus to descend and escort Julius's soul back to heaven, and as she does he is transformed into a star (see also 15.748–750). See also Cicero's initial rejection of the deification of Julius as involving impious practices (*Phil.* 1.13; 2.110; cited in Daniel N. Schowalter, *The Emperor and the Gods*, HDR 28 [Minneapolis: Fortress, 1993], 62 n. 47). For photograph of the arch, see Michael Pfanner, *Der Titusbogen*, Beiträge zur Erschliessung hellenistischer und kaiserzeitlicher Skulptur und Architektur 2 (Mainz: Philipp von Zabern, 1983).

77. Gertrude Grether, "Livia and the Roman Imperial Cult," *AJP* 67 (1946): 222–52.

78. For a polemical description by Philo of Gaius Caligula on his divine status, see *Legat.* 162–165.

79. Eugénie S. Strong, *Apotheosis and after Life: Three Lectures on Certain Phases of Art and Religion in the Roman Empire* (Freeport, NY: Books for Libraries Press, 1969), 67–70. See "Apotheosis," in *A Dictionary of Greek and Roman Antiquities*, ed. W. Smith and C. Anthon, 2nd ed. (London: Murray, 1875), 105–6.

ers, such as Scipio (the elder) Africanus (*Rep.* 6.13).[80] Cicero relates that Romulus disappeared when the sun darkened and was "set up [*conlocatus*] among the number of the gods" (2.10.17). Later, a common peasant, Proculus Julius (encouraged by the senators to clear them from possible incrimination), attested in a public assembly that Romulus appeared to him on a hill (later called Quirinal) and gave orders to build him there a shrine and that "he was a god and called Quirinus" (*se deum esse et Quirinum vocari*; 2.10.20). What is striking, however, is the length to which Cicero argues against this tradition being a myth or fable, since Romulus had already established culture and education "with very little opportunity for the invention of fables"; this time was well after Homer and not so long before Cicero's own times (2.10.18–20).

The basis for the apotheosis of Romulus, according to Cicero, was his "ingenuity and virtue" (*ingenium et virtus*; *Rep.* 2.10.20) and his establishment of two foundations of the republic, the auspices and the senate (2.10.17). Service to the state is central at the end of Cicero's *Republic*, "Scipio's Dream" (in book 6). This dream provided an *apocalyptic* description of the heavenly abodes of deceased, worthy human spirits as gods under the "supreme God" (*princeps deus*; 6.26). Central in the dream is how to attain this heavenly reward (6.13, 15, 16, 18, 20, 25, 26, 29), which is the spirit's proper "seat and home" (*sedem et domum*; 6.29). The elder Scipio explains: "All those who have preserved, aided, or enlarged their fatherland have a special place prepared for them in the heavens…. Their rulers and preservers come from here and here they return" (6.13).[81] When

---

80. Translations of Cicero's *De republica* and *De legibus* are from Keyes, whereas *Tusculanae disputationes* translations are ours. Cicero's hope in apotheosis was influenced by the Roman poet Ennius (239–170 BCE), who had sung earlier of apotheosis of the elder Scipio (Seneca, *Ep.* 108.34, as cited in Strong, *Apotheosis*, 243 n. 37). See also Cicero's statements affirming the apotheosis of Romulus and others in *Tusc.* 1.12.28, in agreement with Ennius's statement: "Romulus in heaven passes time with the gods" (*Romulus in caelo cum diis agit aevum*). At the death of his daughter, Cicero had longed for her apotheosis and had intended to build a temple for her (Cicero, *Att.* 12.36, as cited in Strong, *Apotheosis*, 243 n. 38). This temple never was realized.

81. Cicero's views on this point correspond with the Orphic view, according to Max Radin, "Apotheosis," *The Classical Review* 30.2 (1916): 44–46. He argues, "We have only to remember the Orphic conception, emphasized in a hundred ways by writers from Euripides to Aristotle, to the effect that the human soul does not merely become divine at the death of the body, but that it always was divine, and that at bodily death it returns to its divine condition…. To the masses, no doubt, each deification of

asked about whether the deceased are alive, Scipio answered, "Surely all those are alive [*vivunt*] … who have escaped the bondage of the body so as from a prison; but that life of yours, which men so call, is really death" (6.14). Indeed, the heavenly abodes, emphasizes Cicero clearly, are a place of life; the "life" (*vita*) that loves "justice and duty [*iustitiam ... et pietatem*] … is the way to heaven [*via est in caelum*]" and is a gathering place of those now "living in that place [*illum incolunt locum*]" (6.16.16).[82] In Cicero's *Tusculanae disputationes* (1.12.28), he addresses directly life after death in apotheosis by listing Greek and Roman heroes, and then asks, "Isn't heaven nearly filled with human offspring?" The view of Cicero's *Republica* is continued in *De legibus*, when he (as himself in the dialogue) places into religious law for his ideal state, among others, this law: "They shall worship as gods both those who have always been regarded as dwellers in heaven, and also those whose merits [*merita*] have admitted them to heaven" (2.8.19). Such a belief in attaining divinity greatly impacted Augustus; the "elaborate directions for his [own] burial and the deification which he was accorded exemplify Cicero's doctrine, in the *Dream of Scipio*, that a great statesman should seek the reward of glory in the memory of following generations and in the afterworld."[83]

The political bases for apotheosis in Cicero are similar to those found in Manilius's *Astronomica* (written before and after Augustus's death in 14 CE) and Ovid's *Metamorphoses*. In the *Astronomica*, Manilius lists Greek heroes, sages, and Roman warriors ("whose host now is the largest"—1.777) who attained to the heavens in apotheosis on the basis of their triumphs, extensive rule, strength of mind, judgment, foundation of cities, military accomplishments—in sum, "by their own virtue" (*virtute sua*; 804 [Goold]).[84] In the *Metamorphoses*, Ovid describes Romulus's "placement in heaven" *Metamorphoses*. (*inponere caelo*) by his father Mars (14.805–

---

an emperor merely added a new denizen to Olympus. But to some it was more intelligible to consider the process, a return of an incarnated deity to his former state. Thus Julius Caesar was worshipped as *Iuppiter Iulius*, Livia was Ceres. Later, Hadrian, too, was Jupiter" (45).

82. It may be within this framework that in 2 Cor 5:4 Paul too speaks of mortality being swallowed up "by life" (ὑπὸ τῆς ζωῆς) when entering the eternal dwellings (5:1–2).

83. Mason Hammond, *City-State and World State in Greek and Roman Political Theory until Augustus* (Cambridge: Harvard University Press, 1951), 156.

84. For the hope of obtaining immortality through civic benefactions, see the discussion and personal examples in Reggie M. Kidd, *Wealth and Beneficence in the Pas-*

828). Father Jupiter allowed his apotheosis in fulfillment of his promise to Mars. As for the timing of the taking away of Romulus, Mars reasoned that at that time Rome was now on a sure foundation of rule, not resting on one man alone (Romulus had established the rule of senate). So, immediately when Romulus was giving judgment to the citizens and "the Father" (Jupiter) hid the sky with dark clouds," Mars descended "through the air" (*per aera*) and translated Romulus from earth in a form "more dignified for the high seats of honor" (*pulvinaribus altis dignior*; 14.827).[85] Next in turn, Romulus's wife, Hersilia, was apotheosized (14.829–851). Ovid then depicts the apotheosis of Julius Caesar (15.745–750) and Augustus in advance (15.839–870). Julius Caesar's apotheosis is secured by his "civic deeds" (*domi gestae*) that offered a more significant "triumph" (*triumphus*) than his wars that bring peace, although Julius's "greater work" (*maius opus*) is being father of the emperor Augustus (15.745–761), who "showered blessings upon the human race." The basis of Augustus's apotheosis is the blessings he brings in the form of "services" (*merita*; 15.838) and "good deeds" (*bene facta*; 15.850; see also 15.758–759). In Ovid, then, one finds a full expression of apotheosis that would appear repeatedly in the imperial propaganda, in which the emperors were taken skyward and given "heavenly seats" (*aetherias sedes*; 15.839).

The deification of rulers and their placement on seats with the gods at death was an ancient belief. In Egypt, Ramesses II is shown deified seated on a throne, attended to by three gods.[86] Eugénie S. Strong's lectures surveying art depictions of *Apotheosis and the Afterlife* in the Mediterranean world reveals how widespread and diverse the belief of apotheosis was. But among the many themes found in Strong's lectures is occasionally the sitting of the deified one. Reliefs found near Sparta show "the dead man [probably a hero] enthroned with his wife receiving offerings from the survivors."[87] Daniel Schowalter summarizes well the benefit of such a belief

---

toral Epistles: A "Bourgeois" Form of Early Christianity?, SBLDS 122 (Atlanta: Scholars Press, 1990), 120–24; see especially the bibliography and comments in n. 32.

85. Seneca's *Apocolocyntosis* mocks Claudius's apotheosis thoroughly, but has him pleading initially with Hercules on the basis of sitting in judgment before the temple of Hercules (7), as Romulus had been doing before his apotheosis. Also, a favorable witness is found for Claudius, who argues that "blessed Claudius be a god … and that a note to that effect be added to Ovid's *Metamorphoses*" (9 [Heseltine and Rouse]); Ovid also describes the apotheosis of Julius and Augustus.

86. See image in Gilbert Bilezikian, "Tree of Life," *BEB* 2:2104–5.

87. Strong, *Apotheosis*, pls. XVI and XX.

among the Roman emperors: "Instead of journeying to the underworld and being among the shades of the dead as was the lot of other human beings, good emperors were thought to rise up to the stars and join the gods of heaven."[88] The emperors transcended the common Roman beliefs (or worries) about life after death, which might involve existing among the *manes* (shadows of the dead) or nothing at all (nihilism).[89] Tangible "proof" of Julius Caesar's apotheosis was seen in the comet that followed Julius Caesar's death. It was thought to signify his heavenly journey and placement among the stars; the comet is featured on imperial prints (e.g., BMC 323).

Greek heroes were divinized. Although debate continues whether the hero cult or the Greek pantheon was the oldest form of Greek religion,[90] what is paramount for Paul's Letter to the Philippians is simply that Philippi actively enjoyed cults to both. Conquerors as heroes—most famously Alexander the Great, then later followed by Roman conquering generals and successful governing officials—were also deified and worshiped in the Greek East with such divine honors while living (or shortly after death).[91] A short list of Roman leaders would include Flamininus, the liberator of Greece (196 BCE); Pompey, who received several temples (ca. 60 BCE); Cicero, for his governorship of Cilicia but who refused such honors and chastised Verres for presumably accepting such honors (ca. 50 BCE); and

---

88. Schowalter, *Emperor*, 62. He cites Manilius, *Astronomica* 1.799–804, who understood the emperors to be "peers with the gods" but one astral tier lower than them.

89. For a review of Roman beliefs on afterlife, see Keith Hopkins, *Death and Renewal*, Sociological Studies in Roman History 2 (Cambridge: Cambridge University Press, 1983), 226–35.

90. Lewis Richard Farnell, *Greek Hero Cults and Ideas of Immortality: The Gifford Lectures Delivered in the University of St. Andrews in the Year 1920* (repr., Oxford: Clarendon, 1970); Carla M. Antonaccio, "Contesting the Past: Hero Cult, Tomb Cult, and Epic in Early Greece," *AJA* 98 (1994): 389–410; and Jan N. Bremmer, "The Rise of the Hero Cult and the New Simonides," *ZPE* (2006): 15–26.

91. For a review of those receiving divine honors in the Greek East, see Dominique Cuss, *Imperial Cult and Honorary Terms in the New Testament*, Paradosis: Contributions to the History of Early Christian Literature and Theology 23 (Fribourg: Fribourg University Press, 1974), 24–27, and Sara Karz Reid, *The Small Temple: A Roman Imperial Cult Building in Petra, Jordan* (Piscataway, NJ: Gorgias, 2005), 150–51. Reid relates that King Obodas of the Nabateans was worshiped as a god probably only after his death and apotheosis.

Mark Antony.[92] The logic of apotheosis must have been that since their divinity was celebrated on earth, so it should continue in their departure at death, in which they were numbered among the heavenly gods. This tradition continued with the emperors, beginning with Julius Caesar. Augustus, however, established a precedent for the refusal the divine honors (especially in Rome).[93] Yet this did not stop ruler worship and the imperial cult of the living emperors from flourishing in the Greek East.[94] The official consecration of deceased and worthy emperors and family members (listed above) allowed, then, a formal cult to be initiated in Rome, which was felt in the pervasive imperial cults, which quickly spread and augmented what was already occurring in the East.[95] Strong rightly concludes, "The belief in the immortality of the soul and in the soul's return to the heavenly seats, was to gain fresh luster from the Apotheosis of the [Roman imperial] ruler."[96]

There are several interrelated factors that contributed to this Roman doctrine and its attachment to the imperial elite. The influence of the divine king figure with the Ptolemies in Egypt and the Greco-Syria Seleucids among the Greeks in the East resulted in divine honors being awarded to ruling and conquering Roman political figures in their lifetime, as described above. Then, too, the deification of the former emperor allowed the adoptive son the right to claim the status of "son of a god" (*divi filius*). Ovid rehearses the logic well: "So then, that his son might not be born of mortal seed, Caesar must needs be made a god" (*Metam.* 15.760–761). And so, the title *divi filius*, "son of a god," is repeatedly found on imperial coinage in the first century. Also, the death and consecration of Augustus played out prominently in the coinage of Tiberius, who commemorated its anniversary in his decennial and vicennial mintages, and in Nero, who celebrated the event's half-centenary.[97]

---

92. For discussion and citation of sources, see Strong, *Apotheosis*, 63–64, and Cuss, *Imperial Cult and Honorary Terms*, 27–35.

93. See Duncan Fishwick, "Dio and Maecenas: The Emperor and the Ruler Cult," *Phoenix* 44.3 (1990): 267–75.

94. For discussion see Paul Zanker, *The Power of Images in the Age of Augustus*, trans. Alan Shapiro, Jerome Lectures 16 (Ann Arbor: University of Michigan Press, 1988), 297–306.

95. On the diversity of expression in the imperial cults, see Reid, *Small Temple*, 149–50.

96. Strong, *Apotheosis*, 63.

97. Michael Grant, *Roman Anniversary Issues: An Exploratory Study of the Numismatic and Medallic Commemoration of Anniversary Years 49 B.C.–375* (Cambridge:

"Every Knee Bowed" 271

Imperial apotheosis favored the social elite and reflected the pyramidal social and religious hierarchy. The imperial belief trumped the hopes and expectations of the average, servile person, who in common Greco-Roman conceptions of afterlife would face an uncertain future life, if any at all.[98] Thus, Paul's description of Jesus as servant and dying an ignominious death of crucifixion in Phil 2:7–8 would have spoken directly counter to notions of imperial apotheosis. The widespread curriculum of Homer would have encouraged beliefs in either Tartarus (Hades) or a more blessed state in the Elysian fields, which virtually no one attained (see Plato, *Gorg.* 523A–524A, developing Homer's mythology).[99] The Roman poets and the astronomer Manilius continued the Greek traditions of descriptions of afterlife of heroes. Vergil, after surveying the landscape of Tartarus with its punishments on sinners through the sight of Aeneas (*Aen.* 6.548–627), refers to the Elysian fields as "a land of joy" with "happy seats [*sedes beatas*] of the Blissful Groves" (6.69 [Fairclough]).

In Manilius, however, a grander vision attends the place of the Roman emperors. He speculates that the Milky Way is that heavenly place, closest to the abode of the gods, where the souls of heroes, once "freed from the body ... live the infinite years of paradise and enjoy celestial bliss" (1.759–761).[100] Then Manilius offers a lengthy description in 1.762–804 of such male heroes, sages, and Roman warriors, among whom only one woman, Cloelia, is mentioned. The list ends with Julius and Augustus: "and the Julian who boasted descent from Venus. Augustus has come down from

---

Cambridge University Press, 1950), 163. In summary, Grant concludes: "The events of the life and principate of Augustus dominated the anniversary coinages of later epochs" (162).

98. For the range of Roman beliefs, see Hopkins, *Death and Renewal*, 226–35. The elitist distinction is seen in Vergil's *Aen.* 6, where first the deceased Anchises describes to his son Aeneas the common fate of humans before showing him his descendants from divine Romulus, who are likened to "a progeny of gods..., all denizens of heaven, all tenants of the celestial heights" (785–787 [Fairclough]).

99. Radin explains that the verb "to apotheosize" (ἀποθεόω) is found used to describe the burial of ordinary people (*CIG* 2831) and thus, "the ceremonial interment of the lowliest citizen was as much a restoration to his divine nature as the formal *consecratio* of the Master of the World, τοῦ κόσμου κύριος, as Antoninus Pius called himself (*Dig.* 14,2,9)" ("Apotheosis," 45). In the lexical entries of LSJ, both the verb ἀποθεόω, "deify," and the noun ἀποθέωσις, "deification," have possible meanings of consecrating a burial location or burial, respectively.

100. The translation in this paragraph is from Goold.

heaven and heaven one day will occupy, guiding its passage through the zodiac with the Thunderer [Jupiter] at his side; in the assembly of the gods he will behold mighty Quirinius and him whom he himself has dutifully added as a new deity to the powers above [i.e., Julius], on a higher plane than shines the belt of the Milky Way. There is the gods' abode [*deis sedem*], and here is theirs [the heroes], who, peers of the gods in excellence, attain to the nearest heights" (1.798–804).

This imperial privilege of divinization to the highest seated position above the lot of the common folk is exploited by the courtesan of Nero, Lucan, in his *Pharsalia* (or *Bellum Civile*), dated around 61 CE. Lucan, who eventually fell out of favor with Nero, described (in "advance") Nero's supposed apotheosis in terms very similar to Seneca's tragedy *Hercules Oetaeus* (which depicted Hercules's apotheosis) and Vergil's *Georg.* 1.32–39 (describing Augustus's apotheosis) and yet trumping them.[101] Nero, superior to Hercules and Augustus, not only gains entrance into the highest heavenly abodes but assumes Jupiter's prerogative of assigning the seat: Nero will himself decide his own divine position and role.[102] "Not only the new god's rights and privileges, but also the site of his [Nero's] residence become a question of importance. In like manner the chorus in the *Hercules Oetaeus* had been concerned about Hercules's position in the sky [*Herc. Ot.* 1565–1671].... Lucan, insisting upon the pre-eminence of Nero, explicitly asserts that nature will allow him to select the seat of his divine power" (*Phar.* 1.53–54).[103] Because of the presumption and currency of apotheosis as political propaganda, the passage in Lucan, *Phar.* 1.45–63, which exemplifies this, is worth quoting at length:

> When your watch on earth is over and you seek the stars at last, the celestial palace you prefer will welcome you, and the sky will be glad. Whether you choose to wield Jove's scepter, or to mount the fiery chariot of Phoebus and circle earth with your moving flame ... every god will give place to you, and Nature will leave it to you to determine what deity you wish to be, and where to establish your universal throne. But choose not your seat either in the Northern region or where the

---

101. Lynette Thompson, "Lucan's Apotheosis of Nero," *CP* 59, no. 3 (1964): 148–50. Vergil's description of Augustus's apotheosis in *Georg.* 1.32–39 does not specify a specific position but provides several possible roles.

102. Seneca, *Herc. Ot.* 2.1564–1570, describes the final "seat" of Hercules at the appointment of Jove.

103. Thompson, "Lucan's Apotheosis of Nero," 149.

sultry sky of the opposing South sinks down: from these quarters your light would look aslant at your city of Rome.... Maintain therefore the equipoise of heaven by remaining at the centre of the system. May the region of the sky be bright and clear, and may no clouds obstruct our view of Caesar! In that day let mankind lay down their arms and seek their own welfare, and let all nations love one another; let Peace fly over the earth and shut fast the iron gates of warlike Janus. But to me you are divine already. (Duff)

The point in this survey is to understand that in Philippi there would have been ample exposure to Roman imperial understandings of rulers and heroes dying and rising and being seated in the heavenly realms among the stars, that is, obtaining imperial astral apotheosis. Significantly, Paul frames the whole of Philippians with multiple references to Jesus Christ (sixteen times in 1:1–23) as he broached the topic of life and death and his own possible "leaving in death to be with the Christ" (1:23). Why populate the opening with repeated references to Jesus? Why discuss Christ's pattern of suffering servitude to the point of death before being exalted by God? Arguably, Paul was preparing to show how believers should adopt the viewpoint of Christ's movement from life to death to heavenly life after death. The hymn shows that God has exalted Jesus and his name to a superior position (see also Eph 1:20–23; 1 Tim 6:14–16).

That Paul has evoked precisely here the prevailing imperial ideology of astral exaltation finds support immediately in 2:15, when he affirms that believers are "God's children" (τέκνα θεοῦ) who "shine as stars in the world" (φαίνεσθε ὡς φωστῆρες ἐν κόσμῳ). Then, too, Paul explains his own pursuit of following Christ's pattern of suffering/death before resurrection (3:10–11). He then urges the Philippian believers not to focus on earthly things, "because our citizenship belongs in heaven, from where we also await a Savior, the Lord Jesus Christ" (3:19–20). So, believers are encouraged to act courageously in their heroic deeds and set their minds on Christ Jesus, who is in the heavens above every divine being. Then immediately in 3:21 Paul describes how our humble bodies will be transformed into glorious bodies like Christ's, once again recalling the progression of 2:5–11, where Paul effectively subordinates all other views of afterlife and all divine claims to the claim that God has lifted up Jesus Christ as Lord such that all gods will kneel before him. Thus, although Paul does not disclose precisely how believers' lives after death will be like or unlike imperial astral afterlife, his affirmations—that (1) Christ is in heaven, (2) believers are "stars" now, (3) they await a resurrection, (4) they have a heavenly citizenship, (5) they expect a transformation into glorious bodies like the human heroic person Jesus, and (6) they will be present with Christ at death—find analogy in the views of afterlife surveyed above.[104] But while Paul's network of themes are similar to imperial views of afterlife, importantly he subordinates these views to God's purposes in Jesus by his affirmations in 2:10–11; and precisely here he makes a strong allusion to Isa 45:23.

The Intertextuality of Isaiah 45–46 and Submission Scenes

Why did Paul interweave the intertextuality of Isa 45:23 with religious views of the heavenly, earthly, and subterranean gods? In Phil 2:10 Paul vividly presents for the Philippian Christians a scene of the regional gods in the posture of "bowing the knee" that reflected profound submission.[105] This posture was associated with the broader political topos of *proskynesis* (προσκύνησις)—giving homage to a kingly figure, generally despised in Roman sentiment, even though required by the emperors Caligula and Domitian.[106] J. Rufus Fears indicates, "Proskynesis was the act of a social inferior, and normally an eastern king would perform *proskynesis* only before the image of a deity."[107]

---

104. Passages such as 2 Cor 5:1–10 and Eph 2:4–7 are also valuable in this regard; see also Heb 12:22–24.

105. See Paul's own submission when saying κάμπτω τὰ γόνατά μου πρὸς τὸν πατέρα, "I bow my knees to the Father" (Eph 3:14).

106. See the review of the concept and literature cited in E. A. Fredricksmeyer, "Divine Honors for Philip II," *TAPA* 109 (1979): 48 (esp. n. 33) and M. P. Charlesworth, "Some Observations on Ruler-Cult Especially in Rome," *HTR* 28 (1935): 16–20. He concludes that "there is nothing to show that during the first two centuries of the Principate *proskynesis* was ever regarded, by itself, as a cult-act, though it was certainly looked upon at first as a piece of flattery, degrading to the self-respect of the flatterer, foreign and un-Roman." Dio Cassius, *Hist. Rom.* 68.18.2, describes a gift to the emperor Trajan of a horse that was trained to lower its front feet and bow its head. On the mixed meaning of *proskynēsis* before Alexander the Great, who eventually demanded it, see the discussion in Balsdon, "'Divinity' of Alexander," 371–82, and in Hans-Josef Klauck, *The Religious Context of Early Christianity: A Guide to Graeco-Roman Religions*, trans. B. McNeil (Minneapolis: Fortress, 2003), 271–73.

107. J. Rufus Fears, "The Solar Monarchy of Nero and the Imperial Panegyric of Q. Curtius Rufus," *Historia* 25 (1976): 495.

Homer's supplicants in the *Odyssey* and *Iliad* lowered themselves and wrapped their arms around the knees of the beseeched.[108] To an unseen god, this would not be possible; instead one sees the people of God bowing the knee to the Lord, as in Ezra's national prayer of confession (1 Esd 8:73). The nature of bowing the knees indicates ultimate submission, even defeat in death (Judg 7:5–6; 4 Kgdms 9:24; see also 2 Kgdms 22:40). For instance, the military captain of fifty men bowed his knees to Elijah after the previous two captains and men were consumed by fire (4 Kgdms 1:13). Bowing the knee as a gesture involved not merely religious obeisance (3 Kgdms 19:18; Rom 11:4) but political fidelity. The people of God bowed their knees to the Lord God and to their earthly king (1 Chr 29:20).

Bowing in submission is befitting the original context of Isa 45:23, in which before the Lord God "every knee will bow and every tongue swear." In his earlier Epistle to the Romans, Paul at 14:11 formally quotes Isaiah in support of his claim that "we all will stand before the judgment seat of God." After quoting Isa 45:23, which retains its focus on God, then Paul concludes, "So then each of us concerning ourselves will give an account to God" (Rom 14:12).

> For we will all stand before the judgment seat [βῆμα] of God. For it is written,
> "As I live, says the Lord, every knee shall bow to Me,
> And every tongue shall give praise to God."
> So then each one of us will give an account of himself to God. (NASB)

In Phil 2:10–11, however, the scene is radically altered by the addition of Jesus into Isaiah's vision: "at the name of Jesus every knee will bow" and "every tongue confess that Jesus Messiah is Lord to the glory of God." Several points must be considered here regarding Paul's use of Isaiah and its recontextualization.[109]

First, "Whenever Paul referred only to 'Jesus' (not 'Jesus Christ' or 'the Lord Jesus'), he had especially in mind the earthly, historic Jesus, often

---

108. Victoria Pedrick, "Supplication in the Iliad and the Odyssey," *TAPA* 112 (1982): 125–40.

109. On distinguishing citation, recontextualization, and reconfiguration of written materials, see Vernon K. Robbins, *The Tapestry of Early Christian Discourse: Rhetoric, Society, and Ideology* (London: Routledge, 1996), 102–8. Recontextualization does not formally cite the source text and rather places it within a new context, as here.

as one who suffered and died (Rom 3:26; 2 Cor 4:11; 11:4; Gal 6:17; Eph 4:20; Phil 2:10; 1 Thess 1:20; 4:14)."[110] One reason for stressing Jesus as human may be that, according to Peter Oakes, there was no "divine figure in the Philippians' Graeco-Roman background who was likely to be heard receiving a homage of this type."[111] What this means, then, is that Jesus in 2:10 "is being painted in terms of an emperor.... The authority clearly eclipsed that of the gods too but the imagery employed would in the first instance evoke the idea of an imperial figure on his throne receiving homage from all those who had now been put under his authority."[112] In the Greek East, however, persons did bow down to gods.[113] Moreover, Paul strongly alludes to Isa 45, and in Hebrew Scripture there is a tradition of gods bowing before Yahweh as God (e.g., Dagon before the ark of the covenant in 1 Sam 5:4).

Second, Paul's strong allusion to Isa 45:23 is quite apropos to his argument subordinating the gods to Jesus. Isaiah 45 is one of the most antipagan gods texts in all of Scripture.[114] Six times in Isa 45, speaking on behalf of YHWH the prophet declares, "I am God/the Lord, and there is no other" (LXX Isa 45:5[2x], 6, 18, 21, 22). He speaks to "those raising their wood graven images" (οἱ αἴροντες τὸ ξύλον γλύμμα αὐτῶν) and "praying as to gods that do not save" (προσευχόμενοι ὡς πρὸς θεούς, οἳ οὐ σῴζουσιν, 45:20). Isaiah 45:18–25 presents this argument most poignantly with "an elaborate hymnic introduction that stresses the orderliness of creation"[115]

---

110. Fredrick J. Long, *2 Corinthians: A Handbook on the Greek Text*, Baylor Handbook on the Greek New Testament (Waco, TX: Baylor University Press, 2015), 83–84.

111. Oakes, *Philippians*, 150.

112. Oakes, *Philippians*, 150.

113. Balsdon, "'Divinity' of Alexander," 374–77.

114. Throughout Isa 40–55 the people of Israel are envisioned as being in bondage to the Babylonians, a tragic conundrum that would appear to indicate that the God of Israel has been thoroughly discredited and that the gods of Babylon are superior to the God of Israel. Yet, ironically, these chapters present a resounding rejection of this worldview. Though Israel is in bondage, Israel's God has *not* been discredited. On the contrary, there is *none* superior to the God of Israel. If anyone wishes to be delivered from the fate awaiting them in the form of King Cyrus and his armies, they must look to the God of Israel and to no other. For more on the literary and historical context of Isa 45 see John N. Oswalt, *The Book of Isaiah: Chapters 40–66*, NICOT (Grand Rapids: Eerdmans, 1998), 213. Although Oswalt bases his comments primarily on the MT, the overall summary of the context of Isa 45 we have provided here is not materially different in the LXX.

115. Paul D. Hanson, *Isaiah 40–66*, IBC (Louisville: John Knox, 1995), 110.

by affirming the Lord as "the maker of the heaven" (ὁ ποιήσας τὸν οὐρανόν) and "the God who displayed the earth and made it" (ὁ θεὸς ὁ καταδείξας τὴν γῆν καὶ ποιήσας αὐτήν). Consequently, in Isa 46:1–2 the gods Bel ("lord") and Nebo (a Babylonian god) "kneel down" and "bend the knee" (כרע and קרס) before Yahweh's ability to save his people; the gods have themselves been defeated and taken captive.[116] The Hebrew verb כרע in 46:1–2 is the same as in 45:23. Thus, Paul fittingly has utilized Isaiah while updating the gods depicted in defeat and submission to Jesus. In the end, the gods must "confess that Jesus Christ is Lord."[117]

Third, Paul's affirmation of Jesus's suffering death before exaltation is something like we see in Rev 5. There Jesus's identity as slain Lamb does not disqualify him from receiving full divine honor, which he does, and also occurs in the face of the impotence and submission of the regional gods. At Rev 5:3 we find the closest wording to Phil 2:10 and the heavenly, earthly, and subterranean gods right before the slain Lamb is enthroned. First, at Rev 5:3 the impotence of any other "divine" being is shown—"no one was able in heaven nor upon the earth nor under the earth to open the scroll" (οὐδεὶς ἐδύνατο ἐν τῷ οὐρανῷ οὐδὲ ἐπὶ τῆς γῆς οὐδὲ ὑποκάτω τῆς γῆς ἀνοῖξαι τὸ βιβλίον). However, in 5:13 "all of creation which is in the heaven and upon the earth and under the earth and in the sea and all things in them" (καὶ πᾶν κτίσμα ὃ ἐν τῷ οὐρανῷ καὶ ἐπὶ τῆς γῆς καὶ ὑποκάτω τῆς γῆς καὶ ἐπὶ τῆς θαλάσσης καὶ τὰ ἐν αὐτοῖς πάντα) speaks praise to the Lamb.[118] Notice that 5:3 lacks "in the sea," and 5:13 stresses "all creation" and includes the sea. Moreover, it is only the slain Lamb who can receive and open the scroll and be received to the position at God's right hand on the throne (5:7), whereas no other "divinity" can (5:3). The result of the

---

116. Undoubtedly, the Hebrew plays on the meaning of these verbs to signify both kneeling submission and inability due to falling under the weight/burden of their burdens. In the end, these idols "have themselves gone into captivity" (46:2 NASB) due to a military victory on Yahweh's part.

117. To translate the Hebrew absolute use of the niphal verb שׁבע, "I swear" (HALOT, s.v. "שׁבע I"), the LXX uses ἐξομολογέω with a range of meanings, "I confess, admit; I acknowledge, give thanks, praise; I agree, consent" (LSJ). Paul follows the LXX, yet has rendered ἐξομολογέω transitive by explicating the content of what is confessed: "Jesus Christ is Lord." The hymn's concluding prepositional phrase, "for the glory of God, the Father" (εἰς δόξαν θεοῦ πατρός), likely modifies the compound purpose clauses in 2:10–11.

118. Holloway points to Rev 5:13 as equating a similar expression to the one found in Phil 2:10c (*Philippians*, 128 n. 116).

Lamb's exaltation is praise to God and to the Lamb together on the throne (5:13). Thus, in both Phil 2:6–11 and Rev 5 we observe power structures being completely reversed in the wisdom God revealed in Christ crucified (see 1 Cor 2:6–8).

Fourth and finally, consistent with Rom 14:11–12, Paul envisions every knee bowing to Jesus in a scene of submission and judgment similar to 2 Cor 5:10. Although not explicitly mentioning the judgment seat (βῆμα) in Phil 2:10–11, this is probably implied. However, in Paul's recontextualization of Isaiah, Christ has been exalted above very name to whom obeisance and confession could be made, including especially the gods in their regional specificity along with divinized heroes or emperors. But what exactly is the mechanism of the confession and bended knees? When and how does this occur? Here Paul strongly implies that a victory has been awarded to Christ and that submission and confession (not necessarily profession) will occur. This is remarkably similar to the humiliating defeat of Christ's death on the cross achieved over the rulers and the authorities, depicted as a triumph in Col 2:14–15. If a victory is implied in Phil 2:10–11, the bended knee and confession would have corresponded to depictions of surrendered supplicants as seen in Roman victory art. Marjorie C. MacKintosh explains the ubiquity of the topic, "The submission of the barbarians is a frequent subject in Roman relief work. It signals both the end of the conflict between Rome and her enemies and the humiliation of that enemy who dared to challenge the might of Rome. Its main figures are the victorious Roman emperor, the surrendering leaders of the enemy, and the onlooking soldiers, sometimes of both sides."[119]

Several prominent artifacts come to mind. First, the elaborate onyx engraved Gemma Augustea (ca. 9–12 CE) depicts Augustus enthroned and Jupiter-like seated next to the goddess Roma and being crowned by the goddess Oikoumene or Tyche. Beneath them is the victory scene with a trophy being erected and one vanquished barbarian kneeling in submission. The first Boscoreale Cup, possibly copying a lost monument, also represents a submission scene of conquered kneeling men submitting before the seated Augustus.[120] Finally, decades later Trajan's Column commemorates the Dacian Wars (101–102 and 105–106 CE) and was erected

---

119. Marjorie C. MacKintosh, "Roman Influences on the Victory Reliefs of Shapur I of Persia," *California Studies in Classical Antiquity* 6 (1974): 187.

120. Fred S. Kleiner, "The Boscoreale Cups: Copies of a Lost Monument?," *JRA* 10 (1997): 377–80.

in 113 CE. Basically unchanged (excepting Trajan's statue being replaced by Peter), the continuous freeze spirals two hundred meters around the column and chronicles the progression of both wars, with the first coming to a climax with a dramatic surrender scene (scene 75). Before the seated Trajan rows of Dacians surrender, those closest kneeling besides their dropped shields. The final scene, 78, shows winged Victory inscribing the events on a shield between two erected trophies. Coins were struck commemorating the event (*RIC* 2, Trajan 678 and 679).

Conclusions

We have argued that, religiously, Paul makes explicit reference to the gods in Phil 2:10 who kneel down in submission to Jesus. Too often Jewish or Christian backgrounds are favored when reading Paul over against Greco-Roman pagan ones. Yet Paul was writing to mixed audiences who included many (who had been) steeped in paganism. Moreover, our tendencies to generalize ("*all things*" will bow down) or spiritualize ("angels," "spirits," or "demons" bow down) Paul's statements betray our theologizing or modernized reading and translation of texts.[121] Consequently, as interpreters we must consider how Paul himself was contextualizing a Jewish Jesus for his original audience(s) in quite diverse settings.

---

121. One Bible translator related to me in email the importance of recovering the original religious context/message of the Scripture in translation: "While working as a linguist-translator among a Bantu language group, the indigenous translators and I would often work many hours on a text to translate it, not only into their language, but also into their world view perspective. They believed in a High Creator God and three lesser gods confined to the three terrestrial domains: earth, water, and forest. We did not see this to be in conflict with many of passages that we worked with, either in the OT or in the NT. When we translated texts showing the High God's power over the lesser gods, the translators were excited and owned the texts as if they had been written in their own mother tongue. These rough draft texts were eagerly shared and taught to the people. However, when these drafts were brought to the consultant, it was demanded that a recognition of lesser gods be taken out of the text. After this, the translators gradually disowned these texts, for they had been denuded of their power and had lost all vitality for their situation in life. Ironically, the worldview perspective of this Bantu people group is closer to that of biblical cultures and cosmologies than that of the consultant, whose worldview reflected a rationalistic, post-Enlightenment, and European perspective."

Paul's depiction of heavenly, earthly, and subterranean gods submitting to Jesus aligns with his argumentative aims in Philippians. In broad terms, Wayne Meeks's assessment is sound: "The letter's most comprehensive purpose is the shaping of a Christian *phronēsis*, a practical moral reasoning that is 'conformed to [Christ's] death in hope of his resurrection.'"[122] Paul's primary argument in Philippians is that believers should understand their fundamental citizenship in a manner worthy of the gospel of Christ by embracing the mindset of Christ Jesus in their common life together.[123] In this way, 2:6–11 is crucial to Paul's overarching purpose in the letter to shape the Philippians into a community that embraces a mindset of privilege renouncing, self-emptying, other-serving humility, and cross-shaped (costly) obedience to God for the sake of others. Embracing this mindset led to Jesus's ultimate vindication and ultimately to his victory. Jesus is the ultimate human hero. As the Philippians adopt this same mindset in their life together, they may be sure that such a humble, costly disposition will ultimately be vindicated in ways analogous to the vindication of Jesus. This is what it means for Paul's audience to "have this mind among yourselves, which is yours in Christ Jesus" (2:5) and to order their citizenship "in a manner worthy of the gospel of Christ" (1:27).[124]

While it is true that the overarching purpose of 2:6–11 is not to offer systematic teaching on Christology, this has not prevented scholars from rightly teasing out not only its christological significance but also its significance for theology (proper).[125] It is precisely at the same time *because*

---

122. Wayne A. Meeks, "The Man from Heaven in Paul's Letter to the Philippians," in *The Future of Early Christianity: Essays in Honor of Helmut Koester*, ed. Birger Pearson (Minneapolis: Fortress, 1991), 333.

123. This is not to say that this is the *only* purpose of Philippians; it is simply to acknowledge this as the *overarching* or *primary* purpose of the letter. Subthemes and purposes might include, for example, (1) thanking the Philippians for the gifts they sent to Paul, (2) an update about Paul's circumstances, and (3) joy in the midst of suffering. For a concise discussion of the function of Phil 2:6–11 within the larger context of the epistle see Fowl, *Philippians*, 106–8.

124. Among the many scholars who recognize 1:27–30 as Paul's "thesis statement" for Philippians are Flemming, *Philippians*, 36; Ben Witherington III, *Paul's Letter to the Philippians: A Socio-rhetorical Commentary* (Grand Rapids: Eerdmans, 2011), 97; Fowl, *Philippians*, 59. Holloway refers to 1:27a as a "thematic exhortation" (*Philippians*, 103). Fee notes that "this paragraph thus holds the keys to much in this letter," and Fowl refers to it as "a linchpin in the argument of the epistle" (*Philippians*, 161).

125. See for example Richard Bauckham, *Jesus and the God of Israel: God Cruci-*

Jesus Christ was "in the form of God" (ἐν μορφῇ θεοῦ) and "equal with God" (ἴσα θεῷ) that he emptied himself and humbled himself by becoming obedient to the point of death on a cross.[126] In other words, 2:6–8 narratively describes the identity and character of *God*. To be "in the form of God" is to be kenotic and cruciform in character. This is well articulated by N. T. Wright:

> The real humiliation of the incarnation and the cross is that one who was himself God, and who never during the whole process stopped being God, could embrace such a vocation. The real theological emphasis of the hymn, therefore, is not simply a new view of Jesus. It is a new understanding of God. Against the age-old attempts of human beings to make God in their own (arrogant, self-glorifying) image, Calvary reveals the truth about what it means to be God. Underneath this is the conclusion, all important for the present Christological debate: incarnation and even crucifixion are seen to be *appropriate* vehicles for the dynamic self-revelation of God.[127]

This way of understanding *true* divinity runs counter to what has been commonly conceived of as "normal" divinity—grasping for power, might, acclaim, and heroic status—and exploiting these things for one's own advantage. The one who was *truly* divine did not act this way, and because of this he received all that 2:9–11 articulates, including homage of the heavenly, the earthly, and the subterranean gods.[128] The Philippians should

---

fied and Other Studies on the New Testament's Christology of Divine Identity (Grand Rapids: Eerdmans, 2008), 1–60; Larry Hurtado, *Lord Jesus Christ: Devotion to Jesus in Earliest Christianity* (Grand Rapids: Eerdmans, 2003), 98–153; Michael J. Gorman, "'Although/Because He Was in the Form of God': The Theological Significance of Paul's Master Story (Phil 2:6–11)," *JTI* 1 (2007): 147–69; Gorman, *Inhabiting the Cruciform God: Kenosis, Justification, and Theosis in Paul's Narrative Soteriology* (Grand Rapids: Eerdmans, 2009), 9–39; Wright, *Climax*, 56–98.

126. Recognizing the possibility that the participle ὑπάρχων in 2:6 functions both as a concessive participle *and* as a causal participle. For a sustained and compelling argument that this is indeed the best way to understand it see Gorman, *Inhabiting*, 18–28.

127. Wright, *Climax*, 84. For further discussion of the worship of Jesus and therefore "rethinking God," see also N. T. Wright, *Paul: In Fresh Perspective* (Minneapolis: Fortress, 2005), 83–107.

128. However, this does not mean that the causal nature of the link between the two halves of the hymn in some way signals the promotion of Jesus to a new status

adopt this same mindset (2:5) and thereby abandon any submission on their part to the prevailing gods, especially divinized imperial ones, and instead understand that their proper "citizenship is in heaven from where we await the Savior, the Lord Jesus Christ" (3:20).

If, as we have argued, the substantive adjectives of 2:10 make reference to the Greco-Roman divinities, Paul is claiming that Jesus, by acting in ways consistent with *true* divinity, not only casts doubt on the traditional, normal understandings of divinity but also *receives honor and acclaim*—staples of traditional notions of divinity—*precisely from the "gods" themselves*. Jesus's way of being "godlike" is vindicated as the true way and brings submission to those who in false ways most clearly were understood to possess godlikeness. If the purpose of 2:9–11 is to teach that embracing a mindset of self-emptying sacrificial love for the sake of others will ultimately be vindicated analogously to Jesus's vindication, there is no better way than to announce that even the gods themselves will kneel before the truly godlike One.

Bibliography

Antonaccio, Carla M. "Contesting the Past: Hero Cult, Tomb Cult, and Epic in Early Greece." *AJA* 98 (1994): 389–410.

Aristides, Aelius. *P. Aelius Aristides: The Complete Works*. Vol. 1, *Orations I–XVI*. Translated by Charles Allison Behr. Leiden: Brill, 1981.

Audollent, Auguste M. H. *Defixionum tabellae quotquot innotuerunt, tam in Graecis Orientis quam in totius Occidentis partibus praeter Atticas in Corpore Inscriptionum Atticarum editas*. Paris, 1904.

Balsdon, J. P. V. D. "The 'Divinity' of Alexander." *Historia* 1 (1950): 363–88.

Bauckham, Richard. *Jesus and the God of Israel: God Crucified and Other Studies on the New Testament's Christology of Divine Identity*. Grand Rapids: Eerdmans, 2008.

---

as a reward for Jesus's self-emptying and self-humbling, as if divine identity could be attained or granted by any sort of action. Rather than promotion, 2:9–11 indicates that the self-emptying and self-humbling of Jesus as the authentic revelation of divinity that he *already* possessed has been publicly recognized and vindicated by God the Father. Therefore the worship of this one who is "in the form of God" and possesses "equality with God" is entirely appropriate. Against the promotion view of 2:9–11, see Fowl, *Philippians*, 104.

Beare, Frank W. *The Epistle to the Philippians*. HNTC. Peabody, MA: Hendrickson, 1959.

Betz, Hans Dieter. *The Greek Magical Papyri in Translation, Including the Demotic Spells*. Chicago: University of Chicago Press, 1986.

Bilezikian, Gilbert. "Tree of Life." *BEB* 2:2104–5.

Bockmuehl, Markus. *The Epistle to the Philippians*. BNTC 11. Peabody, MA: Hendrickson, 1998.

Bremmer, Jan N. "The Rise of the Hero Cult and the New Simonides." *ZPE* (2006): 15–26.

Carr, Wesley. *Angels and Principalities: The Background, Meaning, and Development of the Pauline Phrase Hai Archai Kai Hai Exousiai*. SNTSMS 42. Cambridge: Cambridge University Press, 1981.

———. "The Rulers of This Age: 1 Corinthians 2:6–8." *NTS* 23 (1976): 20–35.

Charlesworth, M. P. "Some Observations on Ruler-Cult Especially in Rome." *HTR* 28 (1935): 5–44.

Cicero. *On the Republic, On the Laws*. Translated by Clinton W. Keyes. LCL. Cambridge: Harvard University Press, 1928.

———. *Pro Archia, Post Reditum in Senatu, Post Reditum ad Quirites, De Domo Sua, De Haruspicum Responsis, Pro Plancio*. Translated by N. H. Watts. LCL. Cambridge: Harvard University Press, 1923.

Craddock, Fred B. *Philippians*. Interpretation. Atlanta: John Knox, 1985.

Cumont, Franz. *The Mysteries of Mithra*. Translated by Thomas J. McCormack. 2nd rev. ed. Chicago: Open Court, 1903.

Cuss, Dominique. *Imperial Cult and Honorary Terms in the New Testament*. Paradosis: Contributions to the History of Early Christian Literature and Theology 23. Fribourg: Fribourg University Press, 1974.

Deissmann, Adolf. *Light from the Ancient East: The New Testament Illustrated by Recently Discovered Texts of the Graeco-Roman World*. Translated by L. R. M. Strachan. 2nd ed. London: Hodder & Stoughton, 1910.

Dibelius, Martin. *Die Geisterwelt im Glauben des Paulus*. Göttingen: Vandenhoeck & Ruprecht, 1909.

Dickey, Eleanor. *Ancient Greek Scholarship: A Guide to Finding, Reading, and Understanding Scholia, Commentaries, Lexica, and Grammatical Treatises, from Their Beginnings to the Byzantine Period*. Oxford: Oxford University Press, 2010.

Faraone, Christopher A. "The Collapse of Celestial and Chthonic Realms in a Late Antique 'Apollonian Invocation' (PGM I 262–347)." Pages

213–32 in *Heavenly Realms and Earthly Realities in Late Antique Religions*. Edited by Ra'anan S. Boustan and Annette Yoshiko Reed. Cambridge: Cambridge University Press, 2004.

Farnell, Lewis Richard. *Greek Hero Cults and Ideas of Immortality: The Gifford Lectures Delivered in the University of St. Andrews in the Year 1920*. Repr., Oxford: Clarendon, 1970.

Fears, J. Rufus. "The Solar Monarchy of Nero and the Imperial Panegyric of Q. Curtius Rufus." *Historia* 25 (1976): 494–96.

Fee, Gordon D. *New Testament Exegesis: A Handbook for Students and Pastors*. 3rd ed. Louisville: Westminster John Knox, 2002.

———. *Paul's Letter to the Philippians*. NICNT. Grand Rapids: Eerdmans, 1995.

Fishwick, Duncan. "Dio and Maecenas: The Emperor and the Ruler Cult." *Phoenix* 44.3 (1990): 267–75.

Flemming, Dean. *Philippians: A Commentary in the Wesleyan Tradition*. New Beacon Bible Commentary. Kansas City, MO: Beacon Hill, 2009.

Fowl, Stephen E. *Philippians*. THNTC. Grand Rapids: Eerdmans, 2005.

Fredricksmeyer, E. A. "Divine Honors for Philip II." *TAPA* 109 (1979): 39–61.

Gordon, R. L., and Francisco Marco Simón, eds. *Magical Practice in the Latin West: Papers from the International Conference Held at the University of Zaragoza, 30 Sept.–1 Oct. 2005*. RGRW 168. Leiden: Brill, 2010.

Gorman, Michael J. "'Although/Because He Was in the Form of God': The Theological Significance of Paul's Master Story (Phil 2:6–11)." *JTI* 1 (2007): 147–69.

———. *Cruciformity: Paul's Narrative Spirituality of the Cross*. Grand Rapids: Eerdmans, 2001.

———. *Inhabiting the Cruciform God: Kenosis, Justification, and Theosis in Paul's Narrative Soteriology*. Grand Rapids: Eerdmans, 2009.

Gradel, Ittai. *Emperor Worship and Roman Religion*. OCM. Oxford: Clarendon, 2002.

Grant, Michael. *Roman Anniversary Issues: An Exploratory Study of the Numismatic and Medallic Commemoration of Anniversary Years 49 B.C.–375*. Cambridge: Cambridge University Press, 1950.

Grether, Gertrude. "Livia and the Roman Imperial Cult." *AJP* 67 (1946): 222–52.

Hammond, Mason. *City-State and World State in Greek and Roman Political Theory until Augustus*. Cambridge: Harvard University Press, 1951.

Hanson, Paul D. *Isaiah 40–66.* Interpretation. Louisville: John Knox, 1995.
Harris-McCoy, Daniel E. *Artemidorus' Oneirocritica: Text, Translation, and Commentary.* Oxford: Oxford University Press, 2012.
Hawthorne, Gerald F., and Ralph P. Martin, *Philippians.* Rev. ed. WBC 43. Nashville: Nelson, 2004.
Hellerman, Joseph H. *Reconstructing Honor in Roman Philippi: Carmen Christi as Cursus Pudorum.* SNTSMS 132. Cambridge: Cambridge University Press, 2005.
Hirst, Gertrude. "A Discussion of Some Passages in the Prologue to the Georgics. (I. 14, 15 and 27)." *Transactions and Proceedings of the American Philological Association* 59 (1928): 19–32.
Hofius, Otfried. *Der Christushymnus Philipper 2,6-11: Untersuchungen Gestalt und Aussage eines urchristlichen Psalms.* WUNT 2/17. Tübingen: Mohr Siebeck, 1976. 2nd ed., 1991.
Holloway, Paul A. *Philippians.* Hermeneia. Minneapolis: Fortress, 2017.
Holmes, Michael William. *The Apostolic Fathers: English Translations.* Grand Rapids: Baker, 1999.
———. *The Apostolic Fathers: Greek Texts.* Grand Rapids: Baker, 1999.
Hopkins, Keith. *Death and Renewal.* Sociological Studies in Roman History 2. Cambridge: Cambridge University Press, 1983.
Hurtado, Larry. *Lord Jesus Christ: Devotion to Jesus in Earliest Christianity.* Grand Rapids: Eerdmans, 2003.
Irons, William J. "The Transition from Heathen to Christian Civilization, from the Time of the Antonines to the Fall of the Western Empire." *Transactions of the Royal Historical Society* 7 (1878): 163–75.
Käsemann, Ernst. "Critical Analysis of Philippians 2:5-11." *JTC* 5 (1968): 45–88.
Keener, Craig S. *IVP Bible Background Commentary: New Testament.* Downers Grove, IL: InterVarsity Press, 1993.
Kenyon, F. G., ed. *Greek Papyri in the British Museum.* Vol. 1. London: British Museum, 1893.
Kidd, Reggie M. *Wealth and Beneficence in the Pastoral Epistles: A "Bourgeois" Form of Early Christianity?* SBLDS 122. Atlanta: Scholars Press, 1990.
Klauck, Hans-Josef. *The Religious Context of Early Christianity: A Guide to Graeco-Roman Religions.* Translated by B. McNeil. Minneapolis: Fortress, 2003.
Kleiner, Fred S. "The Boscoreale Cups: Copies of a Lost Monument?" *JRA* 10 (1997): 377–80.

Kline, A. H., trans. *Vergil, Georgics.* https://tinyurl.com/SBL4216h.
Koukouli-Chrysantaki, Chaido. "Colonia Iulia Augusta Philippensis." Pages 5–35 in *Philippi at the Time of Paul and after His Death.* Edited by Charalambos Bakirtzis and Helmut Koester. Harrisburg, PA: Trinity Press International, 1998.
Kreitzer, Larry. "Apotheosis of the Roman Emperor." *BA* 53 (1990): 210–17.
Kremydi-Sicilianou, Sophia. "'Belonging' to Rome, 'Remaining' Greek: Coinage and Identity in Roman Macedonia." Pages 95–106 in *Coinage and Identity in the Roman Provinces.* Edited by Christopher Howgego, Volker Heuchert, and Andrew Burnett. Oxford: Oxford University Press, 2007.
Lightfoot, J. B. *Saint Paul's Epistle to the Philippians.* Classic Commentaries on the Greek New Testament. London: Macmillan, 1913.
Loh, I-Jin, and Eugene A. Nida. *A Handbook on Paul's Letter to the Philippians.* UBS Handbook Series. New York: United Bible Societies, 1995.
Long, Fredrick J. "Ephesians: Paul's Political Theology in Greco-Roman Political Context." Pages 255–309 in *Christian Origins and Classical Culture: Social and Literary Contexts for the New Testament.* Edited by S. E. Porter and A. W. Pitts. TENTS 9. Early Christianity in its Hellenistic Context 1. Leiden: Brill, 2013.
———. *Koine Greek Grammar: A Beginning-Intermediate Exegetical and Pragmatic Handbook.* Accessible Greek Resources and Online Studies. Wilmore, KY: GlossaHouse, 2015.
———. "Roman Imperial Rule under the Authority of Jupiter-Zeus: Political-Religious Contexts and the Interpretation of 'the Ruler of the Authority of the Air' in Ephesians 2:2." Pages 124–33 in *The Language of the New Testament: Context, History and Development.* Edited by S. E. Porter and A. W. Pitts. Linguistic Biblical Studies 6. Early Christianity in Its Hellenistic Environment 3. Leiden: Brill, 2013.
———. *2 Corinthians: A Handbook on the Greek Text.* Baylor Handbook on the Greek New Testament. Waco, TX: Baylor University Press, 2015.
Lozano, Fernando. "*Divi Augusti* and *Theoi Sebastoi*: Roman Initiatives and Greek Answers." *CQ* 57 (2007): 139–52.
Lucan. *The Civil War (Pharsalia).* Translated by J. D. Duff. LCL. Cambridge: Harvard University Press, 1928.
MacKintosh, Marjorie C. "Roman Influences on the Victory Reliefs of Shapur I of Persia." *California Studies in Classical Antiquity* 6 (1974): 181–203.

Manilius. *Astronomica*. Translated by G. P. Goold. LCL. Cambridge: Harvard University Press, 1977.
Marshall, I. Howard. *The Epistle to the Philippians*. London: Epworth, 1991.
Martin, Ralph P. *Carmen Christi: Philippians ii. 5–11; In Recent Interpretation and in the Setting of Early Christian Worship*. SNTSMS 4. Cambridge: Cambridge University Press, 1967.
———. *A Hymn of Christ: Philippians 2:5–11 in Recent Interpretation and in the Setting of Early Christian Worship*. 3rd ed. Repr., Downers Grove, IL: InterVarsity Press, 1997.
Meeks, Wayne A. "The Man from Heaven in Paul's Letter to the Philippians." Pages 329–36 in *The Future of Early Christianity: Essays in Honor of Helmut Koester*. Edited by Birger Pearson. Minneapolis: Fortress, 1991.
Miller, Gene. "ΑΡΧΟΝΤΩΝ ΤΟΥ ΑΙΩΝΟΣ ΤΟΥΤΟΥ: A New Look at 1 Corinthians 2:6–8." *JBL* 91 (1972): 522–28.
Oakes, Peter. *Philippians: From People to Letter*. SNTSMS 110. Cambridge: Cambridge University Press, 2001.
———. "Re-mapping the Universe: Paul and the Emperor in 1 Thessalonians and Philippians." *JSNT* 27 (2005): 301–22.
O'Brien, Peter T. *The Epistle to the Philippians*. NIGTC. Grand Rapids: Eerdmans, 1991.
Oswalt, John N. *The Book of Isaiah: Chapters 40–66*. NICOT. Grand Rapids: Eerdmans, 1998.
Pedrick, Victoria. "Supplication in the Iliad and the Odyssey." *TAPA* 112 (1982): 125–40.
Peterson, Erik. *Heis Theos: Epigraphische, Formgeschichtliche und Religionsgeschichtliche Untersuchungen*. FRLANT 24. Göttingen: Vandenhoeck & Ruprecht, 1926.
———. *Heis theos: Epigraphische, formgeschichtliche und Religionsgeschichtliche Untersuchungen zur antiken "Ein-Gott"-Akklamation: Nachdruck der Ausgabe von Erik Peterson 1926 mit Ergänzungen und Kommentaren von Christoph Markschies, Henrik Hildebrandt, Barbara Nichtweiß u.a. 2012*. Edited by Christoph Markschies, Henrik Hildebrandt, and Barbara Nichtweiss. Ausgewählte Schriften 8. Würzburg: Echter, 2012.
Pfanner, Michael. *Der Titusbogen*. Beiträge zur Erschliessung hellenistischer und kaiserzeitlicher Skulptur und Architektur 2. Mainz: von Zabern, 1983.

Pilhofer, Peter. *Philippi.* Vol. 1, *Die erste christliche Gemeinde Europas.* WUNT 87. Tübingen: Mohr Siebeck, 1995.

———. *Philippi.* Vol. 2, *Katalog der Inschriften von Philippi.* WUNT 119. Tübingen: Mohr Siebeck, 2000.

Price, S. R. F. "From Noble Funerals to Divine Cult: The Consecration of Roman Emperors." Pages 56–105 in *Rituals of Royalty: Power and Ceremonial in Traditional Societies.* Edited by David Cannadine and S. R. F. Price. Past and Present Publications. Cambridge: Cambridge University Press, 1987.

———. "Gods and Emperors: The Greek Language of the Roman Imperial Cult." *JHS* 104 (1984): 79–95.

Radin, Max. "Apotheosis." *The Classical Review* 30.2 (1916): 44–46.

Ramsey, John T., and A. Lewis Licht. *The Comet of 44 B.C. and Caesar's Funeral Games.* APA American Classical Studies 39. Atlanta: Scholars Press, 1997.

Reid, Sara Karz. *The Small Temple: A Roman Imperial Cult Building in Petra, Jordan.* Piscataway, NJ: Gorgias, 2005.

Reumann, John. *Philippians: A New Translation with Introduction and Commentary.* AYB. New Haven: Yale University Press, 2008.

Rives, James B. *Religion in the Roman Empire.* Malden, MA: Blackwell, 2007.

Robbins, Vernon K. *The Tapestry of Early Christian Discourse: Rhetoric, Society, and Ideology.* London: Routledge, 1996.

Scheid, John. *The Gods, the State, and the Individual: Reflections on Civic Religion in Rome.* Translated by Clifford Ando. Philadelphia: University of Pennsylvania Press, 2016.

Schowalter, Daniel N. *The Emperor and the Gods.* HDR 28. Minneapolis: Fortress, 1993.

Seneca. *Satyricon, Apocolocyntosis.* Translated by Michael Heseltine and W. H. D. Rouse. Revised by E. H. Warmington. LCL. Cambridge: Harvard University Press, 1913.

Sève, Michel, and Patrick Weber. "Un monument honorifique au forum de Philippes." *BCH* 112 (1988): 467–79.

Silva, Moisés. *Philippians.* 2nd ed. BECNT. Grand Rapids: Baker Academic, 2005.

Smith, W., and C. Anthon, eds. "Apotheosis." Pages 105–6 in *A Dictionary of Greek and Roman Antiquities.* 2nd ed. London: Murray, 1875.

Strong, Eugénie S. *Apotheosis and after Life: Three Lectures on Certain Phases of Art and Religion in the Roman Empire*. Freeport, NY: Books for Libraries Press, 1969.
Thompson, Lynette. "Lucan's Apotheosis of Nero." *CP* 59.3 (1964): 147–53.
Thurston, Bonnie B., and Judith M. Ryan. *Philippians and Philemon*. SP. Collegeville, MN: Liturgical Press, 2005.
Vergil. *Eclogues, Georgics, Aeneid*. Vol. 1. Translated by H. Rushton Fairclough. London: Heinemann, 1916.
Verhoef, Eduard. "Syncretism in the Church of Philippi." *HTS* 64 (2008): 697–714.
White, R. J. *The Interpretation of Dreams*. Park Ridge, NJ: Noyes, 1975.
Witherington, Ben, III. *Paul's Letter to the Philippians: A Socio-rhetorical Commentary*. Grand Rapids: Eerdmans, 2011.
Wright, N. T. *The Climax of the Covenant: Christ and the Law in Pauline Theology*. Minneapolis: Fortress, 1993.
———. *Paul: In Fresh Perspective*. Minneapolis: Fortress, 2005.
Zanker, Paul. *The Power of Images in the Age of Augustus*. Translated by Alan Shapiro. Jerome Lectures 16. Ann Arbor: University of Michigan Press, 1988.
Zeigler, Joseph. *Isaias*. SVTG 14. Göttingen: Vandenhoeck & Ruprecht, 1967.

Rivals, Opponents, and Enemies: Three Kinds of Theological Argumentation in Philippians

Samuel Vollenweider

Paul has been a highly controversial figure throughout the history of Christianity. Such was also the case during his lifetime. From the beginning of his apostolic career, Paul was faced with critics and opponents.[1] Consequently, readers of his letters always ask a standard question: with what kind of adversaries are each of these texts grappling?[2] In Philippians the matter is not so clear, and scholars have proposed various hypotheses, some of which are not overwhelmingly plausible. In this paper my intention is not so much to add a new variant to this repeatedly disputed matter. In agreement with many other scholars, I will take the view that we have to reckon

---

1. See esp. Matthias Konradt, "Antipaulinismus und Paulinismus im neutestamentlichen Schrifttum," in *Paulus Handbuch*, ed. Friedrich W. Horn, WUNT 238 (Tübingen: Mohr Siebeck, 2013), 552–57. About later developments see Andreas Lindemann, *Paulus im ältesten Christentum: Das Bild des Apostels und die Rezeption der paulinischen Theologie in der frühchristlichen Literatur bis Marcion*, BHT 58 (Tübingen: Mohr Siebeck, 1979), 101–9; 367–71; Gerd Lüdemann, *Paulus, der Heidenapostel*, vol. 2, *Antipaulinismus im frühen Christentum*, FRLANT 130 (Göttingen: Vandenhoeck & Ruprecht, 1983); Jürgen Wehnert, "Antipaulinismus in den Pseudoklementinen," in *Ancient Perspectives on Paul*, ed. Tobias Nicklas, Andreas Merkt, and Joseph Verheyden, NTOA 102 (Göttingen: Vandenhoeck & Ruprecht, 2013), 170–90.

2. For a general overview, compare Jerry L. Sumney, *Identifying Paul's Opponents*, JSNTSup 40 (Sheffield: JSOT Press, 1990); and Stanley E. Porter, ed., *Paul and His Opponents*, Pauline Studies 2 (Leiden: Brill, 2005). For the historical possibility of an orchestrated antimission, see my "Kreuzfeuer: Paulus und seine Konflikte mit Rivalen, Feinden und Gegnern," in *Receptions of Paul in Early Christianity: The Person of Paul and His Writings through the Eyes of His Early Interpreters*, ed. Simon Butticaz, Andreas Dettwiler, and Jens Schröter, BZNW 234 (Berlin: de Gruyter, 2018), 649–76.

with different types of dissenters (used in a wide sense) in Philippians. Apart from the identification of several kinds of opponents, what deserves attention is the way that Paul is arguing with regards to these boundaries. I am going to urge that in Philippians at least three kinds of opponents have to be taken into consideration and that Paul is modeling his arguments specifically with regards to their various positions. Throughout this essay my basic assumption is that Philippians is only one coherent letter.[3]

1. Rivals Although Brothers (Philippians 1:15–18)

The first passage we have to deal with is Phil 1:15–18. In this introductory section of his letter, Paul sketches different attitudes toward his person and, especially, to his situation as a prisoner. His chains result in a considerable missionary success, prompted not only by himself but also by other "brothers" (and sisters?!). He postulates, then, a difference in *motivation* among these preaching Christians. We have, on the one side, "envy and rivalry," "selfish ambition" (or whatever ἐριθεία in v. 17 might mean),[4] and being "not sincere." Paul denigrates this motivation with the damning term *pretense*. By contrast, on the other side, which is entirely positive in orientation, we have "goodwill" and "love": all this is characterized by the term *truth*. We already note here that Paul probably does make use of *friendship* terminology.[5] Friends and nonfriends (they need not necessarily be enemies) are distinguished this way. This distinction is very evident for the negative side: envy, strife, and pretense contradict the fundamentals of true friendship. On the positive side, we do not have direct pagan-Greek parallels to goodwill and love, but we might easily find analogies, such as *prothymia* and *philia*.[6]

However, Paul sets all that aside. What matters only is the proclamation of Christ "in every way" (v. 18). This statement is important for the

---

3. See the discussion and main arguments recently offered by Paul A. Holloway, *Philippians*, Hermeneia (Minneapolis: Fortress, 2017), 10–19, esp. 18–19.

4. See BDAG, s.v. "ἐριθεία": "Its meaning in our lit. is a matter of conjecture"; Ceslas Spicq, *Lexique théologique du Nouveau Testament* (Fribourg: Cerf, 1991), 580–81. See the discussion in John Reumann, *Philippians: A New Translation with Introduction and Commentary*, AYB 33B (New Haven: Yale University Press, 2008), 181–82.

5. See the material offered by Reumann, *Philippians*, 206.

6. The negative motives themselves are not specific. In Pauline literature Christians are warned of envy, rivalry, selfishness, and pretense. Selfishness may lead directly to hell (Rom 2:8; Gal 5:20).

interpretation of the whole passage. Paul places his friends and his non-friends under the same umbrella: they preach the gospel, they all proclaim Christ, and they all seem to be brothers (v. 14). This means that there is a basic community between all of them, irrespective of their motivation. The apostle displays in this case an open heart—regardless of whether people are seeking their own interests or those of Jesus Christ (to put it in the terms of 2:21). This attitude of Paul renders it unlikely that the dissenters in our passage do have any connection to those whom he accuses of perverting the gospel, as in Galatia, or also in Phil 3 (we will come back to this point later). There seems to be a common foundation in terms of the Christian life as well as in terms of theological orientation—regardless of the tensions among the Christians and especially in their relation to Paul.

What is behind all this? Paul is so brief in his narration that we cannot easily detect what was really going on inside and outside in terms of the precise circumstances of his imprisonment.[7] The data given in verse 17 that the dissenters "intend to increase my suffering in my imprisonment" leave us with many questions. Scholars have asked whether Paul's appeal to his Roman citizenship had led to debates within the Christian community.[8] But the text does not support any speculation of this kind. We can only state that Paul interpreted the intention of the dissenters as a case of aggression against him as a prisoner—but this personal view should not be mistaken for the real behavior of these people. We receive also no help for an identification of the locality of Paul's prison. Dissent and dissonance within the community, and especially in its relation to the prisoner Paul, would fit well either with Ephesus, which was not founded by the apostle, or with Rome, where the author of 1 Clement mentions "envy and strife" as the reason for the martyrdom of the apostles Peter and Paul (5:2–5).

Having established the difficulty of discerning the apostle's specific circumstances from his brief comments in the text, I turn now to the theological argumentation, which I will unfold along four lines.

---

7. I do not see any convincing reason to build a bridge to the dissonance of the two women, Euodia and Syntyche, in 4:2–3, rightly refuted by Holloway, *Philippians*, 182 n. 5. Such was the argument, also due to his literary-critical operations, of Christoph Kähler, "Konflikt, Kompromiss und Bekenntnis: Paulus und seine Gegner im Philipperbrief," *KD* 40 (1994): 58–61.

8. See Jean-François Collange, *L'épître de saint Paul aux Philippiens*, CNT 10A (Neuchâtel: Delachaux & Niestlé, 1973), 25–26, 51–52.

1. *Polis*: Apart from *friendship*, the terms that Paul uses also point to the *political* domain. Envy, strife, and pretense were a constant feature of first-century city life. Conversely, the same can be said for a more positive involvement in the ancient city: a loyal and solid citizen displays "goodwill" and "love," that is, *prothymia* and *philia*.

2. *Reference to an external divine power*: here Paul is stressing a *Christocentric* attitude. All circumstances for the apostle, no matter their difficulty, are about Christ and his proclamation (v. 18).

3. *Distance*: Complementary to this Christocentric perspective, Paul's argument is characterized by a programmatic indifference: "What then?" he asks. For the apostle only one matter counts: the nonessentials are marked with εἴτε—εἴτε. Indifference, however, does not mean insensibility—neither in the case of Paul nor among Hellenistic moralists (referring here mainly to the Stoics). Rather, paradoxically, Paul's attitude to his difficult circumstances becomes for him a source of *joy*.

Both lines, his Christocentric orientation and programmatic indifference, are continued and deepened in the following passage, that is, verses 19–26.[9] As far as the Christocentric orientation, the "proclaimed Christ" reappears in the Christ who "will be exalted in my body, whether I live or die." The apostle becomes the instrument of Christ, who reveals himself in his life or in his death.

As far as indifference, it reappears in the attitude that Paul displays either to his surviving or to his dying. Again, it does not matter: his personal outcome will serve Christ in either case (indicated in v. 20 again with εἴτε—εἴτε). Both, dying and living, have their own inherent goodness, and each will have a positive outcome—but in a different way for Paul, on the one hand, and for the addressees, his community, on the other hand. The comparison of death and life in verses 21–26, designed in the form of a rhetorical comparison (*synkrisis*), aims at working out the teleology of both options.

4. *Competition*: Here, in Phil 1, all missionary success that is achieved by the brothers is generated by the apostle's chains.

In sum, Paul distances himself from his own opinions and displays a certain kind of conciliatory tolerance. In giving something much greater space, he performs a specific theological movement: his focus shifts away

---

9. For details, see my article, "Die Waagschalen von Leben und Tod. Phil 1,21–26 vor dem Hintergrund der antiken Rhetorik," in *Horizonte neutestamentlicher Christologie*, WUNT 144 (Tübingen: Mohr Siebeck, 2002), 237–61.

from his own subjective attitude to the divine position. The positive counterpart to Paul's indifference is his desire to enhance the greatness of God and his Christ.

Do we have analogies to this theological figure elsewhere in Paul's writings? Indeed, 1 Cor 15:9–11 shows a quite similar movement. Compared to the great apostles of Jerusalem Paul is, on the one hand, "the least of the apostles," whereas, on the other hand, he had "worked harder than any of them." But all this does not count (see again the εἴτε—εἴτε): totally central is the proclamation. As in Phil 1, "friendly competition" is in sight.[10] Again the focus shifts from the human subject to the divine. Paul underlines that all is performed by "the grace of God that is with me." Our passage here is linked with a highly competitive thrust. The apostle was an extremely competitive character, and he lived in a world in which competition was a fundamental pillar of the whole culture. The advice of old Peleus to his son, characteristic of the Greco-Roman nobility, has become formative for the ancient cultural world: "ever be bravest, and pre-eminent above all" (Homer, *Il.* 11.784; 6.208).[11]

2. Exponents of This World (Philippians 1:27–30)

We turn now to the next passage where Paul mentions others whose position is contrary to his own and to the Christian communities, that is, Phil 1:27–30. Verse 28 refers to "opponents" (ἀντικείμενοι). In a construction, the grammar of which is not definitely clear, the apostle links these opponents with future destruction,[12] whereas the Philippian Christians might expect "salvation." There is nowadays little doubt that these opponents have to be identified with the representatives of the pagan environment of the Philippian community and here are probably to be identified with especially the Roman authorities. The term itself does not point to a specific semantic

---

10. For the difference between friendly competition and hostile competition, see Thomas Schmeller, "Paulus und die Konkurrenz," *Wissenschaft und Weisheit* 67.2 (2004): 163–78.

11. Compare to the corresponding nobility code: Joachim Latacz, "Achilleus: Wandlungen eines europäischen Heldenbildes," in *Homers Ilias: Studien zu Dichter, Werk und Rezeption*, Beiträge zur Altertumskunde 327 (Berlin: de Gruyter, 2014), 267–346, esp. 310–12.

12. For ἀπώλεια, see Matt 7:13; Rom 9:22; 2 Pet 2:1; Rev 17:8; Albrecht Oepke, "ἀπώλεια," *TDNT* 1:396–97; Moisés Silva, "ἀπώλεια," *NIDNTTE* 1:359–60; and the excursus "The Fate of the Wicked according to Paul," in Holloway, *Philippians*, 107–8.

field (military or political) but relates much more to biblical language in general (see, e.g., Exod 23:22; Isa 66:6). The Philippians should "in no way be intimidated" by their opponents. The fearlessness of the Christians in the present (v. 28a) will become an important eschatological "sign": the upright attitude of the Christians in the face of their opponents indicates the future "destruction" of their opponents and testifies to their own "salvation" as the eschatological outcome (v. 28b). In verse 29, Paul elaborates on further considerations for the Philippian readers as they adopt this fearless attitude in the face of considerable difficulties: the believers are invited to interpret their (possible) suffering as a gift of God, experienced for the sake of Christ. Paul links the suffering of the Philippians with his own struggle (*agōn*) and with Christ's own suffering (v. 30).

If we take the *antikeimenoi* in verse 28 in the broad sense of "opponents of God and his people," it is attractive to build a bridge to 2:15. There, the Christians are depicted "as lights in the world" "in the midst of a crooked and perverse generation." The notion is here even more general, with its allusions to apocalyptic traditions and especially to Dan 12:3. This "wicked generation," which we are familiar with from Jesus's sayings (Matt 17:17 // Luke 9:41; see also Acts 2:40), refers no longer to Israel (Deut 32:5) but to humankind in general. All those who are outside the Christian community are the lost ones, like darkness opposed to light.

These two references to the outsiders are scattered throughout the central part of Philippian, starting with 1:27. At first glance, these references to opponents seem to be quite marginal. But the whole picture changes if we interpret large portions of Philippians as an implicit reflection on the identity of the Christian community within the Roman colony of Philippi. If verse 27 is read as a programmatic admonition to the Christian community in general, it is depicted as a political body with its own constitution, its own reign, and its own rules of behavior and citizenship. It has often been argued that the letter to the Philippians models the church in terms of a *polis*, that is, of an ideal *polis*, as indicated by the meaning of *politeuesthai*. This word should not be taken as referring to the generalized walk and conduct of the believer, but, rather, much more as an admonition to "live as citizen."[13] This view fits well with the call for unity in verse 27–30

---

13. See, e.g., my article: "Politische Theologie im Philipperbrief?," in *Paulus und Johannes*, ed. Dieter Sänger and Ulrich Mell, WUNT 198 (Tübingen: Mohr Siebeck, 2006), 457–69; Angela Standhartinger, "Die paulinische Theologie im Spannungsfeld römisch-imperialer Machtpolitik. Eine neue Perspektive auf Paulus, kritisch geprüft

and 2:1–4, where Paul is echoing the political rhetoric of *homonoia*. The praise of Christ might be easily interpreted this way; it offers a pattern not only for an ideal ruler but also in general for Christian behavior in the *ekklēsia*. Finally, the political associations are supported by the reference to the *heavenly politeuma* at the end of chapter 3.

Seen from this perspective, our whole passage might be read as an exposition of a counterimage to the Greco-Roman society and its cities in general, and, specifically, to the Colonia Iulia Augusta Philippensis. Paul makes clear where and how Christian life collides with patterns and standards of its cultural environment. On the other hand, the Christian community realizes everything that Greco-Roman society imagines to be the ideal city. The *polis* of the believers, therefore, surpasses the real cities here on earth; it is rooted in heaven, with its divine city.

We return to our question about the opponents and about Paul's approach to them. I will, again, unfold this along the four lines mentioned above.

1. *Polis*: Apart from the specific terminology, it seems quite clear that the city is threatened from the outside by *enemies*. This threat calls for the unity and solidarity of its citizens; they need to be united in their defense. We might refer not only to 1:27–2:4 but also to the blamelessness of the "children of God" in 2:15, which offers no weak spot for any attack from an enemy.

2. *Reference to an external divine power*: At first glance we do not encounter this notion here. Rather, what we are observing is a striking shift in focus from a selfish perspective to the perspective of the *others*: "Be concerned not only about your own interests, but about the interests of others as well" (2:4). The whole passage calls for this kind of Christian solidarity. But when we combine this call to humility with the praise of Christ in 2:6–11, it is quite attractive to read Paul's hymn as a counterprogram to the pagan endeavor toward status and prestige—a basic cultural orientation of the ancient urban elites, which might have been even intensified by the Roman profile of Philippi, especially when the Greeks in the city and its territory took over the values of the Roman upper class. Christian life, therefore, is not about prestige because it consists essentially in an abandonment of status. But this renunciation is only one side of the coin:

---

anhand des Philipperbriefs," in *Religion, Politik und Gewalt*, ed. Friedrich Schweitzer, Veröffentlichungen der Wissenschaftlichen Gesellschaft für Theologie 29 (Gütersloh: Gütersloher Verlagshaus, 2006), 364–82.

humility is complemented by divine elevation. Christ's *kenosis* frees space for God's activity. The immediate implications of the hymn of Christ found in 2:12–13 are put in terms of paradoxical rhetoric that results in a theocentric statement ("it is God who is at work in you"). So, when the focus shifts from the subject to the others, there is room for divine activity. One may detect a glimpse of this theocentric notion in 1:28, where Paul is referring to God's salvific activity ("and this from God").

3. *Distance*: Again we do not meet indifference in our passage but quite the opposite: suffering. In fact, this suffering of the Philippians might imply social and financial marginalization as opposed to robust or heavy treatment. But Paul calls for a new understanding of suffering and makes it possible, therefore, to overcome its negative and depressive force: it is suffering for Christ's sake, and it is a gift of God. And here, again, it becomes the source of *joy* (2:17–18).

4. *Competition*: This element is, again, not obviously on the surface of the text, but nevertheless it is an important one. In 1:26 Paul refers once more to the last judgment and is proud of being an agent of the Philippians' honors. In 2:16 he expresses hope that he himself would be honored by God thanks to his community. And even in the admonition to unity in 2:3, competition (ὑπερέχειν) is converted to humility.

3. Traitors in Their Own Ranks (Phil 3:2–21)

We turn to the last passage where dissenters are mentioned: Phil 3:2–21. The passage deals with adversaries who are called "dogs," "evil workers," "mutilators" (v. 2), and "enemies of the cross of Christ" (v. 18). The whole passage is as rich as it is difficult, and we will focus only on the elements that are most important for our guiding question. Paul's evaluation of these rivals is extremely negative: their eschatological fate is "destruction," the same outcome as for the pagan adversaries (1:28). The portrait of the opponents is mainly designed as a counterpart to his own apostolic person. Because Paul himself pursues the goal of a kind of self-praise—combined with a call to imitate him (v. 17)—the question arises as to whether his image of the opponents still has any historical traits.[14] Despite all the styl-

---

14. See Christine Gerber, "ΚΑΥΧΑΣΘΑΙ ΔΕΙ, ΟΥ ΣΥΜΦΕΡΟΝ ΜΕΝ … (2 Kor 12,1). Selbstlob bei Paulus vor dem Hintergrund der antiken Gepflogenheiten," in *Paul's Graeco-Roman Context*, ed. Cilliers Breytenbach, BETL 277 (Leuven: Peeters, 2015), 238–42, referring to Brian Dodd, *Paul's Paradigmatic "I": Personal Example as*

ization, however, there are some special features that reveal the historical profile of the opponents.

There is clear evidence that the opponents are Judeo-Christian missionaries. What is decisive is the keyword *circumcision* in verse 2c, which certainly has to do with their theological or ecclesiological self-image, completely independent of the question whether they explicitly tried to enforce it on pagans. Circumcision represents, as a title of dignity, the election of Israel as God's own people; Paul turns over the mark of honor to shame ("mutilation"), here following an anti-Jewish topos (see also Gal 5:12). Probably the apostle, with the equally polemical topos in verse 19, namely with "belly" and "shame," also alludes to the importance of food commandments and circumcision in their proclamation.[15] Paul countered their excellent Jewish origins with his own ethnic excellence (vv. 5-7). The "workers" (v. 2b) point to Christian missionaries; even the violent invective makes followers of Christ more likely than non-Christian Jews. There is substantial reason to identify these opponents with Jewish Christian missionaries of the same type as in Galatia. What is more, it seems that Paul does not react to real activities of such missionaries but that he leads a preemptive strike, that is, he reckons with the future possibility of such interventions. The hypothetical opponents are, therefore, "phantoms."[16]

Once again we apply our catalogue of four dimensions to this passage.

1. *Polis:* The climax of our passage, formulated in elevated style (vv. 19-21), consists in the opposition of "earthly things" and the "citizenship in heaven." The opponents of chapter 3 are neither rivals (i.e., under the umbrella of the shared and common gospel) nor external enemies,

---

Literary Strategy, JSNTSup 177 (Sheffield: Sheffield Academic, 1999), 171-95; Eve-Marie Becker, "Polemik und Autobiographie. Ein Vorschlag zur Deutung von Phil 3,2-4a," in *Polemik in der frühchristlichen Literatur*, ed. Oda Wischmeyer and Lorenzo Scornaienchi, BZNW 170 (Berlin: de Gruyter, 2011), 233-54.

15. This opinion, shared by many researchers, is not refuted by the observation that Paul also uses a well-known polemical topos with the "belly," which is especially directed against the Epicureans. See Karl Olav Sandnes, *Belly and Body in the Pauline Epistles*, SNTSMS 120 (Cambridge: Cambridge University Press, 2002). Against Sandnes (159-64), it is not necessary to understand this polemical tradition as an alternative to the reading of Jewish rituals.

16. Thus the wording of Morna Hooker, "Philippians: Phantom Opponents and the Real Source of Conflict," in *Fair Play: Pluralism and Conflicts in Early Christianity; Essays in Honour of Heikki Räisänen*, ed. Ismo Dunderberg et al., NovTSup 103 (Leiden: Brill, 2001), 377-95.

but, rather, they are internal destroyers of the community and betrayers of the gospel (see also Gal 1:6). For any city this is the worst type of possible adversary.

2. *Reference to an external divine power*: This basic figure can easily be picked up in three arguments and formulations, respectively. First, Paul speaks about the leap from "*my own* righteousness" to "the righteousness *from God* based on faith" (v. 9). Second, "dynamics" is much better than the acquisition or maintenance of status: the metaphor of running in verses 12–14 builds up an impressive counterimage to the ethnic privileges of verses 4–7, which are rooted in the flesh (v. 3). This dynamic movement, which includes letting go all these privileges, is based on the communion with Christ, along with his resurrection and his passion (v. 10). Third, our passage ends with an epideictic reference to Christ's "power by which he is able to subject all things to himself" (v. 21).

3. *Distance*: The whole passage works with an "Umwertung aller Werte," a fundamental reshaping of all values. There is much pathos in Paul's argument, especially in the terminology of verses 7–8. Paul offers himself as a pattern for Christian behavior (v. 17). One has to abandon all privileges based on ethnos or on the achievement and maintenance of status.

4. *Competition*: Our passage is one of the most obvious expressions of Paul's competitive character (vv. 3–6). All his former strife for ethnic and personal excellence is denigrated in extremely negative manner. But, on the other hand, the apostle hopes to be honored at the last judgment (v. 14).

There are several analogous passages in Paul where he is engaged in a severe dispute with "false brothers," "false apostles," and "deceitful workers." Apart from Galatians—with a discourse about justification that could be correlated to the one in Phil 3 about God's justice—the Fool's Speech (2 Cor 11–12) deserves special attention. We meet in this passage an analogous combination of hard rejection and polemics, of personal ambition (11:13–15, 22–29), of a deep break with self-praise and, instead, a strong advocacy of the inhabitation of an external divine power (12:9–10).

4. What Makes a Rival a Traitor? Some Conclusions

Finally, we come back to a question that was raised at the beginning in view of Philippians: while Paul is tolerant toward his opponents in Phil 1, nevertheless he draws a strict line regarding a different set of opponents in Phil 3. Where is this only a matter of rivalry or (more or less) friendly competition for him, and where does it become a fundamental issue, acquiring, so to speak, the *status confessionis*? Looking at Paul's understanding of the gospel, it can be said that where a different gospel is proclaimed other than the gospel that he himself represents, there is no possibility of tolerance. According to his testimony, this is the case in Galatia (Gal 1:6) and in Corinth (2 Cor 11:4), and analogously, as we have seen, at least in two instances in Philippi (Phil 1:27–30; 3:2–21), but not where he introduces his letter (1:15, 17–18). What is, therefore, the otherness of the gospel that generates a self-destructive effect, according to Gal 1:7?

The answer must be differentiated: in view of the teachers active in the Galatian communities, content obviously plays a central role, in particular, the importance of the commandments of the Torah for belonging to the people of God. In Corinth, however, at least superficially, it is not fundamental theology that is called for, but rather a call to work at community relationships:[17] what is at stake is the unique biography of the community, which consists in the exclusive relationship between it and its founder. It is shattered by the foreign missionaries (see 2 Cor 11:1–3, where Paul appears almost as "bride" leader). But, in the case of the city where the Epistle to the Philippians was written, neither problem arises: neither is there a Torah-oriented proclamation, nor is it a church founded by the apostle himself whose relationship with his converts had been disturbed by rivals. In Corinth, one passes into the other: internal dissonances ("divisions," 1 Cor 1:10–13; 11:18–19), which do not shake the basis of the common gospel but nevertheless mutate under the influence of external actors into threatening cracks in the foundation—at least in the view of Paul writing 2 Corinthians.

In light of the differences of situation and approach outlines above, we come to some conclusions.

1. In all our passages we discovered ecclesiological motifs that were shaped from the world of *political* discourse and from the experience of ancient cities. Some of the motifs often attributed to the paradigm of friendship[18] are probably better placed in the sphere of political domain.

---

17. See Reimund Bieringer, "Die Gegner des Paulus im 2. Korintherbrief," in *Studies on 2 Corinthians*, ed. Bieringer and Jan Lambrecht, BETL 112 (Leuven: Peeters, 1994), 181–221.

18. See, e.g., L. Michael White, "Morality between Two Worlds: A Paradigm of

Early Christians modeled their communities (ἐκκλησίαι) by means of political conceptions and discourses. The city pattern does not necessarily need to be an alternative to the paradigm of voluntary associations[19] because ancient associations duplicate in many respects city structures.

Our three types of opponents and dissenters, respectively, fit well in the category of the city life. (1) Within the field of politics, we meet rivals and adversaries negatively labeled by the other side. Nevertheless, they are accepted as fighting for the same city, its freedom and its constitution. (2) Each *polis* has enemies outside; there is an urgent need to stand firmly against this threat. (3) The most dangerous type of opponents is those who act from within as destroyers and betrayers.

2. The central basic figure that Paul is articulating in Philippians (as in other letters, at least partially) is the one that we might call an *eccentric* one. Christian life consists mainly in dedicating oneself to a divine reality or agent—namely, Christ and/or God—and, linked with that, devoting oneself to other human beings, especially to the community as a whole. This dedication transforms the notion of status and honor fundamentally. We might read, therefore, Philippians as an argument against the gravity of social status and prestige in a Roman colony.[20] The source and nature of real honor is a quite different one: several times Paul refers not by accident to the divine judgment, where he hopes and expects being honored by God, together with his community (1:6, 10–11; etc.).

This eccentric figure, comprehensible especially in the hymn of Christ in chapter 2, fits well with the strong presence of *epideictic* rhetoric in Philippians (esp. 2:5–11, 19–24, 25–30; 3:2–21).[21] All these encomiastic elements aim ultimately at the praise *soli Deo Gloria* (see Phil 2:11c).

Friendship in Philippians," in *Greeks, Romans, and Christians: Essays in Honor of Abraham J. Malherbe*, ed. David L. Balch, Everett Ferguson, and Wayne A. Meeks (Minneapolis: Fortress, 1990), 201–15; Stanley K. Stowers, "Friends and Enemies in the Politics of Heaven: Reading Theology in Philippians," in *Pauline Theology*, ed. Jouette M. Bassler (Minneapolis: Fortress, 1991), 1:105–21.

19. See Richard S. Ascough, *Paul's Macedonian Associations: The Social Context of Philippians and 1 Thessalonians*, WUNT 2/161 (Tübingen: Mohr Siebeck, 2003).

20. For the background see the instructive monograph of Peter Oakes, *Philippians: From People to Letter*, SNTSMS 110 (Cambridge: Cambridge University Press, 2001).

21. See Ralph Brucker, *"Christushymnen" oder "epideiktische Passagen"? Studien zum Stilwechsel im Neuen Testament und seiner Umwelt*, FRLANT 176 (Göttingen:

Bibliography

Ascough, Richard S. *Paul's Macedonian Associations: The Social Context of Philippians and 1 Thessalonians*. WUNT 2/161. Tübingen: Mohr Siebeck, 2003.

Becker, Eve-Marie. "Polemik und Autobiographie: Ein Vorschlag zur Deutung von Phil 3,2–4a." Pages 233–54 in *Polemik in der frühchristlichen Literatur*. Edited by Oda Wischmeyer and Lorenzo Scornaienchi. BZNW 170. Berlin: de Gruyter, 2011.

Bieringer, Reimund. "Die Gegner des Paulus im 2. Korintherbrief." Pages 181–221 in *Studies on 2 Corinthians*. Edited by Bieringer and Jan Lambrecht. BETL 112. Leuven: Peeters, 1994.

Brucker, Ralph. *"Christushymnen" oder "epideiktische Passagen"? Studien zum Stilwechsel im Neuen Testament und seiner Umwelt*. FRLANT 176. Göttingen: Vandenhoeck & Ruprecht, 1997.

Collange, Jean-François. *L'épître de saint Paul aux Philippiens*. CNT 10A. Neuchâtel: Delachaux & Niestlé, 1973.

Dodd, Brian. *Paul's Paradigmatic "I": Personal Example as Literary Strategy*. JSNTSup 177. Sheffield: Sheffield Academic, 1999.

Gerber, Christine. "ΚΑΥΧΑΣΘΑΙ ΔΕΙ, ΟΥ ΣΥΜΦΕΡΟΝ ΜΕΝ … (2 Kor 12,1): Selbstlob bei Paulus vor dem Hintergrund der antiken Gepflogenheiten." Pages 213–51 in *Paul's Graeco-Roman Context*. Edited by Cilliers Breytenbach. BETL 277. Leuven: Peeters, 2015.

Holloway, Paul A. *Philippians*. Hermeneia. Minneapolis: Fortress, 2017.

Hooker, Morna. "Philippians: Phantom Opponents and the Real Source of Conflict." Pages 377–95 in *Fair Play: Pluralism and Conflicts in Early Christianity; Essays in Honour of Heikki Räisänen*. Edited by Ismo Dunderberg et al. NTS 103. Leiden: Brill, 2001.

Kähler, Christoph. "Konflikt, Kompromiss und Bekenntnis: Paulus und seine Gegner im Philipperbrief." *KD* 40 (1994): 47–64.

Konradt, Matthias. "Antipaulinismus und Paulinismus im neutestamentlichen Schrifttum." Pages 552–57 in *Paulus Handbuch*. Edited by Friedrich W. Horn. WUNT 238. Tübingen: Mohr Siebeck, 2013.

Vandenhoeck & Ruprecht, 1997): "Keine lobende Aussage wird ungebrochen als solche stehengelassen" (345; vgl. 301–2; 320–21; 335; 340; 137–41).

Latacz, Joachim. "Achilleus: Wandlungen eines europäischen Heldenbildes." Pages 267–346 in *Homers Ilias: Studien zu Dichter, Werk und Rezeption*. Beiträge zur Altertumskunde 327. Berlin: de Gruyter, 2014.

Lindemann, Andreas. *Paulus im ältesten Christentum: Das Bild des Apostels und die Rezeption der paulinischen Theologie in der frühchristlichen Literatur bis Marcion*. BHT 58. Tübingen: Mohr Siebeck, 1979.

Lüdemann, Gerd. *Paulus, der Heidenapostel*. Vol. 2, *Antipaulinismus im frühen Christentum*. FRLANT 130. Göttingen: Vandenhoeck & Ruprecht, 1983.

Oakes, Peter. *Philippians: From People to Letter*. SNTSMS 110. Cambridge: Cambridge University Press, 2001.

Oepke, Albrecht. "ἀπώλεια." *TDNT* 1:396–97.

Porter, Stanley E., ed. *Paul and His Opponents*. Pauline Studies 2. Leiden: Brill, 2005.

Reumann, John. *Philippians: A New Translation with Introduction and Commentary*. AYB 33B. New Haven: Yale University Press, 2008.

Sandnes, Karl Olav. *Belly and Body in the Pauline Epistles*. SNTSMS 120. Cambridge: Cambridge University Press, 2002.

Schmeller, Thomas. "Paulus und die Konkurrenz." *Wissenschaft und Weisheit* 67.2 (2004): 163–78.

Silva, Moisés. "ἀπώλεια." *NIDNTTE* 1:359–60.

Spicq, Ceslas. *Lexique théologique du Nouveau Testament*. Fribourg: Cerf, 1991.

Standhartinger, Angela. "Die paulinische Theologie im Spannungsfeld römisch-imperialer Machtpolitik: Eine neue Perspektive auf Paulus, kritisch geprüft anhand des Philipperbriefs." Pages 364–82 in *Religion, Politik und Gewalt*. Edited by Friedrich Schweitzer. Veröffentlichungen der Wissenschaftlichen Gesellschaft für Theologie 29. Gütersloh: Gütersloher Verlagshaus, 2006.

Stowers, Stanley K. "Friends and Enemies in the Politics of Heaven: Reading Theology in Philippians." Pages 105–21 in vol. 1 of *Pauline Theology*. Edited by Jouette M. Bassler. Minneapolis: Fortress, 1991.

Sumney, Jerry L. *Identifying Paul's Opponents*. JSNTSup 40. Sheffield: JSOT Press, 1990.

Vollenweider, Samuel. "Die Waagschalen von Leben und Tod. Phil 1,21–26 vor dem Hintergrund der antiken Rhetorik." Pages 237–61 in *Horizonte neutestamentlicher Christologie*. WUNT 144. Tübingen: Mohr Siebeck, 2002.

———. "Kreuzfeuer: Paulus und seine Konflikte mit Rivalen, Feinden und Gegnern." Pages 649–76 in *Receptions of Paul in Early Christianity: The Person of Paul and His Writings through the Eyes of His Early Interpreters*. Edited by Simon Butticaz, Andreas Dettwiler, and Jens Schröter. BZNW 234. Berlin: de Gruyter, 2018.

———. "Politische Theologie im Philipperbrief?" Pages 457–69 in *Paulus und Johannes*. Edited by Dieter Sänger and Ulrich Mell. WUNT 198. Tübingen: Mohr Siebeck, 2006.

Wehnert, Jürgen. "Antipaulinismus in den Pseudoklementinen." Pages 170–90 in *Ancient Perspectives on Paul*. Edited by Tobias Nicklas, Andreas Merkt, and Joseph Verheyden. NTOA 102. Göttingen: Vandenhoeck & Ruprecht, 2013.

White, L. Michael. "Morality between Two Worlds: A Paradigm of Friendship in Philippians." Pages 201–15 in *Greeks, Romans, and Christians: Essays in Honor of Abraham J. Malherbe*. Edited by David L. Balch, Everett Ferguson, and Wayne A. Meeks. Minneapolis: Fortress, 1990.

From Rome to the Colony of Philippi: Roman Boasting in Philippians 3:4–6 in Its Latin West and Philippian Epigraphic Context

James R. Harrison

1. Prolegomenon: An Evaluation of Proposed Rhetorical Contexts for Paul's Boasting in Philippians 3:4–6

1.1. The Latin Epigraphic Context of Boasting at Philippi

Paul's boasting in Phil 3:4–6 has been little examined in its Roman epigraphic context. But, in a masterful analysis of the honorific inscriptions of the Roman colony, Joseph Hellerman has investigated Christ's *cursus pudorum* (course of shame) in Phil 2:5–11 against the *cursus honorum* (course of honor) of the military and civic elites at Philippi.[1] In regard to Phil 3:4–6, Hellerman highlighted how "ascribed honour precedes acquired honour,"[2] instancing two Philippian inscriptions as samples

---

1. Joseph H. Hellerman, *Reconstructing Honor in Roman Philippi: Carmen Christi as Cursus Pudorum*, SNTSMS 132 (Cambridge: Cambridge University Press, 2005), 121–27. On honor more generally, see Carlin A. Barton, *Roman Honor: The Fire in the Bones* (Berkeley: University of California Press, 2001); J. E. Lendon, *Empire of Honour: The Art of Government in the Roman World* (repr., Oxford: Oxford University Press, 2002). For discussion of honor in the apostle Paul, see the references listed in James R. Harrison, "Paul and Ancient Civic Ethics: Redefining the Canon of Honour in the Graeco-Roman World," in *Paul's Graeco-Roman Context*, ed. C. Breytenbach, BETL 227 (Leuven: Peeters, 2015), 76 n. 5.

2. Hellerman, *Reconstructing Honor*, 125. For discussion of the honor inscriptions in the Roman colony of Philippi, see 88–109. For discussion of other Hellenistic-Roman conventions at Philippi (e.g., benefaction, reciprocity, friendship, patron-client relations), see Lukas Bormann, *Philippi: Stadt und Christengemeinde zur Zeit des Paulus*, NovTSup 58 (Leiden: Brill, 1995), 161–205. Surprisingly, there exists no

of the phenomenon, and proposing that a similar rhetorical dynamic is occurring in Paul's boasting in his Jewish heritage in verses 4–6. In another important contribution to the epigraphic discussion, Peter Pilhofer has examined verse 5 against the backdrop of significant symbols of Roman status at Philippi. Pilhofer argues that Philippian readers would have drawn analogies between Paul's Jewish boasts and (what he proposes are) their Roman counterparts. There would have been correspondence, Pilhofer claims, between (1) Paul's being "circumcised on the eighth day" and the Roman assumption of the toga (*virilis*), (2) his membership of "the people of Israel" and being born into the Roman

---

monograph by classicists of Greco-Roman boasting focusing on the literary and epigraphic evidence. See, however, the following articles from ancient historians: E. A. Judge, "Paul's Boasting in Relation to Contemporary Professional Practice," in *Social Distinctives of the Christians in the First Century: Pivotal Essays by E. A. Judge*, ed. David M. Scholer (Peabody, MA: Hendrickson, 2008), 57–71; Judge, "The Conflict of Educational Aims in the New Testament," in *The First Christians in the Roman World: Augustan and New Testament Essays*, ed. James R. Harrison, WUNT 229 (Tübingen: Mohr Siebeck, 2009), 706–8; Christopher Forbes, "Comparison, Self-Praise and Irony: Paul's Boasting and the Conventions of Hellenistic Rhetoric," *NTS* 32 (1986): 1–30; L. Pernot, "*Periautologia*, problèmes et méthodes de l'éloge de soi-même dans la tradition éthique et rhétorique gréco-romaine," *REG* 111 (1998): 101–24. On the Greco-Roman context of boasting in Paul's letters, see Jorge Sánchez Bosch, *"Gloriarse" segun San Pablo: Sentido y teología de kauchaomai*, AnBib 40 (Rome: Biblical Institute Press, 1970), not seen by me; Hans Dieter Betz, *Der Apostel Paulus und die sokratische Tradition: Eine exegetische Untersuchung zu seiner "Apologie" 2 Korinther, 10–13*, BHT 45 (Tübingen: Mohr Siebeck, 1972); S. H. Travis, "Paul's Boasting in 2 Corinthians 10–12," *SE* 6 (1973): 527–32; J. Paul Sampley, "Paul, His Opponents in 2 Corinthians 10–13," in *The Social World of Formative Christianity: Essays in Tribute to Howard Clark Kee*, ed. Jacob Neusner et al. (Philadelphia: Fortress, 1988), 162–77; Terrance Callan, "Competition and Boasting: Toward a Psychological Portrait of Paul," *ST* 40 (1986): 137–56; Jennifer A. Glancy, "Boasting of Beatings (2 Corinthians 11:23–25)," *JBL* 123 (2004): 99–135; M. Wocjiechowski, "Paul and Plutarch on Boasting," *JGRChJ* 3 (2006): 99–109; K. C. Donahoe, "From Self-Praise to Self-Boasting: Paul's Unmasking of the Rhetorico-Linguistic Phenomena in 1 Corinthians" (PhD diss., St Andrews University, 2008); Matthew R. Malcolm, *Paul and the Rhetoric of Reversal: The Impact of Paul's Gospel on His Macro-Rhetoric*, SNTSMS 155 (Cambridge: Cambridge University Press, 2013), 155–61; Peter-Ben Smit, "Paul, Plutarch and the Problematic Practice of Self-Praise (περιαυτολογία): The Case of Phil 3:2–21," *NTS* 60 (2014): 341–59; Duane F. Watson, "Paul and Boasting," in *Paul and the Greco-Roman World: A Handbook*, ed. J. Paul Sampley (London: Bloomsbury T&T Clark, 2016), 1:90–112.

citizenship (Acts 21:25–28), (3) his birth into the "tribe of Benjamin" and the Philippian tribe of Voltinia,[3] and (4) his self-designation of "Hebrew of the Hebrews" and the Roman patronymic (e.g., son of Caius). So far as I am aware, no other serious Latin epigraphic exploration of boasting in our passage has been undertaken since Hellerman and Pilhofer. However, as brief as these incisive contributions to Phil 3:4–6 have been, they help us to see more clearly how Paul engages a Philippian audience through a boasting style modeled on the rhetoric of local Roman honorific epigraphy.[4]

What is required, however, is a full investigation of the first-century Philippian honorific inscriptions within their epigraphic context of late republican and early imperial Rome, the culture of which the Roman colony of Philippi, like other colonies in the Greek East, mimicked. Such a comparison allows us a better appreciation of the subtleties of boasting in the epigraphic genre and, therefore, of Paul's eulogistic conventions in their Latin context. What dangers did excessive boasting arouse in the Roman world at a local level? What light might these republican traditions throw on the aspirations of Roman soldiers and civic leaders later on in the early imperial colony of Philippi? How does Paul's gospel of justifying grace address this new situation (Phil 3:7–11)?

However, before we examine the epigraphic evidence from Rome and Philippi relating to Roman boasting culture, there are two further stands of evidence, each identified by scholars as pertinent to Phil 3:4–6, that are worthy of discussion for a full understanding of Paul's approach to boasting in our pericope. Thus we turn to a brief examination of Plutarch's *De se ipsum citra invidiam laudando* and the Greek rhetorical genre of the encomium, as well as to the Jewish "zeal" terminology (Phil 3:6) and Sirach's "Hymn in Honor of Ancestors" (Sir 44:1–50:24). Curiously, however, Sirach's famous hymn has been inadequately explored in relation to Phil 3:4–6, even though there is nothing else comparable to its power and scope as far as Jewish encomiastic culture.

---

3. Joseph H. Hellerman writes: "More than half of the inscriptions from Philippi contain the abbreviation *VOL.*, which boasts of membership in the Roman tribe Voltinia." Joseph H. Hellerman, *Philippians*, EGGNT (Nashville: Broadman & Holman, 2015), 177.

4. Peter Pilhofer, *Philippi*, vol. 1, *Die erste christliche Gemeinde Europas*, WUNT 87 (Tübingen: Mohr Siebeck, 1995), 123–27.

1.2. Plutarch's *De se ipsum citra invidiam laudando* and the Greek Rhetorical Genre of the Encomium

Boasting in the Philippian and Corinthian epistles has been profitably investigated against the backdrop of Plutarch's treatise on self-eulogy, *De se ipsum citra invidiam laudando* ("On Praising Oneself Inoffensively" [539a–547f]).[5] M. Wocjiechowski, although he does not discuss Phil 3:4–6, argues that Plutarch allows boasting to a limited degree (e.g., Plutarch, *De ipsum laud.* 2 [539e–f], 5–6 [541c–e], 16 [545a]),[6] as did the apostle Paul (1 Cor 9:15; 2 Cor 1:12; 11:10, 18, 21; 11:21–12:4). This includes boasting in others (1 Thess 2:19; 2 Thess 1:4; 1 Cor 15:31; 2 Cor 7:4; 8:4; Phil 2:16), a tactic also endorsed by Plutarch (*De ipsum laud.* 9 [542b–c]).[7] Paul's piety, Wocjiechowski proposes, is determinative for his overall attitude toward boasting, flowing from the Old Testament, where God alone is the source of all glory (1 Cor 1:29, 31; 2 Cor 10:8; Phil 3:3; Gal 6:14; Rom 5:11, 17).[8] Although Paul is sometimes forced into eulogistic self-comparison (2 Cor 12:11: "you forced me to it"), he nevertheless regards human boasting as fundamentally misconceived (1 Cor 9:16; 13:3; 2 Cor 10:12, 13, 15–17), as does Plutarch in particular circumstances (*De ipsum laud.* 1 [539a–d]; see *De tranq. anim.* 10 [470c]). Instead Paul chooses to boast in his weaknesses (2 Cor 12:7) and the cross (Gal 6:14)—a tactic of self-denigration

---

5. The self-eulogy in Phil 3:4–6 is to be distinguished from those occasions in Philippians where Paul commends others (e.g., 2:19–24; 4:2–3). See Efrain Agosto, "Paul's Use of Greco-Roman Conventions of Commendation" (PhD diss., Boston University, 1996), 188–92, 196–203. Additionally, Agosto, *Servant Leadership: Jesus and Paul* (Saint Louis: Chalice, 2005); Agosto, "Paul and Commendation," in Sampley, *Paul and the Greco-Roman World*, 143–68.

6. For Wocjiechowski on Plutarch, see "Paul and Plutarch on Boasting," 105–7. For further discussions of Plutarch, see Hans Dieter Betz, "*De laude ipsius* (Moralia 539A–547F)," in *Plutarch's Ethical Writings and Early Christian Literature*, SCHNT 4 (Leiden: Brill, 1978), 367–93; Lorenzo Miletti, "Il *De laude ipsius* di Plutarco e la teoria 'classica' dell'autoelogi," in *Plutarco: Linguaggi e Retorica; Atti del XII Convegno della International Plutarch Society*, ed. Paola Volpe Cacciatore (Naples: D'Auria Editore, 2014), 81–99.

7. Wocjiechowski, "Paul and Plutarch on Boasting," 104.

8. Wocjiechowski, "Paul and Plutarch on Boasting," 102–3. For discussion of the Jewish and Roman attitude to glory and its relation to Romans, see James R. Harrison, *Paul and the Imperial Authorities at Thessalonica and Rome: A Study in the Conflict of Ideology*, WUNT 273 (Tübingen: Mohr Siebeck, 2011), 201–69.

only rarely entered into by the ancients (e.g. Plutarch, *De ipsum laud.* 13 [544b]; see Quintilian, *Inst.* 11.1.21).⁹

By contrast, Peter-Ben Smit highlights Plutarch's distinction between occasions where self-praise is employed primarily as a rhetorical tactic in competition with one's opponents,¹⁰ over against those other occasions where self-praise is entirely justified (*De ipsum laud.* 14–17 [544d–546a]). Paul's use of self-praise, Smit concludes, is not offensive because it coheres with rhetorical conventions and strategies employed by the ancient orators of his day. Scott Ryan, ranging more widely than just the treatise of Plutarch, argues that Paul follows the instructions for the encomium (a celebratory speech) that were prescribed in the ancient *Progymnasmata* (preliminary exercises in speech writing).¹¹ Thus, in the case of both Smit and Ryan, Paul establishes his own ethos, affirms his concern for others, and, last, asserts his probity in the face of unjustified attack. Further, as Smit demonstrates, the apostle mitigates any potential offense by focusing on his own limitations (e.g., Phil 3:6: "persecuting the church") and also by highlighting the personal exempla of others (2:5–11, 25–30; 4:2–3).¹²

---

9. Wocjiechowski, "Paul and Plutarch on Boasting," 107–8.

10. For references in Plutarch, see Smit, "Paul, Plutarch and the Problematic Practice of Self-Praise," 349–51.

11. Scott C. Ryan argues that Paul follows Plutarch's exception (*De ipsum laud.* 3 [540c], 5 [541a–c]), which permits boasting when one is addressing a personal charge or bolstering one's reputation for the greater good. Thus, as Ryan elaborates, Paul demonstrates his intimate familiarity with Greco-Roman rhetorical conventions in Phil 3:4–6, including the encomium prescribed in the ancient *Progymnasmata*. But Paul's dismissal of his Jewish credentials in Phil 3:8 as σκύβαλα ("waste," "refuse") and his offer of an alternative form of rectitude (3:9–11) is, according to Ryan, a dramatic rhetorical move. Scott C. Ryan, "The Reversal of Rhetoric in Philippians 3:1–11," *PRSt* 39 (2012): 67–77. It seems to me, however, that Paul's rhetoric in v. 8 is so extreme in this instance that the entire encomium genre of the *progymnasmata* (preliminary exercises in speech writing) is undermined. Furthermore, the rectitude that is articulated is not self-generated but a divine benefaction (Phil 3:9: τὴν ἐκ θεοῦ δικαιοσύνην). For examples of the encomium genre in the ancient textbooks of prose and rhetoric, see George A. Kennedy, trans. and ed., *Progymnasmata: Greek Textbooks of Prose Composition and Rhetoric*, WGRW 10 (Atlanta: Society of Biblical LIterature, 2003): "The Exercises of Aelius Theon," 109–12; "The *Preliminary Exercises* Attributed to Hermogenes," 15–18; "The *Preliminary Exercises* of Aphthonius the Sophist," 35–40; "The *Preliminary Exercises* of Nicolaus the Sophist," 47–58; "Commentary on the *Progymnasmata* of Aphthonius Attributed to John of Sardis," 116.1–142.6.

12. Smit, "Paul, Plutarch and the Problematic Practice of Self-Praise," 352–58.

Moreover, in undertaking such a calculated rhetorical risk, the apostle does not fall into the trap of rivalry in self-praise, a possibility mentioned by Plutarch (*De ipsum laud.* 18–22 [546c–547f]). Paul instead avows that his real concern always was the well-being of the Philippians.[13]

In sum, Wocjiechowski, Smit, and Ryan have helpfully clarified Paul's boasting in Phil 3:4–16 in its ancient oratorical context. However, they do not bring us any closer to the local Roman conventions of boasting at Philippi (or, for that matter, those at the Roman colonies of Pisidian Antioch and Corinth, each visited by Paul) and, concomitantly, how the apostle interacted with these conventions in the wider eulogistic context of the Latin West. Given the prominence of the eulogistic genre in the inscriptions of the Mediterranean basin, what difference did Paul's highly unconventional approach to boasting make to the Western intellectual tradition in this regard?

1.3. The Jewish Context of Boasting: The Zeal and Priestly Traditions in Sirach 44.1–50.24 and the *Vita* of Josephus

Consideration should also be given to scholarly discussion on the Jewish background of boasting in Phil 3:4–6.[14] Does (what seems to be) the Jewish context (Phil 3:1–3) and content of Paul's boasting (3:4–6) make our study of the Philippian epigraphic context of our pericope unlikely to be exegetically fruitful? At first glance, this might seem to be the case. Boasting is excluded in the Old Testament and Second Temple Judaism (1 Kgs 20:11; 1 Sam 2:2–3; Judg 7:2; Prov 11:7; 25:14; 27:1; Pss 49:6; 52:1; 93:3–4; 115:1; Sir 48.4; 3 Macc 2:17; Philo, *Congr.* 107; T. Jud. 13.2–3). Humans were only permitted to glory in God's works and their relationship with him (Deut 10:21; 1 Chr 16:27–29; 29:11; Ps 5:11–12; Sir 1:11; 9:16; 10:22; 17:9; 39:8; 50:20).[15] Furthermore, if the (real or hypothetical) opponents in Phil

---

13. Smit, "Paul, Plutarch and the Problematic Practice of Self-Praise," 358.

14. For discussion of Jewish attitudes toward boasting in Second Temple Judaism and their relevance for the Epistle to the Romans, see Simon J. Gathercole, *Where Is Boasting? Early Jewish Soteriology and Paul's Response in Romans 1–5* (Grand Rapids: Eerdmans, 2002); Judith M. Gundry, "'Or Who Gave First to Him, So That He Shall Receive Recompense?' (Rom 11,35): Divine Benefaction and Human Boasting in Paul and Philo," in *The Letter to the* Romans, ed. Udo Schnelle, BETL 126 (Leuven: Peeters, 2009), 26–53.

15. Rudolf Bultmann, "καυχάομαι," *TDNT* 3:645–53; Ceslas Spicq, "καυχάομαι, καύχημα, καύχησις," *TLNT* 3:295–302; Wocjiechowski, "Paul and Plutarch on Boast-

3:1–3 are identified as Jewish, then a critique of Roman boasting could be ruled out in advance. Surely we should be approaching Phil 3:4–6 from an exclusively Jewish viewpoint?

But there is evidence for a more positive evaluation of boasting in a Jewish context: namely, the zeal tradition. Dane Ortlund has recently argued, on the basis of an extensive examination of the zeal traditions of Second Temple Judaism,[16] that Paul's zeal in persecuting the church did not just originate with his rejection of the false messianic and nomistic beliefs of the early Christians. Nor did it only arise from his own version of nomistic righteousness as a Pharisee (i.e., "Jewish set-apartness").[17] Rather, Ortlund suggests, Paul alludes to the zeal motif in Phil 3:6 as indisputable evidence of what he had personally achieved before his conversion. Thus the allusion functions as a testimony to Paul's strong sense of moral superiority to his Jewish contemporaries in the heated public competition for a Phinehas-like nomistic righteousness (ἐγώ μᾶλλον: Phil 3:4; 3:9: μὴ ἔχων ἐμὴν δικαιοσύνην τὴν ἐκ νόμου; see Gal 1:13–14 [v. 14: ζηλωτὴς ὑπάρχων τῶν πατρικῶν μου παραδόσεων]; Acts 22:3b [ζηλωτὴς ὑπάρχων τοῦ θεοῦ]; see MT Num 25:11, 13; LXX Num 25:13 [ἐζήλωσε τῷ θεῷ]).[18] But Paul's use of venerable zeal motifs from a Jewish context, we will argue, also ideologically engaged the Roman aristocratic quest for ancestral and personal glory over their civic rivals, which were unmasked for posterity to see in the epigraphic evidence of Rome and its colony at Philippi.

---

ing," 99–100. Note the comment of Spicq ("καυχάομαι," 297–98): "The peculiar contribution of the OT to the semantics of *kauchaomai* is to give this verb a religious meaning and to pose the radical contrast between human vainglory and divine honor."

16. Dane C. Ortlund, *Zeal without Knowledge: The Concept of Zeal in Romans 10, Galatians 1, and Philippians 3*, LNTS 472 (London: T&T Clark, 2012), 24–114.

17. Ortlund, *Zeal without Knowledge*, 146–47.

18. For full argument, see Ortlund, *Zeal without Knowledge*, 150–64. Callan argues that Paul was psychologically a competitor, manifesting the zeal for God similar to Phinehas (MT Num 25:11, 13; MT Ps 106:30–33; Sir 45:23–25; 1 Macc 2:54; 4 Macc 18:12; Josephus, *Ant.* 4.152–155; Pseudo-Philo, L.A.B. 46–48; m. Sanh. 9:6; Sifre Num. 151) in his pre-Christian state as a persecutor of the church ("Competition and Boasting," 139–40). For full exposition of the zeal motif, see James D. G. Dunn, *The Theology of Paul the Apostle* (Grand Rapids: Eerdmans, 1998), 350–53; Dunn, *The Epistle to the Galatians*, BNTC 9 (Peabody, MA: Hendrickson, 1993), 60–62. By contrast, Ortlund argues that Dunn fails to see the Godward orientation of zeal (*Zeal without Knowledge*, 164–65).

But there remains a surprising lacuna in the scholarly discussion of the Jewish background to Paul's self-encomium in Phil 3:4-6: Sirach's Hymn in Honor of Ancestors (Sir 44:1–50:24).[19] How does this rich Jewish eulogistic hymn intersect with the boasting culture of Rome and Philippi? Ortlund helpfully traces the zeal terminology employed in Sirach (9:1, 11; 30:24; 37:10; 40:4; 45:18, 23; 48:2; 51:18), dismissing the first six examples as merely cases of "jealousy."[20] But he goes on to argue that the final three zeal references (Sir 45:23; 48:2; 51:18) denote the ethical and obedient life of the covenantal Jew under God's law.[21] As such, the emphasis coheres with the overall tenor of Sir 44–52, where "the emphasis is on Israel's past heroes as moral exemplars, emphasizing not so much their maintenance of Israel's set-apartness as their individual obedience."[22] Is Paul similarly setting himself forth as an exemplum of Jewish covenantal righteousness and zeal, culminating in his triumph over his Pharisaic rivals by virtue of his moral perfection (Phil 3:6: ἄμεμπτος), with a view to repudiating it subsequently in Christ?

However, Ortlund draws no explicit connection between Phil 3:6 and Sirach's hymn and its conception of zeal. Rather, in the view of Ortlund, Ps 106 (LXX 105) provides for Paul the exegetical clue regarding zeal and righteousness in Phil 3:6 and 9. The psalm's vignette of the zeal of Phinehas and, crucially, its mention of the divine crediting of righteousness to Phinehas (MT Ps 106:30-31; see MT Gen 15:6; Rom 4:3-25; Gal 3:1-7), explains why Paul opted for the LXX intertextual echo at this juncture. For Paul, Ps 106:30-31 finds christological fulfillment in the gift of divine righteousness, conveyed either through the faithfulness of Christ or by the

---

19. On Sirach's hymn as an encomium, see Burton L. Mack, *Wisdom and the Hebrew Epic: Ben Sira's Hymn in Praise of the Fathers* (Chicago: University of Chicago Press, 1985), 128-37; Thomas R. Lee, *Studies in the Form of Sirach 44–50*, SBLDS 75 (Atlanta: Scholars Press, 1986). On Sirach generally, see B. M. Metzger, *An Introduction to the Apocrypha* (New York: Oxford University Press, 1957), 77-88; David A. deSilva, "The Wisdom of Ben Sira: Honor, Shame, and the Maintenance of the Values of a Minority Culture," *CBQ* 58 (1996): 433-55; deSilva, *Introducing the Apocrypha: Message, Context, and Significance* (Grand Rapids: Baker, 2002), 153-97; Elisa Uusimäki, "The Formation of a Sage according to Ben Sira," in *Second Temple Jewish Paideia in Context*, ed. Jason M. Zurawski and Gabriele Boccaccini, BZNW 228 (Berlin: de Gruyter, 2017), 59-69.

20. Ortlund, *Zeal without Knowledge*, 70-73.

21. Ortlund, *Zeal without Knowledge*, 73-76.

22. Ortlund, *Zeal without Knowledge*, 72-73.

believer's faith in Christ, or, perhaps in a case of deliberate ambiguity, by means of both (Phil 3:9).[23]

Of course, it is also possible that Paul did not refer to the rendering of Phinehas in Sir 45:23-25 in his theological discussion of zeal and righteousness in Phil 3:1-11 (esp. v. 6 [κατὰ ζῆλος διώκον τὴν ἐλλησίαν]; v. 9: μὴ ἔχων ἐμὴν δικαιοσύνην ἀλλὰ τὴν διὰ πίστεως Χριστοῦ) because he did not know of this encomiastic tradition.[24] But, as we have argued, Paul's bypassing of Sir 45:23-25 is more dictated by the focus of MT Ps 106:30-31 on the ratification of the Abrahamic covenantal promises by divine grace through faith (MT Gen 15:6; Ps 106:30-31; see Phil 3:9). But in the hymn of Sirach, the figures of Aaron (Sir 45:6-22) and Phinehas (45:23-25) embody an eternal high priesthood (Sir 45:24; see 45:7a, 15a) and function as priestly precursors to the glorious high priest, Simon the Just, son of Onias (Sir 50:1-24), who is exuberantly eulogized as the culmination of Old Testament temple and sacrificial piety, securing God's mercy and peace for Israel "as in the days of old" (Sir 50:23-24).[25] Furthermore, a priestly emphasis to "zeal" would not have sat easily with the Pharisaic righteousness to which Paul appealed in his own self-eulogy in Phil 3:6. One wonders, then, what Roman auditors, familiar with their own encomiastic conventions, might have made of this Jewish eulogistic hymn to Israel's heroes of eternal priesthood. It is, as I have noted, the most positive boasting tradition in the Jewish intertestamental writings.

First, David deSilva suggests that Sirach's hymn is profitably compared with the Greek encomia, where the aim is to praise virtuous people and provoke imitation of them.[26] Thus a significant rhetorical bridge with Greco-Roman encomiastic culture exists. Second, more than imitation is

---

23. For full argumentation, see Ortlund, *Zeal without Knowledge*, 150-64. On the *pistis Christou* debate in relation to Phil 3:9, see Michael F. Bird and Preston M. Sprinkle, eds., *The Faith of Jesus Christ: Exegetical, Biblical, and Theological Studies* (Peabody, MA: Hendrickson, 2009).

24. For an excellent discussion of Sir 45:23-25, see Dongshin D. Chang, "Phinehas, the Sons of Zadok, and Melchizedek: An Analysis of Some Understandings of Priestly Covenant in the Late Second Temple Period" (PhD diss., University of Manchester, 2013), 85-87.

25. On whether Sir 50:1-24 refers to high priest Simon I (post-300 BCE) or Simon II (ca. 200 BCE), see James C. Vanderkam, *From Joshua to Caiaphas: High Priests after the Exile* (Minneapolis: Fortress, 2004), 137-57.

26. DeSilva, "Wisdom of Ben Sira."

involved here: rather, the memorialization of the wisdom and the name of the pious Jewish ancestral figures is paramount (Sir 44:14–15):

> Their bodies are buried in peace,
> > but their name lives on,
> > generation after generation.
> The assembly declares their wisdom,
> > and the congregation proclaims their praise.[27]

It is therefore likely, as we will see, that resonances with the Roman quest for ancestral glory, recorded eternally for posterity, would have been evoked by this Jewish emphasis on memorialization.

Second, as noted, there is a strong priestly focus to the encomium in Sir 44:1–50:24. This emphasis would also have registered socially with Philippian auditors. The imperial priests were prominent citizens in the Roman colony. At the port city of Philippi, Neapolis (Acts 16:11: i.e., modern Kavala), there are inscribed sarcophagi of Julio-Claudian priests and priestesses, as well as a *flamen* of Vespasian.[28] There is reference in an inscription to a "*flamen* of divine Augustus" and "patron of [the] colony," named Caius Oppius Montanus, also based at Kavala.[29] These status-conscious priests, who lived and died at the beautiful port city of Neapolis,[30] are the eminent and wealthy citizens of the colony of Philippi, who maintained the rituals of the imperial cult, ensuring the patronage of Rome and the blessing of her gods and ruler. Thus the drive for social precedence among the priestly elites at Philippi had its counterpart in the Jewish world.

Furthermore, from the time of the Hasmonean dynasty onward, there had emerged within Second Temple Judaism a highly competitive culture among the elites, especially among the aristocratic priestly families who aggressively promoted their own social, educational, and religious status.

---

27. DeSilva aptly writes: "In a book in which one's memory, or the name and reputation one leaves behind, becomes a major motivation for choosing covenant loyalty and integrity rather than more shady paths to wealth, enjoyment and power, it is strategic to display that collective memory at work" (*Introducing the Apocrypha*, 186).

28. Julio-Claudian priests: Claudius (Peter Pilhofer, *Philippi*, vol. 2, *Katalog der Inschriften von Philippi*, 2nd ed., WUNT 119 [Tübingen: Mohr Siebeck, 2009], 001). Julio-Claudian priestesses: Augusta (002; see 226). Flamen of Vespasian (004; see 719).

29. Pilhofer, *Philippi*, 2.031; see 241, 700.

30. Charalambos Bakirtzis and Helmut Koester, eds., *Philippi at the Time of Paul and after His Death* (Harrisburg, PA: Trinity Press International, 1998), 10.

This was presaged to some degree by encomiastic texts such as Sirach's hymn, which reflected Sadducean emphases,[31] but it also became more obvious in the first century CE in the self-eulogies of some of its priestly representatives. For example, in his *Vita* (1–9), Jewish historian Josephus speaks effusively of his own educational upbringing as a priest.[32] What is especially interesting is that Josephus displays a pronounced ancestral self-consciousness, parading the primacy of his socially well-placed house in the same self-magnifying manner as the aristocrats of Rome and the elites of the provincial colonies. But, in addition to this, Josephus also highlights his own pedagogic progress over against his pedestrian contemporaries (see Gal 1:13–14), adding thereby further gloss to the aristocratic and royal pedigree (necessarily abbreviated in the extract below):

> My family is not an ignoble one, tracing its descent far back to priestly ancestors. Different races base their claim to nobility on various grounds; with us a connection with the priesthood is the hallmark of an illustrious line. Not only, however, were my ancestors priests, but they belong to the first of the twenty-four courses—a peculiar distinction—and to the most eminent of its constituent clans. Moreover, on my mother's side I am of royal blood; for the posterity of Asamonauus, from whom she sprang, for a very considerable period were kings, as well as high priests, of our nation.... Distinguished as he was by his noble birth, my father Matthias was even more esteemed for his upright character, being among the most notable men in Jerusalem, our greatest city. Brought up with Matthias, my own brother, by both parents, I made great progress in my education, gaining a reputation for an excellent memory and understanding. While still a mere boy, about fourteen years old, I won universal applause for my love of literature; insomuch that the chief priests and the leading men of the city used constantly to come to me for precise information on some particular in our ordinances.[33]

---

31. Metzger, *Introduction to the Apocrypha*, 87.

32. Note the perceptive comment of Helen K. Bond regarding the upbringing of the New Testament high priest Caiaphas: "Caiaphas' family would have brought him up to have a sense of his own position as an aristocrat and member of a distinguished priestly clan. In a society where everything was conducted on a face-to-face basis, he would have been taught to recognise the importance of reputation, honour, and the family name" (*Caiaphas: Friend of Rome and Judge of Jesus?* [Louisville: Westminster John Knox, 2004], 25–26).

33. Loeb translation. For other examples of boasting in the "grand Roman style" in Josephus's *Vita*, see Bond, *Caiaphas*, 80–83, 187–88. For examples of boasting in

Last, Steve Mason makes an important observation concerning the inherent virtue exuded by the person possessing a priestly and aristocratic pedigree like that of Josephus: "For Josephus, as for all aristocrats and especially those in Rome, a distinguished ancestry ... was the normally expected source of a sterling character, since character was considered more or less fixed along blood lines."[34] In other words, virtue was assigned as a static construct to the aristocratic elites from the day of their birth, and they exercised this inherent virtue in the *cursus honorum* as either priests, generals, or benefactors during their adult life.

Where does this leave us in terms of Jewish boasting and Paul's own exercise in boasting in Phil 3:4–6? We have suggested that the strong Jewish rejection of human boasting and the redirection of all glory toward God characterized Paul's general attitude toward the issue. Nevertheless, we have suggested that Sirach's priestly hymn and the Jewish zeal traditions would have been congruent with elements of Roman boasting, especially those touching on the virtue of the priestly elites at Philippi and the undying ancestral glory of the noble houses at Rome,[35] even though the conceptual worlds underpinning each tradition were vastly different. Josephus's own boasting demonstrates the same rhetorical features as his Roman contemporaries. We are not suggesting that the Roman world would have been in any way familiar with Jewish encomiastic texts such as Sirach. Nor are we implying, as with the old Reformed caricatures of

---

various Jewish honorific inscriptions from the diaspora, mimicking the eastern Mediterranean epigraphic eulogies for beneficence, see B. Lifshitz, *Donateurs et fondateurs dans les synagogues juives* (Paris: Gabalda, 1967), 13, 33, 36. These stand in sharp contrast to the more circumspect Palestinian honorific inscriptions for beneficence in Palestine, where the honorand is only spoken of as "remembered for good" (by God). See Susan Sorek, *Remembered for Good: A Jewish Benefaction System in Ancient Palestine*, Social World of Biblical Antiquity 2/5 (Sheffield: Sheffield Phoenix, 2010). On reciprocity culture in Jewish society, see Seth Schwartz, *Were the Jews a Mediterranean Society? Reciprocity and Solidarity in Ancient Judaism* (Princeton: Princeton University Press, 2010). On the degree to which Josephus's speech reflects an accurate account of his family tree as opposed to being a distinguished invention, see the discussion of Steve Mason, *Life of Josephus*, FJTC 9 (Leiden: Brill, 2001), 3–15.

34. Mason, *Life of Josephus*, 3.

35. Mason writes: "Whereas in Rome the priestly offices themselves were not hereditary, though they were largely restricted to the aristocracy, Josephus boasts here as elsewhere (*Apion* 2.185) that the Judeans perfectly integrate priesthood and aristocracy" (*Life of Josephus*, 4). For citation of Josephan texts that demonstrate "the importance of the priesthood for Josephus' literary identity," see Mason, *Life of Josephus*, 4.

Judaism, that such eulogistic traditions within Second Temple Judaism had extinguished a proper understanding of divine grace by Paul's time.[36] But we are proposing that Paul's Roman auditors, listening to the apostle's boasting in his Jewish pedigree in Phil 3:4–6 for the first time, would have immediately recognized a rhetorically well-crafted *cursus honorum* of Roman style aimed at securing Paul's social and religious advantage over his rivals. In other words, no matter the stance that we adopt to the question regarding the identity of Paul's opponents in Phil 3:1–3, we should be open to the likelihood that Paul's rhetoric is polyvalent in its reference, critiquing Roman boasting in general as much as its more specialized Jewish versions.

1.4. Conclusion

Paul's self-eulogy in Phil 3:4–6 has strong affinities with not only the Latin epigraphic boasting traditions of Philippi but also in the encomiastic traditions of the ancient *Progymnasmata* and in Plutarch's *De se ipsum citra invidiam laudando*. We have seen that the Old Testament dismissed human boasting as fundamentally misconceived, a position with which Paul agrees. However, various Old Testament zeal traditions, Sirach's Hymn in Honor of Ancestors, and Josephus's *Vita* indicated that there were eulogistic traditions in Second Temple Judaism that were congruent with elements of Greco-Roman boasting. The remainder of this chapter will explore boasting as a social phenomenon in the Latin epigraphy of Rome, the Italian peninsula more generally, and Philippi. Last, the phenomena of the *damnatio memoriae* ("condemnation of memory") and the arousal of *invidia* ("jealousy") will be explored for the insight that they provide into the unraveling of honor rituals, whether that is the loss of significant honor or the acquisition of too much honor. Paul's own radical disavowal of boasting will be explored in this wider context. Upon a close exegetical analysis of Phil 3:5–6, it will be argued that Paul sets out his Jewish *cursus honorum* in a rhetorical manner that would have resonated with a Latin West and Philippian audience, but undermines its rationale through a concerted focus on the soteriological career of Christ and, concomitantly, his personal reevaluation of the protocols of status in light of that paradigm.

---

36. See now the state-of-the-art discussion of John M. G. Barclay, *Paul and the Gift* (Grand Rapids: Eerdmans, 2015), 11–328.

2. Boasting in Late Republican and Early Imperial Rome: The Latin Epigraphic Evidence

2.1. Honorific Inscriptions from Republican Rome: The Traditional *Cursus Honorum*

Historically the Roman nobility were identified by their notability due to their ancestral wealth, their prestigious military victories in service of the state, their establishment of overseas networks of *clientelae*, and the acquisition of prestigious posts in the *cursus honorum*. But, above all, for a Roman house to be classified as a *nobilis* ("noble"), a family member had to acquire the highest office (i.e., the dictatorship, consulship, or consular tribunate).[37] In the republican era, the epitaphs and honorific inscriptions of the Roman *nobiles* and the local aristocrats from the Italian peninsula were set out in a stylized manner, though their precise design depended on the context of the inscription, its eulogistic aim, and its genre (epitaph, dedication, honorific text?). The eulogistic inscriptions of the Latin West could variously list the honorand's filiation, tribe, magistracies (sometimes highlighting a second consulship), military victories, and beneficence.[38] In terms of eulogistic conventions, the composers of the Roman inscriptions employed repetitions (numbers, lists, categories) as a mnemonic, and

---

37. See Matthias Gelzer, *The Roman Nobility*, trans. Robin Seager (Oxford: Basil Blackwell, 1969), 27–53.

38. For tribe, see E. H. Warmington, *Remains of Old Latin IV: Archaic Inscriptions*, LCL (Cambridge: Harvard University Press, 1953), "Epitaphs," 17 (Veline tribe), 105 (Terentine and Falernian tribes); "Honorary Inscriptions," 16 (Clustumine tribe). For magistracies, see Warmington, *Remains of Old Latin*, "Honorary Inscriptions," 4: "consul for the second time." See "Inscriptions on Public Works," 6: "In reward for these works the Senate made him censor twice and ordered that his son be exempt from military service." For military victories, see Warmington, *Remains of Old Latin*, "Dedicatory Inscriptions," 82–85; "Honorary Inscriptions," 1, 5–7. For beneficence, see Warmington, *Remains of Old Latin*, "Honorary Inscriptions," 8, 16 ("the whole borough as, through his services, released and preserved from the greatest daners and difficulties"); "Inscriptions on Public Works," 6, 7, 9, 11, 55. Note, however, the social shame that occurs when a benefactor is not able to fulfill his vow ("disheartened, dishevelled, despairing in his smitten fortunes") and has to have his sons instead pay for his promised gift to Hercules ("Dedicatory Inscriptions," 78).

the language of primacy to ensure that the glory of the honorand and his house was appropriately magnified.[39]

Sometimes carefully chosen vignettes of the excellence (*virtus*) of the honorand brought the inscriptional boasting to a fitting conclusion. For example, the eulogistic inscription of Lucius Mummius, consul of 146 BCE and the conqueror of Achaea, concludes in this manner after lauding his military conquest of Corinth and subsequent triumph at Rome in 145 BCE: "In recompense for these exploits prosperously achieved, he, the commander, is the dedicator of this temple and statue of Hercules the conqueror; which he had vowed in the war."[40] Here we see that the military victory of Mummius was understood in light of his piety to the gods, whereupon he reciprocates Hercules's beneficence to him on the battlefield with his (previously vowed) countergift of a temple to the demigod.

Supremely, the Res gestae divi Augusti in the Campus Martius represented the culmination of this eulogistic rhetorical genre.[41] After relentlessly listing his achievements in the previous thirty-three chapters, in Res gest. 34.3 Augustus highlights his alternative to the classical canon of four cardinal virtues (i.e., temperance [*sophrosyne*], prudence [*phronesis*], courage [*andreia*], and justice [*iustitia*]) with a striking vignette,[42] noting that they were inscribed as a personal honorific on a golden shield placed in the Curia Julia: namely, *virtus* (manliness), *clementia* (clemency), *pietas* (piety), and *iustitia* (justice). Such vignettes of virtue are crucial for the assessment of the ethos of an honorand in epigraphic boasting. What type of moral assessment would Roman auditors have brought to bear regarding Paul's final claim in his *cursus honorum* that, as far as "righteousness" went, he was ἄμεμπτος ("blameless")? Would such a truncated claim have impressed in Roman society, where multiple cardinal virtues were de rigeur?

---

39. For discussion, see Harrison, *Paul and the Imperial Authorities*, 223–25.

40. Warmington, *Remains of Old Latin*, "Dedicatory Inscriptions," 82.

41. See James R. Harrison, "Augustan Rome and the Body of Christ: A Comparison of the Social Vision of the *Res Gestae* and Paul's Letter to the Romans," *HTR* 106 (2013): 1–36.

42. See Helen F. North, "Canons and Hierarchies of the Cardinal Virtues in Greek and Latin Literature," in *The Classical Tradition: Literary and Historical Studies in Honor of Harry Caplan*, ed. Luitpold Wallach (Ithaca, NY: Cornell University Press, 1966), 165–83. For the Italian municipal construction of aristocratic virtue in the honorific inscriptions, see Elizabeth Forbis, *Municipal Virtues in the Roman Empire: The Evidence of Italian Honorary Inscriptions* (Leipzig: Teubner, 1996).

The remainder of this section will address how virtue, inherited and acquired, was addressed in the *elogia* of the Scipionic epitaphs for insight into Roman perceptions of Phil 3:4–6. We will then explore how with the advent of the Augustan principate and the accession of his Julio-Claudian heirs, the traditional *cursus honorum* was reconfigured along imperial lines, so that the upwardly mobile, powerful freedmen, and the military forces could achieve posts of eminence in the Roman empire. This will help us understand Roman boasting better in a Philippian context. Last, we will discuss the very rare cases of the unraveling of honor rituals in the Latin inscriptions across the Mediterranean basin, with a view to understanding how Paul's dismissal of his Jewish *cursus honorum* in Phil 3:7–11 might have been perceived by an honor-and-dishonor-sensitive culture.

2.1.1. Ancestral Virtue, the Generational Replenishment of Glory, and the Failure to Achieve: The Epitaphs of the House of the Republican Scipios

The epitaphs of the republican Scipionic family and local Italian aristocracies set out the pedigrees (filiation, magistracies, military victories and official posts, priesthoods, board memberships, etc.) of the deceased members.[43] The ethos evinced by the Scipionic epitaphs points to the vitality of the Roman nobleman's quest for ancestral glory. Two epitaphs in particular demonstrate this. Gnaeus Cornelius Scipio Hispanus (*praetor peregrinus*, 139 BCE) lists the magistracies of his pedigree[44] and then adds this highly revealing *elogium*: "By my good conduct I heaped virtues on the virtues of my clan: I begat a family and sought to equal the exploits of my father. I upheld the praise [*laudem*] of my ancestors, so that they were glad that I was created of their line. My honours have ennobled [*nobilitavit honor*] my stock."[45] This epitaph sums up succinctly the worldview of the

---

43. For examples of Sciponic decrees with pedigrees, see Warmington, *Remains of Old Latin*, "Epitaphs," 1–2, 3–4, 7, 10. For discussion, see R. E. Smith, *The Aristocratic Epoch in Latin Literature* (Sydney: Australasian Medical, 1947), 8–10. The next four paragraphs, reduced and adapted, are borrowed from James R. Harrison, "Paul and the Roman Ideal of Glory in the Epistle to the Romans," in *The Letter to the Romans*, ed. Udo Schnelle, BETL 226 (Leuven: Peeters, 2009), 350–51.

44. The *cursus honorum* is as follows: "Gnaeus Cornelius Scipio Hispanus, son of Gnaeus, praetor, curule aedile, quaestor, tribune of soldiers (twice); member of the Board of Ten for Judging Law-suits; member of the Board of Ten for making sacrifices" (Warmington, *Remains of Old Latin*, 10).

45. Warmington, *Remains of Old Latin*, 10. For all the Sciponic epitaphs, see

Roman *nobiles* (nobles). The ancestral virtues of the noble house had to be replenished generation by generation. The praise accorded the ancestors placed enormous expectations on each new generation of nobles. Each noble had to equal (and, hopefully, surpass) by virtuous conduct the achievements of the ancestors,[46] with the exploits of the immediate father being the starting point. If the replication of ancestral merit was successfully carried out by each new generation, the *nobilitas* of the family was rendered even more noble and virtuous. Remarkably, the dead ancestors are depicted as still vitally interested in the replenishment of the family honor attached to their line.[47] Would they have been disappointed that Gnaeus fell short of the consulship?

What happens, however, if the noble's life was prematurely cut short by his death before he could add to his ancestral glory? The answer is given with moving simplicity in the epitaph of a young Scipio who had only achieved "the honoured cap of Jupiter's priest" before he died: "Death caused all your virtues, honour, good report and valiance, your glory [*gloria*] and your talents to be short-lived. If you had been allowed long life in which to enjoy them, an easy thing it would been for you to surpass by great deeds the glory of your ancestors [*gloriam maiorum*]. Wherefore, O Publius Cornelius Scipio, begotten son of Publius, joyfully does earth take you to her bosom."[48] Here we see how the Scipios han-

---

Warmington, *Remains of Old Latin*, "Epitaphs," 1–10. Note the comment of Mario Erasmo: "That his dead ancestors would be happy … with his moral character illustrates a readership joined, rather than separated by death. Thus the epitaph reflects a need for accuracy since self-representation would have an objective assessment by ancestors who now form the contemporary family of the deceased, as would his descendants who will join him and their ancestors and face a similar reckoning of their accomplishments and virtues." Mario Erasmo, *Reading Death in Ancient Rome* (Columbus: Ohio State University Press, 2008), 170.

46. Note that Cicero also speaks of the *nobilis* surpassing his own accomplishments: "Do your utmost to surpass yourself in enhancing your own glory" (*Fam.* 12.7.2 [Williams]).

47. Note the comment of Donald Charles Earl regarding the role of *virtus* in Plautus and the Scipionic elogia: "[*Virtus*] consists in the gaining of pre-eminent *gloria* by the winning of office and the participation in public life. It concerns not only the individual but the whole family, not only its living members but the dead members and the unborn posterity as well." Donald Charles Earl, "Political Terminology in Plautus," *Historia* 9 (1960): 242.

48. Warmington, *Remains of Old Latin*, "Epitaphs," 5. Smith observes: "We see the constancy of the ideal, consisting still in public honours and public office, to the extent

dled their less successful members, when their advancement in the *cursus honorum* (course of honour: i.e., magistracies) was cut short either by death, as was the case with Publius Cornelius Scipio above,[49] or by a lack of significant magistracies.

Another variation on the theme is found in the *elogium* of Lucius Cornelius Scipio on a tablet from a sarcophagus: "Great virtues and great wisdom holds this stone with tender age. Whose life but not his honour fell short of honours, he that lies here was never outdone in virtue; twenty years of age to burial-places was he entrusted. Seek you not honour; which unto this man was not entrusted."

Whereas the previous *elogium* spoke of the noble's progress in virtue and glory, which had been cut short by death, there is no sense in this *elogium* that this young man was somehow deficient in virtue: his honor remains undiminished by his death and was never outdone the public contest for virtue despite the brevity of his life. Why was this the case? The answer seems to be that honor and virtue are assigned the well-born at birth and that members of this class continuously draw on a repository of moral and social excellence, no matter the brevity of their life or their failure to attain magisterial posts in the *cursus honorum* ("seek you not honour, which unto this man was not entrusted"). The idea of a repository of virtue on which one might draw has resonance in a Reformed understanding of imputed righteousness, though its accession through a messianic claimant crucified by their imperial prefect Pontius Pilate would have repulsed Roman auditors.

We turn now to the reconfiguration of the traditional republican *cursus honorum* under the Julio-Claudian rulers.

2.1.2. The Julio-Claudian Era, Imperial Patronage, and the Reconfigured *Cursus Honorum*

With the triumph of the Julian house at Actium (31 BCE), not only was Augustus the unchallenged military victor over all his enemies, but also he became the benefactor of the world by virtue of the vast wealth he now wielded (Res gest. 15–24). In particular, he outcompeted the old nobility

---

that even where the dead man took no part in public life, the only comment is on what he would have done had he lived longer" (*Aristocratic Epoch*, 10).

49. See also Warmington, *Remains of Old Latin*, "Epitaphs," 8: "Cornelius Scipio Asiagenus Nevershorn, son of Lucius, grandson of Lucius, sixteen years of age."

in the acquisition of clients through his unparalleled patronage at Rome and in the far-flung provinces, either sponsoring their careers in the army or appointing loyal provincial elites in imperial posts. The imperial *cursus honorum* of Augustus continued to flourish under his heirs. One such example is the Julio-Claudian legate C. Ummidius Durmius Quadratus, who erected his inscription below at Casinum, Latium Italy (first century CE).[50] He is well known to us from Tacitus as the legate of the province of Syria, one of the most important and prestigious provincial commands of the empire at the time of Nero (*Ann.* 12.45, 48, 54; 13.8–9; 14.26).[51] He probably died around 60 CE.

The inscription sets out his offices "in descending order (from the latest to the oldest), though some are out of order,"[52] highlighting the consulship first:

> To Gaius Ummidius Durmius Quadratus, son of Gauis, son of the Teretina tribe, consul, one of the 15 men in charge of the performance of the sacred rites, legate of Tiberius Caesar Augustus of the province of Lusitania, legate of the divine Claudius [*divi Claudi*] at Illyricum, legate of Syria of the same emperor and of Nero Caesar Augustus, proconsul of the province of Cyprus, quaestor of the divine Augustus [*divi Aug[usti]*] and Tiberius Caesar Augustus, curule aedile, prefect of the public treasury, one of the ten men in charge of hearing legal cases, caretaker of the public records office, prefect for the distribution of grain by decree of the Senate.

What is obvious is how Quadratus meticulously sets out his *cursus honorum* within the patronal frameworks of the Julio-Claudian house.[53] His

---

50. Brian K. Harvey, *Roman Lives: Ancient Roman Life as Illustrated by Latin Inscriptions*, Focus Classical Sources (Newburyport, MA: Focus Publishing/Pullins, 2004), 2 (*CIL* 10.5182).

51. Harvey, *Roman Lives*, 19: "Only the emperor's most trusted friends and family members held this post."

52. Harvey, *Roman Lives*, 17.

53. Early in Augustus's reign, there remains an example of a *cursus honorum* belonging to the consular senator Lucius Munatius Plancus (22 BCE), who unrestrainedly boasts in his own achievements and claims a triumph with no reference to the *princeps* (Harvey, *Roman Lives*, 1). As Harvey argues, "Plancus' career exemplifies the heights to which a senator could aspire *before* Augustus' creation of the empire in 27 BCE. Plancus was among the *last* senators not directly connected with the imperial family to receive three supreme acclamations: that of imperator, censor, as well as the

career has been sponsored by the imperial rulers at critical junctures, including his nominations to the legateships of Lusitania, Illyricum, and Syria, and his post as quaestor. Not only is Quadratus duly acknowledging the fact that the traditional *cursus honorum* is now redefined imperially, sponsored by the grace of the Roman ruler, but also he spotlights how he is a close and trusted *amicus* of the Julio-Claudian house by virtue of such prestigious appointments. He is especially careful with the honorifics of each ruler, acknowledging the apotheosis of Augustus and Claudius (*divus*), while respecting, in terms of the absence of the same nomenclature on the inscription, Tiberius's own refusal of divine honors.[54] Thus the inscription captures both personally achieved and deflected honor. Last, as far as we can discern, the entire career of Quadratus is set out, covering all his posts.[55] Here we see how honors under the Julio-Claudian honor system were "redimensioned" in that, in contrast to the republican inscriptions, "honorific inscriptions for the living now came to include the titles of all offices ever held by them."[56] The type of military career outlined in the inscription of Quadratus accords well with the ethos of the military and elite inscriptions found at Philippi in the early Roman empire.

2.1.3. Conclusion

The *cursus honorum* of the Roman noble and Italian aristocrat was an identifiable epigraphic genre in the Latin West, with its own rhetorical features (e.g., the language of primacy, mnemonic patterns, defining vignettes of achievement). The Scipionic epitaphs are fascinating by virtue of their strong emphasis on the surpassing of ancestral glory and the

---

right to hold a triumph" (*Roman Lives*, 16). After the public honoring of Plancus, however, such acclamations were restricted to the Roman ruler and his family members. The acknowledgment of the Julio-Claudian ruler in sponsoring one's career, therefore, became the convention in the epigraphic rhetoric of the *cursus honorum*.

54. Although Tiberius refused divine honors, the imperial cult in his honor nevertheless flourished during his reign. See Bruce W. Winter, *After Paul Left Corinth: The Influence of Secular Ethics and Social Change* (Grand Rapids: Eerdmans, 2001), 270–71.

55. Harvey mentions that the post of legionary legate (*legatus legionis*) is omitted but is uncertain whether this is because of lack of space on the stone or because Quadratus never held the post (*Roman Lives*, 18).

56. Karl Galinsky, *Augustan Culture: An Interpretative Introduction* (Princeton: Princeton University Press, 1996), 385.

intense interest that the dead ancestors evinced in the next generation's replication of the virtue of the house. The virtue of the Scipionic ancestors became a repository of merit for those in the house who, due to their premature death, were unable to achieve significant posts. In the early empire, however, the upwardly mobile in the new Julio-Claudian *cursus honorum* redefined their identity in light of the grace of the Roman ruler to them in their rise to power through the acquisition of significant posts.

But what happens when honor rituals go astray or where the inscriptions themselves explicitly raise the issue of people who are not worthy of honor? Because such epigraphic occurrences are so infrequent in the eulogistic corpus, they are worth considering, given Paul's startling counterparadigm to the Roman *cursus honorum* encapsulated in Christ's cruciform *cursus pudorum*.

3. The Experience of Dishonor and *Invidia*: The Social Underside of the Roman Boasting System

In light of Paul's dramatic portrait of the *cursus pudorum* of Christ in Phil 2:5–11 and, relatedly, Paul's disavowal of his *cursus honorum* (3:5–6) in 2:7–11, it is worth pursuing examples of the unraveling of the rituals of honor in the Greco-Roman boasting system. We will focus on the very rare instances of such epigraphic dishonor: (1) the arousal of *invidia* through the exploits of a proconsul and his proprietor in the Roman colony of Corinth; (2) the erasure of an inscription on an obelisk in a notorious case of *damnatio memoriae* and the eventual relocation of the reinscribed monument from Alexandria to Rome several generations later; and, last, (3) the provision of burial sites, though with exclusions of interment, at Sassina (Umbria, Italy).

3.1. The Exploits of Antonius and Hirrius

An inscription in elegiacs from an unknown poet, found on a stone at Corinth and recounting the exploits of Hirrius as proprietor in 102 BCE, is "the first recorded erasure in a Roman private inscription."[57] As we will

---

57. Allen Brown West, *Latin Inscriptions 1896–1926*, vol. 8.2 of *Corinth: Results of Excavations Conducted by the American School of Classical Studies at Athens* (Cambridge: Harvard University Press, 1931), 4.

see, strategies for handling *invidia* (envy, jealousy) combine with blatantly exaggerated boasting in the inscription. The inscription is set out below:

> Learn you of an exploit such as no man has attempted and no man [will hazard hereafter], so that we may make wide renown of a hero's achievements. Under the command of [M]arcus [Ant]onius, proconsul, a fleet was carried over the Isthmus and sent across the sea. Marcus himself set out upon his voyage to Sida. Hirrus, as proprietor, stationed his fleet at Athens because of the season of the year. All this was accomplished in a few days with little turmoil; sound strategy and safe deliverance attended it. He who is upright has praise [*laud*[*a*]*t*] for him, and he who is otherwise, looks askance at him. Let men envy [*invid*[*ea*]*nt*] so long as they have reverence for what is seemly.[58]

The Latin name [Ant]**oni** [M]**arci** is an erasure, with its original letters having been chiseled off the stone. Seven letters, bolded above, are shown with sublinear dots by the editor of the Latin Corinthian inscriptions,[59] indicating that the letters are faintly legible on the stone. The bracketed letters above, missing entirely, are also restored by the editor. Why has the name of Marcus Antonius, *praetor pro consule* of 102 BCE and consul of 99 BCE, been erased? Although it might be a case of mistaken identity,[60] the most likely answer is that our proconsul was Mark Antony's grandfather. When Antony's memory was damned from any further mention in 30 BCE after the fall of Alexandria, his name was erased from the consular Fasti (*CIL* 1.422, 439).[61] Remarkably, it seems that Antonius's *damnatio memoriae* was even extended to his ancestral predecessors, including the famous forebear of our inscription in 102 BCE.[62] The inscription honors

---

58. For the Latin text and commentary, see West, *Latin Inscriptions 1896–1926*, 1 (*CIL* 1.2662). For the English translation, see Warmington, *Remains of Old Latin*, "Honorary Inscriptions," 7. For full discussion of the inscription, see Elizabeth R. Gebhard and Matthew W. Dickie, "The View from the Isthmus, ca. 200 to 44 B.C," in *Corinth the Centenary, 1896–1996*, vol. 20 of *Corinth: Results of Excavations Conducted by the American School of Classical Studies at Athens*, ed. Charles K. Williams II and Nancy Bookidis (Athens: American School of Classical Studies at Athens, 2003), 272–77.

59. West, *Latin Inscriptions 1896–1926*, 4.

60. Arthur E. Gordon, *Illustrated Introduction to Latin Epigraphy* (Berkeley: University of California Press, 1982), 90.

61. Cited in West, *Latin Inscriptions 1896–1926*, 4.

62. West notes that a person unknown restores the erased names in the official

the haulage of a fleet across the Corinthian Isthmus, with Antonius's fleet setting out for Sida in Asia Minor to fight the Cilician pirates, while the fleet of Hirrus remained in Athens owing to, as Cicero informs us (*De or.* 1.82), difficulty in navigation.[63]

The inflated rhetoric used regarding the Diolkos crossing,[64] however, is telling: "an exploit such as no man has attempted and no man [will hazard hereafter]." As Allen Brown West notes,[65] fleets had long since crossed the Corinthian Isthmus using the Diolkos from Greek times (Thucydides, *Hist.* 8.7–8; Polybius, *Hist.* 5.101.4 [see 4.19]). Whatever mitigating precedents might be appealed to justify the excessive boasting employed here,[66] we should not dilute the rhetorical force of the primacy, spanning the past and future, that is being claimed here.

In lines 9–10 of our inscription, the part of our text that crucially deals with *invidia*, we face problems because of the fragmentary state of the text and the hazardous nature of the restorations suggested by editors of the text. West indicates by sublinear dots that some letters are (in his opinion) faintly legible on the stone, but he provides no English translation. The Loeb translation, by E. H. Warmington, merely restores the Latin text as the editors imagine that it might have been and, accordingly, provide their English translation. By contrast, Elizabeth Gebhard and Matthew Dickie (very frustratingly) provide no restorations of the fragmentary Latin text at all, rendering only what is certain, but they give an English translation, which they show is provisional guesswork by means of question marks. The differing results are set out below.

(1) West Latin text (with restorations and the bolded letters below indicating the editor's sublinear dots), but with no English translation provided:

---

records at Rome (Tacitus, *Ann.* 3:18; Dio Cassius, *Hist. Rom.* 59.20) (*Latin Inscriptions*, 4), but this is not the case at Corinth.

63. See Philip de Souza, *Piracy in the Graeco-Roman World* (Oxford: Oxford University Press, 1999), 104–9. See also West, *Latin Inscriptions 1896–1926*, 1: "sound strategy and safe deliverance."

64. On the Diolkos, see David. K. Pettigrew, "The *Diolkos* of Corinth," *AJA* 115 (2011): 549–74; Pettigrew, *The Isthmus of Corinth: Crossroads of the Mediterranean World* (Ann Arbor: University of Michigan Press, 2016), 125–30.

65. West, *Latin Inscriptions 1896–1926*, 3.

66. Pettigrew states: "The extraordinary nature of the event is not entirely exaggerated, for the portage was the only certain transfer of ships by a Roman commander and probably the first since 217 B.C.E." ("*Diolkos* of Corinth," 567).

Q[u]ei probus **est** lauda[t], quei **contra** est inv[idet illum].
Invid[ea]nt, dum q[uos cond]**ecet** id **v**[ideant].

(2) Warmington Latin text (with restorations) and English translation:

Q[u]ei probus est lauda[t], quei contra est
    inv[idet illum];
Invid[ea]nt, dum q[uod cond]ecet id v[enerant].

He who is upright has praise for him, and he who is otherwise,
    looks askance at him.
Let men envy so long as they have reverence for what is seemly.

(3) Gebhard and Dickie Latin text (without restorations) and English translation:

q[u]ei probus est lauda[t], quei contra est in[
invid[ea]nt, dum q[u]ecet id v[.

The man who is upright praises, he who is, in contrast, envious (?), denigrates (?), but let them envy, provided that they see (?) what hurts (?) them.

We will bypass the restorations of West, since he has not provided an English translation. If the Loeb restorations and translation are correct, the inscription warns its readers not to let envy discount the achievements of Antonius by diminishing the praise rightly owed to him. The damaging effects of *invidia*, aroused by individuals of great achievement, are mollified if the envious exhibit reverence for what is seemly. Does this imply that a certain measure of *invidia* can be appropriate on occasion, provided that a consciousness of public decorum and personal conduct prevails over the strong emotion of jealousy, preventing it from spiraling out of control? By contrast, the English translation of Gebhard and Dickie sees the text as concluding with "the wish that those who do not find the deed praiseworthy may suffer for their envy."[67] Which interpretation is correct? Given the fragmentary nature of the text in lines 9–10 and the differing views of the editors regarding the restorations and the potential presence of letters that are (at best) faintly legible, we cannot be sure.

---

67. Gebhard and Dickie, "View from the Isthmus," 272.

Minimally, therefore, this inscription points to a fascinating interplay between the erasure of honor through a *damnatio memoriae* (effected by a later hand) and the arousal of *invidia* in the face of an individual's towering achievement (asserted by the original composer of the elegiacs on behalf of the proposer of the inscription). This sums up effectively the dark underside of the Roman boasting system. But whether a curse is being invoked against certain people who are consumed by *invidia*, or whether only the constraints of public decorum are being prescribed against *invidia* in this instance, is impossible to determine with confidence because of the indeterminacy of the Latin text in lines 9–10.

3.2. The *Damnatio Memoriae* of Gaius Cornelius Gallus

In terms of the *damnatio memoriae*, Gaius Cornelius Gallus, an *amicus* (friend) of Augustus, had made a very public gambit for primacy of status as a Roman general and the prefect of Egypt. He had disseminated his honorific statues throughout Egypt, inscribed inscriptions on the pyramids, and erected a boastful trilingual inscription at Philae (15 April 29 BCE), listing his victories in Egypt (30 BCE) in the grand rhetorical style of republican luminaries.[68] These victories had significantly contributed to the defeat of Antony and Cleopatra,[69] and, as prefect of Egypt, his conquest of territory extended farther than all previous Roman generals, including Augustus himself, reaching as far as the Thebaid in Ethiopia.

However, because of Gallus's hubristic behavior, Augustus immediately renounced his friendship with Gallus (*amicitiam renuntiare*), leading to his exile and suicide in 26 BCE. Tragically for Gallus, he did not recognize (or perhaps deliberately ignored?) that a significant shift in the acquisition of social and political status had occurred with the advent of the Augustan principate. The traditional republican noble quest for glory

---

68. For full discussion, see James R. Harrison, "The Erasure of Honour: Paul and the Politics of Dishonour," *TynBul* 66 (2016): 166–72. See Friedhelm Hoffmann, who translates and comments on the hieroglyphic version of the inscription, demonstrating how the Egyptian priests depicted Gallus with traditional Egyptian motifs. Friedhelm Hoffmann et al., eds., *Die dreisprachige Stele des C. Cornelius Gallus: Übersetzung und Kommentar* (Berlin: de Gruyter, 2009), 45–118. For a translation of the Latin text, see David C. Braund, *Augustus to Nero: A Sourcebook on Roman History 31 BC–AD 68* (London: Croom & Helm, 1985), 425 (*CIL* 3.14147 = *ILS* 8995 = *OGI* 2.654).

69. F. Cairns, *Sextus Propertius: The Augustan Elegist* (Cambridge: Cambridge University Press, 2006), 73.

could not be allowed to infringe on the primacy of Augustus and his unchallenged place of honor, lest the Roman state be plunged again into another round of civil war. The relentless enthusiasm of the Roman senate and people to press on Augustus unprecedented powers in 27 BCE and 23 BCE, proposals that Augustus strongly resisted, underscores the dramatic change in public perception that had occurred regarding the status of the Julian ruler and the members of his house.

The memory of Gallus's public dishonoring, in which Augustus consigned all public recognition of the prefect's status (or any claims thereunto) to oblivion, would reverberate for generations to come. An Egyptian obelisk of Gallus, whose honorific inscription at its the base had been erased in a *damnatio memoriae* (condemnation of memory) at Alexandria, was later recycled by the Roman ruler Caligula and rededicated in the Piazza di S. Pietro at the Vatican to the honor of Augustus and Tiberius.[70] The double brackets in the inscription, cited below, indicate the modern scholarly restoration of the obelisk's erased original, dedicated to Cornelius Gallus, which was ascertained from the telltale holes to which the bronze letters were originally attached:

[[By order of imperator Caesar, son of a god,
Gaius Cornelius Gallus, son of Gnaeus [vac.],
chief engineer [*praef[ectus] fabr[um]*] of Caesar, son of a god [vac.],
[vac.] built the Forum Julium. [vac.]]][71]

Here we see how interminably long the rituals of dishonor could last. The original honorific inscription of Gallus, celebrating his building of

---

70. The new honorific inscription erected in the Piazza di S. Pietro by Caligula, incised in two identical versions on the eastern and western sides, states: "Sacred to the divine Caesar Augustus, son of the divine Julius, to Tiberius Caesar Augustus, son of the divine Augustus." Inscription translated by Tyler Lansford, *The Latin Inscriptions of Rome: A Walking Guide* (Baltimore: Johns Hopkins University Press, 2009), 15.3B.

71. Translated by Lansford, *Latin Inscriptions of Rome*, 15.3B. On Gallus's erased inscription, see F. Magi, "Le iscrizioni recentemente scoperte sull'obelisco vaticano," *Studi Romani* 11 (1963): 50–56; Magi, "L'obelisco do Caio Cornelio Gallo," *Capitolium* 29 (1963): 488–92. See also Géza Alföldy, *Der Obeliskaufdem Petersplatzin Rom: Ein historisches Monument der Antike* (Heidelberg: SB Heidelberger Akademie der Wissenschaften, phil.-hist. Klasse, 1990), not seen by me. For further discussion, see Harriet I. Flower, *The Art of Forgetting: Disgrace and Oblivion in Roman Political Culture* (Chapel Hill: University of North Carolina Press, 2006), 125–32.

the Forum Julium in 30 BCE in Alexandria, was erased on his *damnatio memoriae* in 26 BCE. Remarkably, the erased obelisk remained unused in Alexandria until the advent of Tiberius's reign (14–37 CE). Moreover, it was only with the accession of Caligula to power that the relocation of the obelisk to Rome could be seriously considered.

3.3. Burial Conventions and the Dishonorable at Sassina

In the honorific inscription of Horatius Balbus, the local benefactor presents a graveyard to his town, Sassina:

> Horatius Balbus son of … is the giver to members of his township and other residents therein, at his own expense, of sites for burial, except such as had bound themselves to serve as gladiators and such as had hanged themselves with their own hand or had followed a filthy profession for profit; to each person a site, 10 ft. in frontage and 10 ft. in depth, between the bridge over the Sapis and the upper monument which is on the boundary of the Fangonian estate.[72]

What is interesting here is the exclusion of certain despised professions and those who had died in a particularly dishonorable way from burial. It poses a pointed question regarding what would have been public attitudes toward a socially despised crucified criminal in a Roman context and those who would continue to associate with his legacy of dishonor (Mark 15:29, 32; John 19:38–39; see also 1 Cor 1:18–25; Gal 3:13; 5:11; Phil 2:8b; Heb 12:2).

3.4. Conclusion

Only very occasionally did issues of dishonor appear in the honorific inscriptions, congregating around *damnatio memoriae* and the inevitable erasures of inscriptions on the stones. In the case of Gaius Cornelius Gallus, the time between the original honorific inscribing of his obelisk, the subsequent erasure of its text because of the dishonor of Gallus, and its eventual reinscribing and relocation in honor of another honorand, could span decades, so great was the opprobrium experienced and remembered. Conversely, significant civic and military achievement in a *cursus*

---

72. Warmington, *Remains of Old Latin*, "Epitaphs," 106.

honorum could provoke *invidia* among one's peers, who experienced their own gradual decline in fame due to the ascendant star of their political rival. Finally, exclusions of the dishonorable due to their profession were implemented in burial practice, another case of the hierarchy of honor in Roman society that determined the ultimate worth of individuals from the apex to the base of the social pyramid at their exit from life.

It is now time to investigate the Philippian honorific inscriptions from the first century to the early second century CE, spanning the Julio-Claudian and Flavian periods. What do we learn about boasting in a Roman colony of the Greek East, and to what degree does it reflect the ethos of Latin West boasting?

4. The Roman *Cursus Honorum* and the Honorific Inscriptions of Philippi

Our selection of datable Philippian inscriptions will only extend from the principate of Augustus to the reign of Hadrian, limiting in the main our investigation to the New Testament period, thereby excluding the heavy concentration of second–third century CE epigraphic evidence available at the city. Consequently, we will consider none of the later senatorial epigraphic evidence, restricting our selection to the members of the equestrian order, soldiers of the garrison of Rome, legionaries and soldiers of auxiliary troops, and municipal magistrates. Apart from the municipal inscriptions, the strong military ethos of the Philippian inscriptions is readily apparent, demonstrating how the values of Roman soldiers and their boasting culture shaped the morality of Philippi, as well as impacting on the non-Roman constituency of the colony (Thracians, Greeks, and Macedonians).[73]

4.1. The *Cursus Honorum* of the Equestrian Honorand

An inscription from the Claudian era, possibly from the north side of the Forum of Philippi, speaks of two equestrian Burreni Firmi, possibly

---

73. See the discussion of the Philippian military inscriptions in Dierk Mueller, "Military Images in Paul's Letter to the Philippians" (PhD diss., University of Pretoria, 2013), 84–93. For Paul's use of military imagery in Philippians, see Phil 1:20; 2:19–24, 25–30; 3:12–15; 4:3, 10–19, and the discussion of Mueller, "Military Images," 155–384.

brothers,[74] setting out their *cursus honorum* thus: "[Burrenus Fir]mus, son of Quintus, of the tribe Voltinia, military tribune [of the IV legion Macedonica] ... [prefect] ... prefect of nations ... pre[fect of his fathe]r Quintus Burrenu[s] Firmus, [son] of T[i]berius, [of the tribe Voltinia ...]."[75] If Cédric Brélaz is correct, the dead Quintus Burrenus Firmus is being honored by his brother, who is erecting the funerary monument. As was the case with the inscriptions at Rome, it is important to mention one's tribe, in this case the Voltinia tribe of Philippi, mentioned twice in the inscription. The living brother had commenced his career as a military tribune in Legio IV Macedonica, which had fought successively in Spain and Germany, only to be disbanded before the reign of Vespasian.[76] The double prefecture of a cohort in his career is interesting, the latter ("prefect of the nations") being a post of an ordinary military and administrative nature "over the peoples not entirely pacified," probably Africans.[77] However, the full equestrian career, due to damage of the stone, is not recoverable, so we do not know what prestigious posts followed in the case of Quintus Burrenus Firmus. What is clear is that equestrians in the military forces competed for status and took advantage of whatever rhetorical flourishes in boasting that their often-brief careers allowed them.

We see the same competition for status in another Julio-Claudian equestrian inscription of the Burreni Firmi: there one family member from the Voltinia tribe is "prefect of workers," while the other was "*two times* military tribune, prefect of a cohort."[78] Such repetitions of posts in an epigraphic *cursus honorum* highlight the primacy of the honorand. Significantly, the military careers of male equestrians could also be mentioned even when the epitaph was in honor of a daughter, in this case, Sertoria Optata, age twenty-seven. Here the person who made the sarcophagus and had its epitaph composed, Manius Cassius Valens from the Voltina tribe, states his own military career, so that the male honor

---

74. See *CIPh* 2.1.161. Brélaz includes new inedited inscriptions from Philippi not found in Pilhofer's collection (*Philippi*, vol. 2). The translations presented below draw from Pilhofer and Brélaz.

75. *CIPh* 2.1.48; Pilhofer, *Philippi*, 2.046.

76. *CIPh* 2.1.160. In a Julio-Claudian inscription mentioning the two brothers Mucii from the tribe of Fabia, the living relative erects a monument for his deceased brother, who is eulogized as "primopilus of VI Legion Ferrata, prefect of a cohort" (*CIPh* 2.1.59, inscription A).

77. *CIPh* 2.1.160–61.

78. *CIPh* 2.1.49.

of this equestrian family is upheld, notwithstanding the social anonymity of the young female honorand: "prefect of workers in charge nearby to the consul, duumvir *iure dicundo*, quaestor."[79] What is remarkable is the prestigious civic career that Valens subsequently accomplished (duumvir *iure dicundo*, quaestor), having only been a military prefect beforehand.[80] We are seeing here the versatile career paths provided for civic elites in the Roman colonies in the imperial age, the transition to the civic arena probably being effected by a powerful Philippian or imperial patron sponsoring Valens, though unnamed in this instance.

However, other equestrians, such as P. Cornelius Asper Atiarius Montanus, were explicit in highlighting imperial patronage. Montanus's inscription, erected after 54 CE in modern Kavala (ancient Neapolis), the harbor city of Philippi and the preferred place of residence of the elite Philippian priests, sets out the details of his *cursus honorum*. It rises progressively in a crescendo of equestrian (*equus publicus*), decurion, and priestly (*pontifex*) status, until the impressive vignette of the Claudian patronage of Montanus as a priest (*flamen*) in the imperial cult is unveiled at the end: "Here is lying P. Cornelius Asper Atiarius Montanus, honoured [as an eques] with an *equus publicus* and the decoration of decurion and duumviral [status], *pontifex*, *flamen* of divine Claudius at Philippi, age 23 years."[81] It is therefore not surprising to learn that Montanus's daughter, Cornelia Asprilla, would later become a "priestess of the divine Augusta," given the substantial social prestige of the Cornelii family at Philippi, strengthened as it was by their family alliance with the prestigious Atiarii house from the same city.[82]

On the south side of a large equestrian funerary monument from the reign of Nero or Vespasian, erected on the Via Egnatia leading to the city of Philippi, we read the following dedication: "Caius Vibius Quartus, son of Caius, of the tribe Cornelia, soldier of the V legion Macedonica, decurion of the Ala Scubulorum, prefect of the cohort III Cyreneica, tribune

---

79. *CIPh* 2.1.50 (end of first century–early second century CE).

80. *CIPh* 2.1.163.

81. *CIPh* 2.1.53; Pilhofer, *Philippi*, 2.001. See also the Julio-Claudian inscription of the paving of Philippi (*CIPh* 2.1.66): "… -lus, military tribune … flamen of divine Augustus." *Equus publicus* literally means "horse bought by the state."

82. *CIPh* 2.1.167–68. On Cornelia Asprilla, see *CIPh* 2.1.118 (ca. 80–90 CE; not in Pilhofer's volume).

of the II legion Augusta, prefect [of the Ala…]."[83] As a member of the Cornelia tribe, Quartus belonged to those individuals from Philippi who had recently acquired the citizenship. There is a funerary inscription also erected to the same Quartus at Thessalonica, recounting the same military posts (soldier, decurion, tribune, prefect), but, significantly, adding two new functions at the end of its *cursus honorem*, unknown to us in our Philippian inscription due to its damaged text. The two additional posts are the prefecture of two cavalry units (Ala Gallorum, Ala Gaetulorum), as well as the prestigious post of prefect of the emperor's Alexandrian fleet.[84] These epigraphic additions to the spectacular career of this Thessalonian soldier, now a Roman citizen at Philippi, explains a remarkable fact: how Quartus, a mere soldier from Thessalonica, was promoted to the equestrian order at Philippi.[85] Seemingly, talent alone accounts for his upward mobility.

An inscription from the reign of Trajan is revealing for the role assigned to virtue, infrequently mentioned in the Philippian equestrian inscriptions: "honour[ed [as an equites] with] [*equus pub*]*licus*, by [imperator Caesa]r Nerva Traja[n Augustus Germanicus], [flamen of di]vine Ve[spa]sian … [in remembrance for the a]ffection [[*propter a*]*morem*] which he manifests towards his citizens, an[d] his [benefice]nce [[*benevole*]*ntiam*] and his generos[ity] [*liberalita*[*tem*]] … from the revenue of farm[s]."[86] Here we see a strong emphasis on the moral virtue of the unknown honorand emerge in a way that is consonant with the benefaction inscriptions of the Greek East. The Greek inscriptions, in contrast to the clipped *cursus honorum* of the Latin West inscription, which asserts the virtue of the local elites by means of the posts listed, refer to specific ethical qualities of the benefactor. This Latin inscription more reflects the Greek epigraphic ethos.[87] The virtues mentioned function as circumlocutions for gifts of money (*amor, benevolentia, liberalitas*), offered to his citizens from the revenues of farms, emanating, it would seem, from a foundation that the benefactor had established as member of the Philippian elite.[88] These

---

83. *CIPh* 2.1.63; Pilhofer, *Philippi*, 2.58.
84. *IG* 2.1.1175.
85. *CIPh* 2.1.187.
86. *CIPh* 2.1.68 (not in Pilhofer's volume).
87. *CIPh* 2.1.195: "On retrouve, dans ce passage, le lexique caractéristique de l'évergétisme municipal."
88. *CIPh* 2.1.196.

epigraphic virtues and the honorific award of *equus publicus* (a military horse from the state or its monetary equivalent) function as public recompense from the still-living and nonapotheosized Hadrian for the faithful service of this equestrian as an imperial priest of the apotheosized Vespasian ("divine"). Other municipal posts were undoubtedly mentioned in the large lacuna of lines 4–8 of the inscription and would have helped us to appreciate more fully the reasons for the imperial honors conferred on the honorand.[89]

4.2. The *Cursus Honorum* of the Soldier of the Garrison of Rome

The military careers of soldiers provided significant opportunities for boasting because the composer of the inscription could provide striking vignettes of the honors conferred by the imperial ruler. In an inscription from the reign of Hadrian, the honorand, Gaius Annicius, lists at the outset his inherited Roman tribal status (Voltina) because, as Joseph H. Hellerman notes,[90] it allowed the honorand "to proclaim one's citizen status" of Rome. From there we see the progression of Gaius's personally achieved military magistracies, until he highlights the patronal intervention of Trajan (or, equally likely, the Roman ruler's military or colonial representative). Having served his time and obtained a discharge, Gaius was voluntarily enlisted again (*evocatus*) by Trajan and was subsequently decorated by the ruler with military ornaments, which, due to the fragmentary nature of the text, are not specified: "To Gaius Annicius, son of Lucius, of the tribe V[oltina] … soldier of the eighth praetor[ian] cohort … [be]*neficiarius*, optio in charge of the prison … [in the cen]turia, standard-bearer [*signifer*] of *curator* [?], ben[*eficiarus praefecti pr*]aetorio, *evocatus* of the emperor, [decorated by the divine] Tr[aj]an, honoured with ornam[ents…]."[91] In an inscription from the reign of Domitian—whose name, in the ritual of *damnatio memoriae*, has been erased from the stone—the conspicuous success of the military career of the soldier Cnosus is set out fulsomely. Unexpectedly, however, the emperor Domitian had invited Cnosus, who had served out his time, to enlist voluntarily in his service again, an honor conveyed by the phrase "*evocatus* of the emperor." The inscription does not specify

---

89. *CIPh* 2.1.195.
90. Hellerman, *Philippians*, 177.
91. *CIPh* 2.1.74 (not in Pilhofer's volume).

what the military service was,⁹² but it spawns remarkable honorific decorations from the ruler (necklaces, bracelets, breast jewelry, a gold crown). What then follows after this unspecified service are three successive posts of the centurionate, each held in Rome, commanding the night watchmen (*vigiles*), discharged soldiers (*statores*), and the urban cohort. Having set out the accolades of Cnosus received from the emperor, the inscription concludes with irrefutable evidence of the personal esteem evinced toward him by his veteran soldiers under his command. They were all discharged honorably, thereby reflecting the greater honor of their commander:

> To Lucius Tatinius Cnosus, son of Lucius, of the tribe Voltina, soldier of the fourth praetorian cohort, *singularis* and *beneficiarius tribuni*, optio, *beneficiarius praefecti praetorio*, *evocatus* of the emperor, decorated with necklaces, with bracelets, with breast jewellry and with a gold crown [[by imperator Domitian Caesar Augustus]], centurion of the fourth cohort of the watchmen [*vigiles*], centurion of the *statores*, centurion of the eleventh urban cohort, the veterans who have served under his orders in the watchmen [cohort] and who have received their honourable leave.⁹³

4.3. The *Cursus Honorum* of the Legionaries and Soldiers of Auxiliary Troops

A massive monument, inscribed with the inscription cited below and housed now in the Archaeological Museum of Kavala, was originally found in a village to the northwest of Philippi.⁹⁴ It depicts the military career of Tiberius Claudius Maximus, who was the captor of King Decebalus, the last Dacian chieftain (r. 87–106 CE). Decebalus committed suicide rather than be captured when Trajan reduced the Dacian capital Sarmizegetusa to ruins in 106 CE. This remarkable inscription, accompanied by two reliefs, offers us one of the most detailed accounts of the career of a Roman soldier available to us in antiquity, and readers are referred to the

---

92. See *CIPh* 2.1.219, for suggestions regarding what Cnosus's mission might have been.

93. *CIPh* 2.1.85; Pilhofer, *Philippi*, 2.202. For definitions of the complex posts recorded in this inscriotion, see Mueller, "Military Images," 89–90.

94. For full discussion, see Michael Speidel, "The Captor of Decebalus: A New Inscription from Philippi," *JRS* 60 (1960): 142–53; *CIPh* 2.1.226–36.

excellent discussion of Michael Speidel in this regard.[95] The inscription is set out below:

> Tiberius Claudius Maximus, veteran, has erected [this monument] in [his] lifetime. He served as a knight in the VII legion Claudia Pia Fidelis, was named [*factus*] quaestor of knights, *singularis* of the legate of same legion, standard-bearer [*vexillarius*] of knights; he was similarly decorated for his courage [*ob virtute*] during the Dacian war by imperator Domitian; he was named [*factus*] *duplicarius* in the second Ala Pannoniorum by the divine Trajan, by whom he was also named [*factus*] scout during the Dacian war and he was decorated two times for his courage [*virtus*] during the Dacian war and the Parthian war, and he was named [*factus*] *decurio* in the same Ala by the same [emperor] because he had captured Decebalus and had brought his head to him at Ranistorum; as a volunteer [he received] his honourable leave from Terent[ius Scau]rianus, consul of the ne[w] provinc[e] of [Mesopotamia].[96]

Several features, for our purposes, are worth noting. First, very surprisingly, the name of Domitian, in contrast to the inscription of Gaius Annicius above, has not been erased in a *damnatio memoriae*.[97] Why the inscription was not erased at this juncture is not readily explainable: did the enormity of Maximus's victory, reinforced visually by the reliefs on the large monument, deter people from detracting from this very public honor of Maximus by erasing Domitian's name? Second, the reference to Maximus's courage (*virtus*) here is entirely conventional and does not approximate the moral worldview articulated in the Scipionic inscriptions of Rome. Third, the standard features of rhetoric in the *cursus honorum*, noted above, appear in this inscription as well: the repetitive use of numbers and motifs (e.g., decoration, naming) as a mnemonic. However, the mention epigraphically of unspecified decorations twice in the Dacian and once in Parthian wars is cleverly reinforced visually in the relief of two *torques* (necklaces) and two *armillae* (armbands, in the popular rendering of snakes, as other soldiers' tombstones show).[98]

---

95. Speidel, "Captor of Decebalus."
96. *CIPh* 2.1.94; Pilhofer, *Philippi*, 2.522. Pilhofer, as opposed to Brélaz, restores "Mesopotamia," although he concedes it could equally be Syria or Dacia.
97. Noted by Speidel, "Captor of Decebalus," 146.
98. Speidel observes that Maximus is "one of the most decorated Roman soldiers

From Rome to the Colony of Philippi   341

But, above all, the vignette of the capture and beheading of Decebalus, mentioned succinctly in the inscription, is rendered in graphic detail in the monument's relief. It depicts the light-cloaked cavalryman Maximus charging forth toward his enemy on his horse, holding in his left hand two spears and an oval shield, while he grasps in his right hand his sword, drawn and ready for deadly use. The enemy, Decebalus, identified as a Dacian chieftain by his trousers and pointed Dacian cap, cradles his hexagonal shield on his left arm, having fallen backwards on his haunches. But his sickle-sword falls from his right hand, because he has just cut his throat to avoid capture. In a graphic touch, his mouth is wide open, as he gasps his last breaths.[99] Importantly, we see here how the Roman colony of Philippi reflects the culture of Rome in its military ethos, because Trajan's column also portrays the capture of Decebalus and, additional to the Philippian relief, the emperor displays the severed head of the Dacian chieftain to his troops on the column.[100] Not only is the complexity of Maximus's military career superbly set out, but also the clever interplay between the visual reliefs and the epigraphic *cursus honorum* brings a new dimension to Philippian boasting.

4.4. The *Cursus Honorum* of the Municipal Magistrates

The inscriptions of the municipal magistrates at Philippi do not have the same wide range of prestigious posts that the soldiers at Philippi were able to acquire because of their access to the imperial military *cursus honorum*. Nevertheless, such elite officials could erect expensive monuments, paid by a family will, not only for themselves but also for other family members (e.g., brother, father), listing in the process the magistracies achieved each individual (aedile, quaestor, duumvir). Where such magistracies of a family member were not able to be listed (e.g., Caius Decimius Maximus, below), his tribe (Voltina) was again appealed to as a mark of honor: "[Lucius Decimiu]s Bassus, son of Lucius, of the tribe Volitina, aedile at Philippi has erected [this monument] by a will for himself as well as for his father Lucius Decimius, son of Lucius, of the tribe Voltina, [quaestor,

---

known" ("Captor of Decebalus," 148). For the relief, see Speidel, "Captor of Decebalus," 145, pl. XIII, and discussion, 148–49.
    99. Speidel, "Captor of Decebalus," pl. XV.1.
    100. For the reliefs, see Speidel, "Captor of Decebalus," pl. XIV ("Trajan's column, scene CXLV") and pl. XV.2 ("Trajan's column, scene CXLVII").

duumvir at Philippi] and for his brother Caius Decimius Maximus, son of Lucius, of the tribe Voltina, for the sum of 30,000 sesterces."[101]

Finally, in a first-century CE municipal inscription from Philippi, we see the reappearance of a phenomenon already commented on: namely, the bolstering of family honor on the socially inauspicious death of a young woman, a feature also observed in the Scipionic *elogia*, where the death of a young son created a vacuum on the progression of ancestral honor. However, in the first-century CE inscription below, the sarcophagus was probably built by the husband of Tatinia, Titus Valerius Fulcinius Maior, for his deceased wife. He retrieves family honor by setting out expansively his own prestigious *cursus honorum*, culminating in the important civic position of *irenarch*, approximating our justice of the peace, which he held in the city: "Here is lying [Ta]tinia Tertulla, daughter of Publius, aged 24 years, 5 months. Titus Valerius Fulcinius Maior, son of Titus, of the tribe Voltinia, honoured with the ornaments of a decurion, aedile, decurion, quaestor, duumvir *iure dicundo* and *munearius*, *irenarch* at Philippi, aged 63 years."[102]

4.5. Conclusion

We have seen that boasting in the Roman colony has duplicated the rhetorical conventions and military ethos of boasting at Rome, though the strong moral self-justification underlying some of the Scipionic inscriptions from Rome is much less prominent in the Philippian inscriptions. There is also less evidence for the *damnatio memoriae* at Philippi: an erasure is present on one inscription of Domitian, but it does not occur in another inscription of the same emperor. We speculated that the towering reputation of the honorand in this instance perhaps caused viewers of the inscription at Philippi to reconsider dishonoring his monument by chiseling out the name of the reviled Domitian. The reconfiguration of the republican *cursus honorum* around the patronage of the imperial ruler is especially noteworthy in the eulogistic inscriptions of Philippi, as it was in the imperial example we cited from the Latin West. The male-centered focus of honor is very evident at Philippi, apart from the cases of imperial priestesses. In the case of the Philippian epitaph of a young daughter,

---

101. *CIPh* 2.1.119 inscription A; Pilhofer, *Philippi*, 2.213.
102. *CIPh* 2.1.133; Pilhofer, *Philippi*, 2.127b.

her social anonymity was supplemented by the honor accrued from the magistracies of the male dedicator of the inscription, ensuring the celebration of ancestral glory. Finally, the magnificent monument of Tiberius Claudius Maximus reminds us that Roman boasting was as much visual as epigraphic, with reliefs on the stone conveying its message as effectively for the illiterate as its inscribed text did for the literate.

5. Philippians 3:5–6 in Its Latin West and Philippian Context

5.1. Preliminary Considerations

Before we move to a consideration of our pericope in its Roman eulogistic context, several preliminary questions need to be addressed. I subscribe to a Roman imprisonment for Philippians, composed under house arrest around 61–62 CE, as opposed to an Ephesian or Caesarea Maritima incarceration.[103] While various rhetorical genres have been suggested for Philippians (e.g., deliberative or consolatory rhetoric, friendship epistle, etc.), it is preferable, as Grindheim suggests,[104] to allow that various rhetorical topoi influenced

---

103. For the most recent defense of the Roman origin of the captivity epistles, see Ben Witherington III, "The Case of the Imprisonment That Did Not Happen: Paul at Ephesus," *JETS* 60 (2017): 525–32. Additionally, see Markus Bockmuehl, *The Epistle to the Philippians*, BNTC 11 (Peabody, MA: Hendrickson, 1998), 25–32. For the suggestion of an Ephesian imprisonment for Philippians, see the powerfully argued thesis of M. A. Flexsenhar III, "Slaves of Christ: Caesar's Household and the Early Christians" (PhD diss., University of Texas at Austin, 2016).

104. Sigurd Grindheim, "Paul's Critique of the Jewish Confidence in the Election of Israel in 2 Corinthians 11:16–12:10 and Philippians 3:1–11" (PhD diss., Trinity International University, 2002), 141. On deliberative rhetoric, see Duane F. Watson, "A Rhetorical Analysis of Philippians and Its Implications for the Unity Question," *NovT* 30 (1988): 57–88; G. Walter Hansen, *The Letter to the Philippians*, PNTC (Grand Rapids: Eerdmans, 2009), 12–15. On friendship, see Hansen, *Letter to the Philippians*, 6–12, and the literature cited in 6 n. 18; Gordon D. Fee, *Paul's Letter to the Philippians*, NICNT (Eerdmans: Grand Rapids, 1995), 1–14; Ben Witherington III, *Friendship and Finances in Philippi: The Letters of Paul to the Philippians* (Valley Forge, PA: Trinity Press International, 1994). On consolation, see Paul. A. Holloway, *Consolation in Philippians: Philosophical Sources and Rhetorical Strategy*, SNTSMS 112 (Cambridge: Cambridge University Press, 2001); Holloway, *Philippians*, Hermeneia (Minneapolis: Fortress, 2017). Generally, see Jeffrey T. Reed, *A Discourse Analysis of Philippians: Method and Rhetoric in the Debate over Literary Integrity*, JSNTSup 136 (Sheffield: Sheffield Academic, 1997), 154–287.

Paul in writing Philippians without trying to conform his epistle to a particular genre. Further, if we consult the letter types enumerated in the handbooks of the epistolary theorists, it is more likely that Philippians represents a "mixed genre" rhetorically, which, as we shall see, incorporated citizenship as one of its potential *topoi*.[105] We will suggest that Paul draws on the epigraphic genre of the Roman *cursus honorum* in Phil 3:5–6, but, like other forms of public rhetoric, this only reflects his adoption of one persuasive strategy at this juncture of the letter.

Paul's dramatic shift in tone in Phil 3:2 in describing his "opponents," over against his more measured characterizations in 1:28 and 2:15, could arguably indicate that Philippians consisted of fragments of two or three letters as opposed to being a unified whole.[106] In 1985 Donald Garland concluded that scholarship had reached an impasse on the issue of epistle's unity.[107] Two years later, Duane F. Watson examined Philippians against the backdrop of the ancient rhetorical conventions and demonstrated that the letter had an integrated rhetorical structure throughout, overturning the arguments for literary fragmentation.[108] Importantly for our purposes, Watson also demonstrated that the tonal shift in Phil 3:2 is better explained as a conventional rhetorical tactic "designed to regain audience attention and receptivity."[109]

Last, amid the plethora of suggestions made regarding the purpose of Philippians, none of which we can afford to ignore in such a rhetorically complex letter, I will adopt Bruce Winter's proposal that the letter is a call to live as good citizens in the Roman empire.[110] I would add, how-

---

105. Ps.-Libanius, Epistolary Styles 4.25. See n. 111 below.

106. On the literary unity of Philippians, see the new consensus in Holloway, *Philippians*, 10–19. Also Bockmuehl, *Epistle to the Philippians*, 20–25.

107. David E. Garland, "The Composition and Unity of Philippians: Some Neglected Factors," *NovT* 27 (1985): 144.

108. Watson, "Rhetorical Analysis of Philippians."

109. Watson, "Rhetorical Analysis of Philippians," 86–87.

110. Bruce W. Winter, *Seek the Welfare of the City: Christians as Benefactors and Citizens* (Grand Rapids: Eerdmans, 1994), 85. The various suggestions made regarding the purpose of Philippians include, e.g., the consolidation of Christian unity: Davorin Peterlin, *Paul's Letter to the Philippians in the Light of Disunity in the Church*, NovTSup 79 (Leiden: Brill, 1995); suffering as a valid experience of existence in Christ: Robert Jewett, "Conflicting Movements in the Early Church as Reflected in Philippians," *NovT* 12 (1970): 362–90, and suffering as the occasion of the letter: L. Gregory Bloomquist, *The Function of Suffering in Philippians*, JSNTSup 78 (Sheffield: Sheffield

ever, that this summons occurs in a culture where boasting is culturally de rigeur. But this ethos of self-promotion, in Paul's estimation, is totally antithetical to the exemplum of the cross and his own experience of God's justifying grace. Therefore, Paul highlights a central piece of advice early on in the letter (Phil 1:27-28a): "Only live as citizens [1:27a: πολιτεύσθε; see 3:20: ἥνων γάρ τὸ πολίτευμα ἐν οὐρανοῖς] worthy of the gospel of Christ, so that whether I come and see you or am absent and hear about you, I will know that you are standing firm in one spirit, striving side by side with one mind for the faith of the gospel, and are in no way intimidated by your opponents."[111] As Paul Holloway extrapolates, this "would have struck a chord with the Philippians, whose social identity turned on being citizens of a Roman colony (*Colonia Iulia Augusta Philippensis*) and as such citizens of Rome."

Ironically, Paul, in advocating that the Philippian believers should live worthily of the gospel, was proclaiming Christ as the risen and reigning Lord of all creation over against to the current Roman ruler, Nero, and the apotheosized Claudius, a cruciform *cursus pudorum* instead of the Philippian *cursus honorum*, and a heavenly citizenship in comparison to Rome's earthly citizenship. Furthermore, Paul provides several portraits of what the believing good citizen should look like by means of a series of striking exempla, each with relevance to the Roman contcxt of Philippi:

1. A unified and blemish-free community in Christ at Philippi, an ethos different from many ancient cities, which were often torn

---

Academic, 1993); securing a proper attitude to Paul's possible martyrdom: Brian J. Capper, "Paul's Dispute with Philippi: Understanding Paul's Attitude in Phil 1-2 from His Thanks in 4:10-20," *TZ* 49 (1993): 193-214. Additionally, see Hansen, *Letter to the Philippians*, 25-30; Bockmuehl, *Epistle to the Philippians*, 32-40; Fee, *Paul's Letter to the* Philippians, 34-40.

111. Note that Pseudo-Libanius (Epistolary Styles 92) gives an example of the "mixed" letter style, the genre I have suggested for Philippians above, choosing the same "citizenship" topos as Phil 1:27a: "The mixed letter. I know that you live a life of piety, that you conduct yourself as a citizen in a manner worthy of respect [σεμνῶς πολιτεύῃ], indeed, that you adorn the illustrious name of philosophy itself, with the excellence of an unassailable and pure citizenship [τῇ ἀνεπιλήπτου τε καὶ ἁγνῆς πολιτείας ἀρετῇ]. But in this one thing alone do you err, that you slander your friends. You must avoid that, for it is not fitting that philosophers engage in slander."

apart by internal *stasis* and intercity rivalries (Phil 2:1–4, 12–18; 4:2–3).[112]

2. The humility and obedience of Christ, the dishonored slave-benefactor, who is the divinely vindicated risen Lord of all and decorated with the name above all names (2:5–11).[113]
3. Timothy, the faithful son, who honors his spiritual father-in-Christ in his service of Christ (2:19–24).[114]
4. Epaphroditus, the endangered benefactor, who risks his life for his dependents (Phil 2:19–24; 4:18).[115]
5. Paul's humility in his erasure of his inherited and personally achieved honor and its replacement with a righteous status acquired by divine grace (3:1–11).[116]
6. Paul the heavenly citizen and earthly martyr for Christ (3:17–20).
7. The community model of Paul's partnership with the Philippian believers in a *societas evangeli* (4:10–20), where the apostle provides the labor and the skills, and the Philippians financially sponsor the apostle in his evangelistic mission.[117]

But how should we understand Paul's description of his opponents in Phil 3:2, depicted, it seems, in a highly Jewish manner? What sense does this

---

112. See Andrew Lintott, *Violence, Civil Strife and Revolution in the Classical City* (London: Croom & Helm, 1982); Peter T. Manicas, "War, *Stasis*, and Greek Political Thought," *Comparative Studies in Social History* 24 (1982): 673–88; David Armitage, *Civil Wars: A History in Ideas* (New York: Knopf, 2017); Carsten Hjort Lange, "*Stasis* and *Bellum Civile*: A Difference in Scale?," *Critical Analysis of Law* 4 (2017): 129–40.

113. See *CIPh* 2.1.85 (Pilhofer, *Philippi*, 2.202) and *CIPh* 2.1.94 (Pilhofer, *Philippi*, 2.522) for the extravagant decorations and nomenclature allocated to victorious generals at Philippi.

114. Note the *pietas* of Lucius Scipio toward his father, Lucius Cornelius Scipio Long-Beard (Warmington, *Remains of Old Latin*, "Epitaphs," 1–3, 3–4).

115. On the endangered benefactor, see Frederick W. Danker, *Benefactor: Epigraphic Study of a Graeco-Roman and New Testament Semantic Field* (Saint Louis: Clayton, 1982), 417–35. We only have (potentially) one fragmentary Philippian example of the genre: Pilhofer, *Philippi*, 2.437 (*periculo*). For a good military and civic example from Aphrodisias, see Joyce Reynolds, *Aphrodisias and Rome*, JRS Monographs 1 (London: Society for the Promotion of Roman Studies, 1982), 30.

116. Harrison, "Erasure of Honour."

117. See Julien M. Ogereau, *Paul's Koinonia with the Philippians: A Socio-historical Investigation of a Pauline Economic Partnership*, WUNT 2/377 (Tübingen: Mohr Siebeck, 2014).

make in a Roman colony? How can we argue that Paul is polemicizing against Roman boasting in Phil 3:5–6 when the referent, as traditionally argued, is Jewish?

5.2. Paul's Opponents in Philippians 3:2: Who Is Paul Arguing Against?

In Phil 3:2 Paul warns against τοὺς κύνας ("the dogs"), τοὺς κακοὺς ἐργάτας ("the evil workers"), and τὴν κατατομήν ("the mutilators"). The widespread argument that Paul is polemicizing against real Judaizers (or Jewish missionaries) present at Philippi is very well known and need not be rehearsed here again.[118] However, it is worth pondering whether Paul's terminology in Phil 3:2 has a Greco-Roman target in view, as opposed to being a clever strategy of polemicizing against the Judaizers by means of a well-known Jewish slur against the gentiles. Mark Nanos, in a detailed discussion of the evidence, has challenged the consensus, positing that the language of "dogs" in the Old Testament and the rabbinic literature does not have a gentile referent, as the proponents of the Judaizer consensus assert.[119] Rather, in the case of the Old Testament, Josephus, and Philo, the word is employed polemically to refer to dog-like behavior as opposed to ethnic gentiles. Moreover, if the examples from the rabbinic corpus cited by Nanos are sufficiently representative, then the later Jewish literature does not call gentiles "dogs" either. Instead, Nanos argues that in Phil 3:2 Paul is either polemicizing against the presence of Cynic philosophers at Philippi or is attacking local pagan cults whose iconography included dogs (Silvanus, Diana, Hecate, Cybele).[120]

---

118. For Christian Judaizers, see Fee, *Paul's Letter to the Philippians*, 293–97; Peter T. O'Brien, *The Epistle to the Philippians*, NIGTC (Grand Rapids: Eerdmans, 1991), 352–57; Hansen, *Letter to the Philippians*, 216–20. For Jewish missionaries, see Gerald F. Hawthorne, *Philippians*, WBC 43 (Waco, TX: Word, 1983), xliv–xlvii, 124–26.

119. Mark D. Nanos, "Paul's Reversal of Jews Calling Gentiles 'Dogs' (Philippians 3:2): 1600 Years of an Ideological Tale Wagging an Exegetical Dog?," *BibInt* 17 (2009): 448–82; Nanos, "Out-Howling the Cynics: Reconceptualizing the Concerns of Paul's Audience from His Polemics in Philippians 3," in *The People beside Paul: The Philippian Assembly and History from Below*, ed. Joseph A. Marchall, ECL (Atlanta: SBL Press, 2015), 183–221.

120. Kathy Ehrensperger ("'Join in Imitating Me' [Phil 3.17]: Embodying Christ in the Face of 'the Enemies of the Cross'" [paper delivered at the 2017 Society of New Testament Studies Meeting in Pretoria, South Africa]) also agreed with Nanos's case, pointing to the rock carvings in the vicinity of Philippi depicting Diana and her dogs.

Often an appeal is made to Jesus's encounter with the Syro-Phoenician woman (Mark 7:24–29) to bolster the Judaizer interpretation, spotlighting Jesus's use of the diminutive τὰ κυνάρια (little dogs, puppies) in Mark 7:27. Later rabbinic references to the dishonorable position of gentile "dogs" at the eschatological banquet (Midr. Ps. 4.11) and their exclusion from any access to the torah (b. Hag. 13a) are also seen as confirming the derogatory reference to dogs in Phil 3:2.[121] However, as I have argued elsewhere, Jesus was more likely using the term positively, drawing on the widespread gentile affection for their domestic pets, and thereby offering the gentile woman eschatological hope rather than initial rejection.[122]

It is beyond the scope of this chapter to assess the evidence of both sides of this debate. But, if the evidence for the term *dogs* being a Jewish derogatory referent for gentiles is not incontrovertible, we should allow the possibility that Paul is rejecting Greco-Roman boasting in verses 5–6, targeted with a specific Philippian reference rhetorically, as much as he is attacking the strand of Jewish priestly and ancestral boasting exemplified by Josephus's *Vita* 1–9. In other words, there is a polyvalence in Paul's polemic in verses 5–6. I suspect that this is rendered even more likely if we take seriously the viewpoint of those scholars who argue that in Phil 3:2 Paul is only arguing hypothetically about a potential threat of Judaizing beliefs at Philippi some time in the indefinite future, as opposed to Judaizing interlopers actually being present in the city, as was the case at Galatia.[123] This widens Paul's front to a generalized polemic, operating on several ideological fronts, as opposed to being exclusively Jewish in focus.

Out of 187 cave reliefs at the acropolis of Philippi, thirty-three reliefs show Diana with a dog. See Paul Collart and Pierre Ducrey, *Philippes I: Les reliefs rupestres*, BCHSupp 55 (Athens: École française d'Athènes, 1975), 8–13, 15–16, 18–19, 24, 26, 37, 40, 43, 50, 54–55, 59–60, 62–63, 65–66, 69, 70–71, 73–78. Thus Ehrensperger, very reasonably in a Philippian cultic context, concludes that the labels in Phil 3:2 refer to gentiles and their pagan practices as opposed to being Jewish derogatory terms for gentiles.

121. Michael F. Bird, *Jesus and the Origins of the Gentile Mission*, LNTS 331 (London: T&T Clark, 2006), 48 n. 18.

122. Bockmuehl proposes that Paul provides a general warning here, though its immediate occasion may have been provoked by "some event at Rome or some news about a church other than Philippi" (*Epistle to the Philippians*, 184).

123. James R. Harrison, "'Every Dog Has Its Day,'" *NewDocs* 10:136–45. On the potential future threat, see Grindheim, *Paul's Critique of the Jewish Confidence*, 150–56.

5.3. Paul's *Cursus Honorum* (Phil 3:5–6) in Roman and Jewish Context

We turn now to the items of boasting in the *cursus honorum* that the apostle successively parades before the Philippians, moving adeptly from his inherited honor (v. 5) to his personal achievements (vv. 5b–6). Although each item is Jewish, we must not forget that this *cursus honorum* unveils autobiographically the grounds for Paul's own boasting, in which he had previously claimed superiority of merit over his Jewish contemporaries of his pre-Christian past in a heated quest for nomistic holiness (Gal 1:14). However, we should not assume that Paul somehow has lost his pastoral grip in confining himself to the particularities of Jewish boasting at the expense of the ubiquity of Roman eulogistic culture and its beguiling self-assertion at Philippi (Phil 2:3–4), including its impact on his gentile converts. Several intersections of Paul's Jewish *cursus honorum*, I suggest, occur within the Philippian inscriptions that are more than just stylistic.

5.3.1. "Circumcised on the Eighth Day" (Verse 5)

In the Philippian and Latin West inscriptions, there is regular citation of numbers of magistracies, commands, victories, and honors in order to establish the superiority of the honorand over their rivals. The only place where a number appears in Paul's *cursus honorum* is ὀκταήμερος. At first blush, it does not approximate the claim to primacy routinely associated with numbers in the Roman inscriptions of the Latin West and the Roman colonies. However, in a Jewish boasting context, the force of the number ὀκταήμερος is no less impressive than its Roman counterparts. Indeed, it functions in a rhetorically similar manner. Paul's parents had abided by the exact time requirements of the Abrahamic covenant (Gen 17:12; Lev 12:3), in contrast to Ishmael, who was circumcised in his thirteenth year (Gen 17:25). Paul as a Jew was sharply differentiated from those gentiles who, only much later in life, voluntarily became proselytes of Yahweh. Indeed, Jub. 15:11–14 makes it plain that a child not circumcised in the eighth day "has broken my covenant." Nor was Paul a distant descendant of those gentiles forcibly circumcised by the Maccabean conquerors and their heirs (1 Macc 2:45–46; Jospehus, *Ant.* 13.258, 318–319). Paul's Philippian readers would have expected him to boast in circumcision as one of the defining Jewish distinctives mentioned by Roman authors (Suetonius, *Dom.* 12.2; Petronius, *Sat.* 102.14; Tacitus, *Hist.* 5.5.2; Juvenal, *Sat.* 14.99; Horace, *Sat.* 1.9.69–70; Persius, *Sat.* 5.184; Martial, *Ep.* 7.30.5), even if they did not immediately understand the full significance of ὀκταήμερος. In sum, the "eighth day" secured Paul's covenantal righteousness from the very beginning of his life, establishing his boast to ascendancy over those who had entered God's family later in life as converted gentiles or who, as Jews, may not have been properly circumcised according to the covenantal calendrical prescription.

5.3.2. "A Member of the People of Israel" (Verse 5)

From the day of his birth, Paul was identified with the covenantal people of God by his racial descent. We have seen the intriguing Philippian inscription of Caius Vibius Quartus, who simultaneously had his *cursus honorum* erected at Thessalonica, his birth city, and at Philippi, of which city he had subsequently became a citizen, and, remarkably, had finally acquired equestrian status there after commencing his career as a soldier elsewhere.[124] Quartus was a citizen of two cities (Thessalonica, Philippi), as was the apostle Paul (Tarsus, Rome), in a world where the major cities outshone the Roman provinces.[125] But, in the case of Paul and other first-century Jews, there was a category of ethnic association other than his city or province: namely, ἐκ γένους Ἰσραήλ. God's chosen people were linked by physical descent to the patriarch Jacob ("Israel": Gen 32:28; 35:10), and, in the case of the non-Jewish proselytes and Godfearers, were adopted by grace as family members into Israel. In sum, Paul's membership of Israel is by birth and not by conversion.[126] We are witnessing here in Paul's *cursus honorum* the one defining boast that is not comparable to anything Roman that is at Philippi: Paul belonged to "the nation of the theocracy, the people in covenant relation with God."[127] Whatever mythological origins Romans assigned to their city (Aeneas, Romulus and Remus) and the priestly cult that ensured its continued blessing at home and in its overseas colonies, the only divinely elect person was the Roman ruler, whereas the entire theocratic nation, spanning the ages, had been chosen from the time of

---

124. *CIPh* 2.1.63; Pilhofer, *Philippi*, 2.58.
125. Jae Won Lee, "Paul, Nation, and Nationalism," in *The Colonized Apostle: Paul through Postcolonial Eyes*, ed. Christopher D. Stanley, Paul in Critical Contexts (Minneapolis: Fortress, 2011), 225.
126. Hawthorne, *Philippians*, 132.
127. Hawthorne, *Philippians*, 132.

its Abrahamic inception to its Palestinian and synagogal diaspora expressions at the time of Paul.[128]

5.3.3. "Of the Tribe of Benjamin" (Verse 5)

We have already seen in many of the Philippian inscriptions the frequent mention of the tribe of the honorand. In Pilhofer's Philippian epigraphic corpus, the Caleria, Cornelia, M(a)ecia, Pollia, and Sergia tribes are only mentioned once, the Fabia and Quirina tribes only twice, but the Voltinia tribe appears some seventy-five times.[129] The same emphasis on tribes was also found in the Latin inscriptions from Rome.[130] Occasionally, even where no magistracy status has accrued to the one of the family's honorands, the tribe is nevertheless mentioned (e.g., Caius Decimius Maximus).[131] By contrast, in the Scipionic inscriptions at Rome, the failure to achieve a magistracy due to premature death was deflected, as we have seen, by the mention of the achievements of a prestigious ancestor, as opposed to mention of the tribe: "Lucius Cornelius Scipio, son of Lucius, grandson of Publius, quaestor, tribune of soldiers, died at the age of thirty-three years: his father vanquished King Antiochus."[132] Thus membership of a Philippian tribe was the fundamental marker of Philippian citizenship and was legitimately boasted in by less successful family members.

But in the case of Paul, membership of the "tribe of Benjamin" (see Rom 11:1) was highly prestigious. Benjamin is one of the only two tribes that maintained covenantal loyalty to God, in contrast to the ten faithless tribes of Israel (1 Kgs 12:21). It was the tribe from which the first king of Israel, Saul, Paul's namesake (Acts 13:9), had come (1 Sam 9:2–3), and which inherited the territory of the city of Jerusalem (Judg 1:21), the site of the temple. Paul's tribal qualifications are impeccable. They were, in a Jewish context, inherited by blood kinship and not by enrollment in

---

128. For an insightful discussion of Paul's ethnic terminology, see Christopher D. Stanley, "Paul the Ethnic Hybrid: Postcolonial Perspectives on Paul's Ethnic Categorizations," in Stanley, *Colonized Apostle*, 110–26.
129. Pilhofer, *Philippi*, 2: indexes, 6, Römisches, s.v. "tribus," 1144.
130. Above, n. 38.
131. See above, n. 101.
132. Warmington, *Remains of Old Latin*, "Epitaphs," 7.

geographical region, as was the case at Rome and Philippi.¹³³ The heavy emphasis on the Voltinia tribe at the expense of other tribes in the Philippian inscriptions, for reasons we can only guess, is similar to Paul's boast in the tribe of Benjamin. Finally, Holloway has claimed that Paul's mention of his tribe in this instance is precipitated by his "response to the imagined claims of his opponents" (2 Cor 11:22; Rom 11:22) rather than, as Pilhofer has argued, by local references to the Voltinia tribe in the Philippian inscriptions.¹³⁴ Hollway's objection, however, abstracts Paul's rhetoric from a *cursus honorum* modeled on the grand epigraphic boasting style of Romans in the Latin West. To reduce Paul's rhetoric on this occasion to a riposte against hypothetical opponents overlooks the significance of tribal identity for the colonial Philippians and for the residents of Rome.

5.3.4. "A Hebrew of the Hebrews" (Verse 5)

Paul refers to his status as a Ἑβραῖος, denoting an Aramaic-speaking and (most probably) a Hebrew-speaking Jew (Acts 21:40; 22:2; 26:14) in terms of his mother tongue. As a Roman colony, Philippi, like Corinth and Pisidian, strove to ensure the continued use of Latin in its public and private inscriptions, even though the city was in the Greek East. Latin was preserved as the language of government, administration, and honorific ritual in the colony, promoting its Roman identity in an act of faithfulness to its founder city, Rome. The aristocratic values passed down among the Roman *nobiles* from grandfather to father and son, evidenced in the Scipionic eulogistic epitaphs of the Latin West, reflected a similar chain of oral tradition and culture that was kept by Paul's parents in a Jewish context at Tarsus. G. Walter Hansen correctly notes that Paul's parents would have stood against any attempt to hellenize the Jews, as did the faithful Jews of the Maccabean period (1 Macc 1:11–15). Thus they ensured that their son was trained in the Hebrew Scriptures and traditions of the fathers at Jerusalem (Gal 1:14; see Acts 5:34; 22:3; 23:6; 26:4–5), along with his sister, who also had maintained her own Jewish culture and mother tongue by residing in the same city (23:16).¹³⁵ The Philippian auditors of Paul's letter, when informed about the import of Paul's puzzling phrase here,

---

133. John Reumann, *Philippians: A New Translation with Introduction and Commentary*, AYB 33B (New Haven: Yale University Press, 2008), 483.

134. Holloway, *Philippians*, 158.

135. Hansen, *Letter to the Philippians*, 224–25. He concludes: "Paul was a *Hebrew*

would have appreciated as Romans the traditional claim to ancestral piety implicit in this boast.

5.3.5. "According to the Law a Pharisee" (Verse 5)

At the outset of this chapter, we suggested that scholars have not sufficiently situated Jewish boasting, despite its disavowal in the Masoretic Text, within the priestly tradition of Sirach's "Hymn in Honor of Ancestors" and Josephus's own boasting as a priestly aristocrat in his *Vita*. The eulogistic priestly culture evinced in these Jewish documents matches well the boastful ethos of the inscriptions of the aristocratic priests residing at the port city of Philippi, ancient Neapolis (modern Kavala). However, as a Pharisee, Paul bypasses the priestly aristocratic elites, Roman and Jewish, both groups of which he would have been familiar with during his preconversion life and in his subsequent missionary travels. Paul's choice to bypass at this juncture the Jewish priestly tradition of boasting in his *cursus honorum* reflects not only his own autobiographical and apologetic interests, but also the traditional rivalry between the Pharisees and Sadducees for social prominence that Paul would have experienced over the years. The apostle magnifies his own Pharisaic tradition at the expense of the priestly elites, diminishing his social and religious rivals by ignoring them.[136] However, it also underscores the strict Pharisaic attachment to the Mosaic law and oral tradition (Gal 1:14; Acts 26:5; Josephus, *B.J.* 2.162–166; *Ant.* 18.18–25; *Vita* 191), which extended the quest for holiness beyond the precincts of the Jerusalem temple to the everyday life of the lay communities of the law-obedient Pharisees.[137] It would have allowed Paul to boast subsequently in his own nomistic performance (Phil 3:6b) before he radically reconfigures the Jewish quest for righteousness under a new rubric. According to Paul, the gift of God's righteousness, the personal experience of which is based on the believer's faith (Phil 3:9b: τὴν ἐκ θεοῦ

---

of Hebrews: he had not lost his use of Hebrew, his mother tongue, nor deviated from his cultural heritage" (225).

136. Francis Wright Beare writes: "Paul does not use the name Pharisee as a reproach but as a title of honour." Francis Wright Beare, *The Epistle to the Philippians* (London: A&C Black, 1959), 107.

137. G. B. Caird, *Paul's Letters from Prison in the Revised Standard Version*, New Clarendon Bible (Oxford: Oxford University Press, 1976), 135–36.

δικαιοσύνην ἐπὶ τῇ πίστει), was unexpectedly secured through the cruciform faithfulness of Christ (Phil 3:9b: διὰ πίστεως Χριστοῦ; see Phil 2:8).[138]

The aristocratic priestly elites of Kavala and elsewhere, with their cultic maintenance of the beneficence of the gods toward the Julio-Claudian rulers, are therefore given no credence by the apostle in a Philippian context.[139] This does not mean that Paul totally ignores the priestly and sacrificial context of Philippian society. Rather he reconfigures its imagery, democratizing its terminology throughout the body of Christ. The only sacrifice and priestly service that matters for the Philippians, Paul avers, is the one emanating from their faith (Phil 2:17b: ἐπὶ τῇ θυσίᾳ καὶ λειτοθργίᾳ τῆς πίστεως ὑμῖν ["upon the sacrifice and priestly service of your faith"]),[140] which the potential death of the imprisoned Paul may crown, as a martyr, with the drink offering of his own shed blood (Phil 2:17a; 1:7, 20–22). The Philippian gifts to Paul through Epaphroditus are described with sacrificial imagery, each word of which carries strong resonances of the Old Testament cult (Phil 4:18: "a fragrant offering, a sacrifice acceptable and pleasing to God [θυσίαν δεκτήν, εὐάρεστον τῷ θεῷ])." Thus, although Paul, as a Pharisee, dismisses the priestly boasting of contemporary aristocratic priests like Josephus, he nevertheless employs sacrificial imagery in the epistle, widely drawn from the Septua-

---

138. The subjective genitive ("faithfulness of Christ": Bockmuehl, *Epistle to the Philippians*, 210–11; O'Brien, *Epistle to the Philippians*, 398–400; Bonnie B. Thurston and Judith M. Ryan, *Philippians and Philemon*, SP 10 [Collegeville, MN: Liturgical Press, 2005], 124) is preferred in Phil 3:9 to the objective genitive ("faith in Christ": Hawthorne, *Philippians*, 141–42; Hansen, *Letter to the Philippians*, 241–42; Reumann, *Philippians*, 494–96; Moisés Silva, *Philippians*, WEC [Chicago: Moody, 1988], 186–87).

139. *Flamen* of divine Julius: Pilhofer, *Philippi*, 2.700–703. *Flamen* of divine Augustus: Pilhofer, *Philippi*, 2.031, 241, 531a, 700, 702–3. *Sacerdos* of divine Augusta: Pilhofer, *Philippi*, 2.002, 226. *Flamen* of divine Claudius: Pilhofer, *Philippi*, 2.001. *Flamen* of divine Vespasian: Pilhofer, *Philippi*, 2.719. *Flamen* of divine Titus: Pilhofer, *Philippi*, 2.004. Note the general references to *sacerdos*: Pilhofer, *Philippi*, 2.019, 163–64, 166, 177, 407, 509e, 519, 581, 703d, 703e. *Pontifex*: CIPh 2.1.53, 60, 152, 157, 184. Occasionally the priest to particular deities are mentioned: Pilhofer, *Philippi*, 2.642a (flamen of Apollo); Pilhofer, *Philippi*, 2.175, 455a (*sacerdos* of Isis). Jane Lancaster Patterson makes no reference to the Philippian sacrificial context, Roman or indigenous. Jane Lancaster Patterson, *Keeping the Feast: Metaphors of Sacrifice in 1 Corinthians and Philippians*, ECL 16 (Atlanta: SBL Press, 2015), 81–116.

140. There is only one mention of a sacrifice in an inscription to Septimius Severus and his family (θυσία: Pilhofer, *Philippi*, 2.349; *CIPh* 2.1.24), though there is a lacuna either side of the word.

gint. This reconfigures not only the cultic operations of the Sadducean hierarchy at Jerusalem and its holiness system but also the elite social status of the imperial priests at Kavala and elsewhere in Philippi by its virtue of Paul's focus on the priesthood of all believers.

5.3.6. "As to Zeal, a Persecutor of the Church" (Verse 6)

We have already discussed the zeal tradition of Phinehas and how it shaped the boasting tradition of Sirach's "Hymn in Honor of Ancestors." It should be no surprise that the same eulogistic tradition surfaces in verse 6. The Greek inscriptions from Philippi, however, do not appeal to the ζῆλος tradition, but, if they did, it would undoubtedly be a reference to the zeal of benefactors in fulfilling their promises of beneficence. The Greek East context of zeal is entirely different from Second Temple Judaism. Nevertheless, it is highly significant that Paul appeals to the tradition, notwithstanding its absence at Philippi. Having bypassed the priestly tradition in preference for his own Pharisaic vocation, Paul returns to the Jewish boasting tradition, exemplified in Sirach's exposition of the zeal motif in its priestly representative of Phinehas (Sir 45:23–25),[141] though Paul's exposition in verse 6 more likely derives from the reference to MT Ps 106:30–31. What makes Paul's zeal exposition distinctive is the way that he links the zeal tradition not directly to Phinehas but to his own persecution of the church (Gal 1:13, 23; 1 Cor 15:9; 1 Tim 1:13).

At one level, this is totally understandable, linking the (then) Saul's orchestrated violence against Christian believers (Acts 8:3; 9:1; 22:4–6; 26:10–11) with the violent nomistic zeal of the original Phinehas (MT Num 25:5–14). But, at another level, we have to ask whether the implied priestly paradigm of Phinehas is appropriate for Paul's persecuting activity. The priestly perspective is nonetheless present, as Markus Bockmuehl's fine summary of Paul's motivations demonstrates: "It *probably* arose out of a nationalist dedication to the purity of Israel, which he perceived Christianity to be threatening with its criticism of the Temple (see Acts 6:14 with 8:1), its openness to an inclusion of the Gentiles, and arguably it endorsement of a crucified Messiah."[142] But what resonances might this vignette from Paul's pre-Christian life have had with the Philippian inscriptions?

---

141. On the other heroes of zeal in Israelite history, see Reumann, *Philippians*, 485.
142. Bockmuehl, *Epistle to the Philippians*, 200.

Occasionally the Philippian inscriptions do provide vignettes of intense violence, as the inscription and relief of the magnificent monument of Tiberius Claudius Maximus demonstrates.[143] In the same way that Maximus protected the Roman Empire against the incursion of King Decebalus, the Dacian chieftain, in the reign of Trajan, so the (then) Saul, acting with the holy violence of the Old Testament priest Phinehas, protected the people of Israel from the defilement of a heretical Jewish movement. It not only diluted Israel's purity boundaries but also made foolish the nation's eschatological hope of messianic redemption by proclaiming a divinely cursed and crucified pretender (see Gal 3:13 [Deut 21:23]; Phil 2:8b). A new Maccabean defender of the Israelite faith, modeling himself on Phinehas's zeal for the law, had arisen to defend the priestly and Pharisaic heritage of early first-century Judaism. In sum, the very gravity of such a threat posed by the early Christians deserved to be rhetorically highlighted in the same manner as the Philippian inscriptions.

5.3.7. "As to Righteousness under the Law, Blameless" (Verse 6)

We turn to the final vignette of achieved virtue in Paul's *cursus honorum*, which also rhetorically draws on the Latin West epigraphic tradition. As we have seen, Roman boasting sometimes reserved the most important boast until the conclusion,[144] or postponed an incomparable achievement until the end. We have already agreed with the suggestion of Ortlund, noted above (section 1.3), that the emphasis is on what Paul had achieved before his conversion. The emphasis is decidedly moral and is not just referring to his detailed compliance with boundary markers and purity concerns. At the very least, Paul's blamelessness includes such concerns but also exceeds them in scope.

Furthermore, Bockmuehl is correct in saying that the general Pharisaic assumption was that the 613 Old Testament commandments could be kept: but this only occurred within the boundaries of the torah provisions for the purification of defilement and according to the stipulations for the

---

143. See above, n. 98.

144. Note, however, that the *cursus honorum* of an honorific inscription could be composed in ascending or descending order of importance, as the rhetoric demanded. See J. R. Harrison, "Paul and the *Agōnothetai* at Corinth: Engaging the Civic Values of Antiquity," in *The First Urban Churches*, vol. 2, *Roman Corinth*, ed. James R. Harrison and L. L. Welborn, WGRWSup 8 (Atlanta: SBL Press, 2016), 271–326.

sacrificial atonement for sin.¹⁴⁵ As a small confirmatory aside, the word ἄμεμπτος (blameless) is also applied to Zechariah and his wife, Elizabeth, walking blamelessly (ἄμεμπτοι) in all the commandments and regulations of the Lord (Luke 1:6). Paul, too, also assumes that Christians will demonstrate that they are ἄμεμπτοι and ἀκέραιοι (innocent) by not murmuring and arguing (Phil 2:15; see v. 14). Bockmuehl is also careful to allow that Paul exceeded this covenantal understanding of blamelessness in righteous living, given that Paul strove to outcompete his contemporaries (Gal 1:14).¹⁴⁶ In sum, the state of being ἄμεμπτος, in the context of nomistic righteousness for the Jew of Second Temple Judaism, is a complex phenomenon. It is only achievable within the strict boundaries of one's covenantal and soteriological relationship with God, but also it represents a standard of holiness toward which one should continuously strive.¹⁴⁷ But how should Paul's pre-Christian claim to be ἄμεμπτος be understood in the context of Roman boasting at Philippi?

We have already seen that the moral terminology of the Philippian inscriptions functions conventionally, being a circumlocution for the gifts of the benefactor.¹⁴⁸ More interesting are the cases of failed members of the Scipionic house at Rome, where the honorand either draws on the repository of ancestral fame of the house or is affirmed as being able to surpass easily ancestral virtue should the circumstances had been otherwise. Notwithstanding, this hardly approximates Paul's claim to be ἄμεμπτος.

However, a striking compliment in a nonelite epitaph from the Sabine territory of Italy is made regarding Manlia Sabina, her own voice on the tombstone articulating her moral status as a pious daughter and wife. It approaches Paul's claim to be ἄμεμπτος: "My parent I loved as being my parent, my husband I cherished in the second place after my parent. Thus was my life's account proved right [*veitae constitit ra(tio meae)*]—a spotless one [*casta*]."¹⁴⁹ The metaphorical reckoning mentioned in the Latin is derived from the mercantile world: the phrase *ratio constat* indicates (in

---

145. Bockmuehl, *Epistle to the Philippians*, 202–3.
146. Bockmuehl, *Epistle to the Philippians*, 202.
147. Thurston and Ryan (*Philippians and Philemon*, 122) comment: "Paul asserts that his Torah observance was faultless, *not* that he was sinless. It is a subtle but important distinction."
148. E.g., above, n. 86.
149. Warmington, *Remains of Old Latin IV*, "Epitaphs," 63.

modern parlance) that the reconciliation of accounts agrees or is proven right.[150] The feminine adjective, *casta*, has a wide range of ethical and cultic nuances in addition to "spotless," ranging from the sexual virtues to faithfulness in protocols of religious cult: thus it can mean morally "pure," "unpolluted," "guiltless," "chaste," "virtuous," "pious," "religious," "holy," and "sacred."[151] The interesting question, unanswered by the inscription, is *who* makes the final reckoning that results in Sabina being so confident about the accuracy of her declaration. Does her moral status come from the estimate of her family, or from her community, or from her own cultic faithfulness, or from her own purity of conscience, or from posterity reading her tombstone? No answer is hinted at. But we gain insight into how Paul's gospel of the justification of the ungodly provided a radically different assessment of and answer to human perceptions of their moral rightness in a Roman context.[152] The inscription also affords us acute insight into the moral heights to which Roman boasting culture could aspire.

5.4. Conclusion

We have seen that in the seven Jewish boasts of Paul cited in Phil 3:5–6, there is not only resonance with the grand epigraphic rhetorical genre of the *cursus honorum* at Philippi and in the Latin West, but also there were specific intersections with the ethos of the Philippian and Latin West inscriptions in six of the boasts. We turn now to the issue of epigraphic dishonor and how Paul releases believers from its crippling social effects by means of (paradoxically) the dishonor of the cross and—as an exem-

---

150. See Charlton Lewis and Charles Short, *A Latin Dictionary, Founded on Andrews' Edition of Freund's Latin Dictionary, Revised, Enlarged, and in Great Part Rewritten by Charlton T. Lewis, Ph.D. and. Charles Short, LL.D* (Oxford: Clarendon, 1879), s.v. *consto*, I.B.4.

151. See Lewis and Short, *Latin Dictionary*, s.v. *castus-a-um*.

152. Note in this regard the confident assertion of the freedwoman Larcea Horaea from Traiectum (on the Liris) on her epitaph in circa 45 BCE (*CIL* 1.1570): "From when I was a girl I supervised the house for 20 years—the whole of it. My final day gave its judgement, and death took my spirit, and did not remove the splendour of my life." Translated by M. Dillon and L. Garland, *Ancient Rome: Social and Historical Documents from the Early Republic to the Death of Augustus*, 2nd ed. (London: Routledge, 2015), 6.65.

plum to believers—by his own radical disavowal of Greco-Roman and Jewish expressions of boasting.

6. Paul's Reevaluation of Boasting in Light of the Shame of the Cross and Its Honorific Reversal by God

We have highlighted the rare instances where the rituals of Roman boasting went astray and culminated in the experience of dishonor and, worse, the public erasure of memory. We can only make brief suggestions regarding how Paul addressed the issue in Phil 3:7-11. First, and most remarkably, Paul erases the memory of his Jewish boasts, formerly considered as gains (Phil 3:7a: μοι κέρδη). In a type of Roman *damnatio memoriae* ("forgetting what is past": 3:13 [ὀπίσω ἐπιλανθανόμενος]), the apostle consigns his gains to the loss column in his accounting of merit (Phil 3:8a: ζημίαν εἶναι; see v. 7b). This radical reevaluation of Paul's boasting stocks stands in contrast to the mercantile reckoning of boasting in our nonelite inscription cited above.[153]

This does not mean that Paul discounts elsewhere the advantages that the Jews possessed in terms of their salvation-history primacy (Rom 1:16b; 3:1-2; 9:1-5; 10:2a; 11:1-2a, 16, 28) or their eschatological soteriological future by virtue of God's covenantal remembrance (Rom 11:26-28).[154] But they no longer counted as advantages about which one could boast before God or before others. Disconnected from the culmination of righteousness in Christ, these gains would always count as loss (Rom 9:30-10:4). In a remarkable rhetorical strategy, Paul devalues their reputational potency by labeling them "garbage" (σκύβαλα: Phil 3:8).[155]

---

153. See n. 145. On the mercantile metaphor in Phil 3:7, see Reumann, *Philippians*, 488; Bockmuehl, *Epistle to the Philippians*, 207-8; Hansen, *Letter to the Philippians*, 233-37.

154. William S. Campbell writes regarding Paul's Jewish boasts in Phil 3:5-6: "However, although Paul repositions these treasured values in the light of Christ, in his perspective, they certainly retained some value." William S. Campbell, "'I Rate All Things as Loss': Paul's Puzzling Accounting System. Judaism as Loss or the Re-evaluation of All Things in Christ?," in *Unity and Diversity: Interpreting Paul in Context: Collected Essays* (Eugene, OR: Cascade, 2015), 214.

155. Paul's use of σκύβαλα (Phil 3:8) has, some scholars allege, the register of *shit* or *crap*. However, Jeremy F. Hultin has recently challenged this conclusion. After a comprehensive examination of the ancient evidence, Hultin demonstrates that the term does not necessarily have the vulgar tone of the English word *shit* in a wide range

Thus the social danger aroused in antiquity by excessive accomplishment and honor—the blight of *invidia* from one's enemies—is pinpricked by Paul's refusal to lend any credence to the boasting represented by the stylized *cursus honorum*. This type of boasting was not just the preserve of the social elites but extended to a much wider celebrity circuit reaching down to the base of the social pyramid in antiquity.[156] An equally shocking approach, widely discussed by scholars, is where Paul boasts in his weaknesses (2 Cor 11:16–12:10), deliberately constructing a *cursus honorum* that is shameful and foolish in order to debunk human self-advertisement.

Further, the continuing Jewish zeal for God (Rom 10:2: ζῆλον θεοῦ), apart from Christ, remains "unenlightened" (10:2: οὐ κατ' ἐπίγνωσιν). Being ignorant of the true righteousness that comes from God's beneficence (Rom 10:3a: ἀγνοοῦντες γὰρ τὴν θεοῦ δικαιοσύνη), the Jews had vainly tried to establish their own (Rom 10:3: τὴν ἰδίαν [δικαιοσύνην] ζητοῦντες στῆσαι; Phil 3:9: μὴ ἔχων ἐμὴν δικαιοσύνην τὴν ἐκ νόμου) instead of submitting to God's free gift of righteousness in Christ (Rom 10:3: τῇ δικαιοσύνῃ τοῦ θεοῦ οὐχ ὑπετάγησαν; Phil 3:9: ἀλλὰ τὴν διὰ πίστεως Χριστοῦ). Paul's rejection of his *cursus honorum*, both in terms of its ancestral privileges and personal attainments, would have shocked contemporary Romans, as well as Jews. But it originates from his deep consciousness of the electing grace of God, extended to him on the Damascus road amid the self-deception that he was perfectly fulfilling the nomistic righteousness of God in persecuting Christian believers snared by the vile heresy of a crucified messiah. Moreover, the use of the present tense of ἡγέομαι in Phil 3:8 points to a continuing reevaluation of all things in Christ, including even his subsequent Christian accomplishments as an apostle.[157] In a Roman and Jewish context, therefore, the ancient boasting system had been overthrown by the apostle. Humility, as legacy of Paul's thought, would become enshrined in the Western intellectual tradition.

---

of writers: a more neutral translation such as *refuse, garbage,* or *excrement* conveys the register better. Jeremy F. Hultin, *The Ethics of Obscene Language in Early Christianity and Its Environment*, NovTSup 128 (Leiden: Brill, 2008), 150–54.

156. See James R. Harrison, *Paul and the Ancient Celebrity Circuit: The Cross and Moral Transformation* (Tübingen: Mohr Siebeck, forthcoming).

157. Campbell, "'I Rate All Things as Loss,'" 212; Ralph P. Martin, *Philippians: An Introduction and Commentary*, TNTC (London: Inter-Varsity Press, 1959), 145.

Second, Paul's reevaluation of all things formerly worthy of boasting has been effected by the soteriological work of Christ's cross. The parallelism between Phil 2:5–11 and 3:4–11, unobserved by most commentators, makes this clear:[158]

Philippians 2:5–11	Philippians 3:4–11
The preexistent Christ's equality to God	Paul's illustrious ancestry and achievements
Christ's cruciform humiliation and self-emptying	Paul's reckoning of all advantage as loss
God's resurrection and exaltation of Christ	Paul's privilege of being conformed to Christ's death in power and suffering, with a view to the eschatological resurrection

Thus the divine interplay between the vicarious dishonor of the cross and the vindicatory honor of Christ's resurrection overturns all human criteria of worth and status.

Last, we have seen from the Philippian military inscriptions that Tiberius Claudius Maximus was named for prestigious military posts and decorated with extraordinary honors, as were other soldiers in the Roman colony.[159] In contrast, Christ, as Lord of all, is given by the Father the name above every name, but his honorific exaltation, unlike the victorious Philippian generals, came through the shame of the cross. Paul, in renouncing all boasting in honor, inherited and achieved, and by embracing conformity to Christ's dishonorable death, with a view to the eschatological resurrection and the divine honor beyond, showed how

---

158. For discussion, see Michael Brynes, *Conformation to the Death of Christ and the Hope of Resurrection: An Exegetico-Theological Study of 2 Corinthians 4:7–15 and Philippians 3:6–11*, TGST 99 (Rome: Gregorian University Press, 2003), 229–30; Gerard F. Hawthorne, "The Imitation of Christ: Discipleship in Philippians," in *Patterns of Discipleship in the New Testament*, ed. R. N. Longenecker (Grand Rapids: Eerdmans, 1996), 163–69, at 173–74; Rachael Tan, "Conformity to Christ: An Exegetical and Theological Analysis of Paul's Perspective on Humiliation and Exaltation in Philippians 2:5–11" (PhD diss., Southern Baptist Theological Seminary, 2017), 139–82. I have adapted Tan's comparative table (p. 21) above.

159. Above, n. 98.

well he understood and modeled himself on the pattern of Christ's soteriological career.

Bibliography

Agosto, Efrain. "Paul and Commendation." Pages 143–68 in *Paul and the Greco-Roman World: A Handbook*. Vol. 1. Edited by J. Paul Sampley. London: Bloomsbury T&T Clark, 2016.

———. "Paul's Use of Greco-Roman Conventions of Commendation." PhD diss., Boston University, 1996.

———. *Servant Leadership: Jesus and Paul*. Saint Louis: Chalice, 2005.

Alföldy, Géza. *Der Obeliskaufdem Petersplatzin Rom: Ein historisches Monument der Antike*. Heidelberg: SB Heidelberger Akademie der Wissenschaften, phil.-hist. Klasse, 1990.

Armitage, David. *Civil Wars: A History in Ideas*. New York: Knopf, 2017.

Bakirtzis, Charalambos, and Helmut Koester, eds. *Philippi at the Time of Paul and after His Death*. Harrisburg, PA: Trinity Press International, 1998.

Barclay, John M. G. *Paul and the Gift*. Grand Rapids: Eerdmans, 2015.

Barton, Carlin A. *Roman Honor: The Fire in the Bones*. Berkeley: University of California Press, 2001.

Beare, Francis Wright. *The Epistle to the Philippians*. London: A&C Black, 1959.

Betz, Hans Dieter. "*De laude ipsius* (Moralia 539A–547F)." Pages 367–93 in Plutarch's Ethical *Writings and Early Christian Literature*. SCHNT 4. Leiden: Brill, 1978.

———. *Der Apostel Paulus und die sokratische Tradition: Eine exegetische Untersuchung zu seiner "Apologie" 2 Korinther, 10–13*. BHT 45. Tübingen: Mohr Siebeck, 1972.

Bird, Michael F. *Jesus and the Origins of the Gentile Mission*. LNTS 331. London: T&T Clark, 2006.

Bird, Michael F., and Preston M. Sprinkle, eds. *The Faith of Jesus Christ: Exegetical, Biblical, and Theological Studies*. Peabody, MA: Hendrickson, 2009.

Bloomquist, Gregory L. *The Function of Suffering in Philippians*. JSNTSup 78. Sheffield: Sheffield Academic, 1993.

Bockmuehl, Markus. *The Epistle to the Philippians*. BNTC 11. Peabody, MA: Hendrickson, 1998.

Bond, Helen K. *Caiaphas: Friend of Rome and Judge of Jesus?* Louisville: Westminster John Knox, 2004.
Bormann, Lukas. *Philippi: Stadt und Christengemeinde zur Zeit des Paulus.* NovTSup 58. Leiden: Brill, 1995.
Bosch, Jorge Sánchez. *"Gloriarse" segun San Pablo: Sentido y teología de kauchaomai.* AnBib 40. Rome: Biblical Institute Press, 1970.
Braund, David C. *Augustus to Nero: A Sourcebook on Roman History 31BC–AD 68.* London: Croom & Helm, 1985.
Brynes, Michael. *Conformation to the Death of Christ and the Hope of Resurrection: An Exegetico-Theological Study of 2 Corinthians 4:7–15 and Philippians 3:6–11.* TGST 99. Rome: Gregorian University Press, 2003.
Bultmann, Rudolf. "καυχάομαι." *TDNT* 3:645–53.
Caird, G. B. *Paul's Letters from Prison in the Revised Standard Version.* New Clarendon Bible. Oxford: Oxford University Press, 1976.
Cairns, F. *Sextus Propertius: The Augustan Elegist.* Cambridge: Cambridge University Press, 2006.
Callan, Terrance. "Competition and Boasting: Toward a Psychological Portrait of Paul." *ST* 40 (1986): 137–56.
Campbell, William S. "'I Rate All Things as Loss': Paul's Puzzling Accounting System; Judaism as Loss or the Re-evaluation of All Things in Christ?" Pages 203–23 in Campbell, *Unity and Diversity: Interpreting Paul in Context: Collected Essays.* Eugene, OR: Cascade, 2015.
Capper, Brian J. "Paul's Dispute with Philippi: Understanding Paul's Attitude in Phil 1–2 from His Thanks in 4:10–20." *TZ* 49 (1993): 193–214.
Chang, Dongshin D. "Phinehas, the Sons of Zadok, and Melchizedek: An Analysis of Some Understandings of Priestly Covenant in the Late Second Temple Period." PhD diss., University of Manchester, 2013.
Cicero. *The Letters to His Friends.* Translated by W. Glynn Williams. 3 vols. LCL. Cambridge: Harvard University Press, 1927–1929.
Collart, Paul, and Pierre Ducrey. *Philippes I: Les reliefs rupestres.* BCHSupp 55. Athens: École française d'Athènes, 1975.
Danker, Frederick W. *Benefactor: Epigraphic Study of a Graeco-Roman and New Testament Semantic Field.* Saint Louis: Clayton, 1982.
deSilva, David A. *Introducing the Apocrypha: Message, Context, and Significance.* Grand Rapids: Baker, 2002.
———. "The Wisdom of Ben Sira: Honor, Shame, and the Maintenance of the Values of a Minority Culture." *CBQ* 58 (1996): 433–55.

Dillon, M., and L. Garland. *Ancient Rome: Social and Historical Documents from the Early Republic to the Death of Augustus*. 2nd ed. London: Routledge, 2015.

Donahoe, K. C. "From Self-Praise to Self-Boasting: Paul's Unmasking of the Rhetorico-Linguistic Phenomena in 1 Corinthians." PhD diss., St Andrews University, 2008.

Dunn, James D. G. *The Epistle to the Galatians*. BNTC 9. Peabody, MA: Hendrickson, 1993.

———. *The Theology of Paul the Apostle*. Grand Rapids: Eerdmans, 1998.

Earl, Donald Charles. "Political Terminology in Plautus." *Historia* 9 (1960): 235–43.

Ehrensperger, Kathy. "'Join in Imitating Me' (Phil 3.17): Embodying Christ in the Face of 'the Enemies of the Cross.'" Paper delivered at the 2017 Society of New Testament Studies meeting in Pretoria, South Africa.

Erasmo, Mario. *Reading Death in Ancient Rome*. Columbus: Ohio State University Press, 2008.

Fee, Gordon D. *Paul's Letter to the Philippians*. NICNT. Grand Rapids: Eerdmans, 1995.

Flexsenhar, Michael A., III. "Slaves of Christ: Caesar's Household and the Early Christians." PhD diss., University of Texas at Austin, 2016.

Flower, Harriet I. *The Art of Forgetting: Disgrace and Oblivion in Roman Political Culture*. Chapel Hill: University of North Carolina Press, 2006.

Forbes, Christopher. "Comparison, Self-Praise and Irony: Paul's Boasting and the Conventions of Hellenistic Rhetoric." *NTS* 32 (1986): 1–30.

Forbis, Elizabeth. *Municipal Virtues in the Roman Empire: The Evidence of Italian Honorary Inscriptions*. Leipzig: Teubner, 1996.

Galinsky, Karl. *Augustan Culture: An Interpretative Introduction*. Princeton: Princeton University Press, 1996.

Garland, David E. "The Composition and Unity of Philippians: Some Neglected Factors." *NovT* 27 (1985): 141–75.

Gathercole, Simon J. *Where Is Boasting? Early Jewish Soteriology and Paul's Response in Romans 1–5*. Grand Rapids: Eerdmans, 2002.

Gebhard, Elizabeth R., and Matthew W. Dickie. "The View from the Isthmus, ca. 200 to 44 B.C." Pages 261–78 in *Corinth the Centenary, 1896–1996*. Vol. 20 of *Corinth: Results of Excavations Conducted by the American School of Classical Studies at Athens*. Edited by Charles K. Williams II and Nancy Bookidis. Athens: American School of Classical Studies at Athens, 2003.

Gelzer, Matthias. *The Roman Nobility*. Translated by Robin Seager. Oxford: Basil Blackwell, 1969.
Glancy, Jennifer A. "Boasting of Beatings (2 Corinthians 11:23–25)." *JBL* 123 (2004): 99–135.
Gordon, Arthur E. *Illustrated Introduction to Latin Epigraphy*. Berkeley: University of California Press, 1982.
Grindheim, Sigurd. "Paul's Critique of the Jewish Confidence in the Election of Israel in 2 Corinthians 11:16–12:10 and Philippians 3:1–11." PhD diss., Trinity International University, 2002.
Gundry, Judith M. "'Or Who Gave First to Him, So That He Shall Receive Recompense?' (Rom 11,35): Divine Benefaction and Human Boasting in Paul and Philo." Pages 26–53 in *The Letter to the* Romans. Edited by Udo Schnelle. BETL 126. Leuven: Peeters, 2009.
Hansen, G. Walter. *The Letter to the Philippians*. PNTC. Grand Rapids: Eerdmans, 2009.
Harrison, James R. "Augustan Rome and the Body of Christ: A Comparison of the Social Vision of the *Res Gestae* and Paul's Letter to the Romans." *HTR* 106 (2013): 1–36.
———. "The Erasure of Honour: Paul and the Politics of Dishonour." *TynBul* 66 (2016): 161–84.
———. "'Every Dog Has Its Day.'" *NewDocs* 10:136–45.
———. *Paul and the Ancient Celebrity Circuit: The Cross and Moral Transformation*. Tübingen: Mohr Siebeck, forthcoming.
———. "Paul and Ancient Civic Ethics: Redefining the Canon of Honour in the Graeco-Roman World." Pages 75–118 in *Paul's Graeco-Roman Context*. Edited by C. Breytenbach. BETL 227. Leuven: Peeters, 2015.
———. "Paul and the *Agōnothetai* at Corinth: Engaging the Civic Values of Antiquity." Pages 271–326 in *Roman Corinth*. Vol. 2 of *The First Urban Churches*. Edited by James R. Harrison and L. L. Welborn. WGRWSup 8. Atlanta: SBL Press, 2016.
———. *Paul and the Imperial Authorities at Thessalonica and Rome: A Study in the Conflict of Ideology*. WUNT 273. Tübingen: Mohr Siebeck, 2011.
———. "Paul and the Roman Ideal of Glory in the Epistle to the Romans." Pages 323–63 in *The Letter to the Romans*. Edited by Udo Schnelle. BETL 226. Leuven: Peeters, 2009.
Harvey, Brian K. *Roman Lives: Ancient Roman Life as Illustrated by Latin Inscriptions*. Focus Classical Sources. Newburyport, MA: Focus Publishing/Pullins, 2004.

Hawthorne, Gerald F. "The Imitation of Christ: Discipleship in Philippians." Pages 163–79 in *Patterns of Discipleship in the New Testament*. Edited by R. N. Longenecker. Grand Rapids: Eerdmans, 1996.

———. *Philippians*. WBC 43. Waco, TX: Word, 1983.

Hellerman, Joseph H. *Philippians*. EGGNT. Nashville: Broadman & Holman, 2015.

———. *Reconstructing Honor in Roman Philippi: Carmen Christi as Cursus Pudorum*. SNTSMS 132. Cambridge: Cambridge University Press, 2005.

Hoffmann, Friedhelm, et al., eds. *Die dreisprachige Stele des C. Cornelius Gallus: Übersetzung und Kommentar*. Berlin: de Gruyter, 2009.

Holloway, Paul. A. *Consolation in Philippians: Philosophical Sources and Rhetorical Strategy*. SNTSMS 112. Cambridge: Cambridge University Press, 2001.

———. *Philippians*. Hermeneia. Minneapolis: Fortress, 2017.

Hultin, Jeremy F. *The Ethics of Obscene Language in Early Christianity and Its Environment*. NovTSup 128. Leiden: Brill, 2008.

Jewett, Robert. "Conflicting Movements in the Early Church as Reflected in Philippians." *NovT* 12 (1970): 362–90.

Judge, E. A. "The Conflict of Educational Aims in the New Testament." Pages 693–708 in *The First Christians in the Roman World: Augustan and New Testament Essays*. Edited by James R. Harrison. WUNT 229. Tübingen: Mohr Siebeck, 2009.

———. "Paul's Boasting in Relation to Contemporary Professional Practice." Pages 57–71 in *Social Distinctives of the Christians in the First Century: Pivotal Essays by E. A. Judge*. Edited by David M. Scholer. Peabody, MA: Hendrickson, 2008.

Kennedy, George A., trans. and ed. *Progymnasmata: Greek Textbooks of Prose Composition and Rhetoric*. WGRW 10. Atlanta: Society of Biblical Literature, 2003.

Lange, Carsten Hjort. "*Stasis* and *Bellum Civile*: A Difference in Scale?" *Critical Analysis of Law* 4 (2017): 129–40.

Lansford, Tyler. *The Latin Inscriptions of Rome: A Walking Guide*. Baltimore: Johns Hopkins University Press, 2009.

Lee, Jae Won. "Paul, Nation, and Nationalism." Pages 223–35 in *The Colonized Apostle: Paul through Postcolonial Eyes*. Edited by Christopher D. Stanley. Paul in Critical Contexts. Minneapolis: Fortress, 2011.

Lee, Thomas R. *Studies in the Form of Sirach 44–50*. SBLDS 75. Atlanta: Scholars Press, 1986.

Lendon, J. E. *Empire of Honour: The Art of Government in the Roman World*. Repr., Oxford: Oxford University Press, 2002.

Lewis, Charlton, and Charles Short. *A Latin Dictionary, Founded on Andrews' Edition of Freund's Latin Dictionary, Revised, Enlarged, and in Great Part Rewritten by Charlton T. Lewis, Ph.D. and. Charles Short, LL.D.* Oxford: Clarendon, 1879.

Lifshitz, B. *Donateurs et fondateurs dans les synagogues juives*. Paris: Gabalda, 1967.

Lintott, Andrew. *Violence, Civil Strife and Revolution in the Classical City*. London: Croom & Helm, 1982.

Mack, Burton L. *Wisdom and the Hebrew Epic: Ben Sira's Hymn in Praise of the Fathers*. Chicago: University of Chicago Press, 1985.

Magi, F. "Le iscrizioni recentemente scoperte sull'obelisco vaticano." *Studi Romani* 11 (1963): 50–56.

———. "L'obelisco do Caio Cornelio Gallo." *Capitolium* 29 (1963): 488–92.

Malcolm, Matthew R. *Paul and the Rhetoric of Reversal: The Impact of Paul's Gospel on His Macro-Rhetoric*. SNTSMS 155. Cambridge: Cambridge University, 2013.

Manicas, Peter T. "War, *Stasis*, and Greek Political Thought." *Comparative Studies in Social History* 24 (1982): 673–88.

Martin, Ralph P. *Philippians: An Introduction and Commentary*. TNTC. London: Inter-Varsity Press, 1959.

Mason, Steve. *Life of Josephus*. FJTC 9. Leiden: Brill, 2001.

Metzger, B. M. *An Introduction to the Apocrypha*. New York: Oxford University Press, 1957.

Miletti, Lorenzo. "Il *De laude ipsius* di Plutarco e la teoria 'classica' dell'autoelogi." Pages 81–99 in *Plutarco: Linguaggi e Retorica; Atti del XII Convegno della International Plutarch Society*. Edited by Paola Volpe Cacciatore. Naples: D'Auria Editore, 2014.

Mueller, Dierk. "Military Images in Paul's Letter to the Philippians." PhD diss., University of Pretoria, 2013.

Nanos, Mark D. "Out-Howling the Cynics: Reconceptualizing the Concerns of Paul's Audience from His Polemics in Philippians 3." Pages 183–221 in *The People beside Paul: The Philippian Assembly and History from Below*. Edited by Joseph A. Marchall. ECL. Atlanta: SBL Press, 2015.

———. "Paul's Reversal of Jews Calling Gentiles 'Dogs' (Philippians 3:2): 1600 Years of an Ideological Tale Wagging an Exegetical Dog?" *BibInt* 17 (2009): 448–82.

North, Helen F. "Canons and Hierarchies of the Cardinal Virtues in Greek and Latin Literature." Pages 165–83 in *The Classical Tradition: Literary and Historical Studies in Honor of Harry Caplan*. Edited by Luitpold Wallach. Ithaca, NY: Cornell University Press, 1966.

O'Brien, Peter T. *The Epistle to the Philippians*. NIGTC. Grand Rapids: Eerdmans, 1991.

Ogereau, Julien M. *Paul's Koinonia with the Philippians: A Socio-historical Investigation of a Pauline Economic Partnership*. WUNT 2/377. Tübingen: Mohr Siebeck, 2014.

Ortlund, Dane C. *Zeal without Knowledge: The Concept of Zeal in Romans 10, Galatians 1, and Philippians 3*. LNTS 472. London: T&T Clark, 2012.

Patterson, Jane Lancaster. *Keeping the Feast: Metaphors of Sacrifice in 1 Corinthians and Philippians*. ECL 16. Atlanta: SBL Press, 2015.

Pernot, L. "*Periautologia*, problèmes et méthodes de l'éloge de soi-même dans la tradition éthique et rhétorique gréco-romaine." *REG* 111 (1998): 101–24.

Peterlin, Davorin. *Paul's Letter to the Philippians in the Light of Disunity in the Church*. NovTSup 79. Leiden: Brill, 1995.

Pettigrew, David. K. "The *Diolkos* of Corinth." *AJA* 115 (2011): 549–74.

———. *The Isthmus of Corinth: Crossroads of the Mediterranean World*. Ann Arbor: University of Michigan Press, 2016.

Pilhofer, Peter. *Philippi*. Vol. 1, *Die erste christliche Gemeinde Europas*. WUNT 87. Tübingen: Mohr Siebeck, 1995.

———. *Philippi*. Vol. 2, *Katalog der Inschriften von Philippi. 2. Auflage*. 2nd ed. WUNT 119. Tübingen: Mohr Siebeck, 2009.

Reed, Jeffrey T. *A Discourse Analysis of Philippians: Method and Rhetoric in the Debate over Literary Integrity*. JSNTSup 136. Sheffield: Sheffield Academic, 1997.

Reynolds, Joyce. *Aphrodisias and Rome*. JRS Monographs 1. London: Society for the Promotion of Roman Studies, 1982.

Reumann, John. *Philippians: A New Translation with Introduction and Commentary*. AYB 33B. New Haven: Yale University Press, 2008.

Ryan, Scott C. "The Reversal of Rhetoric in Philippians 3:1–11." *PRSt* 39 (2012): 67–77.

Sampley, J. Paul. "Paul, His Opponents in 2 Corinthians 10–13." Pages 162–77 in *The Social World of Formative Christianity: Essays in Tribute to Howard Clark Kee*. Edited by Jacob Neusner et al. Philadelphia: Fortress, 1988.

Schwartz, Seth. *Were the Jews a Mediterranean Society? Reciprocity and Solidarity in Ancient Judaism.* Princeton: Princeton University Press, 2010.
Silva, Moisés. *Philippians.* WEC. Chicago: Moody, 1988.
Smit, Peter-Ben. "Paul, Plutarch and the Problematic Practice of Self-Praise (περιαυτολογία): The Case of Phil 3:2–21." *NTS* 60 (2014): 341–59.
Smith, R. E. *The Aristocratic Epoch in Latin Literature.* Sydney: Australasian Medical, 1947.
Sorek, Susan. *Remembered for Good: A Jewish Benefaction System in Ancient Palestine.* The Social World of Biblical Antiquity 2/5. Sheffield: Sheffield Phoenix, 2010.
Souza, Philip de. *Piracy in the Graeco-Roman World.* Oxford: Oxford University Press, 1999.
Speidel, Michael. "The Captor of Decebalus: A New Inscription from Philippi." *JRS* 60 (1960): 142–53.
Spicq, Ceslas. "καυχάομαι, καύχημα, καύχησις." *TLNT* 3:295–302.
Stanley, Christopher D. "Paul the Ethnic Hybrid: Postcolonial Perspectives on Paul's Ethnic Categorizations." Pages 110–26 in *The Colonized Apostle: Paul through Postcolonial Eyes.* Edited by Christopher D. Stanley. Paul in Critical Contexts. Minneapolis: Fortress, 2011.
Tan, Rachael. "Conformity to Christ: An Exegetical and Theological Analysis of Paul's Perspective on Humiliation and Exaltation in Philippians 2:5–11." PhD diss., Southern Baptist Theological Seminary, 2017.
Thurston, Bonnie B., and Judith M. Ryan. *Philippians and Philemon.* SP 10. Collegeville, MN: Liturgical Press, 2005.
Travis, S. H. "Paul's Boasting in 2 Corinthians 10–12." *SE* 6 (1973): 527–32.
Uusimäki, Elisa. "The Formation of a Sage according to Ben Sira." Pages 59–69 in *Second Temple Jewish Paideia in Context.* Edited by Jason M. Zurawski and Gabriele Boccaccini. BZNW 228. Berlin: de Gruyter, 2017.
Vanderkam, James C. *From Joshua to Caiaphas: High Priests after the Exile.* Minneapolis: Fortress, 2004.
Warmington, E. H. *Remains of Old Latin IV: Archaic Inscriptions.* LCL. Cambridge: Harvard University Press, 1953.
Watson, Duane F. "Paul and Boasting." Pages 90–112 in *Paul and the Greco-Roman World: A Handbook.* Edited by J. Paul Sampley. Vol. 1. London: Bloomsbury T&T Clark, 2016.
———. "A Rhetorical Analysis of Philippians and Its Implications for the Unity Question." *NovT* 30 (1988): 57–88.

West, Allen Brown. *Latin Inscriptions 1896–1926*. Vol. 8.2 of *Corinth: Results of Excavations Conducted by the American School of Classical Studies at Athens*. Cambridge: Harvard University Press, 1931.

Winter, Bruce W. *After Paul Left Corinth: The Influence of Secular Ethics and Social Change*. Grand Rapids: Eerdmans, 2001.

———. *Seek the Welfare of the City: Christians as Benefactors and Citizens*. Grand Rapids: Eerdmans, 1994.

Witherington, Ben, III. "The Case of the Imprisonment That Did Not Happen: Paul at Ephesus." *JETS* 60 (2017): 525–32.

———. *Friendship and Finances in Philippi: The Letters of Paul to the Philippians*. Valley Forge, PA: Trinity Press International, 1994.

Wocjiechowski, M. "Paul and Plutarch on Boasting." *JGRChJ* 3 (2006): 99–109.

Contributors

Richard S. Ascough is a Professor in the School of Religion at Queen's University in Kingston, Canada. His research and teaching focuses on the history of early Christianity and Greco-Roman religious culture, with particular attention to various types of associations. He has published widely in the field, with more than forty articles and essays and ten books, including *Associations in the Greco-Roman World* (with John Kloppenborg and Philip Harland; Baylor University Press; de Gruyter, 2012) and *1 and 2 Thessalonians: Encountering the Christ Group at Thessalonike* (Sheffield Pheonix, 2014).

Cédric Brélaz has been Professor of History of Antiquity at the University of Fribourg since 2016. His monographs are *La sécurité publique en Asie Mineure sous le Principat (Ier–IIIème s. ap. J.-C.)* (Schwabe, 2005) and *La colonie romaine*, vol. 2 of *Corpus des inscriptions grecques et latines de Philippes* (École française d'Athènes, 2014). He has also edited three books on the military life, colonial heritage, and public security of the Greek and Roman world (Fondation Hardt, 2008; Picard, 2013; de Boccard, 2017).

Kathy Ehrensperger (PhD, 2002) is Research Professor of the New Testament in Jewish Context, at the Abraham Geiger College, University of Potsdam. Recent publications include *Paul and the Dynamics of Power* (T&T Clark, 2008) and *Paul at the Crossroads of Cultures* (T&T Clark, 2013).

Ryan Kristopher Giffin (MA, Nazarene Theological Seminary) is a PhD Candidate in Biblical Studies at Asbury Theological Seminary and Adjunct Professor of Biblical Literature at MidAmerica Nazarene University.

James R. Harrison studied Ancient History at Macquarie University and graduated from the doctoral program in 1997. Professor Harrison is the

Research Director at the Sydney College of Divinity. His recent publications include *Paul's Language of Grace in Its Graeco-Roman Context* (Mohr Siebeck, 2003; repr., Wipf & Stock, 2017) and *Paul and the Imperial Authorities at Thessalonica and Rome* (Mohr Siebeck, 2011); he coedited with S. R. Llewelyn volume 10 of *New Documents Illustrating Early Christianity* (Eerdmans, 2012).

Paul A. Holloway (PhD University of Chicago, 1998) is University Professor of Classics and Ancient Christianity in the University of the South in Sewanee, Tennessee. Prior to coming to "Sewanee," he was Senior Lecturer in the Department of Theology and Religious Studies at the University of Glasgow, Scotland. His recent publications include: *Philippians: A Commentary* (Fortress, 2017) and *Coping with Prejudice: 1 Peter in Social-Psychological Perspective* (Mohr Siebeck, 2009).

Fredrick J. Long (PhD, Marquette University; MA Classics, University of Kentucky; MDiv, Asbury Theological Seminary) is Professor of New Testament and Director of Greek Instruction at Asbury Theological Seminary as well as the International Coordinator of Gamma Rho Kappa Greek Honor Society. He is the author of several books, including *Ancient Rhetoric and Paul's Apology: The Compositional Unity of 2 Corinthians* (Cambridge University Press, 2004), *2 Corinthians: A Handbook on the Greek Text* (Baylor University Press, 2015), *Koine Greek Grammar: A Beginning-Intermediate Exegetical and Pragmatic Handbook* (GlossaHouse, 2015), and *In Step with God's Word: Interpreting the New Testament with God's People* (GlossaHouse, 2017).

Peter Oakes (MA, Cambridge University; DPhil, Oxford) is Professor and Greenwood Senior Lecturer in New Testament at the University of Manchester. He is editor for the *Journal for the Study of the New Testament* Booklist. His three monographs are *Galatians* (Paideia, 2015), *Reading Romans in Pompeii: Paul's Letter at Ground Level* (Fortress, 2013), and *Philippians: From People to Letter* (Cambridge University Press, 2007).

Julien M. Ogereau (PhD 2014) studied Theology, New Testament, and Early Christian Studies at the Sydney College of Divinity and Macquarie University, Sydney. He was a research associate with the Excellence Cluster 264 Topoi at Humboldt-Universität zu Berlin from 2014 to 2016 and an LMUexcellent Research Fellow at the Ludwig-Maximilians-Universität München from 2017 to 2018. Recent publications include *Paul's Koinonia* *with the Philippians* (Mohr Siebeck, 2014) and *Authority and Identity in Emerging Christianities in Asia Minor and Greece* (Brill, 2018).

Angela Standhartinger studied Protestant Theology at Frankfurt am Main, Munich, and Heidelberg and finished her habilitation at Frankfurt in 1998. She is professor for New Testament Studies at the Philipps-Universität in Marburg, Germany. Her recent publications include "Better Ending: Paul at the Roman Colonia Philippi in Acts 16," in *Delightful Acts: New Essays on Canonical and Non-canonical Acts* (ed. Harold W. Attridge, Dennis R. MacDonald, and Clare K. Rothschild; Mohr Siebeck, 2017) and "Apocalyptic Thought in Philippians," in *The Jewish Apocalpytic Tradition and the Shaping of New Testament Thought* (ed. Benjamin E. Reynolds and Loren T. Stuckenbruck; Fortress, 2017).

Samuel Vollenweider studied Theology and Classical Studies at the Universities of Zurich, Tübingen and Heidelberg. He is professor of New Testament studies in Zurich. His recent publications include studies on Paul and on early Christian theology (*Horizonte neutestamentlicher Christologie*, Mohr Siebeck, 2003) and on Hellenistic philosophy and early Christianity (*Epiktet: Was ist wahre Freiheit?*, Mohr Siebeck, 2011). He coedited with Ulrich Luz and Thomas Söding the volume, *Exegese-ökumenisch engagiert: Der "Evangelisch-Katholische Kommentar," in der Diskussion über 500 Jahre Reformation*, Neukirchener Verlag, 2016).

L. L. Welborn (PhD, 1992) studied New Testament and early Christianity at Vanderbilt University and the University of Chicago and is currently Professor of New Testament and Early Christianity at Fordham University and Honorary Professor of Ancient History at Macquarie University. Recent publications include *Paul, the Fool of Christ: A Study of 1 Corinthians 1–4 in the Comic-Philosophic Tradition* (T&T Clark, 2005), *An End to Enmity: Paul and the "Wrongdoer" of Second Corinthians* (de Gruyter, 2011), and *Paul's Summons to Messianic Life: Political Theology and the Coming Awakening* (Columbia University Press, 2015).

Primary Sources Index

Old Testament		7:12	312
		14:3	146
Genesis			
15:6	314–15	1 Samuel	
15:20	253	2:2–3	312
17:12	349	5:4	276
17:25	349	9:2–3	351
32:28	350		
35:10	350	2 Kingdoms	
35:31	146	22:40	275
Exodus		1 Kings	
3:8	252	12:21	351
3:17	252	20:11	312
20:6	246		
23:22	296	3 Kingdoms	
		19:18	275
Leviticus		4 Kingdoms	
12:3	349	1:13	275
Numbers		9:24	275
12:6–8	146		
24:17	36	1 Chronicles	
25:5–15	355	16:27–29	312
25:13	313	29:11	312
Deuteronomy		Nehemiah	
5:8	248	9:10	146
10:21	312	9:38	146
21:23	356		
32:5	296	Psalms	
		5:11–12	312
Judges		49:6	312
1:21	351	52:1	312
7:5–6	275	93:3–4	312

Psalms (cont.)
- 106 — 314
- 106:30–31 — 314–15, 355
- 106:30–33 — 313
- 115:1 — 312
- 148 — 250
- 148:1–6 — 250
- 148:7–12 — 250
- 148:13–14 — 250

Proverbs
- 11:7 — 312
- 25:14 — 312
- 27:1 — 312

Isaiah
- 40–55 — 296
- 42:4b — 39
- 45–46 — 274
- 45:5 — 276
- 45:6 — 276
- 45:18 — 276
- 45:18–25 — 276
- 45:20 — 276
- 45:21 — 276
- 45:22 — 276
- 45:23 — 232, 243, 246, 274–77
- 46:1 — 243
- 46:1–2 — 277
- 49:1 — 39
- 49:6b — 39
- 66:6 — 296

Jeremiah
- 1:5 — 39

Daniel
- 12:3 — 296

Deuterocanonical Books

Sirach
- 1:11 — 312
- 9:1 — 314
- 9:11 — 314
- 9:16 — 312
- 10:22 — 312
- 17:9 — 312
- 30:24 — 314
- 37:10 — 314
- 39:8 — 312
- 40:4 — 314
- 44:1–50:24 — 311, 314, 316
- 44:14–15 — 316
- 45:6–22 — 315
- 45:7a — 315
- 45:15 — 315
- 45:23–25 — 315
- 45:24 — 315
- 45:18 — 314
- 45:23 — 314
- 45:23–25 — 313, 315, 355
- 48:2 — 314
- 48:4 — 312
- 50:1–24 — 315
- 50:20 — 312
- 50:23–24 — 315
- 51:18 — 314

1 Maccabees
- 1:11–15 — 352
- 2:45–48 — 349
- 2:54 — 313

1 Esdras
- 8:73 — 275

3 Maccabees
- 2:17 — 312

4 Maccabees — 313
- 18:12

Pseudepigrapha

Jubilees
- 15:11–14 — 349

Testament of Judah
- 13.2–3 — 312

Primary Sources Index

Testament of Solomon		Philo, *De somniis*	
18.3	251	1.181	144
21.1	251		
		Philo, *De specialibus legibus*	
Dead Sea Scrolls		1.13–15	144
		2.45	144
1QH[a]			
11 II, 19–22	144	Philo, *Legatio ad Gaium*	
19 XI, 11–14	144	282	42
		44	201
1QS[b]			
4, 24–26	144	Pseudo-Philo, *Liber antiquitatum biblicarum*	
		46–48	313
Ancient Jewish Writers			
		New Testament	
Josephus, *Antiquitates Judaicae*			
4.151–155	313		
13.258	349	Matthew	
13.318–319	349	7:13	295
18.12–15	353	17:17	296
18.192–236	147	26:59	127
18.203	147	27:20	127
18.235	147		
18.257	201	Mark	
18.261–68	201	1:33	127
		3:17	44
Josephus, *Bellum Judaicum*		7:24–29	348
1.648	146	7:27	348
2.162–166	353	10:45	38
3.120	130	15:1	127
		15:16	127
Josephus, *Contra Apionem*		15:29	333
2.185	318		
		Luke	
Josephus, *Vita*		1:6	357
1–9	317–18, 348	9:41	296
192	353	22:26–27	38
Philo, *De agricultura*		John	
65	144	18:28	127
		18:33	127
Philo, *De confusione linguarum*	144	19:9	127
		19:38–39	333
Philo, *De congress ereditionis gratia*			
107	312		

Acts		18:3	47
2:40	296	18:4	164
2:47	127	18:7	164
5:34	352	18:12–17	167, 171
8:1	355	19:29–40	171
8:3	355	19:35	167
9:1	355	21:25–28	309
12	126	21:30	127
13:6–12	161	21:40	352
13:9	351	22:2	352
13:14	164	22:4–6	355
13:44–50	171	22:3	31, 352
13:50	170	22:25–29	172
15:22	127	23:6	352
16	64, 126, 226	23:16	352
16:6	139	23:35	127, 147
16:11	316	25:8–12	167
16:11–40	11	25:10–12	172, 190
16:12	166, 167, 173	26:4–5	352
16:12–14	154	26:5	353
16:13	43, 72, 164, 181	26:10–11	355
16:13–14	163	26:14	352
16:13–15	14	26:30–32	167
16:14	41, 88, 164, 355	27:1–3	147
16:15	37	28:16	50
16:16–19	170	28:16–31	147
16:17	175	28:19	190
16:19	157, 170	28:30	50
16:19–40	170		
16:20	167, 170	Romans	
16:20–21	26	1:1	39, 65
16:21	235	1:8	146
16:22	170	1:16b	359
16:22–23	171	2:8	292
16:23–36	166	3:1–2	359
16:33	88	3:26	276
16:35–38	166	4:3–25	314
16:37	165, 170	5:11	310
17:1	164, 181	5:17	310
17:4	164	8:22	247
17:5–9	171	8:29	23
17:7–8	167	9:1–5	359
17:10	164	9:22	295
17:17	164	10:2	359–60
18:2–3	165	10:3	36

11:1	351	2 Corinthians	
11:1–2a	359	1:8	147
11:4	275	1:8–10	126
11:7	127	1:12	310
11:13	65	3:18	23, 310
11:16	359	3:20	13
11:19	359	4:5	267
11:22	352	4:11	276
11:26–28	359	5:1–10	274
14:12	275	5:17	23, 310
15:20	125	5:21	23, 310
15:25–28	126	6:5	195
15:26	212	7:4	310
16:23	127	8–9	126
		8:1	149
1 Corinthians		8:1–2	140
1–4	46	8:1–4	12
1:2	73	8:1–5	13, 181
1:10–13	301	8:2	71, 86
1:18–25	333	8:4	310
1:26	86	10:8	310
1:29	310	10:12	310
1:31	310	10:13	310
2:6–8	250	10:15–17	310
4:12	195	11–12	300
4:15	42	11:1–13	301
7:8–12	127	11:4	276, 301
9:5	64	11:7–9	139
9:15	310	11:8	195
9:22	72	11:9	13, 208, 212
10:8	310	11:10	308
10:25	157	11:13–15	300
11:18–19	301	11:16–12:10	46–47, 360
12:28–29	64	11:18	308
14:23	127	11:19	208
15:9	355	11:21	308
15:9–11	295	11:21–12:4	310
15:31	310	11:22	352
15:32	126	11:22–29	300
15:42–44	23	11:23	126
15:49	23	12:7	310
16:1–4	126	12:9–10	300
16:2	42	13:2	127

Galatians
1:13	355
1:13–14	313, 317
1:14	313, 349, 352, 357
1:15a	39
1:15–16	39
1:16	39, 301
1:22–23	66
1:23	355
2:10	126
2:11–14	139
3:1–7	314
3:13	333, 356
3:28	39
4:13–18	139
5:11	333
5:12	299
5:20	292
6:14	310
6:16	300
6:17	276

Ephesians
1:19–23	255
1:20–22	247
1:20–23	273
2:2	252
2:4–7	274
3:10	250–52, 255
3:14	274
4:10	248
6:12	252

Philippians
1	294, 295
1:1	13, 66, 144
1:1–23	273
1:3–7	206
1:3–11	194
1:4	24
1:5	140, 193, 207, 212
1:6	302
1:7	140, 191, 193, 201, 241, 354
1:7–8	181
1:10–11	302
1:12	40, 66, 202, 207
1:12–14	241
1:12–18	191, 202
1:13–14	127
1:13	48–49, 127–29, 131–32, 145, 147, 190, 195, 197, 228, 234
1:14	40, 48, 127, 228, 293
1:14–18	241
1:15	301
1:15–17	124
1:15–18	292
1:17	241, 292, 293
1:17–18	301
1:18	24, 292, 294
1:19	140
1:19–26	294
1:19–30	241
1:20	24, 40, 228, 234, 293, 334
1:20–22	354
1:21	228
1:21–23	234
1:21–26	294
1:22	24
1:23	23, 228, 273
1:24–25	24, 234
1:25	24
1:25–26	125
1:26	191, 209, 212, 296, 298
1:27	46, 75, 125, 191, 203, 209, 222, 231, 280, 296, 345
1:27–28a	345
1:27–30	206, 222, 280, 295, 296, 301
1:27–2:4	297
1:28–30	76, 139
1:28	234, 296, 298, 344
1:29	296
1:30	205, 296
2:1–4	297, 346
2:2, 29	24
2:3–4	40, 349
2:3	298
2:4	12, 297
2:5	40, 280
2:5–11	12–13, 160, 222, 240, 245, 273, 302, 311, 327, 346, 361

2:6	23, 40, 232, 240	3:1–2	43
2:6–8	232, 240, 281	3:1–3	312–13, 319
2:6–11	209, 231, 239–41, 246, 278, 280, 297	3:1–11	315, 346
2:7a	23, 40	3:2	43, 298–99, 344, 346, 347–48
2:7–8	240, 271	3:2–21	298, 301, 302
2:7–11	327	3:3	300, 310
2:8–9	234	3:3–6	300
2:8	49, 228, 333, 354, 356	3:4	313
2:9	229, 230, 235, 263	3:4–6	307–9, 313–14, 318–19, 322
2:9–11	23, 27, 40, 222, 231–33, 281, 282	3:4–7	22, 300
		3:4–11	361
2:10	24, 210, 230, 235, 239, 242, 247, 250–52, 254, 255, 274, 276, 279, 282	3:4–16	312
		3:5	167, 232, 308, 350–55
		3:5–6	327, 343–44, 347–49, 358
2:10–11	195, 240, 242, 245, 274, 275, 277	3:5–7	299
		3:5–8	40
2:11	23, 26, 230, 235, 248, 302	3:6	311, 313, 314, 315, 355–58
2:12–13	298	3:7	359
2:12–18	346	3:7–8	300
2:13	40	3:7–11	309, 322, 359
2:14	13, 357	3:8	22, 359
2:14–16a	206	3:9	23, 300, 313, 314–15, 354, 360
2:15	209, 273, 296–97, 344, 357	3:9–10a	40
2:16	209, 298, 310	3:10	23, 40, 300
2:17	24, 228, 241, 354	3:10–11	23, 273
2:17–18	125, 298	3:11	40
2:18	24	3:12–14	300
2:19	125	3:12–15	40, 334
2:19–24	302, 346	3:13	24, 40, 66, 359
2:19–24	40, 302, 334	3:14	45, 300
2:19–30	206	3:17	24, 40, 66, 210, 298, 300
2:21	293	3:17–20	346
2:23	125	3:18	298
2:24	125	3:18–19	234
2:25	40, 125, 181, 208, 212, 227	3:19	167, 299
2:25–30	40, 42, 140, 144, 302, 310, 311, 334	3:19–20	273
		3:19–21	299
2:26	124	3:20	13, 40, 143–44, 167, 191, 202, 222, 230–31, 234, 282, 345
2:27	124–25	3:20–21	12, 235
2:28	24	3:21	23, 40, 230, 273, 300
2:28–29	212	4:1	24, 66
2:30	124	4:1	40
3	293, 297	4:2	13, 14, 66, 227
3:1	24, 40, 66	4:2–3	293, 310, 346,

Philippians (cont.)

4:3	40, 46, 334
4:4	24
4:5	210
4:7	222
4:8	40, 66
4:9	206, 210
4:10	24, 140
4:10–14	84, 212
4:10–18	181
4:10–19	40, 334
4:10–20	12, 13, 14, 42, 346
4:11	208, 212, 213
4:12	195
4:14	193, 197
4:14–20	194
4:15	66, 83, 143, 179, 189, 193, 207–8, 212, 229
4:15–16	139
4:15–20	147, 83, 84
4:16	208, 212
4:17–18	212, 213
4:18	83, 140, 191, 212, 346, 354
4:19	191
4:20	49, 212
4:21	40
4:22	48, 50, 190, 195, 197, 229, 235, 241

Colossians

2:9	250
2:10	250
2:14–15	250, 278
2:15	251

1 Thessalonians

1:9	232
2:2–3	139
2:7	65
2:9	149, 195
2:11	42
2:19	310
4:11–12	210
4:13	127
5:6	127

2 Thessalonians

1:4	310

1 Timothy

1:13	355
6:14–16	273

Titus

1:11	127

Hebrews

3:2–5	127
12:2	333

2 Peter

1:13–14	94
2:1	295

1 John

2:2	127
5:19	127

Revelation

3:10	127
5	277, 278
5:3	246, 248, 277
5:7	277
5:13	246–48, 277–78
12:9	127
17:8	295

Rabbinic Works

b. Hagigah

13a	348

m. Sanhedrin

9.6	313

Midrash Psalms

4.11	348

Sifre Numbers

151	313

Primary Sources Index   383

Early Christian Literature

Athanasius, *Historia Arianorum*
75
97

1 Clement
   5:2–5   293

Codex theodosianus
   13.1.1, 5   99
   13.3.5   99
   16.2.8, 10, 14–15   99

Ignatius, *To the Trallians*
   5.2   250
   9.1   247, 249–50

John Chrysostom, *De Lazaro*
   4.4   97

John Chrysostom, *Homiliae in Matthaeum*
   85.4   97

John Chrysostom, *Homiliae in epistulam ad Philippenses*
   2   127
   2.1   250

Julian, *Epistulae*
   42   99

Melito, *Peri Pascha*
   414   146

Polycarp, *To the Philippians*
   2   247
   2.1   250
   3   182
   4.1   88
   9.1   148, 182
   11.1   89
   11.1–2   147–48
   11.1–4   88, 89
   13   148

Socrates, *Historia ecclesiastica*
   6.9.3   105

Tertullian, *Adversus Marcionem*
   3.24.3   143

Tertullian, *De corona militis*
   13.3–4   143

Tertullian, *De praescriptione haereticorum*
   36.1–2 182

Greco-Roman Literature

Aelius Aristides, *Orations*
   43.18   261

Aristotle, *De generatione anamalium*
   755b36   146

Artemidorus, *Onirocritica*
   2.34.1–26   261–62
   2.34.31   262
   2.35.48   262
   2.36.153–154   262
   2.37.155–156   262
   2.38.25–26   262
   2.39.45   262
   2.40.1   262
   3.56   91

Ausonius, *Epitaphia*
   31   18, 19

Cicero, *Ad Atticum*
   3.23.1   123

Cicero, *De amicitia*
   16.58   84

Cicero, *De domo suo*   242

Cicero, *De legibus*   242
   2.2.5   231
   2.8.19   267

Cicero, *De oratore*
  1.82   329

Cicero, *De republica*
  2.10.17   266
  2.10.18–20   266
  2.10.20   266
  2.11.21   265
  6.13   266
  6.14   267
  6.15   266
  6.16   266
  6.18   266
  6.20   266
  6.25   266
  6.26   266
  6.29   266
  6.16.16   267

Cicero, *Epistulae ad familiares*
  12.7.2   323
  12.16   124

Cicero, *In Verrem*
  4.65   128
  5.92   128

Cicero, *Orationes philippicae*
  1.13   265
  2.110   265

Cicero, *Tusculanae disputationes*
  1.12.28   266, 267

Dio Cassius, *Historiae romanae*
  51.4.6   155, 224
  56.46.2   265
  56.46.3   265
  60.3   52
  60.5.2   265
  68.18.2   274

Dio Chrysostom, *Borysthentica* (Oration 36)
  22–23   144

  29–32   144

Homer, *Iliad*   275
  6.208   295
  11.748   295

Homer, *Odyssey*   275
  5.184–186   247, 255–56

Horace, *Satires*
  1.8.69–70   349

Julius Pollux, *Onomasticon*
  1.23.4—24.10   256

Justinian, *Corpus Iuris Civilis*
  3.25.6   211

Justinian, *Digest*
  17.2.63.10   211
  17.2.65.10   211

Juvenal, *Satires*
  14.99   349

Kennedy, *Progymnasmata*
  Aelius Theon 109–112   311
  Apthonius 35–40   311
  Hermogenes 15–18   311
  John of Sardis 116.1—142.6   311
  Nicolaus 47–58   311

Lucan, *Pharsalia*
  1.45–63   272–73
  1.53–54   272

Lucian, *Deorum concilium*   251

Manilius, *Astronomica*
  1.759–61   271
  1.762–804   271
  1.777   267
  1.798–804   272

Martial, *Epigrammaton*
- 7.30.5 — 349
- 10.19.21 — 18

Ovid, *Metamorphoses*
- 14.805–828 — 267–78
- 14.829–851 — 268
- 14.827–829 — 268
- 15.745–750 — 268
- 15.745–761 — 268
- 15.748–750 — 265
- 15.758–759 — 268
- 15.760–761 — 270
- 15.838 — 268
- 15.839–870 — 268
- 15.839 — 268
- 15.850 — 268

Petronius, *Satyricon*
- 102.14 — 349

Plato, *Gorgias*
- 523a–524a — 271

Plautus, *Mostellaria*
- 1.3.304 — 84

Pliny the Elder, *Naturalis Historiae*
- 12.12 — 50

Pliny the Younger, *Epistulae*
- 10.96 — 80

Plutarch, *An seni respublica gerenda sit*
- 2 (784d) — 143
- 18 (793b) — 143
- 18 (793c) — 143
- 20 (794c) — 143
- 25 (796b) — 143
- 25 (796c) — 143

Plutarch, *De se ipsum citra invidiam laudando*
- 1–21 (539a–547f) — 310
- 2 (539a–d) — 310
- 3 (540c) — 311
- 5 (541a–c) — 311
- 5–6 (541c–e) — 310
- 9 (542b–c) — 310
- 13 (544b) — 311
- 14–17 (544d–546a) — 311
- 16 (545a) — 310
- 11–22 (546c–547f) — 312

Plutarch, *De tranquillitate animi*
- 10 (470c) — 310

Plutarch, *Praecepta gerendae rei publicae*
- 7 (803d) — 143
- 14 (810d) — 143

Polybius, *Historiae*
- 4.19 — 329
- 5.101.4 — 329

Pseudo-Libanius, *Epistolary Styles*
- 4.25 — 344
- 92 — 345

Quintilian, *Institutio oratoria*
- 11.1.21 — 311

Res gestae divi Augusti
- 15–24 — 324
- 19–21 — 242
- 28.1 — 160
- 34.3 — 321

Seneca, *Ad Lucillium*
- 81.18 — 84

Seneca, *Apolocyntosis*
- 9 — 268
- — 265

Seneca, *Epistulae morales*
- 108.34 — 265

Seneca, *Hercules Oetaeus*
- 1565–71 — 272

Strabo, *Geographika*
6.2.11	260
7.4	141
7, frag. 17a	180
12.3.6, 11	166

Suetonius, *Vitae caesarum*
Aug. 100.4	264
Tib. 37.1	129
Dom. 12.2	349

Tacitus, *Annales*
2.37–38	31
4.2	129
12.45, 48, 54	325
13.3	52
13.8–9	325
14.6	325

Tacitus, *Historiae*
2.92	50
2.93.2	129
5.5.2	349

Thucydides, *Historiae*
8.7–8	329

vetera Scholia in Aeschylum in Persas
499b, line 2	258

vetera Scholia in Aristophanem
1126, line 2	258

vetera Scholia in Homeri
5.418.7–11	257

vetera Scholia in Lycophronem
679.15–16	258

vetera Scholia in Pindarum
Ode 8, 106g1–4	258

Virgil, *Aeneid*
6.548–627	271
6.69	271

Virgil, *Georgics*
1.25–39	262–63
1.32–39	272
6.785–87	271

Inscriptions and Papyri

AÉ
1937.250	130
1940.216	130
1969–1970.602	130
1973.538	130
2012.1377	174
2012.1382	177

AGRW
33	192
34	192
38	200
42	191
44	191
131	199, 215
138	200, 216
141	200, 217
180	199, 214
184	200, 215
223	198, 213

ASAA 41–42 (1963–1964)
351	259

Ascough, *AGRW*
44	41
55	41
152	41
155	41
157	41
158	41
209	41

Baillet, *Inscriptions grècques et latines des tombeaux des rois où syringes à Thèbes*
1473	130
1688	130

Primary Sources Index

BGU
  1.34   91

Braund, *Augustus to Nero*
  425   331

CID
  2.31   91
  2.34   91

CIG
  2831   271

CIL
  1.1570   358
  1.2662   328–31
  3.633   191
  3.703   191
  3.704   191
  3.707   191
  3.14147   331
  5.5188   51
  5.5195   51
  6.4226   51
  6.5197   51
  6.8958   52
  6.9037   52
  6.9097   52
  10.5182   325
  13.7709   130

CIPh 2.1
  5   158, 174
  6   133, 158, 169, 174
  8a   158
  17   168
  23   163, 174
  24   354
  32   92
  37   101, 104, 161
  38   32–33, 101, 161
  41   101
  42   101
  43   33–34
  47   167
  48   335
  49   335
  50   336
  53   336
  54–55   174
  63   104, 159, 337, 350
  64   167
  66   157, 174, 336
  68   160, 169, 337
  74   338
  76   176
  78   176
  81   176
  85   338–39, 346
  94   339–41, 346
  111   176
  112   176
  114   176
  117   92
  118   336
  119   341–42
  126   159
  129   167
  133   342
  134   174
  144   176
  151   134
  158   168, 176
  168   168, 176
  193   174, 176
  225   174

CPR
  9.77   91

Crawford, *Roman Statutes*
  25   168

DAW
  38.94   259

Ἐπιγραφές κάτω Μακεδονίας, τεύχος Α'
  438   109

Επιγραφές κάτω Μακεδονίας, τεύχος Β'
336   109

ETAM
15.141–42   102

FD
3.4.77   91
5.19   91
5.23   91

Galsterer, *Die römischen Steininschriften aus Köln*
260   130

Gordon, *Album of Dated Latin Inscriptions*
1.122   51

Greek Papyri in the British Museum (P.Lond.)
2851   130

GRA 1
68   191
69   191
70   191
71   191

IDelos
1519   198

IDidyma
107   199, 214

IEph
22   200, 215

IErythrai
63   263

IG
1^3.84   96
2.1.1175   337
2.2^2.212   96
2.2^2.13343   91

2.3^2.10051   29
4.3.1491   102
10.2.1.292   37
10.2.382   130
10.2.495   130
10.2.583   130
12.5.697   129
12.8.595   91
12.8.163   198
12.Supp.165   259
12.Supp.438   96

IGRR
1.945   252
3.394   130

IGUR
3.1203   260
3.1309   260

IK
10.1114   259
10.1115   259
49.81   29
56.73   259
56.135   259
67.111   94

IKaunos
1.a   263
1.c   263

IKosS
side A   198

ILS
8995   331

ILycia
2.9.16   259

ILydiaHM
7.1   260

Primary Sources Index 389

IMakedD	
920	191
1104	191
IMT Kyz Kapu Dağ	
1825	259
ISmyrna	
643	259
JHS 18 (1898)	
307.3	159
JÖAI (1915)	
45	
259	
Lansford, *Latin Inscriptions of Rome*	
15.3B	332
MAMA	
3.77	260
3.82	91
6.13	102
6.222	94
6, list 150.186	259
7.89	105
OGI	
2.656	331
Paton, *The Greek Anthology*	
2.264	192
P.Col.	
7.150, 161	97
P.Giss.	
1.101	91
PGM	
12.67–72	253
12.325–31	253, 254
17a.2–6	253, 254

Pilhofer, *Philippi 2*	
001	26, 316, 336, 354
002	25, 316, 354
004	26, 37, 316, 354
016	167
018	27
019	354
022	37, 94,
028a	27, 173,
029	16, 20, 41–42, 167, 177, 191
030a	134
031	25, 316, 354
037	27, 38
043	27,
167	
045	15, 18, 38, 167, 191
046	335
048	15, 34, 37
049	34
053	34, 354
054	27
057	27
058	104, 243, 337, 350
068	35
071	37
072	37
074	27
074b	38
079	24
080	24
089	35
091	191
094	28, 35
095	192
098	37
104	101
108	35
111–112	179
110	108
111	100
112	38
114	108
115	110
119	167
123	108

Pilhofer, Philippi 2 (cont.)

125	110	229	41
125a	106	232a	26
125b	106	240	104
127b	342	241	25, 316, 354
129	44	245–58	92
131	37	246	27, 174
132	28, 92	247	101
133	28, 35, 177, 191	248	37, 94
136	24	249	25
142	28, 191	250	92
143	28, 191	251	28, 34, 92
144	28, 191	252	28, 37
148	28, 173	255	28, 174
152	354	256	27
157	354	258	103
161	27, 28	268	38, 109
163–64	38, 354	274	108
163–66	173	276	27
164–66	42, 178	281	26
164	28, 42	282	26, 38
166	28, 354	283	26
166a	178	289	27
167	37	296	19, 24, 45
174	27	301	37, 167
175	28, 174, 354	307	28, 37
177	39, 354	308	108
178	174	311	44
184	354	322	37
186	174	328	38
190–93	174	329	148
191	27, 28, 174	332	28
192	28	333	94
199	41	338–39	176
202	52, 134, 338–39, 346	338–40	28
203	134	338–42	28
207	26	340	178, 191
208	28	341–42	176
209	191	344	94
213	341–42	348	37
215	96	349	17, 21–22, 178, 354
223	174	350	27, 191
225	28	357	104
226	316, 354	359	27, 174
227	20, 24	381a	43, 163
		384	174

Primary Sources Index 391

384b	24	509a	28, 178
386	41	509b	174
387	43	509e	28 354,
387a	163	512	16, 18, 19, 24, 27, 177
388	28	514	28, 174, 177
392	38	515	173. 177
407	354	516	22
408	176	517	22, 28
410	37, 191	518	22
412	27	519	16, 20–21, 354
414	16, 26, 27	522	346
417	176	524	16, 21, 176, 177
432	37	524–25	28
437	15	525	16, 21, 24, 94, 176, 191
408	28	528	38
429	24	529	18, 28, 191
432	94	531a	29, 354
437	346	535	178
439	16, 28, 29	536–37	38
439	16	543	16
451	16, 20	545	28
452	25	547	29
455	26, 28	552	339–41
455a	29, 354	558	39
456	16	559	26
463	27	568	16, 19, 178
473	28, 174	568b	28
474	28	580	28, 176
476	37, 46	581	28, 174, 354
485	28	582	39, 39
492	35	588	16, 174
493	35	597	16, 29, 177, 178
497	26	617	35–36, 52
499	28	618	28
500–01	28	619	176
500	28	621	176
500a	29	622	28
501a	29	623	28
501b	29, 176	624	28
501c	29, 176	625	28
501d	29	626	28
502	24	626a	28
505	27, 38	629	28
506	28, 174	630–32	110
508	28	636	177

Pilhofer, Philippi 2 (cont.)

639	27
642a	27, 174, 354
644	16, 18, 177
647	37
650	28
651	27
652	27
660	16, 28
663	37
664	37
665	37, 44
667	26
669	26, 27
671a	28
672	28
678	28
680	37, 44
681	27, 39
682	27
689	37
697	36–37, 191
700–03	25, 354
700	316, 354
702–03	354
703	26, 44
703d	354
703e	28, 354
705	134
719	26, 316, 354
721	38
729	27
754	28

P.Lond.

46	252

P.Oxy.

1.108	91
20.2284	130
46.3312	50

P.Paris

574.3037–45	252

P.Ross.Georg.

31	130

RECAM

2.449	105

Reynolds, *Aphrodisias and Rome*

30	

RICM

26–29	109
64	102
70	109
86	102
111	94
115	96
116	104
117	104
120	102
123	94
124	107
132	102
153–54	109
159–60	109
161	109
221	110
224	103
225	110
226	110, 148
22–78	109
205	109
221	110
225	110
226	110
229	90
231	94, 97, 98
232	93, 94, 97
233	110
234	108
235–39	110
235	107
237	99
238	104, 105, 110
241	96, 110
242	110

246	100, 109	5.2.1096	259
248	95	5.2.1109	200, 216
249	108	5.2.1731	259
250	108		
252	109	Vindolanda Tablet 2.154	123, 128–31,
267	102	128, 145	

Rizakis, *Achaïe, II: La cité de Patras*
363	166

Robert et al., *Le martyre de Pionios*
15	172

Samama, *Les médecins*
026	99
027	99
070	99

SEG
19.444	101
19.450	108
19.483	192
21.815	260
27.259	103
30.584	95
33.466	46
45.795	97, 105
48.716	192
59.691	174

SIG
3.1140	192

SIRIS
122	191
123	191
124	191

Stud.Palmyr.
8.958	97

TAM
2.521	259
5.2.996	200, 216
5.2.1002	199, 215

Warmington, *Remains of Old Latin*
Dedicatory Inscriptions 78	320
Dedicatory Inscriptions 82–85	320
Dedicatory Inscriptions 82	320
Epitaphs 1–10	323
Epitaphs 1–2, 3–4, 7, 10	322
Epitaphs 1–2, 3–4	346
Epitaphs 5	323
Epitaphs 7	351
Epitaphs 8	324
Epitaphs 63	357
Epitaphs 106	333
Honorary Inscriptions 1, 5–7	320
Honorary Inscriptions 7	328–31
Honorary Inscriptions 8, 16	320
Inscriptions on Works 6, 7, 9, 11, 55	320

West, *Latin Inscriptions 1896–1926*
1	328–31

Coins

BMC
323	265, 269

RIC 2
678	279
679	279

RPC 1
307	7
307–8	8
1646–49	7
1646	7, 8, 224
1647	8
1648	8

RPC 1 (cont.)

1649	8, 224
1650	9–10
1651	10–11, 52, 123, 131–34
1653–54	245
1653	245
1653–55	10

Modern Authors Index

Abrahamsen, Valerie A.   14, 21, 29, 42, 53, 96, 112, 140, 149
Adam-Veleni, P.   104, 112
Agosto, Efrain   310, 362
Akkan, Y.   15, 58
Aland, Kurt   143 149
Alcock, Susan E.   225, 236
Alfen, Peter G. van   175, 182
Alföldy, Géza   332, 362
Amandry, Michel   175, 182
Ameling, Walter   104, 114
Ando, Clifford   69, 76, 204, 217, 240, 288
Andreau, Jean   89, 122
Andringa, William van   92, 122
Anthon, C.   265, 288
Antonaccio, Carla M.   269, 282
Arband, S.   124, 134
Armitage, David   346
Arzt-Graber, Peter   74, 76, 143, 149, 362
Ascough, Richard S.   13, 17–18, 20, 37, 41–43, 54, 86–87, 112, 140, 149, 189–220, 163–64, 166, 178, 182, 189, 192, 197, 203–5, 208, 213, 217, 302–3
Aubert, Jean-Jacques   94, 112
Audollent, Auguste   260, 282
Bagnall, R. S.   218
Baillet, Jules   130, 134
Bakirtzis, Charalambos   2, 6, 43, 54, 82, 94, 96, 104, 110, 121, 140, 149, 244, 286, 316, 362
Balch, David L.   302, 305
Balsdon, J. P. V. D.   244, 274, 276, 282
Banchich, Thomas M.   99, 112
Barclay, John M. G.   81, 112, 319, 362
Barnes, Timothy D.   109, 112

Bartels, Jens   161, 182
Barton, Carlin A.   307, 362
Baslez, Marie-Françoise   153, 182
Bassler, Jouette M.   302, 304
Bauckham, Richard   280–82
Bauer, Walter   89, 112
Beard, Mary   142, 150
Beare, Francis Wright   248–49, 283, 353, 362
Becker, Eve-Marie   299, 303
Behr, Charles Allison   261, 282
Berger, Adolf   101, 112
Berges, Dietrich   94, 112
Benoist, Stéphane   158, 183, 187
Berthelot, Katell   231, 237
Bertrand, Audrey   177, 183
Betz, Hans Dieter   194, 207, 217, 253, 283, 307, 310, 362
Beyer, H. W.   223, 237
Bieringer, Reimund   301, 303
Bilezikian, Gilbert   268, 283
Bingham, Sandra   126, 135
Bird, Michael F.   315, 348, 362
Bloomquist, L. Gregory   12, 24, 54, 344, 362
Boccaccini, Gabriele   314
Bockmuehl, Marcus   24, 50, 54, 247, 283, 343–45, 348, 354–55, 358–59, 362
Bolden, Ron   9, 11,
Bond, Helen K.   317, 363
Bonnekoh, Pamela   107, 112
Bookidis, Nancy   328, 364
Bormann, Lukas   12, 54, 64, 66, 68, 77, 82, 112, 132, 135, 140–41, 225, 236, 307, 363

Bornhäuser, D. Karl 232, 236
Bosch, Jorge Sánchez 307, 363
Boustan, Ra'anan S. 251, 284
Bowden, W. 103, 110, 113
Bowersock, G. W. 99, 113, 172, 187
Bowman, Alan K. 128, 135
Boyd, Michael 93, 96
Bradford, John 47, 54,
Bransbourg, Gilles 175, 182
Braund, David C. 331, 363
Brélaz, Cédric 2–3, 32, 54, 102, 113, 141, 153, 155, 156, 159, 162, 164–66, 169, 172, 175, 179–80, 183, 335
Bremmer, Jan N. 269, 283
Brewer, R. R. 231, 236
Breytenbach, Cilliers 90, 113, 119, 153, 182, 298, 303, 307
Briones, David E. 13, 54, 193, 212, 217
Brown, M. J. 50–52, 55
Bru, Hadrien 102, 113, 165, 184
Bruce, F. F. 135
Brucker, Ralph 302–3
Bryen, Ari Z. 172, 184
Brynes, Michael 361, 363
Buckler, W. H. 125–26, 135
Bultmann, Rudolf 312, 363
Burnett, Andrew 133, 136, 244, 286
Brunt, P. A. 227, 236
Butticaz, Simon 291
Cadwallader, Alan H. 45, 55
Caird, G. B. 353, 363
Cairns, F. 331, 363
Calder, W. M. 126, 135
Callan, Terrance 307, 313, 363
Cameron, Ron 18, 55
Campbell, William S. 359, 360, 363
Cannadine, David 264, 288
Capper, Brian J. 194, 201, 207, 217, 345, 363
Carr, Wesley 249–50, 283
Casiday, Augustine 105
Cassidy, Richard J. 124, 135, 230, 237
Cauwenberghe, C. Hoët-van 183
Cavalier, Laurence 170–71, 188
Cébeillac-Gervasoni, M. 159–61, 184, 187

Chang, Dongshin D. 315, 363
Chaniotis, Angelos 171, 185
Chankowski, Véronique 89, 94, 122
Charlesworth, M. P. 274, 283
Christol, Michel 180, 184
Chryssanthaki-Nagle, K. 131, 135
Cohick, Lynn H. 223, 237
Colin, Frédéric 163, 183
Colognesi, Luigi C. 170, 186
Collange, J.-F. 45, 55, 126, 135, 293, 303
Collart, Paul 2, 4, 15–18, 27, 30, 37, 55, 82, 91, 94–95, 113, 131, 135, 155, 176, 178, 184, 226, 237, 348, 363
Colpe, C. 124, 134
Colson, F. H. 201, 219
Concannon, C. W. 45, 55
Coogan, Michael D. 197, 217
Corsten, Thomas 94, 113
Cottier, Michel 98, 118
Coupry, Jacques 2–3, 55, 91, 93, 98, 113
Courtils, Jacques des 170, 188
Craddock, Fred B. 247, 283
Crawford, Michael H. 168, 184
Cribiore, Raffaella 99–100, 113
Cumont, Franz 242, 283
Cuss, Dominique 269–70, 283
Dąbrowa, Edward 153, 187
Daguet-Gagey, Anne 182, 183
Dam, Raymond van 105, 122
Dana, Dan 162, 184
Danker, Frederick W. 346, 363
Daumet, Pierre G. H. 94, 115
Daumet, Honoré 3, 55
Deissmann, Adolf 48, 55, 125, 135, 197, 217, 252–53, 283
Demandt, Alexander 101–2, 113
Dement'eva, Vera V. 75, 77
Demougin, Ségolène 102, 120
Demaille, Julien 155, 184
Descat, Raymond 171, 188
DeSilva, David A. 314–16, 363
Destephen, Sylvain 90, 93, 99, 113
Dettwiler, Andreas 291, 305
Devillers, Olivier 174, 185
De Vos, Craig Steven 12, 140, 205, 219

Dickie, Matthew W. 328, 330
Dickson, John P. 203, 205, 207, 209–10, 217
Dibelius, Martin 248, 255, 283
Dickey, Eleanor 257, 283
Dillon, M. 358, 364
Dimitsas, M. G. 94, 113
Dinahet, Marie-Thérèse Le 86–87, 96, 116
Dodd, B. 298, 303
Dodd, Brian J. 23, 55
Dodd, C. H. 84, 114
Doi, Masaoki 100, 116
Donahoe, K. C. 307, 364
Drake, H. A. 93, 114
Drew-Bear, Thomas 180, 184
Ducoux, Henri 3, 58
Ducrey, Pierre 4, 27–28, 30, 153–54, 176, 184, 348
Duff, J. D. 273, 286
Dumézil, Bruno 90, 93,113
Duncan, G. S. 126, 135
Dunderberg, Ismo 299, 303
Dunn, James D. G. 313, 364
Durry, M. 132, 135
Earl, Donald Charles 323, 364
Eck, Werner 82, 102, 104, 108, 114
Edwards, Douglas R. 69, 77
Egger, R. 129, 135
Ehrensperger, Kathy 12, 40, 64–65, 71, 77, 139, 347, 364
Ehrhardt, Norbert 95, 114
Erasmo, Mario 324, 364
Fairclough, H. Rushton 289
Faraone, Christopher A. 251, 261, 283
Farnell, Lewis Richard 269, 284
Fears, J. Rufus 274, 284
Fee, Gordon D. 197, 202, 208, 210, 218, 232–33 237, 240, 250, 284, 343, 345, 364
Feher, Géza 4, 55
Feine, Paul 125, 135
Feissel, Denis 96–98, 106
Feldman, Louis H. 218
Ferguson, Everett 302

Fernoux, Henri-Louis 179, 185
Feyel, Christophe 161, 185
Feyel, Michel 2, 55 113
Fishwick, Duncan 270, 284
Flemming, Dean 241, 280, 284
Flexsenhar III, Michael A. 48–49, 52, 55, 228, 237, 343, 364
Flower, Harriet I. 332, 364
Forbes, Christopher 307, 364
Forbis, Elizabeth 321, 364
Förster, Hans 69, 77, 143, 149, 167, 185
Fournier, Julien 5, 15, 55, 164, 169, 173, 184
Fowl, S. E. 240–41, 247, 280, 282, 284
Fox, Robert Lane 89, 116
Fredricksmeyer, E. A. 274, 284
Frey, Jörg 190, 219
Friesen, Steven J. 5, 55, 81, 82–83, 104, 114, 121, 157, 160, 176, 185–86, 228, 237
Gabba, Emilio 170, 186
Gabrielsen, Vincent 74,
Gaebler, H. 132, 135
Galinsky, Karl 326, 364
Galsterer, B. 130, 135
Galsterer, H. 130, 135, 240, 243, 285
Garland, David E. 344, 358
Garland, L. 358, 364
Garnsey, Peter 204, 218, 227, 237
Garrison, Roman 88, 114
Gathercole, Simon J. 312, 364
Gebhard, Elizabeth R. 328, 330, 364
Gelzer, Matthias 31, 55, 320, 365
Geoffrion, Timothy C. 231, 237
Gerber, Christine 298, 303
Gerhard, Friedrich 223, 237
Gibson, Elsa 89, 114
Giffin, Ryan Kristopher 24, 239–89
Gill, David 164, 184
Glancy, Jennifer A. 307, 365
Goddard, Christophe J. 93, 114
Goldsworthy, Adrian 130, 136
Gonzales, Antonio 102, 120, 121
Goold, G. P. 267, 271, 287
Gordon, Arthur E. 51, 328, 365

Modern Authors Index

Gordon, Joyce S.   51, 56
Gordon, R. L.   251, 284
Gorman, Michael J.   23, 56, 240, 281, 284
Goukowsky, Paul   161, 185
Gounari, Emmanuela   4–5, 44, 47–48, 56
Gournaris, Georgios   4–5, 44, 56
Gounaropoulou, Loukretia   109, 114
Gradel, Ittai   264, 284
Grant, Michael   270–71, 284
Gregory, Andrew F.   87, 119
Gregory, A. P.   15, 56
Grether, Gertrude   265, 284
Grindheim, Sigurd   343, 348, 365
Guillaumin, Jean-Yves   102, 120, 121
Gundry, Judith M.   312, 365
Haehling, Raban von   146, 150
Halfmann, Helmut   161, 185
Hammond, Mason   267, 284
Hanges, James Constantine   190, 218
Hansen, G. Walter   343, 345, 347, 352, 359, 365
Hanson, Paul D.   276, 285
Harker, Andrew   200, 218
Harland, Philip A.   198, 213
Harris-McCoy, Daniel E.   262, 285
Harrison, James R.   15, 22, 26, 48, 56, 79, 82, 111, 114–15, 119, 307, 310, 321–22, 331, 346, 348, 356, 360, 365–66
Hartog, Paul   88, 114–16
Harvey, B. K.   51, 53, 56, 325–26, 365
Hasselhoff, Görge K.   67, 77
Hattersley-Smith, Kara   103, 110, 115
Hatzopoulos, Miltiades B.   109, 114
Hawthorne, Gerard F.   23, 45, 56, 197, 202, 208, 218, 247, 285, 347, 350, 361, 366
Heinrich-Tamaszka, O.   100, 120
Heinrichs, Johannes   104, 114
Hellerman, Joseph H.   13, 31, 33, 41, 56, 64, 70, 75, 77, 161, 185, 204, 218 307–8, 338, 366
Hellmann, M.-C.   95, 115
Hengel, Martin   80–81, 115
Henten, J. W. van   203, 218
Herzer, Jens   74, 143, 151
Heseltine, Michael   288
Heuzey, Léon   3, 56, 94, 115
Heuchert, Volker   133, 136, 244, 286
Hildebrandt, Henrik   248, 287
Hirst, Gertrude   262–63, 285
Hock, Ronald F.   85, 115
Hoddinott, Ralph F.   98, 100, 105, 107, 115
Hoey, A. S.   18, 57
Hoffmann, Friedhelm   331, 366
Hofius, Otfried   246, 249, 251, 254, 285
Holloway, Paul A.   11–13, 24, 49–50, 57, 139, 241, 277, 280, 285, 292–93, 295, 303, 343–44, 352, 366
Holmes, Michael William   249, 285
Hooker, Morna   299, 303
Hopkins, Keith   271, 285
Horn, Friedrich W.   291, 303
Horsley, G. H. R.   37, 41, 50, 57, 94, 115
Horst, P. W. van der   203, 218
Howgego, Christopher   9, 133, 135, 244, 286
Huck, Olivier   163, 183
Hultin, Jeremy F.   359, 366
Hurtado, Larry   281, 285
Huttner, U.   111, 115
Illiadis, George   29, 57
Inglebert, Hervé   90, 93, 113–14
Irons, William J.   241, 285
Ismard, Paul   177, 185
Itgenshorst, T.   31, 57, 113
James, Sarah A.   157, 186
Jellonek, Szymon   7, 9–10, 57
Jewett, Robert   344, 366
Johnson, Gary J.   82, 90, 115
Jones, A. H. M.   97, 100–103, 107–8, 115
Jones, Christopher P.   172, 187
Joshel, Sandra R.   89, 115,
Judge, Edwin A   50–51, 57, 79, 80–82, 115, 307, 366
Jung, Franz   144, 150

Modern Authors Index 399

Kähler, Christoph 293, 303
Karadedos, G. 141, 150
Karyakina, Maria 40, 57
Käsemann, Ernst 248, 285
Kaster, Robert A. 100, 116
Katsari, Constantina 94, 113, 185
Keener, Craig S. 37, 43, 255, 285
Keith, Alison 69, 76
Kennedy, George A. 311, 366
Kennedy, Harry A. A. 83, 116
Kenyon, F. G. 252, 285
Keown, Mark J. 206, 218
Keyes, Clinton W. 266, 283
Kidd, Reggie M. 267–68, 285
Kirbihler, François 161, 174, 185
Klauck, Hans-Josef 274, 285
Kleiner, Fred S. 278, 285
Kline, A. S. 263, 286
Kloppenborg, John S. 213
Knapp, Robert 86, 116
Kobayashi, Masao 100, 116
Koch, Paul 103, 116
Koester, Helmut 2, 43, 82–83, 110, 112, 116, 140, 149, 244, 286, 316, 362
Konradt, Matthias 291, 303
Konstantinas, P. Mentzu, 89, 118
Köster, Beate 143, 149
Koukouli, C. 107, 116
Koukouli-Chrysantaki, C. 43–44, 57, 131, 140–41, 143, 150, 155, 186, 244–45, 285
Kourkoutidou-Nikolaidou, E. 103, 116
Krause, Jens-Uwe 124, 135, 147, 150, 124
Kreitzer, Larry J. 23, 57, 264, 286
Kremydi-Sicilianou, S. 8, 57, 133, 135–36, 145, 150, 244–45, 286
Kritikakou-Nikolaropoulou, K. I. 94, 118
Krohn, Niklot 100, 120
Kroll, J. H. 131, 136
Kroll, W. 116
Kruse, Thomas 74–75, 77
Kuhn, Annika B. 82, 118
Kuhn, Christina T. 171, 185
Kurek-Chomycz, D. 46, 58

Kyrtatas, Dimitris J. 89, 116
Labarre, Guy 86–87, 96, 102, 113, 165, 184
Laffi, Umberto 170, 186
Lagogianni-Georgakarakos, M. 103, 116
Lakonidou, Athena 141, 150
Lallemand, Jacqueline 97, 116
Lambrecht, Jan 301, 303
Lamer, Hans 91, 117
Lamoine, Laurent 160, 161, 184, 187
Lamoreaux, Jason T. 14, 27–30, 58, 205, 218
Landucci, Franca 141, 150
Lane Fox, Robin J. 89, 141, 150, 155, 185
Lange, Carsten Hjort 346, 366
Lansford, Tyler 332, 366
Lapalus, E. 4, 58
Latacz, Joachim 295, 304
Latte, K. 91, 117
Lavan, Luke 103, 113
Lee, Jae Won 350, 366
Lee, Thomas R. 314, 366
Lemerle, Paul 2–4, 44–45, 58, 82, 90–91, 96, 98, 108–9, 117, 154, 178, 186
Lendon, J. E. 309, 367
Levick, Barbara 169, 186, 226, 237
Lewis, Charlton 358, 367
Lewis, Peter E. 9, 11, 58
Licht, A. Lewis 264, 288
Liertz, Uta-Maria 160, 187
Lifshitz, B. 318, 367
Lightfoot, J. B. 83, 117, 127, 136, 247, 286
Lincoln, Andrew T. 203, 218
Lindemann, Andreas 291, 305
Lintott, Andrew 346, 367
Loh, I.-Jin 248, 286
Long, Fredrick J. 24, 240, 246, 251, 276, 286
Longenecker, Bruce W. 81, 117, 361
Lozano, Fernando 245, 263–64, 286
Lüdemann, Gerd 291, 304
Lüderitz, Gert 203, 218
Lychounas, Michalis 228, 237

MacKintosh, Marjorie C. 278, 286
Macheiner, W. 124, 134
Mack, Burton L. 314, 367
MacMullen, Ramsay 93, 117
Magi, F. 332, 367
Maier, Harry O. 89, 117
Malay, H. 15, 58
Malcolm, Matthew R. 307, 367
Malherbe, Abraham J. 80–81, 117, 126, 136, 237
Malina, Bruce J. 225, 237
Manicas, Peter T. 346, 367
Mann, J. C. 225, 237
Mantovani, Dario 172, 187
Marc, Jean-Yves 92,
Marchal, Jospeh A. 6, 12–14, 132, 136, 147, 154, 186, 205, 217, 347, 367
Marki, Efterpi 107, 117
Markschies, Christoph 248, 287
Marrou, Henri-Irénée 99, 117
Marshall, I. Howard 247, 287
Marshall, Peter 84, 117
Martin, R. P. 23, 58, 246–48, 285, 287, 360, 367
Martindale, John R. 101, 117
Mason, Hugh J. 87, 117, 367
Mason, Steve 318, 364
Matthews, John 30–31, 58
Maurice, Lisa 100, 117
McCormack, Thomas J. 242
McNeil, B. 274
McKechnie, Paul 82, 90, 109, 117
McKnight, Scot 223
Meeks, Wayne A. 80–81, 117, 280, 287, 302,
Meggitt, Justin J. 81, 117
Meimaris, Yiannis E. 94, 118
Meinhold, Peter 89, 118
Mell, Ulrich 63, 295
Melville, R. D. 211, 218
Mentzu, Konstantinas P. 89, 91, 94–96, 98–99, 118
Meriç, R. 15, 58
Merkt, Andreas 291, 305
Metzger, B. M. 314, 316–17, 367

Meyer, Heinrich A. W. 83, 118
Michaelis, Wilhelm 127, 136, 197, 218
Miletti, Lorenzo 310, 367
Miller, Anna C. 179, 186
Miller, Gene 250, 287
Miller, Merrill P. 18, 54
Millis, Benjamin W. 157, 186
Minnen, Peter van 165, 186
Mitchell, Stephen 89–90, 94, 113, 115, 118, 175, 185
Modica, Joseph B. 223, 237
Mouritsen, Henrik 82, 118
Mueller, Dierk 13, 39–40, 58, 334, 339, 367
Müller-Wiener, M. 6, 58
Mark D. Nanos 347, 367
Nasrallah, Laura S. 6, 7, 59, 104, 121, 132, 136, 154, 186
Neusner, Jacob 307, 368
Niebuhr, Karl-Wilhelm 74, 77
Nichtweiß, Barbara 248, 287
Nicklas, Tobias 291, 305
Nida, Eugene A. 248, 286
Nigdelis, Pantelis M. 94, 118
Nijf, Onno M. van 86–87, 98, 118
Nock, Arthur Darby 18, 58
Noethlichs, Karl Leo 146, 150
Nollé, Johannes 94, 112
Norman, A. F. 87, 100, 118
Norris, Frederick W. 105, 122
North, John 142, 149
North, Helen F. 321, 368
Nuffelen, Peter van 175, 186
Oakes, Peter 12, 16, 25, 27, 50–51, 59, 77, 81–82, 87–89, 118, 132, 136, 139, 150, 157, 169, 186, 195, 204–5, 218, 225–26, 229–33, 241, 243–44, 276, 287, 302, 304, 237–38, 243
Oates, J. F. 218
O'Brien, Peter T. 202–4, 208, 219, 229, 238, 241, 247, 249, 287, 347, 354, 368
Oepke, A. 295, 304
Oertel, Friedrich 97, 118
Ogereau, Julien M. 2, 12, 14, 59, 64, 69, 77, 81, 83–85, 104, 111,

113, 118-19, 139, 145, 150, 158, 178, 186, 193-95, 207-8, 219, 346, 368
Öhler, Markus 190, 219
Omerzu, Heike 147, 150, 172, 186
Orlandos, Anastasios K. 95, 119
Ortland, Dane C. 313, 368
Ostmeyer, Karl-Heinrich 143, 150
Oswalt, John N. 276, 287
Pallas, D. I. 98-99, 119
Papazoglou, F. 133, 136
Parissaki, Maria-Gabriella G. 164, 184
Park, Young-Ho 179, 186
Pate, C. Marvin 221-22, 238
Paton, W. R. 219
Patterson, Jane Lancaster 354, 368
Paulsen, H. 89, 112
Pearson, Birger 287
Pedrick, Victoria 275, 287
Peerbolte, L. J. Lietaert 208, 219
Pellecchi, Luigi 172, 187
Pelekanidis, Stylianos 96, 98, 100, 105, 107-8, 119
Pennas, Charalambos 96, 105-7, 119
Perdrizet, Paul 18, 59, 94-95, 119
Pernot, L. 307, 368
Pervo, Richard I. 125, 136, 146, 151
Peterlin, Davorin 12, 19, 37-38, 59, 81, 86, 119, 344, 368
Peterman, G. W. 13, 84, 88, 119
Peterson, Erik 247-48, 287
Pettigrew, David. K. 287, 329, 368
Pfanner, Michael 265, 287
Pilhofer, Peter 2, 4, 11-12, 15-22, 24-29, 31, 34-46, 52-53, 59, 66, 77, 82, 84, 88-90, 96, 98-101, 103-9, 120, 132, 136, 140-41, 143, 148, 151, 154, 158, 163, 166-67, 173-74, 176-79, 187, 191-92, 207, 225-26, 238, 244-45, 288, 308, 316, 335-40, 342, 346, 350-51, 354, 368
Pitts, A. W. 240, 251, 286
Plummer, Robert L. 206-7, 210, 219
Portefaix, Lilian 14, 21-22, 29-30, 59
Porter, Stanley E. 165, 187, 240, 251, 286, 291, 304

Portier-Young, Anathea 71, 77
Potter, David S. 204
Price, Jonathan 232, 237
Price, Simon R. F. 142, 150, 264, 288
Provost, Samuel 93, 96, 120
Quinn, Josephine Crawley 157, 187
Radin, Max 266, 288
Radt, S. 188
Ramsey, John T. 264, 288
Rankin, Edwin M. 91, 120
Rankov, Boris 130, 136
Rapp, Claudia 105, 120
Rapske, Brian 124, 136
Ravizza, Mariangela 172, 187
Reed, Annette Yoshiko 251, 284
Reed, Jeffrey T. 343, 368
Reid, Sara Karz 269, 270, 288
Reumann, John 24, 44, 50, 59, 126, 132, 136, 194, 196-97, 202, 208, 210, 219, 247, 288, 292, 304, 352, 354-55, 359, 368
Reynolds, Benjamin E. 74, 78
Reynolds, Joyce 346, 368
Rich, John 15, 59
Riggs, Christina 200, 218
Ristow, Sebastian 100, 120
Rives, James B. 239, 288
Rizakis, Athanase 16, 33, 59, 102, 120, 159-60, 162, 166, 169, 184, 187, 226, 238
Rizos, Efthymios 100, 110, 120
Robbins, Vernon K. 275, 288
Robert, Louis 90-91, 95, 120, 172, 187
Robert, Louis and Jeanne 94-95, 105
Robinson, T. A. 15, 60
Roger, Jacques 3, 60
Rosenbaum, Hans-Udo 143
Rouse, W. H. D. 289
Ruppel, Walter 143, 151
Ruyt, Claire De 91-92, 121
Ryan, Judith M. 197, 202, 219, 247, 289, 354, 357
Ryan, Scott C. 311, 368
Salac, A. 16, 20, 60
Salomies, Olli 160, 187

Samaran, C. 90, 120
Samama, Évelyne 99–100, 121
Sampley, Paul J. 14, 45, 60, 194, 207, 219, 307, 362, 368
Sandnes, Karl Olav 299, 304
Sänger, Dieter 63, 185, 295
Sänger, Patrick 67, 74, 77, 143, 149, 167, 185
Sarikakis, T. 133, 136
Sarrazanas, C. 3
Sartre, Maurice 153, 187
Scheid, John 102, 120, 239, 288
Schellenberg, Ryan S. 47, 60
Schließer. Benjamin 190, 219
Schmeller, Thomas 295, 304
Schmidt, Tassilo 75, 77
Schnelle, Udo 312, 322, 365
Schoedel, William R. 88, 121
Schoell, R. 97, 116
Scholer, David M. 51, 79, 116, 307, 366
Schowalter, Daniel 157, 160, 185–86, 228, 237, 265, 269, 288
Schröter, Jens 291, 305
Schwartz, Seth 318, 369
Schweitzer, Friedrich 297, 304
Scornaienchi, Lorenzo 299, 303
Seager, Robin 31, 320
Seeck, O. 101, 121
Sergienko, Gennadi A. 13–14, 60
Sève, Michel 4–5, 32–34, 44, 60, 91, 121, 140, 151, 153, 156, 158, 170, 187–88, 233, 238, 245, 288
Shapiro, Alan 133, 270, 289
Sherwin-White, Adrian N. 227, 238
Short, Charles 358, 367
Silva, Moisés 247, 288, 295, 304, 354, 369
Simón, Francisco Marco 251, 284
Sion-Jenkins, Karin 174, 185
Smit, P.-B. 307, 311–12, 369
Smith, Rowland 99, 121, 213
Smith, R. E. 322–24, 369
Smith W. 265, 288
Sodini, Jean-Pierre 88, 95
Sodini, Pierre 86–87, 89, 95–96, 121, 188
Solin, Heikki 160, 187
Sorek, Susan 318, 369
Souza, Philip de 329, 369
Spawforth, Anthony J. S. 226, 238
Speidel, Michael 129, 137, 339–41, 369
Spicq, Ceslas 292, 304, 312–13, 369
Spiliopoulou-Donderer, I. 103, 121
Sprinkle, Preston M. 315, 362
Standhartinger, Angela 12, 65–67, 74, 78, 143, 147, 151, 296–97, 304
Stanley, Christopher D. 351 369
Stefanidou-Tiveriou, Thea 104, 121
Stegemann, Ekkehard W. 81, 121
Stegemann, Wolfgang 81, 121, 146, 151
Sterck-Degueldre, J.-P. 163, 188
Stowers, S. K. 50, 60, 302, 304
Strachan, L. R. M. 252, 283
Strong, Eugénie S. 265–66, 270, 289
Strothmann, Meret 67, 77
Stuckenbruck, Loren 74
Sumney, Jerry L. 291, 304
Sweetman, Rebecca J. 156, 188
Tan, Rachael 361, 369
Taylor, Lily Ross 39, 60
Tellbe, Mikael 12, 60, 140, 151, 196, 203, 205, 219
Theissen, Gerd 80–81, 121
Thompson, Lynette 272, 289
Thomsen, Christian A. 74, 77
Thurston, Bonnie B. 197, 202, 219, 247, 289, 354, 357, 369
Tirologos, G. 102, 113, 121, 165, 184
Tran, Nicolas 86–87, 89, 92, 122
Travlos, Ioannes N. 95
Toynbee, J. M. C. 18, 60
Travis, S. H. 307, 369
Trebilco, Paul 164, 184
Tsochos, Charalampos 148, 151
Tuckett, Christopher M. 87, 118
Unwin, James 45, 60
Urso, Gianpaolo 161, 185
Uusimäki, Elisa 314, 369
Vanderkam, James C. 315, 369

Vanséveren, Sylvie 163, 183
Verboven, Koenraad 94, 122
Verheyden, Joseph 291, 305
Verhoef, Eduard 2, 13, 60, 205, 244, 289
Veyne, Paul 86, 122
Vielhauer, Philipp 88, 122
Vincent, Marvin R. 83, 122, 202, 219
Vollenweider, Samuel 41, 61, 63, 78, 294, 296, 304
Volpe, Paola 310, 367
Vos, Craig Steven de 12, 61, 151, 171, 188, 205, 219
Wallace-Hadrill, Andrew 15, 224, 238
Wallach, Luitpold 321
Walters, James C. 157, 160, 185–86
Walton, Steve 164, 183
Ware, James P. 165, 188, 202, 206, 220,
Warmington, E. H. 320–24, 328–29, 332–33, 346, 351, 357, 369
Watson, D. F. 307, 343–44, 369
Watts, N. H. 242, 283
Weaver, P. R. C. 50–52, 61, 196, 220
Weber, Ekkehard 172, 188
Weber, Patrick 4, 32–34, 60, 91, 121, 140, 151, 156, 170, 188, 233, 238, 245, 288
Wehnert, Jürgen 291, 305
Welborn, L. L. 26, 15, 47, 61, 81–82, 84, 111, 119, 122, 356
Welte, Michael 143, 149
Weiß, Alexander 81–82, 109, 122
West, Allen Brown 327–28, 370
White, John L. 124, 137, 188
White, L. Michael 301–2, 154
White, Peter 123, 137
White, R. J. 262, 289
Williams II, Charles K. 328, 363–64
Willet, Rinse 169, 188
Willis, W. H. 160, 218
Wilson, Andrew 157, 187
Winter, Bruce W. 203, 205–6, 209, 220, 326, 344, 370
Wipszycka, Ewa 97, 99, 103, 122
Wischmeyer, Oda 299, 303

Witherington, Ben, III 41, 50, 61, 202, 220, 280, 289, 343, 370
M. Wocjiechowski 307, 310–12, 370
Wojtkowiak, Heiko 74, 78
Wright, N. T. 241, 281, 289
Yarbrough, O. Larry 154, 188
Yonge, C. D. 144, 151
Yuge, Toru 100, 116
Zajac, Barbara 7, 57
Zanker, Paul 8, 10, 61, 133, 137, 270, 289
Zannis, Angelos G. 162, 188
Zeigler, Joseph 246, 289
Zurawski, M. 314, 369
Zimmermann, Christiane 90, 113

www.ingramcontent.com/pod-product-compliance
Lightning Source LLC
Chambersburg PA
CBHW021929290426
44108CB00012B/768